DEATH

DEATH: CURRENT PERSPECTIVES

THIRD EDITION

Edited by

Edwin S. Shneidman, Ph.D.

Professor of Thanatology

*Director, Laboratory for the Study of
Life-Threatening Behavior*

*University of California at Los Angeles
School of Medicine*

MAYFIELD PUBLISHING COMPANY

Library of Congress Catalog Card Number: 83-062824
International Standard Book Number: 0-87484-713-3

Manufactured in the United States of America
Mayfield Publishing Company
285 Hamilton Avenue
Palo Alto, California 94301

Sponsoring editor: Franklin C. Graham

Manuscript editor: Deborah L. Cogan

Managing editor: Pat Herbst

Art director and designer: Nancy Sears

Cover photograph: Mark Gottlieb

Part-opening illustrations: Martha Breen Bredemeyer

The dedication illustration is from an original work by Judith Malkin Watkyns, rendered by Mary Burkhardt.

Production manager: Cathy Willkie

Compositor: Lienett Company

Printer and binder: National Press/Kingsport Press

The quotation on pages 366–67 is from René Fueloep-Miller, *Fyodor Dostoevsky,* transl. by Richard Winston and Clara Winston. Copyright 1950 by Charles Scribner's Sons; copyright renewed 1978. Reprinted with the permission of Charles Scribner's Sons.

To
Judith Malkin Watkyns
1944–1971
my former Teaching Assistant
gentle and generous
even in her death

CONTENTS

PREFACE

The very act of revising a book carries with it the requirement for an explanation. A new edition of an old work demands that a few words be said in defense of it.

The arithmetic of the present edition is this: 23 articles were retained and 27 articles were dropped from the previous edition; 16 articles were added, making a total of 39 articles in all.

My intention has been to bring the topic of death "up to date." In the very recent past there have been developments and writings of sufficient importance to make a revision of this source book advisable. These recent developments include:

The reports of the President's Commission for the Study of Ethical Problems in Medicine and Biomedical and Behavioral Research. These reports reflect the increased interest of the lay and professional communities in the legal-ethical-moral aspects of death, dying, and suicide. In this context, some important questions are raised: Who owns the living body? What are the rights of the dying person? Who should speak for the muted (comatose, neonatal) dying person?

Some new and fascinating scholarship (by which I mean thoughtful essays) on death, notably by Ernest Becker, Phillipe Ariès, and Susan Sontag—all included in this edition.

Some emerging fresh conceptualizations about suicide, especially the work of Jean Baechler, Ronald Maris, Louis Wekstein, and Jack D. Douglas (the last included in this volume).

A surge of interest in the quality of life during the process of dying. This includes an interest in clinical thanatology as well as in palliative care units in hospitals and home care for the dying. There is a definite place in medicine (and the other health sciences) for recognition of the importance of *caring* for a person who is dying, in addition to efforts at *curing* the life-threatening disease. The deeply personal statements of two learned physicians, Dr. Martin Grotjahn (new to this edition) and Dr. Erich Lindemann, lend a fresh and poignant note to this volume.

A growing sense of urgency about "big-death" and a growing anxiety about the ineptitude of political leaders in forestalling death on a global scale. The last section of this volume, "Twentieth-Century Megadeath," includes pieces by Gil Elliot, Elie Wiesel, Robert Jay Lifton, and George F. Kennan; they should be required reading for every citizen.

A number of people helped me personally, especially Carol J. Horky, my incomparable assistant, and Deborah Allen, an unusually helpful under-graduate volunteer.

I wish to thank Charles A. Corr, from Southern Illinois University at Edwardsville; Walter L. Moore, Jr., from Florida State University, and Robert L. Wrenn, from the University of Arizona, for their counsel in preparing this edition.

Finally, I acknowledge my gratitude to Frank Graham, editor of Mayfield Publishing Company, who cheerfully applied a combination of extraordinary skills to the preparation of this revision.

E.S.S.

DEATH

INTRODUCTION

Perhaps the single most impressive fact about death today—independent of the unchangeable truth that death can never be circumvented—is how much (and in how many different ways) various aspects of death and dying are currently undergoing dramatic changes. Nowadays, there are many breezes in the thanatological wind.[1] We are experiencing a cultural revolution in many areas of our living. In the last short generation, dozens of our folkways (in dress, behavior, civility, morality, sexuality) and even some of our mores have been changed, often in breathtaking ways. The ethics, and sociology, and psychology, and morality of death have not been exempt from these culturewide changes. This book attempts to reflect these changes in relation to death—changes that have led us to new, and often startling, insights into the very process of dying; into the intricate interactions between the dying and those who care for the dying; into the impact of death on those left behind; even into the need for reexamining such fundamental questions as: When does death occur? When should death occur?

In order to place these current trends in thanatology in context, this volume examines death from many perspectives, ranging from cultural strategies for dealing with death as a philosophical concept to individual tactics for dealing with death as an inevitable reality.

What will be discussed here are the threads of change that weave through the various chapters and constitute some of the more important developments in the current thanatological scene.

Consider this paragraph:[2]

"Haul in the chains! Let the carcass go astern!" The vast tackles have done their duty. The peeled white body of the beheaded whale flashes like a marble sepulchre; though changed in hue, it has not perceptibly lost anything in bulk. It is still colossal. Slowly it floats more and more away, the water around it torn and splashed by the insatiate sharks, and the air above vexed with rapacious flights of screaming fowls, whose beaks are like so many insulting poniards in the whale. The vast white headless phantom floats further and further from the ship, and every rod that it so floats, what seem square roods of sharks and cubic roods of fowls, augment the murderous din. For hours and hours from the almost stationary ship that hideous sight is seen.

Beneath the unclouded and mild azure sky, upon the fair face of the pleasant sea, wafted by the joyous breezes, the great mass of death floats on and on, till lost in infinite perspectives.

What is to be especially noted in this superlative passage is the breathtaking shift in mood between the first eight sentences and the last—from horror and rapaciousness to the most pacific calm. Indeed, the last sentence itself contains the same dramatic contrast as seen in the shift in tone between the first three phrases, and the last two. Such a combination of opposites is called an *oxymoron*. The best known examples of oxymorons in the English language are from *Romeo and Juliet:* ". . . Feather of lead, bright smoke, cold fire, sick health" and, of course, ". . . Parting is such sweet sorrow." I have dwelled on the subject of oxymorons because it so aptly describes death in our time. Death is oxymoronic, a paradox made up of contrasting values, opposite trends, and even contradictory facts.

We live in an oxymoronic century. At the same time we have created the most exquisitely sophisticated technological procedures for saving one individual's life, we have also created lethal technological devices of at least equal sophistication, with the capacity of exterminating millions, of expunging cultures, of jeopardizing time itself by not only erasing the present but also threatening the future—what Melville, in *White Jacket*, called ". . . the terrible combustion of the entire planet." On the one hand, marvelous devices for emergency surgery, kidney dialysis, and organ transplantations promise life; on the other hand, megadeath bombs constantly aimed from above the clouds and beneath the waves promise death. No one is safe; there is no place to hide (see Kahn's *On Thermonuclear War* [1960] and Lifton's *Death in Life* [1967]).

We live in paradoxical times. On the one hand, there has been more killing by the state than ever before: over 110 million deaths since 1900 in brutish wars, deliberate famines, planned starvations, police and government executions (see Elliot's *The Twentieth Century Book of the Dead* [1972]); on the other hand, there has been no century where so much effort has been put into saving individual lives and increasing the general span of life.

Even the scientific marvels of our age for saving individual lives are part of the oxymoronic nature of death in our times, for they exist side by side with the frustrating and unfulfilled promises of medicine to save us from the dread maladies of heart disease and cancer. Dubos has referred to this failure of medicine in his book *The Mirage of Health* (1971), and others have called it "the mythology of American medicine." We have been overpromised in part because we have oversought. But great strides have been made: in the United States, life expectancy has been extended 28 years in the last 75 years, from 47 years in 1900 to 75 years in 1975 (see Dublin's *After Eighty Years* [1966]). However, it is important to note that this remarkable increase has been due not so much to medicine's miracles for adults, as to everyday public health practices in the areas of infant mortality (reduced from 150 to 25 per 1,000 births in this century), sanitation, immunization, and environmental control—unpretentious activities when compared with the dramatic surgical and medical cures that can increase the life span of a relatively few specially selected individuals.

The elimination of diphtheria, scarlet fever, and typhoid fever and the reduction of mortality from tuberculosis were a million times more effective in increasing general longevity than heart transplants. Conquering the causes of death over 40—cancer, cardiovascular diseases, and accidents—will do an incalculable amount of psychological good, but will not have enormous impact on the total duration of life for the populace as a whole, adding no more than perhaps five or fix years to the present average of 75 (Dublin, 1966). Probably the most significant changes in mortality are to be found less in medical and hospital care than they are in health education: simply in voluntary and controllable changes in our routine daily patterns of eating, exercising, and smoking.

Nowadays the great challenge seems to lie in improving the kind of lives we lead. It seems more important than extending life by a year or two to enhance the quality of those seventy or eighty years by elevating the current level of our common courtesy, moral rights, education, employment, and contentment. This refocusing on the quality, rather than the quantity, of life has profound implications for our changing views on death and for our treatment of the dying.

Certainly one of the most refreshing currents in the changing thanatological wind is the increasing emphasis on a "humanistic" approach to death—an approach that seems to parallel the humanistic trends in other sectors of society today. This new approach is seen, for example, in an increasing concern that the dying individual live as fully and as richly as possible until death and that communication with the dying be tailored to specific human needs, and in the recognition of a need for special therapies to help those who have suffered the loss of someone close. Indeed, this humanistic trend in the treatment of the dying and those immediately affected by death is causing a complete reexamination of the premises on which we have traditionally based our views of death and dying.

A very impressive aspect of thanatology in the current scene is the dynamic and changing nature of its vital issues. Consider, for example, the swirl of debate around organ transplantation, tied directly to the definition of "death"—does death occur when the heart stops? When the vital signs are gone? Or when the cradle of consciousness, the brain, ceases to generate electrical energy? (The last-named criterion is the one emphasized in the famous Harvard report on "brain death" [Beecher et al., 1968]). One expert (Glaser, 1970) summed it up this way: "The brain is our master control; the heart is just a pump." Or, to put it another way: "No brain, no personality," (Murray, 1951).

And if there is controversy over the definition of "death"—or "How does one take a live heart from a dead person?"—there is a potential moral and legal storm over the issue of voluntary euthanasia. If, as has been said, war is too important to be left to generals, then is a life too precious (or too miserable) to be left solely to the judgment of doctors? Should a weakened citizen, too ill to kill himself, have the right to say, "Enough!" And, consider what we read and know of occasional heinous derelictions in some nursing homes, what are the chances, without any opportunity for redress, of abuses in the practice of voluntary euthanasia? For young readers especially, these questions may become real issues before their time to die.

One additional current trend can be mentioned. Today there is a new permissiveness regarding death, almost an urgency to speak and think about it. In this century death has become, as Gorer (1965) says, the new pornography—a subject banned from polite society and social discourse. Yet, in the last few years there has been a spate of books on death; death has become a respectable field of inquiry, particularly in the social and behavioral sciences; and death has become an acceptable topic of study in the college curriculum.

The cultural revolution that we are experiencing today is effecting sweeping changes in the pattern and texture of our lives, changes that are now reaching to the very threshold of our deaths. The scope and impact of these changes concerning death are the concern of this book.

Notes

1 Thanatology is the study of death and dying, after Thanatos, the mythological Greek god of death, twin of Hypnus, the god of sleep.

2 This passage is from the chapter "The Funeral" in Herman Melville's masterpiece, *Moby Dick*.

References

Beecher, Henry K., *et al.*, A Definition of Irreversible Coma. *Journal of the American Medical Association*, 1968, 205, 85–88.

Dublin, Louis I. *After Eighty Years.* Gainesville: University of Florida Press, 1966.

Dubos, Rene. *The Mirage of Health.* New York: Harper, 1971.

Elliot, Gil. *The Twentieth Century Book of the Dead.* New York: Ballantine Books, 1972.

Glaser, Robert J. Innovations and Heroic Acts in Prolonging Life. In Orville G. Brim, Jr., *et al.* (eds.), *The Dying Patient.* New York: Russell Sage Foundation, 1970.

Gorer, Geoffrey. *Death, Grief and Mourning.* New York: Anchor Books, 1965.

Kahn, Herman. *On Themonuclear War.* Princeton: Princeton University Press, 1960.

Lifton, Robert Jay. *Death in Life: Survivors of Hiroshima.* New York: Vantage Books, 1967.

Murray, Henry A. Some Basic Psychological Assumptions and Conceptions. *Dialectica*, 1951, 5, 266–292.

PART I
DIMENSIONS
OF DEATH

Contents

"Death" is a word that has a dozen meanings. Some of these meanings describe various "dimensions" of death. (It almost sounds as though Death were a reified corpse being measured for a coffin.)

In contemporary discussions on the topic, these dimensions include the distinction between death and dying, and the all-important distinction between "my death" and "your death" (i.e., all other deaths); the pivotal role played by the denial of death; the twentieth-century pornography of death; the ways in which some deaths are more "appropriate" than others; the sociology (specifically, the social inequality) of death; and the demography (the factual figures) of death.

These six chapters are written by a historian, two anthropologists, a psychiatrist, a sociologist, and a public health specialist.

This part teaches us that no single-sentence definition of death is likely to encompass the diverse meanings and multiple dimensions contained in that elusive concept.

1 · The Relation Between Life and Death, Living and Dying

Arnold Toynbee

Arnold Toynbee, an internationally famous English historian, is best known for A Study of History, *a ten-volume work written between 1934 and 1954. In the moving Epilogue of his book* Man's Concern with Death, *from which the following essay is excerpted, Professor Toynbee introduces us to the concept that the suffering of death is a dyadic event, involving two parties. These passages serve excellently to introduce the other selections in this section.*

Premature death may be incurred in various ways. It may be inflicted by human hands deliberately either by public enterprise (war and the execution of judicial death sentences) or by private enterprise (murder). It may be inflicted by nonhuman living creatures (bacteria, sharks, man-eating tigers). It may be caused by hunger, thirst, exposure to the elements—defeats of man by nonhuman nature that have been becoming less frequent in the economically "developed" minority of mankind, though the reduction of the rate of premature deaths from these causes among this minority is being offset by an increase in the rate of premature deaths caused by accidents—particularly in the form of miscarriages of our increasingly high-powered machinery which, in its application to our means of locomotion, has enabled us to "annihilate distance" at the price of a high toll of deaths in road vehicles and in aeroplanes. (The toll taken by the now obsolescent railway train was comparatively light.)

Since death is irretrievable, the deliberate infliction of premature death by one human being on another is surely a heinous offense—and this not only in murder and in war, but also in the execution of judicial death sentences. Murder has been almost universally condemned—though there have been, and still are, some exceptional societies in which a youth does not qualify for being accepted as a man until he has taken another man's life. Killing in war has, till now, been almost universally regarded as being respectable—though a misgiving about its respectability is betrayed in the euphemistic use of the word "defense" to signify war and preparation for war, however aggressive the intention. For instance, the Spartan official formula for a mobilization order with the object of invading a foreign country was "to declare a state of defense" (*phouran phainein*); and the costs of genocidal atomic weapons are entered under the rubric "defense" in the budgets of present-day states. The infliction of premature death by process of law has been approved of still more widely and confidently than the infliction of it by act of war. When the abolition of the death penalty has been mooted, this has usually aroused violent controversy; yet the abolition of it is now an accomplished fact in some states in the present-day world. The reason for this obstinately resisted abandonment of an age-old practice is that "while there is life there is hope." A change of heart may be experienced by even the most apparently hardened criminal.

We ought not to be reconciled to premature death when this is caused by human design or callousness or incompetence or carelessness. Yet there are cases in which even premature death is acceptable—the cases in which it has been risked and suffered voluntarily for the benefit of some fellow human being or of mankind in general. Voluntary premature death in war is the form of heroic self-sacrifice that has been both the most frequently performed and the most enthusiastically applauded; yet this is also the form of heroism that is the most ambivalent, since a man who is killed in war dies prematurely in the act of trying to inflict premature death on some of his fellow human beings. There is nothing questionable about the heroism of the premature death of someone who sacrifices his or her life in trying to save a fellow human being from meeting death by, say, drowning or burning; and we can also accept, while we lament, the premature death of pioneers and inventors who have deliberately risked their lives in the cause of making life better for mankind as a whole.

Many men have sacrificed their lives prematurely in winning for mankind, by daring and dangerous experimentation, the art of domesticating wild animals, the art of navigation, the art of aviation. (Scaling the Matterhorn, reaching the poles, and breaking out of the earth's air-envelope into outer space do not seem to me to be objectives for which lives ought to have been risked and lost.) Many physicians have sacrificed their lives prematurely by tending the victims of deadly contagious diseases, or by experimenting perilously on themselves. My grandfather, who was a doctor, killed himself, unintentionally, when he was at the height of his powers, by experimenting on himself, in the early days of the use of anaesthetics, in order to discover what the right degree of dosage was. So there are circumstances in which premature death is not unacceptable, however grievous it may be.

What are we to say about the premature death of the spirit in a human body that still remains physically alive? I am familiar with this form of premature death too—the death-in-life of insanity and senility. I have been at very close quarters with a human being who lived on physically to a higher age than I have reached now for more than thirty years—about three-eighths of his total span of physical life—after he had suffered the death of the spirit. I have also known intimately three persons—two of them dominating personalities and the third a robust one—who have succumbed to senility in old age. This premature death of a human spirit in advance of the death of its body is more appalling than any premature death in which spirit and body die simultaneously. It is an outrage committed by nature on human dignity. "Slay us," nature or God, if you choose or if you must, but slay us "in the light."[1] Allow the light of reason—the faculty that makes a human being—to survive in us till the end of the life of the body. The spectacle of insanity and senility has always appalled me more than the witnessing or the hearing of a physical death. But there are two sides to this situation; there is the victim's side, as well as the spectator's; and what is harrowing for the spectator may be alleviating for the victim.

It will not, of course be alleviation for him if the failure of his mental faculties overtakes him only gradually and then only to a degree that leaves him aware of what is happening to him. I can think of no worse fate than this, and I have seen it befall my oldest and closest friend—a man three months younger than myself. Our friendship had begun at school when we were thirteen years old and had continued for more than sixty years before he died. One could hardly suffer a greater loss than I suffered in losing him. Yet I could not and cannot regret his death, grievously though I miss him; for his death was, for him a merciful release from a distress that was irremediable and that was becoming excruciating for him. As for those other three friends of mine, they did not suffer as my poor school fellow suffered; for their mental eclipse was, not partial, but total—as complete as if they had been dead physically as well as mentally—and, for two of the three, this mental death, so far from being a torment, was a release from acute unhappiness. One of these two had previously been in a constant state of painful anxiety, fretfulness, and tension; and, for her, senility brought with it a serenity that she had not enjoyed since her early years. The other, who was love incarnate, had been inconsolable for the loss of her husband till she was released from her unbearable grief by oblivion—a mental death which was a merciful anticipation of the physical death that was tardy in coming to her rescue.

This two-sidedness of death is a fundamental feature of death—not only of the premature death of the spirit, but of death at any age and in any form. There are always two parties to a death; the person who dies and the survivors who are bereaved.

Death releases its prey instantly from all further suffering in this world —and from any further suffering at all, if one does not believe in personal immortality or in metempsychosis, but believes either that death spells annihilation or that it spells reabsorption into the Ultimate Spiritual Reality from which the life of a human personality is a temporary aberration.

Lucretius believed that death spells annihilation, and that it therefore confers on the dead a total and everlasting immunity from suffering, either mental or physical. He preaches the nihilist gospel of salvation with a passionate conviction and a fervent concern for the relief of his fellow mortals that make this passage of his poem[2] particularly memorable.

> Death, then is null for us—null and irrelevant—in virtue of the conclusion that the spirit of man is mortal. We felt no ill in that past age in which the Phoenicians were flocking to battle from all quarters—an age in which the whole earth was rocked by the fearful turmoil of war, rocked till it quaked horrifyingly under the lofty ceiling of the air; an age in which the fate of all mankind was trembling in the balance. One of the two contending powers was going to win worldwide dominion on both land and sea, and none could foresee which of the two would be the winner. Well, we felt no ill in

that age, and we shall feel no ill, either, when we have ceased to exist—when once soul and body, whose union constitutes our being, have parted company with each other. We shall have ceased to exist; that is the point; and this means that, thenceforward, nothing whatsoever can happen to us, that nothing can awaken any feeling in us—no, not even if land were to fuse with sea, and sea with sky . . .[3]

We can feel assured that, in death, there is nothing to be afraid of. If one is nonexistent, one is immune from misery. When once immortal death has relieved us of mortal life, it is as good as if we had never been born . . .[4]

So, when you see someone indulging indignantly in self-pity [at the thought of his body's destiny after death], you may be sure that, though he himself may deny that he believes that, in death, he will retain any capacity for feeling, his profession of faith does not ring true. It is belied by a latent emotion that is subconscious. As I see it, he is not really conceding his premise and its basis. He is not removing and ejecting himself from life radically. Unconsciously he is making some vestige of himself survive . . . He is not dissociating himself fully from his castaway corpse; he is identifying himself with it and is infusing into it his own capacity for feeling, under the illusion that he is standing there beside it. This is the cause of his indignant self-pity at having been created mortal. He fails to see that, in real death, he will have no second self that will be still alive and capable of lamenting to itself over its own death, or of grieving, as he stands, in imagination, over his prostrate self, that he is being mangled by beasts of prey or is being cremated.[5]

Lucretius goes on to put his finger on the difference between the fate of the dead and the fate of the survivors. He pictures a dead man's wife and children saying, as they stand by his funeral pyre:

"Poor wretch, what a wretched fate. One cruel day has deprived you of all the blessings of life." But, in this pass, they do not go on to say: "However, death has simultaneously released you from any desire for these blessings." If they realised this truth clearly and matched it in what they said, they would be able to release their souls from a heavy burden of anguish and fear. "You," they would say, "are now oblivious in death, and in that state you will remain until the end of time, exempt from all pain and grief. It is we who are the sufferers; it is we who, standing by you, reduced to ashes on the appalling pyre, have mourned you to the limit of human capacity for grief, and find ourselves still inconsolable. Our sorrow is everlasting. The day will never come that will relieve our hearts of it."[6]

From this Lucretius draws the following conclusion in the lines that immediately follow.

So this man [who feels an indignant self-pity in contemplating his future after death] has to be confronted with the question: What is there that is particularly bitter in this future, if it is just a return to sleep and quiet? What is there in this prospect that should make anyone pine away in everlasting grief?[7]

This lapse of a sensitive spirit into such obtuse complacency pulls up Lucretius's reader with a jerk. Is a man who is feeling distress at the prospect of his own death going to be totally relieved by the realization that his death will automatically bring with it an immunity from suffering from himself? Is he going to feel no concern for the grief of his bereaved wife and children? Is his certainty of "everlasting" peace and quiet for himself in death going to console him for the "everlasting" sorrow of the survivors?

It may be answered that, though the poet has used—and perhaps deliberately used—the same word "everlasting" to describe the respective states of the survivors and of the dead, the application of the word to the survivors is an exaggeration, considering that they, in their turn, are going to attain, sooner or later, "the return to sleep and quiet" that death brings to every mortal in the end. Meanwhile, they are going, on Lucretius's own showing, to experience the extreme of suffering; and Lucretius has denied himself the license to play this suffering down on the ground that it will be only temporary; for in a later passage,[8] he argues, eloquently and convincingly, that the fancied everlasting torments of the damned in hell after death are fabulous projections of genuine torments—mostly self-inflicted—which we experience in this life. "It is here, in this world," he sums up the argument of this passage in its last line, "that people make life hell through their own stupidity." Yet he has admitted that bereavement makes life hell, here in this world, for the bereaved. Is he prepared to write off their torment, too, as the self-inflicted penalty for a stupidity that is avoidable and reprehensible?

The truth is that Lucretius has been preoccupied by his characteristically impetuous effort to deprive death of its sting and the grave of its victory for the person who is dreading the prospect of death for himself. He has overlooked the crucial fact that, in death, there are two parties to the event. "For none of us liveth to himself and no man dieth to himself."[9] Man is a social creature; and a fact of capital importance about death's sting is that it is two-pronged. Lucretius may have succeeded in excising the sting for the person who dies, but he has failed to excise it for the dead's survivors. It looks, indeed, as if he has been blind to the significance of the pain of bereavement that he has described incidentally in such moving words. Euripides had been more perceptive. After asking if the experience that we call dying is not really living, and if living is not really dying,[10] he immediately goes on to observe that the spectators of a death are not saved from suffering by their awareness that the dead are exempt from all suffering and from all ills.

When, therefore, I ask myself whether I am reconciled to death, I have to distinguish, in each variant of the situation, between being reconciled to death on my own account and being reconciled to it on the account of the other party. Supposing that I am really reconciled to the prospect of my own death at a ripe old age, am I also reconciled to the prospect of the sorrow and the loneliness that death is going to bring upon my wife if she survives me? Supposing that I feel that people who have risked and suffered premature death deliberately for the sake of fellow human beings have found a satisfactory fulfilment of the possibilities of life for themselves, am I reconciled to the loss that their premature deaths have inflicted on mankind, including me? (This question is the theme of George Meredith's novel *Beauchamp's Career.*) Supposing that I feel that the oblivion conferred by senility or insanity has been a boon for someone who was suffering spiritual agony so long as he was in full possession of his mental and spiritual faculties, am I reconciled to my loss of this friend through his lapse into a death-in-life? And, apart from my personal loss, am I reconciled to the brutal affront to human dignity that nature has committed in choosing this humiliating way of releasing a human being from spiritual suffering?

Finally, am I reconciled to the prospect that I may survive my wife, even supposing that she lives to a ripe old age in full possession of her faculties and without suffering more than the minimum of physical pain that is the normal accompaniment of death even in its easiest forms, with the exception of instantaneous deaths and deaths in sleep? The hard fact is that the ways of dying that impose the lightest ordeal on the person who dies are, by their very nature, the ways that inevitably make the shock for the survivors the severest. I have mentioned an old friend of mine whose unbearable grief for the death of her husband was eventually obliterated by the oblivion of senility. The shock that she had suffered had been extreme. She had found her husband lying dead in his bed one morning. He had appeared to be in normal health the day before; but for some years his heart had been weak, and he had died from heart failure in his sleep—peacefully and almost certainly painlessly; I myself recently had the experience of receiving a severe shock from learning of the sudden death of someone with whom my life had once been intimately bound up, though, in this case too, the death had not been a lingering one or been physically painful, and had come at an age—six months younger than mine—at which death is to be expected.

If one truly loves a fellow human being, one ought to wish that as little as possible of the pain of his or her death shall be suffered by him or by her, and that as much of it as possible shall be borne by oneself. One ought to wish this, and one can, perhaps, succeed in willing it with one's mind. But can one genuinely desire it in one's heart? Can one genuinely long to be the survivor at the coming time when death will terminate a companionship that is more precious to one than one's life—a companionship without which one's life would be a burden, not a boon? Is it possible for love to raise human nature to this height of unselfishness? I cannot answer this question for anyone except myself, and, in my own case, before the time comes, I can only guess what my reaction is likely to be. I have already avowed a boastful guess that I shall be able to meet my own death with equanimity. I have now to avow another guess that puts me to shame. I guess that if, one day, I am told by my doctor that I am going to die before my wife, I shall receive the news not only with equanimity but with relief. This relief, if I do feel it, will be involuntary. I shall be ashamed of myself for feeling it, and my relief will, no doubt, be tempered by concern and sorrow for my wife's future after I have been taken from her. All the same, I do guess that, if I am informed that I am going to die before her, a shameful sense of relief will be one element in my reaction.

My own conclusion is evident. My answer to Saint Paul's question "O death, where is thy sting?" is Saint Paul's own answer: "The sting of death is sin." The sin that I mean is the sin of selfishly failing to wish to survive the death of someone with whose life my own life is bound up. This is selfish because the sting of death is less sharp for the person who dies than it is for the bereaved survivor.

This is, as I see it, the capital fact about the relation between living and dying. There are two parties to the suffering that death inflicts; and, in the apportionment of this suffering; the survivor takes the brunt.

Notes

1 *Iliad*, Book XVII, line 647.
2 Lucretius *De Rerum Natura*, Book III, lines 830–930, minus lines 912–18, which have been misplaced in the surviving manuscripts.
3 *Ibid.*, lines 830–42.
4 *Ibid.*, lines 866–69.
5 *Ibid.*, lines 870–87.

Ernest Becker

Ernest Becker (1924–1974) won the Pulitzer Prize for general nonfiction in 1974 for The Denial of Death. *After receiving a Ph.D. in Cultural Anthropology from Syracuse University, Dr. Becker taught at the University of California at Berkeley, San Francisco State College, and Simon Fraser University in Canada. He was the author of* The Birth and Death of Meaning, Revolution in Psychiatry, The Structure of Evil, Angel in Armor, *and* Escape from Evil. *Becker's main theme in this unusual book is that our entire lives are organized around our fear and denial of death. The chapter "The Terror of Death" is a discussion of this deep-seated fear especially in relation to its opposite, heroism.*

It is not for us to confess that in our civilized attitude towards death we are once more living psychologically beyond our means, and must reform and give truth its due? Would it not be better to give death the place in actuality and in our thoughts which properly belongs to it, and to yield a little more prominence to that unconscious attitude towards death which we have hitherto so carefully suppressed? This hardly seems indeed a greater achievement, but rather a backward step . . . but it has the merit of taking somewhat more into account the true state of affairs. . . .

—Sigmund Freud[1]

The first thing we have to do with heroism is to lay bare its underside, show what gives human heroics its specific nature and impetus. Here we introduce directly one of the great rediscoveries of modern thought: That of all things that move man, one of the principal ones is his terror of death. After Darwin the problem of death as an evolutionary one came to the fore, and many thinkers immediately saw that it was a major psychological problem for man.[2] They also very quickly saw what real heroism was about, as Shaler wrote just at the turn of the century:[3] heroism is first and foremost a reflex of the terror of death. We admire most the courage to face death; we give such valor our highest and most constant adoration; it moves us deeply in our hearts because we have doubts about how brave we ourselves would be. When we see a man bravely facing his own extinction we rehearse the greatest victory we can imagine. And so the hero has been the center of human honor and acclaim since probably the beginning of specifically human evolution. But even before that our primate ancestors deferred to others who were extrapowerful and courageous and ignored those who were cowardly. Man has elevated animal courage into a cult.

Anthropological and historical research also began, in the nineteenth century, to put together a picture of the heroic since primitive and ancient times. The hero was the man who could go into the spirit world, the world of the dead, and return alive. He had his descendants in the mystery cults of the Eastern Mediterranean, which were cults of death and resurrection. The divine hero of each of these cults was one who had come back from the dead. And as we know today from the research into ancient myths and rituals, Christianity itself was a competitor with the mystery cults and won out— among other reasons—because it, too, featured a healer with supernatural powers who had risen from the dead. The great triumph of Easter is the joyful shout "Christ has risen!", an echo of the same joy that the devotees of the mystery cults enacted at their ceremonies of the victory over death. These cults, as G. Stanley Hall so aptly put it, were an attempt to attain "an immunity bath" from the greatest evil: death and the dread of it.[4] All historical religions addressed themselves to this same problem of how to bear the end of life. Religions like Hinduism and Buddhism performed the ingenious trick of pretending not to want to be reborn, which is a sort of negative magic: claiming not to want what you really want most.[5] When philosophy took over from religion it also took over religion's central problem, and death became the real "muse of philosophy" from its beginnings in Greece right through Heidegger and modern existentialism.[6]

We already have volumes of work and thought on the subject, from religion and philosophy and—since Darwin—from science itself. The problem is how to make sense out of it; the accumulation of research and opinion on the fear of death is already too large to be dealt with and summarized in any simple way. The revival of interest in death, in the last few decades, has alone already piled up a formidable literature, and this literature does not point in any single direction.

THE "HEALTHY-MINDED" ARGUMENT

There are "healthy-minded" persons who maintain that fear of death is not a natural thing for man, that we are not born with it. An increasing number of careful studies on how the actual fear of death develops in the child[7] agree fairly well that the child has no knowledge of death until about the age of three to five. How could he? It is too abstract an idea, too removed from his experience. He lives in a world that is full of living, acting things, responding to him, amusing him, feeding him. He doesn't know what it means for life to disappear forever, nor theorize where it would go. Only gradually does he recognize that there is a thing called death that takes some people away forever; very reluctantly he comes to admit that it sooner or later takes everyone away, but this gradual realization of the inevitability of death can take up until the ninth or tenth year.

If the child has no knowledge of an abstract idea like absolute negation, he does have his own anxieties. He is absolutely dependent on the mother, experiences loneliness when she is absent, frustration when he is deprived of gratification, irritation at hunger and discomfort, and so on. If he were abandoned to himself his world would drop away, and his organism must sense this at some level; we call this the anxiety of object-loss. Isn't this anxiety, then, a natural, organismic fear of annihilation? Again, there are many who look at this as a very relative matter. They believe that if the mother has done her job in a warm and dependable way, the child's natural anxieties and guilts will develop in a moderate way, and he will be able to place them firmly under the control of his developing personality.[8] The child who has good maternal experiences will develop a sense of basic security and will not be subject to morbid fears of losing support, of being annihilated, or the like.[9] As he grows up to understand death rationally by the age of nine or ten, he will accept it as part of his world view, but the idea will not poison his self-confident attitude toward life. The psychiatrist Rheingold says categorically that annihilation anxiety is not part of the child's natural experience but is engendered in him by bad experiences with a depriving mother.[10] This theory puts the whole burden of anxiety onto the child's nurture and not his nature. Another psychiatrist, in a less extreme vein, sees the fear of death as greatly heightened by the child's experiences with his parents, by their hostile denial of his life impulses, and more generally, by the antagonism of society to human freedom and self-expansiveness.[11]

As we will see later on, this view is very popular today in the widespread movement toward unrepressed living, the urge to a new freedom for natural biological urges, a new attitude of pride and joy in the body, the abandonment of shame, guilt, and self-hatred. From this point of view, fear of death is something that society creates and at the same time uses against the person to keep him in submission; the psychiatrist Moloney talked about it as a "culture mechanism," and Marcuse as an "ideology."[12] Norman O. Brown, in a vastly influential book that we shall discuss at some length, went so far as to say that there could be a birth and development of the child in a "second innocence" that would be free of the fear of death because it would not deny natural vitality and would leave the child fully open to physical living.[13]

It is easy to see that, from this point of view, those who have bad early experiences will be most morbidly fixated on the anxiety of death; and if by chance they grow up to be philosophers they will probably make the idea a central dictum of their thoughts—as did Schopenhauer, who both hated his mother and went on to pronounce death the "muse of philosophy." If you have a "sour" character structure or especially tragic experiences, then you are bound to be pessimistic. One psychologist remarked to me that the whole idea of the fear of death was an import by existentialists and Protestant theologians who had been scarred by their European experiences or who carried around the extra weight of a Calvinist and Lutheran heritage of life-denial. Even the distinguished psychologist Gardner Murphy seems to lean to this school and urges us to study *the person* who exhibits the fear of death, who places anxiety in the center of his thought; and Murphy asks why the living of life in love and joy cannot also be regarded as real and basic.[14]

THE "MORBIDLY-MINDED" ARGUMENT

The "healthy-minded" argument just discussed is one side of the picture of the accumulated research and opinion on the problem of the fear of death, but there is another side. A large body of people would agree with these observations on early experience and would admit that experiences may heighten natural anxieties and later fears, but these people would also claim very strongly that nevertheless the fear of death is natural and is present in everyone, that it is the basic fear that influences all others, a fear from which no one is immune, no matter how disguised it may be. William James spoke very early for this school, and with his usual colorful realism be called death "the worm at the core" of man's pretensions to happiness.[15] No less a student of human nature than Max Scheler thought that all men must have some kind of certain intuition of this "worm at the core," whether they admitted it or not.[16] Countless other authorities—some of whom we shall parade in the following pages—belong to this school: students of the stature of Freud, many of his close circle, and serious researchers who are not psychoanalysts. What are we to make of a dispute in which they are two distinct camps, both studded with distinguished authorities? Jacques Choron goes so far as to say that it is questionable whether it will ever be possible to decide whether the fear of death is or is not the basic anxiety.[17] In matters like this, then, the most that one can do is to take sides, to give an opinion based on the authorities that seem to him most compelling, and to present some of the compelling arguments.

I frankly side with this second school—in fact, this whole book is a network of arguments based on the universality of the fear of death, or "terror" as I prefer to call it, in order to convey how all-consuming it is when we look it full in the face. The first document that I want to present and linger on is a paper written by the noted psychoanalyst Gregory Zilboorg; it is an especially penetrating essay that—for succinctness and scope—has not been much improved upon, even though it appeared several decades ago.[18] Zilboorg says that most people think death fear is absent because it rarely shows its true face; but he argues that underneath all appearances fear of death is universally present:

> For behind the sense of insecurity in the face of danger, behind the sense of discouragement and depression, there always lurks the basic fear of death, a fear which undergoes most complex elaborations and manifests itself in many indirect ways. . . . No one is free of the fear of death. . . . The anxiety neuroses, the various phobic states, even a considerably number of depressive suicidal states and many schizophrenias amply demonstrate the ever-present fear of death which becomes woven into the major conflicts of the given psychopathological conditions. . . . We may take for granted that the fear of death is always present in our mental functioning.[19]

Hadn't James said the same thing earlier, in his own way?

> Let sanguine healthy-mindedness do its best with its strange power of living in the moment and ignoring and forgetting, still the evil background is really there to be thought of, and the skull will grin in at the banquet.[20]

The difference in these two statements is not so much in the imagery and
style as in the fact that Zilboorg's comes almost a half-century later and is
based on that much more real clinical work, not only on philosophical
speculation or personal intuition. But it also continues the straight line of
development from James and the post-Darwinians who saw the fear of death
as a biological and evolutionary problem. Here I think he is on very sound
ground, and I especially like the way he puts the case. Zilboorg points out
that this fear is actually an expression of the instinct of self-preservation
which functions as a constant drive to maintain life and to master the
dangers that threaten life:

> Such constant expenditure of psychological energy on the business of
> preserving life would be impossible if the fear of death were not as
> constant. The very term "self-preservation" implies an effort against
> some force of disintegration; the affective aspect of this is fear, fear of
> death.[21]

In other words, the fear of death must be present behind all our normal
functioning, in order for the organism to be armed toward self-preservation.
But the fear of death cannot be present constantly in one's mental functioning, else the organism could not function. Zilboorg continues:

> If this fear were as constantly conscious, we should be unable to
> function normally. It must be properly repressed to keep us living with
> any modicum of comfort. We know very well that to repress means
> more than to put away and to forget that which was put away and the
> place where we put it. It means also to maintain a constant
> psychological effort to keep the lid on and inwardly never relax our
> watchfulness.[22]

And so we can understand what seems like an impossible paradox: the
ever-present fear of death in the normal biological functioning of our instinct
of self-preservation, as well as our utter obliviousness to this fear in our
conscious life:

> Therefore in normal times we move about actually without ever
> believing in our own death, as if we fully believed in our own
> corporeal immortality. We are intent on mastering death. . . . A man
> will say, of course, that he knows he will die some day, but he does
> not really care. He is having a good time with living, and he does not
> think about death and does not care to bother about it—but this is a
> purely intellectual, verbal admission. The affect of fear is repressed.[23]

The argument from biology and evolution is basic and has to be taken
seriously; I don't see how it can be left out of any discussion. Animals in order
to survive have had to be protected by fear-responses, in relation not only to
other animals but to nature itself. They had to see the real relationship of
their limited powers to the dangerous world in which they were immersed.
Reality and fear go together naturally. As the human infant is in an even more

exposed and helpless situation, it is foolish to assume that the fear response of animals would have disappeared in such a weak and highly sensitive species. It is more reasonable to think that it was instead heightened, as some of the early Darwinians thought: early men who were most afraid were those who were realistic about their situation in nature, and they passed on to their offspring a realism that had a high survival value.[24] The result was the emergence of man as we know him: a hyperanxious animal who constantly invents reasons for anxiety even where there are none.

The argument from psychoanalysis is less speculative and has to be taken even more seriously. It showed us something about the child's inner world that we had never realized: namely, that it was more filled with terror, the more the child was different from other animals. We could say that fear is programmed into the lower animals by ready-made instincts; but an animal who has no instincts has no programmed fears. Man's fears are fashioned out of the ways in which he perceives the world. Now, what is unique about the child's perception of the world? For one thing, the extreme confusion of cause-and-effect relationships; for another, extreme unreality about the limits of his own powers. The child lives in a situation of utter dependence; and when his needs are met it must seem to him that he has magical powers, real omnipotence. If he experiences pain, hunger, or discomfort, all he has to do is to scream and he is relieved and lulled by gentle, loving sounds. He is a magician and a telepath who has only to mumble and to imagine and the world turns to his desires.

But now the penalty for such perceptions. In a magical world where things cause other things to happen just by a mere thought or a look of displeasure, anything can happen to anyone. When the child experiences inevitable and real frustrations from his parents, he directs hate and destructive feelings toward them; and he has no way of knowing that malevolent feelings cannot be fulfilled by the same magic as were his other wishes. Psychoanalysts believe that this confusion is a main cause of guilt and helplessness in the child. In his very fine essay Wahl summed up this paradox:

> ... the socialization processes for all children are painful and
> frustrating, and hence no child escapes forming hostile death wishes
> toward his socializers. Therefore, none escape the fear of personal
> death in either direct or symbolic form. Repression is usually ...
> immediate and effective. . . .[25]

The child is too weak to take responsibility for all this destructive feeling, and he can't control the magical execution of his desires. This is what we mean by an immature ego: the child doesn't have the sure ability to organize his perceptions and his relationship to the world; he can't control his own activity; and he doesn't have sure command over the acts of others. He thus has no real control over the magical cause-and-effect that he senses, either inside himself or outside in nature and in others: his destructive wishes could explode, his parents' wishes likewise. The forces of nature are confused, externally and internally; and for a weak ego this fact makes for quantities of exaggerated potential power and added terror. The result is that the child—at least some of the time—lives with an inner sense of chaos that other animals are immune to.[26]

Ironically, even when the child makes out real cause-and-effect relationships they become a burden to him because he overgeneralizes them. One such generalization is what the psychoanalysts call the "talion principle." The child crushes insects, sees the cat eat a mouse and make it vanish, joins with the family to make a pet rabbit disappear into their interiors, and so on. He comes to know something about the power relations of the world but can't give them relative value: the parents could eat him and make him vanish, and he could likewise eat them; when the father gets a fierce glow in his eyes as he clubs a rat, the watching child might also expect to be clubbed—especially if he has been thinking bad magical thoughts.

I don't want to seem to make an exact picture of processes that are still unclear to us or to make out that all children live in the same world and have the same problems; also, I wouldn't want to make the child's world seem more lurid than it really is most of the time; but I think it is important to show the painful contradictions that must be present in it at least some of the time and to show how fantastic a world it surely is for the first few years of the child's life. Perhaps then we could understand better why Zilboorg said that the fear of death "undergoes most complex elaborations and manifests itself in many indirect ways." Or, as Wahl so perfectly put it, death is a *complex symbol* and not any particular, sharply defined thing to a child:

> ... the child's concept of death is not a single thing, but it is rather a composite of mutually contradictory paradoxes ... death itself is not only a state, but a complex symbol, the significance of which will vary from one person to another and from one culture to another.[27]

We could understand, too, why children have their recurrent nightmares, their universal phobias of insects and mean dogs. In their tortured interiors radiate complex symbols of many inadmissible realities—terror of the world, the horror of one's own wishes, the fear of vengeance by the parents, the disappearance of things, one's lack of control over anything, really. It is too much for any animal to take, but the child has to take it, and he wakes up screaming with almost punctual regularity during the period when his weak ego is in the process of consolidating things.

THE "DISAPPEARANCE" OF THE FEAR OF DEATH

Yet, the nightmares become more and more widely spaced, and some children have more than others: we are back again to the beginning of our discussion, to those who do not believe that the fear of death is normal, who think that it is a neurotic exaggeration that draws on bad early experiences. Otherwise, they say, how explain that so many people—the vast majority— seem to survive the flurry of childhood nightmares and go on to live a healthy, more-or-less optimistic life, untroubled by death? As Montaigne said, the peasant has a profound indifference and a patience toward death and the sinister side of life; and if we say that this is because of his stupidity, then "let's all learn from stupidity."[28] Today, when we know more than Montaigne, we would say "let's all learn from repression"—but the moral would have just as much weight: repression takes care of the complex symbol of death for most people.

But its disappearance doesn't mean that the fear was never there. The argument of those who believe in the universality of the innate terror of death rests its case mostly on what we know about how effective repression is. The argument can probably never be cleanly decided: if you claim that a concept is not present because it is repressed, you can't lose; it is not a fair game, intellectually, because you always hold the trump card. This type of argument makes psychoanalysis seem unscientific to many people, the fact that its proponents can claim that someone denies one of their concepts because he represses his consciousness of its truth.

But repression is not a magical word for winning arguments; it is a real phenomenon, and we have been able to study in many of its workings. This study gives it legitimacy as a scientific concept and makes it a more-or-less dependable ally in our argument. For one thing, there is a growing body of research trying to get at the consciousness of death denied by repression that uses psychological tests such as measuring galvanic skin responses; it strongly suggests that underneath the most bland exterior lurks the universal anxiety, the "worm at the core."[29]

For another thing, there is nothing like shocks in the real world to jar loose repressions. Recently psychiatrists reported an increase in anxiety neuroses in children as a result of the earth tremors in Southern California. For these children the discovery that life really includes cataclysmic danger was too much for their still-imperfect denial systems—hence open outbursts of anxiety. With adults we see this manifestation of anxiety in the face of impending catastrophe where it takes the form of panic. Recently several people suffered broken limbs and other injuries after forcing open their airplane's safety door during take-off and jumping from the wing to the ground; the incident was triggered by the backfire of an engine. Obviously underneath these harmless noises other things are rumbling in the creature.

But even more important is how repression works: it is not simply a negative force opposing life energies; it lives on life energies and uses them creatively. I mean that fears are naturally absorbed by expansive organismic striving. Nature seems to have built into organisms an innate healthy-mindedness; it expresses itself in self-delight in the pleasure of unfolding one's capacities into the world, in the incorporation of things in that world, and in feeding on its limitless experiences. This is a lot of very positive experience, and when a powerful organism moves with it, it gives contentment. As Santayana once put it: a lion must feel more secure that God is on his side than a gazelle. On the most elemental level the organism works actively against its own fragility by seeking to expand and perpetuate itself in living experience; instead of shrinking, it moves toward more life. Also, it does one thing at a time, avoiding needless distractions from all-absorbing activity; in this way, it would seem, fear of death can be carefully ignored or actually absorbed in the life-expanding processes. Occasionally we seem to see such a vital organism on the human level: I am thinking of the portrait of *Zorba the Greek* drawn by Nikos Kazantzakis. Zorba was an ideal of the nonchalant victory of all-absorbing daily passion over timidity and death, and he purged others in his life-affirming flame. But Kazantzakis himself was no Zorba—which is partly why the character of Zorba rang a bit false—nor are most other men. Still, everyone enjoys a working amount of basic narcissism, even though it is not a lion's. The child who is well nourished and loved develops, as we said, a sense of magical omnipotence, a sense of his own indestructibility, a feeling of proven power and secure support. He can imagine himself, deep down, to be eternal. We might say that his repression of the idea of his own death is made easy for him because he is fortified against it in his very narcissistic vitality. This type of character probably helped Freud to say that the unconscious does not know death. Anyway, we know that basic narcissism is increased when one's childhood experiences have been securely life-supporting and warmly enhancing to the sense of self, to the feeling of being really special, truly Number One in creation. The result is that some people have more of what the psychoanalyst Leon J. Saul has aptly called "Inner Sustainment."[30] It is a sense of bodily confidence in the face of experience that sees the person more easily through severe life crises and even sharp personality changes; it almost seems to take the place of the directive instincts of lower animals. One can't help thinking of Freud again, who had more inner sustainment than most men, thanks to his mother and favorable early environment; he knew the confidence and courage that it gave to a man, and he himself faced up to life and to a fatal cancer with a Stoic heroism. Again we have evidence that the complex symbol of fear of death would be very variable in its intensity; it would be, as Wahl concluded, "profoundly dependent upon the nature and the vicissitudes of the developmental process."[31]

But I want to be careful not to make too much of natural vitality and inner sustainment. As we will see in Chapter Six, even the unusually favored Freud suffered his whole life from phobias and from death-anxiety; and he came to fully perceive the world under the aspect of natural terror. I don't believe that the complex symbol of death is ever absent, no matter how much vitality and inner sustainment a person has. Even more, if we say that these powers make repression easy and natural, we are only saying the half of it. Actually, they get their very power from repression. Psychiatrists argue that the fear of death varies in intensity depending on the developmental process, and I think that one important reason for this variability is that the fear is transmuted in that process. If the child has had a very favorable upbringing, it only serves all the better to hide the fear of death. After all, repression is made possible by the natural identification of the child with the powers of his parents. If he has been well cared for, identification comes easily and solidly, and his parents' powerful triumph over death automatically becomes his. What is more natural to banish one's fears than to live on delegated powers? And what does the whole growing-up period signify, if not the giving over of one's life-project? I am going to be talking about these things all the way through this book and do not want to develop them in this introductory discussion. What we will see is that man cuts out for himself a manageable world: he throws himself into action uncritically, unthinkingly. He accepts the cultural programming that turns his nose where he is supposed to look; he doesn't bite the world off in one piece as a giant would, but in small manageable pieces, as a beaver does. He uses all kinds of techniques, which we call the "character defenses": he learns not to expose himself, not to stand out; he learns to embed himself in other-power, both of concrete persons and of things and cultural commands; the result is that he comes to exist in the imagined infallibility of the world around him. He doesn't have to have fears when his feet are solidly mired and his life mapped out in a ready-made maze. All he has to do is to plunge ahead in a compulsive style of drivenness in the "ways of the world" that the child learns and in which he lives later as a kind of grim equanimity—the "strange power of living in the moment and ignoring and forgetting"—as James put it. This is the deeper reason that Montaigne's peasant isn't troubled until the very end, when the Angel of Death, who has always been sitting on his shoulder, extends his wing. Or at least until he is prematurely startled into dumb awareness, like the "Husbands" in John Cassavetes' fine film. At times like this, when the awareness dawns that has always been blotted out by frenetic, ready-made activity, we see the transmutation of repression redistilled, so to speak, and the fear of death emerges in pure essence. This is why people have psychotic breaks when repression no longer works, when the forward momentum of activity is no longer possible. Besides, the peasant mentality is far less romantic than Montaigne would have us believe. The peasant's equanimity is usually immersed in a style of life that has elements of real madness, and so it protects him: an undercurrent of constant hate and bitterness expressed in feuding, bullying, bickering and family quarrels, the petty mentality, the self-deprecation, the superstition, the obsessive control of daily life by a strict authoritarianism, and so on. As the title of a recent essay by Joseph Lopreato has it: "How would you like to be a peasant?"

We will also touch upon another large dimension in which the complex symbol of death is transmuted and transcended by man—belief in immortality, the extension of one's being into eternity. Right now we can conclude that there are many ways that repression works to calm the anxious human animal, so that he need not be anxious at all.

I think we have reconciled our two divergent positions on the fear of death. The "environmental" and "innate" positions are both part of the same picture; they merge naturally into one another; it all depends from which angle you approach the picture: from the side of the disguises and transmutations of the fear of death or from the side of its apparent absence. I admit with a sense of scientific uneasiness that whatever angle you use, you don't get at the actual fear of death; and so I reluctantly agree with Choron that the argument can probably never be cleanly "won." Nevertheless something very important emerges: there are different images of man that he can draw and choose from.

On the one hand, we see a human animal who is partly dead to the world, who is most "dignified" when he shows a certain obliviousness to his fate, when he allows himself to be driven through life; who is most "free" when he lives in secure dependency on powers around him, when he is least in possession of himself. On the other hand, we get an image of a human animal who is overly sensitive to the world, who cannot shut it out, who is thrown back on his own meagre powers, and who seems least free to move and act, least in possession of himself, and most undignified. Whichever image we choose to identify with depends in large part upon ourselves. Let us then explore and develop these images further to see what they reveal to us.

Notes

1 S. Freud, "Thoughts for the Times on War and Death," 1915, *Collected Papers*, Vol. 4 (New York: Basic Books, 1959), pp. 316–317.

2 Cf., for example, A. L. Cochrane, "Elie Metschnikoff and His Theory of an *'Instinct de la Mort,'*" *International Journal of Psychoanalysis* 1934, 15:265–270; G. Stanley Hall, "Thanatophobia and Immortality," *American Journal of Psychology*, 1915, 26:550–613.

3 N. S. Shaler, *The Individual: A Study of Life and Death* (New York: Appleton, 1900).

4. Hall, "Thanatophobia," p. 562.

5 Cf., Alan Harrington, *The Immortalist* (New York: Random House, 1969), p. 82.

6 See Jacques Choron's excellent study: *Death and Western Thought* (New York: Collier Books, 1963).

7 See H. Feifel, ed., *The Meaning of Death* (New York: McGraw-Hill, 1959), Chapter 6; G. Rochlin, *Griefs and Discontents* (Boston: Little, Brown, 1967), p. 67.

8 J. Bowlby, *Maternal Care and Mental Health* (Geneva: World Health Organization, 1952), p. 11.

9 Cf. Walter Tietz, "School Phobia and the Fear of Death," *Mental Hygiene*, 1970, 54:565–568.

10 J. C. Rheingold, *The Mother, Anxiety and Death: The Catastrophic Death Complex* (Boston: Little, Brown, 1967).

11 A. J. Levin, "The Fiction of the Death Instinct," *Psychiatric Quarterly*, 1951, 25:257–281.

12 J. C. Moloney, *The Magic Cloak: A Contribution to the Psychology of Authoritarianism* (Wakefield, Mass.: Montrose Press, 1949), p. 217; H. Marcuse, "The Ideology of Death," in Feifel, *Meaning of Death*, Chapter 5.

13 LAD, p. 270.

14 G. Murphy, "Discussion," in Feifel, *The Meaning of Death*, p. 320.

15 Williams James, *Varieties of Religious Experience: A Study in Human Nature*, 1902 (New York: Mentor Edition, 1958), p. 121.

16 Choron, *Death*, p. 17.

17 *Ibid.*, p. 272.

18 G. Zilboorg, "Fear of Death," *Psychoanalytic Quarterly*, 1943, 12:465–475. See Eissler's nice technical distinction between the anxiety of death and the terror of it, in his book of essays loaded with subtle discussion: K. R. Eissler, *The Psychiatrist and the Dying Patient* (New York: International Universities, Press, 1955), p. 277.

19 Zilboorg, "Fear of Death," pp. 465–467.

20 James, *Varieties*, p. 121.

21 Zilboorg, "Fear of Death," p. 467. Or, we might more precisely say, with Eissler, fear of annihilation, which is extended by the ego into the consciousness of death. See *The Psychiatrist and the Dying Patient*, p. 267.

22 *Ibid.*

23 *Ibid.*, pp. 468–471 *passim*.

24 Cf. Shaler, *The Individual.*

25 C. W. Wahl, "The Fear of Death," in Feifel, pp. 24–25.

26 Cf. Moloney, *The Magic Cloak*, p. 117.

27 Wahl, "Fear of Death," pp. 25–26.

28 In Choron, *Death*, p. 100.

29 Cf., for example, I. E. Alexander *et al.*, "Is Death a Matter of Indifference?" *Journal of Psychology*, 1957, 43:277–283; I. M. Greenberg and I. E. Alexander, "Some Correlates of Thoughts and Feelings Concerning Death," *Hillside Hospital Journal*, 1962, No. 2:120–126; S. I. Golding *et al.*, "Anxiety and Two Cognitive Forms of Resistance of the Idea of Death," *Psychological Reports*, 1966, 18: 359–364.

30 L. J. Saul, "Inner Sustainment," *Psychoanalytic Quarterly*, 1970, 39:215–222.

31 Wahl, "Fear of Death," p. 26.

3 ·   The Pornography of Death

Geoffrey Gorer

Geoffrey Gorer is a noted English anthropologist who has written about Africa, Bali and Angkor, Himalayan villages, and the American people. His first book was about the Marquis de Sade. This selection, which is taken from his book Death, Grief and Mourning, *has already become a classic of its kind. In it, Gorer proposes and brilliantly explicates the dramatic thesis that death is treated in our society as obscene and pornographic; that while sex was the pornography of the Victorians, death is the pornography of our times.*

> Birth, and copulation, and death.
> That's all the facts when you come to brass tacks;
> Birth, and copulation, and death.
>
> —T. S. Eliot, *Sweeney Agonistes* (1932)

Pornography is, no doubt, the opposite face, the shadow, of prudery, whereas obscenity is an aspect of seemliness. No society has been recorded which has not its rules of seemliness, of words or actions which arouse discomfort and embarrassment in some contexts, though they are essential in others. The people before whom one must maintain a watchful seemliness vary from society to society: all people of the opposite sex, or all juniors, or all elders, or one's parents-in-law, or one's social superiors or inferiors, or one's grandchildren have been selected in different societies as groups in whose presence the employment of certain words or the performance of certain actions would be considered offensive; and then these words or actions become charged with affect. There is a tendency for these words and actions to be related to sex and excretion, but this is neither necessary nor universal; according to Malinowski, the Trobrianders surround eating with as much shame as excretion; and in other societies personal names or aspects of ritual come under the same taboos.

Rules of seemliness are apparently universal; and the nonobservance of these rules, or anecdotes which involve the breaking of the rules, provoke that peculiar type of laughter which seems identical the world over; however little one may know about a strange society, however little one may know about the functions of laughter in that society (and these can be very various) one can immediately tell when people are laughing at an obscene joke. The topper of the joke may be "And then he ate the whole meal in front of them!" or "She used her husband's name in the presence of his mother!" but the laughter is the same; the taboos of seemliness have been broken and the result is hilarious. Typically, such laughter is confined to one-sex groups and is more general with the young, just entering into the complexities of adult life.

Obscenity then is a universal, an aspect of man and woman living in society; everywhere and at all times there are words and actions which, when misplaced, can produce shock, social embarrassment, and laughter. Pornography on the other hand, the description of tabooed activities to produce hallucination or delusion, seems to be a very much rarer phenomenon. It probably can only arise in literate societies, and we certainly have no records of it for nonliterate ones; for whereas the enjoyment of obscenity is predominantly social, the enjoyment of pornography is predominantly private. The fantasies from which pornography derives could of course be generated in any society; but it seems doubtful whether they would ever be communicated without the intermediary of literacy.

The one possible exception to this generalization is the use of plastic arts without any letterpress. I have never felt quite certain that the three-dimensional *poses plastiques* on so many Hindu temples (notably the "Black Pagoda" at Konarak) have really the highfalutin worship of the life force or glorification of the creative aspect of sex which their apologists claim for them; many of them seem to me very like "feelthy" pictures, despite the skill with which they are executed. There are too the erotic woodcuts of Japan; but quite a lot of evidence suggests that these are thought of as laughter provoking (i.e., obscene) by the Japanese themselves. We have no knowledge of the functions of the Peruvian pottery.

As far as my knowledge goes, the only Asian society which had a long-standing tradition of pornographic literature is China; and, it would appear, social life under the Manchus was surrounded by much the same haze of prudery as distinguished the nineteenth century in much of Europe and the Americas, even though the emphasis fell rather differently; women's deformed feet seem to have been the greatest focus of peeking and sniggering, rather than their ankles or the cleft between their breasts; but by and large life in Manchu China seems to have been nearly as full of "unmentionables" as life in Victoria's heyday.

Pornography would appear to be a concomitant of prudery, and usually the periods of the greatest production of pornography have also been the periods of the most rampant prudery. In contrast to obscenity, which is chiefly defined by situation, prudery is defined by subject; some aspect of human experience is treated as inherently shameful or abhorrent, so that it can never be discussed or referred to openly, and experience of it tends to be clandestine and accompanied by feelings of guilt and unworthiness. The unmentionable aspect of experience then tends to become a subject for much private fantasy, more or less realistic, fantasy charged with pleasurable guilt or guilty pleasure; and those whose power of fantasy is weak, or whose demand is insatiable, constitute a market for the printed fantasies of the pornographer.

Traditionally, and in the lexicographic meaning of the term, pornography has been concerned with sexuality. For the greater part of the last two hundred years copulation and (at least in the mid-Victorian decades) birth were the "unmentionables" of the triad of basic human experiences which "are all the facts when you come to brass tacks," around which so much private fantasy and semiclandestine pornography were erected. During most of this period death was no mystery, except in the sense that death is always a mystery. Children were encouraged to think about death, their own deaths and the edifying or cautionary deathbeds of others. It can have been a rare individual who, in the nineteenth century with its high mortality, had not witnessed at least one actual dying, as well as paying their respect to "beautiful corpses"; funerals were the occasion of the greatest display for working class, middle class, and aristocrat. The cemetery was the center of every old-established village, and they were prominent in most towns. It was fairly late in the nineteenth century when the execution of criminals ceased to be a public holiday as well as a public warning.

In the twentieth century, however, there seems to have been an unremarked shift in prudery; whereas copulation has become more and more "mentionable," particularly in the Anglo-Saxon societies, death has become more and more "unmentionable" *as a natural process*. I cannot recollect a novel or play of the last twenty years or so which has a "deathbed scene" in it, describing in any detail the death "from natural causes" of a major character; this topic was a set piece for most of the eminent Victorian and Edwardian writers, evoking their finest prose and their most elaborate technical effects to produce the greatest amount of pathos or edification.

One of the reasons, I imagine, for this plethora of deathbed scenes—apart from their intrinsic emotional and religious content—was that it was one of the relatively few experiences that an author could be fairly sure would have been shared by the vast majority of his readers. Questioning my old acquaintances, I cannot find one over the age of sixty who did not witness the agony of at least one near relative; I do not think I know a single person under the age of thirty who has had a similar experience. Of course my acquaintance is neither very extensive nor particularly representative; but in this instance I do think it is typical of the change of attitude and "exposure."

The natural processes of corruption and decay have become disgusting, as disgusting as the natural processes of birth and copulation were a century ago; preoccupation about such processes is (or was) morbid and unhealthy, to be discouraged in all and punished in the young. Our great-grandparents were told that babies were found under gooseberry bushes or cabbages; our children are likely to be told that those who have passed on (fie! on the gross Anglo-Saxon monosyllable) are changed into flowers, or lie at rest in lovely gardens. The ugly facts are relentlessly hidden; the art of the embalmers is an art of complete denial.

It seems possible to trace a connection between the shift of taboos and the shift in religious beliefs. In the nineteenth century most of the inhabitants of Protestant countries seem to have subscribed to the Pauline beliefs in the sinfulness of the body and the certainty of the afterlife. "So also is the resurrection of the dead. It is sown in corruption; it is raised in incorruption: it is sown in dishonour; it is raised in glory." It was possible to insist on the corruption of the dead body, and the dishonour of its begetting, while there was a living belief in the incorruption and the glory of the immortal part. But in England, at any rate, belief in the future life as taught in Christian doctrine is very uncommon today even in the minority who make church going or prayer a consistent part of their lives; and without some such belief natural death and physical decomposition have become too horrible to contemplate or to discuss. It seems symptomatic that the contemporary sect of Christian Science should deny the fact of physical death, even to the extent (so it is said) of refusing to allow the word to be printed in the *Christian Science Monitor.*

During the last half century public health measures and improved preventive medicine have made natural death among the younger members of the population much more uncommon than it had been in earlier periods, so that a death in the family, save in the fullness of time, became a relatively uncommon incident in home life; and, simultaneously, violent death increased in a manner unparalleled in human history. Wars and revolutions, concentration camps, and gang feuds were the most publicized of the causes for these violent deaths; but the diffusion of the automobile, with its constant and unnoticed toll of fatal accidents, may well have been most influential in bringing the possibility of violent death into the expectations of law-abiding people in time of peace. While natural death became more and more smothered in prudery, violent death has played an evergrowing part in the fantasies offered to mass audiences—detective stories, thrillers, Westerns, war stories, spy stories, science fiction, and eventually horror comics.

There seem to be a number of parallels between the fantasies which titillate our curiosity about the mystery of sex, and those which titillate our curiosity about the mystery of death. In both types of fantasy, the emotions which are typically concomitant of the acts—love or grief—are paid little or no attention, while the sensations are enhanced as much as a customary poverty of language permits. If marital intercourse be considered the natural expression of sex for most of humanity most of the time, then "natural sex" plays as little role as "natural death" (the ham-fisted attempts of D. H. Lawrence and Jules Romains to describe "natural sex" realistically but high-mindedly prove the rule). Neither type of fantasy can have any real development, for once the protagonist has done something, he or she must proceed to do something else, with or to somebody else, more refined, more complicated, or more sensational than what had occurred before. This somebody else is not a person; it is either a set of genitals, with or without secondary sexual characteristics, or a body, perhaps capable of suffering pain as well as death. Since most languages are relatively poor in words or constructions to express intense pleasure or intense pain, the written portions of both types of fantasy abound in onomatopoeic conglomerations of letters meant to evoke the sighs, gasps, groans, screams and rattles concomitant to the described actions. Both types of fantasy rely heavily on adjective and simile. Both types of fantasy are completely unrealistic, since they ignore all physical, social or legal limitations, and both types have complete hallucination of the reader or viewer as their object.

There seems little question that the instinct of those censorious busy-body preoccupied with other people's morals was correct when they linked the pornography of death with the pornography of sex. This, however, seems to be the only thing which has been correct in their deductions or attempted actions. There is no valid evidence to suggest that either type of pornography is an incitement to action; rather are they substitute gratifications. The belief that such hallucinatory works would incite their readers to copy the actions depicted would seem to be indirect homage to the late Oscar Wilde, who described such a process in *The Picture of Dorian Gray*. I know of no authenticated parallels in real life, though investigators and magistrates with bees in their bonnets can usually persuade juvenile delinquents to admit to exposure to whatever medium of mass communication they are choosing to make a scapegoat.

Despite some gifted precursors, such as Andréa de Nerciat or Edgar Allan Poe, most works in both pornographics are aesthetically objectionable; but it is questionable whether, from the purely aesthetic point of view, there is much more to be said for the greater part of the more anodyne fare provided by contemporary mass media communication. Psychological Utopians tend to condemn substitute gratifications as such, at least where copulation is involved; they have so far been chary in dealing with death.

Nevertheless, people have to come to terms with the basic facts of birth, copulation, and death, and somehow accept their implications; if social prudery prevents this being done in an open and dignified fashion, then it will be done surreptitiously. If we dislike the modern pornography of death, then we must give back to death—natural death— its parade and publicity, readmit grief and mourning. If we make death unmentionable in polite society—"not before the children"—we almost ensure the continuation of the "horror comic." No censorship has ever been really effective.

Avery Weisman

Avery Weisman is a psychoanalyst, physician, and professor of psychiatry at the Harvard Medical School and the Massachusetts General Hospital where he heads Project Omega—the study of dying persons. He is one of the most thoughtful writers in the field of thanatology today. One of his most felicitous contributions to the field of thanatology is the concept of an "appropriate death"—a consummatory end that each person would seek were he or she able to do so. In this paper from his book On Dying and Denying, *Dr. Weisman contrasts appropriate death with appropriated death (suicide) and discusses how the dying person can be helped toward achieving a more appropriate death.*

From On Dying and Denying: A Psychiatric Study of Terminality *by Avery Weisman, Copyright © 1972 by Behavioral Publications, Inc., New York. Reprinted by permission.*

Every idea about death is a version of life. Concepts of heaven and hell, damnation and redemption, resolution of suffering, and rewards for deeds, good and ill, are simply extensions of what is already here. To look far into the future is largely an unrevealing pastime. Those events which we glimpse in the distant future are contemporary occasions, seen through the wrong end of a telescope. Even with thorough knowledge of someone's habits, thoughts, and style of life, we cannot accurately predict how and when he will come to the end of his life. Nor can we do this for ourselves. Like living, dying cannot be reduced to a small package of maxims. To tell another person what he ought to do, think, or be is an affront at any time; but to do this when he nears the end of life is sanctimonious cruelty.

We need not be very perceptive to realize that the unceasing destruction afflicting mankind supports the belief that death is senseless, unfair, painful, and tragic. Wars and calamities of nature somehow change our image of death, even giving it a bitter meaning. Where individual death is concerned, however, few of us would ever be prepared to die, if we did not die until we chose. Human beings struggle, suffer, falter, and ask for more. But when the margin between life and death blurs, as in many illnesses, people are then willing to slip quietly into oblivion. Indeed, were it possible for a few people in every generation to live on forever, we would soon cease thinking of them as members of the human race. This elite group might even be feared, like some monstrosity who could not die. Although in the flush of health, we may want to live on, and spontaneously assume that this is possible, the gift of immortality, were it available, might turn out to be a curse.

Appropriate death is a form of purposeful death, but not every instance of purposeful death is an appropriate death. To be willing to die does not mean that someone is able to die, or that his death would be appropriate. Death may be appropriate, but not acceptable; acceptable, but not appropriate. Obviously, appropriate death for one person might be unsuitable for another.

Finally, what might seem appropriate from the outside, might be utterly meaningless to the dying person himself. Conversely, deaths that seem unacceptable to an outsider, might be desirable from the inner viewpoint of the patient.

APPROPRIATED DEATH

Appropriate death has a superficial resemblance to rational suicide, i.e., self-elected death compatible with the ego ideal. In olden times, suicide was an option that ensured honor for certain steadfast people. Many famous men took their own life, instead of surrendering their principles or compromising integrity. A legendary contrast in two manners of suicide is that of Seneca who chose death by his own hand, as opposed to his pupil, Nero, who had to be forced into suicide.

Actually, suicides of great men are often misinterpreted as great and rational deeds, worthy of the man. But we may forget that a great man may be subject to deep depressions and fully capable of destroying himself without the exoneration of "good reasons." The schoolbook jingle that "Lives of great men all remind us/We can make our lives sublime . . ." hides another fact, that the deaths of great men also show how mortal and fallible they can be. Who has the audacity to approve or disapprove of how anyone chooses to die, unless by his death, he nullifies whatever potential being alive holds? We can readily conjure up events that might justify self-destruction, but there are also circumstances in which murder could be condoned. An act of destruction might resolve conflict and relieve suffering, but for whom—the victim or the executioner?

It can be argued that to deprive man of his right to terminate life is an abridgement of his freedom. Yet, few suicides, rescued after an attempt, complain about their freedom, though they might regret being saved. The reasons that people assign to a suicide may be "good," but not the correct reasons. A man who is suicidal at 3 A.M. may find the idea unthinkable at 9 A.M., even though his reasons remain the same. One part of his personality decrees death for every other part. In a sense, suicide is an external agency that victimizes; the option to destroy oneself is not an expression of freedom, but one of despair. We lament a suicide; arguments for its freedom and rationality are only sophistries. Suffering of any origin is deplorable; any of us might choose to die before being completely tyrannized by disease or despotism. Few of us can predict with unerring certainty what we would do if . . . Suicide must be construed as an emergency exit, not the main approach to a style of life. The suicide, for his own private reasons and intentionality, appropriates death for himself; he does not seek appropriate conditions in which to die. His death usually negates his ego ideal, and in other respects, as well, may be the antithesis of the conditions and circumstances for an appropriate death.

It is conceivable that at at the very end of life, people can undergo changes in outlook, so that the meaning of having existed acquires a special significance. Appropriate death does not require complete knowledge about the dying person; few of us could satisfy these preconditions, even about ourselves! Appropriate death does require that we understand the contemporaneous experience that we call dying-in-the-here-and-now. The Greek word *kairos*, an auspicious moment that leads to a decisive change, can also be applied to the event called dying. It is not an idealized image of death, nor does it delete the painful implications of dying to and from a number of things. The here-and-now significance of dying is very concrete, and should not be confused with the imaginary then-and-there of a "promised land." The dying person can, at best, only foresee a wisp of future time. Hence, the now-and-here has a pungency that draws upon every level and period of his existence. Like some memento, it is a unit of reality that may encompass a lifetime.

CONDITIONS OF AN APPROPRIATE DEATH

Someone who dies an appropriate death must be helped in the following ways: He should be relatively pain free, his suffering reduced, and emotional and social impoverishments kept to a minimum. Within the limits of disability, he should operate on as high and effective a level as possible, even though only tokens of former fulfillments can be offered. He should also recognize and resolve residual conflicts, and satisfy whatever remaining wishes are consistent with his present plight and with his ego ideal. Finally, among his choices, he should be able to yield control to others in whom he has confidence. He also has the option of seeking or relinquishing significant key people.

Obviously, these conditions of an appropriate death are like the highest aspirations of mankind! Few people are ever fortunate enough to realize these goals. Consequently, it may seem most unlikely that people about to die could reach or even care about appropriate death, if the requirements are so unrealistic. On the other hand, our preconception that death can *never* be appropriate may be a self-fulfilling idea. If we believe that death is bad, and dying people, by a magical contagion, are tainted, then appropriate deaths are never possible. By discouraging therapeutic intercessions, therefore, we may contribute deep alienation, hopelessness, and loneliness.

Given a measure of consciousness, control and competence to work with, we can encourage appropriate death, or at least a purposeful death. Patients can, for example, be protected from needless procedures that only dehumanize and demean, without offering suitable compensation. We can, moreover, ask people how much consciousness is desirable. Some patients prefer solitude toward the end in order to collect their thoughts. Others, more gregarious, need family and friends. As life ebbs away, some patients want to doze, while others prefer to be alert, and to simulate the regular periods of sleep and wakefulness that healthy people enjoy.

If we refuse to think of appropriate death as a quixotic vision beyond reach, we will protect the patient's autonomy and personal dignity. Much, of course, depends upon the concern of the key participants. Although most people tremble at the notion of dying, it is wholly practical that they can offer a substantial contribution to the mutual task. An appropriate death, in brief, is a death that someone might choose for himself—had he a choice. The central idea, of course, is that to foster an appropriate death, one must realize that death is not an ironic choice without an option, but a way of living as long as possible. Our task is therefore to separate death and its prejudices from each other.

5 · The Social Inequality of Death

Calvin Goldscheider

Calvin Goldscheider's work explicates, in a fascinating and frightening manner, the social inequalities of death. In this selection Professor Goldscheider focuses on the inequalities as they relate specifically to race and socioeconomic status.

From Calvin Goldscheider, Population, Modernization, and Social Structure, *pp. 259–265. Copyright ©1971 by Little, Brown and Company. Reprinted by permission.*

SOCIOECONOMIC STATUS AND MORTALITY

On April 14, 1912, the maiden voyage of the *Titanic* met with disaster. However, not all the passengers died at sea. The official casualty lists revealed that only 4 first-class female passengers (3 voluntarily chose to stay on the sinking ship) of 143 were lost; among second-class passengers, 15 of 93 females drowned; among third-class female passengers, 51 out of 179 died.[1] The social class selectivity among females on the *Titanic*—from 3 percent to 45 percent who died—dramatically illustrates the general inequality in death associated with social class levels.

The unequal distribution of death for various social classes has been observed regularly since the turn of the twentieth century. Sir Arthur Newsholme wrote in 1910 about England that "no fact is better established than the deathrate, and especially the deathrate among children, is high in inverse proportion to the social status of the population." In a review of infant mortality conditions in the United States during the first quarter of this century, Woodbury notes that low socioeconomic status, particularly low-income earnings, is the "primary cause" of excess mortality.[2]

Let us review briefly the relationship between social class and mortality for several European countries, where data have been more accurate and more readily available for a longer period of time, and for the United States. The countries to be considered include Scotland, England and Wales, The Netherlands, Denmark, the United States, and one underdeveloped country, Chile.

In Scotland, infant and fetal mortality rates for all social classes (defined by father's occupation) have declined over the last three decades, but the mortality differential between the lowest and highest social class has widened. In 1939, the fetal deathrate of the lowest occupation class was 1¼ times as high as that of the highest occupational class grouping; in 1963, it was 2⅓ times as high. Similarly, in 1939, the highest social class had a neonatal mortality rate of 30 per 1,000 live births, whereas the lowest social class had a neonatal mortality rate of 40 per 1,000 live births; in 1963, the gap widened with the highest social class having a neonatal mortality rate of 9.5, and the lowest social class a rate of 22.3. Moreover, the gap between these two class extremes was most evident in the postneonatal period, where socioeconomic environmental conditions clearly outweigh biological factors. In 1939, postneonatal deaths in the lowest occupational class were six times that of the highest occupational class, whereas in 1963, the differential more than doubled, and postneonatal deathrates were more than thirteen times as great among the lowest than among the highest social classes.[3]

Since 1911, British statistics have repeatedly shown this same inverse relationship between parental social class (father's occupation) and infant mortality. Although significant declines in infant mortality *within* each social class during the first half of the twentieth century have been reported, the relative differences *between* classes have not decreased.[4] The gap is indeed large: mortality among infants born into families of unskilled laborers is 2½ times that of infants born into families of professionals and rates of infant deaths among the lowest class lag thirty years behind infant deathrates among the highest class.[5] This has occurred in Britain and Scotland even when medical care is readily available to the entire population and where maternity hospital accommodations are ample. Moreover, some evidence shows that the steep mortality gradient from the highest to the lowest occupational class has widened in England and Wales, as in Scotland, precisely during the same period when the gap between the incomes of these class extremes has decreased.

The Danish evidence reveals the same pattern of considerable mortality differences from one occupational group to another. In a 1967 report, data derived in 1954-1955 show that 2½ times as many children of "domestic workers" (lowest occupational rank) died in their first year of life when compared to the children of self-employed persons in professional services.[6] The widening of class inequalities in life chances, particularly between the highest and lowest social classes, has also been observed for Denmark.

The Netherlands data provide an interesting confirmation of the persistence of inequality in deathrates between social classes. Infant mortality in The Netherlands (15 per 1,000 live births in 1964) is one of the lowest recorded in the world (second only to Sweden) and probably one of the lowest recorded in world history. After World War II, the Netherlands became one of the western European welfare states characterized by social security for the great masses, moderate wages increasing with the living standard, relatively little unemployment, and no real poverty. Yet, despite the fact that infant loss has reached low levels, the classic rule still prevails: unfavorable social conditions increase prenatal and postnatal mortality. Mortality is lowest in the highest social class and increases more or less progressively with decreases in social class. Data for 1961-1962 show a wide mortality range by social class in the Netherlands. Neonatal and postneonatal mortality among children with parents in the highest occupational class was about 20 percent below the averages for the country as a whole, whereas in the lowest occupational class, the mortality rates were 10 percent above the national average. The influence of father's occupation on infant mortality is unmistakable. Infant mortality in the lowest social class shows a lag of about seven years in reaching the level attained by the highest social class. The lag would be even greater if the highest income group included in the highest occupational class were compared with the lowest income group in the lowest occupational class. The decline in infant mortality has been fairly uniform for all occupational groups and, at least over the last decade, no appreciable increase in the gap between the highest and lowest class has been observed.[7]

Most European data available on social class differences in general mortality are based on the occupation of father. For overall mortality, it is difficult to separate deaths associated with the "risks" or hazards of various occupations from deaths due to the social and economic implications of life-styles associated with occupational class. But the data on infant mortality classifed by the occupation of father unmistakably reflect life-style and social class factors. In addition, information in England on social class differentials in mortality of women classified by the occupation of their husbands show the same mortality gradient by social class. In these cases, the relationship found could only be a function of differential social and economic life styles indicted by occupational groupings.[8]

Comparable data on socioeconomic class differences in mortality are unavailable for the United States. The several community, ecological studies (ranking census tracts by some measure of socioeconomic status and correlating census tract mortality measures), direct studies for New York State and California, and preliminary national estimates based on death record-census matching of 1960 have all noted the inverse relationship of social class indicators and mortality. These findings, based on various methodologies, gain in reliability not only because of the consistency of results but because of the overall similarity with the European evidence, which is based on more accurate data for a longer period of time. Several United States studies illustrate similar findings using the three methodologies cited.

First, one of the most carefully executed ecological-correlation studies, of Providence, Rhode Island, found infant mortality to be less a sensitive indicator of socioeconomic status as it was in the past. However, when neonatal mortality was separated from postneonatal mortality, i.e., where the major causes of death are farther removed from the physiological processes of gestation and birth, the findings point clearly to an inverse relationship between postneonatal mortality and socioeconomic status.[9]

In a 1961-1963 special study of health problems associated with poverty in New York City, sixteen poverty areas were identified by low income and high frequency of social problems. In 1961-1963, infant mortality in New York City was 26 per 1,000 live births, but in the sixteen poverty areas the rate was 35 per

1,000. The maternal mortality rate for the sixteen poverty areas was almost 2½

times that of the rest of New York City. When health districts were grouped by housing quality in New York City, districts with poor housing had an infant mortality rate over twice that of districts with good housing and a maternal mortality rate almost four times as high.[10]

Studies of upstate New York, for the 1950–1952 period, reaffirm the inverse relationship between level of father's occupation and infant deaths. Neonatal mortality ranged from 14 per 1,000 births among the children of professionals to 20 per 1,000 among the children of laborers; postneonatal mortality (28 days to 11 months per 1,000 survivors to 28 days among births) ranged from 3.5 to 3.7 among professionals and managers to 9.6 among nonfarm laborers.[11]

Finally, carefully matched death and census records (350,000) in the United States resulted in the following estimates of mortality (twenty-five years of age and older) by years of school completed and family income.[12]

1. Among white males with no schooling, mortality was about 10 percent higher than among the college educated; among females mortality was about 50 percent higher among those with no schooling than among those with some college education. The inverse gradient characterizes both sexes and most age groups.

2. Among white males with family incomes below $2,000 a year, mortality was over 50 percent higher than among males with incomes $10,000 a year or more; among females mortality was slightly less than 50 percent greater among those with the lowest family incomes than among those with the highest family incomes.

3. A strong inverse relationship between mortality and level of educational attainment was found for the 1960 nonwhite population. Among nonwhite males, from twenty-five to sixty-four years of age, mortality was 31 percent higher for those with less than five years of schooling when compared to males with some high school or college education. Poorly educated nonwhite females from twenty-five to sixty-four years of age had mortality rates 70 percent higher than better-educated nonwhite females.

Health can be measured not only by length of life but also by positive elements of good health. Information from the United States National Health Survey clearly confirms the generally accepted positive relationship between poor health and low income.[13] People in families with a total income of less than $2,000 a year (in 1961) had twenty-nine restricted days of activities per year, per person; for those with family incomes of $2,000 to $4,000 a year, disability days dropped to eighteen, and in families with incomes of $4,000 a year and over the number was thirteen. To some extent income may be low because of greater illness just as illness may be low because of higher income—but it is clear that the two misfortunes exist together.

The National Health Survey in the United States further reveals that lower income persons, despite their increased level of illness and greater need for health care, receive fewer health services than people with higher incomes. Information gathered between 1963 and 1964 shows that 59 percent with family incomes below $2,000 a year consulted a physician at least once during the preceding year, compared with 66 percent of those with annual incomes between $4,000 and $7,000 a year and 73 percent of those with annual incomes of $10,000 a year. Finally, twice as many of those with higher incomes ($7,000 a year or more) avail themselves of medical specialists when compared to those with lowest income status (below $2,000 a year).

In sum, the evidence from several European countries and the United States points consistently to the social inequality of death for members of different social strata. Some evidence, by no means universal or documented fully, also indicates an increased mortality discrepancy between the highest and lowest classes since World War II, paralleling the findings for racial mortality differentials in the United States and South Africa. Sufficient materials are not yet available to account for these increased mortality discrepancies, if they do in fact exist. Two points of conjecture are worthy of intense and rigorous testing. First, social class mobility may result in the movement out of the lower classes of persons who are healthier and more motivated to achieve a positive state of health. In the process, the lower classes, over time, may become composed of social and physical "rejects," whose mortality patterns may be consequently higher. This selective upward mobility may have increased after World War II, and, in part, may account for increased discrepancies between the lowest and higher classes. A second possibility relates to processes of urbanization and changing environmental densities since the end of World War II. The increasing urbanization of the lower classes, especially Negroes, as a result of rural-to-urban and interurban mobility, and the increasing concentration of urban residents among the poor in substandard housing and deprived social environments, may have increased mortality rates between classes and races. Although static areal measures show lower mortality rates in overall urban areas, more refined measures that subdivide urban areas into homogeneous socioeconomic sections are needed. A contributing and interrelated factor beyond the changing social-environmental situation of millions of poor persons relates to the differential availability of health and medical facilities and services and, more significantly perhaps, differential motivation to utilize services when they are available. Whether these motivational elements have changed in the last decades requires careful research. These suggestions for research may illuminate the specific problem of the social inequality of death, its persistence and increase, and in the process may suggest alternative solutions for diminishing such inequalities.

Notes

1 Cited in Aaron Antonovsky, "Social Class, Life Expectancy and Overall Mortality," *Milbank Memorial Fund Quarterly*, 45 (April 1967), pt. 1, p. 31.

2 Both Newsholme and Woodbury are cited in Edward G. Stockwell, "Infant Mortality and Socio-Economic Status: A Changing Relationship," *Milbank Memorial Fund Quarterly*, 40 (January 1962), pp. 102–103.

3 The data for Scotland are based on a report by Dr. Charlotte Douglas reviewed in U.S. Department of Health, Education and Welfare, *Report of the International Conference on the Perinatal and Infant Mortality Problem of the U.S.*, National Center for Health Statistics, ser. 4, no. 3 (June 1966), p. 3. (Similar findings are cited for France and Hungary.) Although Dr. Douglas notes the difficulty in understanding the widening class differential in infant mortality in Scotland, she suggests that nutrition, housing, economic conditions, and general life-styles conspire to produce the class gap.

4 See the summary by Dr. Katherine M. Hirst, in ibid., pp. 4–5; Cf. K. Hirst et al., *Infant and Perinatal Mortality in England and Wales*, National Center for Health Statistics, ser. 4, no. 12 (November 1968), pp. 31–32; Helen Chase, *International Comparison of Perinatal and Infant Mortality*, National Center for Health Statistics, ser. 3, no. 6 (March 1967), p. 67.

5 See R. K. Kelsall, *Population* (London: Longmans, Green, 1967), pp. 47–50; for earlier reports, see R. M. Titmuss, *Birth, Poverty and Wealth* (London: H. Hamilton Medical Books, 1943); J. N. Morris and J. A. Heady, "Social and Biological Factors in Infant Mortality," *Lancet*, 268 (March 1955), pp. 554–560; and several studies cited in Kelsall, *Population*, p. 98.

6 P. C. Matthiessen et al., *Infant and Perinatal Mortality in Denmark*, National Center for Health Statistics, ser. 3, no. 9 (November 1967), pp. 15–16, and tables S and 12, p. 55. The same pattern was observed in earlier years.

7 Data on the Netherlands were derived from J. H. de Haas-Posthuma and J. H. de Haas, *Infant Loss in the Netherlands*, National Center for Health Statistics, ser. 3, no. 11 pp. 16–24, and table 11. Social class differences in mortality remain practically the same when adjustment is made for parity and age of mother. See ibid., p. 32.

8 Cf. Harold Dorn, "Mortality" in *The Study of Population*, ed. Philip Hauser and Otis D. Duncan (Chicago: University of Chicago Press, 1959)

9 Stockwell, "Infant Mortality and Socio-Economic Status," pp. 101–111.

10 Eleanor Hunt and Earl Huyck, "Mortality of White and Non-White Infants in Major U.S. Cities," *Health, Education and Welfare Indicators* (January 1966), pp. 1–18.

11 Chase, *International Comparison of Perinatal and Infant Mortality*, pp. 67–68.

12 Evelyn Kitagawa and Philip Hauser, "Education Differentials in Mortality by Cause of Death, United States, 1960," *Demography*, 5:1 (1968), pp. 318–353; Evelyn Kitagawa, "Social and Economic Differentials in Mortality in the United States, 1960" (paper presented to the General Assembly, International Union for the Scientific Study of Population, London, 1969).

13 Data from the National Health Survey has been presented in Forrest E. Linder, "The Health of the American People," *Scientific American*, 214 (June 1966), pp. 21–29.

6 · When, Why, and Where People Die

Monroe Lerner

Monroe Lerner is a professor at The Johns Hopkins University, where he is a member of the department of medical care and the department of behavioral sciences. This selection, which first appeared in the The Dying Patient, edited by Orville Brim, Jr., and others, is both current and encyclopedic in its discussion of the many facts of mortality statistics.

Perhaps one of man's greatest achievements in his endless quest to extend the limits of his control over nature has been his success in increasing the average duration of his lifetime. This success has been particularly substantial in the modern era, beginning with the mid-seventeenth century, and during the second third of the twentieth century it extended even to the far corners of the globe. During this period, and possibly for the first time in human history, the lifetimes of a substantial proportion of the world's population have been extended well beyond even the economically productive years, so that most people can now reasonably expect to survive at least into their retirement period.

The ability to do this has always been highly valued, at least as an ideal, and perhaps especially in those societies able at best to struggle along only at the subsistence margin and with almost no economic surplus to support life during the barren years. But even in other circumstances, more than one conception of the "good society" has had a component notion that survival beyond the productive years could be within the realm of possibility for all. Nevertheless, only in the technologically advanced Western nations of today does the *average* duration of life reach, and even in some instances exceed, the famous biblical standard of threescore and ten. If the average duration of life—life expectancy, to use the technical term of statisticians and actuaries—is conceived of as an important indicator of man's control over nature and at the same time also as a crucial element in the moral evaluation of society, then surely man's difficult journey down the long paths of history may be described as social progress rather than merely as evolution.

In any case, whether progress or evolution, man certainly has extended his average lifetime. This [selection] first traces that process, as much as it is possible to do so from the inadequate historical data, and only in the most general terms, from prehistory down to the present situation in the United States. Life expectancy, however, is in one sense simply a refined measure of mortality, and for some purposes it is more useful to deal with mortality rates rather than with life expectancy. Mortality, then, becomes the focus of the remainder of the present discussion.

Later, mortality trends in the United States are traced from 1900 to the present, for the total population and separately by age and sex. Young people—infants, children, and young adults—and females of all ages have clearly been the chief beneficiaries of this process, although other segments of the population have also gained substantially. The major communicable diseases—tuberculosis, influenza and pneumonia, gastritis and duodenitis, the communicable diseases of childhood, and so on—have declined as leading causes of death, to be replaced by the "degenerative" diseases, that is, diseases associated with the aging process—heart disease, cancer, and stroke—and by accidental injury.

Populations may be perceived not only as consisting of sex and age groups, but also as individuals and families ranged along a multidimensional, socioeconomic continuum. The problem then becomes: How do people at various points or in various sections of this continuum fare with regard to mortality risk or, in a more literal meaning of the term than was intended by the German sociologist Max Weber who coined it, what are their life chances?

Perhaps the most meaningful way of dealing with this question, if the objective is to identify large groups or strata in the population who actually do experience gross or at least identifiable differences in mortality risk, is to assume the existence of three major socioeconomic strata in this country, each characterized by a distinctive and unique life-style—the white-collar middle class, the blue-collar working class, and the poverty population. Various structural factors in the life-styles of these populations are conducive to different outcomes in mortality risk. In general, the poverty population experiences relatively high mortality rates at the younger ages and from the communicable diseases, while the white-collar middle class, especially its male members, experiences relatively high mortality rates at midlife and in the older ages, from the "degenerative" diseases. The blue-collar working class, to the extent that it avoids both types of disabilities, appears for the moment at least to be experiencing the lowest mortality rates among the three strata.

Finally, the place where death occurs—that is, in an institution, at home, or elsewhere—has long been a neglected area of mortality statistics. From national data presented later in this [selection], it seems clear that the proportion of all deaths in this country occurring in institutions has been rising steadily, at least for the last two decades and probably for much longer than that. It may now be as high as, or higher than, two-thirds of all deaths. Almost 50 percent of all deaths occurring outside an institution in 1958 were due to heart disease, and especially to the major component of this cause-of-death category, arteriosclerotic heart disease, including coronary disease, which accounted for 37 percent of the total. Cancer, stroke, and accidents comprised the remaining major components of the total, accounting for another 30 percent of the out-of-institution deaths.

HISTORY AND THE DURATION OF
HUMAN LIFE

Scholars can only estimate, in the absence of direct data, what the average duration of life must have been during prehistory. Such estimates have been made, however, and they appear to be roughly consistent with the fragmentary data available from the few surviving contemporary primitive groups, in Africa and elsewhere, whose conditions of life resemble those of our remote ancestors at least in some of their major relevant aspects. Prehistoric man lived, according to these estimates, on the average about eighteen years (Dublin, 1951:386–405); life during the prehistory was, in the Hobbesian sense, indeed nasty, short, and brutish. Violence was the usual cause of death, at least judging from the many skulls found with marks of blows, and man's major preoccupation was clearly satisfying his elemental need for survival in the face of a hostile environment including wild beasts and other men perhaps just as wild. Survivorship in those days was very seldom beyond the age of forty. Persons who reached their midtwenties and more rarely their early thirties were *ipso facto* considered to have demonstrated their wisdom and were, as a result, often treated as sages.

With the rise of the early civilizations and the consequent improvements in living conditions, longevity must surely have risen, reaching perhaps twenty years in ancient Greece and perhaps twenty-two in ancient Rome. Life expectancy is estimated to have been about thirty-three years in England during the Middle Ages, about thirty-five in the Massachusetts Bay Colony of North America, about forty-one in England and Wales during the nineteenth century, and 47.3 in the death-registration states of the United States in 1900.[1] Thus a definite upward progression in life expectancy has been evident in the Western world throughout its history, and this progression is, furthermore, one in which the pace has clearly accelerated with the passage of time.

The upward progression has continued during the twentieth century and, at least in the United States, its rate of increase has accelerated even further. Thus, life expectancy continued to rise in this country after 1900, even if somewhat erratically; by 1915 it had reached a temporary peak at 54.5 years. The 1918 influenza epidemic caused a sharp drop in life expectancy, to just below forty years, a level probably typical of "normal" conditions in the United States during the first half of the nineteenth century (Lerner and Anderson, 1963:317–326). But thereafter the upward trend in life expectancy resumed and, between 1937 and 1945 and following the development of the sulfa drugs and the introduction of penicillin during World War II, its increase was extraordinarily rapid. From 1946 to 1954, however, although life expectancy in this country continued upward, the *rate* of increase tapered off. And from 1954, when life expectancy was 69.6 years, to 1967[2] when it had reached only to 70.2, the gain was at a snail's pace compared to what it had been during the earlier period.

In broader perspective, that is, during the first two-thirds of the twentieth century that we have now experienced, life expectancy rose by almost twenty-three years, an average annual gain of about one-third of a year. This is a breathtaking pace compared to any period of human history prior to this century, and it clearly could not be sustained over a long period of time without enormous social disruption. In line with this, however, life expectancy in the country may now have reached a plateau at, or just above seventy years.

Where does the United States stand in life expectancy compared with other nations, and what can we anticipate as the reasonable upper limit, or goal, that this country *should* be able to attain in the present state of the arts? Although international comparisons of this type appear to be a hazardous undertaking, in large part because of the substantial obstacles to comparability, a number of other nations clearly have higher life expectancies than we do, and at least in some instances the differences are fairly substantial. Even cursory observation of a recent international compendium of demographic statistics (United Nations, 1967:562–583) reveals, for example, that in Australia, Denmark, The Netherlands, New Zealand, Norway, and Sweden life expectancy may be as much as two to three years higher than the comparable figure in the United States. Countries such as Belgium, France, East Germany, the Federal Republic of Germany, Switzerland, England and Wales, and many others, also exceed us in life expectancy, but not by so wide a margin. Surely this country should at least be able to reach the level of those listed above, if not to exceed them. It is possible that these countries may be nearing an upper limit, however, one that may persist unless some major medical breakthrough occurs. Returning to our own country, future projections of life expectancy and mortality made prior to 1954 now appear to have been much too conservative (Dorn, 1952); on the other hand, those made subsequent to 1954 were clearly too optimistic. Tarver (1959), for example, projected a life expectancy of about 73.5 years in 1970, but it now appears that we may be a long time in reaching this goal.

Life expectancy by definition is equivalent to the average duration of life. But how are the numbers obtained for this measure? Starting with a hypothetical cohort of one hundred thousand persons at birth, the mortality rates by age and by sex of a given population in a given year are applied to this cohort as it ages and moves through its life cycle, reducing it in number until no survivors of the original cohort remain (Spiegelman, 1968:293). The number of years lived by the *average* person in this cohort is termed the given population's life expectancy. Clearly then, the life expectancy figure thus obtained is simply the inverse of mortality experience; it depends entirely upon age-and-sex-specific mortality rates. Employment of the measure of "life expectancy" as an indicator of the mortality experience of a population is useful for comparison purposes both currently and across time. This is especially true because this measure eliminates the disturbing influence on the mortality rate of variation in the age-and-sex composition of populations. It is precisely because of this characteristic that life expectancy was used in the preceding discussion to make comparisons across the long span of history. For discussion of the immediate past and current situations, however, it is perhaps best to shift the locus of the discussion from life expectancy to mortality.

MORTALITY IN THE UNITED STATES, 1900 TO 1967: TRENDS AND DIFFERENTIALS, OVERALL AND BY AGE AND SEX

Paralleling inversely the increase in life expectancy from 1900 to the present, the mortality rate (deaths per 1,000 population) of the United States population has declined sharply during this century. Thus in 1900 the mortality rate was 17.2 per 1,000 population, but by 1954 had dropped to 9.2 per 1,000, the lowest ever recorded in the United States. Since that time it has fluctuated between 9.3 and 9.6, and in 1967 the rate was 9.4, representing a decline of about 45 percent since 1900. These figures understate the extent of the "true" decline, however, primarily because the age composition of the United States population has changed drastically since 1900. This change has generally been in the direction of increasing the high-mortality-risk age segments of the population as a proportion of the total and at the expense of the low. With age composition held constant, that is, using the 1940 age composition of the United States population as a standard, the hypothetical "age-adjusted" death rate in this country declined between 1900 and 1967 from 17.8 to 7.2 per 1,000, a drop of about 60 percent.

Age and sex

The pattern of mortality rates by age in this country during 1900 was generally similar to that prevailing today (see Table 1). Thus in 1900 the mortality rate

TABLE 1

MORTALITY RATES PER 1,000 POPULATION BY AGE AND SEX,
UNITED STATES, 1900 AND 1966

Age (in years)	1900			1966		
	Both sexes	Males	Females	Both sexes	Males	Females
All ages	17.2	17.9	16.5	9.5	11.0	8.1
Under 1	162.4	179.1	145.4	23.1	25.7	20.4
1–4	19.8	20.5	19.1	1.0	1.0	0.9
5–14	3.9	3.8	3.9	0.4	0.5	0.4
15–24	5.9	5.9	5.8	1.2	1.7	0.6
25–34	8.2	8.2	8.2	1.5	2.0	1.0
35–44	10.2	10.7	9.8	3.1	3.9	2.3
45–54	15.0	15.7	14.2	7.3	9.7	5.1
55–64	27.2	28.7	25.8	17.2	23.6	11.2
65–74	56.4	59.3	53.6	38.8	52.0	28.1
75–84	123.3	128.3	118.8	81.6	98.5	69.5
85 and over	260.9	268.8	255.2	202.0	213.6	194.9

was high during infancy, 162.4 per 1,000, in comparison to the rates at other ages; it dropped to the lowest point for the entire life cycle, 3.9, at ages five through fourteen; but thereafter it rose steadily with increasing age until at ages eighty-five and over the mortality rate was 260.9 per 1,000 population. In 1966 the comparable rate was only 23.1 per 1,000 during infancy; the low point was 0.4 at ages five through fourteen; and again the rates rose steadily with increasing age, to 202 per 1,000 at ages eighty-five and over. Between 1900 and 1966 the largest *relative* declines in the mortality rates took place at the younger ages, especially during infancy and childhood. Although the declines at the older ages are less impressive percentages, they are, neverthe-less, very substantial in absolute numbers. For example, at ages eighty-five and over the mortality rate dropped by about 59 deaths per 1,000 population, that is, from 261 to 202 per 1,000.

Although the mortality rates for both males and females in the United States population declined substantially since 1900, the *rate* of decline was much sharper for females. Thus the mortality rate for females dropped from 16.5 in 1900 to 8.1 in 1966, a decline of 51 percent. For males the correspond-ing drop was from 17.9 to 11.0, or by 39 percent. The male death rate has been significantly higher than the female death rate in this country throughout the twentieth century, but the relative excess of male over female rates has increased over the years from 8.5 percent in 1900 to 36 percent in 1966. When these rates are age adjusted to a standard population, the excess of male over female rates in 1966 is considerably larger, about 70 percent.

In 1900, the relative excess of male over female mortality rates by age was largest during infancy, at 23 percent. At ages five through fourteen, the mortality rates for males were actually slightly lower than the comparable rates for females; at ages fifteen through thirty-four, rates were about the same for each sex; and in each of the age groups at thirty-five and over, the mortality rates for males exceeded the comparable rates for females only by a relatively slight amount, that is, by from 5 to 11 percent. By 1966, however, although the mortality rates at each age were lower for each sex than the comparable rates in 1900, the decline in almost all cases was larger for females. As a result, the percentage excess of male mortality rates over female rates was larger in most age groups during 1966 than it had been during 1900. It was largest (an excess of almost 200 percent in 1966), at ages fifteen through twenty-four.

MORTALITY IN THE UNITED STATES, 1900 TO 1967:
TRENDS AND DIFFERENTIALS
BY CAUSE OF DEATH

One of the most significant changes in the mortality experience of this country since 1900 has been the decline in the major communicable diseases as leading causes of death[3] and the consequent increase in *relative impor-tance* of the so-called chronic degenerative diseases, that is, diseases occurring mainly later in life and generally thought to be associated in some way with the aging process. Accidents, especially motor vechicle accidents, have also risen in relative importance as causes of death during this period, but mortality during infancy and maternal mortality, that is, mortality associated with childbearing, have declined sharply.

The communicable diseases

The leading cause of death[4] in 1900 was the category: "influenza and pneumonia, except pneumonia of the newborn." This major communicable disease category was listed as the cause of 202.2 deaths per 100,000 population in 1900 (see Table 2), and it accounted for 11.8 percent of all deaths in that year. By 1966, however, the mortality rate for this category was down to 32.8, it ranked fifth among the leading causes of death, and it now accounted for only 3.4 percent of all deaths during the year.

Tuberculosis (all forms) and the gastritis grouping[5] second and third leading causes of death, respectively, in 1900, were both reduced so significantly and to such low rates during the course of this century that neither category was listed among the ten leading causes of death in 1966. Tuberculosis had caused 194.4 deaths per 100,000 in 1900, or 11.3 percent of all deaths, while the gastritis grouping, with 142.7 deaths per 100,000, had accounted for 8.3 percent of the total. By 1966 the comparable rates for these two categories were 3.9 and 3.3, respectively, with each accounting for substantially less than one-half of 1 percent of all deaths in that year. The percentage declines for each from 1900 to 1966 were by 98 percent.

Diphtheria had been listed as tenth leading cause of death in 1900, with 40.3 deaths per 100,000 population. In 1966 this condition accounted for only forty deaths all told in this country, that is, considering the entire United States population as at risk, so that the death rate was about one death per five million persons. Other major communicable diseases with impressive declines in mortality were some of the other communicable diseases of childhood, such as whooping cough, measles, scarlet fever, and streptococcal sore throat, and syphilis, typhoid and paratyphoid fevers, rheumatic fever, and typhus.

Hillery *et al.* (1968), comparing recent mortality data from forty-one countries, have shown that the communicable diseases ("infectious diseases" in their terminology) as causes of death decline significantly as a proportion of all deaths in each country as these countries move "up" in the demographic transition, that is, as their birth and death rates decline, and as they concomitantly become at least presumably more "advanced" technologically and socially. Thus, in the "transitional" countries (low death rates but high birth rates), communicable diseases account for about one-third of all deaths on the average, while in the demographically "mature" countries (both death rates and birth rates low), the comparable proportion is about one in twelve of all deaths. This finding is generally in conformity with past experience in this country and elsewhere.

TABLE 2

47

THE TEN LEADING CAUSES OF DEATH, BY RANK,
UNITED STATES, 1900 AND 1966

1900

Rank	Cause of death	Deaths per 100,000 population	Percent of all deaths
	All causes	1,719.1	100.0
1	Influenza and pneumonia	202.2	11.8
2	Tuberculosis (all forms)	194.4	11.3
3	Gastritis, duodenitis, enteritis, etc.	142.7	8.3
4	Diseases of the heart	137.4	8.0
5	Vascular lesions affecting the central nervous system	106.9	6.2
6	Chronic nephritis	81.0	4.7
7	All accidents	72.3	4.2
8	Malignant neoplasms (cancer)	64.0	3.7
9	Certain diseases of early infancy	62.6	3.6
10	Diphtheria	40.3	2.3

1966

Rank	Cause of death	Deaths per 100,000 population	Percent of all deaths
	All causes	954.2	100.0
1	Diseases of the heart	375.1	39.3
2	Malignant neoplasms (cancer)	154.8	16.2
3	Vascular lesions affecting the central nervous system	104.6	11.0
4	All accidents	57.3	6.0
5	Influenza and pneumonia	32.8	3.4
6	Certain diseases of early infancy	26.1	2.7
7	General arteriosclerosis	19.5	2.0
8	Diabetes mellitus	18.1	1.9
9	Cirrhosis of the liver	13.5	1.4'
10	Suicide	10.3	1.1

The degenerative diseases

"Diseases of the heart" ranked fourth among the leading causes of death in
this country during 1900; this category caused 137.4 deaths per 100,000 and
accounted for 8.0 percent of all deaths. By 1966, however, it had risen so far in
importance that it had become the leading cause of death, far outranking all
others. Its mortality rate had risen to 375.1 deaths per 100,000 population,
and it accounted for nearly 40 percent of all deaths in that year. Between 1900
and 1966 the unadjusted death rate from this disease rose by 173 percent; the
rise was much less if the age-adjusted rates for these two years are compared,
but even this rise was very substantial.

The pattern of increase for malignant neoplasms (cancer) as a cause of death was generally quite similar. This disease ranked eighth among the leading causes of death in 1900. It accounted for 64 deaths per 100,000 population and less than 4 percent of all deaths. By 1966, however, its rank among the leading causes had risen to second, its rate per 100,000 to 154.8, and its proportion of the total of all deaths exceeded 16 percent. Vascular lesions of the central nervous system, although remaining relatively stable in number of deaths per 100,000 (106.9 in 1900 and 104.6 in 1966), nevertheless rose in rank (fifth to third) and as a proportion of all deaths (6 to 11 percent).

How can we account for the increases, in both absolute and relative terms, in these "degenerative" diseases as causes of death? As the classification implies, these are diseases occurring later in life and closely associated with the aging process. Whereas formerly people died on the average much earlier in life, victims primarily of the communicable diseases, they survive today to a much later age, only to succumb in due time to the degenerative conditions. Hillery and his associates (1968) in their interesting study have generalized this trend also. Thus in their demographically transitional countries (low death rates but high birth rates) the degenerative diseases account for less than one-third of all deaths, whereas in their demographically mature countries (both death rates and birth rates low) these diseases account for just under two-thirds of the total. The net overall gain has clearly been an extension of life by many years.

MORTALITY AND SOCIOECONOMIC STATUS

There appears to be a good deal of confusion in this country today, and perhaps especially among social scientists, demographers, and health statisticians, as to the precise nature of the relationship between mortality and socioeconomic status. This confusion has existed, and perhaps will continue to exist for some time, despite the fact that quite a few studies in the past, and a number of ongoing studies, have attempted to clarify the relationship. Part of this confusion may be occasioned by what is perhaps the changing nature of that relationship, a change which in turn may have been brought about by the tremendous improvements in medical technology and therapies during the past century and by the increasing general affluence of the American population. But part of it results from the lack of a generally accepted method for the construction of an overall index of socioeconomic status (Lerner, 1968).

In turn, the failure of social scientists to develop a generally accepted method for the construction of an overall index reflects their lack of general agreement on the number or composition of social classes or social strata in the United States, especially when this entire culturally diverse country is considered as the unit of analysis. Different numbers of classes or strata have been identified, depending on definitions and operational purposes, but none of these is a real entity. Various measures of socioeconomic status have been related to mortality, and the results of one very large study along these lines are now beginning to appear (Kitagawa, 1968). Nevertheless, the overall pattern continues to remain quite unclear at this writing.

For present purposes—to relate socioeconomic status to mortality—it appears that the most meaningful division of the United States population from a conceptual, rather than an operational, standpoint is into three socioeconomic strata. These strata are set apart from one another, in the most general terms, by a distinctive and unique life-style, even though the boundaries between these strata are not sharp, and there may be a considerable movement of individuals and families among them. The life-styles of these strata, in turn, are dependent upon or associated with income, wealth, occupation and occupational prestige, dwelling, ethnic origin, educational attainment, and many other factors, all of which, in some as yet unspecified way, add up to the total. The life-styles, in turn, are directly relevant to the health level, and more specifically the mortality experience of each stratum. The structural factors in each of the three major life-styles through which the relationship to mortality operates include at least these four: the level of living (food, housing, transportation, or other factors); degree of access to medical care within the private medical care system; occupation of the family head (sedentary or involving physical activity); and the nature of the social milieu for that stratum (that is, its degree of economic or social security).

The highest stratum consists of those who are usually designated as the middle- and upper-class white-collar business executives at all levels and professionals, and all those who are above this category. It even includes the highest echelons of skilled blue-collar workers (tool-and-die makers), foremen, supervisors, or the like. Although the range of variation *within* this stratum is great, the group as a whole shares the essential elements of a "middle-class" way of life, that is, residence in "better" neighborhoods and suburbs, general affluence, and so on.

The second stratum consists of this country's blue-collar working class —mainly the semiskilled and unskilled workers in the mass-production and service industries, but also small farmers and possibly even farm laborers, and lower level white-collar workers. These people are also relatively affluent, but not to the same extent as the middle class. Again, although the range of variation *within* this stratum is great, they also share a unique style of life distinctively different from that of the higher stratum. This group will subsequently be designated in the present discussion as the working class.

The lowest of the three strata includes those who are generally designated as the poverty population. By definition, these people generally do not share in the affluence characteristic of this country. It consists of the poor in large-city ghettoes and the rural poor (residents of Appalachia or the Deep South, as well as others); the Negro, Puerto Rican, Mexican, and French Canadian populations, and the other relatively poor ethnic minorities in this country; Indians on reservations; the aged, migratory laborers; and the dependent poor.

Although, as stated above, this mode of classification of socioeconomic status appears to be the most meaningful from a conceptual standpoint in terms of relating it to mortality, it clearly lacks merit from the operational point of view. This is because there would appear to be no ready way of segregating these groups from one another in the available national statistical data, relating either to population data or health statistics, and especially to study their respective mortality experiences. Nevertheless, here and there some attempts have been made, and some studies, mostly local and regional in character and particularly of the poverty population, have been carried out (cf. Chicago Board of Health, 1965; and Lerner, 1968). What follows, therefore, is to be understood as more of an overall gross impression and prediction, rather than anything else, and one based on a general familiarity with the literature of what would be found if the data were available in the form required by the present framework.

The poverty populations generally are likely to have the highest death rates of the three strata on an overall basis, but especially from the communicable diseases. This has been true historically between rich and poor nations in the modern era and still represents the situation in the world today at various levels of wealth and technological advancement (Pond, 1961; Anderson and Rosen, 1960). Within this country, a considerable amount of evidence exists to show that mortality rates among the poverty population are likely to be highest during infancy, childhood, and the younger adult ages. The communicable diseases of childhood, gastrointestinal diseases, and influenza and pneumonia are still a relatively serious health problem among this population, even where public health facilities and services are relatively adequate, as, for example, in the slums of large cities in this country today. What this population lacks most, perhaps, is adequate access to personal health services within the private medical care system. Although these services are to some degree available under other auspices (Strauss, 1967), they may be relatively ineffective and not oriented to the life-style of their recipients, while the cultural impediments to their use appear to be substantial.

In contrast, the white-collar middle class does enjoy relatively adequate access to personal health services under the private medical care system, and their mortality rates during infancy, childhood, and even young adulthood are substantially lower than that of the poverty populations. This is especially true for mortality from the communicable diseases, but appears to extend almost to the entire spectrum of causes of death. The higher levels of living enjoyed by this stratum in general buttress its advantage during the younger years. During midlife and especially during the later years, however, its mortality rates appear to become substantially higher than those of the rest of the population, primarily for the "degenerative" diseases, especially heart disease, cancer, and stroke.

One possible hypothesis that has been offered in explanation of this phenomenon merits comment here. It may be that, because of improved survival by members of this stratum at the younger ages, many persons are carried into midlife with a lower "general resistance" factor than that which

characterizes persons in the poverty stratum, and that these individuals are perhaps therefore more vulnerable to the diseases and hazards most prevalent at midlife and beyond. At the moment, at least, there seems to be no possible way of testing this hypothesis.

Another hypothesis is that this excess mortality at midlife is a concomitant of the general affluence characterizing the life-styles of the middle class and of their sedentary occupations (executive and white-collar). Both of these, in turn, may result in obesity, excessive strains and tensions, excessive cigarette smoking, and perhaps ultimately premature death. Men aged forty-five through sixty-four (midlife), especially white men, appear to be particularly vulnerable to coronary artery disease and respiratory cancer. Middle-class women, on the other hand, appear to be less affected by these affluence-related forms of ill health than middle-class men, perhaps because of innate resistance, social pressures to avoid obesity, cigarette smoking without inhalation, and generally less stressful lives, or perhaps some combination of these factors. In any case, women in this stratum appear to have the best of all possible worlds, that is, they have none of the health disabilities associated with the sedentary occupations characteristic of their spouses while at the same time enjoying adequate medical care.

The blue-collar working class appears to have the best overall mortality record. This group appears to have relatively low mortality during the younger ages and from the communicable diseases, especially because they do have access to good medical care in the private medical care system. At midlife, moreover, they appear to suffer from relatively few of the disabilities associated with middle-class affluence.

WHERE DEATH OCCURS

Where people die—in a hospital or other institution, at home, or in a public place—has been a relatively neglected aspect of mortality statistics in this country during the past few years. Although this information is contained on each death certificate and relatively little additional effort or expense would be required to code and tabulate it, this has not been done, perhaps because it has not been at all clear that the returns would be commensurate to the additional expense. As a result, the last national tabulation of these data based on the regular vital statistics data-collection system relates to 1958, and these data were far from complete; many of the cross-tabulations that could have been made were not, in fact, carried out. Some of these states and cities here and there have published tabulations since that time, however.

Recently, some new interest has been expressed in this question among public health circles, possibly stimulated by the coming into being of Regional Medical Programs throughout the country. These in turn were set up under the Heart Disease, Cancer, and Stroke Amendments of 1965 (P.L. 89–239), which provided for the establishment of regional cooperative

arrangements for improvement of the quality of medical care through research and training, including continuing education, among medical
schools, research institutions, and hospitals, and in related demonstrations
of patient care. The new legislation was aimed generally at improving the
health, manpower, and facilities available, but one specific purpose was to
make new medical knowledge available, as rapidly as possible, for the treatment of patients (Yordy and Fullarton, 1965). The assumption in public
health circles was that the place of occurrence of some deaths, and the
circumstances, may have been related to an inability to obtain proper medical care either at the moment of death or immediately preceding it, as in cases
of sudden death, or at some point during the illness or condition leading to
death in other cases. The extent to which this assumption is true is, of course,
difficult to test given the present paucity of relevant data.

In 1958, according to the most recent *national* data available (see Table 3),
60.9 percent of all deaths in this country occurred in institutions, that is, in
hospitals, convalescent and nursing homes, and in hospital departments of
institutions or in other domiciliary instittions. This figure represented a
considerable rise over the comparable 49.5 percent recorded in 1949, the
most recent preceding year for which a national tabulation was made. On the
basis of these data it appeared that the proportion was rising by an average of
better than 1 percent annually.

TABLE 3

NUMBER AND PERCENT OF DEATHS OCCURRING IN INSTITUTIONS BY TYPE OF
SERVICE OF INSTITUTION, UNITED STATES, 1949 AND 1958

	1958		1949	
	Number	*Percent*	*Number*	*Percent*
Total deaths	1,647,886	100.0	1,443,607	100.0
Not in institution	644,548	39.1	728,797	50.5
In institution	1,003,338	60.9	714,810	49.5
General hospital	784,360	47.6	569,867	39.5
Maternity hospital	1,862	0.1	2,249	0.2
Tuberculosis hospital	9,097	0.6	13,627	0.9
Chronic disease, convalescent and other special hospitals	24,180	1.5	12,402	0.9
Nervous and mental hospitals	57,675	3.5	45,637	3.2
Convalescent and nursing homes, homes for the aged, etc.	98,444	6.0	22,783	1.6
Hospital department of institutions, and other domiciliary institutions	3,646	0.2	41,841	2.9
Type of service not specified	24,074	1.5	6,404	0.4

National data to test whether the trend continued beyond that year are unavailable, but state and local data appear to indicate that this, in fact, may have been the case. In New York City, for example, the proportion of deaths occurring in institutions rose steadily, with only one very slight fluctuation, from 65.9 percent in 1955 to 73.1 percent in 1967 (see Table 4). These same data indicate that the proportion of deaths occurring at home dropped commensurately during these years, from 31.4 percent to 24.2 percent. The proportion of deaths occurring elsewhere, primarily in public places, remained relatively constant. Data from the Maryland State Department of Health also indicate a substantial upward progression in the proportion of all deaths occurring in institutions, from 64.4 percent in 1957 to 71.8 percent in 1966 (Maryland State Department of Health, 1967).

Most of the deaths occurring in "institutions," as the data of Table 3 indicate, occurred in hospitals, the vast majority of which were general hospitals. Nervous and mental hospitals during each of the two years to which the table relates, however, accounted for somewhat more than 3 percent of all deaths. The proportion occurring in convalescent and nursing homes, homes for the aged, and similar establishments increased substantially between 1949 and 1958, from 1.6 percent to 6.0 percent.[6]

Table 5 shows the percent of deaths, by color, that occurred in institutions in 1949 and 1958, for the entire country and for each geographic division. In

TABLE 4
NUMBER AND PERCENT OF DEATHS BY PLACE OF DEATH,
NEW YORK CITY, 1955-1967

	Number of deaths				Percentage			
	Total	In insti- tution	At home	Other	Total	In insti- tution	At home	Other
1955	81,612	53,746	25,598	2,268	100.0	65.9	31.4	2.8
1956	81,118	54,716	24,193	2,209	100.0	67.5	29.8	2.7
1957	84,141	57,141	24,609	2,391	100.0	67.9	29.2	2.8
1958	84,586	57,946	24,230	2,410	100.0	68.5	28.6	2.8
1959	85,352	58,859	24,127	2,366	100.0	69.0	28.3	2.8
1960	86,252	59,413	24,341	2,498	100.0	68.9	28.2	2.9
1961	86,855	60,061	24,524	2,270	100.0	69.2	28.2	2.6
1962	87,089	60,409	24,315	2,365	100.0	69.4	27.9	2.7
1963	88,621	61,588	24,677	2,356	100.0	69.5	27.8	2.7
1964	88,026	62,391	23,602	2,033	100.0	70.9	26.8	2.3
1965	87,395	62,308	22,879	2,208	100.0	71.3	26.2	2.5
1966	88,418	63,599	22,576	2,243	100.0	71.9	25.5	2.5
1967	87,610	64,083	21,222	2,305	100.0	73.1	24.2	2.6

Source of basic data: Personal communication from Mr. Louis Weiner, New York City Department of Health.

TABLE 5

PERCENT OF DEATHS OCCURRING IN INSTITUTIONS BY COLOR AND
GEOGRAPHIC DIVISION, UNITED STATES, 1949 AND 1958

Geographic division	1958			1949		
	Total	White	Nonwhite	Total	White	Nonwhite
United States	60.9	61.9	53.2	49.5	50.4	43.2
New England	64.2	64.0	72.4	52.2	52.0	67.1
Middle Atlantic	62.8	62.3	68.9	53.2	52.2	69.0
East North Central	63.6	63.2	67.9	51.5	50.9	59.7
West North Central	63.8	63.9	61.5	50.7	50.6	54.4
South Atlantic	55.8	58.6	48.4	42.5	45.3	36.3
East South Central	47.6	51.8	37.3	34.6	37.8	27.6
West South Central	54.9	57.7	44.2	42.8	45.3	34.3
Mountain	63.5	63.4	64.1	55.2	54.9	61.0
Pacific	66.5	66.3	68.8	58.5	58.1	65.5

TABLE 6

TOTAL DEATHS AND PERCENT OCCURRING IN INSTITUTIONS BY CAUSE,
FOR SELECTED CAUSES OF DEATH, UNITED STATES, 1958

Cause of death	Total deaths, number	Percent in institutions
Tuberculosis, all forms	12,361	80.0
Syphilis and its sequelae	3,469	71.7
Dysentery, all forms	407	62.4
Scarlet fever and streptococcal sore throat	139	57.6
Whooping cough	177	60.5
Meningococcal infections	746	87.9
Acute poliomyelitis	255	91.8
Measles	552	63.8
Malignant neoplasms, including neoplasms of lymphatic and hematopoetic tissues	254,426	67.7
Benign neoplasms	4,961	82.5
Asthma	5,035	55.4
Diabetes mellitus	27,501	68.6
Anemias	3,195	72.4
Meningitis, except meningococcal and tuberculous	2,247	91.8
Vascular lesions affecting central nervous system	190,758	65.8
Diseases of heart	637,246	50.4
Arteriosclerotic heart disease, including coronary disease	461,373	48.5
Other hypertensive disease	13,798	68.5
General arteriosclerosis	34,483	61.8
Other diseases of circulatory system	17,204	79.5
Chronic and unspecified nephritis, etc.	13,827	67.6

both years the proportion of deaths occurring in institutions was substantially lower for the nonwhite population than for the white when the country as a whole is considered as the unit. However, for the New England, Middle Atlantic, and East North Central states in both years and the West North Central states in 1949 the reverse pattern was true, that is, the proportion of deaths occurring in institutions was higher for the nonwhite population than for the white. In general, the proportions in both years for the East South Central, West South Central, and South Atlantic states, and especially for their nonwhite populations, were very low in comparison to the rest of the country. In Mississippi, even as late as 1958, only 31.0 percent of the nonwhite deaths occurred in institutions. (These data are not shown in Table 5.)

By cause of death, as Table 6 indicates, the most important categories in which the proportion of deaths occuring in institutions was relatively small were the external causes of death (accidents, suicide, and homicide), diseases of the heart, influenza, and the catchall category "symptoms, senility, and ill-defined conditions." Less than one-half of all deaths following acci-

Cause of death	Total deaths, number	Percent in institutions
Influenza and pneumonia	57,439	68.6
Influenza	4,442	43.1
Pneumonia, except pneumonia of newborn	52,997	70.7
Bronchitis	3,973	61.7
Ulcer of stomach and duodenum	10,801	88.2
Appendicitis	1,845	94.5
Hernia and intestinal obstruction	8,853	90.5
Gastritis, duodenitis, enteritis, etc.	7,838	78.7
Cirrhosis of liver	18,638	79.3
Cholelithiasis, cholecystitis and cholangitis	4,720	90.0
Acute nephritis, and nephritis with edema, etc.	2,203	76.0
Infections of kidney	6,889	85.5
Hyperplasia of prostate	4,627	81.1
Deliveries and complications of pregnancy, childbirth, and the puerperium	1,581	85.5
Congenital malformations	21,411	86.5
Certain diseases of early infancy	68,960	94.5
Symptoms, senility, and ill-defined conditions	19,729	25.2
Accidents	90,604	47.6
Motor-vehicle accidents	36,981	44.0
Other accidents	53,623	50.0
Suicide	18,519	18.5
Homicide	7,815	34.1

dents occurred in the hospital, and the comparable figure was only 44 percent for motor vehicle deaths. Only about one-half of all deaths from diseases of the heart occurred in an institution, and somewhat less than that figure for arteriosclerotic heart disease, including coronary disease. In the case of each of these conditions, as well as for suicide and homicide, it seems likely that the short time interval between onset of the condition and death is probably a major reason for the relatively small proportions occurring in hospitals. Finally, only about one-fourth of all deaths for which a cause could not clearly be delineated (deaths attributed to symptoms, senility, and ill-defined conditions) occurred in hospitals.

Considering the almost 645,000 deaths that occurred outside an institution in 1958, almost one-half (49 percent) were accounted for by diseases of the heart (see Table 7). (Within this category, arteriosclerotic heart disease, including coronary disease, accounted for about 37 percent of the total.) The next three most important causes of death in accounting for all deaths outside of institutions were malignant neoplasms, 13.1 percent; vascular lesions, 10.1 percent; and accidents, 7.4 percent. These first four categories combined accounted for about 80 percent of all deaths occurring outside institutions, but other causes of death—for example, influenza and pneumonia, suicide, general arteriosclerosis, and so on—were also important in the total.

CONCLUSIONS AND IMPLICATIONS

It would appear, at least from the point of view and focus of the preceding discussion, that the implicit goal of the health establishment in this country to "assure for everyone the highest degree of health attainable in the present state of the arts" has been far from realized. For example, with regard to mortality and its derivative, life expectancy, other nations have clearly outdistanced us, and by a substantial margin. It is true that most of these countries are smaller and more homogeneous, and the environmental hazards plaguing them may not be operative in the same manner and to the same degree as they are among us. Nevertheless, we do appear to have fallen short of what has been achieved elsewhere, and it is therefore appropriate to raise questions about the reasons for this apparent failure.

Three broad lines of inquiry have been suggested as possible approaches in this [discussion], and a fourth influencing and possibly underlying the others will be mentioned. When one considers the entire spectrum of causes of death and their "places of occurrence," it is not unreasonable to assume *as a working hypothesis* that many deaths are occurring from causes—disease conditions—that are amenable, at least under optimum conditions in the present state of the arts, to medical management and control. Of course, the sex and age of the patient, the general state of health and degree of "resistance" of the organism, and many other factors should be considered in the evaluation of each case before any death is characterized as needless or

TABLE 7

57

MONROE LERNER

DEATHS OCCURRING OUTSIDE INSTITUTIONS BY CAUSE,
FOR SELECTED CAUSES OF DEATH, UNITED STATES, 1958

Cause of death	Number	Percent
All causes	644,548	100.0
1. Diseases of the heart	316,074	49.0
Arteriosclerotic heart disease, including coronary disease	237,607	36.9
2. Malignant neoplasms, including neoplasms of the lymphatic and hematopoietic tissues	84,724	13.1
3. Vascular lesions affecting the central nervous system	65,239	10.1
4. Accidents, all forms	47,476	7.4
Motor-vehicle accidents	20,709	3.2
Other	26,767	4.2
5. Influenza and pneumonia	18,036	2.8
Pneumonia	15,528	2.4
Influenza	2,508	0.4
6. Suicide	15,093	2.3
7. General arteriosclerosis	13,173	2.0
8. Diabetes mellitus	8,635	1.3
9. Homicide	5,150	0.7

preventable. Furthermore, it may be very difficult to refrain from setting up, as working standards, ideal conditions that are unattainable anywhere, given the realities and the imperatives of social organization, the relatively low priority of health in the hierarchy of human values and "needs," the "mass" nature of society, and the vagaries and irrational elements in what is colloquially described as "human nature." Nevertheless, the social and economic differentials in mortality discussed in this [selection] would appear to argue that there is much room for improvement, that the low mortality rates now attained by some could be attained, theoretically at least, by all.

If this is true, and if our goal is indeed to assure the highest degree of health attainable *for everyone,* then we must ask ourselves whether the social organization for the provision of health services to the population in some degree shares responsibility for the discrepancy between goal and reality. If responsible inquiry is directed toward this problem, the unknowns in this vital area of public policy may be reduced, and we may begin to reexamine the place of health in our presently implicit hierarchy of values as opposed, for example, to education, other forms of welfare, space exploration, urban crowding, rural poverty, national security, and the myriad national concerns to which we allocate community resources. We may even be able to move toward calm and rational discussion of some alternative forms of social organization of the health care system, including their economic and perhaps social costs, hopefully with the result that we ultimately arrive at intelligent decisions.

Notes

1 All life expectancy and mortality figures presented in this section pertaining to the United States in 1900 or subsequent years, unless otherwise specified, are based on various published reports of the National Vital Statistics Division of the National Center for Health Statistics (formerly the National Office of Vital Statistics), U.S. Public Health Service. The reports themselves are not specifically cited here, but the source for each figure is available upon request. Rates for years prior to 1933 are based on the "death-registration states" only. In 1900 this group consisted of ten states, primarily in the northeastern part of the country, and the District of Columbia. However, the number of states included in this registration area gradually increased over the years, and by 1933 all states in the continental United States were part of it. For comparison purposes, figures for the death-registration states are customarily considered as satisfactorily representing the experience of the entire country, and this practice is followed in the present discussion.

2 All 1966 and 1967 figures shown in this selection are provisional. Based on past experience, however, the provisional rates are likely to be identical, or nearly so, to the final rates.

3 Cause of death in United States mortality statistics is currently determined in accordance with World Health Organization Regulations, which specify that member nations classify causes of death according to the International Statistical Classification of Diseases, Injuries and Causes of Death, 1955. Besides specifying the classification, World Health Organization Regulations outline the form of medical certification and the coding procedures to be used. In general, when more than one cause of death is reported, the cause designated by the certifying physician as the underlying cause of death is the cause tabulated (cf. World Health Organization, 1957).

4 The method of ranking causes of death used here follows the procedure recommended by *Public Health Conference on Records and Statistics* at its 1951 meeting. Only those causes specified in the "List of 60 Selected Causes of Death" were included in the ranking, and the following categories specified in that list were omitted: the two group titles, "major cardiovascular-renal diseases" and "diseases of the cardiovascular system"; the single title, "symptoms, senility, and ill-defined conditions"; the residual titles, "other infective and parasitic diseases," "other bronchopulmonic diseases," "other diseases of the circulatory system," and "all other diseases"; and all subtitles represented within a broader title. Causes of death are ranked on the basis of rates unadjusted for age or to a specific Revision of the International List of Diseases and Causes of Death, and the above discussion is based on these "crude" rates. But the *titles* used, and the 1966 rates, are those of the Seventh Revision.

5 The full title of this cause-of-death grouping, in the nomenclature of the Seventh Revision of the International List of Diseases and Causes of Death, is: gastritis, duodenitis, enteritis, and colitis, except diarrhea of the newborn.

6 However, there is some lack of comparability between these two figures, and this increase, although undoubtedly substantial, may not be quite as large as these figures indicate.

References

Anderson, Odin W., and George Rosen.
  1960   An examination of the concept of preventive medicine. *Health Information Foundation, Research Series No. 12.* New York: Health Information Foundation.

Chicago Board of Health; Planning Staff of the Health Planning Project.
  1965   *A Report on Health and Medical Care in Poverty Areas of Chicago and Proposals for Improvement.*

Dorn, Harold F.
  1952   Prospects of further decline in mortality rates. *Human Biology* 24, 4 (December): 235–261.

Dublin, Louis I., in collaboration with Mortimer Spiegelman.
  1951   *The Facts of Life—From Birth to Death.* New York: Macmillan.

Hillery, George A., Jr., *et al.*
  1968   Causes of death in the demographic transition. Paper presented at the Annual Meeting of the Population Association of America, Boston, Mass.

Kitagawa, Evelyn M.
  1968   Race differential in mortality in the United States, 1960 (corrected and uncorrected). Paper presented at the Annual Meeting of the Population Association of America, Boston, Mass., April.

Lerner, Monroe.
  1968   The level of physical health of the poverty population: a conceptual reappraisal of structural factors. Paper presented at Conference on New Dimensions in Health Measurements, sponsored by Washington Statistical Society and American Marketing Association, Washington, D.C., January 25.

Lerner, Monroe, and Odin W. Anderson.
  1963   *Health Progress in the United States: 1900-1960.* Chicago: University of Chicago Press.

Maryland State Department of Health, Division of Biostatistics.
  1967   *Annual Vital Statistics Report: Maryland, 1966.* Also, same annual reports for earlier years to 1957. Baltimore.

Pond, M. Allen.
  1961   Interrelationship of poverty and disease. *Public Health Reports 76* (November): 967–974.

Spiegelman, Mortimer.
  1968   Life tables. Pp. 292–299 in *International Encyclopedia of the Social Sciences.* New York: Free Press.

Strauss, Anselm L.
  1967   Medical ghettos: medical care must be reorganized to accept the life-styles of the poor. *Trans-action* 4(May):7–15 and 62.

Tarver, James D.
  1959   Projections of mortality in the United States to 1970. *The Milbank Memorial Fund Quarterly 37,* 2(April): 132–143.

United Nations.
  1967   *Demographic Yearbook, 1966.* New York.

World Health Organization.
  1957   *Manual of the International Statistical Classification of Diseases, Injuries, and Causes of Death: Based on the Recommendations of the Seventh Revision Conference, 1955.* Vol. I. Geneva, Switzerland.

Yordy, K. D., and J. E. Fullarton.
  1965   The heart disease, cancer, and stroke amendments of 1965 (P.L. 89–239). Reprint from *Health, Education and Welfare Indicators.* November.

PART II
VIEWS ON DEATH:
HISTORICAL AND
CONTEMPORARY

Contents

Although it may be banal to say that death is as old as man, it is nonetheless interesting to reflect that the topic of death is a development that distinguishes man from every other creature. Currently there are many obvious changes in the "thanatological wind." These changes include the increase in general longevity, the secularization of death, organ transplantations, a swirling debate on the topics of euthanasia and "appropriate death," and a general concern with reconceptualizing the psychological dimensions of death in light of changes in our knowledge of the human condition.

To understand the contemporary discussions and disputations about death, we need to know something of the ways in which human beings have attempted to come to grips with the fact of death throughout history, including their religious creeds, their philosophical beliefs, their views of certain diseases (TB and cancer), and their funerary and burial practices.

This part touches upon historical views of death and some contemporary reflections. It includes chapters by a historian, a medievalist, and a novelist-essayist, which, taken together, provide a panoramic view of death in Western society.

60

7 ·   Five Variations on Four Themes

Philippe Ariès

*Philippe Ariès is a French civil servant—a botantist(!)—who
specializes in social history. Among his works are the books
Centuries of Childhood: A Social History of Family Life, Death in
America, and Western Attitudes Toward Death: From the Middle
Ages to the Present. His most recent work, The Hour of Our
Death, has been called "an absolutely magnificent thousand-year
panorama." The section reproduced here is the conclusion of that
book and is a summary of Ariès's view of the changing nature of
death in the Western world over the last one thousand years.*

In the preface, I explained how I was gradually led to
select certain kinds of documentation: literary, liturgical, testamentary, epi-
graphic, and iconographic. I did not study these documents separately or in
any particular order. I studied them simultaneously, in the light of a question
that arose in the course of my first explorations. My hypothesis, which had
already been proposed by Edgar-Morin, was that there was a relationship
between man's attitude toward death and his awareness of self, of his degree
of existence, or simply of his individuality. This is the thread that has guided
me through a dense and confusing mass of documents; this is the idea that
has determined the itinerary that I have followed to the end. It is in terms of
these questions that the information contained in the documents has taken
on a form and a meaning, a continuity and a logic. This has been the key that
has helped me to decipher facts otherwise unintelligible or unrelated.

In *Essais sur l'histoire de la mort*, I held to this system of analysis and
interpretation. I have also used it in the general organization of the present
work. It has inspired the titles of three of the five parts: "The Tame Death,"
"The Death of the Self," and "The Death of the Other." These titles were also
suggested by Vladimir Jankélévitch in his book on death.

But my research for that gave me a greater familiarity with the facts, which
slightly altered my original hypothesis, raised other questions, and opened
up other perspectives. Awareness of one's self or one's destiny was no longer
the only possible point of departure. Other systems of analysis and interpretation appeared along the way, systems that were just as important as the
one I had chosen to guide me and that would have served just as well to give
some order to the formless mass of documentation. I have allowed them to
take shape in my text as I discovered them in the documents, while I
continued my research and reflection. I hope that the reader has noticed
them in passing.

Today, at the end of this seemingly endless itinerary, the assumptions I
started out with are no longer exclusive. Having abandoned my preconceived
ideas along the way, I turn and cast my eye over this thousand-year landscape like an astronaut looking down at the distant earth. This vast space

seems to me to be organized around the simple variations of four psychological themes. The first is the one that guided my investigation, *awareness of the individual.* The others are: the *defense of society against untamed nature, belief in an afterlife,* and *belief in the existence of evil.*

By way of conclusion I shall try to show how the various models defined in the course of this book (the tame death, the death of self, remote and imminent death, the death of the other, and the invisible death) can be explained in terms of variations on these four themes.

THE TAME DEATH

All four themes appear in the first model of the tame death, and all are of equal importance in defining it.

Death is not a purely individual act, any more than life is. Like every great milestone in life, death is celebrated by a ceremony that is always more or less solemn and whose purpose is to express the individual's solidarity with his family and community.

The three most important moments of this ceremony are the dying man's acceptance of his active role, the scene of the farewells, and the scene of mourning. The rites in the bedroom or those of the oldest liturgy express the conviction that the life of a man is not an individual destiny but a link in an unbroken chain, the biological continuation of a family or a line that begins with Adam and includes the whole human race.

One kind of solidarity subordinated the individual to the past and future of the species. Another kind made him an integral part of his community. This community was gathered around the bed where he lay; later, in its rites of mourning, it expressed the anxiety caused by the passage of death. The community was weakened by the loss of one of its members. It expressed the danger it felt; it had to recover its strength and unity by means of ceremonies the last of which always had the quality of a holiday, even a joyous one. Thus, death was not a personal drama but an ordeal for the community, which was responsible for maintaining the continuity of the race.

If the community feared the passage of death and felt the need to recover itself, this was not only because it was weakened by the loss of one of its members. It was also because death—the death of an individual or the repeated deaths caused by an epidemic—opened a breach in the defense system erected against the savagery of nature.

From the earliest times man has refused to accept either sex or death as crude facts of nature. The necessity of organizing work and maintaining order and morality in order to have a peaceful life in common led society to protect itself from the violent and unpredictable forces of nature. These included both external nature, with its intemperate seasons and sudden accidents, and the internal world of the human psyche, which resembles nature in its suddenness and irregularity; the world of the ecstasy of love and the agony of death. A state of equilibrium was achieved and maintained by means of a conscious strategy to contain and channel the unknown and formidable forces of nature. Death and sex were the weak points in the defense system, because here there was no clear break in continuity between culture and nature. So these activities had to be carefully controlled. The ritualization of death is a special aspect of the total strategy of man against nature, a strategy of prohibitions and concessions. This is why death has not been permitted its natural extravagance but has been imprisoned in ceremony, transformed into spectacle. This is also why it could not be a solitary adventure but had to be a public phenomenon involving the whole community.

The fact that life has an end is not overlooked, but this end never coincides with physical death. It depends on the unknown state of the beyond, the solidity or ephemerality of survival, the persistence of memory, the erosion of fame, and the intervention of supernatural beings. Between the moment of death and the end of survival there is an interval that Christianity, like the other religions of salvation, has extended to eternity. But in the popular mind the idea of infinite immortality is less important than the idea of an extension. In our first model, the afterlife is essentially a period of waiting characterized by peace and repose. In this state the dead wait, according to the promise of the Church, for what will be the true end of life, the glorious resurrection and the life of the world to come.

The dead live a diminished life in which the most desirable state is sleep, the sleep of the future blessed who have taken the precaution of being buried near the saints. Their sleep may be troubled owing to their own past impiety, the stupidity or treachery of survivors, or the mysterious laws of nature. In this case they cannot rest; they wander and return. The living do not mind being close to the dead in churches, parks and markets, provided they remain asleep. But it is impossible to forbid these returns; so they must be regulated, channeled. Society permits the dead to return only on certain days set aside by custom, such as carnivals; then it can control their presence and ward off its effects. The Latin Christianity of the Middle Ages reduced the ancient risk of their return by installing them among the living, at the center of public life. The gray ghosts of paganism became the peaceful recumbent figures, whose sleep was likely to remain untroubled thanks to the protection of the Church and the saints; later, thanks to the Masses and prayers said in their behalf.

This conception of life after death as a state of repose or peaceful sleep lasted much longer than one might believe. It is surely one of the most tenacious forms of the old attitude toward death.

Death may be tamed, divested of the blind violence of natural forces, and ritualized, but it is never experienced as a neutral phenomenon. It always remains a misfortune, a *mal-heur*. It is remarkable that in the old Romance languages physical pain, psychological suffering, grief, crime, punishment, and the reverses of fortune were all expressed by the same word, derived from *malum*, either alone or in combination with other words: in French, *malheur, maladie, malchance, le malin* (misfortune, illness, mishap, the devil). It was not until later that an attempt was made to distinguish the various meanings. In the beginning there was only one evil that had various aspects: suffering, sin, and death. Christianity explained all of these aspects at once by the doctrine of original sin. There is probably no other myth that has such profound roots in the collective unconscious. It expressed a universal sense

of the constant presence of evil. Resignation was not, therefore, submission to
a benevolent nature, or a biological necessity, as it is today, as it was no doubt
among the Epicureans or Sotics; rather it is the recognition of an evil inseparable from man.

THE DEATH OF THE SELF

Such is the original situation, as defined by the relationship of our four
themes. Later, as one or more of these fundamental elements varied, the
situation changed.

The second model, the death of the self, is obtained quite simply by a shift
of the sense of destiny toward the individual.

We recall that the model was originally limited to an elite of rich, educated,
and powerful persons in the eleventh century, and still earlier to the isolated,
organized, and exemplary world of monks and canons. It was in this milieu
that the traditional relationship between self and other was first overthrown,
and the sense of one's own identity prevailed over submission to the collective destiny. Everyone became separated from the community and the species by his growing awareness of himself. The individual insisted on assembling the molecules of his own biography, but only the spark of death enabled
him to fuse them into a whole. A life thus unified acquired an autonomy that
placed it apart; its relations with others and with society were transformed.
Friends came to be possessed like objects, while inanimate objects were
desired like living beings. No doubt the balance sheet of the biography should
have been closed at the formidable hour of death, but soon it was carried
beyond, under the pressure of a desire to be more—something death could
not touch. These determined men colonized the beyond like some new
continent, by means of Masses and pious endowments. The chief instrument
of their enterprise, their guarantee of continuity between this world and the
next, was the will. The will served both to justify the love of earth and to make
an investment in heaven, thanks to the transition of a good death.

Individualism triumphed in an age of conversions, spectacular peni-
tences, and prodigious patronage, but also of profitable businesses; an age of
unprecedented and immediate pleasures and of immoderate love of life.

So much for awareness of the individual. It was inevitable that such an
exaltation of the individual, even if it was more empirical than doctrinal,
would cause some changes in the third theme, the nature of the afterlife. The
passion for being oneself and for being more than was manifested during a
single lifetime spread by contagion to the afterlife. The strong individual of
the later Middle Ages could not be satisfied with the peaceful but passive
conception of *requies*. He ceased to be the surviving but subdued *homo totus*.
He split into two parts: a body that experienced pleasure or pain and an
immortal soul that was released by death. The body disappeared, pending a
resurrection that was accepted as a dogma but never really assimilated at the
popular level. However, the idea of an immortal soul, the seat of individuality,
which had long been cultivated in the world of clergymen, gradually spread,
from the eleventh to the seventeenth century, until eventually it gained
almost universal acceptance. This new eschatology caused the word *death* to

be replaced by trite circumlocutions such as "he gave up the ghost" or "God has his soul."

This fully conscious soul was no longer content to sleep the sleep of expectation like the *homo totus* of old—or like the poor. Its immortal existence, or rather its immortal activity, expressed the individual's desire to assert his creative identity in this world and the next, his refusal to let it dissolve into some biological or social anonymity. It was a transformation of the nature of human existence that may well explain the cultural advance of the Latin West at this time.

So the model of the death of the self differs from the older model of the tame death with respect to two of our themes, that of the individual and that of the afterlife. The second and fourth parameters, on the other hand, have hardly moved. Their relative immobility protected the model from too sudden a change. It gave it a centuries-old stability that can be deceptive and that can give the impression that things had not changed at all.

Our fourth theme, belief in evil, remained virtually unchanged. It was necessary to the economy of the will and to the maintenance of a love of life that was based partly on an awareness of its fragility. It is obviously an essential element of permanence.

The second, defense against nature, might have been affected by the changes in the sense of the individual and of the afterlife. It was certainly threatened, but its equilibrium was restored.

The desire to assert one's identity and to come to terms with the pleasures of life gave a new and formidable importance to the hour of death mentioned in the *Ave Maria*, a prayer for a good death that dates from the end of this period. This could very well have upset the relationship of the dying man to his survivors or to society, making death pathetic, as in the romantic era, or solitary, like the death of the hermit, and abolishing the calming ritual that men had created as a defense against natural death. Death might then have become wild and terrifying, because of the force of emotion and the fear of hell. But this did not happen, because a new and totally opposite ceremony took the place of what had been threatened by individualism and its agonies.

The deathbed scene, which had once been the most important part of the ceremony, persisted, sometimes with just a touch more pathos, until the seventeenth and eighteenth centuries, when the pathetic element declined under the influence of an attitude of mingled acceptance and indifference. A series of ceremonies was inserted between death and burial: the funeral procession, which became ecclesiastical in character, and the service at the church in the presence of the body, which was the work of the urban reform movement of the late Middle Ages and the mendicant orders. Death was not abandoned to nature, from which the ancients had claimed it in order to tame it. On the contrary, death was more concealed than ever, for the new rites also included a fact that may seem negligible but that is highly significant. The face of the cadaver, which had been exposed to the eyes of the community, and which continued to be for a long time in Mediterranean countries and still is today in Byzantine cultures, was covered by the successive masks of a sewn shroud, the coffin, and the catafalque or representation.

After the fourteenth century, the material covering of the deceased become a theatrical monument such as was erected for the decor of mystery plays or for grand entrances.

The phenomenon of the concealment of the body and face of the deceased is contemporaneous with the attempts we find in the macabre arts to represent the underground decay of bodies, the underside of life, which was all the more bitter because this life was so well loved. This interest was transitory, but the concealment of the body was permanent. The features of the deceased, once calmly accepted, were henceforth covered because they might be upsetting, that is, frightening. The defense against untamed nature was invaded by a new fear, but this fear was immediately overcome by the taboo to which it gave rise. Once the body was conjured away by the catafalque or representation, the old familiarity with death was restored and everything returned to normal.

The definitive concealment of the body and the prolonged use of the will are the two most significant elements of the model of the death of the self. The first balances the second, maintaining the traditional order of death against the pathos and nostalgia of the individualism illustrated by the will.

REMOTE AND IMMINENT DEATH

This model of the death of the self, with all that it preserved in the way of traditional defenses and a sense of evil, influenced customs until the eighteenth century. However, profound changes were beginning to take place by the end of the sixteenth century, to some extent in actual customs and conscious ideas, but more especially in the secret world of the imagination. These changes, although barely perceptible, are very important. A vast transformation of sensibility was under way. The beginning of a reversal—a remote and imperfect adumbration of the great reversal of today—was starting to appear in representations of death.

Where death had once been immediate, familiar, and tame, it gradually began to be surreptitious, violent, and savage. Already, as we have seen, the old familiarity had been maintained only by means of the artifices of the later Middle Ages: more solemn rites and the camouflage of the body under the presentation.

In the modern era, death, by its very remoteness, has become fascinating; has aroused the same strange curiosity, the same fantasies, the same perverse deviations and eroticism, which is why this model of death is called "remote and imminent death."

What was stirring in the depths of the collective unconscious is something that had hardly moved at all for thousands of years, our second theme, the defense against nature. Death, once tame, was now preparing its return to the savage state. It was a discontinuous movement, made up of violent jolts, long imperceptible advances, and real or apparent retreats.

At first sight it may seem surprising that this period of returning savagery was also characterized by the rise of rationalism, the rise of science and technology, and by faith in progress and its triumph over nature.

But it was at this time that the barriers patiently maintained for thousands of years in order to contain nature gave way at two points that are similar and often confused: love and death. Beyond a certain threshold, pain and pleasure, agony and orgasm are one, as illustrated by the myth of the erection of the hanged man. These emotions associated with the edge of the abyss inspire desire and fear. An early manifestation of the great modern fear of death now appears for the first time: the fear of being buried alive, which implies the conviction that there is an impure and reversible state that partakes of both life and death.

This fear might have developed and spread and, combined with other effects of the civilization of the Enlightenment, given birth (over a century ahead of time) to our culture. This is not the first time that the late eighteenth century seems to lead directly into the twentieth. But instead, something happened that could not have been forseen and that restored the actual chronology.

THE DEATH OF THE OTHER

If the momentum really did carry from the eighteenth to the twentieth century, it hardly seems that way to the unsophisticated observer. The continuity exists on deeper levels, but only rarely does it show above the surface. This is because in the nineteenth century, which saw the triumph of the industrial and agricultural techniques born of the scientific thought of the previous period, romanticism (the word is convenient) gave birth to a sensibility characterized by passions without limit or reason. A revolution in feeling seized the West and shook it to its foundation. All four of our themes were transformed.

The determining factor was the change in the first theme, the sense of the individual. Up to now this theme had alternated between two extremes: the sense of a universal and common destiny and the sense of a personal and specific biography. In the nineteenth century both of these declined in favor of a third sense, formerly confused with the first two: the sense of the other. But this was not just any other. Affectivity, formerly diffuse, was henceforth concentrated on a few rare beings whose disappearance could no longer be tolerated and caused a dramatic crisis: the death of the other. It was a revolution in feeling that was just as important to history as the related revolutions in ideas, politics, industry, socioeconomic conditions, or demography.

An original type of sensibility now came to dominate all others, a type that is well expressed by the English word *privacy*. It found its place in the nuclear family, remodeled by its new function of absolute affectivity. The family replaced both the traditional community and the individual of the late Middle Ages and early modern times. Privacy is distinguished both from individualism and from the sense of community, and expresses a mode of relating to others that is quite specific and original.

Under these conditions, the death of the self had lost its meaning. The fear of death, born of the fantasies of the seventeenth and eighteenth centuries, was transferred from the self to the other, the loved one.

The death of the other aroused a pathos that had once been repressed. The ceremonies of the bedroom or of mourning, which had once been used as a barrier to counteract excess emotion—or indifference—were deritualized and presented as the spontaneous expression of the grief of the survivors. But what the survivors mourned was no longer the fact of dying but the physical separation from the deceased. On the contrary, death now ceased to be sad. It was exalted as a moment to be desired. Untamed nature invaded the stronghold of culture, where it encountered humanized nature and merged with it in the compromise of "beauty." Death was no longer familiar and tame, as in traditional societies, but neither was it absolutely wild. It had become moving and beautiful like nature, like the immensity of nature, the sea or the moors. The compromise of beauty was the last obstacle invented to channel an immoderate emotion that had swept away the old barriers. It was an obstacle that was also a concession, for it restored to this phenomenon that people had tried to diminish an extraordinary glamour.

But death could not have appeared in the guise of the highest beauty if it had not ceased to be associated with evil. The ancient and intimate relationship between death and physical illness, psychic pain, and sin was beginning to break down. Our fourth theme, the belief in evil, which had long been stationary, was preparing to withdraw, and the first stronghold it deserted was the heart and the mind of man, which was believed to be its original and impregnable seat. What a revolution in thought! It is a phenomenon as important as the return of untamed nature within the human psyche, and indeed, the two are related; it is as if evil and nature had changed places.

The first barrier that fell in the eighteenth century—perhaps as early as the seventeenth in England—was belief in hell and in the connection between death and sin or spiritual punishment. (The necessity of physical illness was not yet questioned.) Scholarly thought and theology raised the problem as early as the eighteenth century. By the beginning of the nineteenth century, the debate in Catholic and Puritan cultures was over; belief in hell had disappeared. It was no longer conceivable that the dear departed could run such a risk. At most, among Catholics, there still existed a method of purification: time in purgatory, shortened by the pious solicitude of survivors. No sense of guilt, no fear of the beyond remained to counteract the fascination of death, transformed into the highest beauty.

If hell is gone, heaven has changed too; this is our third theme, the afterlife. We have followed the slow transition from the sleep of the *homo totus* to the glory of the immortal soul. The nineteenth century saw the triumph of another image of the beyond. The next world becomes the scene of the reunion of those whom death has separated but who have never accepted this separation: a re-creation of the affections of earth, purged of their dross, assured of eternity. It is the paradise of Christians or the astral world of spiritualists and psychics. But it is also the world of the memories of nonbelievers and freethinkers who deny the reality of a life after death. In the piety of their love, they preserve the memories of their departed with an intensity equal to the realistic afterlife of Christians or psychics. The difference in doctrine between these two groups may be great, but it becomes negligible in the practice of what may be called the cult of the dead. They have all built the same castle, in the image of earthly homes, where they will be reunited—in dream or in reality, who knows?—with those whom they have never ceased to love.

THE INVISIBLE DEATH

In the nineteenth century the psychological landscape was completely transformed. Neither the nature of the four themes nor the relationships among them were the same. The situation that resulted did not last more than a century and a half. But the model of death that came next, our model, which I have called the invisible death, does not challenge the underlying tendency or the structural character of the changes of the nineteenth century. It continues them, even if it seems to contradict them in its most spectacular effects. It is as if beyond a certain threshold, these tendencies produced the opposite effects.

Our contemporary model of death is still determined by the sense of privacy, but it has become more rigorous, more demanding. It is often said that the sense of privacy is declining. This is because today we demand the perfection of the absolute; we tolerate none of the compromises that romantic society still accepted beneath its rhetoric—or beneath its hypocrisy, as we would say. Intimacy must be either total or nonexistent. There is no middle ground between success and failure. It is possible that our attitude toward life is dominated by the certainty of failure. On the other hand, our attitude toward death is defined by the impossible hypothesis of success. That is why it makes no sense.

The modern attitude toward death is an extension of the affectivity of the nineteenth century. The last inspiration of this inventive affectivity was to protect the dying or the invalid from his own emotions by concealing the seriousness of his condition until the end. When the dying man discovered the pious game, he lent himself to it so as not to disappoint the other's solicitude. The dying man's relations with those around him were now determined by a respect for this loving lie.

In order for the dying man, his entourage, and the society that observed them to consent to this situation, the protection of the patient had to outweigh the joys of a last communion with him. Let us not forget that in the nineteenth century, death, by virtue of its beauty, had become an occasion for the most perfect union between the one leaving and those remaining behind. The last communion with God and/or with others was the great privilege of the dying. For centuries there was no question of depriving them of this privilege. But when the lie was maintained to the end, it eliminated this communion and its joys. Even when it was reciprocal and conspiratorial, the lie destroyed the spontaneity and pathos of the last moments.

Actually, the intimacy of these final exchanges had already been poisoned, first by the ugliness of disease, and later by the transfer to the hospital. Death became dirty, and then it became medicalized. The horror and fascination of death had fixed themselves for a moment on the apparent death and had

then been sublimated by the beauty of the Last Communion. But the horror
returned, without the fascination, in the repellent form of the serious illness
and the care it required.

When the last of the traditional defenses against death and sex gave way, the medical profession could have taken over the role of the community. It did so in the case of sex, as is attested by the medical literature on masturbation. It tried to do so in the case of death by isolating it in the scientific laboratory and the hospital, from which the emotions would be banished. Under these conditions it was better to communicate silently in the complicity of a mutual lie.

It is obvious that the sense of the individual and his identity, what we mean when we speak of "possessing one's own death," has been overcome by the solicitude of the family.

But how are we to explain the abdication of the community? How has the community come to reverse its role and to forbid the mourning which it was responsible for imposing until the twentieth century? The answer is that the community feels less and less involved in the death of one of its members. First, because it no longer thinks it necessary to defend itself against a nature which has been domesticated once and for all by the advance of technology, especially medical technology. Next, because it no longer has a sufficient sense of solidarity; it has actually abandoned responsibility for the organization of collective life. The community in the traditional sense of the word no longer exists. It has been replaced by an enormous mass of atomized individuals.

But if this disappearance explains one abdication, it does not explain the powerful resurgence of other prohibitions. This vast and formless mass that we call society is, as we know, maintained and motivated by a new system of constraints and controls. It is also subject to irresistible movements that put it in a state of crisis and impose a transitory unity of aggression or denial. One of these movements has unified mass society against death. More precisely, it has led society to be ashamed of death, more ashamed than afraid, to behave as if death did not exist. If the sense of the other, which is a form of the sense of the self taken to its logical conclusion, is the first cause of the present state of death, then shame—and the resulting taboo—is the second.

But this shame is a direct consequence of the definitive retreat of evil. As early as the eighteenth century, man had begun to reduce the power of the devil, to question his reality. Hell was abandoned, at least in the case of relatives and dear friends, the only people who counted. Along with hell went sin and all the varieties of spiritual and moral evil. They were no longer regarded as part of human nature but as social problems that could be eliminated by a good system of supervision and punishment. The general advance of science, morality, and organization would lead quite easily to happiness. But in the middle of the nineteenth century, there was still the obstacle of physical illness and death. There was no question of eliminating that. The romantics circumvented or assimilated it. They beautified death, the gateway to an anthropomorphic beyond. They preserved its immemorial association with illness, pain, and agony; these things aroused pity rather than distaste. The trouble began with distaste: Before people thought of abolishing physical illness, they ceased to tolerate its sight, sound, and smells.

Medicine reduced pain; it even succeeded in eliminating it altogether. The goal glimpsed in the eighteenth century had almost been reached. Evil was no longer part of human nature, as the religions, especially Christianity, believed. It still existed, of course, but outside of man, in certain marginal spaces that morality and politics had not yet colonized, in certain deviant behaviors such as war, crime, and nonconformity, which had not yet been corrected but which would one day be eliminated by society just as illness and pain had been eliminated by medicine.

But if there is no more evil, what do we do about death? To this question modern society offers two answers.

The first is a massive admission of defeat. We ignore the existence of a scandal that we have been unable to prevent; we act as if it did not exist, and thus mercilessly force the bereaved to say nothing. A heavy silence has fallen over the subject of death. When this silence is broken, as it sometimes is in America today, it is to reduce death to the insignificance of an ordinary event that is mentioned with feigned indifference. Either way, the result is the same: Neither the individual nor the community is strong enough to recognize the existence of death.

And yet this attitude has not annihilated death or the fear of death. On the contrary, it has allowed the old savagery to creep back under the mask of medical technology. The death of the patient in the hospital, covered with tubes, is becoming a popular image, more terrifying than the *transi* or skeleton of macabre rhetoric. There seems to be a correlation between the "evacuation" of death, the last refuge of evil, and the return of the same death, no longer tame. This should not surprise us. The belief in evil was necessary to the taming of death; the disappearance of the belief has restored death to its savage state.

A small elite of anthropologists, psychologists, and sociologists has been struck by this contradiction. They propose not so much to "evacuate" death as to humanize it. They acknowledge the necessity of death, but they want it to be accepted and no longer shameful. Although they may consult the ancient wisdom, there is no question of turning back or of rediscovering the evil that has been abolished. They propose to reconcile death with happiness. Death must simply become the discreet but dignified exit of a peaceful person from a helpful society that is not torn, not even overly upset by the idea of a biological transition without significance, without pain or suffering, and ultimately without fear.

8 · Various Ways in Which Human Beings Have Sought to Reconcile Themselves to the Fact of Death

Arnold Toynbee

In this selection taken from his remarkable and scholarly book Man's Concern with Death, *Professor Toynbee lists and discusses numerous ways in which human beings have denied, accepted, embraced, or "handled" death.*

From Man's Concern with Death. *Copyright ©1968 by Arnold Toynbee, A. Keith Mant, Ninian Smart, John Hinton, Cicely Yudkin, Eric Rhode, Rosalind Heywood, and H. H. Price. Used with permission of McGraw-Hill Book Company, and Hodder and Stoughton Ltd.*

(a) *Hedonism*. The most obvious way of reconciling oneself to death is to make sure of enjoying life before death snatches it from us. The catchwords *"Carpe diem"*[1] and "Let us eat and drink, for tomorrow we shall die"[2] are notorious, and Herodotus[3] has preserved an Egyptian folktale in which Pharaoh Mycerinus, when the gods had sentenced him to die after enjoying six more years of life, successfully doubled the term arbitrarily allotted to him by turning night into day. This hedonistic solution of the problem of death is, of course, illusory. In reality a human being cannot stay awake, enjoying himself, for twenty-four hours a day, day in and day out, over a span of six years. Nor can he make sure of enjoying himself even for the briefest spells; and, if luck does favor him that far, his foreknowledge that one day he is going to die will be lurking all the time at the back of his mind. The skeleton was simply being brought out of the cupboard in the Egyptian custom, also recorded by Herodotus,[4] of exhibiting a miniature wooden model of a mummy at a feast in order to remind the revellers of the grim fact of death, which they were trying to put out of their minds for the moment. Eating, drinking, and being merry is, like war and revolution, an intrinsically transient activity. It is, in fact, another name for "sowing one's wild oats," and it is only in fairy tales that this conventional escapade is followed by "marrying and living happily after." In prosaic real life, it is followed by the anxieties and fatigues and maladies of adult life—congenital evils of our human condition, which, if they are severe and long drawn out, may make a human being actually look forward to death as an eventual relief on which he can count for certain.

(b) *Pessimism*. The most obvious alternative to the illusory solace of hedonism is to conclude that life is so wretched that death is the lesser evil. In the fifth century B.C., when the Greeks were at the height of their achievement in all fields, the Greek poet Sophocles declared[5] that "it is best of all never to have been born, and second best—second by far—if one has made his appearance in this world, to go back again, as quickly as may be, thither whence he has come." The Greek historian Herodotus attributed the same view to the sixth century B.C. Greek sage Solon.[6] According to Herodotus's story of Solon's conversation with King Croesus, the human beings cited by Solon as having been the happiest, save for one, within his knowledge, were, not Croesus, as Croesus had hoped, but two young men—a pair of brothers—who had died in their sleep at the height of their strength, achievement, and fame, when their mother had prayed to the goddess Hera to bestow on them the best lot that a human being can hope for. The comment that Herodotus puts into Solon's mouth is that the brothers "met with the best possible end that human life can have, and that God took this opportunity for making it manifest that, for a human being, it is better to be dead than to be alive."

"Those whom the gods love, die young."[7] In many military-minded societies, there have been young men who have looked forward, with pride and exaltation, to the prospect of dying prematurely in battle; and it is significant that when, in the seventh and sixth centuries B.C., some Greeks began to transfer their treasure from their community to their own individual lives, the elegiac and lyric poets who gave expression to this psychological revolution harped plaintively on the brevity of the springtime of an individual human being's life, and on the weariness of the long-drawn-out sequel of old age, with its burden of increasing ill health and debility.[8]

However, in this age and in all subsequent ages of ancient Greek history, the Greeks continued to be enthralled by the Homeric epics. These were probably composed, or given their final form, in the eighth century B.C., and the hero of the *Iliad*, Achilles, is not at all reconciled to his foreknowledge that he is doomed to die young, nor does his mother the goddess Thetis take satisfaction, as some Spartan human mothers did in later times, in the prospect of her son's dying young on the field of honor. Young though he still is at the siege of Troy, Achilles has already had time to win matchless glory by his outstanding prowess. But the fame that Achilles has already achieved in a short life does not console him for death's imminence; and his experience after death, in the realm of the shades of the dead, justifies posthumously his reluctance, while alive, to lose his life prematurely. In the eleventh book of the *Odyssey*, his shade is represented as saying to Odysseus that the lot of an agricultural laborer who is the serf of a pauper in the land of the living is preferable to being king of all the dead,[9] and, after making this bitter observation, he strides away, unresigned and indignant, though elated at the same time by the news, given him by Odysseus, of the military prowess of his son.[10]

The repining at the prospect of an early death which is attributed to Achilles in the *Iliad* may have corresponded to the average Greek young man's attitude in real life—even a young man who happened to have been born a Spartan and to have been conditioned by being brought up under the "Lycurgan" regimen. If his mother took the stand of the legendary Spartan mother, his private reaction may have been a wry one. At Sparta, and, *a fortiori*, in other Greek city-states, there is much evidence that the Greeks,

even those who paid lip service to pessimism, got much enjoyment out of life;
were not eager to exchange it for death; and did not let the edge be taken off
their enjoyment by brooding on a death for which they were in no hurry. The
Greeks enjoyed passing the time of day in each other's company, discussing
anything and everything; they enjoyed beauty; and they had a genius for
bringing these two sources of enjoyment together in choral singing and
dancing, theatrical performances, religious processions, and talkative political assemblies.

Compared with Greek pessimism, Indian pessimism has been radical, and
it has also been sincere, as is demonstrated by the single-mindedness and the
austerity with which it has been put into action. Hinduism regards man's
universe as being an illusion; the Buddha, anticipating some of the schools of
modern Western psychologists by about twenty-four centuries, held that the
soul is an illusion too. He saw in the human psyche only a fleeting series of
discontinuous psychological states, which are held together only by desire,
and which can be dissipated if and when desire is extinguished. In the
Buddha's view, the extinction of desire is the proper goal of human endeavor,
because the achievement of this brings with it the extinction of suffering, and,
for the Buddha, life and suffering were synonymous. Not death, but rebirth, is
the arch-ordeal for a human being. The Buddha took it for granted that the
effect of desire, precipitated in the form of karma (the cumulative spiritual
effects of action taken in a succession of lives up to the present), is to keep a
series of rebirths going *ad infinitum,* unless and until, in one of the lives in this
chain, the sufferer, by successfully performing the strenuous spiritual exerci-
ses that the Buddha has prescribed, manages to bring the series to an end by
attaining the state of extinguishedness (nirvana) in which all passion is spent
and rebirth ceases because it is no longer brought on by the momentum of
karma, now that karma has been worked off. In this spiritual struggle to attain
nirvana, death (i.e., the death of the current life in the series) is an unimpor-
tant incident. Nirvana may be attained at death, but it may also be attained
while the former sufferer is still living what will now have been the last of his
successive lives.

One index of pessimism is suicide. In a society in which life is rated at so
low a value that death is held to be the lesser evil, suicide will be held to be
one of the basic human rights, and the practice of it will be considered
respectable and in some cases meritorious or even morally obligatory.

In the Graeco-Roman world, no stigma was attached to suicide, though the
practice of it was not so common as it has been in South and East Asian
countries in which the prevailing religions and philosophies have been of
Indian or Chinese origin. There were cases of Greek statesmen who committed suicide in a political impasse. Demosthenes and King Cleomenes III of
Sparta are examples. Under the Principate, Roman nobles were in some cases
allowed to commit suicide as an alternative to execution. The Greek philosopher Democritus is said by Lucretius to have exposed himself to death
voluntarily (perhaps by starvation) when he found that his mental powers
were failing.[11] But the Greek spectators were surprised and impressed when
Peregrinus Proteus burned himself to death ostentatiously at Olympia.[12] (A

modern Western psychologist might have convicted him, as Lucian does, of exhibitionism.) It is possible that Peregrinus may have been influenced by an Indian precedent that could have been within his knowledge. According to the geographer Artemidorus of Ephesus, an Indian who had accompanied an Indian embassy to the Emperor Augustus had burnt himself to death at Athens. Strabo[13] cites Artemidorus as saying that "some Indians do this because they are finding life a burden, while others — of whom this one is an example — do it because they are finding life so good. The idea is that, when everything has gone as one likes, it is time to be off, for fear that, if one lingers, one may be overtaken by something that one does not like."

According to Artemidorus, this particular Indian "leaped on to the pyre, laughing, with nothing on but a loin cloth and with his body well oiled; and his tomb bears the inscription: 'Zarmanochegas, an Indian from Bargosa (Broach), who made himself immortal by following traditional Indian custom'."

In Hindu society the commonest form of suicide has been *sati*. It used to be deemed a meritorious act for a widow to burn herself to death when her husband died; and, though *sati* was nominally voluntary, it seems often to have been committed under pressure. A widower was under no reciprocal obligation; but male devotees used to throw themselves under the wheels of Juggernaut's car to be crushed to death. In present-day Vietnam, Buddhist monks and nuns have committed suicide by burning themselves as a political protest. In China under the imperial regime, a censor who had felt it to be his official duty to present a memorial to the Emperor, criticizing the Emperor's conduct, might follow up this act by committing suicide—a reconciliation of sincerity with loyalty that would increase the pressure on the Emperor while releasing the censor himself from embarrassment. In Japan, it has been a point of honor to commit suicide, not only as a political protest, but as a sign of respect for a defunct emperor or as atonement for some failure in duty, or for some breach of etiquette, which, in a Westerner's eye, would be a quite inadequate ground for making such drastic and such irrevocable amends, even if the Western observer had no objection to suicide in principle.

There have been cases in which Jews, Phoenicians, and Lycians have committed suicide *en masse* rather than allow themselves to be taken prisoner by a victorious enemy. On the other hand, Christians, whose religion is of Jewish origin, have always felt an inhibition against committing suicide, and have branded a suicide as a *felo de se*, who has debarred himself, by his crime, from being given burial in consecrated ground. The Christian's view of this world as being "a vale of tears" is much the same as the Buddhist's view; but the Christian, unlike the Buddhist, does not consider that he has the right to decide for himself to put an end to his life. For the Christian, this is not man's prerogative; it is God's; and it is impious wilfully to anticipate God's action. If this is a Christian superstition—and it is a superstition in Greek, Roman, Hindu, Buddhist, Confucian Chinese, and Japanese eyes—it is a Christian tradition that dies hard. At the present day, many ex-Christians, who have abandoned almost all the rest of the Christian tradition, still retain the Christian feeling that suicide is shocking.

In a community of Australian natives who live by food gathering and migrate, in search of food, in an annual orbit, the aged will voluntarily drop out and stay behind to die, in order to relieve the community of the burden of continuing to maintain them. In the present-day Western world the average expectation of life has been increased, without any accompanying increase in zest or relief from pressure, while the loosening of family ties has left many old people out in the cold, socially and spiritually. If they had been Australian natives, they would have allowed themselves to die; if they had been Chinese peasants, there would have been a place for them in the home, with their children and grandchildren, as long as they remained alive. Being Christians or ex-Christians, and therefore feeling the traditional Christian inhibition against committing suicide, many old people in the Western world today linger on, lonely and unhappy, until medical ingenuity ceases to be able to keep them physically alive.

The Christian inhibition against suicide applies *a fortiori*, to giving to incurably and painfully ailing human beings the merciful release that humane Christians give, as a matter of course, to animals when these are in the same plight. Hitler was not prevented by the conscience of the German Christian public from murdering millions of Jews; yet the German Christian conscience that did not prove effective for deterring Hitler from committing the crime of genocide did make it impossible for Hitler to carry out his plan of killing off aged, infirm, and feeble-minded Germans in order to relieve physically and mentally fit Germans of the burden of continuing to look after the unfit when Geman energies were being mobilized by Hitler for the waging of the Second World War.

(c) *Attempts to circumvent death by physical countermeasures.* One of the commonest primitive assumptions regarding death is that a dead person's life can be prolonged after death by providing the corpse with the food, drink, paraphernalia, and services that were formerly at the disposal of the person whose living body this corpse once was. The burial with the dead of objects that are useful to the living has been a worldwide practice. Archaeologists have been able to reconstruct a culture from the contents of graves in sites which there has been little or no trace left of the apparatus used by the living. Ancient tombs have been preserved in far greater numbers than ancient dwellings once inhabited by the living. Besides yielding up tools, weapons, ornaments, and clothes, some tombs have been found to contain the remains of slaughtered domestic animals and of human servitors, whose services the dead owner of the tomb was expected still to be able to command.

This naive strategy for circumventing death was carried to extremes in Ancient Egypt. If the tomb representing a dead pharaoh's house was magnified to the dimensions of a gigantic pyramid, if the furniture deposited in his tomb was as lavish in both quantity and quality as the gear that was buried with Tutankhamen; and if the tomb was endowed with lands whose revenues would pay, in perpetuity, for the provision of victals and for the performance of ritual by priests, it was felt that death could be counteracted and overcome by this massive application of physical countermeasures—in fact, by sheer physical force. Still more naive was the assumption that preserving a dead body by arresting its natural decay was tantamount to keeping the life in it. Mummification was practiced not only in Egypt but in Peru. The dryness of the climate in both coastal Peru and Upper Egypt was an assistance to the embalmer's work, yet this fine art was manifestly just as incapable of keeping life in a corpse as the Zoroastrian practice of exposing corpses to putrefy until they have been consumed by scavenging birds and beasts.

Another strategy for the circumvention of death by physical countermeasures has been to seek for the tree of life or for the elixir of immortality. But the fruitlessness of this quest has been recognised in mythology. When Adam and Eve had eaten of the fruit of the Tree of Knowledge, they were expelled from the Garden of Eden by the angel with the flaming sword before they had had time to baffle Yahweh by eating the fruit of the Tree of Life as well. Translated into present-day prosaic terms, this myth signifies that man's acquisition of science and technology has not enabled him to acquire immortality as well. The outcome of the Sumerian hero Gilgamesh's quest for immortality was likewise ironical. After performing a series of Herculean labors, Gilgamesh was on the last stage of his journey home with a branch of the Tree of Life in his hand when he accidentally dropped this into the water, where it was immediately snapped up by a snake. So Gilgamesh arrived home still mortal. His labors had, after all, been in vain.

The futility of trying to circumvent death by taking physical countermeasures was demonstrated dramatically in Ancient Egypt at the fall of the Old Kingdom. The fall of this regime was accompanied by a social revolution in the course of which the tombs of the pharaohs and of their courtiers were rifled and the funerary wealth accumulated in the course of three-quarters of a millennium was impudently plundered. The irony of this ignominious end of such careful and elaborate physical provision for the circumvention of death is one of the themes of surviving Egyptian works of literature written in the age of the Middle Kingdom. Yet this recognition of the futility of the practice did not deter succeeding generations from persisting with it, and the principal beneficiaries of the costly furnishing of Egyptian pharaohs and nobles came to be, not the dead themselves, but living tomb robbers. Tomb robbing became as fine an art as mummification. The robbers penetrated the most massive and most cunningly contrived defences and eluded the watchful eye of the public authorities. They battened on the Egyptian people's invincible naiveté. Yet it is conceivable that the robbers themselves were not altogether immune from the prevailing superstition. We can imagine them going about their professional business with mixed feelings of cynicism and guilt.

(d) *Attempts to circumvent death by winning fame.* Though a dead body cannot be kept alive by physical measures, the memory of the dead, as they were when they were truly alive, can be transmitted to succeeding generations. In an illiterate society the main media of commemoration are the memorization of genealogies and the composition and recital of oral poetry.

When a society has become literate, poetry can be reduced to writing and can
be supplemented by inscriptions engraved on stone or impressed on clay
tablets or written on papyrus or parchment or paper or palm leaves or slivers
of bamboo, to record the foundation of temples and the annals of reigns.
These official records, in turn, can be raised to the level of biographies and
historical works of literature which can take their place side by side with
poetry.

This attempt to circumvent death by commemoration is more sophisticated than the attempt to circumvent it by physical measures; but the outcome
of this attempt is ironical too in ways of its own. For instance, the recorder
eventually wins greater fame than the men of action whose fame has been
preserved by the recorder's pen. Most of what we know about the Athenian
statesman Pericles and the Spartan soldier Brasidas today is due to the fact
that a minor naval commander, Thucydides, was given the leisure for becoming a major historian thanks to his having been cashiered and exiled,
perhaps unfairly, for having failed to prevent Brasidas from capturing Amphi-
polis. When Horace wrote "non omnis moriar,"[14] he underestimated the
length of the time after his death during which his poetry would preserve the
memory of the poet himself. He reckoned that his poetry would continue to
be read as long as the ritual of Rome's official religion continued to be
performed. This ritual was suppressed by the intolerant Christian Roman
Emperor Theodosius I in the last decade of the fourth century of the Christian Era, only four centuries after the date of Horace's death. Yet Horace's
poetry is still being read in the twentieth century by readers whose mother
tongue is not Latin, and, in the earlier decades of the nineteenth century, it
was still being quoted in speeches made in English by members of the
parliament at Westminster.

Horace himself, however, has pointed out the precariousness of this circumvention of death by commemoration — sophisticated and ethereal
though this method is by comparison with the naive circumvention of death
by physical measures.

> Vixere fortes ante Agamemnona
> multi; sed omnes illacrimabiles
> urgentur ignotique longa
> nocte, carent quia vate sacro.[15]

The relics of Agamemnon's predecessors who are not commemorated in
the Homeric epic have now been disinterred by modern archaeologists. They
have proved to have been mightier monarchs than Agamemnon himself, and
whether or not they employed court poets whose works have not yet come to
light, we have now retrieved some of their records—not romantic minstrels'
lays but prosaic official inventories, corresponding to what present-day
governments call "forms." These pre-Agamemnonian Mycenaean official
documents are at least four or five centuries older than the *Iliad* and the
Odyssey, and we have specimens of rudiments of the Sumerian cuneiform
script that date from before the close of the fourth millennium B.C. but

mankind's first five millennia of literacy are dwarfed by the dark night of the preceding million years during which our ancestors were already human yet have not left any surviving memorial except their tools and their cave paintings—and even those Late Palaeolithic paintings are estimated to be not more than about thirty thousand years old. Our thousand past millennia of oblivion are a long span of time, compared to our subsequent 30,000 years of pictorial commemoration and 5000 years of literacy. But mankind's first million years, as well as his latest 5000 years, are dwarfed by the span of 2000 million years which is reckoned to be the expectation of life on the surface of this planet. It is difficult to imagine that any existing works of man, either monumental or literary, will have survived until the day when this planet becomes no longer habitable. Will any of the now current languages then still be intelligible? Will any works written in these still survive? Will not the pyramids, and the still more durable tumuli and railway embankments, have been worn down flatter than the most archaic of the rocks that now crop out on the earth's surface?

(e) *Self-liberation from self-centeredness by putting one's treasure in future generations of one's fellow human beings.* Another way in which human beings have sought to reconcile themselves to the fact of death has been so ubiquitous and so constant that one might almost venture to infer that it is innate in human nature. Down to this day, since the earliest date to which our surviving records reach back, most human beings have reconciled themselves, to some extent, to their mortality as individuals by putting their treasure in their descendants, while some human beings have expanded their concern to embrace all the other representatives of future generations who, though not their physical descendants, will be their successors and will perhaps be their spiritual heirs.

In the genealogy in the eleventh chaper of the Book of Genesis, the high point in the life of Shem and each of his successive descendants is his age when his first child is born. The remainder of his life, from that red-letter day onwards, till his death, is represented implicitly as being an anticlimax.

In Yahweh's successive promises to Abraham, the god never promises his human client personal immortality. What he promises him is progeny. "I will make of thee a great nation";[16] "I will make thy seed as the dust of the earth, so that, if a man can number the dust of the earth, then shall thy seed also be numbered";[17] "look now toward heaven and tell the stars, if thou be able to number them: and he said unto him, so shall thy seed be";[18] "thou shalt be a father of many nations";[19] Abraham shall surely become a great and mighty nation";[20] "in multiplying I will multiply thy seed as the stars of the heaven, and as the sand which is upon the sea shore."[21] Whether or not this prospect of becoming the ancestor of the Hebrew peoples reconciled Abraham to the prospect of his own death, it is evident that the promises that were held to have been made to Abraham by Yahweh were felt, by the authors and editors of the Book of Genesis, to be more valuable and more satisfying than any promise of personal immortality would have been. If the Israelite writers of

these passages believed that, after death, the shades of the dead retained a
shadowy existence in Sheol, they will have shared the feelings of the author of
the eleventh book of the *Odyssey*, who, as has been remarked earlier, describes the shade of Achilles as exulting, in Hades, at the news of his son's
prowess on earth, unreconciled though Achilles himself was to his own state
after death.[22]

It is significant that the belief in the resurrection of the dead did not gain a
foothold in the Jewish community until the second century B.C. This belief
seems to have been introduced to the Jews through their becoming acquainted with a foreign religion, Zoroastrianism. One of the considerations
that led some Jews to believe, from the second century B.C. onwards, in the
eventual resurrection of some individuals is thought to have been their
confidence in Yahweh's sense of justice. They will have felt that this was
bound to move Yahweh to reward those Jews who had suffered martyrdom
in resisting the Seleucid Emperor Antiochus IV's attempt to coerce the
Palestinian Jewish community into adopting the Greek way of life; and these
martyrs would not be adequately rewarded if they were not eventually raised
from the dead to become living participants in the messianic kingdom when
this was eventually established. The belief that, not only the Jewish martyrs,
but all the dead, were destined to rise again seems, in the development of
Judaism, to have come later.

It is also significant that this addition of a new article to the traditional
corpus of Jewish beliefs was not accepted immediately by the Jewish people
as a whole. It was adopted, at first, by the Pharisees only. It was rejected by
the Sadducees on the ground that there was no warrant for it in the written
Mosaic Law, and that the written law alone was valid. The Pharisees were
originally dissenters; the Sadducees represented the "establishment." The
Sadducees were in control of the temple at Jerusalem, and held at least the
key posts in the officiating priesthood. The Sadducees maintained their
dominant position in the Palestinian Jewish community, and persisted in
their rejection of the belief in resurrection of the dead, until the destruction of
the temple in A.D. 70. It was only after this that the Pharisees' hitherto
controversial belief became part of the orthodox faith of the Jewish people as
a whole; and, among the Jews, this general adoption of the belief in the
resurrection of the dead has not weakened the desire for the continuous
survival of the Jewish people as a community that perpetuates itself from
generation to generation of the mortal men and women who are its successive ephemeral representatives.

The pre-Pharisaic Israelites and Jews were not peculiar in reconciling
themselves to the prospect of death by taking comfort in the prospect that
their race would be perpetuated in their descendants. A prospect that has
caused greater anxiety and distress than the prospect of death has been the
prospect of dying without being survived by any descendants. According to
the Book of Genesis,[23] Abraham felt that Yahweh's announcement that he

was going to be Abraham's "exceeding great reward" was meaningless so long as Yahweh suffered Abraham to go childless; and this passionate desire to have descendants, that is attributed to Abraham in this passage, has been widespread. It has been particularly strong in societies, such as the Hindu and the Chinese, in which it has been held to be important for a human being that, after his death, he should be commemorated and venerated in a cult performed by a surviving son and by this son's descendants in their turn.

Where the cult of ancestors is practiced, this is evidence of a concern about what is going to happen after one's own death, but this concern may not be solely a concern for the perpetuation of the race; it may be partly self-centered. The ancestor who has demanded the cult has presumably sought commemoration for himself in the belief that this will have some posthumous value for him; the descendant who performs the cult may be moved to undertake this burden not only by love of a parent or by a feeling of piety toward a more remote ancestor, but also by a belief that dead ancestors have it in their power to benefit or injure their descendants, and that it is therefore advisable for their descendants to give them satisfaction by carrying on the cult. Abraham's longing to have a child is not un-self-regarding either. He points out to Yahweh that, if he dies childless, the heir who will inherit his estate will be, not one of his own kinfolk, but "one born in my house," i.e. a child of one of Abraham's slaves."[24]

This self-regarding aspect of the desire to be survived by a legitimate successor is likely to be prominent in cases in which the estate that the present holder of it will leave behind him at death does not consist just of private property, such as Abraham's flocks and herds, but is the succession to the throne of a kingdom. In this case, no doubt, the self-regarding desire to be succeeded by a descendant may be accompanied by a concern for the public welfare. The reigning sovereign may forebode that, if no near kinsman of his survives to succeed him, his own death may be followed by a dispute over the succession that might give rise to disorder. If the reigning sovereign has imposed on his subjects reforms that are radical and controversial, and if he is conscious that his own ability and willpower have been the principal agencies by which his reforms have been instituted and have been maintained, his desire that his lifework shall outlast his own lifetime may be stronger than his desire that his successor shall be one of his descendants.

The classic case is Peter the Great's treatment of his son and heir Alexei. After disinheriting Alexei, Peter had him flogged to death. One of Peter's motives for committing this dreadful and unnatural crime was a personal antipathy that was mutual; but Peter was also moved by concern for the future public welfare of the Russian state and people, and this concern of Peter's was justified by facts. Alexei was not, by nature, a man of action; he hated being involved in public affairs and was incompetent in them, and he was under the influence of people who were opposed to Peter's reforms and who would have pressed Alexei to undo these if Alexei had survived Peter and had succeeded him. Posterity will agree with Peter that, for Russia, this would have been a calamity.

The extreme step taken by Peter to ensure that the reforms which he had carried out in Russia should not be undone after his death brings out the truth that it is difficult to feel concern for the future welfare of posterity without also trying to give practical effect to this concern by taking steps to influence or even determine what shall happen after one's death insofar as this lies in one's power. If one feels concern for posterity, one will have one's own ideas about what is going to be beneficial for or detrimental to posterity, and one will then be moved to try to ensure the welfare of these future generations as one sees it, and to secure them against suffering harm as one sees that too. Heads of states who have a lifelong tenure of office are, of course, not the only people whose concern for posterity may incline them to try to make their power last longer than their own lifetime by fixing, while they are still alive, what shall happen after they are dead. This possibility also arises whenever any private person makes his or her will, especially if the testator is making bequests, not only to kinsmen and friends of his, but to religious, educational, or charitable institutions. The exercise, by the dead, of this posthumous power has been found so burdensome for posterity that, in some countries, legislation has been enacted that limits a testator's freedom to dispose of his property altogether as he chooses.

However, neither private testators nor rulers with a lifelong tenure have been so successful in governing the life of posterity as the founders of the historic philosophies and higher religions. Hundreds of millions of human beings who are alive at this moment are being swayed, on many issues, great and small, by the commandments and precepts of Marx, Muhammad, Saint Paul, Jesus, the Buddha, Confucius, and the redactors of the Pentateuch. The posthumous power of these spiritual authorities has been, and continues to be, incomparably great. Yet the exercise of this posthumous spiritual power has its ironical aspect.

Some of the authentic commandments and precepts of these religious leaders were drafted and promulgated by them on the spur of the moment for dealing with some urgent but local and temporary situation. Cases in point are Saint Paul's epistles and the chapters of the Qur'an that were issued by the Prophet Muhammad when he was the head of the government of the city-state of Medina. Both Muhammad and Paul would probably have been disconcerted if they could have foreseen how literally and earnestly even the most casual of their pronouncements were going to be taken by millions of devout posthumous adherents of theirs, and this for hundreds of years to come. There are other zealously obeyed commandments and precepts and statements that have been attributed falsely to the religious leader whose name has lent them their authority, and some of these might have shocked their alleged authors. What would Jesus, for instance, have felt if he could have foreseen that, after his death, his followers were going to worship him, in company with Yahweh and with the Holy Spirit, as one of the members of a divine trinity? On the evidence of the Gospels themselves, Jesus was an orthodox Jew. He is reported to have said to an enquirer: "Why callest thou me good? There is none good save one: that is God."[25] This saying is likely not only to be authentic but to have been notoriously authentic at the time when the Gospel according to Saint Mark was composed. If it had not been, it would surely have been expurgated; for it is a contradiction, out of Jesus's own mouth, of his posthumous Christian followers' thesis that he was God himself.

Peter's murder of Alexei also brings out, through being an extreme case, the truth that the future generations in whom a living human being can put his treasure may comprise a far wider circle than his own physical descendants. The choice that confronted Peter was not, in itself, a unique one. The reigning occupant of an hereditary office—whether he is the sovereign of a state or the director-in-chief of a family business—may feel obliged to disinherit his son, or some less close kinsman, because he judges him to be unfit to take over the duties of the office and because his conscience tells him that the interests of the realm or the business—i.e., the interests of people who are not his relatives but for whose welfare he is responsible—ought to take precedence over his family obligations to his "kith and kin." The disinheriting of an heir who is his heir by virtue of kinship does not normally require that he should put his disinherited kinsman to death. The Roman emperors Nerva, Trajan, Hadrian, and Antoninus Pius each in turn handed on the imperial office to a successor who was his son only by the legal fiction of adoption, and in doing this they were making the future welfare of the Empire and its inhabitants their paramount concern; but none of them murdered any disinherited kinsman of his, as Peter murdered Alexei. On the other hand Marcus Aurelius did a bad service to the Empire when he departed from the consistent practice of his four immediate predecessors by bequeathing the imperial office to his actual son Commodus. For Commodus was not only incompetent in public affairs and uninterested in them, as Alexei was. Unlike Alexei, Commodus was a vicious character.

Peter the Great's concern for the welfare of future generations embraced a nation that was already a large one, but that was, at the same time, only one among a number, with some of which it was at enmity. Marcus Aurelius's four predecessors' concern embraced the whole population of an empire that was a world-state in the eyes of its rulers and their subjects, in the sense that the Roman Empire contained within its frontiers as much of the contemporary civilised world as was within its inhabitants' ken. Today, anyone who is concerned with the welfare of future generations has to expand his concern not only from his family to his nation, but from his nation to the whole human race. For, in our day, "the annihilation of distance" by the progress of technology has linked together, for good or for evil, the fortunes of all sections of mankind, while the invention of the atomic weapon has put the human species in danger of extinction once again for the first time since, in the Later Paleolithic Age, man definitively got the upper hand over all other living creatures on the face of this planet except bacteria. No doubt, Lord Russell was thinking in these ecumenical terms if he said, as he is reported to have said, that, when one has reached old age, it is important to care immensely about what is going to happen after one is dead.

In the present state of military potency, political tension, and scientific knowledge, this means putting one's treasures in seventy million future generations of mankind which will have come and gone, after the present generation has died off, before the surface of this planet will have ceased to be habitable for living creatures. Can a human being reconcile himself to the fact of death by putting his treasure in future generations of all mankind in these almost unimaginably large numbers? Can the transfer of one's concern from one's own puny self to so vast a posterity give meaning, value, and zest to life and deprive death of its sting?

It may seem audacious to say that posterity on this scale is not something great enough to draw a human being competely out of himself, and so to reconcile him entirely to his foreknowledge that he himself is going to die. Yet to sink one's self-centeredness in a concern for all future generations of one's fellow human beings would be wholly satisfying only if one knew that mankind was the be-all and end-all of the universe. We do not know this; we have no means of discovering whether or not it is the truth; and it seems unlikely to be the truth, considering that our own planet, solar system, and galaxy are only minute fragments of a physical universe whose bounds, if it has any bounds, are beyond the reach of our powers of observation. Moreover, there is, within the psyche of any single human being, a psychic universe that is apparently proving to be at least as vast, in its own medium, as the physical universe is. Furthermore, the psychic universe, the physical universe, and the relation between the two are not self-explanatory; they are mysterious; they can hardly be the ultimate reality. Can a human being get into touch with this ultimate reality? And, if he can, can he reconcile himself to death by entering into eternal communion with the ultimate reality or by merging himself in it?

(f) *Self-liberation from self-centeredness by merging oneself in ultimate reality.* To get into touch with ultimate reality and to merge oneself in it has been an Indian quest. In India, this has been the principal quest of philosophers of all schools for the last 3,000 years at least. Round about the turn of the sixth and fifth centuries B.C., the quest produced a sharp cleavage between two schools which gave different reports of the findings of introspection and consequently worked out different prescriptions for reaching spiritual goals that were perhaps identical.

The adherents of one school reported that, when a human being succeeds in bringing into the light of consciousness the very center of his psyche, he finds there a "dweller in the innermost"—a soul—that is identical with ultimate reality itself. This finding has been expressed in the three words "That art thou"—"that" meaning ultimate reality, and "thou" meaning a human soul. Was the recognition of the identity of "thou" with "that" held to be tantamount to the merging of "thou" in "that"? Possibly it was; for the recognition of the identity is not just an intellectual discovery; it is the consummation of long and hard spiritual travail.

The opposing school was the school founded by the Buddha. The Buddha's findings were quite different from those of his contemporaries, and, so far from being the final consummation of long and hard spiritual travail, they were a fresh starting point for this. The Buddha reported that in the psyche there was no soul; he found there only a series of discontinuous psychic states, held together and kept moving only by the momentum of the karma engendered by desire. His prescription for merging the self in ultimate reality was not to penetrate to the self's core and recognise the identity of ultimate reality with this; it was to stop the flow of psychic states by extinguishing desire—i.e., self-centeredness—thus attaining the state of "extinguished-ness" (nirvana).

A present-day Western observer is likely to be more conscious of the common ground of these two opposing Indian schools of thought than of the differences that loomed so large in the minds of their respective Indian initiators. Both schools take it for granted that all sentient beings are doomed to go through a round of rebirths which will continue unless and until, in one of the successive lives, the sufferer succeeds in bringing the series of lives to an end. Both schools hold that rebirth is a far greater evil than death, and that to circumvent rebirth, not to circumvent death, ought therefore to be the supreme goal of human endeavors. Both schools also hold that the spiritual exertions required for attaining this goal are long and hard, though their prescriptions for striving to attain it differ. A human being who adheres to either of these schools of Indian philosophy will have little difficulty in reconciling himself to the fact of death. The fact (taken by him for granted) that death is going to be followed by another rebirth will be this man's nightmare. I have never forgotten the radiant smile that came over the face of a Japanese scholar, Professor Anesaki, when, at a conference held in Kyoto in 1929, he announced: "I am from Tokyo, but also from Kyoto, because I am coming here after I am dead." My guess is that Professor Anesaki's smile was evoked by two thoughts: the thought of the natural beauty of the city that was to cherish his mortal remains, and the thought of the ineffable beauty of nirvana.

(g) *The belief in the personal immortality of human souls.* Hindus believe in a suprapersonal immortality (i.e., in the identity of the essence of a human being's psyche with ultimate reality). Buddhists believe in a depersonalized immortality (i.e., in the possibility of extinguishing the self through self-release from self-centeredness). I have suggested that these two beliefs of Indian origin prove, on analysis, to be more closely akin to each other than they might appear to be at first sight and than they have been held to be in Indian philosophical controversies. A further feature that they have in common is that both alike are more credible than the belief in personal immortality.

It is credible that a human being, in his psychic dimension, may be part and parcel of ultimate reality in its spiritual aspect, and it is demonstrable that, in his physical dimension, the same human being is part and parcel of the universe in the material aspect in which we apprehend the universe with our senses and interpret our sense data in scientific terms. On the other hand, no living human being has ever been able to demonstrate conclusively that he has been in psychic communication with a disembodied human psyche (i.e., with the psyche of a human being whose body was, at the time not alive, but was either a corpse or had decomposed into the chemical elements of which the corpse had consisted at the moment at which it had ceased to be a living body). *A fortiori*, no one has ever been able to demonstrate that he has been in psychic communion with an unembodied human psyche that has never yet been embodied or that has, at the time, been temporarily unembodied in an interval between the successive incarnations (a conception that requires the undemonstrated assumption that a psyche can be, and is, repeatedly reembodied in successive living bodies, human or nonhuman, without losing its identity).

Every living human being whom any other living human being has ever encountered has been a psychosomatic entity; and the life of every one of these human psychosomatic entities, like the life of every other sexual living organism inhabiting this planet, has moved, or is in the course of moving, in the time dimension, on a trajectory which describes a course up from birth through infancy to its prime and from its prime through old age down to death, supposing that the human being in question lives out his or her life to the end of its full natural span, and that this particular life is not cut short prematurely by disease, accident, or violent death inflicted by other human beings in war, by law, or by private enterprise.

Death, whatever its cause and its circumstances may be, is an event in which the former living body becomes a corpse which decays (unless its physical decomposition is artificially arrested), while, at the same moment, the psyche passes out of human ken (i.e. ceases to be in communication with the psyche of any human being who is alive at that moment). It is impossible to conceive of a human body being alive without being associated with a human psyche. It has been found possible to imagine a psyche being alive without being associated with a living body. However, this feat of imagination is so difficult that attempts to work outs its implications in detail have run into incongruities, inconsistencies, incompatibilities, and self-contradictions.

When believers in personal immortality have sought to describe the state of disembodied souls, they have found no way of describing this hypothetical state that does not involve the drawing of some analogy with the psychosomatic life on earth of which we have actual experience. The shade that has been consigned to Sheol or to Hades or the underworld as conceived by the Sumerians and their Akkadian and Babylonian cultural heirs is an enfeebled replica of the now dead person who was once alive in psychosomatic form. In fact, the author of the eleventh book of the *Odyssey* takes it for granted that the only condition on which the living visitor, Odysseus, can put himself into communication with the shades of the dead in their shadowy world is by partially and temporarily reendowing them with a modicum of physical life. In order to enable them to talk to him, Odysseus has first to administer to them a physical stimulant. He gives each of them, in turn, a drink of the blood of nonhuman psychosomatic animals—sheep—which Odysseus has slaughtered for this purpose.[26] As for the privileged minority of the departed who are imagined to be enjoying a blissful existence in the Kingdom of the

West or as a star in heaven (if the departed grandee has been an Egyptian pharaoh), or in Elysium (if he has been a pre-Christian Greek hero), or in Valhalla (if he has been a pre-Christian Scandinavian warrior), these favored few are credited with a vitality that is of a superhuman or even godlike exuberance.

This inability to conceive of disembodied spirits in nonpsychosomatic terms also besets those believers in personal immortality who hold that the destiny of the departed is determined, not by their former rank, but by their former conduct. The torments of the damned in hell are depicted on the walls of Etruscan tombs and of Eastern Orthodox Christian refectories in monasteries on Mount Athos, and are described in Dante's *Divina Commedia*, in crassly physical terms—and some of these imaginary torments are so extreme that no living human being could be subjected to them for more than a few seconds without dying of them, though, incongruously, the disembodied spirits that are believed to be suffering these lethal torments are held to have been made immortal in order that their suffering may be everlasting. There have been a number of different conceptions of the nature of the personal immortality of a disembodied or unembodied soul, but they all have one significant feature in common. In some degree, they all involve some incongruities, inconsistencies, incompatibilities, and self-contradictions.

One conception of the immortality of the soul has been that souls are not only immortal but eternal: i.e., that every soul has been in existence eternally before it ever came to be embodied, and that it will remain in existence eternally after having become disembodied once for all. Of all the divers conceptions of the personal immortality of the soul, this is the one that comes nearest to the Indian conception of a suprapersonal or a depersonalized immortality. This belief was held by some pre-Christian Greeks, but never, so far as we can judge, by more than a small sophisticated minority. Another small minority believed that, at death, the soul was annihilated. The majority probably believed, from the beginning to the end of the pre-Christian age of Greek history, that each human soul comes into existence together with the body with which it is associated in life, and that, after death, it continues, as a shade, to lead, in Hades, a shadowy life of the kind depicted in the eleventh book of the *Odyssey*.

The most prominent of the Greek believers in the eternity of souls were the Pythagoreans (an esoteric semiphilosophical semireligious organized fraternity) and the Orphics (an unorganized and unsophisticated sect). Both these Greek sets of believers in the eternity of souls were also believers in the transmigration of souls from one incarnation to another, and this latter belief is so arbitrary and so peculiar that its simultaneous appearace, in the sixth century B.C., in the Greek world and in India can hardly have been fortuitous. One possible common source is the Eurasian nomad society which, in the eighth and seventh centuries B.C., had descended upon India, Southwestern Asia, the steppe country along the north shore of the Black Sea, and the Balkan and Anatolian peninsulas in one of its occasional explosive *völkerwanderungen*.

A belief in the personal immortality of souls which does not involve a belief
in their being eternal as well as immortal is bound up with the attempts,
noted already, to circumvent death by physical countermeasures. The pre-
Christian and pre-Muslim Egyptians, for instance, believed in the conditional
immortality of the souls of the dead—or, strictly speaking, in the conditional
immortality of one of the several souls that were believed to appertain to a
human being. The particular soul known as "ka" was believed to remain in
existence, haunting the dead person's tomb, as long as posterity continued to
keep the tomb in proper spiritual condition by performing the requisite ritual
there and by providing the requisite supplies of food, drink, clothes, and
furniture which were conceived of as being necessities of life after death, as
they had been before death. This belief was held simultaneously with the
incompatible beliefs that the dead person's soul might have migrated to the
Kingdom of the West or might have ascended to heaven to shine there as a
star or might have descended into the underworld presided over by the god
Osiris.

This Egyptian belief in the conditional immortality of souls after death has
also been held, though it has not, in all cases, been worked out so systematically, by all the numerous other peoples that have practiced ancestor worship, e.g., the Chinese.

Three other varieties of a belief in the immortality of souls after death that
does not involve a belief in their preexistence before birth or in their eternity
have been mentioned already. There has been a belief in a dismal habitation
of the souls of the dead, which retain a shadowy existence there. This is the
Hebrew Sheol, the Greek Hades, and the Sumerian counterpart of these.
There has been a belief in a blissful abode for the souls of dead persons who
had been in privileged positions in their lifetime. This is the Egyptian Kingdom of the West and the Kingdom of Heaven, the Greek Elysium, the Scandinavian Valhalla. There has also been a belief in the existence of two alternative
destinations for the souls of the dead—destinations that are determined,
according to this more ethical belief, not be previous rank, but by previous
behavior. The souls of the wicked are consigned, as a punishment, to hell—
an everlasting abode which is not merely dismal, as Sheol or Hades is, but is
excruciating. On the other hand, the souls of the righteous are admitted, as a
reward, to Paradise or heaven—an everlasting abode which is as blissful as
Elysium or Valhalla, but which, unlike them, is attained in virtue of previous
merits, not of previous rank.

For believers in Hades and Elysium, the consignment of a dead person's
soul to the one or the other two alternative abodes is automatic. It is decided
by the dead person's former social rank in his lifetime. For believers in hell
and heaven, the decision depends on the dead person's conduct during his
lifetime; his conduct cannot be assessed without being examined and apprai-
sed; and this requires the passing of a judgment by some authority. The belief
in a judgment of souls after death is a necessary corollary of the belief in
heaven and hell.

This belief in a judgment of souls after death made its appearance at two
widely different dates at two far apart places (far apart, that is to say, before

the very recent "annihilation of distance"). The belief appeared in Egypt perhaps as early as the age of the Old Kingdom in the third millennium B.C., and it also appeared in Northeastern Iran or in the Oxus-Jaxartes basin round about the turn of the seventh and sixth centuries B.C., i.e., in the lifetime of the Prophet Zarathustra, who was the promulgator of the belief in this region. We We have no evidence as to whether the Egyptian and the Iranian belief in a judgment by which the soul, after death, is consigned either to hell or to heaven had a common historical origin. It is noteworthy, however, that the Egyptian and Iranian beliefs have a further feature in common. The judge of the souls of the dead — Osiris in the one case and Ahura Mazdah in the other — is a good god who has triumphed, or who is going to triumph, in a hard struggle with a wicked god or wicked semidivine being. Osiris, after an initial defeat, has been given an eventual victory over his wicked brother and adversary Seth by the prowess of Osiris's son Horus and by the devotion of his sister and wife Isis. Ahura Mazdah is going to be victorious, eventually, over his wicked adversary Ahriman.

The Egyptian belief in a judgment of souls after death, to determine whether they shall be sent to hell or to heaven, was presumably the source of the same belief in the Greek world in the Hellenic Age. Here it was probably a legacy of Egyptian influence in Crete in the Minoan Age. Osiris, in his capacity of serving as the judge of the souls of the dead, has a Cretan counterpart in Rhadamanthus. In Egypt the pyramid texts, inscribed for the benefit of pharaohs in the age of the Old Kingdom, and the later "Book of the Dead," circulated for popular use, are collections of formulae, spells, and instructions designed to help the dead person's soul find its way successfully to a blissful terminus without falling into any of the pitfalls, traps, and obstacles that will beset the soul in the course of its difficult and dangerous passage. The contents of the Orphic tablets are similar and are designed to serve the same purpose.

In both cases the purpose is practical guidance, not edification, and, in so far as purification enters into it, this is purification in the ritual, not in the ethical, sense. In the pre-Christian Greek picture of hell, Tityus, Sisyphus, Tantalus, and Ixion are four classical representatives of the damned who are suffering everlasting torments. The wall paintings in Etruscan tombs show that the Greek picture of hell made a strong impression on the Etruscans; and it may not be fanciful to guess that there may have been an Etruscan component (preserved in subsequent Tuscan folklore), as well as a Christian component, in the medieval Christian Tuscan poet Dante's lurid description of the torments of the damned in the Christian hell.

The Christian and Muslim conceptions of the judgment of souls after death and of the heaven and the hell to which the souls are consigned respectively, in accordance with the verdict, are evidently derived, in the main, not from the pre-Christian religion of Egypt, but from Zoroastrianism —presumably via Pharisaic Judaism, which—unlike the Sadduccan Judaism of the postexilic Jewish "establishment" in Judea—laid itself open to Zoroastrian influences that played upon Judaism after the incorporation of

Babylonia, Syria, Palestine, and Egypt in the Persian Empire in the sixth century B.C.

In Christian belief the individual judgment of souls immediately after death, and their consignment, immediately after judgment, to hell, limbo, or heaven, coexists with the incompatible belief in the universal judgment of all souls—both the souls of the resurrected dead and the souls of the human beings alive at the moment—when the Last Trump sounds to give the signal for the resurrection of the dead and for "the Last Judgment" of living and of resurrected dead human beings alike.

When the belief in personal immortality is associated with a belief in a judgment after death—a judgment that will consign the dead to either eternal bliss or eternal torment—the price of a human being's belief in the survival of his personality after his death is anxiety during his lifetime.

> For we know Him that hath said, "Vengeance belongeth unto me; I will recompense," said the Lord. And again, "The Lord shall judge his people."
> It is a fearful thing to fall into the hands of the living God.[27]

(h) *The belief in the resurrection of human bodies.* A disembodied or unembodied soul is more difficult to imagine than a soul that is associated with a living body in the psychosomatic unity with which we are familiar through our acquaintance with ourselves and with our fellow living human beings. This union of soul with body in a life after death is easier to imagine if it is represented as being a reunion, in which the body with which the soul is now associated is the body — reconstituted, reanimated, and resurrected — with which this soul was associated before soul and body were parted by death and the body consequently became a corpse. On the other hand the reconstitution, reanimation, and resurrection of a corpse is virtually impossible to imagine, considering that, after death, a human body immediately begins to decay and eventually decomposes completely, unless the entrails are removed and the rest of the corpse is preserved artificially by being mummified.

The audience that Saint Paul had attracted at Athens listened to him patiently till he made the statement that God had raised a man from the dead; but this assertion brought the meeting to an end. Some of Paul's listeners laughed, while others, more courteously, told him that they would wait to hear more from him till they found another opportunity.[28] If Paul had stated that Jesus had an immortal soul which had preexisted and would continue to exist eternally, his Greek audience might have been willing to hear him out. Personal immortality of souls was a familiar and not incredible hypothesis for Greeks of Saint Paul's generation, but to be asked to believe in the resurrection of the dead was, for them, tantamount to being given notice by the speaker himself that he was wasting their time by talking nonsense.

Paul might have obtained a better hearing for his declaration of belief in bodily resurrection if he had been preaching in contemporary Egypt; for in

Egypt, since at least as far back in time as the third millennium B.C., it had been believed that one corpse had come to life again—and this after it had been cut up into fourteen pieces that had been scattered and had had to be reassembled. In Egypt this story was told of a god—the god Osiris who, since his own bodily resurrection, had become the judge of souls after death. When Paul told the Athenians that Jesus had been raised from the dead, he referred to Jesus as being a man and said that it was God who had raised him; but at the same time Paul cited this act of God's as evidence that God had appointed Jesus to judge all mankind at a future date that was already fixed,[29] and Paul believed that Jesus was in some sense God, though he did not divulge this belief of his on this occasion. It will be recognized that the role of being a god who is put to death and is resurrected in order to become mankind's judge is attributed to both Osiris and Jesus.

The belief that Jesus has risen from the dead, the belief that he is to judge mankind, and the linking of these two beliefs with each other thus have an Egyptian precedent; but there is also another tenet of Christianity in which a belief in resurrection is linked with a belief in judgment, and this tenet appears to be of Zoroastrian, not Egyptian, origin. According to Christian doctrine, Christ's judgment of mankind is not an *ad hoc* judgment of the souls of the dead individually, immediately after the death of each of us; it is a future judgment of all mankind simultaneously, including the people who will be alive at the time, as well as all those who will have lived and died by then; and the dead will be brought to judgment by a resurrection of their bodies, which will be brought back to life for the occasion and will be reunited with their souls. This belief in the bodily resurrection of all dead human beings is common to Christianity and Islam, and, like the belief in judgment, noted earlier, it seems to have been derived by both religions from Zoroastrianism via Pharisaic Judaism. According to Zoroastrian doctrine, the discrimination between the righteous and the wicked at the last and general judgment is to be made by means of a physical ordeal by fire and molten metal; and this indicates that, according to Zoroastrianism, in accordance with Pharisaic Judaism, Christianity, and Islam, the dead are expected to rise again physically.

Zoroastrianism anticipated Christianity in believing in two judgments: a judgment of each soul individually, immediately after death, and a final judgment of all human beings simultaneously, the dead as well as those alive at the time. This belief is so peculiar and involves such incongruities that there surely must be an historical connection between its appearances in these two different religions: i.e., Christianity must have adopted the belief from Zoroastrianism. Zoroastrianism's priority is indicated, not only by the chronological fact that Zoroastrianism is about six centuries older than Christianity, but also by the connection, in Zoroastrianism, between the belief in a future last and general judgment and the belief in a final and conclusive victory of the good god Ahura Mazdah over the evil spirit Ahriman in the current war between these two spiritual powers. Ahura Mazdah's coming victory over Ahriman is to have the general judgment of mankind as its sequel.

This belief that mankind is to be judged twice over, besides being incongruous—it seems superfluous to recall souls from heaven or hell, as the case may be, to earth in order to have the same verdict passed on them for the second time—also raises the question whether heaven and hell are to be thought of as existing in the psychic dimension or in the physical dimension. The locus of disembodied souls is presumably not physical. Yet the agony and the bliss of the souls of the dead before the general resurrection are depicted in physical imagery; and if, for the last and general judgment, the temporarily disembodied souls of the dead will have been reunited with their resurrected bodies, the heaven and the hell to which they will then be consigned must be physical localities, if the human beings who are sent there after this second judgment have been restored to the psychosomatic state in which they lived on earth before their deaths — not to speak of those who are overtaken, still alive, by the sounding of the Last Trump.

In Christianity and Islam, as in Zoroastrianism, the resurrection of human bodies is associated with a last and general judgment, which will consign —or reconsign—the resurrected dead, and will also consign the living to either heaven or hell. Their common mother religion, Pharisaic Judaism, however, seems—at any rate, to begin with—to have adopted the Zoroastrian belief in bodily resurrection in a version that was less close to the original than the Christian-Muslim version is. In this original Pharisaic Jewish version the resurrection is apparently to be a privilege, not an ordeal. The Jewish martyrs who have given their lives for the Jewish faith and for the Jewish people are to rise again from the dead, not to attend a divine judgment which will consign them either to heaven or to hell, but to participate in the reestablishment on earth of the Kingdom of Judah by "the Lord's Anointed" (the Messiah): a scion of the House of David who will not only reinstate his ancestral kingdom up to its Davidic frontiers, but will transform it into a world-empire that will be the millennial Jewish successor of the successive world-empires of the Assyrians, the Persians, and the Macedonians.

This mundane Jewish adoption of a transcendental Zoroastrian belief brings out the truth that the resurrection of the body does not necessarily imply that the reconstituted psychosomatic human being is going to be immortal. The Messiah himself seems to have been thought of originally as being a mortal man who would be distinguished from his fellow mortals only in being the legitimate Davidic heir to the Kingdom of Judah and in bearing rule over a world-empire that would be still more extensive and more mighty than the realm of the Messiah's ancestor David himself. In the course of nature the Messiah would die, like David and like every one of David's successors and the Messiah's predecessors who, from the tenth to the sixth century B.C. had, each in turn, reigned over the Kingdom of Judah as "the Lord's Anointed," i.e., as the legitimate living representative of the Davidic dynasty. If the Davidic restorer of the Davidic kingdom was destined to be mortal, like his ancestor, the resurrected martyrs would presumably prove to be mortal too. They would be resurrected only to die again eventually —dying, in their exceptional case, for the second time.

It will be seen that, in this first phase, the adoption by the Pharisaic Jews of

the Zoroastrian belief in bodily resurrection was subordinated to the traditional Jewish view—expressed in the legend of Yahweh's successive promises to Abraham—that the supreme blessing for a mortal man was to be
assured, not of securing personal immortality for himself, but of leaving
behind him descendants who would perpetuate his race. It was taken as a
matter of course that the Jewish martyrs would be raised from the dead
expressly for the purpose of witnessing the eventual military and political
triumph of Judah to which they would have contributed by having sacrificed
their lives. It was assumed that they would be well content to "depart in
peace," together with the Messiah himself, when their eyes had seen God's
salvation which He had prepared before the face of all peoples[30] — a salvation that would be the corporate salvation of the Jewish people, and a glory
that would be the political glory of a reestablished Jewish state which, this
time, would be, not a petty local principality, but a veritable world-empire.

(i) *The hope of heaven and the fear of hell.* A Hindu who, as a result of
intense introverted contemplation, has attained, as a personal experience,
the intuition that the essence of his soul is identical with ultimate reality, has
presumably been liberated by this experience from all hopes and fears about
either life or death. He has become aware of a truth that assures him of the
unimportance of life and of death alike. A Buddhist who has learned that it is
possible to make a definitive exit into nirvana from the sorrowful series of
rebirths, and who has also been instructed in the strenuous spiritual exerci-
ses by means of which this goal may be attained, will be too absorbingly
preoccupied with the pursuit of his practical spiritual endeavors to concern
himself with either life or death or to entertain either hopes or fears. On the
other hand, lively hopes and fears about a human being's destiny after death
will be aroused by a belief in personal immortality, whether the believer in
this expects to survive everlastingly as a disembodied soul or expects his soul
to be reunited, at the sounding of the Last Trump, with his resurrected body,
to live on everlastingly thereafter as a reconstituted psychosomatic unity: i.e.,
as a human being constituted like his own present living self and like the
living selves of his contemporaries who, like him, have not yet suffered death.

What is the effect of the belief in personal immortality after death on the
feelings, attitude, and conduct of the believer? To what degree, if any, does it
influence his behavior while he is alive in the psychosomatic form of life
which is the only form of it that is known to us in our experience?

The believer in a conditional personal immortality—an immortality that is
dependent on the perpetual performance of rites by the believer's descendants — is likely to suffer anxiety. He will be anxious to make sure both that
he is going to leave descendants behind him and that these will have both the
will and the means to perform, punctiliously, all that is requisite in order to
maintain the immortality of this ancestor of theirs. The believer in a personal
immortality in the shadowy realm of Sheol or Hades will repine at the brevity
of a human being's full-blooded zestful psychosomatic life on earth—unless,
of course, he undergoes so much suffering before death that he comes to
contemplate even the bleak prospect of Sheol or Hades with resignation. The

grandee who is confident that his own destination is not Sheol or Hades but is Elysium or Valhalla may be nerved by his aristocratic self-assurance to face the prospect of personal immortality after death with equanimity, or even with the pleasurable anticipation with which a Buddhist—the polar opposite of the pagan barbarian warrior—looks forward to his exit into a nirvana in which his personality will have been extinguished.

The believer in a personal immortality which he may be going to spend either in heaven or in hell, according to the verdict that will be passed, after his death, on his conduct while he was alive, ought, if he holds this belief *bona fide*, to be the most anxious of all; and his version of the belief in personal immortality ought to have the greatest effect of all on his present behavior. He is committed to the belief that the credit or debit balance of the account of his good and evil deeds during his brief life on earth is going to decide, once and for all, whether his destiny is to be weal or woe in the everlasting future of sentient personal life that awaits him after death.

In practice, there is in some cases a considerable discrepancy between the belief on the one hand—even when the believer believes himself to be sincere—and the believer's state of mind and behavior on the other hand. I have, for instance, known one believer who was intensely afraid of the prospect of death, though he was conscious of having lived righteously in the main and though he was utterly confident that he was one hundred percent correct in his theological tenets. Logically, he ought to have felt assured that, after death, he would not only go to heaven but would be received there as a VIP. All the same, he was unable to face the prospect of death with equanimity. Conversely, there have been people who have believed that the infallible penalty for the commission of serious sins in this life is condemnation, after death, to everlasting torments in hell, yet who have not been deterred by this belief from committing sins that have been so heinous that, according to the sinner's own belief, his condemnation to suffer everlasting torment in hell will be inescapable.

Such discrepancies between belief and behavior indicate that belief has to be supported by experience if its influence on behavior is to be effective. All beliefs, whatever they may be, that relate to what is going to happen or is not going to happen to a human being after death are, intrinsically beyond the range of experience, and they are perhaps even beyond the range of realistic imagination.

Insofar as the belief in personal immortality after death does captivate a living person's imagination, the believer's mental picture of hell seems generally to be livelier than his mental picture of heaven. The torments of the damned in hell have, on the whole, been depicted and described more vividly than the bliss of the salvaged in heaven. Lucretius, in the third book of his *De Rerum Natura*,[31] in which he is arguing that death spells complete and permanent annihilation, presents this as a consoling thought for the living, because the prospect liberates them from the fear that, after death, they may be condemned to suffer the legendary everlasting torments that are believed, by the credulous, to be being inflicted on the mythical archsinners Tantalus, Tityus, Sisyphus, and Ixion.[32] As Lucretius drives his point home at the close of this passage, it is in this world only that life ever becomes hell, and this only for people who are such fools as to believe in the reality of a life in hell after death.

This fear of hell, which Lucretius is seeking to dispel, is offset, of course, by the hope of reunion, after death, with beloved fellow human beings from whom one has been parted either by dying before them or by surviving them. Bereavement through death is harder to face and to bear than death itself; and the pain of bereavement is mitigated if the separation that death brings with it is believed to be not everlasting but only temporary. The coming reunion is usually pictured as a blissful one in heaven; yet even the torments of hell are eased if they are shared. The most moving passage in Dante's *Inferno* is his depiction of Paolo and Francesca[33] locked in each other's arms in everlasting love as they are swept round together in an everlasting wind of anguish.

Notes

1 Horace, *Odes*, Book I, Ode xi, line 8. Cf. Book I, Ode iv, passim.

2 Isaiah 22:13. Cf. Eccles. 3:22.

3 Herodotus, Book II, chap. 133.

4 *Ibid.*, chap. 78.

5 Sophocles, *Oedipus Coloneus*, lines 1224-26.

6 Herodotus, Book I, chap. 31.

7 Byron, *Don Juan*, IV, xii.

8 E.g., Mimnermus, *Nanno*, Elegies I and II.

9 Homer, *Odyssey*, Book XI, lines 489-491.

10 *Ibid.*, lines 538-540.

11 Lucretius, *De Rerum Natura*, Book III, lines 139-141.

12 Lucian, *De Morte Peregrini*.

13 Strabo, *Geographica*, Book XV, chap. 1, §73 (C.720).

14 Horace, *Odes*, Book III, Ode xxx, line 6.

15 Horace, *Odes*, Book IV, Ode ix, line 25-28. "There were mighty men before Agamemnon— there were any number of them; yet, one and all, these are buried in a long, long night, unknown and unmournable—and this just because they had no inspired bard [to commemorate them, as Agamemnon has been commemorated by Homer]."

16 Gen. 12:2.

17 Gen. 13:16.

18 Gen. 15:5.

19 Gen. 17:4.

20 Gen. 18:18.

21 Gen. 22:17.

22 Homer, *Odyssey*, Book XI, lines 538-540.

23 Gen. 15:2-3.

24 *Ibid.*

25 Mark 10:18.

26 Homer, *Odyssey* Book XI, lines 23-50, 82, 88-89, 98, 153, 232, 390.

27 Heb. 10:30-31.

28 Acts 17:32.

29 Acts 17:31.

30 Luke 2:29-32.

31 Lucretius, *De Rerum Natura*, lines 978-1023.

32 Cf. Homer, *Odyssey*, Book XI, lines 582-600.

33 Dante, *Inferno*, Canto Quinto, lines 73-142.

9 · Illness as Metaphor

Susan Sontag

Susan Sontag is a novelist and essayist. Her nonfiction books include On Photography, Illness as Metaphor, *and two collections of essays,* Against Interpretation *and* Style of Radical Will; *her novels include* The Benefactor *and* Death Kit. *Essentially,* Illness as Metaphor *contrasts the ways in which two diseases—tuberculosis and cancer—have been viewed over the past few centuries. In the following selection from that book, Sontag reveals the metaphors—the connotative feelings—for these two scourges in a totally original and captivating way.*

INTRODUCTION

Illness is the night-side of life, a more onerous citizenship. Everyone who is born holds dual citizenship, in the kingdom of the well and in the kingdom of the sick. Although we all prefer to use only the good passport, sooner or later each of us is obliged, at least for a spell, to identify ourselves as citizens of the other place.

I want to describe, not what it is really like to emigrate to the kingdom of the ill and live there, but the punitive or sentimental fantasies concocted about that situation: not real geography, but stereotypes of national character. My subject is not physical illness itself but the uses of illness as a figure or metaphor. My point is that illness is *not* a metaphor, and that the most truthful way of regarding illness—and the healthiest way of being ill—is one most purified of, most resistant to, metaphoric thinking. Yet it is hardly possible to take up one's residence in the kingdom of the ill unprejudiced by the lurid metaphors with which it has been landscaped. It is toward an elucidation of those metaphors, and a liberation from them, that I dedicate this inquiry.

Two diseases have been spectacularly, and similarly, encumbered by the trappings of metaphor: tuberculosis and cancer.

The fantasies inspired by TB in the last century, by cancer now, are responses to a disease thought to be intractable and capricious—that is, a disease not understood—in an era in which medicine's central premise is that all diseases can be cured. Such a disease is, by definition, mysterious. For as long as its cause was not understood and the ministrations of doctors remained so ineffective, TB was thought to be an insidious, implacable theft of a life. Now it is cancer's turn to be the disease that doesn't knock before it enters, cancer that fills the role of an illness experienced as a ruthless, secret invasion—a role it will keep until, one day, its etiology becomes as clear and its treatment as effective as those of TB have become.

Although the way in which disease mystifies is set against a backdrop of new expectations, the disease itself (once TB, cancer today) arouses thoroughly old-fashioned kinds of dread. Any disease that is treated as a mystery and acutely enough feared will be felt to be morally, if not literally, contagious. Thus, a surprisingly large number of people with cancer find themselves being shunned by relatives and friends and are the object of practices of decontamination by members of their household, as if cancer, like TB, were an infectious disease. Contact with someone afflicted with a disease regarded as a mysterious malevolency inevitably feels like a trespass; worse, like the violation of a taboo. The very names of such diseases are felt to have a magic power. In Stendhal's *Armance* (1827), the hero's mother refuses to say "tuberculosis," for fear that pronouncing the word will hasten the course of her son's malady. And Karl Menninger has observed (in *The Vital Balance*) that "the very word 'cancer' is said to kill some patients who would not have succumbed (so quickly) to the malignancy from which they suffer." This observation is offered in support of anti-intellectual pieties and a facile compassion all too triumphant in contemporary medicine and psychiatry. "Patients who consult us because of their suffering and their distress and their disability," he continues, "have every right to resent being plastered with a damning index tab." Dr. Menninger recommends that physicians generally abandon "names" and "labels" ("our function is to help these people, not to further afflict them")—which would mean, in effect, increasing secretiveness and medical paternalism. It is not naming as such that is pejorative or damning, but the name "cancer." As long as a particular disease is treated as an evil, invincible predator, not just a disease, most people with cancer will indeed be demoralized by learning what disease they have. The solution is hardly to stop telling cancer patients the truth, but to rectify the conception of the disease, to de-mythicize it.

When, not so many decades ago, learning that one had TB was tantamount to hearing a sentence of death—as today, in the popular imagination, cancer equals death—it was common to conceal the identity of their disease from tuberculars and, after they died, from their children. Even with patients informed about their disease, doctors and family were reluctant to talk freely. "Verbally I don't learn anything definite," Kafka wrote to a friend in April 1924 from the sanatorium where he died two months later, "since in discussing tuberculosis . . . everybody drops into a shy, evasive, glassy-eyed manner of speech." Conventions of concealment with cancer are even more strenuous. In France and Italy it is still the rule for doctors to communicate a cancer diagnosis to the patient's family but not to the patient; doctors consider that the truth will be intolerable to all but exceptionally mature and intelligent patients. (A leading French oncologist has told me that fewer than a tenth of his patients know they have cancer.) In America—in part because of the doctors' fear of malpractice suits—there is now more candor with patients, but the country's largest cancer hospital mails routine communications and bills to outpatients in envelopes that do not reveal the sender, on the assumption that the illness may be a secret from their families. Since getting cancer can be a scandal that jeopardizes one's love life, one's chance of promotion, even one's job, patients who know what they have tend to be extremely prudish, if not outright secretive, about their disease. And a federal law, the 1966 Freedom of Information Act, cites "treatment for cancer" in a clause exempting from disclosure matters whose disclosure "would be an unwarranted invasion of personal privacy." It is the only disease mentioned.

All this lying to and by cancer patients is a measure of how much harder it has become in advanced industrial societies to come to terms with death. As death is now an offensively meaningless event, so that disease widely considered a synonym for death is experienced as something to hide. The policy of equivocating about the nature of their disease with cancer patients reflects the conviction that dying people are best spared the news that they are dying, and that the good death is the sudden one, best of all if it happens while we're unconscious or asleep. Yet the modern denial of death does not explain the extent of the lying and the wish to be lied to; it does not touch the deepest dread. Someone who has had a coronary is at least as likely to die of another one within a few years as someone with cancer is likely to die soon from cancer. But no one thinks of concealing the truth from a cardiac patient: there is nothing shameful about a heart attack. Cancer patients are lied to, not just because the disease is (or is thought to be) a death sentence, but because it is felt to be obscene—in the original meaning of that word: ill-omened, abominable, repugnant to the senses. Cardiac disease implies a weakness, trouble, failure that is mechanical; there is no disgrace, nothing of the taboo that once surrounded people afflicted with TB and still surrounds those who have cancer. The metaphors attached to TB and to cancer imply living processes of a particularly resonant and horrid kind.

2

Throughout most of their history, the metaphoric uses of TB and cancer crisscross and overlap. The *Oxford English Dictionary* records "consumption" in use as a synonym for pulmonary tuberculosis as early as 1398.[1] (John of Trevisa: "Whan the blode is made thynne, soo folowyth consumpcyon and wastyng.") But the pre-modern understanding of cancer also invokes the notion of consumption. The OED gives as the early figurative definition of cancer: "Anything that frets, corrodes, corrupts, or consumes slowly and secretly." (Thomas Paynell in 1528: "A canker is a melancolye impostume, eatynge partes of the bodye.") The earliest literal definition of cancer is a growth, lump, or protuberance, and the disease's name—from the Greek *karkinos* and the Latin *cancer*, both meaning crab—was inspired, according to Galen, by the resemblance of an external tumor's swollen veins to a crab's legs; not, as many people think, because a metastatic disease crawls or creeps like a crab. But etymology indicates that tuberculosis was also once considered a type of abnormal extrusion: the word tuberculosis—from the Latin *tūberculum*, the diminutive of *tūber*, bump, swelling—means a morbid swelling, protuberance, projection, or growth.[2] Rudolf Virchow, who founded the science of cellular pathology in the 1850s, thought of the tubercle as a tumor.

Thus, from late antiquity until quite recently, tuberculosis was— typologically—cancer. And cancer was described, like TB, as a process in which the body was consumed. The modern conceptions of the two diseases could not be set until the advent of cellular pathology. Only with the microscope was it possible to grasp the distinctiveness of cancer, as a type of cellular activity, and to understand that the disease did not always take the form of an external or even palpable tumor. (Before the mid-nineteenth century, nobody could have identified leukemia as a form of cancer.) And it was not possible definitively to separate cancer from TB until after 1882, when tuberculosis was discovered to be a bacterial infection. Such advances in medical thinking enabled the leading metaphors of the two diseases to become truly distinct and, for the most part, contrasting. The modern fantasy about cancer could then begin to take shape—a fantasy which from the 1920s on would inherit most of the problems dramatized by the fantasies about TB, but with the two diseases and their symptoms conceived in quite different, almost opposing, ways.

●

TB is understood as a disease of one organ, the lungs, while cancer is understood as a disease that can turn up in any organ and whose outreach is the whole body.

TB is understood as a disease of extreme contrasts: white pallor and red flush, hyperactivity alternating with languidness. The spasmodic course of the disease is illustrated by what is thought of as the prototypical TB symptom, coughing. The sufferer is wracked by coughs, then sinks back, recovers breath, breathes normally; then coughs again. Cancer is a disease of growth (sometimes visible; more characteristically, inside), of abnormal, ultimately lethal growth that is measured, incessant, steady. Although there may be periods in which tumor growth is arrested (remissions), cancer produces no contrasts like the oxymorons of behavior—febrile activity, passionate resignation—thought to be typical of TB. The tubercular is pallid some of the time; the pallor of the cancer patient is unchanging.

TB makes the body transparent. The X-rays which are the standard diagnostic tool permit one, often for the first time, to see one's insides—to become transparent to oneself. While TB is understood to be, from early on,

rich in visible symptoms (progressive emaciation, coughing, languidness, fever), and can be suddenly and dramatically revealed (the blood on the handkerchief), in cancer the main symptoms are thought to be, characteristically, invisible—until the last stage, when it is too late. The disease, often discovered by chance or through a routine medical checkup, can be far advanced without exhibiting any appreciable symptoms. One has an opaque body that must be taken to a specialist to find out if it contains cancer. What the patient cannot perceive, the specialist will determine by analyzing tissues taken from the body. TB patients may see their X-rays or even possess them: the patients at the sanatorium in *The Magic Mountain* carry theirs around in their breast pockets. Cancer patients don't look at their biopsies.

TB was—still is—thought to produce spells of euphoria, increased appetite, exacerbated sexual desire. Part of the regimen for patients in *The Magic Mountain* is a second breakfast, eaten with gusto. Cancer is thought to cripple vitality, make eating an ordeal, deaden desire. Having TB was imagined to be an aphrodisiac, and to confer extraordinary powers of seduction. Cancer is considered to be de-sexualizing. But it is characteristic of TB that many of its symptoms are deceptive—liveliness that comes from enervation, rosy cheeks that look like a sign of health but come from fever—and an upsurge of vitality may be a sign of approaching death. (Such gushes of energy will generally be self-destructive, and may be destructive of others: recall the Old West legend of Doc Holliday, the tubercular gunfighter released from moral restraints by the ravages of his disease.) Cancer has only true symptoms.

TB is disintegration, febrilization, dematerialization; it is a disease of liquids—the body turning to phlegm and mucus and sputum and, finally, blood—and of air, of the need for better air. Cancer is degeneration, the body tissues turning to something hard. Alice James, writing in her journal a year before she died from cancer in 1892, speaks of "this unholy granite substance in my breast." But this lump is alive, a fetus with its own will. Novalis, in an entry written around 1798 for his encyclopedia project, defines cancer, along with gangrene, as "full-fledged *parasites*—they grow, are engendered, engender, have their structure, secrete, eat." Cancer is a demonic pregnancy. St. Jerome must have been thinking of cancer when he wrote: "The one there with his swollen belly is pregnant with his own death" (*"Alius tumenti aqualiculo mortem parturit"*). Though the course of both diseases is emaciating, losing weight from TB is understood very differently from losing weight from cancer. In TB, the person is "consumed," burned up. In cancer, the patient is "invaded" by alien cells, which multiply, causing an atrophy or blockage of bodily functions. The cancer patient "shrivels" (Alice James's word) or "shrinks" (Wilhelm Reich's word).

TB is a disease of time; it speeds up life, highlights it, spiritualizes it. In both English and French, consumption "gallops." Cancer has stages rather than gaits; it is (eventually) "terminal." Cancer works slowly, insidiously: the standard euphemism in obituaries is that someone has "died after a long illness." Every characterization of cancer describes it as slow, and so it was first used metaphorically. "The word of hem crepith as a kankir," Wyclif wrote in 1382 (translating a phrase in II Timothy 2:17); and among the earliest figurative uses of cancer are as a metaphor for "idleness" and "sloth."[3] Metaphorically, cancer is not so much a disease of time as a disease or pathology of space. Its principal metaphors refer to topography (cancer "spreads" or "proliferates" or is "diffused"; tumors are surgically "excised"), and its most dreaded consequence, short of death, is the mutilation or amputation of part of the body.

TB is often imagined as a disease of poverty and deprivation—of thin garments, thin bodies, unheated rooms, poor hygiene, inadequate food. The poverty may not be as literal as Mimi's garret in *La Bohème*; the tubercular Marguerite Gautier in *La Dame aux camélias* lives in luxury, but inside she is a waif. In contrast, cancer is a disease of middle-class life, a disease associated with affluence, with excess. Rich countries have the highest cancer rates, and the rising incidence of the disease is seen as resulting, in part, from a diet rich in fat and proteins and from the toxic effluvia of the industrial economy that creates affluence. The treatment of TB is identified with the stimulation of appetite, cancer treatment with nausea and the loss of appetite. The undernourished nourishing themselves—alas, to no avail. The overnourished, unable to eat.

The TB patient was thought to be helped, even cured, by a change in environment. There was a notion that TB was a wet disease, a disease of humid and dank cities. The inside of the body became damp ("moisture in the lungs" was a favored locution) and had to be dried out. Doctors advised travel to high, dry places—the mountains, the desert. But no change of surroundings is thought to help the cancer patient. The fight is all inside one's own body. It may be, is increasingly thought to be, something in the environment that has caused the cancer. But once cancer is present, it cannot be reversed or diminished by a move to a better (that is, less carcinogenic) environment.

TB is thought to be relatively painless. Cancer is thought to be, invariably, excruciatingly painful. TB is thought to provide an easy death, while cancer is the spectacularly wretched one. For over a hundred years TB remained the preferred way of giving death a meaning—an edifying, refined disease. Nineteenth-century literature is stocked with descriptions of almost symptomless, unfrightened, beatific deaths from TB, particularly of young people, such as Little Eva in *Uncle Tom's Cabin* and Dombey's son Paul in *Dombey and Son* and Smike in *Nicholas Nickleby*, where Dickens described TB as the "dread disease" which "refines" death

> of its grosser aspect . . . in which the struggle between soul and
> body is so gradual, quiet, and solemn, and the result so sure, that
> day by day, and grain by grain, the mortal part wastes and withers
> away, so that the spirit grows light and sanguine with its lightening
> load. . . .[4]

Contrast these ennobling, placid TB deaths with the ignoble, agonizing cancer deaths of Eugene Gant's father in Thomas Wolfe's *Of Time and the River* and of the sister in Bergman's film *Cries and Whispers*. The dying tubercular is pictured as made more beautiful and more soulful; the person dying of cancer is portrayed as robbed of all capacities of self-transcendence, humiliated by fear and agony. . . .

7

Cancer is generally thought an inappropriate disease for a romantic character, in contrast to tuberculosis, perhaps because unromantic depression has supplanted the romantic notion of melancholy. "A fitful strain of melancholy," Poe wrote, "will ever be found inseparable from the perfection of the beautiful." Depression is melancholy minus its charms—the animation, the fits.

Supporting the theory about the emotional causes of cancer, there is a growing literature and body of research: and scarcely a week passes without a new article announcing to some general public or other the scientific link between cancer and painful feelings. Investigations are cited—most articles refer to the same ones—in which out of, say, several hundred cancer patients, two-thirds or three-fifths report being depressed or unsatisfied with their lives, and having suffered from the loss (through death or rejection or separation) of a parent, lover, spouse, or close friend. But it seems likely that of several hundred people who do *not* have cancer, most would also report depressing emotions and past traumas: this is called the human condition. And these case histories are recounted in a particularly forthcoming language of despair, of discontent about and obsessive preoccupation with the isolated self and its never altogether satisfactory "relationships," which bears the unmistakable stamp of our consumer culture. It is a language many Americans now use about themselves.[5]

Investigations carried out by a few doctors in the last century showed a high correlation between cancer and that era's complaints. In contrast to contemporary American cancer patients, who invariably report having feelings of isolation and loneliness since childhood, Victorian cancer patients described overcrowded lives, burdened with work and family obligations, and bereavements. These patients don't express discontent with their lives as such or speculate about the quality of its satisfactions and the possibility of a "meaningful relationship." Physicians found the causes or predisposing factors of their patients' cancers in grief, in worry (noted as most acute among businessmen and mothers of large families), in straitened economic circumstances and sudden reversals of fortune, and in overwork—or, if the patients were successful writers or politicians, in grief, rage, intellectual overexertion, the anxiety that accompanies ambition, and the stress of public life.[6]

Nineteenth-century cancer patients were thought to get the disease as the result of hyperactivity and hyperintensity. They seemed to be full of emotions that had to be damped down. As a prophylaxis against cancer, one English doctor urged his patients "to avoid overtaxing their strength, and to bear the ills of life with equanimity; above all things, not to 'give way' to any grief." Such stoic counsels have now been replaced by prescriptions for self-expression, from talking it out to the primal scream. In 1885, a Boston doctor advised "those who have apparently benign tumors in the breast of the advantage of being cheerful." Today, this would be regarded as encouraging the sort of emotional dissociation now thought to predispose people to cancer.

Popular accounts of the psychological aspects of cancer often cite old authorities, starting with Galen, who observed that "melancholy women" are more likely to get breast cancer than "sanguine women." But the meanings have changed. Galen (second century A.D.) meant by melancholy a physiological condition with complex characterological symptoms; we mean a mere mood. "Grief and anxiety," said the English surgeon Sir Astley Cooper in 1845, are among "the most frequent causes" of breast cancer. But the nineteenth-century observations undermine rather than support late-twentieth-century notions—evoking a manic or manic-depressive character type almost the opposite of that forlorn, self-hating, emotionally inert creature, the contemporary cancer personality. As far as I know, no oncologist convinced of the efficacy of polychemotherapy and immunotherapy in treating patients has contributed to the fictions about a specific cancer personality. Needless to say, the hypothesis that distress can affect immunological responsiveness (and, in some circumstances, lower immunity to disease) is hardly the same as—or constitutes evidence for—the view that emotions cause diseases, much less for the belief that specific emotions can produce specific diseases.

Recent conjecture about the modern cancer character type finds its true antecedent and counterpart in the literature on TB, where the same theory, put in similar terms, had long been in circulation. In his *Morbidus Anglicus* (1672), Gideon Harvey declared "melancholy" and "choler" to be "the sole cause" of TB (for which he used the metaphoric term "corrosion"). In 1881, a year before Robert Koch published his paper announcing the discovery of the tubercle bacillus and demonstrating that it was the primary cause of the disease, a standard medical textbook gave as the causes of tuberculosis: hereditary disposition, unfavorable climate, sedentary indoor life, defective ventilation, deficiency of light, and "depressing emotions."[7] Though the entry had to be changed for the next edition, it took a long time for these notions to lose credibility. "I'm mentally ill, the disease of the lungs is nothing but an overflowing of my mental disease," Kafka wrote to Milena in 1920. Applied to TB, the theory that emotions cause diseases survived well into this century—until, finally, it was discovered how to cure the disease. The theory's fashionable current application—which relates cancer to emotional withdrawal and lack of self-confidence and confidence in the future—is likely to prove no more tenable than its application to tuberculosis.

●

In the plague-ridden England of the late sixteenth and seventeenth centuries, according to historian Keith Thomas, it was widely believed that "the happy man would not get plague." The fantasy that a happy state of mind would fend off disease probably flourished for all infectious diseases, before the nature of infection was understood. Theories that diseases are caused by mental states and can be cured by will power are always an index of how much is not understood about the physical terrain of disease.

Moreover, there is a peculiarly modern predilection for psychological explanations of disease, as of everything else. Psychologizing seems to provide control over the experiences and events (like grave illnesses) over which people have in fact little or no control. Psychological understanding undermines the "reality" of a disease. That reality has to be explained. (It really means; or is a symbol of; or must be interpreted so.) For those who live neither with religious consolations about death nor with a sense of death (or of anything else) as natural, death is the obscene mystery, the ultimate affront, the thing that cannot be controlled. It can only be denied. A large part of the popularity and persuasiveness of psychology comes from its being a sublimated spiritualism: a secular, ostensibly scientific way of affirming the primacy of "spirit" over matter. That ineluctably material reality, disease, can be given a psychological explanation. Death itself can be considered, ultimately, a psychological phenomenon. Groddeck declared in *The Book of the It* (he was speaking of TB): "He alone will die who wishes to die, to whom life is intolerable." The promise of a temporary triumph over death is implicit in much of the psychological thinking that starts from Freud and Jung.

At the least, there is the promise of a triumph over illness. A "physical" illness becomes in a way less real—but, in compensation, more interesting— so far as it can be considered a "mental" one. Speculation throughout the modern period has tended steadily to enlarge the category of mental illness. Indeed, part of the denial of death in this culture is a vast expansion of the category of illness as such.

Illness expands by means of two hypotheses. The first is that every form of social deviation can be considered an illness. Thus, if criminal behavior can be considered an illness, then criminals are not to be condemned or punished but to be understood (as a doctor understands), treated, cured.[8] The second is that every illness can be considered psychologically. Illness is interpreted as, basically, a psychological event, and people are encouraged to believe that they get sick because they (unconsciously) want to, and that they can cure themselves by the mobilization of will; that they can choose not to die of the disease. These two hypotheses are complementary. As the first seems to relieve guilt, the second reinstates it. Psychological theories of illness are a powerful means of placing the blame on the ill. Patients who are instructed that they have, unwittingly, caused their disease and are also being made to feel that they have deserved it.

8

Punitive notions of disease have a long history, and such notions are particularly active with cancer. There is the "fight" or "crusade" against cancer; cancer is the "killer" disease; people who have cancer are "cancer victims." Ostensibly, the illness is the culprit. But it is also the cancer patient who is made culpable. Widely believed psychological theories of disease assign to the luckless ill the ultimate responsibility both for falling ill and for getting well. And conventions of treating cancer as no mere disease but a demonic enemy make cancer not just a lethal disease but a shameful one.

Leprosy in its heyday aroused a similarly disproportionate sense of horror. In the Middle Ages, the leper was a social text in which corruption was made visible; an exemplum, an emblem of decay. Nothing is more punitive than to give a disease a meaning—that meaning being invariably a moralistic one. Any important disease whose causality is murky, and for which treatment is ineffectual, tends to be awash in significance. First, the subjects of deepest dread (corruption, decay, pollution, anomie, weakness) are identified with the disease. The disease itself becomes a metaphor. Then, in the name of the disease (that is, using it as a metaphor), that horror is imposed on other things. The disease becomes adjectival. Something is said to be disease-like, meaning that it is disgusting or ugly. In French, a moldering stone façade is still *lépreuse*.

Epidemic diseases were a common figure for social disorder. From pestilence (bubonic plague) came "pestilent," whose figurative meaning, according to the *Oxford English Dictionary*, is "injurious to religion, morals, or public peace—1513"; and "pestilential," meaning "morally baneful or pernicious—1531." Feelings about evil are projected onto a disease. And the disease (so enriched with meanings) is projected onto the world.

●

In the past, such grandiloquent fantasies were regularly attached to the epidemic diseases, diseases that were a collective calamity. In the last two centuries the diseases most often used as metaphors for evil were syphilis, tuberculosis, and cancer—all diseases imagined to be, preeminently, the diseases of individuals.

Syphilis was thought to be not only a horrible disease but a demeaning, vulgar one. Anti-democrats used it to evoke the desecrations of an egalitarian age. Baudelaire, in a note for his never completed book on Belgium, wrote:

> We all have the republican spirit in our veins, like syphilis in our bones—we are democratized and venerealized.

In the sense of an infection that corrupts morally and debilitates physically, syphilis was to become a standard trope in late-nineteenth- and early-twentieth-century anti-Semitic polemics. In 1933 Wilhelm Reich argued that "the irrational fear of syphilis was one of the major sources of National Socialism's political views and its anti-Semitism." But although he perceived sexual and political phobias being projected onto a disease in the grisly harping on syphilis in *Mein Kampf*, it never occured to Reich how much was being projected in his own persistent use of cancer as a metaphor for the ills of the modern era. Indeed, cancer can be stretched much further than syphilis can as a metaphor.

Syphilis was limited as a metaphor because the disease itself was not regarded as mysterious; only awful. A tainted heredity (Ibsen's *Ghosts*), the perils of sex (Charles-Louis Phillipe's *Bubu de Montparnasse*, Mann's *Doctor Faustus*)—there was horror aplenty in syphilis. But no mystery. Its causality was clear, and understood to be singular. Syphilis was the grimmest of gifts, "transmitted" or "carried" by a sometimes ignorant sender to the unsuspecting receiver. In contrast, TB was regarded as a mysterious affliction, and a disease with myriad causes—just as today, while everyone acknowledges

cancer to be an unsolved riddle, it is also generally agreed that cancer is
multi-determined. A variety of factors—such as cancer-causing substances
("carcinogens") in the environment, genetic makeup, lowering of immuno-
defenses (by previous illness or emotional trauma), characterological
predisposition—are held responsible for the disease. And many researchers
assert that cancer is not one but more than a hundred clinically distinct
diseases, that each cancer has to be studied separately, and that what will
eventually be developed is an array of cures, one for each of the different
cancers.

The resemblance of current ideas about cancer's myriad causes to long-
held but now discredited views about TB suggests the possibility that cancer
may be one disease after all and that it may turn out, as TB did, to have a
principal causal agent and be controllable by one program of treatment.
Indeed, as Lewis Thomas has observed, all the diseases for which the issue of
causation has been settled, and which can be prevented and cured, have
turned out to have a simple physical cause—like the pneumococcus for
pneumonia, the tubercle bacillus for tuberculosis, a single vitamin deficiency
for pellagra—and it is far from unlikely that something comparable will
eventually be isolated for cancer. The notion that a disease can be explained
only by a variety of causes is precisely characteristic of thinking about
diseases whose causation is *not* understood. And it is diseases thought to be
multi-determined (that is, mysterious) that have the widest possibilities as
metaphors for what is felt to be socially or morally wrong.

●

TB and cancer have been used to express not only (like syphilis) crude
fantasies about contamination but also fairly complex feelings about strength
and weakness, and about energy. For more than a century and a half,
tuberculosis provided a metaphoric equivalent for delicacy, sensitivity, sadness, powerlessness; while whatever seemed ruthless, implacable, preda-
tory, could be analogized to cancer. (Thus, Baudelaire in 1852, in his essay
"L'Ecole païenne," observed: "A frenzied passion for art is a canker that
devours the rest. . . .") TB was an ambivalent metaphor, both a scourge and an
emblem of refinement. Cancer was never viewed other than as a scourge; it
was, metaphorically, the barbarian within.

While syphilis was thought to be passively incurred, an entirely involuntary disaster, TB was once, and cancer is now, thought to be a pathology of
energy, a disease of the will. Concern about energy and feeling, fears about
the havoc they wreak, have been attached to both diseases. Getting TB was
thought to signify a defective vitality, or vitality misspent. "There was a great
want of vital power . . . and great constitutional weakness"—so Dickens
described little Paul in *Dombey and Son.* The Victorian idea of TB as a disease
of low energy (and heightened sensitivity) has its exact complement in the
Reichian idea of cancer as a disease of unexpressed energy (and anesthetized
feelings). In an era in which there seemed to be no inhibitions on being
productive, people were anxious about not having enough energy. In our
own era of destructive overproduction by the economy and of increasing

bureaucratic restraints on the individual, there is both a fear of having too much energy and an anxiety about energy not being allowed to be expressed.

Like Freud's scarcity-economics theory of "instincts," the fantasies about TB which arose in the last century (and lasted well into ours) echo the attitudes of early capitalist accumulation. One has a limited amount of energy, which must be properly spent. (Having an orgasm, in nineteenth-century English slang, was not "coming" but "spending.") Energy, like savings, can be depleted, can run out or be used up, through reckless expenditure. The body will start "consuming" itself, the patient will "waste away."

The language used to describe cancer evokes a different economic catastrophe: that of unregulated, abnormal, incoherent growth. The tumor has energy, not the patient; "it" is out of control. Cancer cells, according to the textbook account, are cells that have shed the mechanism which "restrains" growth. (The growth of normal cells is "self-limiting," due to a mechanism called "contact inhibition.") Cells without inhibitions, cancer cells will continue to grow and extend over each other in a "chaotic" fashion, destroying the body's normal cells, architecture, and functions.

Early capitalism assumes the necessity of regulated spending, saving, accounting, discipline—an economy that depends on the rational limitation of desire. TB is described in images that sum up the negative behavior of nineteenth-century *homo economicus:* consumption; wasting; squandering of vitality. Advanced capitalism requires expansion, speculation, the creation of new needs (the problem of satisfaction and dissatisfaction); buying on credit; mobility—an economy that depends on the irrational indulgence of desire. Cancer is described in images that sum up the negative behavior of twentieth-century *homo economicus:* abnormal growth; repression of energy, that is, refusal to consume or spend.

●

TB was understood, like insanity, to be a kind of one-sidedness: a failure of will or an overintensity. However much the disease was dreaded, TB always had pathos. Like the mental patient today, the tubercular was considered to be someone quintessentially vulnerable, and full of self-destructive whims. Nineteenth- and early-twentieth-century physicians addressed themselves to coaxing their tubercular patients back to health. Their prescription was the same as the enlightened one for mental patients today: cheerful surroundings, isolation from stress and family, healthy diet, exercise, rest.

The understanding of cancer supports quite different, avowedly brutal notions of treatment. (A common cancer hospital witticism, heard as often from doctors as from patients: "The treatment is worse than the disease.") There can be no question of pampering the patient. With the patient's body considered to be under attack ("invasion"), the only treatment is counterattack.

The controlling metaphors in descriptions of cancer are, in fact, drawn not from economics but from the language of warfare: every physician and every attentive patient is familiar with, if perhaps inured to, this military terminology. Thus, cancer cells do not simply multiply; they are "invasive." ("Malignant

tumors invade even when they grow very slowly," as one textbook puts it.)
Cancer cells "colonize" from the original tumor to far sites in the body, first
setting up tiny outposts ("micrometastases") whose presence is assumed,
though they cannot be detected. Rarely are the body's "defenses" vigorous
enough to obliterate a tumor that has established its own blood supply and
consists of billions of destructive cells. However "radical" the surgical intervention, however many "scans" are taken of the body landscape, most
remissions are temporary; the prospects are that "tumor invasion" will
continue, or that rogue cells will eventually regroup and mount a new assault
on the organism.

Treatment also has a military flavor. Radiotherapy uses the metaphors of
aerial warfare; patients are "bombarded" with toxic rays. And chemotherapy
is chemical warfare, using poisons.[9] Treatment aims to "kill" cancer cells
(without, it is hoped, killing the patient). Unpleasant side effects of treatment
are advertised, indeed overadvertised. ("The agony of chemotherapy" is a
standard phrase.) It is impossible to avoid damaging or destroying healthy
cells (indeed, some methods used to treat cancer can cause cancer), but it is
thought that nearly any damage to the body is justified if it saves the patient's
life. Often, of course, it doesn't work. (As in: "We had to destroy Ben Suc in
order to save it.") There is everything but the body count.

The military metaphor in medicine first came into wide use in the 1880s,
with the identification of bacteria as agents of disease. Bacteria were said to
"invade" or "infiltrate." But talk of siege and war to describe disease now has,
with cancer, a striking literalness and authority. Not only is the clinical
course of the disease and its medical treatment thus described, but the
disease itself is conceived as the enemy on which society wages war. More
recently, the fight against cancer has sounded like a colonial war—with
similarly vast appropriations of government money—and in a decade when
colonial wars haven't gone too well, this militarized rhetoric seems to be
backfiring. Pessimism among doctors about the efficacy of treatment is growing, in spite of the strong advances in chemotherapy and immunotherapy
made since 1970. Reporters covering "the war on cancer" frequently caution
the public to distinguish between official fictions and harsh facts; a few years
ago, one science writer found American Cancer Society proclamations that
cancer is curable and progress has been made "reminiscent of Vietnam
optimism prior to the deluge." Still, it is one thing to be skeptical about the
rhetoric that surrounds cancer, another to give support to many uninformed
doctors who insist that no significant progress in treatment has been made,
and that cancer is not really curable. The bromides of the American cancer
establishment, tirelessly hailing the imminent victory over cancer; the professional pessimism of a large number of cancer specialists, talking like battle-
weary officers mired down in an interminable colonial war—these are twin
distortions in this military rhetoric about cancer.

●

Other distortions follow with the extension of cancer images in more
grandiose schemes of warfare. As TB was represented as the spiritualizing of

consciousness, cancer is understood as the overwhelming or obliterating of consciousness (by a mindless It). In TB, you are eating yourself up, being refined, getting down to the core, the real you. In cancer, non-intelligent ("primitive," "embryonic," "atavistic") cells are multiplying, and you are being replaced by the non-you. Immunologists class the body's cancer cells as "nonself."

It is worth noting that Reich, who did more than anyone else to disseminate the psychological theory of cancer, also found something equivalent to cancer in the biosphere.

> There is a deadly orgone energy. It is in the atmosphere. You can demonstrate it on devices such as the Geiger counter. It's a swampy quality.... Stagnant, deadly water which doesn't flow, doesn't metabolize. Cancer, too, is due to the stagnation of the flow of the life energy of the organism.

Reich's language has its own inimitable coherence. And more and more—as its metaphoric uses gain in credibility—cancer is felt to be what he thought it was, a cosmic disease, the emblem of all the destructive, alien powers to which the organism is host.

As TB was the disease of the sick self, cancer is the disease of the Other. Cancer proceeds by a science-fiction scenario: an invasion of "alien" or "mutant" cells, stronger than normal cells (*Invasion of the Body Snatchers, The Incredible Shrinking Man, The Blob, The Thing*). One standard science-fiction plot is mutation, either mutants arriving from outer space or accidental mutations among humans. Cancer could be described as a triumphant mutation, and mutation is now mainly an image for cancer. As a theory of the psychological genesis of cancer, the Reichian imagery of energy checked, not allowed to move outward, then turned back on itself, driving cells berserk, is already the stuff of science fiction. And Reich's image of death in the air—of deadly energy that registers on a Geiger counter—suggests how much the science-fiction images about cancer (a disease that comes from deadly rays, and is treated by deadly rays) echo the collective nightmare. The original fear about exposure to atomic radiation was genetic deformities in the next generation; that was replaced by another fear, as statistics started to show much higher cancer rates among Hiroshima and Nagasaki survivors and their descendants.

Cancer is a metaphor for what is most ferociously energetic; and these energies constitute the ultimate insult to natural order. In a science-fiction tale by Tommaso Landolfi, the spaceship is called "Cancerqueen." (It is hardly within the range of the tuberculosis metaphor that a writer could have imagined an intrepid vessel named "Consumptionqueen.") When not being explained away as something psychological, buried in the recesses of the self, cancer is being magnified and projected into a metaphor for the biggest enemy, the furthest goal. Thus, Nixon's bid to match Kennedy's promise to put Americans on the moon was, appropriately enough, the promise to "conquer" cancer. Both were science-fiction ventures. The equivalent of the legislation establishing the space program was the National Cancer Act of

1971, which did not envisage the near-to-hand decisions that could bring **111**
under control the industrial economy that pollutes—only the great destina-   SUSAN SONTAG
tion: the cure.

TB was a disease in the service of a romantic view of the world. Cancer is now in the service of a simplistic view of the world that can turn paranoid. The disease is often experienced as a form of demonic possession—tumors are "malignant" or "benign," like forces—and many terrified cancer patients are disposed to seek out faith healers, to be exorcised. The main organized support for dangerous nostrums like Laetrile comes from far-right groups to whose politics of paranoia the fantasy of a miracle cure for cancer makes a serviceable addition, along with a belief in UFOs. (The John Birch Society distributes a forty-five-minute film called *World Without Cancer*.) For the more sophisticated, cancer signifies the rebellion of the injured ecosphere: Nature taking revenge on a wicked technocratic world. False hopes and simplified terrors are raised by crude statistics brandished for the general public, such as that 90 percent of all cancers are "environmentally caused," or that imprudent diet and tobacco smoking alone account for 75 percent of all cancer deaths. To the accompaniment of this numbers game (it is difficult to see how any statistics about "all cancers" or "all cancer deaths" could be defended), cigarettes, hair dyes, bacon, saccharine, hormone-fed poultry, pesticides, low-sulphur coal—a lengthening roll call of products we take for granted have been found to cause cancer. X-rays give cancer (the treatment meant to cure kills); so do emanations from the television set and the microwave oven and the fluorescent clock face. As with syphilis, an innocent or trivial act—or exposure—in the present can have dire consequences far in the future. It is also known that cancer rates are high for workers in a large number of industrial occupations. Though the exact processes of causation lying behind the statistics remain unknown, it seems clear that many cancers are preventable. But cancer is not just a disease ushered in by the Industrial Revolution (there was cancer in Arcadia) and certainly more than the sin of capitalism (within their more limited industrial capacities, the Russians pollute worse than we do). The widespread current view of cancer as a disease of industrial civilization is as unsound scientifically as the right-wing fantasy of a "world without cancer" (like a world without subversives). Both rest on the mistaken feeling that cancer is a distinctively "modern" disease.

The medieval experience of the plague was firmly tied to notions of moral pollution, and people invariably looked for a scapegoat external to the stricken community. (Massacres of Jews in unprecedented numbers took place everywhere in plague-stricken Europe of 1347–48, then stopped as soon as the plague receded.) With the modern diseases, the scapegoat is not so easily separated from the patient. But much as these diseases individualize, they also pick up some of the metaphors of epidemic diseases. (Diseases understood to be simply epidemic have become less useful as metaphors, as evidenced by the near-total historical amnesia about the influenza pandemic of 1918–19, in which more people died than in the four years of World War I.) Presently, it is as much a cliché to say that cancer is "environmentally" caused as it was—and still is—to say that it is caused by mismanaged emotions. TB was associated with pollution (Florence Nightingale thought it was "induced by the foul air of houses"), and now cancer is thought of as a disease of the contamination of the whole world. TB was "the white plague." With awareness of environmental pollution, people have started saying that there is an "epidemic" or "plague" of cancer.

Notes

1 Godefroy's *Dictionnaire de l'ancienne langue française* cites Bernard de Gordon's *Pratiqum* (1495): *"Tisis, c'est ung ulcere du polmon qui consume tout le corp."*

2 The same etymology is given in the standard French dictionaries. *"La tubercule"* was introduced in the sixteenth century by Ambroise Paré from the Latin *tūberculum*, meaning *"petite bosse"* (little lump). In Diderot's *Encyclopédie*, the entry on tuberculosis (1765) cites the definition given by the English physician Richard Morton in his *Phthisiologia* (1689): *"des petits tumeurs qui paraissent sur la surface du corps."* In French, all tiny surface tumors were once called *"tubercules"*; the word became limited to what we identify as TB only after Koch's discovery of the tubercle bacillus.

3 As cited in the OED, which gives as an early figurative use of "canker": "that pestilent and most infectious canker, idlenesse"—T. Palfreyman, 1564. And of "cancer" (which replaced "canker" around 1700): "Sloth is a Cancer, eating up the Time Princes should cultivate for Things sublime"—Edmund Ken, 1711.

4 Nearly a century later, in his edition of Katherine Mansfield's posthumously published *Journal*, John Middleton Murry uses similar language to describe Mansfield on the last day of her life. "I have never seen, nor shall I ever see, any one so beautiful as she was on that day; it was as though the exquisite perfection which was always hers had taken possession of her completely. To use her own words, the last grain of 'sediment,' the last 'traces of earthly degradation,' were departed for ever. But she had lost her life to save it."

5 A study by Dr. Caroline Bedell Thomas of the Johns Hopkins University School of Medicine was thus summarized in one recent newspaper article ("Can Your Personality Kill You?"): "In brief, cancer victims are low-gear persons, seldom prey to outbursts of emotion. They have feelings of isolation from their parents dating back to childhood." Dr. Claus and Marjorie Bahnson at the Eastern Pennsylvania Psychiatric Institute have "charted a personality pattern of denial of hostility, depression and of memory of emotional deprivation in childhood" and "difficulty in maintaining close relationships." Dr. O. Carl Simonton, a radiologist in Fort Worth, Texas, who gives patients both radiation and psychotherapy, describes the cancer personality as someone with "a great tendency for self-pity and a marked impaired ability to make and maintain meaningful relationships." Lawrence LeShan, a New York psychologist and psychotherapist (*You Can Fight for Your Life: Emotional Factors in the Causation of Cancer* [1977]), claims that "there is a general type of personality configuration among the majority of cancer patients" and a world-view that cancer patients share and "which pre-dates the development of cancer." He divides "the basic emotional pattern of the cancer patient" into three parts: "a childhood or adolescence marked by feelings of isolation," the loss of the "meaningful relationship" found in adulthood, and a subsequent "conviction that life holds no more hope." "The cancer patient," LeShan writes, "almost invariably is contemptuous of himself, and of his abilities and possibilities." Cancer patients are "empty of feeling and devoid of self."

6 "Always much trouble and hard work" is a notation that occurs in many of the brief case histories in Herbert Snow's *Clinical Notes on Cancer* (1883). Snow was a surgeon in the Cancer Hospital in London, and most of the patients he saw were poor. A typical observation: "Of 140 cases of breast-cancer, 103 gave an account of previous mental trouble, hard work, or other debilitating agency. Of 187 uterine ditto, 91 showed a similar history." Doctors who saw patients who led more comfortable lives made other observations. The physician who treated

Alexandre Dumas for cancer, G. von Schmitt, published a book on cancer in 1871 in which he listed "deep and sedentary study and pursuits, the feverish and anxious agitation of public life, the cares of ambition, frequent paroxysms of rage, violent grief" as "the principal causes" of the disease. Quoted in Samuel J. Kowal, M.D. "Emotions as a Cause of Cancer: 18th and 19th Century Contributions," *Review of Psychoanalysis*, 42, 3 (July 1955).

7 August Flint and William H. Welch, *The Principles and Practice of Medicine* (fifth edition, 1881), cited in René and Jean Dubos, *The White Plague* (1952).

8 An early statement of this view, now so much on the defensive, is in Samuel Butler's *Erewhon* (1872). Butler's way of suggesting that criminality was a disease, like TB, that was either hereditary or the result of an unwholesome environment was to point out the absurdity of condemning the sick. In Erewhon, those who murdered or stole are sympathetically treated as ill persons, while tuberculosis is punished as a crime.

9 Drugs of the nitrogen mustard type (so-called alkylating agents)—like cyclophosphamide (Cytoxan)—were the first generation of cancer drugs. Their use—with leukemia (which is characterized by an excessive production of immature white cells), then with other forms of cancer—was suggested by an inadvertent experiment with chemical warfare toward the end of World War II, when an American ship, loaded with nitrogen mustard gas, was blown up in the Naples harbor, and many of the sailors died of their lethally low white-cell and platelet counts (that is, of bone-marrow poisoning) rather than of burns or sea-water inhalation.

Chemotherapy and weaponry seem to go together, if only as a fancy. The first modern chemotherapy success was with syphilis: in 1910, Paul Ehrlich introduced an arsenic derivative, arsphenamine (Salvarsan), which was called "the magic bullet."

PART III
DEFINITIONS
OF DEATH

Contents

The apparently simple question "What is death?" has become increasingly complicated in the recent past, reflecting, in large part, the technological advances in medical science. Sophisticated equipment stimulates complicated definitions. We now are concerned, for example, with the concept of "brain death," which directly involves electrical and electronic equipment almost not imaginable only a few generations ago.

Death threatens our link to a future. And yet—to use Robert Jay Lifton's imagery—we need to keep that link to the future somehow connected and unbroken. In our time (specifically since August 6, 1945—the date of the Hiroshima atom bombing), there has been a brand new (and dire) meaning to death, one never before existing in the history of the world: the possible death of *all*.

In this part we have chapters by a world-class writer, a professor of the humanities, a medical ethicist, a President's Commission chaired by an educator, and a social psychiatrist—reflecting on the essential nature of death, the reasons we fear it, how our concepts of death are changing, and why the possibility of global death gives a new meaning and a new urgency to the entire field of thanatology.

114

10 · Human Dissatisfactions

John Fowles

John Fowles is an English writer. His works of fiction include The Collector, The Magus, The French Lieutenant's Woman, The Ebony Tower, *and* Daniel Martin. *His nonfiction works include* Islands, Trees, *and, central for our interests,* The Aristos. *The word* aristos, *from the ancient Greek, means roughly "the best for a given situation."* The Aristos *is a collection of 761 aphorisms and notes subsumed under twelve chapters. The pronouncements run from two brief lines to almost a full page. It is a veritable catalog of wisdom and harks back to Pascal's* Pensées. *The short section on death contains twenty-eight aphorisms under the more general heading of "Human Dissatisfactions."*

1 Why do we think this is not the best of all possible worlds for mankind? Why are we unhappy in it?

2 What follow are the great dissatisfactions. I maintain that they are all essential to our happiness since they provide the soil from which it grows.

DEATH

3 We hate death for two reasons. It ends life prematurely; and we do not know what lies beyond it.

4 A very large majority of educated mankind now doubts the existence of an afterlife. It is clear that the only scientific attitude is that of agnosticism: we simply do not know. We are in the Best Situation.

5 The Best Situation is one in which we cannot have certainty about some future event; and yet in which it is vital that we come to a decision about its nature. This situation faces us at the beginning of a horse race, when we want to know the name of the winner . . .

6 To Pascal, who first made this analogy with the bet, the answer was clear: one must put one's money on the Christian belief that a recompensatory afterlife exists. If it is not true, he argued, then one has lost nothing but one's stake. If it is true, one has gained all.

7 Now even an atheist contemporary with Pascal might have agreed that nothing but good could ensue, in an unjust society where the majority conveniently believed in hellfire, from supporting the idea, false or true, of an afterlife. But today the concept of hellfire has been discarded by the theologians, let alone the rest of us. Hell could be just only in a world where all were equally persuaded that it exists; just only in a world that allowed a total freedom of will—and therefore a total biographical and biological similarity—to every man and woman in it . . .

8 The idea of an afterlife has persistently haunted man because inequality has persistently tyrannized him. It is only to the poor, the sick, the unfortunate underdogs of history, that the idea appeals; it has appealed to

all honest men's sense of justice, and very often at the same time as the use of the idea to maintain an unequal *status quo* in society has revolted them. Somewhere, this belief proposes, there is a system of absolute justice and a day of absolute judgment by and on which we are all to be rewarded according to our deserts.

9 But the true longing of humanity is not for an afterlife; it is for the establishment of a justice here and now that will make an afterlife unnecessary. This myth was a compensatory fantasy, a psychological safety valve for the frustrations of existential reality.

10 We are ourselves to establish justice in our world: and the more we allow the belief in an afterlife to dwindle away, and yet still do so little to correct the flagrant inequalities of our world, then the more danger we run.

11 Our world has a badly designed engine. By using the oil of this myth it did not for many centuries heat up. But now the oil level is dropping ominously low. For this reason, it is not enough to remain agnostic. We *must* bet on the other horse: we have one life, and it is ended by a total extinction of consciousness as well as body.

12 What matters is not our personal damnation or salvation in the world to come, but that of our fellow man in the world that is.

13 Our second hatred of death is that it almost always comes too soon. We suffer from an illusion, akin to that of the desirability of an afterlife, that we should be happier if we lived for ever. Animal desires are always for an extension of what satisfies them. Only two hundred years ago a man who reached the age of forty was exceeding the average life span; and perhaps two hundred years from now centenarians will be as common as septuagenarians today. But they will still crave a longer life.

14 The function of death is to put tension into life; and the more we increase the length and the security of individual existence then the more tension we remove from it. All our pleasurable experiences contain a faint yet terrible element of the condemned man's last breakfast, an echo of the intensity of feeling of the poet who knows he is going to die, of the young soldier going doomed into battle.

15 Each pleasure we feel is a pleasure less; each day a stroke on a calendar. What we will not accept is that the joy in the day and the passing of the day are inseparable. What makes our existence worthwhile is precisely that its worth and its while—its quality and duration—are as impossible to unravel as time and space in the mathematics of relativity.

16 *Pleasure is a product of death; not an escape from it.*

17 If it were proved that there is an afterlife, life would be irretrievably spoilt. It would be pointless; and suicide, a virtue. The only possible paradise is one in which I cannot know I did once exist.

18 There are two tendencies in the twentieth century; one, a misguided one, is to domesticate death, to pretend that death is like life; the other is to look death in the face. The tamers of death believe in life after death; they indulge in elaborate after death ceremonial. Their attitude to death is euphemistic; it is "passing on" and "going to a better place." The actual process of death and decomposition is censored. Such people are in the same mental condition as the ancient Egyptians.

19 "Passing on": the visual false analogy. We know that passing objects, such as we see repeatedly every day, exist both before and after the passage that we see: and so we come, illogically and wrongly, to treat life as such a passage.

20 Death is in us and outside us; beside us in every room, in every street, in every field, in every car, in every plane. Death is what we are not every moment that we are, and every moment that we are is the moment when the dice come to rest. We are always playing Russian roulette.

21 Being dead is nothingness, not being. When we die we constitute "God's."* Our relics, our monuments, the memories retained by those who survive us, these still exist; do not constitute "God," still constitute the process. But these relics are the fossilized traces of our having been, not our being. All the great religions try to make out that death is nothing. There is another life to come . . .

22 As one social current has tried to hide death, to euphemize it out of existence, so another has thrust death forward as a chief element in entertainment: in the murder story, the war story, the spy story, the western. But increasingly, as our century grows old, these fictive deaths become more fictitious and fulfill the function of concealed euphemism. The real death of a pet kitten affects a child far more deeply than the "deaths" of all the television gangsters, cowboys, and Red Indians.

23 By death we think characteristically of the disappearance of individuals; it does not console us to know that matter is not disappearing, but is simply being metamorphosed. We mourn the individualizing form, not the generalized content. But everything we see is a metaphor of death. Every limit, every dimension, every end of every road, is a death. Even seeing is a death, for there is a point beyond which we cannot see, and our seeing dies; wherever our capacity ends, we die.

24 Time is the flesh and blood of death; death is not a skull, a skeleton, but a clock face, a sun hurtling through a sea of thin gas. A part of you has died since you began to read this sentence.

25 Death itself dies. Every moment you live, it dies. *O Death where is thy sting, Death I will be thy death.* The living prove this; not the dead.

26 In all the countries living above a bare subsistence level, the twentieth century has seen a sharp increase in awareness of the pleasures of life. This is not only because of the end of belief in an afterlife, but because death is more real today, more probable, now that the H-bomb is.

27 *The more absolute death seems, the more authentic life becomes.*

28 All I love and know may be burnt to ashes in one small hour: London, New York, Paris, Athens, gone in less time than it takes to count ten. I was born in 1926; and because of what can happen now in ten seconds, that year lies not forty-one years but a measureless epoch and innocence away. Yet I do not regret that innocence. I love life more, not less.

---

*EDITOR'S NOTE: *Elsewhere in* The Aristos, *under "God," Fowles says: "God is a situation, Not a power, or a being, or an influence. Not a 'he' or 'she' but an 'it.' Not an entity or nonentity but the situation in which there can be both entity and nonentity."*

29 Death contains me as my skin contains me. Without it, I am not what I am. Death is not a sinister door I walk toward; it is my walking toward.

30 Because I am a man death is my wife; and now she has stripped, she is beautiful, she wants me to strip, to be her mate. This is necessity, this is love, this is being-for-another, nothing else. I cannot escape this situation, nor do I want to. She wants me to make love, not like some man-eating spider, to consume me, but like a wife in love, so that we can celebrate our total sympathy, be fertile and bear children. It is her effect on me and my effect on her that make all that is good in my time being. She is not a prostitute or a mistress I am ashamed of or want to forget or about whom I can sometimes pretend that she does not exist. Like my real wife she informs every important situation in my life, she is wholly of my life, not beyond, or against, or opposite to it. I accept her completely, in every sense of the word, and I love and respect her for what she is to me.

11 · Death

Robert Nisbet

Robert Nisbet is Albert Schweitzer Professor of the Humanities, Emeritus, at Columbia University. He is the author of The Quest for Community, Twilight of Authority, History of the Idea of Progress, *and many other books.* Prejudices *consists of the explication of seventy current topics beginning with abortion, alienation, anomie, atheism, authoritarianism, boredom, bureaucracy, etc. Professor Nisbet's definition and brief discussion of death provide us with a current, insightful, brief overview of the topic.*

From Prejudices: A Philosophic Dictionary *by Robert Nisbet. Copyright ©1982 by Robert Nisbet. Reprinted with permission of the author and Harvard University Press.*

Of the recurring crises of the human condition—birth, marriage, death—the last has drawn the vastly greater part of man's ritual propensity, most of it going to the welfare of the dead in the next world. There seems to be an instinctual disposition to repudiate any thought of death being simply the final stage of the individual life cycle. Even the repugnant spectacle of the human body in process of decomposition has not prevented the almost universal belief that there is some human essence which is destined for survival in the hereafter. Whether one leaves food and clothing in the grave or merely utters prayers, the premise is the same. The community that nourished in life, nourishes also in death. Death as part of the community, death as wound to the community, and death as departure from the community has been for at least fifty thousand years the stated or unstated philosophy of virtually the whole of the human race, the only species to bury its dead.

But in spreading parts of the world, starting with the West and reaching its highest incidence in America, this philosophy is eroding. The socially annihilating individualism—that is, the atomization of society, chiefly by the modern state—that has led to the dismemberment and fragmentation of the traditional forms of community, especially kinship, has removed more and more of the communal properties of death, just as it has of birth and marriage. In modern society people are increasingly baffled and psychologically unprepared for the incidence of death among loved ones. It is not that their grief is greater or that the incomprehensibility of death is increased. The bafflement is in considerable part a result of the smaller size of the family, which gives greater emotional value to each of the members. But even more, it is a result of the decline in significance of the traditional means of ritual completion of the fact of death. Death leaves a kind of moral suspense that is terminated psychologically only with greater and greater difficulty. The social meaning of death has changed with the social position of death.

The social position of death in Western society ranges from a kind of obscenity, whose name is as improper in polite circles as sex was among the Victorians, all the way to a kind of celebrity, receiving immense attention in the form of books, articles, television documentaries, and lectures. With one hand people push death under the carpet, but with the other they reach out almost obsessively for help. "The long habit of living," wrote Thomas Browne, "indisposeth us to dying." But however "indisposed" Paleolithic man and all his successors down to the last century or two may have been, such indisposition could not have been as great where death was just as much a part of family life, of community life, as were birth and marriage. No one was unacquainted with the physical fact of death, directly and personally. It is not entirely that death was earlier and more frequent in human society until recent times; it is rather that death was highly visible to everyone, and in as concrete a way as is possible. Human beings knew death so directly, so recurrently, in the much shorter life cycle, that there was inevitably less of the abstract preoccupation with death known today. In our time an astounding number of people have never seen a dead human body. Our ancestors could, within the house, wash, dress, adorn, and otherwise minister themselves to the corpse in anticipation of burial and mourning. Today people leave that to the mortician and, on a constantly widening scale, avoid even sight of the dead person. Inevitably, cremation and instant dispatch of the ashes crowd out burial. Nor can it be claimed that this behavior is mute recognition of the disappearance of available land for cemeteries, for peoples at other times thought nothing of using and reusing graves, and there were charnel houses for the bones. No, the beginning of the end of funerary and mourning rites in modern society is social, a part of that wider tidal movement of modern history that has destroyed so much which lies intermediate between individual and state.

What has happened to death has happened also to birth, childhood, marriage, and senescence in modern Western society. These have never before had the same functional role and meaning they have today. The entire emphasis is now put upon the conjugal couple; the child is idealized and romanticized in a way that would have been beyond belief before the nineteenth century; and "senior citizens" are venerated once a year as mothers and fathers. But the inescapable fact, despite all of the national holiday devotions and everything that has been done for the welfare of children which exceeds all other ages put together, is that the true value of these roles has withered, for they have been extracted from the traditional community, which alone is the source and sustenance of birth, marriage and death, and have been located in the individual. In times past, individuals did not have children; the community did in its act of acceptance through some form of baptism. The physical fact of birth was not nearly so important as the social fact of birth. In the ancient world no child was "born" until ten days or say after parturition, when it was duly and ritually received or, when necessary, rejected. Marriage was not an affair of two individuals uniting and thus forming a new "family"; marriage was basically a rite of adoption whereby, in strict accord with the bans on incestuous union, the girl from one household was ritually cleansed of her former family identity, her name altered so that its new suffix would indicate that fundamentally she was a daughter in the new family, a possession of husband and house father. Ancient Rome gave the customary and legal base to this sense of marriage so far as Western society is concerned, but everywhere, through the greater part of human history, this has been the significance of marriage. There was a conjugal union, to be sure, but its meaning came from the larger community, starting with kindred.

So long as death was concrete, personally experienced over and over in life, public rather than hidden or transferred to mortuary technicians, and above all, familiar ritually in the kinship community, it was comprehensible and acceptable, at least to a greater degree than it is now in American society. One thinks of the linguistic abominations *pass on, pass away,* and *called for,* which so fastidiously avoid the words *die* and *death,* words as noble as any to be found in the English language. But all the while people are queasily avoiding direct personal contact with death, in substance and in name, they are becoming increasingly obsessed by it in the abstract. No doubt the current mania about "health"—evidenced in health maintenance organizations, health clubs, health pursuits of every kind, with jogging the *pièce de résistance*—is but another manifestation of unease with death. No one knows what health is; sickness, yes; and originally the treating of sickness, not the maintenance of health, was the sworn responsibility of the physician.

Lewis Thomas reported that in his own experience with the dying, there is, at the very end of life, a detached acceptance of death, a serenity and release from care never known before. Rare indeed is the final struggle, the agony, the unwillingness to die that so many books and television documentaries favor. Thomas cited the physician Osler to the effect that dying is "not such a bad thing to do after all." Osler took a dour view of people who spoke of the pain and grief of death, except in the minds of family, friends, and onlookers. Thomas speculated on whether there may possibly be, as the result of evolutionary adaptation to the inexorability of death, "some protective physiological mechanism, switched on at the verge of death, carrying (the dying) through in a haze of tranquillity." The idea is plausible and certainly agreeable.

But more important than the physical onset of death in the individual is the place of death in the community, or rather in what is left of community in the increasingly anonymous, impersonal Western society. According to the wisdom of the past, death is, first and last, communal, not individual. If death and mourning are contained within the community, seen as wound and remembrance within the community, individuals cannot help but be fortified in the "long habit of life" so far as its eventual and necessary termination is involved. The modern indulgence in individualism has ill prepared people for the very sober responsibilities of the family, of the community in all its manifestations, and indeed of the nation itself. There is nothing extraordinary in the fact that narcissism and egocentricity are the companions of fear of death—or, for that matter, fear of birth, children, and even marriage—for the origins of all these lie basically in the individualism that Comte called "the disease of the Western world." Philippe Aries showed how over the past ten centuries dread, apprehension, and rejection of death have grown in almost precise relation to the growth of individualism and repudiation of community. He distinguished "death tamed," which is what it was in traditional society for thousands of years, from "untamed death," which is what it has become. Possibly the newly oriented medical profession, beginning to be taught how to minister to death as well as to life and disease, will help contemporary man come to grips with death in the way his forefathers did; perhaps the hospice movement will provide surrogate families to give all the sustentive attention that family once did for the dying; perhaps still other adaptations will make their way into currently apprehensive minds and will prove anodyne in the long run. But nothing is likely to matter very much until death, along with birth and marriage, ceases to be regarded as something happening primarily to the individual instead of to the community. Therefore, until somehow the reality and sense of community have been restored to Western society in national, local, and kinship spheres, people will continue to live in the void—ego-gratifying, hedonistic, narcissistic, subjective, and at the same time, timorous, trepidant, fearful of death.

Nothing betokens life in community more than does mourning, with its rites, forbearances, weeds, and wailing. As Burke noted, true society, namely community, is a partnership of the dead and unborn as well as of the living. Death is bound to be a more acceptable, even desirable, fate if it has been known repeatedly in vicarious form through rites of mourning. Above all, there must be a restoration of ritual, of the drama of birth, life, and death. This must be ritual alone, not any of the subjectivisms which the twentieth century has made so corrosive to the social fabric. Of no account in death and mourning is one's actual state of mind and emotion on the occasion of ritual expression. The actor need not feel on any given day every last emotional drive inherent in his lines; he need only act. A New England widow's ritual devotion to her late husband took the form of weeds and withdrawal from society lasting many months. "You are obviously desolated by loss," said one *naif* to the widow. "Don't be ridiculous," she replied. "My husband and I ceased even speaking to one another fifty years ago." More good may have been done the social bond by those weeds and that withdrawal from society than by all the muttered prayers since the beginning of time. The truly strong religions of the world are not those rich simply in the word but, far more important, in the act.

Robert M. Veatch

Robert M. Veatch is the associate for medical ethics and director of the research group on death and dying at the Hastings (New York) Institute of Society, Ethics and the Life Sciences. Dr. Veatch's article reports a fascinating and poignant case (involving a heart transplant) that reflects on morality, religion, law, science, praxis, and prejudice.

Robert M. Veatch, "Brain Death: Welcome Definition ... or Dangerous Judgment?" Hastings Center Report, Vol. 2, No. 5 (November 1972). Reprinted by permission.

CASE NO. 23   The following case, decided by a Virginia jury, may be a crucial one for medical ethics. It may be used as precedent in deciding *when a patient is dead* and for establishing *where the proper authority lies* for changing public policy regarding such fundamental decisions as those of human life and death. It appears that there were serious mistakes, both in interpretation and in judgment, by all involved. A more thorough exploration is certainly called for.

On May 25, 1968, at the beginning of the era of transplantation, Bruce Tucker was brought to the operating room of the hospital of the Medical College of Virginia. Tucker, a fifty-six-year-old black laborer, had suffered a massive brain injury the day before in a fall. He sustained a lateral basilar skull fracture on the right side, subdural hematoma on the left, and brain stem confusion.

The following timetable is taken from the summary of the case by Judge A. Christian Compton:

6:05 P.M.	Admitted to the hospital.
11:00 P.M.	Emergency right temporoparietal craniotomy and right parietal burr hole.
2:05 A.M.	Operation complete; patient fed intravenously and received "medication" each hour.
11:30 A.M.	Placed on respirator, which kept him "mechanically alive."
11:45 A.M.	Treating physician noted "prognosis for recovery is nil and death imminent."
1:00 P.M.	Neurologist called to obtain an EEG with the results showing "flat lines with occasional artifact. He found no clinical evidence of viability and no evidence of cortical activity."
2:45 P.M.	Mr. Tucker taken to the operating room. From this time until 4:30 P.M. "he maintained vital signs of life, that is, he maintained, for the most part, normal body temperature, normal pulse, normal blood pressure and normal rate of respiration."
3:30 P.M.	Respirator cut off.
3:33 P.M.	Incision made in Joseph Klett, heart recipient.

3:35 P.M.	Patient pronounced dead.
4:25 P.M.	Incision made to remove Tucker's heart.
4:32 P.M.	Heart taken out.
4:33 P.M.	Incision made to remove decedent's kidneys.

Tucker's heart and kidneys were removed by the surgical team. The heart was transplanted to Joseph G. Klett, who died about one week later.

William E. Tucker, brother of the dead man, sued for $100,000 damages, charging the transplant team was engaged in a "systematic and nefarious scheme to use Bruce Tucker's heart and hastened his death by shutting off the mechanical means of support." According to the judge's summary, "a close friend of the deceased was searching for him and made an inquiry at three of the hospital information desks, all without success." Tucker's brother was "at his place of business, located within fifteen city blocks of the hospital, all day on May 25th until he left his business to go find his brother in the afternoon when he heard he had been injured. Among the personal effects turned over to the brother later was a business card which the decedent had in his wallet which showed the plaintiff's (brother's) name, business address and telephone number thereon." The suit charged that the removal of organs was carried out with only minimal attempts to notify the victim's family and obtain permission for use of his organs.

This case is one of the most complicated and significant in the current debate about the brain locus for death. Whether or not it should, in fact, be treated as a "brain death" case we shall consider later, but certainly that is the way the principals in the case and the press have handled it. The Internal Medicine News Service headed the report, " 'Brain Death' Held Proof of Demise in Va. Jury Decision." The *New York Times'* headline said, "Virginia Jury Rules That Death Occurs When Brain Dies." *Internal Medicine News*, in one of the best stories covering the case, claimed—quite accurately—that "the landmark decision is not binding elsewhere but it is certain to be cited as precedent in related cases." In fact, not one news story with which we are familiar saw this as other than a brain death case.

The surgeons who removed Tucker's heart evidently also interpreted it as a case of deciding when a patient is dead. Dr. Hume is quoted as saying that the court's decision in favor of the physicians "brings the law up to date with what medicine has known all along—that the only death is brain death."

Asked to decide whether the physicians were guilty of causing the death of the heart donor, the jury in the Tucker case were in effect being asked to make a public policy judgment about whether the irreversible loss of brain function is to be equated for moral, legal, and public policy purposes with the death of an individual.

The task of defining death is not a trivial exercise in coining the meaning of a term. Rather, it is an attempt to reach an understanding of the philosophical nature of man and that which is essentially significant to man which is lost at the time of death. When we say that a man has died, there are appropriate behavioral changes; we go into mourning, perhaps cease certain kinds of medical treatment, initiate a funeral ritual, read a will, or, if the individual happens to be president of an organization, elevate the vice president to his presidency role. According to many, including those who focus on the definition of death as crucial for the transplant debate, it is appropriate to remove vital, unimpaired organs after, but not before, death. So there is a great deal at stake at the policy level in the definition of death.

CANDIDATES FOR "DEATH"

There are several plausible candidates for the concept of death. All are attempts to determine that which is so significant to man that its loss constitutes the change in the moral and legal status of the individual. The traditional religious and philosophical view in Western culture was that a man died at the time when his soul left the body. This separation of body and soul is difficult to verify experimentally and scientifically and is best left to the religious traditions, which in some cases still focus upon the soul-departure concept of death.

Traditional secular man has focused on the cessation of the flow of the vital body fluids, blood and breath; when the circulatory and respiratory functions cease, the individual is dead. This is a view of the nature of man which identifies his essence with the flowing of fluids in the animal species.

There are also two new candidates. One of these is the complete loss of the body's integrating capacities, as signified by the activity of the central nervous system. This is the now-popular concept frequently though inaccurately given the name "brain death." Most recently in the literature there are those who are beginning to question the adequacy of this notion of brain death, claiming that it already has become old-fashioned. They ask why is it that one must identify the entire brain with death; is it not possible that we are really interested only in man's consciousness: in his ability to think, reason, feel, experience, interact with others, and control his body functions consciously? This is crucial in rare cases where the lower brain function might be intact while the cortex, which controls consciousness, is utterly destroyed.

MORAL, NOT TECHNICAL

The public policy debate about the meaning of death involves a choice among these several candidates for death. The Harvard Ad Hoc Committee to Examine the Definition of Brain Death established operational criteria for what it called irreversible coma, based on very sound scientific evidence. These four criteria are: (1) unreceptivity and unresponsivity; (2) no movements or breathing; (3) no reflexes; (4) flat electroencephalogram ("of great confirmatory value").

What the committee did not do, however, and what it was not capable of doing, was establishing that a patient in irreversible coma is "dead," i.e., that we should treat him as if he were no longer a living being who is the possessor of the same human moral rights and obligations as other human beings. While it may be the case that a patient in irreversible coma, according to Harvard criteria, has shifted into that status where he is no longer to be considered living, the decision that he is "dead" cannot be derived from any amount of scientific investigation and demonstration. The choice among the many candidates for what is essential to the nature of man and, therefore, the loss of which is to be called "death," is essentially a philosophical or moral question, not a medical or scientific one.

This being the case, it is troubling, indeed, to hear physicians say as Dr. Hume did, that the Virginia legal decision "brings the law up to date with what medicine has known all along—that the only death is brain death." If some physicians have believed this (and certainly there is no consensus among medical professionals), they know it from their general belief system about what is valuable in life and not from their training as medical scientists. It is therefore distressing that "expert" witnesses, including Dr. William Sweet of Harvard Medical School, were called by the defense to testify before the jury. Dr. Sweet said, "Death is a state in which the brain is dead. The rest of the body exists in order to support the brain. The brain is the individual." This may or may not be a sound moral philosophical argument. It is certainly not a medical argument. And to ask a chief of neurosurgery at Massachusetts General Hospital to make the moral argument is certainly a kind of special pleading on the part of legal counsel for the defense. This led to the *New York Times'* story which began, "A medical opinion that death occurs when the brain dies; even if the heart and other organs continue to function, has been reinforced by a jury here in a landmark heart transplant suit." The claim that death occurs when the brain dies is opinion to be sure, but it is not, and by the very nature of the case cannot be, medical opinion. To leave such decision making in the hands of scientifically trained professionals is a dangerous move.

Especially in such a fundamental matter as life and death itself, it is very difficult to see how the rest of society can shirk its responsibility in deciding what concept of death is to be used. To be sure, the scientific community can and should be asked to establish the criteria for measuring such things as irreversible coma, once the public, acting through its policy-making agencies in the legislature, has determined that irreversible coma is to be equated with death.

But let us return to the Tucker trial to see how this confusion between social and medical responsibilities developed. In the state of Virginia, according to the judge, there was a definition of death operative and that definition was specifically "the cessation of life; the ceasing to exist; a total stoppage of the circulation of the blood, and a cessation of the animal and vital functions consequent thereto such as respiration and pulsation." On a motion for summary judgment for the defendants, the judge ruled that the lawbook definition of death must take precedence over medical opinion. In this opinion, Judge Compton directed that the court was bound by the legal definition of death in Virginia until it was changed by the state legislature. Three days later, however, after considerable debate, Judge Compton may have backtracked on his commitment to the publicly established concept of death. He instructed the jury:

In determining the time of death, as aforesaid. . . .you may consider the following elements none of which should necessarily be considered controlling, although you may feel under the evidence that one or more of these conditions are controlling: the time of the total stoppage of circulation of the blood; the time of the total cessation of the other vital functions consequent thereto, such as respiration and pulsation; the time of complete and irreversible loss of all functions of the brain; and whether or not the aforesaid functions were spontaneous or were being maintained artificially or mechanically.

This instruction is ambiguous, to say the least. It could be that Judge Compton meant no innovation here. It could be that the "complete and irreversible loss of all function of the brain" might have been merely the "cause" of death traditionally defined, i.e. "a cessation of the animal and vital functions." Presumably if the head injury to Tucker led to the cessation of all brain function and thereby to the cessation of all other vital functions, death could have occurred in the traditional sense without or prior to the intervention of the surgeons. This almost certainly would have been the case if Mr. Tucker had received no medical attention. The (traditional) death would have occurred and the "complete and irreversible loss of all function of the brain" would have been simply a relevant factor.

But it also is possible to interpret the judge's instructions as authorization for the jury to use a new concept of death—one based directly on brain function—in determining the time of the patient's death. If this is the case it is a complete reversal of the judge's earlier statement and a major change in public policy. It would appear that this contradicts Judge Compton's earlier conclusion that "if such a radical change is to be made in the law of Virginia, the application should be made therefore not to the courts but to the legislature wherein the basic concept of our society relating to the preservation and extension of life could be examined and, if necessary, reevaluated." Let us hope that the judge's later instruction to the jury should not be taken as backing down from this important principle.

WHO SHOULD HAVE MADE THE DECISION?

The other candidates for decision making in this case obviously are the relatives of the patient. While it is the state's obligation to establish fundamental policy in this area, it would seem reasonable and in the interest of the state that they would judge that no organs may be removed from an individual after death unless there is some authorization by the individual patient, such as is now called for in the Uniform Anatomical Gift Act, or by the patient's relatives, also as provided by that act. If it is true, in this case, that the relatives of the patient were not consulted and sufficient time was not taken to establish that relatives were available, this would seem to have been a most serious infringement upon the rights of the patient and the patient's family.

The removal of organs in the rare situations where relatives cannot be found raises a serious, if rather unusual, problem for transplant surgeons. It would appear to be far wiser to avoid the risk of abuse in these cases, which will frequently involve indigent and lonely patients, by simply forbidding the use of organs. Certainly four hours (from the time Mr. Tucker was placed on a respirator until the respirator was turned off) was not sufficient time to seek permission from the next of kin.

WAS THIS REALLY A DEFINITION OF DEATH CASE?

Up to this point, we have assumed that the defense, the prosecution, and the press were correct in interpreting this case as one focusing upon the meaning and concept of death. Yet the case record, as presented to the court, leaves open some very serious questions. The medical team was operating with a definition of death which focused on the brain. Medical witnesses for the defense claimed that Mr. Tucker was "neurologically dead" several hours before the transplant operation. Yet according to the records presented of the case, at 11:45 A.M. Mr. Tucker's physician says prognosis is nil and death imminent. At 1:00 P.M. the neurologist took an EEG reading and found it "showing flat lines with occasional artifact" and he "reports no evidence of viability and no signs of cortical activity." Presumably, according to a brain-oriented concept of death, Mr. Tucker was thought to be dead at the time by the surgeons. Yet we are told by the surgeons that at 3:30 P.M. they turned the respirator off. One must ask what possible moral principle would justify turning off a respirator on a dead patient. Presumably if one is dealing with a corpse, the moral imperative would be to preserve the organs for the benefit of the living in the best possible condition—by continuing the respiration process until the heart could be removed. We would find no moral problems with such behavior; in fact, one would say that it would be morally irresponsible to run the risk of damaging the tissue. Yet the respirator was turned off—from which one can only surmise that it must have been done in order to permit the heart and lungs to stop functioning. The only plausible reason for this would be that there was some lingering doubt about whether or not Mr. Tucker was dead. Of course, to introduce this dimension is to place doubt on the claim that the patient was dead at 1:00 P.M. when the EEG showed a flat tracing, "with occasional artifact."

If, however, the purpose was to turn the respirator off in order to allow the patient to die all the way, the case is not one of a new definition of death at all; it is instead the common one of morally, and possibly legally, deciding to continue treatment no longer on an irreversibly terminal patient. The morality of ceasing treatment on such a terminal patient has been accepted widely in medical ethics. Such procedures are practiced and accepted by Catholic, Protestant, and Jewish moral traditions alike. It could be, then, that this is really a case of deciding when it is morally acceptable to stop treatment on a dying patient, rather than a case of deciding when a patient was dead. This seems to be the most plausible and morally acceptable reason for turning off the respirator under law then existing in Virginia. It is very important to note that the jury never announced that the brain-oriented concept of death is now appropriate or that they themselves used such a concept. They were not asked or permitted to do this. They merely concluded that they found the defendants not guilty of wrongful death of the decedent. It may well be that at least some of them reasoned that the physicians did indeed hasten the dying process by turning off the respirator, but given the patient's condition this was an acceptable way to behave, i.e., they may have considered that the physician could have justifiably decided to withdraw the mechanical means of support as "extraordinary for a patient in Tucker's irreversibly dying condition." We do not know this of course, but we also do not know that the jury accepted a brain-oriented concept of death.

At 3.35 P.M., five minutes after the respirator was turned off, the patient was pronounced dead. One would think this was because there had been a cessation of heartbeat and respiratory function and the death was pronounced according to the traditional heart/lung criteria. If this were the case, the physicians would be operating under the traditional moral and legal requirements, and the removal of organs for transplantation, presumably with the permission of the next of kin, would be an acceptable procedure. They would not be using the brain-oriented concept of death at all.

WAS HE NEUROLOGICALLY DEAD?

There is one final problem which must be resolved. The summary of the proceedings raises some doubt as to whether the patient was dead even according to the concept of brain death which focuses upon the brain. The Harvard criteria call for the use of irreversible coma. But the Harvard report appeared in the *Journal of the American Medical Association* dated August 5, 1968, and the surgeons at the Medical College of Virginia had to make their decision two months earlier, on May 25, 1968. Obviously they could not be expected to have followed the Harvard criteria precisely. Nevertheless, Mr. Tucker definitely could not have been declared dead according to the criteria since established by the Harvard Committee and widely used as being the minimal tests for establishing irreversible coma. At the very least, the tests were not repeated twenty-four hours later. The patient was pronounced dead less than two hours and thirty-five minutes after the electroencephalogram reading.

In order to accept the jury's decision in this case and accept it as demonstrating that the physicians were justified in the use of brain evidence of death, one would have to accept four highly questionable premises. The first is that the jury did indeed base its decision on a brain-oriented concept of death. Second, that a man is really dead when he no longer has any capacity for brain activity. The third is that it was reasonable under 1968 conditions to conclude that the patient had irreversibly lost the capacity for any brain activity based on the EEG reading without repetition. Such a conclusion is premature even for the scientific evidence which exists today, [several] years later. Finally, one would have to accept that individual medical professionals should be vested with the authority to change public policy on an area as fundamental as life and death. This no one should be willing to tolerate.

13 · Model Legislation and Statutes on the
Definition of Death

**President's Commission for the Study of Ethical
Problems in Medicine and Biomedical
and Behavioral Research**

*The President's Commission for the Study of Ethical Problems in
Medicine and Biomedical and Behavioral Research was chaired by
Morris B. Abram, a distinguished attorney and former president of
Brandeis University. The remaining members of the Commission,
with one exception, were either M.D.s or Ph.D.s from various
universities or institutes throughout the country. This report is
part of a larger current investigation, in and out of government,
relating to topics of death and dying, including patients' rights to
end their own lives. The section reproduced below is a collection
of current state statutes relating to the determination of death
itself—a necessary background for any discussion of changes in
the current laws.*

From Defining Death: Medical, Legal and Ethical Issues in the
Determination of Death *by the President's Commission for the
Study of Ethical Problems in Medicine and Biomedical and
Behavioral Research. Published by the U.S. Government Printing
Office, 1981.*

I. ANALYSIS OF STATUTES

A. Degree of uniformity

Prior to the recommendation of the Uniform Deter-
mination of Death Act, five prototype statutes were employed by legislatures:
The Kansas law adopted in 1970,[1] the model statute prepared by A. M. Capron
and L. R. Kass in 1972,[2] the proposal put forward in 1975 by the American Bar
Association,[3] the Uniform Brain Death Act, recommended in 1978 by the
National Conference on Commissioners on Uniform State Laws,[4] and the
American Medical Association's 1979 proposal.[5] Of the 25 statutes adopted
prior to 1981 that are still on the books,[6] 18 were based on the first four models
(no state having directly followed the AMA proposal). But in many instances
the statutes as enacted depart in significant ways from the prototypes; in
addition to the seven states with original legislation not cut to any of the
model patterns, almost all of the other 18 contain some verbal variations
(from minor to major). Thus, if anything, the patchwork appearance of the
map in the Report . . . *overstates* the degree of uniformity achieved thus far.

The prospects for true uniformity are not as bleak as this picture might
suggest, however. In the first place, the state adoptions seem to come in
groups. For several years immediately after the first statute was adopted in
Kansas in 1970,[7] other legislatures used that law as their starting point:
Maryland in 1972,[8] and New Mexico and Virginia in 1973.[9] Similarly, four of the
five states that now have on their books a statute resembling the ABA propos-

al acted between 1974 and 1976; the fifth, Wyoming, adopted its law in 1979.[10]

The two adoptions of the Uniform Brain Death Act came in 1979 and 1980,[11]
and both states that have thus far accepted the Uniform Determination of
Death Act did so within a few months' time in 1981.[12] Second, several states
that had enacted statutes, then amended those statutes when "uniform"
proposals were put forward.[13] It is reasonable to expect that legislators in the
twenty-five states that have accepted the brain-based standard as at least one
basis for declaring death would be amenable to adopting the Uniform Determination of Death Act, which recognizes the brain-based standard in the
context of a uniform law that also incorporates the cardiopulmonary
standard.

Finally, the greatest impediment to uniformity has been the multiplicity of
proposals. Nonstandard laws accounted for nearly a third of the total number of 25 state statutes prior to the recent adoption by two states of the new
law recommended in the Commission's Report. The increasing number of
"models" seems to have caused a flood rather than an ebb in the tide of
idiosyncratic bills. Five of the seven nonstandard statutes were enacted since
1977. Moreover, in the absence of a single, uniform proposal, the states
turned increasingly to nonstandard statutes; the five adopted in 1977–80
represent nearly half of all the statutes adopted (other than "Uniform" proposals) during this period.

B. Scope of statutes

1. Single or multiple bases for diagnosis: All of the enacted statutes depart
from the common law rule that death occurs only when blood flow and
breathing have ceased. The statutes divide, however, into several groups
regarding the grounds for determining death that they do recognize. One
third of the 27 laws presently in force articulate a single, brain-based standard for determining death; they are silent on the relationship between this
statutory, neurological "definition" and the common law, cardiopulmonary
"definition."

In contrast are the laws of 13 states which explicitly provide for determinations of death by either the newer, neurological standards or the traditional,
cardiopulmonary standards. (In some instances the statute spells out the
relationships between the two standards, in others it is left to readers to
deduce the relationship.)

Halfway between these poles are the statutes in four states that specify
cessation of brain functions as a standard for determining death but also
accept other, *unspecified* criteria. Rather than being a happy medium, this
approach contains the worst of both worlds. On the one hand, it seems
intended to recognize that the diagnosis of death in most cases will not be
made by physicians directly measuring brain functions. But the means
chosen by these statutory drafters to go beyond the single, neurological
standard creates an impression that there may be any number of phenomena
called death, of which "brain death" is only one. The statutes open up the
grounds for determining death to an unspecified range of medical (or even
nonmedical) criteria; the Connecticut statute, for example, recognizes brain-

based criteria "[w]ithout limiting any other method of determining death."[14] On the other hand, these statutes lack the elegance of the single-standard statutes. The additional, vaguer language was plainly added (sometimes, as in the first of these statutes to be adopted, in California,[15] through legislative amendment to a bill containing only the single, brain-based standard) out of a recognition that death is diagnosed in most cases through cardiopulmonary tests rather than those that are typically thought of as tests of brain functions. But it replaces the elegance of a "brain only" standard (which rests on the equation of an absence of spontaneous respiratory and circulatory functions with a lack of brain functions) with an open-ended recognition of standards of no specified relationship to "brain death."

Finally, the statute adopted in Oregon[16] carries the process of expansion one step further. It recognizes irreversible cessation *both* of respiratory/ circulatory functions and of brain function. But, in addition, it also accepts without limitation "criteria customarily used by a person to determine death."

The proposed Uniform Determination of Death Act specifies both cardiopulmonary and brain standards as alternative bases for declaring death. These standards exhaust the grounds for such a determination and no unspecified, open-ended language is needed or employed.

2. "Whole" versus "higher" brain: The statutes' diversity in accepting one or more standards is matched by the range of wording used to describe the brain standard. All the laws were apparently intended to cover only loss of functioning in the whole brain, not merely in part. This is clearly expressed in about half the states, in terms that vary somewhat, including "total and irreversible cessation of brain function" (2 states), "irreversible cessation of total brain function" (6 states), "irreversible cessation of all functioning of the brain" (1 state), and "irreversible cessation of the functioning of the entire brain, including the brain stem" (2 states). Some of the statutes state merely "no spontaneous brain function" or "an irreversible cessation of brain function," which by their failure explicity to exclude some parts of the brain imply cessation of functioning in the entire organ. A few of these statutes make this requirement more explicit by linking loss of brain functioning with other signs. Virginia's statute, for example, speaks of "the absence of spontaneous brain functions and spontaneous respiratory functions."[17] Spontaneous respiration does not occur in the absence of a functioning brain stem.

The Uniform Determination of Death Act is explicit on this point: it requires irreversible cessation of *all* functions of the *entire* brain, *including the brain stem*.

3. Functions: Despite these elements of diversity in their explicit scope, the enacted statutes have one important point in common: they all provide *standards* for determining whether death has occurred, not the medical criteria or tests for diagnosing whether such standards have been met, and they do so by speaking of the "functions" (or "functioning") of organ systems, not in terms of any cellular *activity* occurring within those organs. The Uniform Determination of Death Act continues this pattern.

C. Applicability

1. Purpose: About half the statutes include some language intended to frame their purpose: for example, "a person is considered medically and legally dead" (4 states), or "for legal and medical purposes" (3 states), or simply "for all legal purposes" (4 states). None of these except for the two statutes that are amendments to the Uniform Anatomical Gift Act, those of Florida[18] ("for purposes of the Act") and Connecticut (which speaks only of potential organ "donors" and not of general "individuals"), seems intended to limit the normal application of the statute.[19]

The other states avoid possible confusion by not stating a "purpose" for a law intended to be generally applied. The Uniform Determination of Death Act likewise contains no such statement of "purposes" or range of application. It applies to all determinations of death.

2. Definition versus permission: Only a few of the statutes are actually written as "definitions" in the usual sense. The Oklahoma statute is perhaps the best example. It begins straightforwardly: "The term 'dead body' means a human body in which there is irreversible total cessation of brain function."[20] Most of the other statutes—including a few, such as those of New Mexico[21] and Iowa[22] that have the appearance of a "definition"—are actually statements of conditions which, when found upon physical examination to be met, establish that an individual has died.

It is important to note, however, that with only a few exceptions the statutes are declaratory and not merely permissive. That is, they establish that an individual who has lost X functions irreversibly (alternatively, one who has lost X or Y functions irreversibly) has died. Several of the nonstandard statutes, however, announce that "a person *may be* pronounced dead" (Georgia),[23] that "brain death . . . *may be* used as a sole basis for the determination that a person has died" (North Carolina),[24] or that "a physician . . . *may* make such a determination if [X] exists" (Oregon).[25] These statutes are responsive to medical needs. They provide a way out of the dilemma created for physicians and families who wish to use vigorous resuscitative measures while also seeing the need to be able to pronounce death when these artificial means produce breathing and blood flow but the individual has lost all brain functions and hence all ability to regain *spontaneous* respiration. But the statutes do not fulfill the need for legal certainty about an individual's *status*, since they make the determination of death permissive.

The Uniform Determination of Death Act avoids this pitfall. It sets forth alternative standards for determining death; when *either* is met, the individual is dead. (This also avoids the awkwardness of many existing statutes which state that a person *"will be considered dead."*) In most instances, such a determination would be accompanied by an explicit declaration of death by a physician or other qualified observer. But when such a contemporaneous determination is for some reason impossible, not undertaken or actually withheld, the determination could be made after the fact (for example, in a legal proceeding where the time of a particular death is a matter of importance) based upon all the evidence, including the medical records and any postmortem examination.

D. Miscellaneous

1. Standard for action: Four variations appear in the model bills to describe the basis on which the criteria and tests used to diagnose death are to be selected and employed. The enacted statutes are almost evenly divided between "ordinary standards of medical practice" and "usual and customary standards of medical practice." These two formulae appear to be synonymous.

Several states require "reasonable medical standards," which is the formula of the Uniform Brain Death Act. Florida blends this with the notion of acceptability and expects determinations to "be made in accordance with currently accepted reasonable medical standards."[26] The Florida provision highlights the problem with "reasonableness" in this context. The latter standard invites lay (jury) evaluation after-the-fact and for this reason it is seldom used in judging the performance of professionals. Instead, the competence of professionals is usually measured by whether they came within the boundaries of the theories and practices accepted by their professional groups.

The Uniform Determination of Death Act requires that determinations of death be based upon "accepted medical standards." Idaho, one of the first two states to adopt the new statute, defined accepted medical standards as "the usual and customary procedures of the community in which the determination of death is made."[27]

2. Authority to act: Most of the existing statutes are framed in terms of a determination by a "medical doctor" or "physician." The Uniform Determination of Death Act does not explicitly require a physician because in some instances (for example, in the case of a death occurring in a remote area) actions may have to be taken based upon a lay determination that breathing and heartbeat have ceased and cannot be revived. Protection against inappropriate action by a lay person under the statute arises from the requirement mentioned above, that all determinations "must be made in accordance with accepted medical standards." Such standards would not countenance a nonphysician diagnosing that all functions of the entire brain had ceased irreversibly for an individual with respirator-supported cardiopulmonary functions but lacking consciousness.

Similarly, the Uniform Determination of Death Act leaves to current medical standards to establish the number and specialized expertise of the physicians who should perform any particular tests. Some of the existing statutes—particularly those that pay direct attention to organ transplantation—specify that *two* physicans must participate in determining death under the brain-based standard. Some even specify the physician's professional qualifications (e.g., Florida: "Board-eligible or board-certified neurologist, neurosurgeon, internist, pediatrician, surgeon, or anesthesiologist"[28] and Virginia: "a consulting physician, who shall be duly licensed and a specialist in the field of neurology, neurosurgery, or electroencephalography"[29]). The protection against conflict of interest—that a physician diagnosing death ought not to participate in the transplantation of organs from the deceased—is spelled out in several statutes.[30] Such provisions are duplicative of § 7(b) of the Uniform Anatomical Gift Act, which has been adopted in all jurisdictions in the United States.[31]

3. Personal beliefs: None of the existing statutes provide for a "conscience clause" for individuals or their families to "opt out" of the law's provisions. This absence is not surprising in a law intended to establish every individual's status in society (as "alive" or "dead"). The Florida statute does provide, however, for notification of the deceased's next of kin "as soon as practicable of the procedures [used] to determine death" and for the recording in the medical record of such notice or "the attempts to identify and notify the next of kin."[32] This provision seems intended to avoid or reduce misunderstanding. The need for such a provision is not immediately apparent if physicians are following accepted medical procedures in dealing with patients' relatives and maintaining medical records; the provision may have resulted from a particular controversy in Florida. In any event, it does not authorize the next of kin to insist that any particular diagnostic approach be employed in preference to another; such matters are left by the statute to medical judgment.

4. Living will: In a number of jurisdictions bills have been introduced that combine provisions "defining" death with those permitting the use of "living wills" or similar directives to physicians to cease treatment should a person become incompetent while suffering from a terminal illness. In North Carolina a "Natural Death Act" combining these features was adopted in 1977.[33] That statute was criticized as "a virtual invitation to litigation, so many are the problems and ambiguities it create[d]."[34] The statute was subsequently rewritten and reenacted as two separate provisions, with most of the problems in the "definition" of death section removed.[35]

4. Liability: The model statute formulated by the American Medical Association insulated from civil liability or criminal prosecution (i) any physician (or "other person authorized by law to determine death") who acted in accordance with the statute, or (ii) any person "who act[ed] in good faith reliance on [such] a determination."[36] Such preclusion of liability provisions appear in the statutes adopted in five states.[37] They are redundant of the protection already provided by the common law and by accepted rules of statutory interpretation. The Uniform Determination of Death Act does not include any preclusion of liability provisions.

II. MODEL LEGISLATION

ABA

The following is the text of the model statute proposed by the American Bar Association in 1975:

For all legal purposes, a human body with irreversible cessation of total brain function, according to usual and customary standards of medical practice, shall be considered dead.

100 *A.B.A. Ann. Rprt.* 231–32 (1978) (February 1975 midyear meeting).

AMA

The following is the amended model state determination of death bill approved at the December 1979 Interim Meeting of the American Medical Association:

IN THE GENERAL ASSEMBLY
STATE OF _____
An Act
To Provide for Determination of Death

Be it enacted by the People of the State of _____, represented in the General Assembly:

Section 1. An individual who has sustained either (1) irreversible cessation of circulatory and respiratory functions, or (2) irreversible cessation of all functions of the entire brain, shall be considered dead. A determination of death shall be made in accordance with accepted medical standards.

(COMMENT: This section is intended to provide a comprehensive statement for determining death in all situations, by clarifying and codifying the common law in this regard. The two bases set forth in the statute are the only medically accepted bases for determining death, and the statute is therefore all inclusive. "All functions" of the brain means that purposeful activity of the brain, as distinguished from random activity in the brain, has ceased. "Entire brain" includes both the brain stem and the neocortex and is meant to distinguish the concept of neocortical death, which is not a valid medical basis for determining death.

It is recognized that physicians may determine death. It is also recognized that in some jurisdictions non-physicians (i.e. coroners) are empowered to determine death. It is the intent of this bill to recognize that under accepted medical standards a determination of death based on irreversible cessation of brain function may be made only by a physician.)

Section 2. A physician or any other person authorized by law to determine death who makes such determination in accordance with Section 1 is not liable for damages in any civil action or subject to prosecution in any criminal proceeding for his acts or the acts of others based on that determination.

Section 3. Any person who acts in good faith in reliance on a determination of death is not liable for damages in any civil action or subject to prosecution in any criminal proceeding for his act.

(COMMENT: While Section 1 is intended to remove legal impediments relating to a declaration of death based on medically accepted principles, sec-

tions 2 and 3 are intended to remove inhibitions from making a declaration of
death based on either of the two standards and also to remove inhibitions of
hospital personnel from carrying out the direction of a physician in this
regard by removing the threat of liability. These sections do not absolve from
liability a person who acts negligently or contrary to accepted medical
standards.)

> *Section 4.* If any provision of this Act is held by a court to be invalid
> such invalidity shall not affect the remaining provisions of the Act, and
> to this end the provisions of this Act are hereby declared to be
> severable.

Capron-Kass

The following is the modified text of a model bill proposed in 1972 by
Professor Alexander M. Capron and Dr. Leon Kass in an article in Volume 121
of the *University of Pennsylvania Law Review* at pages 87–118:

> A person will be considered dead if in the announced opinion of a
> physician, based on ordinary standards of medical practice, he has
> experienced an irreversible cessation of respiratory and circulatory
> functions, or in the event that artificial means of support preclude a
> determination that these functions have ceased, he has experienced an
> irreversible cessation of total brain functions. Death will have occurred
> at the time when the relevant functions ceased.

> A. M. Capron, "Legal Definition of Death." 315 *Ann. N.Y. Acad. Sci.* 349,
> 356 (1978).

Uniform Brain Death Act

The following is a proposal approved and recommended for enactment by
the National Conference of Commissioners on Uniform State Laws at its
Annual Conference on July 28–August 4, 1978:

> *Section 1. [Brain Death.]* For legal and medical purposes, an individual
> who has sustained irreversible cessation of all functioning of the brain,
> including the brain stem, is dead. A determination under this section
> must be made in accordance with reasonable medical standards.

COMMENT: This section legislates the concept of brain death. The Act does
not preclude a determination of death under other legal or medical criteria,
including the traditional criteria of cessation of respiration and circulation.
Other criteria are practical in cases where artificial life-support systems are
not utilized. Even those criteria are indicative of brain death.

"Functioning" is a critical word in the Act. It expresses the idea of *purposeful* activity in all parts of the brain, as distinguished from random activity. In a
dead brain, some meaningless cellular processes, detectable by sensitive
monitoring equipment, could create legal confusion if the word "activity"
were substituted for "functioning."

> *Section 2. [Short Title.]* This Act may be cited as the Uniform Brain
> Death Act.

The following is the text of the statute approved by the National Conference of Commissioners on Uniform State Laws at its Annual Conference on July 26–August 1, 1980, by the American Medical Association on October 19, 1980, by the President's Commission on November 7, 1980, and by the American Bar Association on February 10, 1981, to supersede the existing "model" bills:

> *Section 1. [Determination of Death.]* An individual who has sustained either (1) irreversible cessation of circulatory and respiratory functions, or (2) irreversible cessation of all functions of the entire brain, including the brain stem, is dead. A determination of death must be made in accordance with accepted medical standards.

> *Section 2. [Uniformity of Construction and Application.]* This Act shall be applied and construed to effectuate its general purpose to make uniform the law with respect to the subject of this Act among states enacting it.

> *Section 3. [Short Title.]* This Act may be cited as Uniform Determination of Death Act.

III: STATE LEGISLATION ADOPTED 1970–1981

Editor's Note: Below are reproduced samples of some recently enacted state statutes relating to the definition of death.

Alabama

§ 22–31–1. Standards and procedures for determination of death generally.

(a) A person is considered medically and legally dead if, in the opinion of a medical doctor licensed in Alabama, based on usual and customary standards of medical practice in the community, there is no spontaneous respiratory or cardiac function and there is no expectation of recovery of spontaneous respiratory or cardiac function.

(b) In the case when respiratory and cardiac function are maintained by artificial means, a person is considered medically and legally dead if, in the opinion of a medical doctor licensed in Alabama, based on usual and customary standards of medical practice in the community for the determination by objective neurological testing of total and irreversible cessation of brain function, there is total and irreversible cessation of brain function. Death may be pronounced in this circumstance before artificial means of maintaining respiratory and cardiac function are terminated. In the case described in this subsection, there shall be independent confirmation of the death by another medical doctor licensed in Alabama. (Acts 1979, No. 70–165, § 1.)

§ 22–31–2. Use of other methods.

Nothing in this chapter shall prohibit a physician from using other procedures based on usual and customary standards of medical practice for determining death as the exclusive basis for pronouncing a person dead. (Acts 1979, No. 79–165, § 2.)

§ 22–31–3. Procedure where part of body to be used for transplantation.

(a) When a part of a donor is proposed to be used for transplantation pursuant to article 3 of chapter 19 of this title and the death of the donor is determined as set forth in section 22–31–1, there shall be an independent confirmation of the death by another medical doctor licensed in Alabama. Neither the physician making the determination of death nor the physician making the independent confirmation shall participate in the procedures for removing or transplanting a part.

(b) When a part of a donor is proposed to be used for transplantation pursuant to article 3 of chapter 19 of this title and the death of the donor is determined as set forth in section 22–31–1, complete patient medical records shall be kept, maintained and preserved. (Act 1979, No. 79–165, § § 3,4.)

§ 22–31–4. Liability for acts.

A person who acts in accordance with the terms of this chapter is not liable for damages in any civil action or subject to prosecution in any criminal proceeding for his act. (Acts 1979, No. 79–165, § 5.)

Ala. Code § § 22–31–1 through 22–31–4 (Cum. Supp. 1979) (Effective June 5, 1979)

California

§ 7180. Pronouncement on determining cessation of brain function: Confirmation: Other procedures.

A person shall be pronounced dead if it is determined by a physician that the person has suffered a total and irreversible cessation of brain function. There shall be indepedent confirmation of the death by another physician.

Nothing in this chapter shall prohibit a physician from using other usual and customary procedures for determining death as the exclusive basis for pronouncing a person dead.

§ 7181. Confirmation in event of transplantation under Uniform Anatomical Gift Act: Restriction on physician's participation in removal and transplantation.

When a part of the donor is used for direct transplantation pursuant to the Uniform Anatomical Gift Act (Chapter 3.5, commencing with Section 7150) and the death of the donor is determined by determining that the person has suffered a total and irreversible cessation of brain function there shall be an independent confirmation of the death by another physician. Neither the physician making the determination of death under Section 7155.5 nor the physician making the independent confirmation shall participate in the procedures for removing or transplanting a part.

§ 7182. Patient medical records.

Complete patient medical records required of a health facility pursuant to regulations adopted by the department in accordance with Section 1275 shall be kept, maintained, and preserved with respect to the requirements of this chapter when a person is pronounced dead by determining that the person has suffered a total and irreversible cessation of brain function.

Cal. Health & Safety Code § § 7180–7182 (Deering Supp. 1980) (Added Stats. 1974 ch 1524 § 1, effective September 27, 1974.)

Idaho

54–1819. Definition and procedure for determination of death.

(1) An individual who has sustained either (a) irreversible cessation of circulatory and respiratory functions, or (b) irreversible cessation of all functions of the entire brain, including the brain stem, is dead.

(2) A determination of death must be made in accordance with accepted medical standards which mean the usual and customary procedures of the community in which the determination of death is made. [I.C., § 54–1819, as added by 1981, ch. 258, § 2, p. 549.]

Former § 54–1819 (1977, ch. 130, § 1, p. 276) was repealed by S.L. 1981, ch. 258, § 1.

Kansas

72–202. Definition of death.

A person will be considered medically and legally dead if, in the opinion of a physician, based on ordinary standards of medical practice, there is the absence of spontaneous respiratory and cardiac function and, because of the disease or condition which caused, directly or indirectly, these functions to cease, or because of the passage of time since these functions ceased, attempts at resuscitation are considered hopeless; and, in this event, death will have occurred at the time these functions ceased; or

A person will be considered medically and legally dead if, in the opinion of a physician, based on ordinary standards of medical practice, there is the absence of spontaneous brain function; and if based on ordinary standards of medical practice, during reasonable attempts to either maintain or restore spontaneous circulatory or respiratory function in the absence of aforesaid brain function, it appears that further attempts at resuscitation or supportive maintenance will not succeed, death will have occurred at the time when these conditions first coincide. Death is to be pronounced before any vital organ is removed for purposes of transplantation.

These alternative definitions of death are to be utilized for all purposes in this state, including the trials of civil and criminal cases, any laws to the contrary notwithstanding.

Kan. Stat. Ann. § 77–202 (Cum. Supp. 1979)
(K.S.A. § 77–202; L. 1979, ch. 199. § 11; July 1. Deleted the provision requiring the pronouncement of death before artificial means of supporting respiratory and circulatory functions are terminated.)
(Enacted 1970)

Montana

50–22–101. Definition of death.

A human body with irreversible cessation of total brain function as determined according to usual and customary standards of medical practice, is dead for all legal purposes.

Mont. Rev. Codes Ann. § 50–22–101 (1978)
(Enacted 69–7201 by Sec. 1, Ch. 228, L. 1977, R.C.M. 1947, 69–7201.)
(Adopted April 4, 1977)

Virginia

§ 54–325.7. When person deemed medically and legally dead.

A person shall be medically and legally dead if, (a) in the opinion of a physician duly authorized to practice medicine in this Commonwealth, based on the ordinary standards of medical practice, there is the absence of spontaneous respiratory and spontaneous cardiac functions and, because of the disease or condition which directly or indirectly caused these functions to cease, or because of the passage of time since these functions ceased, attempts at resuscitation would not, in the opinion of such physician, be successful in restoring spontaneous life-sustaining functions, and, in such event, death shall be deemed to have occurred at the time these functions ceased; or (b) in the opinion of a consulting physician, who shall be duly licensed and a specialist in the field of neurology, neurosurgery, or electroencephalography, when based on the ordinary standards of medical practice, there is the absence of spontaneous brain functions and spontaneous respiratory functions and, in the opinion of the attending physician and such consulting physician, based on the ordinary standards of medical practice and considering the absence of spontaneous brain functions and spontaneous respiratory functions and the patient's medical records, further attempts at resuscitation or continued supportive maintenance would not be successful in restoring such spontaneous functions, and, in such event, death shall be deemed to have occurred at the time when these conditions first coincide. Death, as defined in subsection (b) hereof, shall be pronounced by the attending physician and recorded in the patient's medical record and attested by the aforesaid consulting physician.

Notwithstanding any statutory or common law to the contrary, either of these alternative definitions of death may be utilized for all purposes in the Commonwealth, including the trial of civil and criminal cases.

(Code 1950, § 32–364.3:1; 1973, c. 252; 1979, c. 720)
Va. Code § 54–325.7 (Cum. Supp. 1981)
(Effective March 13, 1973)

Notes

1 Kan. Stat. Ann. § 77–202 (Cum. Supp. 1979).

2 Alexander M. Capron and Leon R. Kass, "A Statutory Definition of the Standards for Determining Human Death: An Appraisal and a Proposal," 121 *U. Pa. L. Rev. 87* (1972), as modified in Alexander M. Capron, "Legal Definition of Death," 315 *Ann. N.Y. Acad. Sci.* 349, 356 (1978).

3 100 *A.B.A. Ann. Report* 231–232 (February 1975 Midyear Meeting).

4 12 *Uniform Laws 5* (Supp. 1980).

5 243 *J.A.M.A.* 420 (1980) (editorial).

6 More than 25 statutes were actually adopted prior to 1981 on the determination of death, since several states (e.g., Idaho, North Carolina and West Virginia) have replaced one statute with another.

7 Kan. Stat. Ann. § 77–202 (Cum. Supp. 1979).

8 Md. Code Ann., Art. 43, § 54F (1972).

9 N.M. Stat. Ann., § 12–2–4 (1978); Va. Code § 54.325.7 (1979).

10 Wyo. Stat. § 35–19–101 (Cum. Supp. 1979).

11 Nev. Rev. Stat. § 451.007 (1979); W. Va. Code § 16.10–1 (Supp. 1980).

12 Colo. Rev. Stat. § 12–36–136 (1981); Idaho Code § 54–1819 (Cum. Supp. 1981).

13 Idaho Code § 54–1819 (Cum. Supp. 1981).

14 Conn. Gen. Stat. Ann. § 19–139i (West. Cum. Supp. 1981).

15 Cal. Health & Safety Code § § 7180–7182 (Deering Supp. 1980).

16 Or. Rev. Stat. § 146.087 (1977).

17 Va. Code § 54.325.7 (Cum. Supp. 1981).

18 Fla. Stat. § 382.085 (1980).

19 Conn. Gen. Stat. Ann. § 19–139i (West Cum. Supp. 1981).

20 Okla. Stat. Ann. tit. 63, § 1–301(g) (West Cum. Supp. 1981).

21 N.M. Stat. Ann. § § 12–2–4 and 5 (1978).

22 Iowa Code Ann. § 702.8 (West 1980).

23 Ga. Code Ann. § 88.1715.1 (Cum. Supp. 1980) (emphasis added).

24 N.C. Gen. Stat. § 90–323 (Cum. Supp. 1979) (emphasis added).

25 Or. Rev. Stat. § 146.087 (1977) (emphasis added).

26 Fla. Stat. § 382.085 (1980).

27 Idaho Code § 54–1819 (Cum. Supp. 1981).

28 Fla. Stat. § 382.085 (1980).

29 Va. Code § 54.325 (Cum. Supp. 1981).

30 *See e.g.* Cal. Health & Safety Code § § 7180–7182 (Deering Supp. 1980); Hawaii Rev. Stat. § 327C–1 (Supp. 1980).

31 Uniform Anatomical Gift Act, *see 8 Uniform Laws Annot.* 608 (1972) at § 7(b); Annot. 76 A.L.R. 3d 890.

32 Alexander Morgan Capron, "The Development of Law on Human Death," 315 *Ann. N.Y. Acad. Sci.* 45, 52 (1978).

33 N.C. Adv. Legis. Serv. Ch. 815, § 90–322.

32 Alexander Morgan Capron, "The Development of Law on Human Death" 315 *Ann. N.Y. Acad. Sci.* 45, 52 (1978).

35 N.C. Gen. Stat. § 90–323 (Cum. Supp. 1979).

36 243 *J.A.M.A.* 420 (1980) (editorial).

37 Ala. § 22–31–4 (Cum. Supp. 1979); Conn. Gen. Stat. Ann. § 19–139i(c) (West Cum. Supp. 1981); Fla. Stat. § 382.085(4) [1980]; Ga. § 88–1715.1(b) (Cum. Supp. 1980); Tex. Rev. Civ. Stat. Ann. art. 447t § 3 (Vernon Cum. Supp. 1980).

14 · The Lost Theme

Robert Jay Lifton

Robert Jay Lifton holds the Foundations' Fund for Research in Psychiatry professorship at Yale University. His books include Death in Life: Survivors of Hiroshima *(which won the National Book Award in the sciences in 1969),* Home from the War, The Life of the Self, Explorations in Psychohistory, *and* Boundaries: Psychological Man in Revolution. *The section reproduced below is the prologue to the book entitled* The Broken Connection. *Lifton's principal thesis in this book is that for our mental health we need to retain a continuity, a connection between ourselves and the past and between ourselves and death, and that at the present time (the time of the threat of nuclear extinction) that vital connection is in jeopardy.*

From The Broken Connection *by Robert Jay Lifton. Copyright © 1979 by Robert Jay Lifton. Reproduced by permission of Simon and Schuster, a Division of Gulf and Western Corporation.*

We live on images. As human beings we know our bodies and our minds only through what we can imagine. To grasp our humanity we need to structure these images into metaphors and models. Writers, artists, and visionaries have always known this—as have philosophers and scientists in other ways. Depth psychologists, however, take on the special and perhaps impossible task of bringing order to this dazzling array of images and the equally impressive range of feelings associated with them.

To create this order, psychologists and social theorists make their own choices of models or paradigms. We, too, require prior structures that seem relatively reliable as guides and maps to the terrain of imagery and feeling. In other words, psychologists do not simply interpret or analyze; we also construct; we engage in our own struggles around form. We are much concerned with narrative, and we inevitably contribute to the narrative of whatever life we examine.

But something has gone seriously wrong with everyone's images and models. When we invoke God and the devil, dialectical materialism and the perfectibility of man, or libido and death instinct, we perceive something familiar and perhaps explanatory or even moving—but these images rarely lead to an exhilarating sense of illumination or truth. We have difficulty seeing ourselves and our experienced work in the models handed down to us. At the same time we feel nagged if not threatened by a new wave of millennial imagery—of killing, dying, and destroying on a scale so great as to end the human narrative. We sense that our models should address that threat, but we do not know just how.

In recent work I have suggested a sequence in psychological thought from Freud's model of instinct and defense, to Erikson's of identity and the life cycle, to an emerging paradigm of death and life-continuity taking shape in the work of a number of people including myself. The general contours of this "new" paradigm were an attempt to move toward a new psychology. It is time to examine more closely the theme of death and continuity at the heart of the paradigm and to begin to fill in a few of the details of that "new psychology."

The "lost theme" to be addressed is not quite death itself. These days, in fact, one has the impression, at least in America, that death has been all too much found. Much more elusive is the psychological relationship between the phenomenon of death and the flow of life. Psychological theory has tended either to neglect death or render it a kind of foreign body, to separate death from the general motivations of life. Or else a previous deathless cosmology is replaced by one so dominated by death as to be virtually lifeless. As theorists, we seem to be all too susceptible both to the enormous cultural denial of (or numbness toward) death and to rebound reactions against that denial and numbness. The necessary dialectical focus on death and continuity poses formidable intellectual difficulties and imaginative requirements. And once that focus is taken seriously, the question is no longer how to incorporate death into psychological theory but how to transform the theory.

That transformation is best approached carefully. Though deviating from various Freudian positions, this book is itself a child of the Freudian revolution. In reexamining many of Freud's ideas, I have been surprised at their relevance for important directions he failed to take or even explicitly rejected. Freud is more present than I had intended him to be, and many of my views emerge in respectful, critical dialogue with him.

Books also begin with models and metaphors. This one emerged from compelling questions about death and holocaust that I originally encountered in my Hiroshima study. I was struck then by how little psychological literature seemed to speak to what I had observed. This deficiency was partly a matter of historical lag: there could be no adequate principles for the unprecedented. It also had to do with the limitations of the psychoanalytic paradigm, with Freud's own brilliant conceptual imbalance. Twentieth-century holocaust exposed rather than created that imbalance, and made urgent demands on psychology in general. Contained within those demands, I felt, were possibilities for new directions, significant insight, and even fundamental advance, for I was convinced that the extreme experiences described to me had considerable relevance for everyday existence.

With that in mind, at the end of my Hiroshima study I suggested relationships between survivor patterns and various forms of psychological disorder we encounter in our clinics and among ourselves. More generally, I spoke of a historical shift from Victorian struggles concerning sexuality and moralism to our present preoccupation with absurd death (and my implication, absurd life) and unlimited technological violence. But the elaboration of that shift has been no easy matter. Though I still think of this book as an outcome of my Hiroshima work, I seem to have required a decade or so to further test its ideas, to examine their application to other cataclysms as well as to clinical syndromes, before attempting a comprehensive synthesis. Now I am ready to risk that effort.

The broken connection exists in the tissues of our mental life. It has to do with a very new historical—one could also say evolutionary—relationship to death. We are haunted by the image of exterminating ourselves as a species by means of our own technology. Contemplating that image as students of human nature, we become acutely aware that we have never come to terms with our "ordinary"—that is, prenuclear—relationship to death and life-continuity. We seem to require this ill-begotten imagery of extinction to prod us toward examining what we have so steadfastly avoided. So this book has a double task. It first seeks general principles concerning death imagery and struggles for continuity, and applies these principles to explorations of the individual life cycle, the varieties of psychiatric disorder, and aspects of the historical process. It then goes on to consider some of the consequences of our imagery of extinction or what I call the "nuclear image." My conviction is that neither of these two tasks is properly undertaken separately from the other. You need to know about the mind's general possibilities and most extreme pitfalls around death imagery if you are to begin to understand radical new influences; and by the same token, can no longer look at "ordinary" relationships to death and life-continuity outside a context of ultimate threat. There is a logic, then, to the seemingly outrageous scope of this book. But invoking so broad a spectrum has its special vulnerabilities. One repeatedly introduces large questions that cannot be independently pursued. I have had to restrain myself from more detailed probing of many fascinating questions—whether about adolescence, schizophrenia, violence, or awareness—in order to hold to the general narrative, within which each of these large questions is no more than a fundamental example. My effort throughout is to press toward integrating principles that can have meaning for psychological work and general living in our time.

More specifically, the plan of the book is this. Part I describes a basic set of propositions that make up an open system in the sense of the Greek idea of *sustēma* or composite whole, one that enables its components to stand together. I stress the mutuality of ultimate and proximate levels of the paradigm. The ultimate level has to do with symbolizing our connection to our history and our biology; the proximate level includes more immediate feelings and images; and the two levels combine in the human struggle not merely to remain alive but to feel alive. I discuss man's evolutionary leap as including his knowledge that he dies, his capacity to symbolize, and his creation of culture. All these are of an imaginative piece: man does not create culture out of his need to deny death (the view put forward by both Freud and Rank and many of their modern disciples), but rather as his way of living out his unique awareness that he both dies and continues.

I examine ways in which these proximate and ultimate involvements are expressed over the course of the life cycle. A key principle is that of the formative process: the continuous creation of psychic images and forms, so that every encounter with the environment is newly constructed according to prior and anticipated experience—according to what one "knows" and expects. Here I extend the classical psychoanalytic idea of a symbol as a relatively primitive, conscious substitution of one thing for another (say, sea for mother or pencil for penis) to a more contemporary view of symbolization: the specifically human need to *construct* all experience as the only means of perceiving, knowing, and feeling. My extensive use of Japanese examples, especially when discussing cultural constructs, may strike some readers as a bit odd in a general study written by an American. To be sure, those examples come to mind because of past work and life experience. But it is also true that Japanese culture is particularly vivid and concrete in its attitudes toward death and life-continuity. The examples I choose reflect my conviction that seemingly alien and exotic culture patterns teach us as much about universals as about the particular characteristics of that culture.*

Part II applies this open system to concepts of the fundamental emotions (attachment and love, anxiety and tension, conscience and guilt, anger and violence); to the classical neuroses and to schizophrenia; and to the phenomenon of suicide. I explore the relationship of all these to death imagery, perceived threat, and struggles toward vitality and meaning. I give special emphasis to traumatic disorder (the experience of death-related stress or

---

*As I have emphasized in earlier work, all collective behavior can be understood within a trinity of what is common to all people in all eras (psychobiological universals), what is given stress by a particular culture (cultural emphases), and recent historical directions (especially ways in which they support and conflict with cultural emphases). From this standpoint no shared experience is merely "cultural," "universal," or "historical"—every experience is simultaneously all three. But in the present study I am most concerned with universals, especially in the early sections; and then with the impact of widely shared recent history upon these universals. Inevitably, therefore, I neglect cultural differences. I believe I can be justified in doing so to the extent that the more general point is validly made.

extreme situations) and to the more general issue of depression as central to all mental suffering and the life process in general. I view schizophrenia as embodying the most extreme death-like maneuvers to avoid feeling; and suicide as always containing a vision, however desperate, of revitalization.

Part III examines broader historical phenomena around the theme of death and continuity. I consider collective versions of the "broken connection," of the loss of a sense of continuity (or symbolization of immortality) and the sequence that can potentially result—from dislocation to totalism to victimization and violence. I particularly stress victimizers' struggles with death imagery and aberrant quests for renewal. Then I apply that model to the influences of the nuclear age and its imagery of extinction. Here I examine threats to our sense of historical continuity posed by the mere existence of the weaponry, and some of the resulting patterns of psychic numbing on the one hand and of worship of nuclear diety (the phenomenon of "nuclearism") on the other. Finally I say something about the principle of awareness— perhaps the touchstone of the entire study—as a source of more genuine directions of renewal.

My effort throughout is to explore the place of death in the human imagination, and its bearing on our sense of endings, changes, and beginnings. The spirit of the work is captured in a parable of the Jewish reinterpretation of the Adam and Eve story told by Nahum Glatzer. According to Glatzer, that description of man and woman being extruded from the Garden of Eden was not a "fall" but a "rise." It meant "becoming human," that is, "giving up immortality for knowledge." For becoming human meant surrendering both ignorance of death (the state of other animals) and the expectation of living forever (a prerogative only of God). "Knowledge," in our sense, is the capacity of the symbolizing imagination to explore the idea of death and relate it to a principle of life-continuity—that is, the capacity for culture. The parable thus depicts an *exchange of literal for symbolic immortality*. It suggests an idea of a mortal being who need not remain numbed toward (ignorant of) the fact of death, who can know death and yet transcend it.

That perspective in turn connects us with recent anthropological views of man as the "cultural animal." For, as Robin Fox goes on to claim, "Culture is part of the biology of man ... a characteristic of our species, as much a characteristic as the long neck of the giraffe." The metaphor of the "long neck" can be carried further: Culture, our means of symbolizing death and continuity, takes us to a higher place, permits us to see and imagine more, but also becomes a source of vulnerability in that very extension (if not overextension) of the brain-body axis.

The goal here is theory with an evolutionary spirit but without narrow biological determinism. For instance, Edward O. Wilson's synthesis of "sociobiology" relates to our paradigm in distinguishing the "proximate causation" of functional biology (the characteristics of a particular organ system—say, the digestive or nervous system of wolves or bees) with his own stress on the "ultimate causation" of evolutionary biology: the influence on species and individuals of the "prime movers of evolution," those environmental influences (weather, predators, stressors, living space, food sources, and accessible mates) that maintain continuous procreation and species' survival. Wilson's argument is that from the vast gene pool available in any species, those genes with the greatest survival value are perpetuated via mating arrangements, even when they propel the individual animal toward a sacrificial or "altruistic" death on behalf of group survival. With human beings, however, this argument runs into difficulty precisely around Wilson's neglect of the crucial symbolizing function.

He thus speaks of "a genetic predisposition to enter certain classes and to play certain roles," of "upwardly-mobile genes," "conformer genes," and "genes favoring spite" and the like. What I call symbolization of immortality (the ultimate level in our paradigm) could be understood as equivalent to Wilson's prime movers of evolution (his ultimate level). For in human experience, one must give primacy to the internal environment of the symbolizing mind and its capacity to envision human connection on a variety of levels. This is why we can speak of the evolutionary principle of staying psychologically as well as physically alive. There is room in this view for principles of genetic legacy around the capacity for symbolizing skills of different kinds. But that legacy must be recast into specifically human constructions around living and dying.

As we explore the nuances of our imaginative relationship to death we must question one particular philosophical claim now so widespread as to have become conventional wisdom: the principle that we are incapable of imagining our own deaths. This observation was made by many existential philosophers, as well as by such luminaries as Goethe and Freud. The truth in the claim is apparent enough: we are unable to imagine—that is, experience through imagery—our own nonexistence. But the fallacy lies in letting the matter end there. For while I cannot imagine my nonexistence, I can very well imagine a world in which "I" do not exist. That imaginative capacity is the basis for our theory of symbolic immortality. For as Paul Edwards has put it, "even existential philosophers . . . appoint literary executors."[1]

There is also the crucial question of the literality of the "I" involved. While "I" will cease to exist (which is why I cannot imagine my own death), elements of my "self"—of its (my) impact on others (children, students, friends, and, one may hope, readers)—will continue. These will exist not as a cohesive entity (the self as such) but as a part of a human flow that absorbs and recreates the components of that impact to the point of altering their shape and obscuring their origin. I can well imagine *that* process, and doing so contributes importantly to my acceptance of the idea of my own death.

We have been much too quick to posit imaginative limitations around death and continuity. We have much more to learn, once we make the critical distinction between literal perpetuation of the intact self—an illusion and frequently a dangerous one—and imagined (symbolized) perpetuation of elements of the self through connection with larger forms of human culture. We can then open our imaginations to a post-death (postself) future—and at the same time to the idea of the termination and disintegration of the self, of the individual mind and body.

Heinrich Böll's observation that "The artist carries death within him like a good priest his breviary" has never been more important than in our death-haunted time. And not only for the artist. For the attempt to exclude from the psychological imagination death and its symbolizations tends to freeze one in death terror, in a stance of numbing that can itself be a form of psychological death. Much of this study is devoted to exposing that process as it operates individually and collectively.

In all this the investigator can hardly be neutral. He resides *in* a particular history, and he badly misleads when he assumes a vantage point outside that history. His own advocacies and their relationship to his time and place are very much part of his narrative. Buber's equilibrium of "distance and relation" is the model here. The author's every exploration of death and continuity must both include and extend beyond himself.

PART IV
ASPECTS OF THE
DYING PROCESS

Contents

Consider these questions: Should we lie to a person who is dying? How can we best interact with a terminally ill person? What subtle psychological and social events occur around the dying person, in the home or in the hospital? How and why do both the hospital staff and the patient contribute to the pretense that the patient is not dying? Is outright denial of one's own life-threatening illness healthy? (To be tolerated? To be openly challenged?) Obviously, there are serious and complicated issues in each dying drama.

The varied selections in this part are by a physician, three sociologists, a philosopher, and a psychologist—all concerned with thanatological issues, especially the improvement of the lot of the dying person by way of a better understanding of the dying process.

150

©MgBB '83

Speaking of Death with the Dying

John Hinton

John Hinton is an English physician and professor of psychiatry at Middlesex Medical School. In this selection, taken from his indispensable book Dying, *Dr. Hinton discusses the issues involved in speaking with a terminal patient and notes that how one speaks with the dying is far more important than what one says.*

From Dying *by John Hinton (Pelican Originals, 1967). Copyright © 1967 by John Hinton. Reprinted by permission of Penguin Books, Ltd.*

The frequently debated question "Should the doctor tell?" tends to carry a false implication that the doctor knows all about the patient's approaching death and the patient knows nothing. The resultant discussion and controversy [are] therefore often irrelevant or, at least, tangential to the real problem. Doctors are far from omniscient. Even if they have no doubt that their patients' condition will be fatal, they can rarely foretell the time of death with any accuracy unless it is close at hand. Furthermore . . . patients are not necessarily unaware of what is happening; many have a very clear idea that they are dying.

Rather than putting a choice between telling or not telling, it would be more useful to ask other questions. Should we encourage or divert a patient who begins to speak of matters that will lead to talk of dying? How freely should we speak to him about it? Should we lie to him if we suspect he only wants to be told that all will be well? If he sincerely wishes to know if his illness will be fatal, should his suppositions be confirmed? If he never asks outright, have we a duty to tell him? Is it right to deny knowledge of dying to those who ask, or wrong to tell those who show no wish to know? Should we allow the awareness of dying to grow gradually, or should patients who are mortally ill know this early on, so that they may attain greater acceptance of dying? If they are to be told more openly, how should such knowledge be given? How do people react to being told? These questions—all part of that oversimplified "Should the doctor tell?"—can have no universally accepted answer. Individuals differ, and ethical beliefs or current opinions will influence judgment.

TO SPEAK FREELY?

There are some good reasons for speaking freely about the possibility of dying to those with fatal conditions. An ill person who strongly suspects that he is dying, but is denied the least opportunity to question or discuss this, can feel cruelly isolated if he does not want this conspiracy of silence. He may be surrounded by people whose every manifest word or action is designed to

deny or avoid the fact that he is dying, and he is aware of the artificiality of
their deception. How can he gain the ease of wholly sincere talk with others if
all maintain the pretence that his imminent departure from life, his leaving
them forever, is just not taking place? It would be thought preposterous and
cruel if throughout a mother's first pregnancy and delivery all around con-
spired to treat it as indigestion and never gave her an opportunity to voice her
doubts.

The view that we all have a duty to inform the dying man has some support
on material and spiritual grounds. If a doctor conceals from a patient that he
is mortally ill, the person may fail to order his family affairs or may embark on
business ventures which he would not contemplate if he knew his likely fate.
The doctor's legal responsibility to warn the dying person appears to be a
matter of debate. Most doctors, however, will bear in mind how far a person
needs to set his affairs in order, when considering what they should tell a
dying patient. Imparting advice to a man that it might be a wise precaution to
tidy up business arrangments serves more than that single function. (Kline &
Sobin, 1951). Conveyed with tact, it is a hint that an ill man can discuss further
with his doctor if he is of a mind to know more, or it is advice he can just
accept at its face value.

The spiritual need for a man to know that he is dying may well take
precedence over material matters in the terminal phase. Frequently the
dying person spontaneously turns or returns to his religious beliefs. He may
already have prayed for help in his serious illness, perhaps with rather
unfamiliar voice. If it appears that recovery is unlikely, most ministers hold
strongly that the patient should know this, so that he can prepare for eternal
life.

At times there is an increasing need to be frank with a patient over his
prognosis, because he has short periods of feverish hopes followed by long
periods of despairing misery. He may waste effort and money on unjustified
and quite hopeless treatments, only to have bitter disappointment as proclaimed panaceas fail. If a patient is seriously ill and appears to be getting
worse, while his physician appears content with ineffective remedies, he may
feel that opportunities of cure are being lost. This may lead to a feeling of
frustration or a desperate tour of other doctors. Of course, a second opinion
from a respected source may be a great help to all concerned. This may bring
assurance that no important possibility is being neglected. When a troubled
patient who has been seeking fruitlessly for cure comes to a better understanding with his doctor on the nature of his disease and how much hope is
justifiable, he may regain confidence and find greater peace.

In spite of these arguments which favor frankness with the dying, many
doctors are reluctant to speak with them of death. They feel that most
patients do not wish to raise the subject except to get reassurance, and that
the truth is likely to be hurtful. This common medical attitude is uncomfort-
ably combined with a considerable hesitation over practicing deliberate
evasion and deceit on patients who have put their trust in the doctor, even if
the "white lies" are intended to avoid distress. Some forthright physicians,
however, make plain their belief that it does patients no good to be told that

they are dying (Asher, 1955). It is a viewpoint easy to attack on theoretical grounds; but when truth can give rise to considerable distress, when kindly half-truths do not materially alter the course of death, and when dying people would like to hear that they will recover, it takes a very convinced man to condemn evasion or even the occasional untruth. Many scrupulous people who care for the dying find themselves concealing the truth in a manner they always wished to avoid.

In practice, relatively few doctors tell patients that there is no hope of recovery. In one study of medical opinion, for example, a group of over two hundred doctors, working in hospital and private practice, were asked if they favored informing those patients found to have a cancer very likely to prove fatal (Oken, 1961). Patients so defined would include, of course, some whose symptoms were investigated early while they were in reasonable general health, with death some way off. Such patients might have little reason at this stage to suspect their illness to be mortal, and if a doctor did tell them, it would give some unanticipated bad news. Eighty-eight percent of these doctors would not tell the patient, although some of them would make exceptions. The doctors felt that usually the patient's questions were pleas for reassurance. The other 12 percent usually told the patients that they had cancer, especially if the latter were intelligent and emotionally stable. Most of the doctors felt that they should inform a relative and were glad to share the burden of their knowledge. Incidentally, no less than 60 percent of these same doctors said that they would like to be told if they themselves had an equally sinister form of cancer. This inconsistency of opinion between imparting and receiving such information was explained by the doctors on the basis of their own greater fortitude or responsibilities. It might be so, but it is more likely to be the emotionally determined attitude found among lay and medical people alike. This was indicated by the fact that these physicians were not any more frank with doctors whom they treated for cancer than any other patients with cancer. Equally, lay people are more in favor of themselves being told they have developed a cancer than of recommending that others in a similar condition should be told (Kelly & Friesen, 1950).

Although the majority of practicing doctors may believe that it is better for them to be reticent with the dying, this opinion must be reconsidered in the light of the fact that an equally large proportion of lay people say that they would like to be told. On the surface, it seems quite perverse that 80 or 90 percent of physicians say that they rarely, if ever, tell patients that their illness is mortal (Oken, 1961), whereas about 80 percent of patients say they would like to be told (Gilbertsen & Wangensteen, 1961). If a doctor sees the question in rather unreal black-and-white terms of either pressing unpleasant news of impending death upon a patient or keeping him in happy ignorance of his fate, this will sway him towards expressing an opinion against telling. This travesties the usual situation, however, where the dying person, with gathering doubts and clues, becomes increasingly suspicious that his condition is mortal.

It is often suggested that the very high percentage of people who give the theoretical answer that they would like to know if they had cancer, do so because they feel secure in their present state of good health. They might be less confident if there was an immediate possibility of having a fatal illness. Albeit, almost as high a proportion of patients actually being treated for cancer in Manchester were just as much in favor of being told of their diagnosis (Aitken-Swan & Easson, 1959). They had been told they had a treatable cancer and later on were asked if they approved or disapproved of being informed. Two thirds were glad to have been told, only 7 percent disapproved, and 19 percent denied having been told—the familiar phenomenon of failing to hear or remember what one does not wish to learn. This particular group of patients, however, had curable cancers. Is it the same for those with incurable cancers?

The answer appears to be that they equally wish to know. In the university hospitals at Minnesota it is the practice of doctors to tell their patients the diagnosis (Gilbertsen & Wangensteen, 1961). A group of patients with advanced cancer were asked if they knew their diagnosis and 86 percent did know. Most had been told by their doctor, although some found out in other ways. Many of the remaining 14 percent, who did not know, had asked at one time and been given evasive answers. As many as four-fifths of these very ill patients thought that cancer patients should be told. They said it had helped them understand their own illness and given them peace of mind. It also allowed them to plan for further medical care, religious matters and for other aspects of their families' and their own lives.

HOW TO SPEAK OF DYING?

There are, therefore, several good reasons justifying considerable candor with people who are fatally ill. If this were to be more widely accepted in principle, how and when should such sincere conversation take place? Clearly an abrupt statement to every patient with incurable disease that he is going to die is likely to do more harm than good.

Some wish to know only a little of their illness. As with nonfatal disease, a person may be helped by simple explanations of the illness, together with a general plan of investigating or treating the condition. An intelligent young woman, who was admitted to hospital with an obviously growing lump on one rib, was very troubled while investigations were done and treatment started without anyone telling her what it was. There was not much reassuring information to give her, as it was the sign of a widespread cancer. She wanted to know something, however. She was told that it was a tumor and that the X rays had shown up one or two smaller ones. They would be treated by radiotherapy and, it was correctly said, her condition would improve considerably. This was as much as she wanted to know at that time. She had been very anxious, but after this talk she was less so. She was quite sad for a day or two, and then her spirits recovered. This sort of response of sorrow on learning of having serious disease, followed by greater equanimity as acceptance grows, is the usual understandable reaction.

Some dying patients want to know even less than this sort of edited version of the truth. They may not want to hear a word about the nature of their condition. They may well have a hidden suspicion and gladly enter a tacit conspiracy to avoid the whole subject. They wish others to take over all responsibilities, anxieties, and decisions. This total surrender of all decision to the doctor may be somewhat less common now, especially as doctors tend to lose a little of their former authoritative manner, and more patients refuse to put up with it. But when seriously ill, it can be easier for a patient to relinquish all control, all knowledge, to his doctor. If the dying person indicates openly that he does not want to know, if he shows by his manner or by his talk that he does not wish to regard his illness as fatal, it would be uncharitable to force the truth upon him. The aim is to make dying a little easier, not to apply a dogma of always divulging truth (Alvarez, 1952).

It is not an easy problem when a patient asks about his incurable illness in a way that indicates his need for reassurance or, at least, hope. He is probably more likely to ask such questions as "It's not cancer, is it, doctor?" if his doctor has shown no sign of giving any spontaneous comment about his condition. If a patient does blurt out this loaded question, or suddenly asks, "Will I get better?" of someone ill prepared to answer, the situation is potentially distressing to both. The result is often a hasty untruthful reassurance. If this is given in an atmosphere of doubt and anxiety, present in both their minds, little good will be done to the ill person's morale. If the question has been met with a hasty denial or a misleadingly optimistic view, this may be accepted with gratitude. Sometimes it is taken as a more definite answer than was intended. The ill person may even, by a series of further questions based on the first slanted answer, wring out a more emphatic denial of fatal disease than one would wish to give. This is disturbing, but is not necessarily a catastrophe, even if the patient later comes to realize that his first misgivings were well founded. Nevertheless, an emotional balance achieved on a basis of assurances bound to be proved false, is no stable adjustment. When the original loaded question is put, it is often better not to answer the dying person's anxious inquiry straight away. Returning the question, asking him to describe more fully what anxieties he has in mind, and listening sympathetically to his doubts and fears will meet some of his needs. Then the fuller description may show the basis of his anxiety. It may be a totally unwarranted fear which can be allayed, such as an anticipation of prolonged agony. It may be a well-founded apprehension, but one that can be borne with help. In the long run, especially if there is someone at hand to help with any subsequent doubts, allowing a person to discuss his fears may prove more valuable than a hasty, consoling, but untrue, answer.

In practice, probably the best and easiest way to broach the matter of dying with a mortally ill person is just to allow him to speak of his suspicions or knowledge of the outcome. If necessary, he can be asked how he feels and shown that more than the polite stereotyped answer is wanted. If the patient mentions that he feels upset he can be encouraged to talk about it. Then frequently the doctor will find that there is little for him to "tell," all that is required is for him to listen with sympathy. In these circumstances the dying person does not usually ask for reassurance or praise for his courage. He may glance up for confirmation of mutual understanding. He may want to know a little more to clarify some aspect of the situation. It is quite possible for the doctor to be uncertain of the exact course of an illness and yet, when asked, to give an honest qualified answer without lying or undue prevarication. To many people this brings firmer comfort than the flimsy props of obviously false promises or the chaos of apparently bewildered ignorance. In treating any disease it is common enough to be thinking in terms of probabilities and possibilities rather than certainties. As compensation for our having to endure uncertainty, it is uncommon to be in a position where there is no comforting straw of hope for survival.

If it is unclear if an ill person desires to know the whole truth, it is possible to start by giving gentle hints. A simple explanation of the disease, mentioning the favorable aspects of treatment and touching upon the other serious possibilities, will enable the ill person to take up the aspects he wishes and ignore others (Aldrich, 1963). The beginnings of awareness may be started early. A surgeon before operating upon a suspected cancer will often tell the patient that if the condition is serious he will need to perform an extensive operation. The patient who has such an operation can then pursue the matter with the doctor as much as he wishes. He can apprehend the threat of the illness, or concentrate on the curative value of the treatment.

Many doctors prefer to use an oblique approach for letting the patient know that he may be dying. Without any deception or lies, they aim to allow an awareness of the outcome to grow. If need be, a germ of realization is planted, but hope is never utterly excluded. Discussion can be reasonably frank, but the emphasis is on the favorable aspects (Gavey, 1955). If, indeed, the awareness of dying is going to grow, those who care for the patient must be prepared to keep pace with this increasing realization. They should be ready to listen and let the patient know that some of his surmises are true and some of his fears are unjustified. In this way the dying person should not feel too lonely, too uncertain, nor plunged into acute emotional distress.

Although it is not an infallible guide to how much the dying patient should be told, his apparent wishes and questions do point the way. This means that the manner in which he puts his views should be revealing. It also means that he must be given ample opportunity to express his ideas and ask questions. If the questions are sincere, however, then why not give quiet straight answers to the patient's questions about his illness and the outcome? It makes for beneficial trust (Leak, 1948).

It is to be remembered that while doctors are trying to judge their patients' capacity to stand unpleasant news, many patients are equally making their intuitive judgments of whether their doctor can bear sincere but difficult questions. They often have a very accurate idea of what doctor is quite accustomed or unsuited to being frank about fatal illness to the person most concerned. I have often been told by understanding people, toward the end of their life, that they knew that the doctor looking after them could not easily talk about this. "He feels he's got to get people well, and I couldn't very well talk to him about not getting better," said a woman who knew she would soon die. If a patient is firmly insistent and his doctor is honest, frank conversations do take place. "I asked him what they'd found and then I asked him if it was cancer. And now I know it's cancer, and they haven't been able to take it all away. There's only one in a thousand chance of recovery." The physician who had been questioned by this man said that he felt that he had probably been more perturbed by this conversation than the patient had.

Occasionally those concerned with a patient's care hold conflicting views over his need to be told. Such unpleasant disagreements, when they do occur, are not resolved as often as they should be by discovering what the patient already knows. Nor do those with his interest at heart meet as often as they should to see what common ground they have between their seemingly opposed and entrenched beliefs.

It is perhaps strange that there is so much more agreement over talking frankly to the members of the family about their relative's fatal illness rather than to the patient himself, even if he shows a wish to know. It reverses the usual convention of the doctor keeping confidential the information concerning an adult and telling other people only if the patient agrees. A few doctors, if they tell the patient the serious nature of the illness, do discuss with them who else should be informed. Usually the next of kin is told, but often it is clear that some other responsible member of the family is better able to receive the information and pass on the appropriate knowledge to the rest. As with the patient, the families receiving these tidings often need more than just a bulletin of bad news.

REACTIONS TO SPEAKING OF DEATH

Many patients have said what a relief they have felt when at last they have had a chance to talk openly about the probability that they are dying. As so many gain comfort from this, it is clearly unkind to deny them the opportunity. They do not get the chance because people are fearful of embarking on such conversations. In the book *Awareness of Dying* by Glaser and Strauss (1965), the authors refer to the fact that some people who care for patients are recognized by their colleagues to have an aptitude for speaking easily and honestly to the dying and bring them comfort. I am sure that many more people could do this if the climate of opinion changed toward greater frankness, and more people realized how much they could help in this way. Most nurses, medical students, and young doctors do not receive as much help as they should, during their training, over the problems raised in caring for the dying.

If more people become prepared to speak freely with the dying there will be a need for caution, because although many would benefit, some would react adversely. A proportion of people, nearing the end of life, are very distressed by implicit or explicit references to death's coming. A little exploratory conversation may indicate a patient's likely reaction. He may say quite clearly what he wants. A man who was pretty sure that he had abdominal cancer said, "I want them to tell me if they *are* going to operate. If they aren't, I want them to give me the wire. Then I'll know what to make of it." It was clear

that he was not one who only wanted to know as long as the news was good.

There can be some intuitive judgment of how much particular individuals should be told. Their habitual manner of life can be a useful guide, their style of facing former difficulties or attaining their social position (Ogilvie, 1957). This was illustrated by one equable man who had risen to a position supervising a group of shops. He had always coped well with problems in life, once he knew what was needed to be done. The previous year he had had a kidney removed and had been told that all should be well after the operation. His wife, however, had been told that he had a cancer and also warned, according to his doctor's usual policy, not to tell the patient. When the patient entered hospital again with a spread of his cancer, he insisted on being told the true state of affairs. He took it very well, but regretted that he had not been told before, so that he and his wife could have openly acknowledged that he might have little time to live. Naturally, a patient's expressed wishes and clues from his past life as to his manner of facing difficulties give no perfect prediction. The man who has succeeded in life, developing strong friendships and warm family ties may, in spite of his apparent stability, be unable to cope with the threat of so much loss. The less happy person may be better prepared to give up his life (Aldrich, 1963). Nevertheless, the view that a stable person will probably retain this characteristic when facing death usually proves correct.

In general, learning that an illness is likely to be fatal produces a period of disquiet, even dismay, although this may be effectively concealed. However well the knowledge has been conveyed, it is almost bound to cause some emotional reaction. If frank discussions were often to result in patients becoming severely or persistently distressed, even suicidal, few doctors would wish to speak to them of dying. There does tend to be an exaggerated fear that dying patients will kill themselves if they are told that their illness may be fatal. The chances are that the suicidal acts which occur in those with mortal disease are due to the suffering and the spiritual isolation when the sick are lonely, rather than any despair following a sympathetic discussion of their outlook. Although suicide remains a threatening possibility, inhibiting some from frank discussion with the dying, it is hard to find a case where a humane conversation on these lines precipitated any suicidal act. It is much more likely to have prevented it. "I knew what I'd got," said a young woman who had attempted suicide, "I'd seen it in my notes. I'd looked it up in the medical books and I knew I couldn't recover. I wanted to talk about it with the doctor, but he always seemed too busy, or just called it inflammation."

Clumsy telling of a fatal illness can cause great distress, but this extreme is generally avoidable. There is an account of one Veteran's Administration Hospital in North America where it was the practice to tell the patient the nature of his illness, including fatal illness (Glaser & Strauss, 1965). Many of the patients in this hospital were from a low social class or destitute, and, it seems, not necessarily treated with much dignity. Some of the doctors made a practice of short, blunt announcements to the patients and walking away. Some softened it a little and assured the patient that pain would be controlled. Although they could justify telling the truth because the patients become "philosophical" about it after a few days, this technique seems hard. The sociologists describing the situation wrote that the abrupt disclosure tended to result in a more immediate profound depression. As a result the patients were more apt to try and cope with such potential distress by denying the reality of their situation, rather than being helped to accept it.

In order to evaluate more reliably the effect of telling patients that they have a mortal illness, a careful and courageous investigation was carried out by some of the medical staff at Lund University (Gerle et al., 1960). Some patients with an incurable illness were told and others were not. Personal contact was maintained throughout the further course and treatment of their illness, taking care to note if the greater frankness or reticence was more helpful to them. A psychiatrist made a preliminary assessment of the patients to see if there were any indications of emotional instability in the past or present to contraindicate telling. In the overwhelming majority of those he thought it suitable to tell, the patients maintained their emotional balance and did not regret being told. In some patients it was suspected that they would be upset initially, but later regain composure; and this was largely borne out. Among both those who were told and those who were not, there were equally small groups who never achieved serenity in this last illness. None of the patients in this group, told with care, reacted in a dramatic or excessive way on learning that they had incurable cancer. On the contrary, the social worker, who continued visiting the patient and family throughout the illness, was impressed by the improved family relationships among those who had been told. There appeared to be less tension and desperation at the progressive deterioration in health.

This maintenance of contact and care by people who have imparted tidings of fatal illness is most helpful. People cannot take in all such information of emotional importance immediately. They must be given the opportunity to ask again. Indeed the patient with a serious disease may ask the same questions about his condition again and again, while gradually coming to terms with it. Others deny that they have ever been told (Aitken-Swan & Easson, 1959). There would seem little kindness in insisting that they realize it if they do not want to hold it in their consciousness. At a later time they may wish to know more. It is a chilling, cruel experience to be told of having an incurable disease and then to be apparently dismissed with no further mention of further care, just discarded. Those who confirm a patient's suspicion that he now has little time to live should surely see that he can return to them or some other suitable person who knows of the situation, if he wishes to talk more of the matter. Then he will gain comfort from this honesty.

References

Aitken-Swan, J., and Easson, E. C. Reactions of Cancer Patients on Being Told Their Diagnosis. *British Medical Journal*, 1959, 1, 779.

Aldrich, C. K. The Dying Patient's Grief. *Journal of the American Medical Association*, 1963, 184, 329.

Alvarez, W. C. Care of the Dying. *Journal of the American Medical Association*, 1952, 150, 86.

Asher, R. Management of Advanced Cancer. *Proceedings of the Royal Society of Medicine*, 1955, 48, 373.

Gavey, C. J. Discussion on Palliation in Cancer. *Proceedings of the Royal Society of Medicine*, 1955, 48, 703.

Gerle, B., Lunden, G., and P. Sandblom. The Patient with Inoperable Cancer from the Psychiatric and Social Standpoints. *Cancer*, 1960, 13, 1206.

Gilbertsen, V.A., and Wangensteen O.H. Should the Doctor Tell the Patient That the Disease Is Cancer? In *The Physician and the Total Care of the Cancer Patient*. New York: American Cancer Society, 1961.

Glaser, B. G., and Strauss, A. L. *Awareness of Dying*. Chicago: Aldine, 1965.

Kelly, W. D., and Friesen, S. R. Do Cancer Patients Want to Be Told? *Surgery*, 1950, 27, 822.

Kline, N. S., and Sobin, J. The Psychological Management of Cancer Cases. *Journal of the American Medical Association*, 1951, 146, 1547.

Leak, W. N. The Care of the Dying. *Practitioner*, 1948, 161, 80.

Ogilvie, H. Journey's End. *Practitioner*, 1957, 179, 584.

Oken, D. What to Tell Cancer Patients. *Journal of the American Medical Association*, 1961, 175, 1120.

16 · The Ritual Drama of Mutual Pretense

Barney G. Glaser and Anselm L. Strauss

This selection, taken from the book Awareness of Dying *by Barney G. Glaser and Anselm L. Strauss, reflects some of the "new sociology" concerning death and discusses an "implicit mutual understanding" about death between terminal patients and hospital staffs.*

When patient and staff both know that the patient is dying but pretend otherwise—when both agree to act as it he were going to live—then a context of mutual pretense exists. Either party can initiate his share of the context; it ends when one side cannot, or will not, sustain the pretense any longer.

The mutual-pretense awareness context is perhaps less visible, even to its participants . . . because the interaction involved tends to be more subtle. On some hospital services, however, it is the predominant context. One nurse who worked on an intensive care unit remarked about an unusual patient who had announced he was going to die: "I haven't had to cope with this very often. I may know they are going to die, and the patient knows it, but (usually) he's just not going to let you know that he knows."

Once we visited a small Catholic hospital where medical and nursing care for the many dying patients was efficiently organized. The staff members were supported in their difficult work by a powerful philosophy—that they were doing everything possible for the patient's comfort—but generally did not talk with patients about death. This setting brought about frequent mutual pretense. This awareness context is also predominant in such settings as county hospitals, where elderly patients of low socioeconomic status are sent to die; patient and staff are well aware of imminent death but each tends to go silently about his own business.[1] Yet, as we shall see, sometimes the mutual pretense context is neither silent nor unnegotiated.

The same kind of ritual pretense is enacted in many situations apart from illness. A charming example occurs when a child announces that he is now a storekeeper, and that his mother should buy something at his store. To carry out his fiction, delicately cooperative action is required. The mother must play seriously, and when the episode has run its natural course, the child will often close it himself with a rounding-off gesture, or it may be concluded by an intruding outside event or by the mother. Quick analysis of this little game of pretense suggests that either player can begin; that the other must then play properly; that realistic (nonfictional) action will destroy the illusion and end the game; that the specific action of the game must develop during interaction; and that eventually the make-believe ends or is ended. Little familial games or dramas of this kind tend to be continual, though each episode may be brief.

For contrast, here is another example that pertains to both children and adults. At the circus, when a clown appears, all but the youngest children know that the clown is not real. But both he and his audience must participate, if only symbolically, in the pretense that he is a clown. The onlookers need do no more than appreciate the clown's act, but if they remove themselves too far, by examining the clown's technique too closely, let's say, then the illusion will be shattered. The clown must also do his best to sustain the illusion by clever acting, by not playing too far "out of character." Ordinarily nobody addresses him as if he were other than the character he is pretending to be. That is, everybody takes him seriously, at face value. And unless particular members return to see the circus again, the clown's performance occurs only once, beginning and ending according to a prearranged schedule.

Our two simple examples of pretense suggest some important features of the particular awareness context to which we shall devote this [discussion]. The make-believe in which patient and hospital staff engage resembles the child's game much more than the clown's act. It has no institutionalized beginning and ending comparable to the entry and departure of the clown; either the patient or the staff must signal the beginning of their joint pretense.

Both parties must act properly if the pretense is to be maintained, because, as in the child's game, the illusion created is fragile, and easily shattered by incongruous "realistic" acts. But if either party slips slightly, the other may pretend to ignore the slip.[2] Each episode between the patient and a staff member tends to be brief, but the mutual pretense is done with terrible seriousness, for the stakes are very high.[3]

INITIATING THE PRETENSE

This particular awareness context cannot exist, of course, unless both the patient and staff are aware that he is dying. Therefore all the structural conditions which contribute to the existence of open awareness (and which are absent in closed and suspicion awareness) contribute also to the existence of mutual pretense. In addition, at least one interactant must indicate a desire to pretend that the patient is not dying and the other must agree to the pretense, acting accordingly.

A prime structural condition in the existence and maintenance of mutual pretense is that unless the patient initiates conversation about his impending death, no staff member is required to talk about it with him. As typical Americans, they are unlikely to initiate such conversation; and as professionals they have no rules commanding them to talk about death with the patient, unless he desires it. In turn, he may wish to initiate such conversation, but surely neither hospital rules nor common convention urges it upon him. Consequently, unless either the aware patient or the staff members break the silence by words or gestures, a mutual pretense rather than an open awareness context will exist; as, for example, when the physician does not care to talk about death, and the patient does not press the issue though he clearly does recognize his terminality.

The patient, of course, is more likely than the staff members to refer openly to his death, thereby inviting them, explicitly or implicitly, to respond in kind. If they seem unwilling, he may decide they do not wish to confront openly the fact of his death, and then he may, out of tact or genuine empathy for their embarrassment or distress, keep his silence. He may misinterpret their responses, of course, but . . . he probably has correctly read their reluctance to refer openly to his impending death.

Staff members, in turn, may give him opportunities to speak of his death, if they deem it wise, without their directly or obviously referring to the topic. But if he does not care to act or talk as if he were dying, then they will support his pretense. In doing so, they have, in effect, accepted a complementary assignment of status—they will act with pretense toward his pretense. (If they have misinterpreted his reluctance to act openly, then they have assigned, rather than accepted, a complementary status.)

Two related professional rationales permit them to engage in the pretense. One is that if the patient wishes to pretend, it may well be best for his health, and if and when the pretense finally fails him, all concerned can act more realistically. A secondary rationale is that perhaps they can given him better medical and nursing care if they do not have to face him so openly. In addition, as noted earlier, they can rely on common tact to justify their part in the pretense. Ordinarily, Americans believe that any individual may live —and die—as he chooses, so long as he does not interfere with others' activities, or, in this case, so long as proper care can be given him.

To illustrate the way these silent bargains are initiated and maintained, we quote from an interview with a special nurse. She had been assigned to a patient before he became terminal, and she was more apt than most personnel to encourage his talking openly, because as a graduate student in a nursing class that emphasized psychological care, she had more time to spend with her patient than a regular floor nurse. Here is the exchange between interviewer and nurse:

INTERVIEWER: Did he talk about his cancer or his dying?

NURSE: Well, no he never talked about it. I never heard him use the word cancer . . .

INTERVIEWER: Did he indicate that he knew he was dying?

NURSE: Well, I got that impression, yes . . . It wasn't really openly, but I think the day that his roommate said he should get up and start walking, I felt that he was a little bit antagonistic. He said what his condition was, that he felt very, very ill that moment.

INTERVIEWER: He never talked about leaving the hospital?

NURSE: Never.

INTERVIEWER: Did he talk about his future at all?

NURSE: Not a thing. I never heard a word . . .

INTERVIEWER: You said yesterday that he was more or less isolated, because the nurses felt that he was hostile. But they have dealt with patients like this many many times. You said they stayed away from him?

NURSE: Well, I think at the very end. You see, this is what I meant by isolation . . . we don't communicate with them. I didn't, except when I did things for him. I think you expect somebody to respond to, and if they're very ill we don't . . . I talked it over with my instructor, mentioning things that I could probably have done; for instance, this isolation, I should have communicated with him . . .

INTERVIEWER: You think that since you knew he was going to die, and you half suspected that he knew it too, or more than half; do you think that this understanding grew between you in any way?

NURSE: I believe so . . . I think it's kind of hard to say but when I came in the room, even when he was very ill, he'd rather look at me and try to give me a smile, and gave me the impression that he accepted . . . I think this is one reason why I feel I should have communicated with him . . . and this is why I feel he was rather isolated . . .

From the nurse's account, it is difficult to tell whether the patient wished to talk openly about his death, but was rebuffed; or whether he initiated the pretense and the nurse accepted his decision. But it is remarkable how a patient can flash cues to the staff about his own dread knowledge, inviting the staff to talk about his destiny, while the nurses and physicians decide that it is better not to talk too openly with him about his condition lest he "go to pieces." The patient, as remarked earlier, picks up these signals of unwillingness, and the mutual pretense context has been initiated. A specific and obvious instance is this: an elderly patient, who had lived a full and satisfying life, wished to round it off by talking about his impending death. The nurses retreated before this prospect, as did his wife, reproving him, saying he should not think or talk about morbid matters. A hospital chaplain finally intervened, first by listening to the patient himself, then by inducing the nurses and the wife to do likewise, or at least to acknowledge more openly that the man was dying. He was not successful with all the nurses.

The staff members are more likely to sanction a patient's pretense than his family's. The implicit rule is that though the patient need not be forced to speak of his dying, or to act as if he were dying, his kin should face facts. After all, they will have to live with the facts after his death. Besides, staff members usually find it less difficult to talk about dying with the family. Family members are not inevitably drawn into open discussion, but the likelihood is high, particularly since they themselves are likely to initiate discussion or at least to make gestures of awareness.

Sometimes, however, pretense protects the family member temporarily against too much grief, and the staff members against too immediate a scene. This may occur when a relative has just learned about the impending death and the nurse controls the ensuing scene by initiating temporary pretense. The reverse situation also occurs: a newly arrived nurse discovers the patient's terminality, and the relative smooths over the nurse's distress by temporary pretense.

THE PRETENSE INTERACTION

An intern whom we observed during our field work suspected that the patient he was examining had cancer, but he could not discover where it was located. The patient previously had been told that she probably had cancer, and she was now at this teaching hospital for that reason. The intern's examination went on for some time. Yet neither he nor she spoke about what he was searching for, nor in any way suggested that she might be dying. We mention this episode to contrast it with the more extended interactions with which this [selection] is concerned. These have an episodic quality—personnel enter and leave the patient's room, or he occasionally emerges and encounters them—but their extended duration means that special effort is required to prevent their breaking down, and that the interactants must work hard to construct and maintain their mutual pretense. By contrast, in a formally staged play, although the actors have to construct and maintain a performance, making it credible to their audience, they are not required to write the script themselves. The situation that involves a terminal patient is much more like a masquerade party, where one masked actor plays carefully to another as long as they are together, and the total drama actually emerges from their joint creative effort.

A masquerade, however, has more extensive resources to sustain it than those the hospital situation provides. Masqueraders wear masks, hiding their facial expressions; even if they "break up" with silent laughter (as a staff member may "break down" with sympathy), this fact is concealed. Also, according to the rules ordinarily governing masquerades, each actor chooses his own status, his "character," and this makes his role in the constructed drama somewhat easier to play. He may even have played similar parts before. But terminal patients usually have had no previous experience with their pretended status, and not all personnel have had much experience. In a masquerade, when the drama fails it can be broken off, each actor moving along to another partner; but in the hospital the pretenders (especially the patient) have few comparable opportunities.

Both situations share one feature—the extensive use of props for sustaining the crucial illusion. In the masquerade, the props include not only masks but clothes and other costuming, as well as the setting where the masquerade takes place. In the hospital interaction, props also abound. Patients dress for the part of not-dying patient, including careful attention to grooming, and to hair and makeup by female patients. The terminal patient may also fix up his room so that it looks and feels "just like home," an activity that supports his enactment of normalcy. Nurses may respond to these props with explicit appreciation—"how lovely your hair looks this morning"—even help to establish them, as by doing the patient's hair. We remember one elaborate pretense ritual involving a husband and wife who had won the nurses' sympathy. The husband simply would not recognize that his already comatose wife was approaching death, so each morning the nurses carefully prepared her for his visit, dressing her for the occasion and making certain that she looked as beautiful as possible.

The staff, of course, has its own props to support its ritual prediction that the patient is going to get well: thermometers, baths, fresh sheets, and meals on time! Each party utilizes these props as he sees fit, thereby helping to create the pretense anew. But when a patient wishes to demonstrate that he is finished with life, he may drive the nurses wild by refusing to cooperate in the daily routines of hospital life—that is, he refuses to allow the nurses to use their props. Conversely, when the personnel wish to indicate how things are with him, they may begin to omit some of those routines.

During the pretense episodes, both sides play according to the rules implicit in the interaction. Although neither the staff nor patient may recognize these rules as such, certain tactics are fashioned around them, and the action is partly constrained by them. One rule is that dangerous topics should generally be avoided. The most obviously dangerous topic is the patient's death; another is events that will happen afterwards. Of course, both parties to the pretense are supposed to follow the avoidance rule.

There is, however, a qualifying rule: Talk about dangerous topics is permissible as long as neither party breaks down. Thus, a patient refers to the

distant future, as if it were his to talk about. He talks about his plans for his
family, as if he would be there to share their consummation. He and the
nurses discuss today's events—such as his treatments—as if they had
implications for a real future, when he will have recovered from his illness.
And some of his brave or foolhardy activities may signify a brave show of
pretense, as when he bathes himself or insists on tottering to the toilet by
himself. The staff in turn permits his activity. (Two days before he returned to
the hospital to die, one patient insisted that his wife allow him to travel
downtown to keep a speaking engagement, and to the last he kept up a lively
conversation with a close friend about a book they were planning to write
together.)

A third rule, complementing the first two, is that each actor should focus
determinedly on appropriately safe topics. It is customary to talk about the
daily routines—eating (the food was especially good or bad), and sleeping
(whether one slept well or poorly last night). Complaints and their management help pass the time. So do minor personal confidences, and chatter
about events on the ward. Talk about physical symptoms is safe enough if
confined to the symptoms themselves, with no implied references to death. A
terminal patient and a staff member may safely talk, and at length, about his
disease so long as they skirt its fatal significance. And there are many
genuinely safe topics having to do with movies and movie stars, politics,
fashions—with everything, in short, that signifies that life is going on "as
usual."

A fourth interactional rule is that when something happens, or is said, that
tends to expose the fiction that both parties are attempting to sustain, then
each must pretend that nothing has gone awry. Just as each has carefully
avoided calling attention to the true situation, each now must avert his gaze
from the unfortunate intrusion. Thus, a nurse may take special pains to
announce herself before entering a patient's room so as not to surprise him at
his crying. If she finds him crying she may ignore it or convert it into an
innocuous event with a skillful comment or gesture—much like the tactful
gentleman who, having stumbled upon a woman in his bathtub, is said to
have casually closed the bathroom door, murmuring "Pardon me, sir." The
mutuality of the pretense is illustrated by the way a patient who cannot
control a sudden expression of great pain will verbally discount its significance, while the nurse in turn goes along with his pretense. Or she may brush
aside or totally ignore a major error in his portrayal, as when he refers
spontaneously to his death. If he is tempted to admit impulsively his terminality, she may, again, ignore his impulsive remarks or obviously misinterpret
them. Thus, pretense is piled upon pretense to conceal or minimize interactional slips.

Clearly then, each party to the ritual pretense shares responsibility for
maintaining it. The major responsibility may be transferred back and forth,
but each party must support the others's temporary dominance in his own
action. This is true even when conversation is absolutely minimal, as in some
hospitals where patients take no particular pains to signal awareness of their
terminality, and the staff makes no special gestures to convey its own aware-

ness. The pretense interaction in this case is greatly simplified, but it is still discernible. Whenever a staff member is so indelicate, or so straightforward, as to act openly as if a terminal patient were dying, or if the patient does so himself, then the pretense vanishes. If neither wishes to destroy the fiction, however, then each must strive to keep the situation "normal."[4]

THE TRANSITION TO OPEN AWARENESS

A mutual pretense context that is not sustained can only change to an open awareness context. (Either party, however, may again initiate the pretense context and sometimes get cooperation from the other.) The change can be sudden, when either patient or staff distinctly conveys that he has permanently abandoned the pretense. Or the change to the open context can be gradual: nurses, and relatives, too, are familiar with patients who admit to terminality more openly on some days than they do on other days, when pretense is dominant, until finally pretense vanishes altogether. Sometimes the physician skillfully paces his interaction with a patient, leading the patient finally to refer openly to his terminality and to leave behind the earlier phase of pretense.

Pretense generally collapses when certain conditions make its maintenance increasingly difficult. These conditions have been foreshadowed in our previous discussion. Thus, when the patient cannot keep from expressing his increasing pain, or his suffering grows to the point that he is kept under heavy sedation then the enactment of pretense becomes more difficult, especially for him.

Again, neither patient nor staff may be able to avoid bringing impending death into the open if radical physical deterioration sets in, the staff because it has a tough job to do, and the patient for other reasons, including fright and panic. Sometimes a patient breaks his pretense for psychological reasons, as when he discovers that he cannot face death alone, or when a chaplain convinces him that it is better to bring things out into the open than to remain silent. (Sometimes, however, a patient may find such a sympathetic listener in the chaplain that he can continue his pretense with other personnel.) Sometimes he breaks the pretense when it no longer makes sense in light of obvious physical deterioration.

Here is a poignant episode during which a patient dying with great pain and obvious bodily deterioration finally abandoned her pretense with a nurse:

> There was a long silence. Then the patient asked, "After I get home from the nursing home will you visit me?" I asked if she wanted me to. "Yes, Mary, you know we could go on long drives together . . ." She had a faraway look in her eyes as if daydreaming about all the places she would visit and all the things we could do together. This continued for some time. Then I asked, "Do you think you will be able to drive your car again?" She looked at me, "Mary, I know I am

daydreaming; I know I am going to die." Then she cried, and said, "This is terrible, I never thought I would be this way."

In short, when a patient finds it increasingly difficult to hang onto a semblance of his former healthy self and begins to become a person who is visibly dying, both he and the staff are increasingly prone to say so openly, whether by word or gesture. Sometimes, however, a race occurs between a patient's persistent pretense and his becoming comatose or his actual death —a few more days of sentience or life, and either he or the staff would have dropped the pretense.

Yet, a contest may ensue when only one side wishes to keep up the pretense. When a patient openly displays his awareness but shows it unacceptably, as by apathetically "giving up," the staff or family may try to reinstate the pretense. Usually the patient then insists on open recognition of his own impending death, but sometimes he is persuaded to return to the pretense. For instance, one patient finally wished to talk openly about death, but her husband argued against its probability, although he knew better; so after several attempts to talk openly, the patient obligingly gave up the contest. The reverse situation may also occur: the nurses begin to give the patient every opportunity to die with a maximum of comfort—as by cutting down on normal routines—thus signaling that he should no longer pretend, but the patient insists on putting up a brave show and so the nurses capitulate.

We would complicate our analysis unduly if we did more than suggest that, under such conditions, the pretense ritual sometimes resembles Ptolemy's cumbersomely patched astronomical system, with interactants pretending to pretend to pretend! We shall only add that when nurses attempt to change the pretense context into an open context, they generally do this "on their own" and not because of any calculated ward standards or specific orders from an attending physician. And the tactics they use to get the patient to refer openly to his terminality are less tried and true than the more customary tactics for forcing him to pretend.

CONSEQUENCES OF MUTUAL PRETENSE

For the patient, the pretense context can yield a measure of dignity and considerable privacy, though it may deny him the closer relationships with staff members and family members that sometimes occur when he allows them to participate in his open acceptance of death. And if they initiate and he accepts the pretense, he may have nobody with whom to talk although he might profit greatly from talk. (One terminal patient told a close friend, who told us, that when her family and husband insisted on pretending that she would recover, she suffered from the isolation, feeling as if she were trapped in cotton batting.) For the family—especially more distant kin—the pretense context can minimize embarrassment and other interactional strains; but for closer kin, franker concourse may have many advantages . . . Oscillation between contexts of open awareness and mutual pretense can also cause interactional strains. We once observed a man persuading his mother to abandon her apathy—she had permanently closed her eyes, to the staff's great distress—and "try hard to live." She agreed finally to resume the pretense, but later relapsed into apathy. The series of episodes caused some anguish to both family and patient, as well as to the nurses. When the patient initiates the mutual pretense, staff members are likely to feel relieved. Yet the consequent stress of either maintaining the pretense or changing it to open awareness sometimes may be considerable. Again, both the relief and the stress affect nurses more than medical personnel, principally because the latter spend less time with patients.

But whether staff or patient initiates the ritual of pretense, maintaining it creates a characteristic ward mood of cautious serenity. A nurse once told us of a cancer hospital where each patient understood that everyone there had cancer, including himself, but the rules of tact, buttressed by staff silence, were so strong that few patients talked openly about anyone's condition. The consequent atmosphere was probably less serene than when only a few patients are engaged in mutual pretense, but even one such patient can affect the organizational mood, especially if the personnel become "involved" with him.

A persistent context of mutual pretense profoundly affects the more permanent aspects of hospital organization as well. (This often occurs at county and city hospitals.) Imagine what a hospital service would be like if all terminal patients were unacquainted with their terminality, or if all were perfectly open about their awareness—whether they accepted or rebelled against their fate.[5] When closed awareness generally prevails the personnel must guard against disclosure, but they need not organize themselves as a team to handle continued pretense and its sometimes stressful breakdown. Also, a chief organizational consequence of the mutual pretense context is that it eliminates any possibility that staff members might "work with" patients psychologically, on a self-conscious professional basis. This consequence was strikingly evident at the small Catholic hospital referred to a few pages ago. It is also entirely possible that a ward mood of tension can be set when (as a former patient once told us) a number of elderly dying patients continually communicate to each other their willingness to die, but the staff members persistently insist on the pretense that the patients are going to recover. On the other hand, the prevailing ward mood accompanying mutual pretense tends to be more serene—or at least less obviously tense—than when open suspicion awareness is dominant.[6]

Notes

1   Robert Kastenbaum has reported that at Cushing Hospital, "a Public Medical Institution for the care and custody of the elderly" in Framingham, Massachusetts, "patient and staff members frequently have an implicit mutual understanding with regard to death . . . institutional dynamics tend to operate against making death 'visible' and a subject of open

communication . . . Elderly patients often behave as though they appreciated the unspoken
feelings of the staff members and were attempting to make their demise as acceptable and
unthreatening as possible." This observation is noted in Robert Kastenbaum, "The Interpersonal Context of Death in a Geriatric Institution," abstract of paper presented at the Seventeenth Annual Scientific Meeting, Gerontological Society (Minneapolis: October 29–31, 1964).

2   I. Bensman and I. Garver, "Crime and Punishment in the Factory," in A. Gouldner and H. Gouldner (eds.), *Modern Society* (New York: Harcourt, Brace and World, 1963), pp. 593–96.

3   A German communist, Alexander Weissberg, accused of spying during the great period of Soviet spy trails, has written a fascinating account of how he and many other accused persons collaborated with the Soviet government in an elaborate pretense, carried on for the benefit of the outside world. The stakes were high for the accused (their lives) as well as for the Soviet. Weissberg's narrative also illustrated how uninitiated interactants must be coached into their roles and how they must be cued into the existence of the pretense context where they do not recognize it. See Alexander Weissberg, *The Accused* (New York: Simon and Schuster, 1951).

4   A close reading of John Gunther's poitnant account of his young son's last months shows that the boy maintained a sustained and delicately balanced mutual pretense with his parents, physicians and nurses. John Gunther, *Death Be Not Proud* (New York: Harper and Bros., 1949). Also see Bensman and Garver, *op. cit.*

5   For a description of a research hospital where open awareness prevails, with far-reaching effects on hospital social structure, see Renée Fox, *Experiment Perilous* (New York: Free Press of Glencoe, 1959).

6   EDITOR'S NOTE: Contrast this paper with selections 17, 24, and 25.

17 · Lies to the Sick and Dying

Sissela Bok

Sissela Bok holds a Ph.D. degree in philosophy. She teaches medical ethics in the Harvard-MIT Division of Health Sciences and Technology. This selection is taken from her book Lying: Moral Choice in Public and Private Life. *The book is a brilliant exposition of the philosophical and ethical aspects of non-truthtelling. The selection reprinted here examines that subject in relation to dealing with the dying patient.*

The face of a physician, like that of a diplomatist, should be impenetrable. Nature is a benevolent old hyprocrite; she cheats the sick and the dying with illusions better than any anodynes. . .

Some shrewd old doctors have a few phrases always on hand for patients that will insist on knowing the pathology of their complaints without the slightest capacity of understanding the scientific explanation. I have known the term "Spinal irritation" serve well on such occasions, but I think nothing on the whole has covered so much ground, and meant so little, and given such profound satisfaction to all parties, as the magnificent phrase "congestion of the portal system."

Oliver Wendell Holmes, Medical Essays

This deception tortured him—their not wishing to admit what they all knew and what he knew, but wanting to lie to him concerning his terrible condition, and wishing and forcing him to participate in that lie. Those lies—lies enacted over him on the eve of his death and destined to degrade this awful, solemn act to the level of their visitings, their curtains, their sturgeon for dinner—were a terrible agony for Ivan Ilych.

Leo Tolstoy, The Death of Ivan Ilych

When a man's life has become bound up with the analytic technique, he finds himself at a loss altogether for the lies and the guile which are otherwise so indispensable to a physician, and if for once with the best intentions he attempts to use them he is likely to betray himself. Since we demand strict truthfulness from our patients, we jeopardize our whole authority if we let ourselves be caught by them in a departure from the truth.

Sigmund Freud, Collected Papers, II

DECEPTION AS THERAPY

A forty-six year-old man, coming to a clinic for a routine physical checkup needed for insurance purposes, is diagnosed as having a form of cancer likely to cause him to die within six months. No known cure exists for it. Chemotherapy may prolong life by a few extra months, but will have side effects the physician does not think warranted in this case. In addition, he believes that such therapy should be reserved for patients with a chance for recovery or remission. The patient has no symptoms giving him any reason to believe that he is not perfectly healthy. He expects to take a short vacation in a week.

For the physician, there are now several choices involving truthfulness. Ought he to tell the patient what he has learned, or conceal it? If asked, should he deny it? If he decides to reveal the diagnosis, should he delay doing so until after the patient returns from his vacation? Finally, even if he does reveal the serious nature of the diagnosis, should he mention the possibility of chemotherapy and his reasons for not recommending it in this case? Of should he encourage every last effort to postpone death?

In this particular case, the physician chose to inform the patient of his diagnosis right away. He did not, however, mention the possibility of chemotherapy. A medical student working under him disagreed; several nurses also thought that the patient should have been informed of this possibility. They tried, unsuccessfully, to persuade the physician that this was the patient's right. When persuasion had failed, the student elected to disobey the doctor by informing the patient of the alternative of chemotherapy. After consultation with family members, the patient chose to ask for the treatment.

Doctors confront such choices often and urgently. What they reveal, hold back, or distort will matter profoundly to their patients. Doctors stress with corresponding vehemence their reasons for the distortion or concealment: not to confuse a sick person needlessly, or cause what may well be unnecessary pain or discomfort, as in the case of the cancer patient; not to leave a patient without hope, as in those many cases where the dying are not told the truth about their condition; or to improve the chances of cure, as where unwarranted optimism is expressed about some form of therapy. Doctors use information as part of the therapeutic regimen; it is given out in amounts, in admixtures, and according to timing believed best for patients. Accuracy, by comparison, matters far less.

Lying to patients has, therefore, seemed an especially excusable act. Some would argue that doctors, and *only* doctors, should be granted the right to manipulate the truth in ways so undesirable for politicians, lawyers, and others.[1] Doctors are trained to help patients; their relationship to patients carries special obligations, and they know much more than laymen about what helps and hinders recovery and survival.

Even the most conscientious doctors, then, who hold themselves at a distance from the quacks and the purveyors of false remedies, hesitate to forswear all lying. Lying is usually wrong, they argue, but less so than allowing the truth to harm patients. B. C. Meyer echoes this very common view:

> [O]urs is a profession which traditionally has been guided by a precept that transcends the virtue of uttering truth for truth's sake, and that is, "so far as possible, do no harm."[2]

Truth, for Meyer, may be important, but not when it endangers the health and well-being of patients. This has seemed self-evident to many physicians in the past—so much so that we find very few mentions of veracity in the codes and oaths and writings by physicians through the centuries. This absence is all the more striking as other principles of ethics have been consistently and movingly expressed in the same documents.

The two fundamental principles of doing good and not doing harm—of beneficence and nonmaleficence—are the most immediately relevant to medical practitioners, and the most frequently stressed. To preserve life and good health, to ward off illness, pain, and death—these are the perennial tasks of medicine and nursing. These principles have found powerful expression at all times in the history of medicine. In the Hippocratic Oath physicians promise to:

> use treatment to help the sick . . . but never with a view to injury and wrongdoing.[3]

And a Hindu oath of initiation says:

> Day and night, however thou mayest be engaged, thou shalt endeavor for the relief of patients with all thy heart and soul. Thou shalt not desert or injure the patient even for the sake of thy living.[4]

But there is no similar stress on veracity. It is absent from virtually all oaths, codes, and prayers. The Hippocratic Oath makes no mention of truthfulness to patients about their condition, prognosis, or treatment. Other early codes and prayers are equally silent on the subject. To be sure, they often refer to the confidentiality with which doctors should treat all that their patients tell them; but there is no corresponding reference to honesty toward the patient. One of the few who appealed to such a principle was Amatus Lusitanus, a Jewish physician widely known for his skill, who, persecuted, died of the plague in 1568. He published an oath which reads in part:

> If I lie, may I incur the eternal wrath of God and of His angel Raphael, and may nothing in the medical art succeed for me according to my desires.[5]

Later codes continue to avoid the subject. Not even the Declaration of Geneva, adopted in 1948 by the World Medical Association, makes any reference to it. And the Principles of Medical Ethics of the American Medical Association[6] still leave the matter of informing patients up to the physician.

Given such freedom, a physician can decide to tell as much or as little as he wants the patient to know, so long as he breaks no law. In the case of the man mentioned at the beginning of this chapter, some physicians might feel justified in lying for the good of the patient, others might be truthful. Some may conceal alternatives to the treatment they recommend; others not. In each case, they could appeal to the AMA Principles of Ethics. A great many would choose to be able to lie. They would claim that not only can a lie avoid harm for the patient, but that it is also hard to know whether they have been right in the first place in making their pessimistic diagnosis; a "truthful" statement could therefore turn out to hurt patients unnecessarily. The concern for curing and for supporting those who cannot be cured then runs counter to the desire to be completely open. This concern is especially strong where the prognosis is bleak; even more so when patients are so affected by their illness or their medication that they are more dependent than usual, perhaps more easily depressed or irrational.

Physicians know only too well how uncertain a diagnosis or prognosis can be. They know how hard it is to give meaningful and correct answers regarding health and illness. They also know that disclosing their own uncertainty or fears can reduce those benefits that depend upon faith in recovery. They fear, too, that revealing grave risks, no matter how unlikely it is that these will come about, may exercise the pull of the "self-fulfilling prophecy." They dislike being the bearers of uncertain or bad news as much as anyone else. And last, but not least, sitting down to discuss an illness truthfully and sensitively may take much-needed time away from other patients.

These reasons help explain why nurses and physicians and relatives of the sick and the dying prefer not to be bound by rules that might limit their ability to suppress, delay, or distort information. This is not to say that they necessarily plan to lie much of the time. They merely want to have the freedom to do so when they believe it wise. And the reluctance to see lying prohibited explains, in turn, the failure of the codes and oaths to come to grips with the problems of truth-telling and lying.

But sharp conflicts are now arising. Doctors no longer work alone with patients. They have to consult with others much more than before; if they choose to lie, the choice may not be met with approval by all who take part in the care of the patient. A nurse expresses the difficulty which results as follows:

> From personal experience I would say that the patients who aren't told about their terminal illness have so many verbal and mental questions unanswered that many will begin to realize that their illness is more serious than they're being told . . .
>
> Nurses care for their patients twenty-four hours a day compared to a doctor's daily visit, and it is the nurse many times that the patient will relate to, once his underlying fears become overwhelming . . . This is difficult for us nurses because being in constant contact with patients we can see the events leading up to this. The patient continually asks you, "Why isn't my pain decreasing?" or "Why isn't the radiation treatment easing the pain?" . . . We cannot legally give these patients an honest answer as a nurse (and I'm sure I wouldn't want to) yet the problem is still not resolved and the circle grows larger with the patient alone in the middle.[7]

The doctor's choice to lie increasingly involves coworkers in acting a part they find neither humane nor wise. The fact that these problems have not been carefully thought through within the medical profession, nor seriously addressed in medical education, merely serves to intensify the conflict.[8] Different doctors then respond very differenty to patients in exactly similar predicaments. The friction is increased by the fact that relatives often disagree even where those giving medical care to a patient are in accord on how to approach the patient. Here again, because physicians have not worked out to common satisfaction the question of whether relatives have the right to make such requests, the problems are allowed to be haphazardly resolved by each physician as he sees fit.

THE PATIENT'S PERSPECTIVE

The turmoil in the medical profession regarding truth-telling is further augmented by the pressures that patients themselves now bring to bear and by empirical data coming to light. Challenges are growing to the three major arguments for lying to patients: that truthfulness is impossible; that patients do not want bad news; and that truthful information harms them.

The first of these arguments . . . confuses "truth" and "truthfulness" so as to clear the way for occasional lying on grounds supported by the second and third arguments. At this point, we can see more clearly that it is a strategic move intended to discourage the question of truthfulness from carrying much weight in the first place, and thus to leave the choice of what to say and how to say it up to the physician. To claim that "Since telling the truth is impossible, there can be no sharp distinction between what is true and what is false"[9] is to try to defeat objections to lying before even discussing them. One need only imagine how such an argument would be received, were it made by a car salesman or a real estate dealer, to see how fallacious it is.

In medicine, however, the argument is supported by a subsidiary point: even if people might ordinarily understand what is spoken to them, patients are often not in a position to do so. This is where paternalism enters in. When we buy cars or houses, the paternalist will argue, we need to have all our wits about us; but when we are ill, we cannot always do so. We need help in making choices, even if help can be given only by keeping us in the dark. And the physician is trained and willing to provide such help.

It is certainly true that some patients cannot make the best choices for themselves when weakened by illness or drugs. But most still can. And even those who are incompetent have a right to have someone—their guardian or spouse perhaps—receive the correct information.

The paternalistic assumption of superiority to patients also carries great dangers for physicians themselves—it risks turning to contempt. The following view was recently expressed in a letter to a medical journal:

> As a radiologist who has been sued, I have reflected earnestly on advice to obtain informed consent but have decided to "take the risks without informing the patient" and trust to "God, judge, and jury" rather than evade responsibility through a legal gimmick . . .
>
> [In] a general radiologic practice many of our patients are uninformable and we would never get through the day if we had to obtain their consent to every potentially harmful study.
>
> . . . We still have patients with language problems, the uneducated and the unintelligent, the stolid and the stunned who cannot form an informed opinion to give an informed consent; we have the belligerent and the panicky who do not listen or comprehend. And then there are the Medicare patients who comprise 35 percent of general hospital admissions. The bright ones wearily plead to be left alone . . . As for the apathetic rest, many of them were kindly described by Richard Bright as not being able to comprehend because "their brains are so poorly oxygenated."[10]

The argument which rejects informing patients because adequate truthful information is impossible in itself or because patients are lacking in understanding, must itself be rejected when looked at from the point of view of patients. They know that liberties granted to the most conscientious and altruistic doctors will be exercised also in the "Medical Mills"; that the choices thus kept from patients will be exercised by not only competent but incompetent physicians; and that even the best doctors can make choices patients would want to make differently for themselves.

The second argument for deceiving patients refers specifically to giving them news of a frightening or depressing kind. It holds that patients do not, in fact, generally want such information, that they prefer not to have to face up to serious illness and death. On the basis of such a belief, most doctors in a number of surveys stated that they do not, as a rule, inform patients that they have an illness such as cancer.

When studies are made of what patients desire to know, on the other hand, a large majority, say that they *would* like to be told of such a diagnosis.[11] All these studies need updating and should be done with larger numbers of patients and non-patients. But they do show that there is generally a dramatic divergence between physicians and patients on the factual question of whether patients want to know what ails them in cases of serious illness such as cancer. In most of the studies, over 80 percent of the persons asked indicated that they would want to be told.

Sometimes this discrepancy is set aside by doctors who want to retain the view that patients do not want unhappy news. In reality, they claim, the fact that patients say they want it has to be discounted. The more someone asks to know, the more he suffers from fear which will lead to the denial of the information even if it is given. Informing patients is, therefore, useless; they resist and deny having been told what they cannot assimilate. According to this view, empirical studies of what patients say they want are worthless since they do not probe deeply enough to uncover this universal resistance to the contemplation of one's own death.

This view is only partially correct. For some patients, denial is indeed well established in medical experience. A number of patients (estimated at between 15 percent and 25 percent) will give evidence of denial of having been told about their illness, even when they repeatedly ask and are repeatedly informed. And nearly everyone experiences a period of denial at some point in the course of approaching death.[12] Elisabeth Kübler-Ross sees denial as resulting often from premature and abrupt information by a stranger who goes through the process quickly to "get it over with." She holds that denial functions as a buffer after unexpected shocking news, permitting individuals to collect themselves and to mobilize other defenses. She describes prolonged denial in one patient as follows:

> She was convinced that the X rays were "mixed up"; she asked for reassurance that her pathology report could not possibly be back so soon and that another patient's report must have been marked with her name. When none of this could be confirmed, she quickly asked to leave the hospital, looking for another physician in the vain hope "to get a better explanation for my troubles." This patient went "shopping around" for many doctors, some of whom gave her reassuring answers, others of whom confirmed the previous suspicion. Whether confirmed or not, she reacted in the same manner; she asked for examination and reexamination . . .[13]

But to say that denial is universal flies in the face of all evidence. And to take any claim to the contrary as "symptomatic" of deeper denial leaves no room for reasoned discourse. There is no way that such universal denial can be proved true or false. To believe in it is a metaphysical belief about man's condition, not a statement about what patients do and do not want. It is true that we can never completely understand the possibility of our own death, any more than being alive in the first place. But people certainly differ in the degree to which they can approach such knowledge, take it into account in their plans, and make their peace with it.

Montaigne claimed that in order to learn both to live and to die, men have to think about death and be prepared to accept it.[14] To stick one's head in the sand, or to be prevented by lies from trying to discern what is to come, hampers freedom—freedom to consider one's life as a whole, with a beginning, a duration, an end. Some may request to be deceived rather than to see their lives as thus finite; others reject the information which would require them to do so; but most say that they want to know. Their concern for knowing about their condition goes far beyond mere curiosity or the wish to make isolated personal choices in the short time left to them; their stance toward the entire life they have lived, and their ability to give it meaning and completion, are at stake.[15] In lying or withholding the facts which permit such discernment, doctors may reflect their own fears (which, according to one study,[16] are much stronger than those of laymen) of facing questions about the meaning of one's life and the inevitability of death.

Beyond the fundamental deprivation that can result from deception, we are also becoming increasingly aware of all that can befall patients in the course of their illness when information is denied or distorted. Lies place them in a position where they no longer participate in choices concerning their own health, including the choice of whether to be a "patient" in the first place. A terminally ill person who is not informed that his illness is incurable and that he is near death cannot make decisions about the end of his life: about whether or not to enter a hospital, or to have surgery; where and with whom to spend his last days; how to put his affairs in order—these most personal choices cannot be made if he is kept in the dark, or given contradictory hints and clues.

It has always been especially easy to keep knowledge from terminally ill patients. They are most vulnerable, least able to take action to learn what they need to know, or to protect their autonomy. The very fact of being so ill greatly increases the likelihood of control by others. And the fear of being helpless in the face of such control is growing. At the same time, the period of dependency and slow deterioration of health and strength that people undergo has lengthened. There has been a dramatic shift toward institutionalization of the aged and those near death. (Over 80 percent of Americans now die in a hospital or other institution.)

Patients who are severely ill often suffer a further distancing and loss of control over their most basic functions. Electrical wiring, machines, intravenous administration of liquids, all create new dependency and at the same time new distance between the patient and all who come near. Curable patients are often willing to undergo such procedures; but when no cure is possible, these procedures merely intensify the sense of distance and uncertainty and can even become a substitute for comforting human acts. Yet those who suffer in this way often fear to seem troublesome by complaining. Lying to them, perhaps for the most charitable of purposes, can then cause them to slip unwittingly into subjection to new procedures, perhaps new surgery, where death is held at bay through transfusions, respirators, even resuscitation far beyond what most would wish.

Seeing relatives in such predicaments has caused a great upsurge of worrying about death and dying. At the root of this fear is not a growing terror of the *moment* of death, or even the instants before it. Nor is there greater fear of *being* dead. In contrast to the centuries of lives lived in dread of the punishments to be inflicted after death, many would now accept the view expressed by Epicurus, who died in 270 B.C.:[17]

> Death, therefore, the most awful of evils, is nothing to us, seeing that, when we are, death is not come, and, when death is come, we are not.

The growing fear, if it is not of the moment of dying nor of being dead, is of all that which now precedes dying for so many: the possibility of prolonged pain, the increasing weakness, the uncertainty, the loss of powers and chance of senility, the sense of being a burden. This fear is further nourished by the loss of trust in health professionals. In part, the loss of trust results from the abuses which have been exposed—the Medicaid scandals, the old-age home profiteering, the commercial exploitation of those who seek remedies for their ailments;[18] in part also because of the deceptive practices patients suspect, having seen how friends and relatives were kept in the dark; in part, finally, because of the sheer numbers of persons, often strangers, participating in the care of any one patient. Trust which might have gone to a doctor long known to the patient goes less easily to a team of strangers, no matter how expert or well-meaning.

It is with the working out of all that *informed consent*[19] implies and the information it presupposes that truth-telling is coming to be discussed in a serious way for the first time in the health professions. Informed consent is a farce if the information provided is distorted or withheld. And even complete information regarding surgical procedures or medication is obviously useless unless the patient also knows what the condition is that these are supposed to correct.

Bills of rights for patients, similarly stressing the right to be informed, are now gaining acceptance.[20] This right is not new, but the effort to implement it is. Nevertheless, even where patients are handed the most elegantly phrased bill of rights, their right to a truthful diagnosis and prognosis is by no means always respected.

The reason why even doctors who recognize a patient's right to have information might still not provide it brings us to the third argument against telling all patients the truth. It holds that the information given might hurt the patient and that the concern for the right to such information is therefore a threat to proper health care. A patient, these doctors argue, may wish to commit suicide after being given discouraging news, or suffer a cardiac arrest, or simply cease to struggle, and thus not grasp the small remaining chance for recovery. And even where the outlook for a patient is very good, the disclosure of a minute risk can shock some patients or cause them to reject needed protection such as a vaccination or antibiotics.

The factual basis for this argument has been challenged from two points of view. The damages associated with the disclosure of sad news or risks are rarer than physicians believe; and the *benefits* which result from being informed are more substantial, even measurably so. Pain is tolerated more easily, recovery from surgery is quicker, and cooperation with therapy is greatly improved. The attitude that "what you don't know won't hurt you" is proving unrealistic; it is what patients do not know but vaguely suspect that causes them corrosive worry.

It is certain that no answers to this question of harm from information are the same for all patients. If we look, first, at the fear expressed by physicians that informing patients of even remote or unlikely risks connected with a drug prescription or operation might shock some and make others refuse the treatment that would have been best for them, it appears to be unfounded for the great majority of patients. Studies show that very few patients respond to being told of such risks by withdrawing their consent to the procedure and that those who do withdraw are the very ones who might well have been upset enough to sue the physician had they not been asked to consent beforehand.[21] It is possible that on even rarer occasions especially susceptible persons might manifest physical deterioration from shock; some physicians have even asked whether patients who die after giving informed consent to an operation, but before it actually takes place, somehow expire because of the information given to them.[22] While such questions are unanswerable in any one case, they certainly argue in favor of caution, a real concern for the person to whom one is recounting the risks he or she will face, and sensitivity to all signs of distress.

The situation is quite different when persons who are already ill, perhaps already quite weak and discouraged, are told of a very serious prognosis. Physicians fear that such knowledge may cause the patients to commit suicide, or to be frightened or depressed to the point that their illness takes a downward turn. The fear that great numbers of patients will commit suicide appears to be unfounded.[23] And if some do, is that a response so unreasonable, so much against the patient's best interest that physicians ought to make it a reason for concealment or lies? Many societies have allowed suicide in the past; our own has decriminalized it; and some are coming to make distinctions among the many suicides which ought to be prevented if at all possible, and those which ought to be respected.[24]

Another possible response to very bleak news is the triggering of physiological mechanisms which allow death to come more quickly—a form of giving up or of preparing for the inevitable, depending on one's outlook. Lewis

> . . . there is a pivotal movement at some stage in the body's reaction
> to injury or disease, maybe in aging as well, when the organism
> concedes that it is finished and the time for dying is at hand, and at
> this moment the events that lead to death are launched, as a
> coordinated mechanism. Functions are then shut off, in sequence,
> irreversibly, and, while this is going on, a neural mechanism, held
> ready for this occasion, is switched on . . .[25]

Such a response may be appropriate, in which case it makes the moments
of dying as peaceful as those who have died and been resuscitated so often
testify. But it may also be brought on inappropriately, when the organism
could have lived on, perhaps even induced malevolently, by external acts
intended to kill. Thomas speculates that some of the deaths resulting from
"hexing" are due to such responses. Lévi-Strauss describes deaths from
exorcism and the casting of spells in ways which suggest that the same
process may then be brought on by the community.[26]

It is not inconceivable that unhappy news abruptly conveyed, or a great
shock given to someone unable to tolerate it, could also bring on such a
"dying response," quite unintended by the speaker. There is every reason to
be cautious and to try to know ahead of time how susceptible a patient might
be to the accidental triggering—however rare—of such a response. One has
to assume, however, that most of those who have survived long enough to be
in a situation where their informed consent is asked have a very robust
resistance to such accidental triggering of processes leading to death.

When, on the other hand, one considers those who are already near death,
the "dying response" may be much less inappropriate, much less accidental,
much less unreasonable. In most societies, long before the advent of modern
medicine, human beings have made themselves ready for death once they
felt its approach. Philippe Ariès describes how many in the Middle Ages
prepared themselves for death when they "felt the end approach." They
awaited death lying down, surrounded by friends and relatives. They recol-
lected all they had lived through and done, pardoning all who stood near
their deathbed, calling on God to bless them, and finally praying. "After the
final prayer all that remained was to wait for death, and there was no reason
for death to tarry."[27]

Modern medicine, in its valiant efforts to defeat disease and to save lives,
may be dislocating the conscious as well as the purely organic responses
allowing death to come when it is inevitable, thus denying those who are
dying the benefits of the traditional approach to death. In lying to them, and
in pressing medical efforts to cure them long past the point of possible
recovery, physicians may thus rob individuals of an autonomy few would
choose to give up.

Sometimes, then, the "dying response" is a natural organic reaction at the time when the body has no further defense. Sometimes it is inappropriately brought on by news too shocking or given in too abrupt a manner. We need to learn a great deal more about this last category, no matter how small. But there is no evidence that patients in general will be debilitated by truthful information about their condition.

Apart from the possible harm from information, we are coming to learn much more about the benefits it can bring patients. People follow instructions more carefully if they know what their disease is and why they are asked to take medication; any benefits from those procedures are therefore much more likely to come about.[28] Similarly, people recover faster from surgery and tolerate pain with less medication if they understand what ails them and what can be done for them.[29]

RESPECT AND TRUTHFULNESS

Taken all together, the three arguments defending lies to patients stand on much shakier ground as a counterweight to the right to be informed than is often thought. The common view that many patients cannot understand, do not want, and may be harmed by, knowledge of their condition, and that lying to them is either morally neutral or even to be recommended, must be set aside. Instead, we have to make a more complex comparison. Over against the right of patients to knowledge concerning themselves, the medical and psychological benefits to them from this knowledge, the unnecessary and sometimes harmful treatment to which they can be subjected if ignorant, and the harm to physicians, their profession, and other patients from deceptive practices, we have to set a severely restricted and narrowed paternalistic view—that *some* patients cannot understand, *some* do not want, and *some* may be harmed by knowledge of their condition, and that they ought not to have to be treated like everyone else if this is not in their best interest.

Such a view is persuasive. A few patients openly request not to be given bad news. Others give clear signals to that effect, or are demonstrably vulnerable to the shock or anguish such news might call forth. Can one not in such cases infer implied consent to being deceived?

Concealment, evasion, withholding of information may at times be necessary. But if someone contemplates lying to a patient or concealing the truth, the burden of proof must shift. It must rest, here, as with all deception, on those who advocate it in any one instance. They must show why they fear a patient may be harmed or how they know that another cannot cope with the truthful knowledge. A decision to deceive must be seen as a very unusual step, to be talked over with colleagues and others who participate in the care of the patient. Reasons must be set forth and debated, alternatives weighed carefully. At all times, the correct information must go to *someone* closely related to the patient.

The law already permits doctors to withhold information from patients where it would clearly hurt their health. But this privilege has been sharply

limited by courts. Certainly it cannot be interpreted so broadly as to permit a
general practice of deceiving patients "for their own good." Nor can it be
made to include cases where patients might calmly decide, upon hearing
their diagnosis, not to go ahead with the therapy their doctor recommends.[30]
Least of all can it justify silence or lies to large numbers of patients merely on
the grounds that it is not always easy to tell what a patient wants.

For the great majority of patients, on the contrary, the goal must be
disclosure, and the atmosphere one of openness. But it would be wrong to
assume that patients can therefore be told abruptly about a serious diagnosis
—that, so long as openness exists, there are no further requirements of
humane concern in such communication. Dr. Cicely Saunders, who runs the
well-known St. Christopher's Hospice in England, describes the sensitivity
and understanding which are needed:

> Every patient needs an explanation of his illness that will be
> understandable and convincing to him if he is to cooperate in his
> treatment or be relieved of the burden of unknown fears. This is true
> whether it is a question of giving a diagnosis in a hopeful situation or
> of confirming a poor prognosis.
>
> The fact that a patient does not ask does not mean that he has no
> questions. One visit or talk is rarely enough. It is only by waiting and
> listening that we can gain an idea of what we should be saying.
> Silences and gaps are often more revealing than words as we try to
> learn what a patient is facing as he travels along the constantly
> changing journey of his illness and his thoughts about it.
>
> . . . So much of the communication will be without words or given
> indirectly. This is true of all real meeting with people but especially
> true with those who are facing, knowingly or not, difficult or
> threatening situations. It is also particularly true of the very ill.
>
> The main argument against a policy of deliberate, invariable denial
> of unpleasant facts is that it makes such communication extremely
> difficult, if not impossible. Once the possibility of talking frankly with a
> patient has been admitted, it does not mean that this will always take
> place, but the whole atmosphere is changed. We are then free to wait
> quietly for clues from each patient, seeing them as individuals from
> whom we can expect intelligence, courage, and individual decisions.
> They will feel secure enough to give us these clues when they wish.[31]

Above all, truthfulness with those who are suffering does not mean that
they should be deprived of all hope: hope that there is a chance of recovery,
however small; nor of reassurance that they will not be abandoned when they
most need help.

Much needs to be done, however, if the deceptive practices are to be
eliminated, and if concealment is to be restricted to the few patients who ask
for it or those who can be shown to be harmed by openness. The medical

profession has to address this problem. Those who are in training to take care of the sick and the dying have to learn how to speak with them, even about dying. They will be helped to do so if they can be asked to consider alternative approaches to patients, put themselves in the situation of a patient, even confront the possibility of being themselves near death.

Until the day comes when patients can be assured that they can trust what doctors tell them, is there anything they can do to improve the chances for themselves? How can they try to avoid slipping into a dependent relationship, one in which they have no way of trusting what anyone tells them? Is there any way in which they can maintain a degree of autonomy, even at a time of great weakness?

Those who know who will take care of them when they become seriously ill or approach death can talk this matter over well ahead of time. If they do, it is very likely that their desires will be respected. Growing numbers are now signing statements known as *living wills*, in which they can, if they so wish, specify whether or not they want to be informed about their condition. They can also specify conditions under which they do not want to have their lives prolonged.[32] Still others, who may not have thought of these problems ahead of time, can insist on receiving adequate information once they are in need of care. It is the great majority—those who are afraid of asking, of seeming distrustful—who give rise to the view that patients do not really want to know since they never ask.

The perspective of needing care is very different from that of providing it. The first sees the most fundamental question for patients to be whether they can trust their caretakers. It requires a stringent adherence to honesty, in all but a few carefully delineated cases. The second sees the need to be free to deceive, sometimes for genuinely humane reasons. It is only by bringing these perspectives into the open and by considering the exceptional cases explicitly that the discrepancy can be reduced and trust restored.

Notes

1 Plato, *The Republic*, 389 b.

2 B.C. Meyer, "Truth and the Physician," *Bulletin of the New York Academy of Medicine* 45 (1969): 59–71 . . .

3 W.H.S. Jones, trans. *Hippocrates*, Loeb Classical Library (Cambridge, Mass.: Harvard University Press, 1923), p. 164.

4 Reprinted in M. B. Etziony, *The Physician's Creed: An Anthology of Medical Prayers, Oaths and Codes of Ethics* (Springfield, Ill.: Charles C. Thomas, 1973), pp. 15–18.

5 See Harry Friedenwald, "The Ethics of the Practice of Medicine from the Jewish Point of View," *Johns Hopkins Hospital Bulletin*, 318 (August 1917): 256–61.

6 "Ten Principles of Medical Ethics," *Journal of the American Medical Association* 164 (1957): 1119–20.

7 Mary Barrett, letter, *Boston Globe*, 16 November 1976, p. 1.

8 Though a minority of physicians have struggled to bring them to our attention. See Thomas Percival, *Medical Ethics*, 3d ed. (Oxford: John Henry Parker, 1849), pp. 132–41; Worthington Hooker, *Physician and Patient* (New York: Baker and Scribner, 1849), pp. 357–82; Richard C. Cabot, "Teamwork of Doctor and Patient Through the Annihilation of Lying," in *Social Service and the Art of Healing* (New York: Moffat, Yard & Co., 1909), pp. 116–70; Charles C. Lund, "The

Doctor, the Patient, and the Truth," *Annals of Internal Medicine* 24 (1946): 955; Edmund Davies, "The Patient's Right to Know the Truth," *Proceedings of the Royal Society of Medicine* 66 (1973): 533–36.

9 Lawrence Henderson, "Physician and Patient as a Social System," *New England Journal of Medicine* 212 (1955).

10 Nicholas Demy, Letter to the Editor, *Journal of the American Medical Association* 217 (1971): 696–97.

11 For the views of physicians, see Donald Oken, "What to Tell Cancer Patients. "*Journal of the American Medical Association* 175 (1961): 1120–28; and tabulations in Robert Veatch, *Death, Dying, and the Biological Revolution* (New Haven and London: Yale University Press, 1976), pp. 229–38. For the view of patients, see Veatch, *ibid.;* Jean Aitken-Swan and E. C. Easson, "Reactions of Cancer Patients on Being Told Their Diagnosis," *British Medical Journal* (1959): 779–83; Jim McIntosh, "Patients' Awareness and Desire for Information About Diagnosed but Undisclosed Malignant Disease," *The Lancet* 7 (1976): 300-303; William d. Kelly and Stanley R. Friesen, "Do Cancer Patients Want to Be Told?" *Surgery* 27 (1950): 822–26.

12 See Avery Weisman, *On Dying and Denying* (New York: Behavioral Publications, 1972); Elisabeth Kübler-Ross, *On Death and Dying* (New York: Macmillan Co., 1969); Ernest Becker, *The Denial of Death* (New York: Free Press, 1973); Philippe Ariès, *Western Attitudes Toward Death*, trans. Patricia M. Ranum (Baltimore and London: Johns Hopkins University Press, 1974); and Sigmund Freud, "Negation," *Collected Papers*, ed. James Strachey (London: Hogarth Press, 1950), 5:181–85.

13 Kübler-Ross, *On Death and Dying*, p. 34.

14 Michel de Montaigne, *Essays*, bk. 1, chap. 20.

15 It is in literature that these questions are most directly raised. Two recent works where they are taken up with striking beauty and simplicity are May Sarton, *As We Are Now* (New York: W. W. Norton & Co., 1973); and Freya Stark, *A Peak in Darien* (London: John Murray, 1976).

16 Herman Feifel et al., "Physicians Consider Death," *Proceedings of the American Psychoanalytical Association*, 1967, pp. 201–2.

17 See Diogenes Laertius, *Lives of Eminent Philosophers*, p. 651. Epicurus willed his garden to his friends and descendants, and wrote on the eve of dying: "On this blissful day, which is also the last day of my life, I write to you. My continual sufferings from strangury and dysentery are so great that nothing could augment them; but over against them all I set gladness of mind at the remembrance of our past conversations." (Letter to Idomeneus, *ibid.*, p. 549.)

18 See Ivan Illich, *Medical Nemesis* (New York: Pantheon, 1976), for a critique of the iatrogenic tendencies of contemporary medical care in industrialized societies.

19 The law requires that inroads made upon a person's body take place only with the informed voluntary consent of that person. The term "informed consent" came into common use only after 1960, when it was used by the Kansas Supreme Court in *Nathanson v. Kline* 186 Kan 393, 350 P2d 1093 (1960). The patient is now entitled to full disclosure of risks, benefits, and alternative treatments to any proposed procedure, both in therapy and in medical experimentation, except in emergencies or when the patient is incompetent, in which case proxy consent is required.

20 See, for example, "Statement on a Patient's Bill of Rights," reprinted in Stanley Joel Reiser, Arthur J. Dyck, and William J. Curran, *Ethics in Medicine* (Cambridge, Mass., and London: MIT Press, 1977), p. 148.

21 See Ralph Aphidi, "Informed Consent: A Study of Patient Reaction," *Journal of the American Medical Association* 216 (1971): 1325–29.

22 See Steven R. Kaplan, Richard A. Greenwald, and Arvey I. Rogers, Letter to the Editor, *New England Journal of Medicine* 296 (1977): 1127.

23 Oken, "What to Tell Cancer Patients"; Veatch, *Death, Dying and the Biological Revolution;* Weisman, *On Dying and Denying*.

24 Norman L. Cantor, "A Patient's Decision to Decline Life-Saving Treatment: Bodily Integrity Versus the Preservation of Life," *Rutgers Law Review* 26: 228–64; Danielle Gourevitch, "Suicide

Among the Sick in Classical Antiquity," *Bulletin of the History of Medicine* 18 (1969): 501–18; for bibliography, see Bok, "Voluntary Euthanasia."

25 Lewis Thomas, "A Meliorist View of Disease and Dying," *The Journal of Medicine and Philosophy* 1 (1976): 212–21.

26 Claude Lévi-Strauss, *Structural Anthropology* (New York: Basic Books, 1963), p. 167; See also Eric Cassell, "Permission to Die," in John Behnke and Sissela Bok, eds., *The Dilemmas of Euthanasia* (New York: Doubleday, Anchor Press, 1975), pp. 121–31.

27 Ariès, *Western Attitudes Toward Death*, p. 11.

28 Barbara S. Hulka, J. C. Cassel, et al., "Communication, Compliance, and Concordance between Physicians and Patients with Prescribed Medications," *American Journal of Public Health*, Sept. 1976, pp. 847–53. The study shows that of the nearly half of all patients who do not follow the prescriptions of the doctors (thus forgoing the intended effect of these prescriptions), many will follow them if adequately informed about the nature of their illness and what the proposed medication will do.

29 See Lawrence D. Egbert, George E. Batitt, et al., "Reduction of Postoperative Pain by Encouragement and Instruction of Patients," *New England Journal of Medicine*, 270 (1964): 825–27. See also Howard Waitzskin and John D. Stoeckle, "The Communication of Information about Illness," *Advances in Psychosomatic Medicine*, 8 (1972): 185–215.

30 See Charles Fried, *Medical Experimentation: Personal Integrity and Social Policy* (Amsterdam and Oxford: North Holland Publishing Co. 1974), pp. 20–24.

31 Cicely M. S. Saunders, "Telling Patients," in Reiser, Dyck, and Curran, *Ethics in Medicine*, pp. 238–40.

32 Sissela Bok, "Personal Directions for Care at the End of Life," *New England Journal of Medicine* 295 (1976): 367–69.

18 ·

Death, Uses of a Corpse, and Social Worth

David Sudnow

David Sudnow is associate professor in the sociology department at Brooklyn College. This selection is taken from his book Passing On *and describes the rather startling treatment accorded both the living and the dead as they pass through a hospital's emergency room.*

From David Sudnow, Passing On, © *1967, pp. 95–107. Reprinted by permission of Prentice-Hall, Inc., Englewood Cliffs, New Jersey.*

In County's Emergency Ward, the most frequent variety of death is what is known as the "DOA" [dead on arrival] type. Approximately forty such cases are processed through this division of the hospital each month. The designation "DOA" is somewhat ambiguous insofar as many persons are not physiologically dead upon arrival, but are nonetheless classified as having been such. A person who is initially classified as "DOA" by

the ambulance driver might retain such a classification even though he might die some hours after his arrival at the hospital.

When an ambulance driver suspects that the person he is carrying is dead, he signals the Emergency Ward with a special siren alarm as he approaches the entrance driveway. As he wheels his stretcher past the clerk's desk, he restates his suspicion with the remark "possible," a shorthand reference for "Possible DOA." The use of the term *possible* is required by law which insists, primarily for insurance purposes, that any diagnosis unless made by a certified physician be so qualified. The clerk records the arrival in a logbook and pages a physician, informing him, in code, of the arrival. Often a page is not needed as physicians on duty hear the siren alarm and expecting the arrival wait at the entranceway. The "person" is rapidly wheeled to the far end of the ward corridor and into the nearest available foyer or room, supposedly out of sight of other patients and possible onlookers from the waiting room. The physician arrives, makes his examination and pronounces the patient dead or alive. A nurse then places a phone call to the coroner's office, which is legally responsible for the removal and investigation of all DOA cases.

Neither the hospital nor the physician has medical responsibility in such cases. In many instances of clear death, ambulance drivers use the hospital as a depository for disposing of a body, which has the advantages of being both closer and less bureaucratically complicated a place than the downtown coroner's office. The hospital stands as a temporary holding station, rendering the community service of legitimate and free pronouncements of death for any comers. In circumstances of near-death, it functions more traditionally as a medical institution, mobilizing lifesaving procedures for those for whom they are still of potential value, at least as judged by the ER's [emergency room] staff of residents and interns. The boundaries between near-death and sure-death are not, however, altogether clearly defined.

In nearly all DOA cases, the pronouncing physician, commonly that physician who is the first to answer the clerk's page or spot the incoming ambulance, shows, in his general demeanor and approach to the task, little more than passing interest in the event's possible occurrence and the patient's biographical and medical circumstance. He responds to the clerk's call, conducts his examination, and leaves the room once he has made the necessary official gesture to an attending nurse (the term "kaput," murmured in differing degrees of audibility depending upon the hour and his state of awakeness, is a frequently employed announcement). It happened on numerous occasions, especially during the midnight-to-eight shift, that a physician was interrupted during a coffee break to pronounce a DOA and returned to his colleagues in the canteen with, as an account of his absence, some version of "Oh, it was nothing but a DOA."

It is interesting to note that while the special siren alarm is intended to mobilize quick response on the part of the ER staff, it occasionally operates in the opposite fashion. Some ER staff came to regard the fact of a DOA as decided in advance, and exhibited a degree of nonchalance in answering the siren or page, taking it that the "possible DOA" most likely is "D," and in so doing gave authorization to the ambulance driver to make such assessments. Given that time lapse which sometimes occurs between that point at which the doctor knows of the arrival and the time he gets to the patient's side, it is not inconceivable that in several instances patients who might have been revived died during this interim. This is particularly likely as apparently a matter of moments may differentiate the reviveable state from the irreversible one.

Two persons in "similar" physical condition may be differentially designated as dead or not. For example, a young child was brought into the ER with no registering heartbeat, respiration, or pulse and was, through a rather dramatic stimulation procedure involving the coordinated work of a large team of doctors and nurses, revived for a period of eleven hours. On the same evening, shortly after the child's arrival, an elderly person who presented the same physical signs, with what a doctor later stated, in conversation, to be no discernible differences from the child in skin color, warmth, etc., "arrived" in the ER and was almost immediately pronounced dead, with no attempts at stimulation instituted. A nurse remarked later in the evening: "They (the doctors) would never have done that to the old lady (attempt heart stimulation) even though I've seen it work on them too." During the period when emergency resuscitation equipment was being readied for the child, an intern instituted mouth-to-mouth resuscitation. This same intern was shortly relieved by oxygen machinery and when the woman "arrived," he was the one who pronounced her dead. He reported shortly afterwards that he could never bring himself to put his mouth to "an old lady's like that."

It is therefore important to note that the category "DOA" is not totally homogeneous with respect to actual physiological condition. The same is generally true of all deaths, death involving, as it does, some decisional considerations, at least in its earlier stages.

There is currently a movement in progress in some medical and lay circles to undercut the traditional distinction between "biological" and "clinical" death, and procedures are being developed and their use encouraged for treating any "clinically dead" person as potentially reviveable.[1] This movement, unlike late nineteenth-century arguments for life after death, is legitimated by modern medical thinking and technology. Should such a movement gain widespread momentum, it would foreseeably have considerable consequence for certain aspects of hospital social structure, requiring, perhaps, that much more continuous and intensive care be given "dying" and "dead" patients than is presently accorded them, at least at County. At Cohen Hospital, where the care of the "tentatively dead" is always very intensive, such developments would more likely be encouraged than at County.

Currently, at County, there seems to be a rather strong relationship between the age, social backgrounds, and perceived moral character of patients and the amount of effort which is made to attempt revival when "clinical death signs" are detected, as well as the amount of effort given to forestalling their appearance in the first place. As one compares practices at different hospitals, the general relationship seems to hold, although at the private, wealthier institutions, like Cohen, the overall amount of attention given to "initially dead" patients is greater. At County, efforts at revival are admittedly superficial, with the exception of the very young and occasionally wealthier patient, who by some accident, ends up at County's ER. No instances have been witnessed, at County, where external heart massage was given a patient whose heart was stethoscopically inaudible, if that patient was over forty years of age. On the other hand, at Cohen Hospital heart massage is a normal routine at that point, and more drastic measures, such as injection of adrenalin directly into the heart, are not uncommon. While these practices are undertaken for many patients at Cohen if "tentative death" is discovered early, as it generally is because of the attention "dying" patients are given, at County they are reserved for a very special class of cases.

Generally, the older the patient the more likely is his tentative death taken to constitute pronounceable death. Before a twenty-year-old who arrives in the ER with a presumption of death, attached in the form of the ambulance driver's assessment, will be pronounced dead by a physician, very long listening to his heartbeat will occur, occasionally efforts at stimulation will be made, oxygen administered, and oftentimes stimulative medication given. Less time will elapse between initial detection of an inaudible heartbeat and nonpalpable pulse and the pronouncement of death if the person is forty years old, and still less if he is seventy. As well as can be detected, there appeared to be no obvious difference between men and women in this regard, nor between white and Negro "patients." Very old patients who are considered to be dead, on the basis of the ambulance driver's assessment, were seen to be put in an empty room to "wait" several moments before a physician arrived. When a young person is brought in as a "possible," the ambulance driver tries to convey some more alarming sense to the arrival by turning the siren up very loud and continuing it after he has already stopped, so that by the time he has actually entered the wing, personnel, expecting "something special," act quickly and accordingly. When it is a younger person that the driver is delivering, his general manner is more frantic. The speed with which he wheels his stretcher in, and the degree of excitement in his voice as he describes his charge to the desk clerk, are generally more heightened than with the elderly "DOA." One can observe a direct relationship between the loudness and length of the siren alarm and the considered "social value" of the person being transported.

The older the person, the less thorough is the examination he is given; frequently, elderly people are pronounced dead on the basis of only a stethoscopic examination of the heart. The younger the person, the more likely will an examination preceding an announcement of death entail an inspection of the eyes, attempt to find a pulse and touching of the body for coldness. When a younger person is brought to the hospital and while announced by the driver as a "possible" is nonetheless observed to be breathing slightly, or have an audible heart beat, there is a fast mobilization of effort to stimulate increased breathing and a more rapid heart beat. If an older person is brought in in a similar condition there will be a rapid mobilization of similar efforts; however, the time which will elapse between that point at which breathing noticeably ceases and the heart audibly stops beating, and when the pronouncement of death is made, will differ according to his age.

One's location in the age structure of the society is not the only factor which will influence the degree of care he gets when his death is considered to have possibly occurred. At County Hospital a notable additional set of considerations can be generally termed as the patient's presumed "moral character." The detection of alcohol on the breath of a "DOA" is nearly always noticed by the examining physician, who announces to his fellow workers that the person is a drunk, and seems to constitute a feature he regards as warranting less than strenuous effort to attempt revival. The alcoholic patient is treated by hospital physicians, not only when the status of his body as alive or dead is at stake, but throughout the whole course of medical treatment, as one for whom the concern to treat can properly operate somewhat weakly. There is a high proportion of alcoholic patients at County, and their treatment very often involves an earlier admission of "terminality" and a consequently more marked suspension of curative treatment than is observed in the treatment of nonalcoholic patients. In one case, the decision whether or not to administer additional needed blood to an alcoholic man who was bleeding severely from a stomach ulcer was decided negatively, and that decision was announced as based on the fact of his alcoholism. The intern in charge of treating the patient was asked by a nurse, "Should we order more blood for this afternoon?" The doctor answered, "I can't see any sense in pumping it into him because even if we can stop the bleeding, he'll turn around and start drinking again and next week he'll be back needing more blood." In the DOA circumstance, alcoholic patients have been known to be pronounced dead on the basis of a stethoscopic examination of the heart alone, even though that person was of such an age that were he not an alcoholic he would have likely received much more intensive consideration before being so designated. Among other categories of persons whose deaths will be more quickly adjudged, and whose "dying" more readily noticed and used as a rationale for palliative care, are the suicide, the dope addict, the known prostitute, the assailant in a crime of violence, the vagrant, the known wifebeater, and other persons whose moral characters are considered reproachable.

Within a limited temporal perspective at least, but one which is not necessarily to be regarded as trivial, the likelihood of "dying" and even of being "dead" can thus be said to be partially a function of one's place in the social structure, and not simply in the sense that the wealthier get better care, or at least not in the usual sense of the fact.[2] If one anticipates having a critical heart attack, he best keep himself well-dressed and his breath clean if there is a likelihood he will be brought into the County Emergency Unit as a "possible."

There are a series of practical consequences of publicly announcing that a patient is dead in the hospital setting. His body may be properly stripped of clothing and jewelry, wrapped up for discharge, the family notified of the death, and the coroner informed in the case of DOA deaths. In the Emergency Unit there are a special set of procedures which are partially definitive of death. DOA cases are very interestingly "used" in many American hospitals. The inflow of dead bodies, or what can properly be taken to be dead bodies, is regarded as a collection of "guinea pigs," in the sense that a set of procedures can be performed upon those bodies for the sake of teaching and research.

In any "teaching hospital" (in the case of County, I use this term in a weak sense, a hospital which employs interns and residents; in other settings a "teaching hospital" may mean systematic, institutionalized instruction), the environment of medical events is regarded not merely as a collection of treatable cases, but as a collection of experience-relevant information. It is a continually enforced way of looking at the cases one treats under the auspices of a concern for experience with "such cases." This concern can legitimately warrant the institution of a variety of procedures, tests, and inquiries which lie outside and may even, on occasion, conflict with the strict interests of treatment; they fall within the interests of learning "medicine," gaining experience with such cases and acquiring technical skills. A principle for organizing medical care activities in the teaching hospital, and perhaps more so in a county hospital where patients social value is often not highly regarded, is the relevance of any particular activity to the acquisition of skills of general import. Physicians feel that among the greatest values of such institutions is the ease with which they can selectively organize medical attention so as to maximize the benefits to knowledge and technical proficiency which working with a given case expectably afford. The notion of the "interesting case" is, at County, not simply a casual notion, but an enforced principle for the allocation of attention. The private physician is in a more committed relation to each and every one of his patients, and while he may regard this or that case as more or less interesting, he ideally cannot legitimate the interestingness of his patients' conditions as bases for devoting varying amounts of attention to them. His reward for treating the uninteresting case is, of course, the fee, and physicians are known to give more attention to the patients who will be paying more.

At County Hospital, a case's degree of interest is a crucial fact, and one which is invoked to legitimate the way a physician does and should allocate his attention. In surgery I found many examples. If on a given morning in one operating room a "rare" procedure was scheduled, and in another a "usual" procedure planned, there would be no special difficulty in getting personnel to witness and partake in the "rare" procedure, whereas work in the "usual" case was considered as merely work, regardless of such considerations as the relative fatality rate of each procedure or the patient's physical condition. It is not uncommon to find interns at County interchange among themselves in scrubbing for an appendectomy, each taking turns going next door to watch the skin graft or chest surgery. At Cohen[3], such house staff interchanging was not permissible. Interns and residents were assigned to a particular surgical suite and required to stay throughout the course of the procedure. On the medical wards, on the basis of general observation, it seems that one could obtain a high order correlation between the amount of time doctors spent discussing and examining patients and the degree of unusualness of their medical problems.

I introduce this general feature to point to the predominant orientation, at County, to such matters as "getting practice," and the general organizational principle which provides for the propriety of using cases as the basis for this practice. Not only are live patients objects of practice, so are dead ones.

There is a rule, in the Emergency Unit, that with every DOA a doctor should attempt to insert an "endotracheal" tube. This should be done only after the patient is pronounced dead. The reason for this practice (and it is a rule on which new interns are instructed as part of their training in doing emergency medicine) is that such a tube is extremely difficult to insert, requiring great yet careful force and, insofar as it causes great pain, cannot be "practiced" on live patients. The body must be positioned with the neck held at an angle so that this large tube will go down the proper channel. In some circumstances when it is necessary to establish a rapid "airway" (an open breathing canal), the endotracheal tube can apparently be an effective substitute for the tracheotomy incision. The DOA's body, in its transit from the scene of the death to the morgue constitutes an ideal experimental opportunity. The procedure is not done on all deceased patients, the reason apparently being that it is part of the training one receives on the Emergency Unit, and to be learned there. Nor is it done on all DOA cases, for some doctors, it seems, are uncomfortable in handling a dead body whose charge as a live one they never had, and handling it in the way such a procedure requires. It is important to note that when it is done, it is done most frequently and most intensively with those persons lowly situated in the social structure. No instances were observed where a young child was used as an object for such practice, nor where a well-dressed, middle-aged, middle-class adult was similarly used.

On one occasion a woman, who had seemingly ingested a fatal amount of Clorox, was brought to the Emergency Unit and after her death several physicians took turns trying to insert an endotracheal tube, after which one of them suggested that the stomach be pumped to examine its contents to try to see what effects the Clorox had on the gastric secretions. A lavage was set up and the stomach contents removed. A chief resident left the room and gathered together a group of interns with the explanation that they should look at this woman because of the apparent results of such ingestion. In effect, the doctors conducted their own autopsy investigation without making any incisions.

On several similar occasions, physicians explained that with these cases they didn't really feel like they were prying in handling the body, but that they often did in the case of an ordinary or "natural death" of a morally proper person. Suicidal victims are frequently the object of curiosity, and while among the nursing staff there is a high degree of distaste in working with such patients and their bodies, doctors do not express such a high degree of distaste. There was a woman who came into the Emergency Unit with a self-inflicted gunshot wound, which ran from her sternum downward and backward, passing out through a kidney. She had apparently bent over the rifle and pulled the trigger. Upon her "arrival" in the Emergency Unit she was quite alive and talkative, and while in great pain and very fearful, was able to conduct something of a conversation. She was told that she would need immediate surgery, and was taken off to the OR. She was followed by a group of physicians, all of whom were interested in seeing what damage the path of the bullet had done. One doctor said aloud, quite near her stretcher, "I can't get my heart into saving her, so we might as well have some fun out of it." During the operation, the doctors regarded her body much as they would during an autopsy. After the critical damage was repaired and they had reason to feel the woman would survive, they engaged in numerous surgical side ventures, exploring muscular tissue in areas of the back through which the bullet had passed but where no damage requiring special repair had to be done, with the exception of tying off bleeders and suturing. One of the operating surgeons performed a side operation, incising an area of skin surrounding the entry wound on the chest, to examine, he announced to his colleagues, the structure of the tissue through which the bullet passed. He explicitly announced his project to be motivated by curiosity. One of the physicians spoke of the procedure as an "autopsy on a live patient," about which there was a little laughter.

In another case, a man was wounded in the forehead by a bullet, and after the damage was repaired in the wound, which resembled a natural frontal lobotomy, an exploration was made of an area adjacent to the path of the bullet, on the forehead proper below the hairline. During this exploration the operating surgeon asked a nurse to ask Dr. X to come in. When Dr. X arrived, the two of them, under the gaze of a large group of interns and nurses, made a further incision, which an intern described to me as unnecessary in the treatment of the man, and which left a noticeable scar down the side of the temple. The purpose of this venture was to explore the structure of that part of the face. This area of the skull, that below the hairline, cannot be examined during an autopsy because of a contract between local morticians and the Department of Pathology, designed to leave those areas of the body which will be viewed, free of surgical incisions. The doctors justified the additional incision by pointing out that since he would have a "nice scar as it was, a little bit more wouldn't be so serious."

During autopsies themselves, bodies are routinely used to gain experience in surgical techniques, and many incisions and explorations are conducted that are not essential to the key task of uncovering the cause of the death. On frequent occasions, specialists-in-training came to autopsies having no interest in the patient's death. They would await the completion of the legal part of the procedure, at which point the body is turned over to them for practice. Mock surgical procedures are staged on the body, oftentimes with two coworkers simulating actual conditions, tying off blood vessels which obviously need not be tied or suturing internally.

When a patient died in the Emergency Unit, whether or not he had been brought in under the designation "DOA," there occasionally occurred various mock surgical procedures on his body. In one case a woman was treated for a chicken bone lodged in her throat. Rapidly after her arrival via ambulance a tracheotomy incision was made in the attempt to establish an unobstructed source of air, but the procedure was not successful and she died as the incision was being made. Several interns were called upon to practice their stitching by closing the wound as they would on a live patient. There was a low peak in the activity of the ward, and a chief surgical resident used the occasion to supervisorily teach them various techniques for closing such an incision. In another case the body of a man who died after being crushed by an automobile was employed for instruction and practice in the use of various fracture-setting techniques. In still another instance several interns and residents attempted to suture a dead man's dangling finger in place on his mangled hand.

Notes

1 There is a large popular and scientific literature developing on efforts to "treat the dead," the import of which is to undercut traditional notions of the nonreversibility of death. Some of this discussion goes so far as to propose the preservation of corpses in a state of nondeterioration until such time as medical science will be able to do complete renovative work. See particularly R. Ettinger, *The Prospect of Immortality* (Garden City: Doubleday & Company, Inc., 1964). The Soviet literature on resuscitation is most extensive. Soviet physicians have given far more attention to this problem than any others in the world. For an extensive review of the technical literature, as well as a discussion of biomedical principles, with particular emphasis on cardiac arrest, see V. A. Negovskii, *Resuscitation and Artificial Hypothermia* (New York: Consultants Bureau Enterprises, Inc., 1962). See also, L. Fridland, *The Achievement of Soviet Medicine* (New York: Twayne Publishers, Inc., 1961), especially Chapter Two, "Death Deceived," pp. 56-57. For an account of the famous saving of the Soviet physicist Landau's life, see A. Dorozynski, *The Man They Wouldn't Let Die* (New York: The Macmillan Company, 1956).

For recent popular articles on "bringing back the dead" and treating death as a reversible process, see "The Reversal of Death," *The Saturday Review*, August 4, 1962; "A New Fight Against Sudden Death," *Look*, December 1, 1964.

Soviet efforts and conceptions of death as reversible might be seen to have their ideological basis in principles of dialectics:

> For everyday purposes we know and can say, e.g., whether an animal is alive or not. But, upon closer inquiry, we find that this is, in many cases a very complex question, as the jurists know very well. They have cudgelled their brains in vain to discover a rational limit beyond which the killing of the child in its mother's womb is murder. It is just as impossible to determine absolutely the moment of death, for physiology provides that death is not an instantaneous, momentary phenomenon, but a very protracted process.
>
> In like manner, every organized being is every moment the same and not the same . . .

From F. Engels, *Socialism: Utopian and Scientific* (New York: International Publishers Co., 1935), p. 47.

For a discussion of primitive conceptions of death with particular attention to the passage between life and death, see I. A. Lopatin, *The Cult of the Dead Among the Natives of the Amur Basin* (The Hague: Mouton and Company, 1960), pp. 26-27 and 39-41.

2 The "DOA" deaths of famous persons are reportedly attended with considerably prolonged and intensive resuscitation efforts. In Kennedy's death, for example, it was reported:

> Medically, it was apparent the President was not alive when he was brought in. There was no spontaneous respiration. He had dilated, fixed pupils. It was obviously a lethal head wound.
>
> Technically, however, by using vigorous resuscitation, intraveneous tubes and all the usual supportive measures, we were able to raise the semblance of a heartbeat.

The New York Times, November 23, 1963, p. 2.

3 EDITOR'S NOTE: A private hospital in the same city.

Edwin S. Shneidman

Edwin S. Shneidman is a professor of thanatology at the University of California at Los Angeles and director of the Laboratory for the Study of Life-Threatening Behavior at the Neuropsychiatric Institute of the UCLA Medical Center. In the piece reproduced below, the author presents verbatim transcripts of interviews with dying individuals—dialogues with life-threatening illness—and discusses certain general features of clinical thanatology.

From Voices of Death *by Edwin S. Shneidman. Copyright ©1980 by Edwin S. Shneidman.*

All are born with halters round their necks; but it is only when caught in the swift, sudden turn of death, that mortals realize the silent, subtle, ever-present perils of life.
> —Herman Melville, *Moby Dick*
> (Chapter 60)

It is from Hippocrates, the great physician of antiquity, that we get the term "carcinoma." It comes from the Greek word *karkinos*, meaning crab. It is so called because the large veins surrounding a tumor look like the extended claws of a crab spreading its multijointed appendages over the tumor like so many hostile tentacles. What Hippocrates did not know (except maybe by prescience) is that a metastasizing cancer can reach, crablike, throughout the body, touching, malignantly, several organs at once.

Just as the "voice of the turtle"—the cooing of the turtle*dove*—was heard throughout the land in biblical times, so today the "voice of the crab," when it is understood to mean the voices of victims of cancer, is heard throughout the land. That voice, sometimes weak but usually clear enough, is worth listening to. Here is the sound of one of those voices.

I'm giving up. I want it to be over. I don't expect any miracles anymore. The sweating and the fevers just get me down. And yet I feel good. It's going to be a slow process. Maybe not so much a painful process, but a slow process. I'd like to get out. And then I'd also like to go to sleep and die. I mean, I don't know what to say. I'm just tired. I woke up this morning, I was really frightened. I was saying dear God, dear God, what am I going to do? Dear God, dear God, doesn't answer.

The words are those of Marion, a twenty-two-year-old professional dancer and a hairdresser, a young man dying of acute myelogenous leukemia. I am at his hospital bedside. These quotations are verbatim from a cassette tape. His voice is low; the words are spoken softly, interrupted by his occasional coughs and sighs.

Initially, when he came to the hospital, his behavior was hostile and irascible—"bitchy," as one doctor later said to me. He railed at the nurses in a vituperative way, calling them foul names. The last straw for them was his throwing a full urinal at a nurse. Then I was asked by his doctor to see him. The very beginning of the first session was somewhat unusual: I went into his hospital room, gently touched his hand, addressed him by his first name and said that I understood that he had been a bad boy. It was a big chance to take; he might have been totally alienated by such an abrupt approach. He began to sob; we immediately had a binding psychological relationship.

His behavior on the ward calmed down within hours; he seemed only to need someone to meet him "where he lived," with his terror and anguish and pain. The session reproduced on these pages took place several weeks after the first one—I saw him almost every day—and occurred about ten days before he died. The session continued as follows:

SHNEIDMAN: What was that fear of?

PATIENT: Oh, the unknown and another day, another day. Something else to keep me going. *(Coughing)* Dr. Shneidman, if there was a way I could end it now I would do that. It's taking so long. I don't have much patience, I guess.

S: That's true. This is a trial for you in many deep ways, including that one.

P: Including patience, you mean?

S: Yes. I don't think there has ever been a time in your life that you've had to be so patient.

P: How do you do it? I'm scared. You said you'd say what death was.

S: Pardon me!

P: You said you'd say what death was. You said it was something that I wouldn't know anything about.

S: Yes.

P: If I could only be sure that it would be peaceful. Will it be peaceful?

S: I can guarantee it.

P: Because that's so important. It's almost more important than anything else, that it be peaceful. My mother still wants to believe that maybe something will happen.

S: In what ways have your relationships with your mother changed in the last several days?

P: I've loved her. I let myself love her. *(Weeping)* Without any ties. I let myself love her without feeling that she was going to emasculate me. I've let her love me. I've let her be a mother. She's been so beautiful. I get more comfort from her than from anybody else.*

S: That's beautiful. Do you think it took this state for that to happen?

P: I don't know. I know for me it has, because now there's no reason to be wary of her castrating tendencies because she really means well for me. And she brings me such comfort, and she's so selfless. Crying's not supposed to help. It hurts when you get a fever and

---

*Only a few weeks before, he had refused to talk to his mother or even to permit her to come into his hospital room.

you sweat a lot, which is what I do. . . . And if there is a God, if there is a somebody that I knew I could pray to that maybe could perform this miracle, I'd be most thankful and I'd show it in every way I could. *(Coughing)* It's so farfetched, so unreal. I don't have a chance. I want to live so much. I don't want to die now. I'm half there and I'm half here, maybe more than half there. Because I don't get any encouragement anymore about living from the doctors. Right now, the big thing is just doing as good a job as possible to keep me alive for as long as possible, which is something I really don't want to do. Because if it's over, shouldn't it be over? Shouldn't I be out of the way? My mother keeps saying take each day as it comes. It's very difficult, extremely difficult. I had a lot of trouble doing that before. I'm having even more trouble doing it now. . . . So many people have said how much I touched their lives.

s: I'm sure that's true.

p: All kinds of people, young, old, my contemporaries. I never knew it.

s: How does all that make you feel?

p: I went to bed last night after listening to it, hearing it, and talking about it. I went to bed last night feeling good, and it was very comforting. But then I woke this morning and I was in this terror. It's like I need constant reassurance that I've been a good person and that there's someone there to love me. I guess I don't call that much of a success.

s: How do you mean?

p: I suppose if I'd been that way, I should be much more capable of taking this thing.

s: With more calmness?

p: Yeah. Maybe even fighting it better. I haven't fought it very well. It's almost as if I've wanted to die, from the time I got it. Not wanted to die, but knew I was going to die.

s: Sort of gave in to it?

p: Yeah. . . . I remember a few months ago they did a blood test and a bone marrow and then the doctor gave me a shot which turned out to be Valium and then he told me I had leukemia.

s: How did he tell you? Did he preface it in any way?

p: I think he told me, he told me in a way that was like we caught it at a good time, that we really had a good chance, that they wanted me to go to the hospital.

s: What were your reactions?

p: I called my mother right away.

s: What went through your head? Did you know what that diagnosis meant?

p: *(Coughing)* I recognized the seriousness, but I was in a state of shock.

s: What did you say to your mother?

p: I told her I had leukemia.

s: What was her reaction to that?

p: She cried.... But I really thought I was going to be cured. I mean, they told me I was. They told me I had a really good chance. And they've tried everything. Now a perfectly good person with an awful lot to give is going to die. A young person is going to die. The death is going to be absolutely senseless.

s: You say it in such an objective way about yourself.

p: It is a senseless death. I've asked the same question: why me? I don't get any answers. I suppose if somebody has to get it, it's just a disease and there's statistics and somebody has to get it, so maybe a friend of mine who's sailing along very nicely now thinking how sorry he is for me is going to get killed in an auto accident, because somebody has to get killed in an auto accident.

s: That's an interesting idea, like there's so much misery and so much death and it has to be distributed.

p: Yeah. I wish I could sleep, get some rest, but I dwell so much on it, on the dying. But if I get out I don't want to sleep. I want to get out. I want to do some things, just some things, maybe have a French meal, go to a movie, sleep with my lover again. In a way, though, it might make it more difficult. But why not? Why shouldn't I do it? Why shouldn't I walk outside again? I wonder how much I've missed. Now it's irretrievable. Do you think it's a good idea, even if I'm not a hundred percent right, if the doctors say it's O.K. for me to go out, do you think it's a good idea for me to go?

s: Naturally. Don't you?

p: You know, I'm still sweating. I think it's part of the leukemia, my throat still bothers me a bit, my stomach still bothers me a bit.

s: Well, I'll put the question to you: what do you think?

p: I almost think that almost anything is better than just lying here in this bed. I hate to be a burden to people on the outside but I'll never be completely well. I'm really at a low point.

s: I know, and a difficult one.

p: A really low point.... Do *you* fear death?

s: Yes, of course. Why do you ask?

p: I was just wondering about somebody who is more or less a specialist in the area of death, how he felt about it.

s: Well, I'm as mortal as anybody. I think I'm very close to you. I don't like illness and pain, incapacity, uncertainty, all those things that you don't like.

p: *(Sigh)* I feel peaceful now.

s: I'll come to see you on Monday, around eleven o'clock.

p: I hope I'll be here. I mean, I hope I'll be here physically.

s: That's a necessary requirement. I'll see you then.

In this dying scene certain themes appear which will come up again and again. These include the terror ("I was really frightened"); the unnerving reaction to severe pain ("like to go to sleep and die"); the pervasive uncertainty ("if there is a God"); the fantasies of rescue ("somebody . . . that maybe could perform this miracle"); the resolute aspirations ("I would look upon myself as a better man"); the incredulity ("It's so farfetched, so unreal. . . . It is a senseless death"); the dramatically changing interpersonal relationships ("I've let her love me"); the deep feelings of unfairness ("a perfectly good person . . . is going to die"); the concern with reputation after death ("I don't feel like I'm making much of a tape for you"); and the fight against pain ("I'm giving up. I want it to be over").

There are some of the themes that occur, and recur, when one is terminally ill and (barely) living with the growing threat of death. They are human fantasies, thoughts and emotions—that is to say, they are universal human experiences—that are in us from infancy, but are brought out (in different combinations) when we are severely threatened by the specter of the dreaded unknown.

Although the themes are often the same, there is not *one* way to die. Each person dies in a notably personal way.[1]

In current thanatology there are those—notably Elisabeth Kübler-Ross[2]—who write about a set of five "stages" of dying, experienced in a specified order. My own experiences have led me to radically different conclusions, so that I reject the notion that human beings, as they die, are somehow marched in lock step through a series of stages of the dying process. On the contrary, in working with dying persons, I see a wide panoply of human feelings and emotions, of various human needs, and a broad selection of psychological defenses and maneuvers—a few of these in some people, dozens in others—experienced in an impressive variety of ways.

Loma Feigenberg, an eminent Swedish thanatologist at the Karolinska Hospital, puts it this way:

> Kübler-Ross, whose work and widely read book have unquestionably been of far-reaching importance for the "new" thanatology, has divided dying into stages of its psychological aspects. . . . This system rests on her impressions and she has not presented a proper study in which they are verified. The eagerness and satisfaction with which this division into five stages has been adopted in many quarters are remarkable. It is as though this regular sequence in the confusing variety of dying has given many people a sense of security and confidence.
>
> Avery Weisman wrote recently: "Schematic stages—denial, anger, bargaining, depression, acceptance— are at best approximations, and at worst, obstacles for individualization."
>
> Nor is the question of stages in dying simply of theoretical thanatological interest—it also has a bearing on practical clinical work with the dying. Whatever her intentions may have been, the fact remains that the stages of Kübler-Ross have come to be regarded as a check-list for the process of dying. Each stage is expected to follow the one before it in the given sequence. And if a patient clearly deviates from this pattern, one is now liable to hear from the hospital staff that his dying is "wrong."[3]

The emotional states, the psychological mechanisms of defense, the needs and drives, are as variegated in the dying as they are in the nondying, although they focus—understandably, given the life-threatening situation—on some of the less euphoric aspects of life. They include such reactions as stoicism, rage, guilt, terror, cringing, fear, surrender, heroism, dependency, ennui, need for control, fight for autonomy and dignity, and denial.

It is important for a potential helper to avoid seeing a dichotomy between the "living" and the "dying." Most people who are seriously ill with a life-threatening disease—unless they are in extended coma—are very much alive, often exquisitely attuned to the symphony of emotions within themselves and the band of feelings of those about them. To tell a person that he or she has cancer may change that person's inner mental life irretrievably, but it does not lobotomize that person into a psychologically nonfunctioning human being; on the contrary, it may stimulate that person to consider a variety of concerns and reactions.

Nor is there any natural law—as those who talk about acceptance as the final stage of dying would seem to assert—that an individual has to achieve a state of psychoanalytic grace or any other kind of closure before death sets its seal. The cold fact is that most people die too soon or too late, with loose threads and fragments of life's agenda uncompleted.

My own notion of the psychology of dying—leaning heavily on general personality theory and the careful, detailed long-term approach to the study of human behavior by Dr. Henry A. Murray[4]—is that each individual tends to die as he or she has lived, especially as he or she has previously reacted in periods of threat, stress, failure, challenge, shock and loss. In this context I can paraphrase the nineteenth-century German biologist Haeckel's famous dictum and say that, in a sense, *oncology recapitulates ontogeny*—by which I mean that, roughly speaking, the course of an individual's life while he or she is dying over time, say of cancer, duplicates or mirrors or parallels the course of the life during its "dark periods"; that is, one dies as one has lived in the terrible moments of one's life.

To anticipate how a person will behave as he or she dies, we look at neither the plateaus nor the highlights of the life, but we search, as an eminent cancer doctor has recently put it, "in the hollow of the waves." Dying is stressful, thus it makes sense to look at previous episodes in one's life that would appear to be comparable or parallel or psychologically similar. There are certain deep consistencies in all human beings. An individual lives characteristically as he or she has lived in the past; and dying is living. There are no set phases. People live differently; people die differently—much as they have lived during previous episodes in their lives that were, to them, presages of their final dying period. My assertion is that the psychological history of the individual while he has cancer mirrors or reflects that same person's psychological history, in comparable periods, throughout his lifetime.

A recent article by Dr. John Hinton[5] reports a study of sixty terminally ill cancer patients. The study inquired into the relationship of each patient's personality and state of mind before and during the illness. The results indicated that we need to know the individual's previous patterns of handling life's demands *in detail*—the dozens of ways in which an individual has been strong, long-suffering, aggressive, weak, passive, fearful, and all the rest.

Hinton's findings (although tentative) are thought-provoking:

> Facing problems: This is the quality of previous character described by the husband or wife to indicate that the patient was one who coped effectively with life's demands rather than avoiding issues. It does appear to influence the most during the terminal illness. The uniform trend was for those who had previously coped well to be less depressed, anxious or irritable and to show less social withdrawal. This was one of the more consistent significant findings in the whole study.... Past difficulties in coping also increased the likelihood of current depression and anxiety.... there is support for the frequent impression that a patient's previous manner of living influences the way he dies.

All this suggests that if one could know a great deal about the other person (over the span of the entire life), then one could make accurate statements about future behavior that would not be simply prediction in the ordinary sense but would be more like reasoned extrapolations from that individual's past patterns of behavior.

The stressful periods in one's life do not always relate to illnesses. They might be tied to failures or threats in one's career or love life, the welfare or well-being of one's loved ones. Many a husband has had elevated blood pressure at the time of his wife's surgery, and vice versa. Among some groups whom anthropologists have studied, there is a condition called couvade, in which the husband takes to his bed and experiences labor pains during the time that his wife is giving birth to their child.

In her brilliant book *Illness as Metaphor*, Susan Sontag, who herself has had cancer, has written about two diseases: tuberculosis (and the curiously romanticized connotations that have been associated with that disease) and cancer (and the pejorative ideas that have accrued to it). She begins by invoking the image of two worlds—the world of the well and the world of the ill—in which illness is the night side of life, the more onerous citizenship. Sooner or later everyone is obligated, at least temporarily, to be identified as a citizen of the kingdom of the sick.[6]

To this compelling metaphor I would add yet a third kingdom: the world of the dying. There is a vast difference between being ill (feeling bad and having pain) and suffering from a life-threatening disease. There is an enormous psychological distance between being told one simply has an illness and being informed that one has a terminal inner enemy. "Being ill" and "dying" are quite different. When your life's passport has been stamped "Dying," it is like having it revoked—and it means that your capacity to travel, even back to the land of "just being sick," has been terminated.

In an intensive interpersonal exchange with a dying person, the focus is special. In this situation, the eye is on the calendar. The dying person usually introduces the topics of death and dying; the helper should not run from them. Conscious and unconscious meanings are sometimes blurred by the irrationality of death itself.

As I think of my own psychotherapeutic work with dying persons, it seems to me that I have been guided by the following principles, goals and beliefs:[7]

1. *The goal of increased psychological comfort.* The main goal of working with the dying person—in the visits, the give-and-take of talk, the advice, the interpretations, the listening—is to increase that individual's psychological *comfort.* One cannot realistically be Pollyannish or, sometimes, even optimistic; the helper begins in a grim situation which will probably become even grimmer.

2. *The autonomy of the individual.* This idea is based on respect for the individual. The opportunities to control one's own treatment, to maintain a sense of dignity and to be as free as possible of unnecessary pain[8] should not be snatched from a person simply because he or she is dying. People should not be reduced to patients; their status as citizens and as human beings should be maintained.

The next document is by a university professor* with amyotrophic lateral sclerosis (ALS), a life-threatening neuromuscular disease. In "Notes of a Dying Professor" and "More Notes of a Dying Professor," he related some of his bitter experiences[9]—his shattering interactions with doctors and hospital personnel—and his reflections on (and implied criticisms of) the manner in which he was being treated.

> After his cursory examination I began to realize that he was becoming increasingly non-communicative. And that alarmed me. What is he not telling me? And he became very grave and serious in his general demeanor. I asked him what he thought it was, but could get no reply. . . . He then let me know that I should see a neurologist immediately. . . . The neurologist was cold, aloof, highly efficient. . . . there began the growing sense from him that this was something serious. . . . I kept pressing him for a response but there was absolutely no response at all. And the non-verbal response, the avoidance itself generates considerable anxiety, fear and confusion on the part of any patient in that kind of situation.
>
> I felt treated as an object. Being a patient is one thing, but being an object is even less than being a patient. And I began to feel not only the fear of this unknown dread thing that I have, that nobody knows anything about—and if they know, they're not going to tell me—but an anger and resentment of "Goddamn it, I'm a human being and I want to be treated like one!"

Consider, in this case, what modern medicine has done. It lets us know almost as soon as possible (in ways ranging from the inadvertently cruel to the sympathetically "very regretfully") that we have a truncated period to live. It places over our heads a sword of Damocles with a time device that will cut the life string, and then it conscientiously devotes its considerable scientific

*The late Archie J. Hanlan, Associate Professor of Social Work, University of Pennsylvania.

energies to saving our somatic selves, while often, at the same time, but with no malice, either disregarding our deepest needs or otherwise unwittingly traumatizing our personalities and psyches.

The saddest part of this paradox is that it need not occur. Medicine could (and should) do both: it could treat the soma and at the same time unfailingly interact in a psychologically supporting way. In theory at least, except for the doctor's own possible neuroses, there are no persuasive reasons why doctors cannot recognize their patient's terrors and anxieties and insecurities in stressful situations, communicate so as best to allay those anxieties, and generally interact with their patients—puting aside the cloak of the mystique of the medicine man—exactly as they would want a colleague to interact with them if they themselves had a grave illness.

You don't have to be anybody to die, and you shouldn't have to be highly placed in society to die well. It is obvious that one is more likely to die well if one has ego strength at the beginning of the trial and if one is lucky and has a good support system of loving people in one's life, and lastly, if that system (including especially the way in which the art of medicine is practiced on you) will let you.

3. *The importance of transference.* In any list of Freud's core ideas, the concept of "transference" would have to be included. That notion holds that human beings tend to relate to certain other "figures" in their lives—doctors, teachers, policemen, servants, etc.—in ways that mirror their own deep need for love, or fear of authority, or disdain for weakness, etc. These feelings and needs stem from their early unconscious reactions toward their own parents and siblings; that is, they have a built-in proclivity for quickly transferring rather important feelings to another person. Transference can be both positive ("I like you") or its opposite ("I dislike you").

Here is an extraordinary excerpt from a therapy session illustrating the concept of transference. The patient is a lovely woman in her fifties, dying (now dead) of metastasized cancer of the breast. Her positive transference to me was an obviously comforting force in her dying days. This session occurred on a day when there had been a heavy rainstorm.

P: It's good to be indoors. I don't want to stop coming just because of the rain. I don't want to cancel unless I absolutely have to. Because I think once you start canceling you think, Well, I just don't feel well or I'm just too tired or something like that and just cancel.

S: Your coming here in this heavy rainstorm raises an interesting question which is appropriate to ask in this setting. What do you get out of these sessions?

P: I don't know. I kind of enjoy them. Talking about things that I haven't thought of for ages and ages. I don't seem to be quite as nervous as I was. Of course, I'm taking some Valium. And I like to hear your thoughts. Oh, then you make me think of things that I haven't thought of before. I don't know what I'm supposed to get from these sessions. I've never been in therapy. Comfort, I suppose. I don't know whether it's a combination of drugs and seeing you, but I am more comforted.

s: I'll now ask a question that only a psychotherapist would ask: What do you think of me?

p: I think you're very kind and you're very easy to talk to, and when there are gaps and I don't have much to say, why, you fill them in with interesting things, like when I'm floundering. You don't expect too much of me. And then, I think you understand the way I feel.

s: Do you like me? [Yes.] Why is that?

p: All those things, I guess.

s: Do I remind you of anyone? I don't mean in appearance or superficials or dress or status. [No.] Well, you've attributed to me some admirable human traits. Never mind whether those attributions are realistic. There have been other people in your life who have had those same traits. Who comes to mind when it's put in those terms?

p: Well, I guess probably you're the person I come to see because I'm troubled, so I guess it would be my mother, that I went to when I was in trouble. I didn't go to my father particularly. We loved each other dearly but we weren't able to communicate, but I could communicate very well with my mother, on anything. And we had a very close relationship, mother-daughter and just friends. But I can still talk more freely in front of you about things. There are some things I'd be ashamed to tell Mother. . . . Mother was like my nurse, my nanny, she was everything combined. I loved her very, very much. She was so gentle and so easy to talk to and so understanding. And she talked to me too, if she had any problems, so we talked to each other as if we were contemporaries. I really don't know why Dad and I could never let down the barriers, because we were terribly fond of each other.

s: You were terribly fond of your father; you deeply loved your mother.

p: I didn't see Dad that much. He was often away on business. But Mother was always around, always there when I came home from school, from the time I was very little. I can't ever remember an occasion when she wasn't there.

s: So you had a feeling of safety all through your life—at least until recently. [Yes.] You were blessed; you had relatively few psychological traumas in your childhood.

p: I had practically none. The only time I can remember being mad at Mother—and you'll understand it wasn't exactly Mother's fault—was when Charles [her husband] was ordered overseas for military duty, and I remember that first night when I went back home and Mother came into my room to kiss me good night and I told her that I wasn't ever going to let this happen to my little girl; I wasn't going to take my little girl's husband away like that. I was crying and sort of accusing Mother. And I remember that I apologized later, I went to her room, because I realized that what I had been saying was stupid, that I wasn't going to let the war take my little girl's husband away and blaming it on my mother.

s: It's understandable that you would have at that moment seemed to blame your mother for that loss.

p: Why? Why did I do that?

s: Oh, for a rather simple reason. You had looked to her to give you everything and to protect you from everything. She had done an almost one hundred percent job. In your head you had an absolutely magical feeling about her. She could do anything. You were as certain of your mother's being there as you were of the sun's coming up. And even though you were an adult and married, you were still a little girl, as in some ways you still are. That's in everybody. We never outgrow those feelings. And in that irrational moment, when you were crying, your major premise was, Mother, you can handle everything. It discounts the fact that there was a world war going on.

p: And she failed me.

s: And that makes psychological sense in the unconscious even if it doesn't make conscious sense.

p: No, it certainly doesn't.

s: But that's how the mind works. That's one of the most psychologically honest moments in your life. And then you say, I didn't mean it, but what you really mean is that you didn't mean it consciously, you meant it unconsciously, and it's really a message that contains a great compliment to your mother, because it implies that she's omnipotent. That's a beautiful moment really. It makes absolute sense in that way.

p: Yes, it does now. It didn't make any sense to me at all, all these years—after I said it or even since—until just now. Now I understand it.

s: And me? What omnipotent thing do you expect from me?

p: To cure my cancer, I suppose. . . .

Along these same lines, here, from Vilhelm Moberg's Swedish classic work of fiction, *The Emigrants*, are the words that Anna, Karl Oskar's eldest and favorite child, calls out to him as she is dying of a ruptured stomach:

It hurts to die, Father. I don't want God to fetch me if it is so painful. I want to stay home. Couldn't I stay home—please let me stay home! You're so big and strong, Father, can't you protect me so God can't take me? . . . I am so little. Would you like to die, Father? Do you want God to come and get you?[10]

In this moving passage we see that subtle but vital difference between the omnipotence that the child projects on her parents (and the patient on her therapist) as surrogates of the Almighty, and the *real* or unescapable omnipotence of Nature Itself or God Himself. And we also see the implied threat of the victim to the heretofore supposed omnipotent father (or therapist) that if you will play God, then the real God will punish you: "Do you want God to come and get you [too]?"

4. *The goals are limited.* There is an understandable underlying concern with "success" in the motivational system of any effective therapist. With a dying patient, the therapist must realign his notions of what he can realistically do for that person. It is a process that no matter how auspiciously begun or effectively conducted, often ends in death. We need to appreciate that very few individuals die right on psychological target with all their complexes and neuroses beautifully worked through. The therapist or helper needs to be able to tolerate incompleteness and lack of closure. No one ever untangles all the varied skeins of one's intrapsychic and interpersonal life; to the last second there are physical creations and re-creations that require new resolutions. Total insight is an abstraction; there is no golden mental homeostasis.

The goal of completely resolving life's problems may be an unattainable one. As Avery Weisman says, "The best death is one that an individual would choose for himself if the choice were possible." The dying person can be helped to put affairs in order—although everyone dies more or less psychologically intestate.

Because there are no specific substantive psychological goals (for example, *this* insight or coming to *that* understanding), *the* emphasis is on the relationship and on the helper's continued presence. Nothing *has* to be accomplished. The patient sets the pace, determining even whether or not the topic of death is mentioned—although, if permitted, it usually will be. The "method of successive approximations" is useful, in which a dying person may be permitted to say, over the course of many days, I have a problem, an illness, a tumor, a malignancy, a cancer, a terminal metastasis. Different individuals get in touch with their illness at various points of candor. As helpers, all of us tend to evaluate our own performance in relation to how much we have given comfort in the death of another. In our own minds, we ruminate that the death of a grandparent, or a parent, or a sibling or a friend or a patient has gone well or poorly, and we feel different amounts of pride, guilt, or shame, depending on the role that we ourselves played in that death. It is clear to me, for example, how I feel about Marion, the young man who died of leukemia, described earlier in this chapter.

When I think of Marion, I mourn his death and I have relatively good feelings about having helped him resolve many conflicts within himself and, best of all, having helped to reunite him with his mother. It was a beautiful experience for him and his mother. It was the most important single thing that could have happened within the awful context of his dying.

My memories of another case are not quite triumphant. In fact, I have a sense of rather abysmal failure in one vital aspect of my work with a fifty-year-old woman who died of lymphosarcoma. Our close psychological relationship served to help her. But in my interactions with her I lost sight of a rule which I constantly attempt to teach to others: To work from the beginning with the important survivors-to-be. She had been divorced for years and did not even know (or care) where her ex-husband was; but she had a grown son—and she zealously (or jealously) kept me from talking with him. I met him briefly only once in her hospital room and she was embarrassingly rude to him. It is clear to me now that in spite of her implicit wishes to the contrary,

I should have telephoned him and talked with him early in my contacts with her. You will know how keenly I feel about this when you learn that he died the day after she did. The facts, as nearly as I can learn them, are that he burned to death in his apartment from a fire caused by a short-circuit in his radio. The coroner called it an accident. But the ghastly timing of his death left me with an overwhelmingly uneasy feeling. There is no question but that I should have been in close contact with her only son from the very beginning of my work with her.

Here is a tender, almost humorous rutter for dying (not of cancer, but of simply wearing out of the human body). It was written by a learned physician, pensive in the twilight of his own life. It is by Hans Zinsser, from his autobiography, called *As I Remember Him*. In the unusual paragraphs below, Zinsser is gently berating the various organs of his own body for finally letting him down—but one senses that he also is somehow tolerant of his whole process of catabolism and disrepair, knowing that it is a part of nature's course that this decline inexorably occurs.

Here I am, *me* as always. My mind more alive and vivid than ever before; my sensitiveness keener; my affections stronger. I seem for the first time to see the world in clear perspective; I love people more deeply and more comprehensively; I seem to be just beginning to learn my business and see my work in its proper relationship to science as a whole; I seem to myself to have entered into a period of stronger feelings and saner understanding. And yet here am I— essentially unchanged except for a sort of distillation into a more concentrated me—held in a damaged body which will extinguish me with it when it dies. If it were a horse I was riding that went lame or broke its neck, or a ship on which I was travelling that sprang a leak, I could transfer to another one and leave the old vehicle behind. As it is, my mind and my spirit, my thoughts and my love, all that I really am, is inseparably tied up with the failing capacities of these outworn organs.

Yet, . . . [to] continue apostrophizing in a serio-comic mood, poor viscera, I can hardly blame you! You have done your best, and have served me better than could be expected of organs so abused. When I think of the things that have flowed over and through you! Innumerable varieties of fermented hops and malt and of the grapes of all countries and climates . . . to say nothing of the distillates—Scotch, Irish, Canadian, rye, bourbon, and the yellowish moonshine, colored with chicken droppings from the Blue Hills; and gin, genuine and synthetic; Schliyovitz from the Balkans, Starka from Poland, and the vodka of the Steppes; creme de menthe and cacao, Marie Brizard, Cointreau and Calvados.

No, no, my organs! I cannot feel that you have let me down. It is quite the other way around. Only now it seems so silly that you must take me with you when I am just beginning to get dry behind the ears.[11]

Those failing, "outworn organs" are the paradigm of the dying process. Cancer is simply a dramatic and painful acceleration of this catabolic curve. And as Zinsser says and as everybody knows, when the hardware of the body goes, it takes with it the mind—the psyche, the person as he introspectively knows himself. That is what death is: it is the stopping of the working of someone's mind. You can die but you can never experience death itself. There is death only for the survivor. As the eminent American scientist-philosopher Percy Bridgman said: "*I am always alive.*"

What is striking about these relatively rare memoirs of terminal illness is how their writers wish to communicate not only love and concern, but also—in an almost obsessed way—to share thoughts about the disease and about the dying process itself. These thoughts include the effects of the disease, the ways in which they were told of it, the impact of the diagnosis, concern over the prognosis, and reflections on the dramatic changes in self-image created by the very label of the disease.

The following is from the preface of a book—*Stay of Execution*—that has had wide circulation. It was written by the well-known author and journalist Stewart Alsop:

> This is a peculiar book. I have two reasons, or excuses, for writing it. First I have myself quite often wondered what it would be like to be told that I had an inoperable and lethal cancer, and I suspect a lot of other people have wondered the same thing. If a writer has had an unusual experience likely to interest a good many people, he has an instinct, and perhaps even a duty, to write about it. Second, after I had been told my remaining span of life would be short, I began to think back quite often about the life behind me. . . . In a way, no experience has been more interesting than living in intermittent intimacy with the gentleman W. C. Fields used to call "the man in the white nightgown" and whom I have come to think of as Uncle Thanatos, and sometimes, when I had been feeling very sick, as dear old Uncle Thanatos. Death is, after all, the only universal experience except birth, and although a sensible person hopes to put it off as long as possible, it is, even in anticipation, an interesting experience.

By the very title of Alsop's book he reminds us of the trauma of others for whom a fatal sentence of death has been ordered, seemingly mercifully lifted and then inexorably enforced. What seemed like a reprieve was only a postponement. Further, in that title Alsop implies a basic question, and in his text he explicitly raises it: Are the postponement and the temporary stay worth it? His veiled answer is partially contained in these paragraphs:

> What were the chances of successful remission?
> Better than 50 percent, he said. . . .
> How long would a remission last?
> "We have an AML [Acute Myelocytic Leukemia—the most common type of leukemia in adults] patient here in the hospital tonight," he said cheerfully. "He's been in remission for seven years. . . ."
> But what was the average?

"About fifty percent of our patients with AML who go into remission last a year or more...."

How many died before two years?

Dr. Glick hesitated a moment. "About ninety-five percent," he said, and briskly changed the subject....

The night was a bad night.... I thought about what Dr. Glick had told me....

Would it really be worthwhile to spend a month or more cooped up all alone in a laminar flow room, losing my hair and my flesh, either to die in the room or emerge a bald skeleton and wait for death? Would it not be more sensible to reach for Hamlet's "bare bodkin," in the shape of a bottle of sleeping pills? And then a sense of the reality of death crowded in on me—the end of a pleasant life, never to see Tish or Andrew or Nicky or the four older children again, never to go to Needwood again or laugh with friends, or see the spring come. There came upon me a terrible sense of aloneness, of vulnerability, of nakedness, of helplessness. I got up, and fumbled in my shaving kit, and found another sleeping pill, and at last dozed off.

I never again had a night as bad as that night, nor, I think, shall I ever again. For a kind of protective mechanism took over, after the first shock of being told of the imminence of death, and I suspect that this is true of most people. Partly, this is a perfectly conscious act of will—a decision to allot to the grim future only its share of your thoughts and no more.

The conscious effort to close off one's mind, or part of it, to the inevitability of death plays a part, I suspect, in the oddly cheerful tone of much of what I've written in this book. I instinctively preferred, for example, to recall episodes that had amused me during the war, like my first meeting with Tish, rather than the times when I was unhappy or afraid. In the same way, I remember from my career as a journalist those episodes that amused me, rather than those to which some profound meaning might be attached.

The protective mechanism is also an unconscious reaction, I think. I remember seeing much the same process at work in combat. There is the first sudden shock of realizing that the people on the other side are really trying to kill you.... But, the incredulity soon wears off and a kind of unhappy inner stolidity takes over, coupled with a strong protective instinct that the shell or the bullet or the mine will kill somebody else—not me.

In this way, the unbearable becomes bearable, and one learns to live with death by not thinking about it too much.[12]

In those paragraphs, Alsop, all by himself, seems to have rediscovered Freud's concepts of suppression, repression and denial. In his tender and insightful psychological writing, we see the appearance of the gyroscopic protector, the greatest of all of nature's anesthetics: denial—to push down in consciousness (into the unconscious of the mind) those thoughts and fears that might threaten to overwhelm us.

Let us now turn to another genuine death rutter—one written with the precise intention of being a guide for those who come after. It is by a young psychiatrist, dying of leukemia. (The document was given to me by his former mentor, Dr. Eugene Pumpian-Mindlin.) Here, with only a few emendations, is the young doctor's essay on his own dying.

The idea of this essay was conceived in November but lay fallow until May of the following year [he died two months later] because of my inability to delineate clearly both the objective and the content of this paper. The passage of time has, of itself, provided some jelling of the ideas and content which, for a time, were so amorphous and jumbled in my mind. My reasons for writing this paper are to objectify and clarify my own feelings regarding my illness, to help crystallize my perspective on matters of living and dying, and to inform others in a subjective way about the psychological processes that take place in a person who has a life-threatening disease.

A narration of the chronological events pertaining to my predicament is in order to keep the reader properly oriented. In November I discovered that I had acute myelogenous leukemia. This discovery was quite by accident and did not occur because of any perception of anything seriously amiss. I had noticed one evening that I had a number of petechiae [tiny blood splotches on the skin]. The following day I saw a physician who was a friend, and he recommended, after examining me and finding nothing unusual, that some blood tests be performed. This led to the ultimate diagnosis by bone marrow examination of the true picture. The next day the hematologist who had subsequently examined me and examined the slides of blood and bone marrow very reluctantly told me that I had this disease.

My initial reactions are difficult to describe and still more difficult to recall accurately. However, I do remember feeling that somehow the doctor's remarks could not be directed to me but must be about some other person. Of course, I shook off that feeling very soon during this conversation as the full realization of the import of this diagnosis struck me. I was steeped in a pervasive sense of deep and bitter disappointment. I thought that I had been maliciously cheated out of the realization of all the hopes and aims that I had accrued during my professional career. I was in the third year of my psychiatric residency and on the brink of fully developing a professional identity. Further, and more important, I was also on the threshold of developing a true sense of personal maturity and personal identity. I felt now this would all be denied me and I would never live to realize the fruit of the struggles in which I had been engaged for so long a time.

I immediately went to see my department chief and discovered that

he had already been informed. He was most kind and gracious and
extremely helpful in setting my skewed perspective back on the right
track. For that matter, from that moment onward I never wanted for
good counsel and enormous equanimity and maturity from my
supervisors and teachers, without whom I doubt I could have rallied
as well as I did.

The next subjective feeling I can clearly identify is that I was
increasingly apprehensive following the diagnosis about my inevitable
decreasing body efficiency and thus very likely my decreasing
efficiency and interest in my work. This engendered some little guilt
over my anticipating not being able to do the job I had been doing.
Indeed, because of the drugs it was necessary to take for the illness
and not really because of the illness itself, the capability of usual
performance was sharply curtailed. Luckily when I expressed such
feelings of guilt over not pulling my weight in the organization, this
was immediately squelched by my teachers, who were able to assuage
my unnecessarily hypertrophied super-ego, which has since become of
a much more manageable size. Nonetheless, I did have pangs of
remorse when I finally had to stop seeing long-term patients because
my physical symptoms interfered too much with appointments.
Surprisingly, I did not feel consciously angry or frightened by the
knowledge that I had a life-threatening illness.

I was gravely disappointed and terribly annoyed that this thing
inside my body would interfere with my life. But at no time did I really
feel, as one might put it, "angered at the gods" for having such sport
with me. Nor did I find that I used denial as a defense to any extent
early in the course of the illness, as I did later on when it appeared
that some of the chemotherapeutic measures were having
considerably good effect and I began to feel that I could go on
interminably from drug to drug and not die of my disease. Instead my
attention was directed away from my illness in its early phases by
some very practical matters which might be called "Setting My Affairs
in Order." I was so busy with this that it served quite well to focus on
an aspect of dying which is not connected with the disease process
itself and thus considerably deceased my own anxiety. There was an
enormous mobilization of energy to get things accomplished in this
regard by both me and my wife.

There were a number of changes we needed to make in our lives in
order to fulfill sooner than we had anticipated some of the
expectations we had about how we would live. Although a great many
things actually transpired, I shall mention only two or three as
examples. We first moved from a small rented apartment which was
adequate for our needs at the time to a larger house and we
purchased additional furniture. Because I was deeply interested in
music and particularly in composing, we borrowed a grand piano from
friends who were extremely gracious in allowing us to use it while

they were living in the area and did not find as much use for it as they had in the past.

My wife undertook practically all of the details of this move herself and also redecorated one of the three bedrooms we had in the home so that I might have a private study and library. When we got all these things accomplished, we took stock of the situation and came to the realization that it had not really required a serious illness to do these things because we had not overextended ourselves in any financial sense and we could have done all this before I got sick if we had really set our minds on it. . . . We had, in effect, denied ourselves some of the comfort of a real home and space in which to work for no valid practical reason.

My parents expressed shock, grief and disbelief over the situation. They worried about such things as how does one get such an illness or, perhaps more cogently, why *should* one get such an illness, reflecting, I suppose, a very common fantasy that such a thing must be some kind of a punishment—just or unjust—visited upon the victim. When it came to the question of informing my three young children about my illness, I was met with the question based on the precept "How could you do this to them just before Christmas?" I explained that it was far better for the children to understand precisely what it was that was going on, rather than permit them to develop their own fantasies about it which could very easily be far worse than the truth. The fact that it was close to Christmas was quite beside the point.

As a matter of fact, it gave me an opportunity to clarify personally some of the confusion I was sure existed about the nature of this disease. Indeed, there were a number of fantasies, doubts and fears which very much needed to be dispelled. They were prepared to some extent for a not-very-well father who had an illness that might easily take his life in a short period of time. One common fantasy of all of the children (unexpressed except through probing) was, "Is this thing contagious? Will I get it if I am close to you?" As soon as this was corrected, the children found themselves able to be much closer to me. As it turned out later, nearly all of the children with whom I had therapeutic contact had this same fantasy.

Some of my colleagues may very well have had similar fantasies. If they did, I have not discovered it but can only surmise it because there have been practically no contacts at all with some of the people with whom I worked since the inception of my illness. There has been some speculation on my part (reinforced to some extent by conversations with supervisors) that some of the people with whom I have had fairly close contact in the past found it almost impossible to deal with me and my illness because of their own fears and fantasies concerning death.

One almost amusing idea came to light through one of my supervisors, namely that some of my colleagues might very well be wishing that I would drop dead and get it over with rather than continue to torment them as I was. For others there was a heightened awareness of a close relationship that had never been verbalized in the past. This occurred with two or three of my fellow residents and certainly we were all the better for it. Not only was there some clarification of feelings and a chance openly to discuss them between us, but also this produced a closer relationship.

At all times I tried to make it clear that I in no way wanted to avoid open discussion of my illness. I did not want to play any games of pretending that I was better than I was (although I am prone to do so), nor did I want to avoid responding to questions about how I was from day to day under the assumption that to be reminded of my illness might hurt me. On the contrary, I felt somehow annoyed if I was not asked how things were going with me because I wanted to share with others feelings about my illness. One of my friends and teachers commented that one of the things that bothered him most was the destruction of his fantasies of omnipotence by the knowledge of my illness. In other words, there was nothing he could do to change the situation, although he wanted to very much. I imagine that many of my fellow residents felt the same way and they responded to this in a very constructive manner. They were discussing this one day among themselves and one of them suggested they donate blood, which most certainly I would eventually need, as a means of doing something positive and relieving the terrible feeling that there was nothing that could be done. This was, I think, of enormous help to them and, of course, to me too.

I was also repeatedly assured by my division chief that I should assume only the work that I felt really capable of doing efficiently. He would rather, he said, that I did less than I had been doing and do a good job of that, than try to put in a full day and have to drag around looking rather dreary, reminding other people that I was sick. This made good sense to me, so I was able to stay home part of the time after I started to feel less well without feeling guilty about it. I have been enormously buoyed up by the generous support of the staff and I hope they know how deeply grateful I am to them. At this point I was feeling very dismal about my prospects for any longevity and I was very glad to get all the support that I did. I did not enter the hospital but continued working and began a program of medication as an outpatient. This was a very important step because otherwise I might have been compelled to concentrate almost exclusively on the internal workings of my disabled body and not been able to continue working. As it turned out, this was one of the most important features of the total adaptation to this disease, because everybody made me feel that I was not giving up, despite the reduction in the time I actually spent at work.

The relationship between me and my wife was also exceedingly important at this time. At first, of course, she responded with remorse, sympathy and total understanding. As time progressed and it appeared that I was evincing some durability and I was pretty much my old self despite the shadow I lived under, she was able to express some of the deeper feelings concerning me and my illness which were not really seen by her as separate entities. Since then we have been able to share feelings, more openly than ever before, never to the detriment of either of us. People wrongly assume that a sick person should be "protected" from strong, and particularly negative, feelings. The truth is that there is probably no more crucial time in a person's life when he needs to know what's going on with those who are important to him.

In the several months since the inception of my illness I became increasingly aware of a new sensitivity that had gradually but progressively developed in my interpersonal relationships, both with patients and with all my acquaintances. The sensitivity of which I speak is rather elusive insofar as a clear definition is concerned, but perhaps I can resort to describing it in terms of its effect. One thing I noticed most pointedly was that I was very much more tolerant of the vagaries and inconsistencies of other people's attitudes and behavior than I had ever been before. Perhaps "tolerant" is not a very good word. It might be better to use the word "understanding," because many times I have found myself perceiving very quickly what lay beneath a particular person's attitude or affect which did not seem altogether appropriate to the situation. Thus I found myself much more at ease with people whom I have found difficult to tolerate in the past. Some people commented they found it easy to be with me because I openly invited questions about my illness.

This heightened awareness of affect in others also extended to myself and I found that my own feelings were much more accessible to my conscious recognition than they had been in the past. I also found that all of my senses seemed more acute, though I believe that really I simply paid more attention to what was going on around me and, in a way, I found myself hungering for every sensory experience that I could absorb. In many ways the world seemed to offer more beauty and there was a heightened awareness of sounds and sights, which in the past I may have only casually observed or simply not have paid much attention to at all. Aside from the sensory and affective sensitivity which I had seemed to acquire, there appeared to me to be a culmination of all the learning experience that I had in my professional career, which, in a compressed space of time, became the foundation for practically a new way of life. Another way to put this is that there was quite suddenly an integration of all the values and understanding I had of human experience into some kind of cohesive whole which, although difficult to describe, made extremely good sense to me.

This brings me to a question which I had earlier put aside: What happened to all the anger and depression which should have occurred after the news of my illness? I think I know. It would seem that the struggles I had with myself had not been in vain and it was fortunate that I was where I was at the time all this happened, since I had a great deal of psychological help available to me. At any rate, it would appear that the peace I made with myself during my illness and the maturing ability that I was developing to cope with life crises like this one arose from several dynamic factors. One was the increasing capacity to sublimate the rage and aggression engendered by the impotency I felt regarding this invasion from within. Instead of striking blindly outwardly or, probably more likely, addressing the anger inward and thus becoming depressed, I became intensely involved in musical composition and composed practically like a madman for the first several weeks of my illness, completing one larger work and two smaller ones, which represented in that space of time more output in this field of art than I had ever been able to accomplish in the past.

This outlet proved so effective that it was very seldom that I was conscious of any feelings of despair or depression. Indeed, I suspect that when they began to reach consciousness I would begin furiously (and I use the word quite deliberately) to become creatively involved, and thus dispel the unpleasant affect. Certain instruments lend themselves to this kind of alteration in the discharge of affect better than others. For example, the percussion instruments, which in a sense include the piano, are really excellent ways to deal with the aggressive energy present in everyone. But it is revealing to cite the ways I thought of working with music in these past few months. I would attack the piano, I would literally hammer out a new piece.

> Certainly there are rewarding aspects of facing life-threatening illness. I have learned much about the alterations in my own internal psychological processes, and the subtle metamorphosis in interpersonal relationships which have occurred and are still occurring.
>
> By way of completing this little essay I might comment that in a way I have, at least intellectually, accepted and I hope that I can wholeheartedly embrace the idea that the death of an individual is really no more nor less than a punctuation mark in the endlessly fascinating conversation amongst all living things.[13]

Such a document is an unusual rutter because it describes the tone of a relatively calm voyage through admittedly stormy seas. It is a case where the enormously bad luck of leukemia falls on a relatively—up until then—lucky person: a physician, with a loving wife, an outlet in his music, and actively supporting supervisors and colleagues (and even patients)—in short, a person who has what is necessary for a good passage through the dying period: a strong support system. Consider even such details as the way in which he is treated by his physician and his department chief: "the hematologist . . . very reluctantly told me"; "my department chief . . . was most kind and gracious and extremely helpful." Those are tiny rays of the sun peeking through extremely dark clouds, which are sometimes just enough to make an absolutely gloomy time a little less intolerable.

The extraordinary public death from cancer of Hubert Humphrey can be a guiding example to some of one kind of "appropriate death." His published utterances about his cancer, his state of health and his death probably can stimulate many of us to think about our own way of dying.

Humphrey was an open man. (His autobiography is called *The Education of a Public Man*.)[14] Not only a gregarious man—"It was hard to tell where he left off and the people began," as Carl Sandburg had said of Lincoln—but also, in a pleasant sense, a man owned by the people. His dying was, in a remarkable way, a community experience. Toward the end, around Christmas time of 1977, he did not hide from the press or from his fellow citizens, but considering his state of health, gave rather freely and answered some pointed personal questions. It is the manner of his responding to these questions, the quality of his banter, his candor and his unique use of humor over the course of his illness that were special.

The insidious growth of Humphrey's cancer is now a matter of record.

1966–1968: First appearance of blood in urine (hematuria). Nonmalignant papillomas (small tumors) found in his bladder. Several removed over the next few years. No press announcements; no public utterances about his medical condition.

1973: A cancer-like tumor—a borderline or possible cancer found in his bladder. No press announcement.

Late 1973: Radiation (x-ray) treatments, almost daily for six weeks. Not even his colleagues were aware of this.

January 1974: First public disclosure of his serious bladder difficulties.

September 1976: Another tumor found in bladder. First mention of cancer.

Early October 1976: Surgical removal of his bladder (at the Memorial Sloan-Kettering Cancer Center in New York City). Subsequent chemotherapy. Detailed newspaper coverage.

Mid August 1977: Intestinal blockage. Colostomy performed at the University of Minnesota Hospital. Subsequent public announcement by his physicians of an inoperable pelvic tumor. His situation was then described as terminal.

January 12, 1978: A bulletin from his home in which he is described as noticeably weakened, but resting comfortably. His situation is listed as critical. The bulletin also stated that it was not planned that he would return to the hospital.

January 13, 1978: Hubert Humphrey died in Waverly, Minnesota.

Among Humphrey's public utterances about his own cancer, here is a typical remark which shows him not succumbing either to self-pity or to deep pessimism: "Deep down, I believe in miracles. They have happened to a lot of people who have been given up to die and then restored to health. If you don't overcome self-pity, the game is all over."

This is not to say that there were not moments of despair, but when Humphrey touched on those moments he separated them from everything else he said by using the word "honestly," by which he must have meant personally, candidly. In August of 1977, reflecting on his x-ray treatments in 1973, which had caused spasms in his bladder, he confessed: "I was in so much agony that I honestly wanted to give it up."[15] During that time he was secretly receiving treatments in the morning and going to his tasks in the Senate. Not even his Senate colleagues knew of his excruciating pains.

His public image was that of a fighter. On September 19, 1977, interviewed in Minnesota, he said, "I'm not ready to have somebody cover me up." But by then everybody knew that he was ailing and on a downhill course. On October 25, 1977, he returned to the Senate after an eleven-week absence during which he was hospitalized and operated upon and had permitted an announcement that he had an inoperable malignant pelvic tumor. On the Senate floor he responded to the affection of his colleagues. His remarks were emotional, sentimental, yet optimistic. The key words are "friendship" and "self-reliance": love of others flowing from inner strength.

> The greatest healing therapy is friendship and love, and over this land
> I have sensed it. Doctors, chemicals, radiation, pills, nurses, therapists
> are all very, very helpful. But without faith in yourself and your own
> ability to overcome your own difficulties, faith in divine Providence
> and without the friendship and kindness and generosity of friends,
> there is no healing.[16]

There was yet another characteristic nuance to Humphrey's public statements, especially those unprepared remarks in response to questions from reporters: it was the quality of humor; wry statements with double entendre. Here are two examples:

Late in 1977, after meeting privately with President Carter, Humphrey was asked what the two of them had talked about. His response included the remark that he had assured the President that he would not run against him in 1980. When one thinks about it, one immediately sees that it is a touching statement, said in a light-hearted but profound way.

The second example of this kind of buoyancy covering deeper and more lugubrious meanings occurred when he went home to Minnesota for the last time. This exchange took place, on December 23, 1977, at the Minneapolis airport:

AIDE: Excuse me, we have time for one last question.

REPORTER: Senator, do you want to scotch all those rumors about resignation?

HUMPHREY: Oh, I'm not resigning from anything. I may even join something. The [Senate] pay is good, the working conditions are good, and I like my associates. No, no, I have no intention of resigning. The only way that could happen is if I were totally incapacitated and I'm a long way from that, fellows. Have fun. Merry Christmas.

PHOTOGRAPHER: Same to you, Senator, same to you. Hey, Senator, God bless you.[17]

Five months before Hubert Humphrey died, his doctors announced to the press—we must assume with his approval—that they had found a metastasized tumor that had spread to his pelvic bone; further, that the condition was medically inoperable, and that his situation was terminal. That announcement came from the University of Minnesota Hospital on August 18, 1977. Thereafter, the world either had to shun Humphrey as a leper and pariah (because of the social stigma of terminal cancer) or, because of who he was and the way in which he conducted himself, accept him as he was. The fact is, he was accepted and *premourned*—by President Carter at Camp David, by the entire Senate and by large segments of the populace—as perhaps no one else in American history has been. If, as Vice President Mondale said after Humphrey's death, he was an A-OK guy, Humphrey made it also A-OK to come out of the closet with cancer.

As important as Humphrey's providing a role model on how to die was the impact of his behavior on our ideas of the loathsomeness of cancer. In his dying months, he helped decontaminate cancer.

In his political and personal losses, Humphrey displayed both a certain realism and a touch of incredulity that never quite crossed over into incapacitating bitterness, and, withal, a certain buoyant optimism. In the end Humphrey was an undiluted winner.

The historic photograph (of January 15, 1978) of the assemblage behind Humphrey's catafalque in the rotunda of the Capitol—including Mrs. Humphrey, Carter, Ford, Nixon, Kissinger—shows many interesting facets. Among them is the deep contrast between the man who wanted to be President and the man who had beaten him for the presidency. It is a contrast that has only sharpened with time. There is Nixon, looking funereal and defeated, and the unseen Humphrey, nobly canonized within his coffin.

Humphrey salvaged some redeeming elements from his defeats by using his own special approach to the hollows in the waves of life. He saved for himself (and bequeathed to the rest of us) some worthwhile elements in his dying. There was a consistency in his living while he was well and his living when he was ill. But in Humphrey it is not so much the consistency we admire, as it is the style of it.

Humphrey did not lie to us about his cancer. He did not conceal from us its ravaging effects. We all knew that he wore a colostomy bag. But he did all this with a dignity and a good humor that absolutely undercut the baleful metaphors associated with that disease. In his openness and sharing, he helped change our notions of cancer itself. He is an important figure in the history of medicine.

1 A. Draper, C. W. Dupertuis and J. L. Caughley, *Human Constitution in Clinical Medicine* (New York: Hoeber, 1944).

2 Elisabeth Kübler-Ross, *On Death and Dying* (New York: Macmillan, 1969).

3 Loma Feigenberg, *Terminal Care: Friendship Contracts with Dying Cancer Patients* (New York: Brunner/Mazel, 1980).

4 Henry A. Murray, *Explorations in Personality* (London and New York: Oxford University Press, 1938); also, E. S. Shneidman, ed., *Endeavors in Psychology: Selections from the Personology of Henry A. Murray* (New York: Harper & Row, 1981).

5 John Hinton, "The Influences of Previous Personality on Reactions to Having Terminal Cancer," *Omega*, 1975, Vol. 6, No. 2, pp. 95–111.

6 Susan Sontag, *Illness as Metaphor* (New York: Farrar, Straus & Giroux, 1978).

7 Edwin S. Shneidman, "Some Aspects of Psychotherapy with Dying Persons," in Charles A. Garfield, ed., *Psychosocial Care of the Dying Patient* (New York: McGraw-Hill, 1978).

8 Cicely Saunders, "St. Christopher's Hospice," in E. S. Shneidman, ed., *Death: Current Perspectives* (Palo Alto, Cal.: Mayfield Publishing Co., 1976), pp. 516–522.

9 Archie Hanlan, "Notes of a Dying Professor" and "More Notes of a Dying Professor," *Pennsylvania Gazette*, March 1972, Vol. 70, No. 3, pp. 18–24; and February 1973, Vol. 71, No. 4, pp. 29–32. Reprinted with permission of Mrs. Mary S. Hanlan. Also published as part of Archie J. Hanlan, *Autobiography of Dying* (New York: Doubleday & Co., 1978).

10 From Vilhelm Moberg, *The Emigrants (Utvandrara)* (1951; New York: Popular Library, 1978).

11 From Hans Zinsser, *As I Remember Him* (Boston: Little, Brown, 1940). pp. 439–440.

12 From Stewart Alsop, *Stay of Execution*, pp. 9–11. Copyright ©1973 by J. B. Lippincott Co.

13 Eugene Trombley, "A Psychiatrist's Response to a Life-Threatening Illness," *Life-Threatening Behavior*, 1972, Vol. 2, No. 1, pp. 26–34.

14 Hubert H. Humphrey, *The Education of a Public Man* (Garden City, N.Y.: Doubleday and Co., 1976).

15 *Reader's Digest*, August 1977.

16 *The New York Times*, October 26, 1977. Copyright © by the New York Times Company.

17 *Minneapolis Tribune*, December 23, 1977.

PART V
THE SICK AND
DYING PERSON

Contents

For many, the greatest fear of death is mostly in the dying. Just as there is a great difference—to use Susan Sontag's terms—between the world of the well and the world of the sick, so too there is a great difference between being sick (no matter how sick) and being sick-and-dying. With respect to those who are sick-and-dying, clinical thanatology has two main goals: to help survivors survive better and, primarily, to help the terminally ill die better.

In our generation we have learned a great deal about how to help both persons who are mourning and persons who are dying manage their travail better than they might if left entirely on their own psychological resources. The dying person deserves our special attention.

This part contains six chapters. The two that are not by experienced thanatologists are by learned physicians, both psychiatrists—one written in the context of his terminal disease and the other on the occasion of his turning eighty and facing, in his own mind, his final years.

220

20 · Common Fallacies About Dying Patients

Avery Weisman

In this selection from Dr. Weisman's book On Dying and Denying, *he attacks some of the myths and fallacies concerning the attitudes and actions of the dying. (See also the note for Chapter 4.)*

The plight of the dying awakens everyone's sense of dread and annihilation. Yet, as Swift said, "It is impossible that anything so natural, so necessary, and so universal as death, should ever have been designed by providence as an evil to mankind." Nevertheless, our common belief, augmented by cultural bias, is that death is a deplorable, evil, unnecessary and premature event. Death is encased by custom. Our rituals, formal and spontaneous, reflect an enormous concern about being in the presence of the dying and the soon-to-be dead.

In this section I use the physician as the prototype for anyone who is forced to consider the interface between life and death. As a professional, however, the physician influences the way that other people approach death. Because dying people are simply living people who have reached an ultimate stage, the doctor's misconceptions may distort their image of death.

Medicine is only partially scientific. Much of what a practitioner does depends upon empirical procedures, ethical precepts, sanctioned mythology, and much, much magic. Were any doctor to depend wholly upon scientific knowledge, he would be as constrained and disabled as anyone who could act only upon proven principles: He would be lost and ineffectual.

To be a responsive and responsible physician is almost an impossible profession, in the presence of incurable disease and dying. Just at the time when a doctor needs his skill and knowledge, they fail him, out of the nature of things. He is forced to improvise, and at times, his art becomes artifice.

Fortunately, patients tend to endow physicians with the aura of the priest and medicine man, both of whom can perform magic. The advantage of magic over science is that it does not need to be true. Magic and sorcery have nothing to do with truth and proof. They are strategies for dealing with special beliefs about reality. Medical practice draws upon folk-wisdom, and it is as indebted to folk-fallacies as to folk-truths. In the realm of death and dying, magical formulas and incantations frequently pass as principles. Consequently, physicians can readily, even inadvertently, call upon their prejudices and act upon preconceptions. As a result, fallacies about dying patients may be perpetuated from one generation to the next, insulated by a tradition that exempts these beliefs from investigation.

Here are a few typical, widespread fallacies about the dying:

1. Only suicidal and psychotic people are willing to die. Even when death is inevitable, no one wants to die.

2. Fear of death is the most natural and basic fear of man. The closer he comes to death, the more intense the fear becomes.

3. Reconciliation with death and preparation for death are impossible. Therefore, say as little as possible to dying people, turn their questions aside, and use any means to deny, dissimulate, and avoid open confrontation.

4. Dying people do not really want to know what the future holds. Otherwise, they would ask more questions. To force a discussion or to insist upon unwelcome information is risky. The patient might lose all hope. He might commit suicide, become very depressed, or even die more quickly.

5. After speaking with family members, the doctor should treat the patient as long as possible. Then, when further benefit seems unlikely, the patient should be left alone, except for relieving pain. He will then withdraw, die in peace, without further disturbance and anguish.

6. It is reckless, if not downright cruel, to inflict unnecessary suffering upon the patient or his family. The patient is doomed; nothing can really make any difference. Survivors should accept the futility, but realize that they will get over the loss.

7. Physicians can deal with all phases of the dying process because of their scientific training and clinical experience. The emotional and psychological sides of dying are vastly overemphasized. Consultation with psychiatrists and social workers is unnecessary. The clergy might be called upon, but only because death is near. The doctor has no further obligation after the patient's death.

Fallacies lead physicians into inconsistencies, and to judgments that confuse the clinical with the moralistic. Precepts help to rationalize assumptions and to shelter the doctor from undue anxiety. Assumptions, particularly false assumptions, decide conclusions in advance. For example, these seven fallacies are, in effect, tacit justifications for not getting involved with death. Were the physician openly to confess his reluctance, he might paraphrase the fallacies like this: "Anyone who is willing to die must be out of his mind. Death is a dreadful business, because I am afraid of dying. I have done everything for this patient that I know. I wish I could do more. I don't want to be blamed, but I can't stand being around anyone who is going to die, especially if I know him. Even though we all know what is going to happen, let's pretend that all is well or soon will be. Maybe he doesn't know, after all. He hasn't ever asked me about his sickness, and certainly never mentioned dying. If he suspects, and he may, I suppose he would rather not know. Leave well enough alone. If we did force him to talk about the future, maybe he'd be more discouraged, or even take matters into his own hands. The family is pretty helpless, too, but I'll make sure that his pain is under control. Why did that family think I was going to upset him when we first found out what was wrong? We've never mentioned it, so far as I can tell. Now, the best thing to do is keep him comfortable, let him die in peace. We don't want to make anyone suffer unnecessarily. The facts are there, but it will do no good to dwell on death. The family seems to be taking it pretty well, but they'll get over it, they always do. Nature will take its course, if things can just be kept quiet. I don't need a psychiatrist to tell me what I know already. When the time comes, I'll ask the family minister to get in on this and offer some consolation. He'll be taking over soon, anyway!"

Dying patients who are attended by physicians who feel this way are probably fortunate. The scene is sympathetic, compared with the bleak prospect of dying alone and unattended. My point, however, is not to argue the merits of one kind of doctor as opposed to the management of another. Compassion and concern are in this mythical doctor's words, but the management he advocates is primarily intended to comfort and console himself.

Only someone who is extremely apprehensive himself would fail to see that many dying patients accept death with equanimity and without mental disturbance. To regard acceptance of death as a sign of being suicidal or psychotic amounts to believing that anyone who attempts suicide is insane and, therefore, beyond help, just as psychotics are beyond help—egregious fallacies, all.

To be more specific about these seven fallacies: the first three rationalize withdrawal and establish more distance between doctor and patient. The fourth fallacy infers that the patient is also disinclined to talk about death. Unwise confrontation is, by definition, apt to cause mental disturbance. We cannot assume, as this doctor does, that someone who asks no questions has no questions to ask. He may have no opportunity to ask, or he may be afraid to ask, lest he repel people on whom he depends. Families cannot decide judiciously about what to tell. They rely upon the expert for advice and can be swayed according to the doctor's beliefs. The fifth and sixth fallacies presuppose that when the patient is not regarded as responsible, with eyes to see and ears to hear, his silence is assumed to mean that he is both ignorant and complacent. Withdrawal does not necessarily mean serenity, nor is open accessibility equivalent to inflicting "unnecessary suffering." It is commonly heard that physicians do not talk about death with very sick patients in order to keep up their hope. But they usually add that the patients are probably already aware of their condition, and so do not need to be told! If there are rationalizations ready for any contingency, how can anyone be wrong?

Let us continue: survivors do not always get over a serious loss and return to "normal," without first suffering a great deal. Sometimes, bereavement leads to serious somatic and psychological symptoms during the next year or two.[1] Mourners may become patients. Yet, some doctors continue to believe that anticipatory bereavement is peripheral to more genuine medical concerns.

What is "unnecessary suffering," that is so often cited as a reason for nonintervention? Who is to judge what varieties of suffering are necessary or not? Whose suffering are we concerned about? During the terminal phase, not many patients ask for miracles, only for evidence of care and concern.

The most damaging and lethal fallacy in this, as in most other situations, is that of stereotyping people and problems. When we categorize anyone, doctor or patient, we reduce them to a least common denominator, and they become less than what they are or could be. The alternative, then, is to look for the exceptions, and meanwhile, to treat everyone as a special case.

Note

1 Colin M. Parkes, "The Psychosomatic Effects of Bereavement," in *Modern Trends in Psychosomatic Medicine*, ed. Oscar W. Hill (London: Butterworth, 1970).

21 · Children and Death

Judith Stillion and Hannelore Wass

Judith Stillion is professor and chairperson of the Department of Psychology, Western Carolina University, Cullowhee, North Carolina. Hannelore Wass is professor of educational psychology and an associate in the Center for Gerontological Studies and Programs at the University of Florida in Gainesville.

INTRODUCTION

Children and *death*—the two words seem contradictory. Children symbolize life and growth whereas death marks decay, the end of growing and being. Why, then, when the subject is so foreign to the nature of children should we try to educate them about the inevitability of death? In the twentieth century the answer of U.S. culture to this question has been, we should not. Many well-intentioned adults fear that facing the facts of death straightforwardly with children will rob them of their essential innocence and, therefore, of their childhood. Some adults go so far as to believe that children, confronted with the concept of death, will become so terrified that they will not be able to face living in a courageous way. A third reason that adults fail to face the question of death with children relates to the adult's own needs for denial and repression of the inevitability of death. Finally, many adults feel that since death is an unknown it is unrealistic to try to teach anyone to prepare for it.

HISTORICAL PERSPECTIVE

That death and children have not always been so foreign to each other is evident in children's games, prayers, and chants that have been passed on from generation to generation. Peek-a-boo, a game that delights infants, is said to be derived from an old English word meaning "dead" or "alive" (1). It teaches babies their first lessons in object permanence. One of the first games children learn, ring-around-the-rosie, with its chant, "ashes, ashes, all fall down," grew out of children's reaction to death during the great plague of the Middle Ages (2). Even today children very commonly learn as their first prayer, "now I lay me down to sleep, I pray the Lord my soul to keep. If I should die before I wake, I pray the Lord my soul to take." Public awareness of death anxiety has caused the latter line to be changed by many teaching agents. However, its original form serves as a reminder that in earlier days children were supposed to recognize life as transient and death as a constant possibility at a very young age. A rope-skipping chant familiar to many children contains the lines, "Doctor, Doctor, will I die? Yes, my dear, but do not cry," or a variation of this rhyme, "Doctor, Doctor, will I die? Yes, my child, and so will I." Many other games, including hide-and-seek and many tag games, have been offered as evidence of children's lasting tendency to explore the contradictory nature of life and death (2, 3).

Until this century children were common witnesses to death. Infant mortality was high, and it was a rare firstborn who did not experience the death of a younger sibling. Similarly, life expectancy was significantly shorter. According to Lerner (4), life expectancy in 1900 in the United States was 47.3 years. Children often attended the funerals of their parents as well as siblings before they reached adulthood. In earlier days death occurred most often at home and children were aware of it in all its aspects. They helped care for the sick family member, were often present at the moment of death, and were included in the planning of the funeral and attended it. In short, children lived continuously with the fact of death from infancy through adulthood.

As medicine became more specialized and sophisticated, as infectious diseases and others were conquered, death became more and more remote. The past two generations are the first in known history in which many middle-aged adults have not experienced the death of an immediate family member.

ADULTS' DEATH DENIAL AND THE CHILD

Death has come to be viewed as an unwelcome stranger rather than an expected companion, and many adults refuse to discuss it or even think about it. Their denial of death has extended to their children. In a survey by Wass 144 high school seniors were asked, among other questions: "When you were a child how was death handled in your family?" Death was never talked about responded 39 percent. An additional 26 percent said that death was talked about only when absolutely necessary, and even then only briefly. The majority of students reported that this death taboo in the family was true for the present time as well. It is safe to say that in the United States parents, as a rule, do not discuss the topic of death with their children. This avoidance of death stems largely from the adults' own discomfort and anxiety concerning dying and death. It is difficult, for example, for the mother of a four-year-old to provide a calm and well-deliberated answer to the child's totally unexpected question "Mommy, do I have to die?" What mother is not horrified at the prospect of her child's death? Even if she managed a straightforward answer such as "Yes, everybody has to die sometime, but we hope you will not die for a long long time, not for many many years," she is likely to communicate a great deal of anxiety to the questioning child. Such transmission of anxiety from adults to children may be unavoidable, and the best we can strive for is to keep the amount of anxiety at a manageable level. In addition to anxiety, adults frequently feel frustrated and sometimes angry about these death questions, and when these feelings are communicated the child may come to feel guilty as well as anxious.

Avoidance of the topic of death on the part of parents is well intentioned. Most parents have a great need to shield their children from the harsh realities of death. In fact, until recently adults generally believed that children are not concerned about death and that those who are need psychiatric help. The fact, however, as shown in many studies and supported by the authors' experiences, is that children are very much concerned. This interest in death is a normal part of human development. The question of life and death is an existential question and an expression of the child's basic curiosity and search for meaning. Children, like other people, seek to understand themselves, their relationship with others, and the world in which they find themselves. Even very young children ask existential questions such as: Where do babies come from? Where was I before I was born? Do I have to die? Who deaded Grandpa? And in their everyday world, children experience death by coming in contact with dead insects, birds, and other animals. With their all-encompassing curiosity, children try to understand the difference between the warmth, motion, and vitality that marks life and the cold, pallor, and silence that marks death. All too often when they broach their questions to adults they are met with not only evasive but often incomplete answers or disapproving silence. In this way a child learns that death is a taboo subject, and a child may well come to believe that death must be a horrifying, terrible thing, too awful even to mention.

Attempting to protect the child from the facts of death is a futile exercise. In addition to their real life experiences with dead animals, children observe death on television news and inordinate amounts of fictional death in movies and television plays. Much of the death portrayed by the media creates a totally unrealistic picture in the mind of child viewers. For example, Wiley Coyote on "Road Runner" is smashed, mashed, blown up, dropped into ravines, shot, stabbed, and run over, and yet he emerges with nothing worse than a frazzled coat and a new determination to catch the Road Runner.

In the human television world, children frequently see a central character on a soap opera die a drawn-out death only to appear on a different soap opera within a week or two. On "cops and robbers" shows characters die violently every night but are seen on other shows the next day or week. Perhaps even more disturbing, actors such as Freddie Prinze die and their deaths are publicized, but they continue to appear on reruns and syndications for years following their deaths. What impression of the nature of death can a child glean from such exposure? While realistic attempts to deal with death, bereavement, and grief are not widespread in our media, at least one notable exception is that of the Emmy award-winning show produced by Family Communications, in which death and grief were both explored at a level preschool children could understand and to which they could relate (5).

CHILDREN'S VIEWS OF DEATH

In order to answer children's questions concerning death, an adult must be aware of the child's age, experience, and prior understanding. In general, children's understandings of death seem to follow the cognitive developmental model rather closely. This model, developed by the acclaimed Swiss psychologist Jean Piaget, states that a child's level of reasoning is dependent upon both maturation and learning. Children pass through certain cognitive stages as their mental structures mature and as they interact with the world around them (6). Thus a child of three confronted with the death of a parent will not react or understand in the same manner as will a child of twelve, even if he or she is given the same explanations and treatment.

Developmental stages in understanding death

Nagy (7), in the now classical study done with Hungarian children between the ages of three and ten years of age, concluded that there are three stages in children's understanding of death and that these three stages are age-related. The *first stage* in understanding death encompasses the age ranges of three to five years and is similar to what Piaget calls the preoperational stage (6) in that it reflects the egocentric mind of the preschool child. Because children know that they need to eat and breathe, they cannot imagine a human body without those characteristics. Therefore, they describe death either as a kind of sleep or as a gradual or temporary state. While there is a recognition that death differs from life (for example, most young children know that dead people are buried in the ground [8]), there is an incomplete and almost wistful tone to the child's understanding. Nagy (9) illustrates this point by recording a preschool child's remarks:

> CHILD: It can't move because it's in the coffin.
> ADULT: If it weren't in the coffin, could it?
> CHILD: It can eat and drink. (p. 274)

Similarly, a small child may urge a parent to take a dead puppy to the doctor to make it well.

This stage in the child's cognitive development is also characterized by magical thinking. The lines between fact and fantasy are often blurred, and for small children many things are possible. A small child believes that flowers whisper and that mountains open up if you tell them to, and that princes turn into frogs and vice versa. Fairy tales support the child's unrealistic concept of death: The beautiful princess sleeps for a hundred years and then a prince awakens her with a kiss (10). While young children are saddened by death, they do not yet grasp the finality and irreversibility of death at this first stage.

The *second stage*, beginning around age five or six and lasting through age eight, is comparable to the stage of concrete operations in Piagetian theory. Piaget describes this stage as the age of the scientist. During this period, children are consumed with questions concerning the workings of the world around them. They are sorting out impressions, classifying objects, and discovering laws of cause and effect (6). Their understanding of death reflects the growing awareness of the way the world operates. They now recognize that death is final. Nagy's children frequently personified death as a skeleton or powerful monster, perhaps in an attempt to bring the topic into a more easily understandable cause-effect relationship. Death personified comes to get you, but if you are fast enough or clever enough you may get away. At this stage, children worry about the mutilation of the body brought about by the death monster. This is well illustrated in poems written by children (11). Obviously the six- to eight-year-old child, while recognizing that death is final, also sees it as capricious. The child has not yet incorporated the ideas that death is inevitable, natural, and universal. A typical conversation with one of Nagy's (9) children reveals this lack of understanding:

ADULT: Do you often think of death?
CHILD: I often do. But such things as when I fight with death and hit him on the head and death doesn't die. (p. 273)

Nagy described the *third stage* of death as that of mature understanding. In Piaget's theory this stage reflects the complex integration of the formal operational stage of cognitive development. Nagy's study indicates that this stage may begin as early as nine years of age. Children who have reached this level of reasoning realize that death is inescapable and universal; "Death is the termination of life. Death is destiny. Then we finish our earthly life. Death is the end of life on earth" (9, p. 273). In addition, children view death as personal. It is no longer something done to people from the outside (except in case of accident) but rather the result of a natural, internal destruction process that will happen to everyone including themselves. Childers and Wimmer (12) conducted a study of the awareness of two aspects of death, universality and irrevocability, in children from ages four to ten. Of the four-year-olds, 11 percent recognized that death is universal, but by the age of nine, 100 percent recognized death as universal. Of the ten-year-olds, 63 percent as compared to 33 percent of four-year-olds recognized death as irrevocable.

However, even strict Piagetian theorists do not maintain that very young children have no concept of death. Being and nonbeing seem to be one of the first differences to which a child attends and tries to understand. Kastenbaum (13) tells the story of a sixteen-month-old boy who is engrossed in watching a caterpillar moving along a path. When the foot of a passing adult crushes the caterpillar, the child looks to his father and says, "No more."

Kastenbaum maintains that the solemnity of the tone and the facial expression of the child are powerful indications that the child comprehends (at least at a preconceptual level) the state of death. Such everyday experiences with death can provide the impetus for an informal death education program within the home.

The influence of life experiences in understanding death

Children vary by age in their understanding of death, but their views are also shaped by their life experiences. For example, two fifteen-year-olds sharing similar backgrounds and IQs can vary greatly in understanding depending upon their religious background and their firsthand dealings with death or lack of them. One fifteen-year-old might have learned at a young age that talking about death made the adults in his family uncomfortable. By circumstance he may not have confronted death among family or close friends. He may even have trained himself to deny curiosity about the subject. When contrasted with a fifteen-year-old who has had to cope with the death of a parent, sibling, or friend, there may be as much difference in comprehension of the topic as we would expect to find between the five- and the nine-year-old of Nagy's study. A replication of Nagy's study (14) showed that children in the United States, in contrast to the Hungarian children of nearly thirty years ago, express concepts of death that could be classified into four categories:

1. Relative ignorance of the meaning of death (ages zero-four).
2. Death as a temporary state. Death is not irreversible and the dead have feelings and biological functions (ages four-seven).
3. Death is final and irreversible but the dead have biological functioning (ages five-ten).
4. Death is final. It is the cessation of all biological functioning (ages six and beyond).

Other attempts to replicate Nagy's findings in this country (12, 14-16) have generally found a relationship between age and breadth of death awareness but have not found the personification of death among six- to nine-year-olds that Nagy found. This may lend support to the idea that cultural beliefs and experiences also shape concepts of death. Nagy's children were all firsthand witnesses of a terrifying, bloody war in which death could be delivered from the skies unexpectedly. Most of them undoubtedly knew families who had lost loved ones during the war. Perhaps it was more natural for those children to try to make the concept of death more understandable by personifying it. However, their words may also reflect a personification tendency more prevalent in Europe than in the United States.

Family and social class influences

The importance of the family in the development of ideas and feelings about death was also demonstrated in a study by Wass and Scott (17). They found that children aged eleven to twelve whose fathers were college educated theorize and verbalize more about death than do children whose fathers only completed high school. Interesting also was the wide variability found in the sample concerning concepts of death. They ranged from an "immature" belief that death is a long rest to a "mature" belief that death is a natural, irreversible, and universal event. It is important to note that the need to discuss death and dying should be viewed as a sign of normal, healthy development rather than as an indication of morbid preoccupation with abnormal material. Older children in particular welcome the chance to discuss their views of death and dying. The protocols that follow are typical of responses made by eleven- and twelve-year-olds who were invited to tell what they thought and felt about what happens when one dies.

GIRL, AGE TWELVE: I would like to die of old age. Just go to sleep and never wake up, a nice quiet way to go. I would like to be buried. Then whatever the spirits wanted to do with me they could do.

BOY, ELEVEN YEARS: I think if death came slowly I would just fade out. But if it was instant, I would suddenly be gone. I believe that after you die, you have another life and you might come back from anything like a cockroach to a royalty.

GIRL, ELEVEN YEARS: I think when someone knows they are going to die, they are very scared. I would be. I think after someone dies they just lie there forever and disintegrate. I hope I never die.

GIRL, TWELVE YEARS: When you die, you lay there wondering if you will go to Heaven or Hell. I get scared and don't want to die. Whenever I think about it, I get all spooked out. I don't know about you, but I am going to Heaven.

GIRL, TWELVE YEARS: When I die, some people will probably come and put me in a coffin with cobwebs in it; and they'll put me in a dark hearse, and the spiders will probably eat me before they get me in the ground. Next they'll put the coffin in a real deep hole and let me rot!

GIRL, TWELVE YEARS: I think you would be surrounded by darkness. You would be absolutely without movement. You couldn't talk or see or use any of your senses. You would be that way forever. It's like taking a very long rest.

BOY, TWELVE YEARS: Well, to me death is a natural thing. Everybody has to die sometime. Nobody can live forever. I know that my mother and father will die sometime. I just hope it's not soon. Then, later, I myself will be threatened by this natural thing called death (17).

A 1974 study (18) supported the impact of the environment in children's conceptualization of death. These authors studied 199 children between the ages of three and nine. They grouped the children by age according to socioeconomic class. The results showed that lower class children, whose environment is more violent, tend to be more aware of death at younger ages. They concluded that "The lower class children's fantasy content indicates that they are attempting to deal in a realistic, sensible manner with their environment" (p. 19).

In summary, whereas there is ample support for the cognitive-developmental approach to children's concepts of death, it should be remembered that development involves more than maturation; it results from an interaction of biological readiness with environmental factors. Life experiences, intelligence levels, family attitudes and values, self-concepts, and many other as yet unexamined factors all seem to play a part in each child's individual attainment of meaning for death.

LOSS, ANXIETY, AND DEATH IN CHILDREN

Children begin to experience loss at a very young age. Birth itself might be regarded as a form of loss as it involves giving up one state of being (the protective womb) to enter another (the world, which requires many adaptations). Weaning represents the loss of the major source of comfort, security, and pleasure in an infant's life. Toilet training also is a milestone away from the comfortable dependency of babyhood. Each loss might be thought of as representing a "small death" to the child and each loss brings with it anxiety. The toddler moves out of the soft security of his mother's lap in an uncertain, vaguely worried way. The five-year-old worries over the loss of her first tooth until the adult mollifies her by assuring that the "tooth fairy" will pay for the loss. The early teen watches with anxiety as the well-known, compact child body begins to assume new proportions.

The process of growing is intimately tied in with loss; and loss produces anxiety. The very young child, from infancy through preschool, manifests this anxiety over separation. The need for mother is almost equivalent to the need for survival and so to be separated arouses a form of death anxiety in the infant. The child between five and nine years old, who is rapidly gaining a strong self-image, shows mutilation anxiety (fear of destruction of some part of his or her body) but is not yet able to verbalize death anxiety per se. It is the adolescents, with their newly acquired ability to think symbolically, who can torture themselves with the concept of nonbeing.

Even strong adults cannot regard nonbeing with equanimity. As children become more mature in their view of death, it is reasonable to suppose that they also become more anxious. Wahl (19) has suggested that many of his child patients' "anxieties, obsessions and other neurotic symptom formations are genetically related to the fear of death or its symbolic equivalents . . ." (p. 27). Von Hug (20) found support for Wahl's suggestion when he obtained a curvilinear relationship between age and death anxiety in normal children but a linear relationship with neurotic children. However, there is evidence that supports the environmental point of view, namely that a child's death anxiety is also largely influenced by the environment. Wass and Scott (17) found that children with college-educated fathers theorized more about death than those whose fathers only completed high school. And children who theorized showed less death anxiety than those who did not theorize.

Positive self-regard is generally viewed as a sign of mental health. Bluebond-Langner (21) suggested that the self-concept may be an important factor in children's concepts of death. It may relate importantly to children's management of death anxiety. This hypothesis is supported in the Wass and Scott study (17) in which it was found that the self-concepts of eleven- and twelve-year-olds were inversely related to their death anxieties, that is, the higher their self-concepts the lower their death anxiety.

It seems possible that healthy children can grow toward low death anxiety, especially if they are provided with adult models who have worked through their own attitudes toward death and who encourage children to express their fears rather than repress or deny them. Neurotic children, on the other hand, tend to grow more anxious as their concept of death matures.

Implications for parents

During the early years, parents can help most by merely being available to children and assuring the child that he or she is loved and will not be abandoned (22). Children need honest answers no matter how unpleasant, offensive, or seemingly morbid their questions may be, Grollman (23) points out that parents should answer their children's questions factually and uncompromisingly and at a level they can understand. To tell fairy tales about death to children is not only misleading but may create serious problems in trust between the parents and the child as the child grows older. One of the problems with parental answers is that they are frequently spiritual answers to children's physical-chemical questions. Children want to know what happens after a person has died, but they are equally curious about the physical aspects of dying, particularly in the middle years. They ask questions such as: Why do people die with their eyes open? Why does the blood turn blue? Do people get buried alive? Could a doctor say a person is dead when he really isn't? How long does it take for the body to disintegrate? If parents do not know the answers to such questions it is all right to admit to ignorance. It would be wise to consult a physician or books. Evasiveness or refusal to answer children's questions may also lead to heightened anxiety (22).

Adolescents may clothe themselves in an illusion of invulnerability in order to deny anxiety brought about by their mature understanding of death (24). Kastenbaum (25) has reported that about 75 percent of the adolescents he studied shut the idea of death out of their minds. They were interested in living fully in the present, seeking their identity in the here and now. Adults working with teenagers may find invitations to discuss death go unanswered. However, meaningful dialogues on grief and life after death are also possible if and when the adolescent seeks them out.

Terminally ill children

How they view death   Since children's firsthand knowledge of death is a powerful environmental influence for learning about death, it would follow that the terminally ill child should have a far different conception of death than would a healthy child of the same age and intelligence. At least one researcher, Bluebond-Langner (21), makes a case for the idea that terminally ill children not only become aware that they are dying but also understand death as adults do. She discusses five stages in the process of the acquisition of information that are progressive and lead to concomitant changes in self-concept. These changes are dependent upon significant cumulative events occurring throughout the course of the illness but follow the sequence as outlined below:

Information acquisition	Self-concept changes
"It" is a serious illness	Seriously ill
Names of drugs and side effects	Seriously ill, but will get better
Purposes of treatment and procedures	Always ill, but will get better
Disease as a series of relapses and remissions minus death	Always ill, and will never get better
Disease as a series of relapses remissions plus death	Dying

Death anxiety   Other researchers working with terminally ill children have found support for Bluebond-Langner's view (21) that many know of the seriousness of their illness. Waechter (26) reported that anxiety scores of a group of fatally ill children were twice as high as those of other hospitalized children. She suggested that the fatal nature of a child's illness is communicated to the child by the changed way that persons react to him or her after the diagnosis is made. She stated that it is meaningless to argue about whether a child should be told that his or her illness is fatal. Rather, "the questions and concerns which are conscious to the child should be dealt with in such a way that the child does not feel further isolated and alienated from his parents and other meaningful adults" (26, p. 172). Her study reported a significant relationship between children's projective anxiety scores and the degree to which the child has been allowed to discuss his fears and prognosis. She concluded that accepting and permitting dying children to discuss any aspect of their illness may decrease feelings of isolation, alienation, and the sense that the illness is too horrible to discuss completely. Her final plea is that helping professionals not allow the existence of "a curtain of silence around the child's most intense fears" (p. 171).

In another supporting study (27) fatally ill children between the ages of six and ten who were treated as outpatients were compared to a group of chronically but not fatally ill outpatient children. The dying children told stories that revealed significantly more preoccupation with threats to body function and body integrity as well as significantly higher general anxiety than the stories of the less severely ill children.

Most of the studies examining the attitudes of fatally ill children have included storytelling or the use of projective techniques in order to circumvent the child's initial reluctance to discuss death. Vernick and Karon (28) state that "the initiative for talking about death must come from the adult who is in possession of more emotional strength" (p. 395). These authors are representative of many health workers who feel that fatally ill children know more than they feel safe in saying. Yudkin (29) points out that children signal deep anxiety about the possibility of death in many unspoken ways: "Depression out of keeping with the effects of the illness itself; unspoken anger and resentment toward his doctors; resentment toward his parents of a child old enough not to be affected by mere separation in the hospital. These all suggest anxiety about death" (p. 39).

In children under five years of age, death awareness often takes the form of separation anxiety. Natterson and Knudson (30) define death awareness as the "individual's consciousness of the finiteness of his personal existence" (p. 457). Young children, totally dependent on their parents for physical and emotional comfort, often equate separation of parents to physical death. Such separation fear is not dependent upon strong ego and intellectual development. Separation anxiety is most commonly seen in children who have not yet attained language skills but may be the most prevalent fear up to five years of age (31). Terminally ill children between the ages of six and ten often display mutilation fear. Children during this period are still working to develop a concept of death but they have well-developed body images. Threats to that image, whether from medical intervention or from the disease itself, cause severe anxiety. The third and final maturational step in death awareness is death anxiety per se. When death is certain, death anxiety must be regarded as a rational fear rather than as a neurotic symptom.

Viewpoints for working with terminally ill children   The medical profession in the past decade has begun to address itself to caring for the psychological health of dying children as well as their physical health. Many health practitioners (32-35) are advocating open honesty in dealing with dying children. Certainly, if it is true that a child may well understand that he is going to die long before he can say it (31), it would seem productive to open lines of communication as fully as possible so as to prevent loneliness, depression, and inward anger in the dying child.

However, the stance of total honesty is not shared by all health professionals. Evans and Edin (34) reflect the more widespread practice of attempting to shield the dying child from death and the fears involved in dying. They believe that this approach is advisable for the following reasons: (a) the fear of death is real and cannot be dissipated by discussion; (b) suppression and rejection cannot be used as mechanisms for dealing with fear if open discussion is encouraged; and (c) children need the support of their parents during terminal illness and parents frequently cannot cope with their children's awareness of imminent death. Evans and Edin appear to favor a less direct method of dealing with children rather than encouraging them to meet the fears head on.

There is a midway position between total honesty and encouraging denial, which is reflected by Green (36). He encourages doctors to remain open to children's questions and to plan for time to talk with their parents. Basically three questions are generally asked by the child between the ages of six and twelve. The first is: "Am I safe?" The second is: "Will there be a trusted person to keep me from feeling helpless, alone, and to overcome pain?" and the third is: "Will you make me feel alright?" (p. 496). Successfully dealing with these three questions may be enough to allow the child to explore his own potential for growth in the time remaining. Even young children need an atmosphere of psychological safety in which to express themselves. Green relates a story of a four-year-old who, though sheltered from the prognosis of his terminal illness, nevertheless told the doctor that he was afraid to die. Allowing the child to express that fear is an important part of total care for the dying child as it results in direct comfort to the child and in freeing up of energy that the child can then use to fight the illness or to engage in intensive living in the time remaining.

Care giving and the dying child   In caring for a dying child the natural core conflict of compassion and nurturance for one in pain versus repulsion against impending shock of separation and loss is heightened (37). Somehow death of a child evokes depths of anger, guilt, and frustration that adult deaths do not raise. Perhaps the child's death awakens one of our deepest fears: death before fulfillment (36). Furthermore, patients' failure to get well often leads to feelings of frustration on the part of the health care workers, since one of their primary goals and needs is to restore health. Frustration may lead to feeling angry toward the dying one, which in turn leads to guilt feelings. Since one of the reactions to grief is to become angry at those who invoked the guilt feelings, "a self-sustaining emotional chain reaction" may ensue (37, p. 509). This reaction may be fully conscious, partially conscious, or unconscious to the care giver, but it affects treatment of the dying child, perhaps leading to overprotection and overindulgence or to isolating the child emotionally and caring only for his or her physical needs.

Helping parents   How much more pronounced these feelings must be in the caring parents of the dying child! One father, in a letter to a friend, expressed his anguish in the following way:

> As you are probably interested, Brian is quite bad. We wait each day for him to die. His discomfort and ours is now so great that I believe we now hope each day for him to die. But the human body does not die easily. We're like weeds in a garden. It's ironic, but waiting for a baby to die is quite similar to having a baby: you wait helplessly, you can't do anything to speed it up or slow it down, it's too late to change the course of things, you call home wondering what stage you're in, doctors and hospitals are involved, you wonder what you're going to do with the other kids when it happens, you have to call the grandparents, your friends are anxious, you want it to happen and you don't want it to happen, you're afraid and yet you desire relief from the long wait. So alike and yet so different. (38)

Friedman (39), in discussing care of the terminal child, points out that there is probably no other area in which "anticipatory guidance" is so helpful in promoting rapport between the physician and the patient's parents. A few authors (40, 41) have offered suggestions for working with parents of the dying child. At the base of all suggestions are the dual principles of open honesty and support. A summary of points to be covered with parents after the initial diagnosis is known includes the following:

1. Recognize the depth of shock and despair the parents must be feeling.

2. Explain the basis for the diagnosis and the nature and type of disease.

3. Explain the fatal outcome and type of therapy to be undertaken. Make every attempt to gain parental support both in the physical and emotional care of the child.

4. Assure parents that medical support will always be available in times of need.

5. Try to help parents anticipate problems involved in the initial telling of others and during the child's illness. Go over possible reactions of siblings (e.g., anger, jealousy, fear, guilt).

6. Discuss causes of the problem with emphasis on relieving possible parental guilt.

7. Emphasize any hope possible. If there is hope for remission, dwell on that. If there is not, discuss scientific research going on, if appropriate. If nothing is available, emphasize the support the child will get throughout the illness from the medical staff. While the good physician will discourage excessive optimism (42), parents must be allowed some hope, especially during the early stages of a disease.

8. Discuss anticipatory grief both as an attempt to educate parents about their own feelings in the coming days and to prepare them to recognize stages their child may be passing through.

9. Stress the importance of maintaining continuity in raising the child. It is essential that parents assume the child will live to adulthood and raise him or her consistent with their prior values and ideals. The alternative is that parents in their grief and guilt will indulge the child, who in turn will become confused and often test new limits until parents are forced to discipline him or her. This often leads to greater feelings of guilt both for the child and the parents. Children need the security of consistency in their parents' behavior.

10. Try to assess family's strengths and weaknesses and encourage building on the strengths. It is important to ask each parent how the other will accept the death, thus encouraging empathy and visualizing problems in advance.

11. Finally, there is evidence that a follow-up talk after the death of the child is often appreciated by the family in order to provide closure for the family and to permit them to express feelings after the death.

Parents are an integral part of total treatment of the dying child. Morrissey (43) showed that high-quality parent participation leads to better adjustment in hospitalized children. Not only can parents be of help to the ward staff throughout their child's illness, but also by doing this they work off some of their own anxiety, guilt, and grief before the child's death (30). In almost all cases of children who survived four months or more after the initial hospitalization, the caregiving parents (usually the mother) reacted with calm acceptance and some were even able to express relief at their child's death. There was a triphasic response among mothers whose children survived at least four months. In the first phase there was shock and denial often accompanied by anger, excessive weeping, and a tendency toward overprotection. In the second phase there was an acceptance of the situation coupled with the parent's willingness to expend energy in realistic ways that offered hope of saving the child. During this phase the psychological separation of the mother from the child often began. The third phase coincided with the terminal phase of the child's illness. Mothers directed their energy toward other sick children as well as their own. Sublimation was often evident in their desire to give physical and psychological comfort to parents of other terminally ill children. It is noteworthy that in cases where mothers reacted hysterically or clung to hope unrealistically, their child's death usually occurred less than three months after the fatal prognosis was given. It would appear that four months is the critical period for the working through of anticipatory grief (30).

CHILDREN AND GRIEF

There are at least three distinct types of grief reactions that are appropriate to examine in a discussion of children and death. The first is preparatory grief, the emotional reaction of a child becoming aware that he or she is dying. The second is bereavement as a child faces the fact of the death of a loved one. The third is anticipatory grief as the parents of the terminally ill child attempt to cope with the realization that their child is dying.

Preparatory grief

Preparatory grief seems to be a universal aspect of the dying process if the person has adequate warning of his or her condition. It involves the following emotions: denial ("This cannot be happening to me"); anger ("How can you let this happen to me?"); resentment ("Why me? Why not you?"); fear ("What will dying be like? Will I suffer? Will I be alone? What will happen after I die?"). Sometimes guilt also is a part of preparatory grieving, as in the case of children who feel that their disease is punishment for earlier behavior. The idea of death as punishment as well as the child's assumption of parents' omnipotence is chillingly portrayed in Hailey's *Airport* (44) when the child in the crashing plane is heard to say "Mummy! Daddy! Do something! I don't want to die . . . Oh, Gentle Jesus, I've been good . . . Please, I don't want to . . ." (p. 142). If care givers can recognize the complexity of these interrelated emotions and encourage the child to verbalize them according to his needs, the child may be able to work through some of them, thus freeing up energy to be spent in more positive ways. Even if the child cannot work through the emotions, he or she will not feel so cut off and alone during the illness. Often, creation of a positive climate for communication with a dying child stems from the way the disease is presented to the child in the beginning. Foley and McCarthy (35) describe a typical physican's explanation to a leukemic child as follows:

> You have a serious blood disease, leukemia. Ten years ago, there was no treatment for leukemia and many people died. Now there are a number of drugs which can be used to treat leukemia. There are several types of leukemia and the type that you have is the one for which there are the most drugs.
>
> Treatment to keep the leukemia cells away will last three years. You'll miss at least a month of school, the time needed to get the disease in control. The main problem right now is infection. If you stay free of infection you will be out of the hospital in about five days, if an infection occurs, you'll be hospitalized for at least two weeks."
> (pp. 1115–1116)

Allowing children to ask questions after such an explanation and making time to talk even when they have no questions creates the setting of mutual trust so necessary for growth during the final period of life.

Death as loss

Death is above all else loss. The young child (aged three to five) usually has experienced only temporary loss, as when a parent leaves for a short time. These children do not understand permanent loss but they know the discomfort of being without their caretakers. Bowlby's work (45) suggests that since preschool grieving and adult grieving are very similar in their intensity, the longing and mourning that are intrinsic to the grief process may be largely instinctive rather than cognitive. Spitz (46) described a syndrome that he called "hospitalism," in which the young child from infancy through preschool reacts to separation from his mother first with anger, then with a kind of quiet, resigned despair. Some of the children actually refused nutrition, turned their faces to the wall, and died. This was not learned behavior. Rather it was a natural response on the part of the child who had suffered an overwhelming loss.

Dying children suffer not only from physical separation from their home and parents but also from pain and loss of function as the disease progresses. Older children (six years and beyond) begin to have the cognitive capacity to grieve over the loss of the future. They can understand that their tomorrows are numbered. It is difficult for the child as well as the adult to make sense of such an intrinsically unfair situation. However, many children have a need to discuss these feelings. If, when they first mention them, they are met with embarrassment, disapproval, or emotional outburst, the children learn that this is not a safe area for discussion. They must deny those feelings in themselves and retreat into the loneliness of their own loss without the support of those they love. Preparatory grief is real and it can become debilitating. Many health workers today agree that the final cruelty added to the already unbelievably cruel dying situation is to encourage these children to pretend they are *not* suffering the greatest loss of all. In dying the child loses everything: possessions, friends, parents, personality, and self. It is right to grieve then, if he or she realizes even a bit of this loss. Health workers can facilitate the grieving process not by silence but by being available to listen, empathize, and support the child in attempting to cope with the illness.

The bereaved child

Just as dying children profit from being able to communicate their feelings of grief, loss, anger, and bewilderment, so children who have lost a loved one profit from communication. The death of a parent can be particularly tragic for a child (47). Mingled with all the other negative emotions is a feeling of betrayal. It is almost as though the young child feels that if the parent had loved him or her enough, the parent would not have left. Bereavement is accompanied by physical symptoms including feelings of panic, insomnia, lack of appetite, nightmares, and others. Unresolved grief, especially in children, can lead to ongoing somatic illness as well as deep psychological problems. In one study (48) 41 percent of the population of 3216 depressed adult patients had lost a parent through death before age fifteen. In a later study (49) 27 percent of patients in a highly depressed group reported the loss of a parent before the age of sixteen as compared with 12 percent of adults in a nondepressed group. Furthermore, an appreciably larger number of patients in the highly depressed group lost a parent before the age of four. It appears that the loss of a parent is a traumatic psychological event for a child and that the earlier that loss occurs, the more potentially devastating the effect can be.

Parness (50), in working with preschool children who have sustained the loss of a parent or sibling, points out that "very young children have resiliency and fortitude in the face of some of the painful and unpredictable experiences life has to offer" (p. 7). However, she goes on to say that death and loss must be worked through with children. She points out that teachers and mental health workers can encourage healthy coping in children by beginning work with the assumption of loss as a universal human emotion. The adult must also be willing to share feelings of grief honestly and in a positive way that communicates faith in the children's "resources, resiliency, and power over their future lives—in spite of the unexpected" (50, p. 7).

Parental anticipatory mourning

The final type of grief to be considered in this chapter is parental anticipatory mourning. Futterman and Hoffman (51) defined it as "a set of processes that are directly related to the awareness of the impending loss, to its emotional impact and to the adaptive mechanisms whereby emotional attachment to the dying child is relinquished over time" (p. 130). It involves the following steps:

1. *Acknowledgement:* growing awareness of the approach of the inevitable moment of death accompanied by alternating feelings of hope and despair.

2. *Grieving:* the emotional reaction to loss that starts off as an intense undifferentiated response but gradually mellows in quality and the intensity becomes subdued.

3. *Reconciliation:* one step advanced from mere acceptance, it involves attempting to find meaning for the child's life and death and moving beyond that to a stage where the parents can be grateful for their blessings.

4. *Detachment:* this is the process whereby the parents gradually withdraw their emotional investment from the child.

   One parent has described a very rapid detachment reaction in the following way: "As soon as the doctor told me that B. had neuroblastoma (a fatal form of the infantile cancer) I looked at him in the bed and felt like he was already dead. Later on, hope revived for a while with a change in medication, but as the disease progressed, I protected myself from too much feeling by viewing him as already lost to us" (38).

   This process, so necessary to the mental health of the parents, sometimes can result in the tragic condition referred to as the "living dead" (52). If parents complete the detachment process too soon or if the child has an unexpected late remission, the family may have completed the detachment process and the child may find himself dying alone or receiving an unwelcome greeting from a family that has already resolved his death.

5. The final stage in anticipatory grieving is called *memorialization*. It involves idealizing the child and results in the parents' developing a mental image of the child which will live beyond his death.

PROFESSIONALS AND THE FAMILY OF THE DYING CHILD

Professionals working with parents of terminally ill children can do little to lessen the sorrow that is the dominant emotion from the time the diagnosis is made until the child dies. They can, however, help the parents to anticipate and deal effectively with accompanying emotions such as anger, guilt, and anxiety.

Powerful feelings of anger often threaten to overcome parents of fatally ill children. The obvious unfairness of the situation coupled with their impotence to do anything to change it leads to feelings of frustration that can be destructive. The important question for helping professionals must be: How can the parents be helped to express their anger in positive ways? Sometimes, especially in cases of genetically transmitted diseases, one parent will turn his or her anger on the other one, thus adding to the stress of the situation (53). Other family members, including siblings and grandparents, may also have to bear the brunt of displaced parental anger. Other common recipients of anger include God, the doctors, nurses, and other caretakers, and even inanimate objects such as the hospital bed and machines used in treating the child. If parents turn their explosive anger inward, it can result in depression, suicidal urges, and even psychotic breakdown.

Parents need to be helped to find appropriate channels for venting anger. Such channels might include ongoing group or individual therapy, joining an organization to raise funds for medical research, forming parent support groups, and physical activities to discharge tension.

The second major emotion that parents should be helped to anticipate is guilt. Since the child's birth the parents' role has been that of protection and nurturance. When parents are not able to protect their child from a fatal disease, they may feel irrational guilt. In addition, if the parent-child relationship has been strained, the parents may feel guilt for the negative feelings they have had toward the child. As the illness proceeds, guilt may be compounded as the parents experience recurring wishes for the child to die. Guilt is also exacerbated as the parents become aware of hidden feelings of relief that it is not they who have the fatal illness. Folk tales and scattered heroic stories tell of parents who willingly give their lives for their children. However, it is the exceptional person who would willingly choose to exchange places with one who is suffering through a lingering death, even if that person is one's own child. Guilt can be tolerated better if the parent can be encouraged to express these feelings openly. The helping professional can then accept the parents' feelings of guilt and join them in attempting to understand those feelings as natural parts of most intimate relationships.

Commonly, parents of fatally ill children experience a third emotion, anxiety, which arises from at least five sources (53):

1. *Lack of mastery of the protective parental role*, resulting in the need to reorganize self-concept, self-esteem, and feelings of potency. Any major threat to the stable self-concept arouses anxiety.

2. *Inability to cope with the situation effectively*, resulting in feelings of an imminent breakdown. Whenever environmental stress threatens to overwhelm a person, the major emotion is that of anxiety. It is hard to envision a situation more stressful than having to watch your child suffer and die.

3. *Feelings of isolation and loneliness* caused by the parents' new identity as the parent of a doomed child. Parents have said that after finding out the diagnosis they did not want to see friends who had healthy children. They experienced feelings of resentment that the world continued to go on as though nothing had happened while their whole world was collapsing. In short, they felt that theirs was a unique position in the world, which no one else could understand; they were alone.

4. *Separation anxiety* as the parents anticipated the child's death and its psychological cost. Parents have reported feelings of loss so keen that it felt as though they had lost a limb or some other part of themselves.

5. *Death anxiety* as the realization of their own inevitable death hits home more acutely than ever before because of identification with the child.

Anxiety is best counteracted by action, and much of a parent's anxiety can be constructively channeled into caring for the dying child (54). However, parents need to know that sleeping and eating disturbances often accompany anxiety and that anxiety, like anger, can be displaced, resulting in irrational fears concerning their own health or the health of their other children.

Siblings and the dying child

Siblings of a dying child also suffer, often in lonely confusion, as they watch their brother or sister die and their parents grieve. Often parents react to grieving children in an overprotective and secretive manner. Green and Solnit (55) have coined the term "vulnerable child" syndrome to refer to such children. Studies done with adults who lost a sibling in childhood have indicated some support for this syndrome. As early as 1943, Rosenweig and Bray (56) found that patients suffering from schizophrenia had a higher than expected number of siblings who died in childhood. Perhaps the one axiom that will promote the best adjustment in the brothers and sisters of the dying child is quite simply, include them. They need to know some details about the illness if they are old enough; they need to visit the sibling in the hospital and be encouraged to express their thoughts, fears, and guilt feelings just as the parents are. Young children especially need to be reassured that no hostile thought of theirs is responsible for their brother or sister's illness, as magical thinking is still very much a part of their cognitive method of operation.

SUMMARY

Death is a natural event and it is normal for children to want to know about and understand it. Many parents have a need to protect their children from the harsh realities of life, but by doing so they contribute to misconceptions and increased anxieties.

The understanding of what death and dying means develops as the child grows older. The preschool child is believed to understand death as a temporary stage, a long sleep or departure. During the early school years, the child comes to recognize that death is final, but at the same time it is also personified, seen perhaps as a skeleton or a powerful monster who capriciously snatches people and kills them. Usually by the age of nine the child understands that death is final but also natural and universal. A number of studies have shown that there is extreme variability with respect to the age at which a child reaches a mature understanding of death. These variations are due to cultural and subcultural factors, family background, personal encounters, and very likely a number of other as yet unidentified factors.

Children experience loss at a young age. Loss produces anxiety. As children become more aware of the reality of death, it is reasonable to assume that they become more anxious. Caring and patient adults can help alleviate a good deal of a child's death anxiety.

The terminally ill child usually becomes aware of his or her dying and experiences fears, but researchers find that these fears are often unspoken or couched in symbolic language. In the very young terminal child the fear of separation from parents is the predominant fear. Older children fear mutilation of their bodies.

Caring for the dying child is the most difficult task. The death of a child evokes depths of anger, guilt, frustration, and helplessness that are difficult to cope with. An important aspect of care of the terminal child is for physicians or other care givers to work with parents to help them cope with this impending loss and the feelings these bring about. When parents are an integral part of the total treatment of the dying child, it is found that parents are able to work off some of their own anxiety, guilt, and grief, while at the same time filling a need for closeness on the part of the dying child as well as assisting the staff.

There are at least three different identifiable types of grieving. First, preparatory grief or the emotional reaction of children who become aware of their own dying. Second is bereavement, as a child faces the loss of a loved one, and third is anticipatory grief, or the feeling that parents of the terminally ill child experience as they attempt to cope with the fact of their child's impending death.

References

1 Crase, D. R., & Crase, D. Helping children understand death. *Young Children,* 1976 (November), 21–25.

2 Kastenbaum, R. J. *Death, society and human experience.* St. Louis: Mosby, 1977.

3 Maurer, A. Maturation of concepts of death. *British Journal of Medicine and Psychology,* 1966, *39,* 35–41.

4 Lerner, M. When, why, and where people die. In E. S. Shneidman (Ed.), *Death: Current perspectives.* Palo Alto: Mayfield Publishing, 1976, 138–162.

5 Sharapan, H. Mister Rogers' neighborhood: Dealing with death on a children's television series. *Death education: 1,* 1977, 131–136.

6 Piaget, J. *The origins of intelligence in children.* New York: Harcourt, Brace and World, 1932.

7 Nagy, M. The child's theories concerning death. *The Journal of Genetic Psychology,* 1948, *73,* 3–27.

8 Koocher, G. P. Talking with children about death. *American Journal of Orthopsychiatry,* 1974, *44,* 404–411.

9 Wilcox, S. G., & Sutton, M. *Understanding death and dying: An interdisciplinary approach.* Port Washington, NY: Alfred Publishing, 1977.

10 Wass, H. How children understand death. *Thanatos,* 1976, *1,* 4, 18–22.

11 Arnstein, F. I met death one clumsy day. *English Journal,* 1972, *61,* 6, 853–858.

12 Childers, P., & Wimmer, M. The concept of death in early childhood. *Child Development,* 1971, *42,* (4), 1299–1301.

13 Kastenbaum, R. Childhood: The kingdom where creatures die. *Journal of Clinical Child Psychology*, 1974, 3, (2), 11–14.

14 Melear J. D. Children's conceptions of death. *Journal of Genetic Psychology*, 1973, *123*, (2), 359–360.

15 Gartley, W., & Bernasconi, M. The concept of death in children. *The Journal of Genetic Psychology*, 1967, *110*, 71–85.

16 Hansen, Y. Development of the concept of death: Cognitive aspects. *Dissertation Abstracts International*, 1973, 34, (2–3), 853.

17 Wass, H., & Scott, M. Middle school students' death concepts and concerns. *Middle School Journal*, 1978, 9, (1), 10–12.

18 Tallmer, M., Formaneck, R., & Tallmer, J. Factors influencing children's concepts of death. *Journal of Clinical Child Psychology*, 1974, 3, (2), 17–19.

19 Wahl, C. W. The fear of death. In H. Feifel (Ed.), *The meaning of death*. New York: McGraw-Hill, 1959.

20 Von Hug, H. H. The child's concept of death. *Psychoanalytic Quarterly*, 1965, *34*, 499–516.

21 Bluebond-Langner, M. Meanings of death to children. In H. Feifel (Ed.), *New meanings of death*. New York: McGraw-Hill, 1977.

22 Wass, H., & Shaak, J. Helping children understand death through literature. *Childhood Education*, 1976, (November-December), 80–85.

23 Grollman, E. A. (Ed.) *Explaining death to children*. Boston: Beacon Press, 1967.

24 McCandless, B. R. *Adolescents—Behavior and development*. Hinsdale, Ill.: Dryden Press, 1970.

25 Kastenbaum, R. Time and death in adolescence. In H. Feifel (Ed.), *The meaning of death*. New York: McGraw-Hill, 1959.

26 Waechter, E. H. Children's awareness of fatal illness. *American Journal of Nursing*, 1971, 71, 1168–1172.

27 Spinetta, J. J., & Maloney, L. J. Death anxiety in the outpatient leukemic child. *Pediatrics*, 1975, *56*, (6), 1034–1037.

28 Vernick, J., & Karon, M. Who's afraid of death and leukemia ward? *American Journal of Diseases of Children*, 1965, *109*, 393–397.

29 Yudkin, S. Children and death. *The Lancet*, 1967, 37–41.

30 Natterson, J. M., & Knudson, A. G. Observations concerning fear of death in fatally ill children and their mothers. *Psychosomatic Medicine*, 1960, *23*, (6), 456–465.

31 Spinetta, J. J., Rigler, D., & Karon, M. Personal space as a measure of a dying child's sense of isolation. *Journal of Consulting and Clinical Psychology*, 1974, *42*, (6), 751–756.

32 Singher, L. J. The slowly dying child. *Clinical Pediatrics*, 1974, *13*, (19), 861–867.

33 Karon, M., & Vernick, J. An approach to the emotional support of fatally ill children. *Clinical Pediatrics*, 1968, 7, (5), 274–280.

34 Evans, A. E., & Edin, S. If a child must die . . . *The New England Journal of Medicine*, 1968, *278*, (3), 138–142.

35 Foley, G. V., & McCarthy, A. M. The child with leukemia in a special hematology clinic. *American Journal of Nursing*, 1976, 76, (7), 1115–1119.

36 Green, M. Care of the dying child. In *Care of the child with cancer*. Proceedings of a conference conducted by the Association for Ambulatory Pediatric Services in conjunction with the Children's Cancer Study Group A on November 17, 1966. Edited by A. B. Bergman, & C. J. A. Schultle, 1966, 492–497.

37 Rothenburg, M. B. Reactions of those who treat children with cancer. In Cancer. Proceedings of a conference conducted by the Association for Ambulatory Pediatric Services in conjunction with the Children's Cancer Study Group A on November 17, 1966. Edited by A. B. Bergman, & C. J. A. Schultle, 1966.

38 Dorsel, T. Personal communication, 1976.

39 Friedman, S. B. Care of the family of the child with leukemia. Proceedings of a conference conducted by the Association for Ambulatory Pediatric Services in conjunction with the Children's Cancer Study Group A on November 17, 1966. Edited by A. B. Bergman, & C. J. A. Schultle, 1966.

40 Ablin, A. R., Binger, C. M., Stein, R. C., Kushner, J., Zoger, S., & Mikkelson, C. A conference with the family of a leukemic child. *American Journal of Disabled Child*, 1971, *122*, 362–364.

41 Friedman, S. B., Chodoff, P., Mason, J. W., & Hamburg, D. A. Behavioral observations on the parents anticipating the death of a child. *Pediatrics*, 1963, *33*, 610–625.

42 Lascari, A. D., & Stephbens, J. A. The reactions of families to childhood leukemia: An evaluation of a program of emotional management. *Clinical Pediatrics*, 1973, *12*, (4), 210–214.

43 Morrissey, J. R. Children's adaptation to fatal illness. *Social Work*, 1963, *8*, 81–88.

44 Hailey, A. *Airport*. New York: Doubleday, 1968.

45 Bowlby, J. *Attachment and loss. Vol. II: Separation anxiety and anger*. New York: Basic Books, 1960.

46 Spitz, R. A. Hospitalism: An inquiry into the genesis of psychiatric conditions in early childhood. In *The Psychoanalytic Study of the Child, Volume I*. New York: International University Press, 1945.

47 LeShan, E. *Learning to say goodbye: When a parent dies*. New York: Macmillan, 1976.

48 Brown, F. Depression and childhood bereavement. *Journal of Mental Science*, 1961, *107*, 754–777.

49 Beck, A. T., Sethi, B. B., & Tuthill, R. Childhood bereavement and adult depression. *Archives of General Psychiatry*, 1963, *9*, 129–136.

50 Parness, E. Effects of experiences with loss and death among preschool children. *Children Today*, 1975, *4*, 2–7.

51 Futterman, E. H., & Hoffman, I. Transient school phobia in a leukemic child. *Journal of the American Academy of Child Psychiatry*, 1970, *9*, (3), 477–494.

52 Easson, W. M. *The dying child*. Springfield, Ill.: Thomas, 1970.

53 McCollum, A. T., & Schwartz, H. A. Social work and the mourning parent. *Social Work*, 1972, *17*, (1), 25–36.

54 Martinson, I. M. *Home care for the dying child: Professional and family perspectives*. New York: Appleton-Century-Crofts, 1976.

55 Green, M., & Solnit, A. J. Reactions to the threatened loss of a child. A vulnerable child syndrome. Paediatric management of the dying child. *Paediatrics*, 1964, *37*, 53–66.

56 Rosenweig, S., & Bray, D. Sibling death in anamnesis of schizophrenic patients. *Archives of Neurology and Psychiatry*, 1943, *49*, (1), 71–92.

ANNOTATED BIBLIOGRAPHY

We must all face death, our own or that of a loved one or both. Preparation for facing death is not only possible but appears to be necessary in light of physical and emotional hazards that can arise from ineffectual handling of death and grief. Since children are aware of death from an early age, parents and helping professionals need only create a climate of tolerance toward the subject and direct children's natural curiosity. In addition, parents' and teachers' books can be excellent sources of information and comfort. The topic of death has concerned humankind from time immemorial, and for this reason death has been written about not only in the context of various theologies, philosophies, and recently the sciences, but also in the general literature, including children's books. There are, of course, the all-time favorites in which the subject of death is imbedded in the main theme but not specifically concentrated upon, such as the following books:

Armstrong, W. *Sounder*. New York: Harper & Row, 1969.
Buck, P. *The big wave*. New York: John Day, 1948.
Cleaver, V. *Where the lilies bloom*. Philadelphia: Lippincott, 1969.
Gipson, F. *Old yeller*. New York: Harper & Row, 1956.
Hunt, I. *Up a road slowly*. Chicago: Follett, 1966.
Lawson, R. *Rabbit hill*. New York: Viking Press, 1944.
O'Dell, S. *Island of the blue dolphins*. Cambridge: Riverside, 1960.
Rawlings, M. *The yearling*. New York: Scribners, 1939.
Salten, F. *Bambi*. New York: Grosset & Dunlap, 1929.
Speare, E. *The bronze bow*. New York: Houghton Mifflin, 1961.
Sperry, A. *Call it courage*. New York: Macmillan, 1940.
White. E. B. *Charlotte's web*. New York: Harper & Row, 1952.

Also, in recent years in particular, a number of gifted authors have chosen death as the main theme of their stories. These books can be informative as well as therapeutic not only for children but for adults as well. Wass and Shaak (22) have compiled a brief selected annotated bibliography of such books by age groups. That bibliography is reproduced below.

Preschool through age 7

Brown, M. W. *The dead bird*. Glenview, Ill.: Scott, 1965. A group of children find a bird and feel its heart not beating. They have a funeral for it before returning to their play. Life continues.

Buck, P. *The beech tree*. New York: John Day, 1958. The metaphor of a beech tree is used by an elderly man to help explain his impending death.

De Paola, T. *Nana upstairs and nana downstairs*. New York: Putnam's, 1973. Tommy is heartbroken when his bedridden great-grandmother, with whom he has spent many happy hours, dies. He comes to realize that both the Nana that lived upstairs and the Nana that lived downstairs are "upstairs" in Heaven. The hope of life after death brings satisfaction.

Fassler, J. *My grandpa died today*. New York: Behavioral Publications, 1971. A description of Grandpa sleeping away to a peaceful death in his rocking chair is presented. Knowing his Grandpa was not afraid to die, David is able to continue "running and laughing and growing up with only fond memories of Grandpa." Written in simple story line but with such factual detail that it could be classed as a nonfiction book.

Grollman, E. *Talking about death*. Boston: Beacon, 1970. The finality of death is presented uncompromisingly in simple direct language without softening the blow. Grollman's intent is to protect the child from destructive fantasy and a distorted view of death as well as guilt that often arises when a child is denied information.

Harris, A. *Why did he die?* Minneapolis: Lerner, 1965. A mother's heartfelt effort to speak to her child about death is portrayed. Death is likened to the leaves falling in autumn with new leaves to come in the spring, and to a worn-out motor. Emphasis is on the fact that, no matter what happens, memories of the deceased will never die.

Kantrowitz, M. *When Violet died*. New York: Parents', 1973. A story of the funeral preparations and ceremony for a dead bird, emphasizing the children's reactions, fascination and fun children get out of ceremonies, even funerals. The children are consoled in the continuity of life as shown through their pregnant cat. Life goes on!

Kuskin, K. *The bear who saw the spring*. New York: Harper & Row, 1961. A story of changing seasons and the changes living things go through as they are born, live, and die.

Miles, M. *Annie and the old one*. Boston: Little, Brown, 1971. Annie's Navajo grandmother says she will be ready to die after the new rug is woven. Annie tries to keep the rug from being finished, but her wise grandmother tells her that is wrong, that the "earth from which good things come is where all creatures finally go." Death is a part of life.

Stein, S. B. *About dying*. New York: Walker, 1974. A "shared" and open story about everyday dying, the kind every child meets early in his own life—the death of a pet and a grandparent. Actual photographs accompany the text of death, funeral, and mourning of Snow, a pet bird, and the Grandpa who had given him to the children. The accompanying adult text serves as a resource for handling the questions and discussions arising from the child's natural curiosity. The book explains reality, guiding a child toward the truth even if it is painful, and gives the children the inner strength to deal with things as they are. Preventive mental health!

Tresselt, A. *The dead tree*. New York: Parents', 1972. The life cycle of a tall oak tree is poetically described, showing that in nature nothing is ever wasted or completely dies.

Viorst, J. *The tenth good thing about Barney*. New York: Atheneum, 1971. The rituals of burial and mourning are observed for Barney, a pet cat. The child is led to understand that dying is as usual as living. Death is a part of life. Some readers may question whether young children will be able to comprehend the abstract idea of Barney's future role as fertilizer.

Warburg, S. S. *Growing time*. Boston: Houghton Mifflin, 1969. Jamie learns to accept the reality and meaning of the death of his dog with the help of his sympathetic and understanding family. He finds out that "death is not easy to bear." Something you love never dies; it lives in your heart.

Zolotow, C. *My grandson Lew*. New York: Harper & Row, 1974. The shared remembrances between a mother and a small child of a sadly missed grandfather keep both mother and son from being lonely. Memories keep the deceased alive in your mind.

Ages 8 through 11

Cleaver, V. *Grover*. Philadelphia: Lippincott, 1970. Ten-year-old Grover is forced to handle the changes that the suicide of his ailing mother brought about in his own groping ways, as his father is too grief-stricken to help. He finds out that there is no formula for overcoming grief other than time, friends, and maturity.

Cohen, B. *Thank you, Jackie Robinson*. New York: Lothrop, 1974. The story of the slowly deepening friendship between twelve-year-old Sam Greene and the elderly black cook in Mrs. Greene's restaurant. After following their "main man"—Jackie Robinson—Sam is bereft when Davy suffers a fatal heart attack. Because their relationship seems solid, readers too will mourn Davy's death and sympathize with an honestly grieving Sam.

Lee V. *The magic moth*. New York: Seabury, 1972. A very supportive family bravely copes with ten-year-old Maryanne's illness and death from a heart defect. A moth bursting from its cocoon as Maryanne dies and seed sprouting just after her funeral symbolize that "life never ends—it just changes."

Orgel, D. *Mulberry music*. New York: Harper & Row, 1971. The efforts of a young girl's parents to protect her from the knowledge of her adored grandmother's impending death result in turmoil, both within the girl and around her, when in her rash and rebellious actions the girl searches for her beloved grandmother. Keeping the truth of an impending death from a child can cause misunderstanding and fear.

Smith. D. B. *A taste of blackberries*. New York: Crowell, 1973. Jamie dies of a bee sting. His best friend is confronted with grief at the loss and comes to terms with a guilty feeling that somehow he might have saved Jamie. After a period of grief, life goes on.

Zim, H., & Bleeker, S. *Life and death.* New York: Morrow, 1970. This is an answer book for questions young people have about death. The physical facts, customs, and attitudes surrounding life and death are discussed. Death is described as part of living.

Age 12 and over

Corburn, J. *Anne and the sand dobbies.* New York: Seabury, 1967. Danny's father tries to answer questions about the death of Danny's sister.

Gunther, J. *Death be not proud.* New York: Harper & Row, 1949. The author writes of the courage of his seventeen-year-old son while facing death. The book is a celebration of life. It is more difficult for his parents than for Johnnie to accept his death.

Hunter, M. *A sound of chariots.* New York: Harper & Row, 1972. Bridie McShane's happy early childhood during World War I in Scotland is interrupted by the death of her beloved father whose favorite child she was. As she matures, her life is marred by her sorrow, leading her to morbid reflections on time and death, which she finally learns to deal with through her desire to write poetry.

Klein, S. *The final mystery.* New York: Doubleday, 1974. The meaning of death is explored and how people of different religions have coped with it. The ongoing war against death is discussed.

Rhodin, E. *The good greenwood.* Philadelphia: Westminster, 1971. A tense and moving story of Mike who lost his good friend, Louie. After time and grief pass, Mike came to realize that Louie was really dead and was not going to reappear around the next corner. He came to remember Louie for the clown and dreamer that he was and for the good times they had together. He was not building another Louie as the grownups were, one that was almost perfect.

22 · Being Sick and Facing 80: Observations of an Aging Therapist

Martin Grotjahn

Martin Grotjahn is a psychoanalyst, now retired; he is emeritus professor of psychiatry at the University of Southern California School of Medicine and emeritus training analyst at the Southern California Psychoanalytic Institute. In the piece below, Dr. Grotjahn shares his reflections on "Being Sick and Facing 80" out of the wellsprings of his personal experience, wisdom, insight, and psychoanalytic training.

From The Race Against Time: Psychotherapy and Psychoanalysis in the Second Half of Life, *edited by Robert A. Nemiroff and Calvin A. Colarusso. Copyright ©1983 by Plenum Publishing Co. Reprinted by permission of Dr. Grotjahn and Drs. Nemiroff and Colarusso.*

I do not mind being 79, but to be soon 80 is a different matter. I have doubts that I will live that long since I am sick and definitely handicapped. Death, however, remains inconceivable for me as being nothing—totally nothing, a black hole in the universe.

I have been sick—kidney stones, gallstones, appendicitis—but sickness came and left my life, and I continued more or less as before.

This, my last sickness, is different. It stays with me and I have to live with it. It is here to stay with me and in time to come it will win.

For all my life I looked forward to growing old with great expectation. In my fantasy it seemed I would become wise, slightly detached from the worries of this world, beyond desire and temptation, without frustration and therefore without anger, rage, and fits of temper. Finally, I would be without guilt, without obligations and duties. I just would be alive. That would be true freedom, freedom from inner drive, freedom from outer temptation or threat. I thought as an old man I would finally be what I was supposed to be: I, myself, and *free.*

I assumed that I had reached maturity by now and had reached a time in my growth where I could deal reasonably well with inner and outer reality. The assignment of my age is now to achieve wisdom, which is the ability to deal with the unavoidable reality of death. That seems to be the last assignment—and it seems to escape my reach. So far as I am concerned, old age seems to be combined with a certain amount of physical deterioration and illness—but the mind should and could grow some more, if given a little time longer. If I could express my wish in that matter, I'd say I need one more year—or two.

Facing 80 (in 1984), I probably have to realize that I am already old—to my surprise. I don't really feel it. I do feel sick at times.

I started to work with the aged, individually and in groups, a long time ago (1936). I became a consultant for gerontology in two universities—but I never felt old. Other people around me got old, but I did not. I could walk as well and as far as always. I never noticed whether the road went up the mountain or came down.

I could think and work out clinical experience as well as ever or better than before. I became 60, 65, and even 70, not feeling much change. This is remarkable for me since I always have been and still am my favorite patient and constantly under my increased self-observation. I think I stand in good and constant communication with my unconscious. My self-awareness had become my trusted working tool for understanding patients and myself. When I could understand myself, I could understand others. When I was in a resistance every patient seemed to follow me and work slowed down, and even stopped.

Never have I felt the need to consult any therapist after my training analysis fifty years ago. Since then I always felt I could take care of myself and of *us,* meaning besides myself also my wife and my son. As I took care of them, they took care of me.

My marriage continued where my analysis left off. It was not necessarily in the form of a dialogue, but mostly in the form of a continued self-analysis. I analyzed myself as if I were my own favorite patient—and I analyzed my patients as if they were myself—more or less.

Anyhow, feeling young or old, I decided to work less when I was 75. I wanted to have more time for contemplation, more time for doing nothing. I tried to do more of nothing. I tried not to follow any ambitions left in me from former times—but there was always another essay to write, another lecture to give, another book to think about, and another city to visit.

My son Michael, who sometimes seems to have learned already what I still have to learn, asked me: "Did you ever sit down and do nothing?" That did it—and I started to do more of nothing.

Then suddenly it happened. I got an "asthma" attack, which I never had experienced in my life. I was not especially surprised or alarmed. I had been allergic to dust, especially when the wind blew from the desert. I reacted sometimes with severe vasomotoric rhinitis. I had often wondered why I did not have asthma since my brother and sister suffered with it.

That night I could not sleep, and an indescribable terror overpowered me. I felt I was being annihilated and destroyed. I was facing absolute, stark, timeless, formless nothingness. Ernst Simmel told me once that he did not mind dying so much as being dead. I felt beyond dying. I know death fear—but this time death was already in me, it stopped my breathing and stopped my heart.

I lived through that night—or, rather, my wife lived me through. She did not do anything—she just was there with me, and I was not alone. We waited for death to come, or for the morning—whichever might come first. I told her about this anxiety but nobody else. I thought it was embarrassing and shameful for a psychiatrist to feel anxiety. In the morning we went to my doctor. In his office I already regretted having come. I felt better and did not feel I had the right to bother him. The "asthma" was almost gone—if there ever was a man with "imagined health," it was I.

My doctor was not fooled—he was shocked. One look at my electrocardiogram showed a total left bundle branch block which had not been there at previous occasions. My doctor suspected that I was having a coronary occlusion right there. He also knew me well enough not to tell me. I probably would have walked away, not believing him. So he called an ambulance first—and when I saw those men with the litter and the oxygen, he told me, and I didn't see any way to protest against the hospitalization. I went to the intensive care unit, in the ambulance, with sirens blaring, and with my wife in hot pursuit of us, desperately trying to keep up with the ambulance.

I still did not feel old—I did not even feel sick. I felt annoyed about the whole circus performance.

I needed a second, much more serious congestive heart failure to realize that something was seriously wrong with my heart. That did it: At first I felt sick, then old. I had angina pectoris attacks, spells of dyspnea, later palpitations—and most of all, overpowering, humiliating anxiety attacks, which I considered most inappropriate for a psychiatrist. The typical angina pain developed only a few weeks later.

It was a panic without visual images, far beyond any words—a certainty of impending death. Only the kind face of my wife would reassure me (and nitroglycerin of course relieved me promptly of pain). The fact that my son appeared—he is, like my wife, also a physician—gave me courage and hope, as well as it showed me that other people took my condition seriously. So I was not only hysterical, I was also sick!

My physicians were still worried and decided on all kinds of tests and they recommended a pacemaker as a "precaution." The procedure gave me a pneumothorax and considerable additional discomfort.

Then a slow recovery followed: As long as I live within my restrictions of most limited walking and a strict low-sodium diet, I live in quiet comfort—but now definitely like an old man. I do not work anymore and I walk little. Peculiarly enough, I feel all right about it. All of a sudden, fifty years of work in psychiatry, psychoanalysis, and group therapy seems to be enough. Now I have no more worries about patients, no more guilt that I don't understand somebody well enough, no more bad conscience that I do not know how to help them more. I feel free from the guilt which goes with our work: the feeling of never being as good as one ought to be to help somebody. Let other people worry now. I am through with work and worry—I am a free man.

I sit in the sun watching the falling leaves slowly sail across the waters of the swimming pool. I think, dream, draw, sit—I feel (almost) free of this world of reality. This fall, this southern California "winter" seems more beautiful than I have ever seen it.

Whoever would have told me that I would be quietly happy just sitting here—reading a little, writing a little, and mostly enjoying life in a quiet and modest way—I would of course not have believed. That a walk across the street to the corner of the park would satisfy me more than a long walk only two years ago when I thought a four-hour walk was just not enough—that surprises me.

I have time now. I do not know how much time is left for me to live, but I am in no hurry: I am in no hurry to get anywhere, not even to the end of time. That can wait. When that time comes, I will try to accept it. I have no illusions; it will not be easy.

Right now I live in the moment and I want to sit here a little while longer, quietly, and hoping not to sit in anybody's way.

I always thought old age is an achievement in itself. I now know better: To get sick and to live on, *that* is an achievement.

HOW TO FACE THE NOTHINGNESS OF BEING DEAD

When I was born, the old and wise woman from the neighborhood came to foretell my future. She listened to the screams of my rage and said: "He will love the yellow of eggs—but he will learn nothing." My mother loved the poetry of these words and I have heard them often.

I did not do badly in the almost 80 years of my life. I even learned a little how to live from the people who did not know it and came to me to learn. But now I am stuck again. I am not ready to die, not ready to say goodbye to this life. I am not ready to say goodbye to myself. That seems to be the worst: to say goodbye to myself.

Through all the years I have built myself and in that way I am a self-made man, or a "self-found" one.

I know dying is unpleasant—but to be dead is *nothing*. I like that even less.

Sure, I am a narcissist—who in our profession is not? I think of all the investment I have made in myself—the analysis, the endless training, the continued self-analysis, the drive to understand, to give insight, and the wealth of knowledge accumulated in a lifetime; all this I should give up?

Fifty-five years of marriage were built with care, study, insight, learning, and patience, and grew to ever-deepening love. I am a most impatient person of genuine bad temper, but I worked on myself, tried to deepen my insight—to become a better therapist and a better person—and finally all should turn to ashes? Just because my heart does not want to do its part anymore? One does not need to be a narcissist to find that unacceptable. To say goodbye to myself and vanish into nothingness? Well, it shall be done. Nobody claimed it would be easy.

I would not want to live my life all over again. I would not want to go to a Prussian school again, to worry about being loved or not. I am equally certain that I would only accept the offer to live a much longer life—in relative health. I would so much like to see "who wins"—or what happens next.

How come so many of my friends accepted death as a matter of course? It may be just that—that death may happen to me too: I hope it will not be tonight and not tomorrow either.

My friend James got angry, very angry; he knew that scotch and a tranquilizer took the edge off his rage. And when there was no more rage in the course of a long night, there was no more James either.

My friend Byron did not want to die, but he was obsessed by the idea that he did not need to be in pain. So he took sedation, ever and ever heavier sedation, until he felt no pain any more. He finally felt nothing, not even himself, and so he was dead.

Maria wanted to die before her arms became paralyzed. She had a degeneration of her spinal cord. And so she took a heavy overdose of sedation, made love as she had planned, said goodbye to herself, and was gone.

I knew a murderer for whom to kill was the ultimate fulfillment, an indescribable lust. When he was told he would have to die, and was made ready for execution, he turned to me and wanted to know whether he would hear his blood rushing out of his neck. That, he knew, would be the moment of greatest lust. I did not know the answer; but I did not interfere with his lustful hope.

My friend George could not die and wanted me to help him. I told him as long as he needed help to die, he was not ready and I would be on the side of life. When he would be ready, he would not need me and would die. He heard me and even understood me, and died that night.

The poor little rich girl Juliana suffered and suffered, fought, and suffered some more. She had no illusion and finally followed her husband silently, obediently, submissively, into the unavoidable nothing.

If I think that millions of people will greet the sun tomorrow morning and I may not, I get mad. Well, I am old. I had a good and full life. I tried my best, and I should be ready to leave, or at least I should be able to learn how to accept the end and wait quietly. I loved and was loved—and that I shall not take with me? Then I will not go!

I still love the yellow of eggs—but I do not learn my last lesson. I live quietly; it is now a life of moderation and meditation—but I live. It is the nothingness I fear. I remember the nothingness of narcosis, and I know there is nothing to remember—there is no suffering and no boredom, there is not even a feeling for nothingness. It will not be terrible—it will be nothing.

DREAMS OF DEATH

Last night I dreamt about my father, who had been my mother when I was a child. He died over fifty years ago (1931). He did not say anything in my dream—he never did talk much. Silence was his answer.

Dreams of death are often beautiful. It always has struck me as sad that when people finally have beautiful dreams, they are dreams of death. In these dreams, people dream about beautiful castles, which represent the houses of the parents, frequently of the dead parents. I dream frequently of the university in the city of God, the city of learning for me. In these dreams I have the vague feeling I don't belong there, or I do not find my room, or my room has been given away to other people. When I dream about beautiful landscapes, fountains, and streams, I associate immediately with fantasies about the marvelous life hereafter—in which I seem to believe only in my dreams.

How banal and naive death symbols may be even in the dreams of a person so complex and supposedly sophisticated as an aging therapist! They are dreams of traveling: riding the train from here to hereafter; the slow emptying of the train, meaning the departure of so many friends; collecting books and notes, symbolizing all my knowledge I want to take along and can't; jumping out of the train and over a deep and dangerous looking trench; being in that part of Berlin where my father died many years ago.

The following dream was dreamt in the night after a visit to my physician, who was as pleased with my state of health as I was:

I was riding in a train, going from a suburb of Berlin (the city of my birth) to the terminal in a dilapidated part of Berlin. I was aware that the train got slowly empty of people. I had made myself comfortable, unpacked several books, many papers, notes, pens and pencils, and writing paper. I realized that I would have to leave the train at the next stop. I had increasing anxiety to get my belongings together, stuffing them in several briefcases, looking back to see whether I left anything. The train stopped, the door opened, and there was a deep, bottomless trench, or empty space, between the train and the station platform. I thought that other people got out there and so would I. I stepped back and then ran with full speed to the door. I made a gigantic jump, landing with all my stuff "on the other side."

I realized it was late when I left the station and I could not walk to visit my father; I wanted to take a taxi, but there were none. There were only a few horse-drawn carriages, as I remember them in Berlin from the time before the war back in 1914. They did not stop when I tried to flag them down—so I woke up highly annoyed.

A patient of mine succeeded in visiting me while I was in the intensive care unit of the hospital. (I do not remember his visit.) A year later, when he visited me at home, he told me a "most banal" dream. He saw an airplane overhead. Suddenly it took a nosedive, could not pull out of it, and crashed into a tree.

"Just like that tree in front of your window." The pilot got out of the plane as if nothing had happened to him. When the man started to tell the dream he was not aware of its meaning; when he, however, mentioned the tree in front of my window, the meaning became clear to him.

I have learned how to wait and I too have learned how to be silent. When my time comes I hope it will not be up to me to accept it or not. There will be no choice I hope, no alternative, not even an acceptance. There will be nothing. Come to think of it, that is what my father finally meant I should do: I should do nothing—and quietly enjoy my existence as long as it lasts.

LOVE IN A MARRIAGE OF FIFTY-FIVE YEARS

We—that is, my wife and I—have known and loved each other for a long time—it was fifty-seven years ago that we met for the first time and we have been married for almost that long (fifty-five years). We never regretted our love, even if it was not always easy. The greatest conflict between us was always that I am never, and my wife is always, worried. I don't want to worry, because it diminishes my hope and confidence in the future: My wife must worry because—she says—"I am not happy if I have nothing to worry about."

People often ask us: "How did you manage to live together for such a long time? In our time of divorce?" My wife feels embarrassed by this question and about the fact that other people remark about it. She does not think our marriage was an endurance test she won.

It seems to me that people do not "solve" problems or conflicts—not even in psychoanalysis. People live out of them, or away from them—they don't really forget them. As they go through a new phase of their lives, new conflicts arise and the old ones become less important. A long psychotherapy is sometimes justified because in such situations a therapist tries to keep his patient going long enough until he has grown and turns to new periods in his life, leaving old conflicts behind. A friend of mine said it perfectly: "Old analysts do not die; they shrink away."

Of course, it helped that our marriage was blessed by good luck—for which I give my wife full credit—and I take some credit myself. It is one thing to be lucky—it is of equal importance to be ready for it, to use it, and to go on from there to the next stroke of good luck. The first chance to escape is always the best—the first chance to success will never return.

We have not lived our lives together without grief, unhappiness, even despair. But the peculiar fact remains that all these tough times have brought us closer together. I once asked her: "How would you live without me?" And she answered with that calm smile of the ageless woman, "After you have gone, I will follow you soon. Don't worry."

When I read about the joy of sex in old age I have to laugh. It amuses me to guess the researcher's age and experience according to his claims. When an old man talks to young or younger would-be sexologists, he rarely tells the truth. Old men are as unreliable as informants as boys in puberty showing off. And old women talk about other people's sexuality—but never, or very rarely, about their own. What old people know and what they say to each other, if they have the courage to face the facts of old age, is quite different from what they told the researcher or wrote as answers in his questionnaire.

Sex in old age—and with that I mean age closer to the 80s than to the 70s—seems to be split in pre-genital indulgences and, I feel tempted to say, "post-genital" or "post-ambivalent" feelings, in the form of tender love, which is mostly a sexual love. It is nevertheless true love, as it is often deep and of everlasting strength.

Old people love less—and mean it more. Old people have intercourse less often—after a couple of coronaries, or when taking diuretics—but they feel deeply, nevertheless.

This is a great lesson old people could teach the younger generation. There is nothing to regret or to envy the younger ones for. To love and to feel loved in old age anticipates that the old ones I am talking about have not become lonely, frustrated, bitter, and despaired.

The enjoyment of looking remains strong and alive in old age. A young and pretty nurse in an intensive care unit is sent by the gods, and appreciated as that. When she combines her attractiveness with good humor—and that includes tolerance and kindliness—everybody will be happier for it in a quiet way.

Sex cannot be repressed, nor can it be sublimated—it certainly can be controlled or disciplined. Sex has to be enjoyed. But sexuality may certainly become less important in later years. Then tenderness in love and friendship can grow like never before. I feel it in relationship to my son and my friends—the few ones which are still around—but most of all I feel it to my wife, Etelka. I also feel it from her. (She is almost as old as I am, but nobody is to know that.) Her name means for me the strange one—the one who came from the dark into the light—the ageless, the understanding one. She always had a kind of superior attitude toward me, which I tried to change for many years and later accepted. It is that kind of benevolent superiority which experienced and mature women develop most frequently when they have been mothers. They then identify with the Mother—and begin to feel that men identify forever with the Son.

When our son left us to start his own family, Etelka changed her attitude toward me somewhat. She no longer treated me as the older of two, but I had become now the only one. I remained still, definitely, one to be taken care of. When I once asked her, "What would you do if I would grow up overnight?" she only smiled, and left the question unanswered. To have felt the nearness of death together was a binding, loving experience—even if I do not recommend it for that purpose.

To feel the nearness of death has done something else to me: It has taught me how to cry—how to feel tears welling up in my eyes. I have often wondered why I never could cry—neither on the death of my father, my brother, my mother, my sister, nor anybody else. Tears of homesickness seemed ridiculous to me.

When I came home from the hospital, I had become old. Etelka smiled at me and said: "I have adopted you."

It is this kind of tender love which I needed and to which I tried to respond in kind. To have that kind of love makes us both happy. Life had become worth living all over again when such tenderness is the final prize.

My story would be incomplete if I did not mention my son, who has become my friend in these times of sickness. He saw me when I was closer to death than to life in the intensive care unit. It seems that to feel the nearness of death washes away all aspects of ambivalence in old and in young. With a different intensity, this is also true in my feelings to my friend who was with me and still is.

I hope when my time comes to say goodbye to this world and to myself, and when I sink into nothingness, I will have enough presence of mind left to say my last words. I would like to say once more and for the last time to my wife: "I love you."

23 · Reactions to One's Own Fatal Illness

Erich Lindemann

Dr. Lindemann was, for many years, professor of psychiatry at Harvard and medical director of the Wellesley project, a landmark study in community psychiatry. He is most noted for his pioneer work in crisis intervention (which began with his working with the survivors of the infamous Coconut Grove fire). He died of cancer in Palo Alto, California, in 1974. The preliminary remarks (in italics), below, were written by his widow, Elizabeth B. Lindemann.

Reprinted with permission of Jason Aronson, Inc., from Beyond Grief: Studies in Crisis Intervention *by Erich Lindemann and Elizabeth Lindemann. Copyright © 1979 by Jason Aronson, Inc.*

Even if he had said nothing worthwhile, the scene would have been impressive: the professor who was also a patient standing in the narrow, windowless room in the basement of the Stanford Medical School, where he had recently been undergoing radiation therapy, before a small group of residents, technicians, and nurses. He had had a sacral chordoma for six years and would have two more years of unspeakable suffering. He could have been excused for withdrawing, but giving came as naturally to him as breathing.

Those present on that February morning in 1972 heard him thank them for their unsuccessful efforts at curing him. If they had been trying to avoid thinking about what having terminal cancer meant to some of the people they were treating, they now heard of several ways to help these patients come to better terms with prospective death.

David Satin has called this chapter "the ultimate expression of Dr. Lindemann's characteristic openness with others and the clearest statement of his companionship and sharing with the patient as his therapeutic stance."

I am delighted to have the opportunity to express my appreciation for the fact that I am able to be here, without much discomfort, and able to be an active participant in academic life again. I came here last November looking for help; I was quite crippled as far as my activities went because of pain and general discomfort. It would be only natural for me, since I am in that branch of medicine that deals with experiences and subjective states, to talk a bit about how patients feel, in general, when they are confronted with approaching death, mediated through a malignancy or other conditions; and say a little how a particular kind of person, of my age and attitude and values, reacted to the confrontation with the situation. I should like to mention that it was Mrs. Lutzker, the department social worker, who first suggested that I talk about this theme. Her daily presence in the radiation service was one of the very important items of the treatment experience, to which I shall refer later.

How does one get to the problem, confrontation with death? At the Massachusetts General Hospital, where I worked for thirty years, we came to it through our interest in how people react to losing part of their body —partial death. We studied women who had had a hysterectomy. They found themselves reacting with surprising distress to this event: Instead of being grateful to their surgeon, they were furious with him! One of these women was admitted to our psychiatry service after having knocked her surgeon flat on the floor on the follow-up visit; she was so scared that her fist would fly out again that she said, "Help me against this violent impulse!" And so we became interested, and our first study was of a series of women who had had hysterectomies, comparing them with patients who had had cholecystectomies. And it turned out that indeed they experienced a heightened level of violence and hostile feelings, in most cases quite unspecific and not directed to the surgeon—being irritable, snappy, disliking people more, not being able to stand scenes in the movies where violence was displayed, etc.

The second stage of our interest occurred when the surgeons had to deal with a large number of people after the Coconut Grove fire in Boston who had severe burns and would not cooperate. They were very angry with their well-meaning surgeons, kicked the nurses away, tore off their transplantations and their infusions, and were just nasty patients. On inspection it turned out that those people who were upset in this manner were people who were confronted with death, but not their own: They were afraid that their wife or husband, as the case might be, had been caught in the fire; often they didn't yet know what had happened. They had a high level of uncertainty, and they were concerned with the flood of imagery which comes to the griever about somebody lost.

We then had an opportunity to study what a grieving person does. One of these grievers, before we had learned how to help them, jumped out of a window. It turned out that he wanted to be with his wife. Other patients then gave us a whole variety of the basic ingredients of the grief process. And only when we helped them to do their grieving—once they knew with certainty that the loved one had died in the fire—were we able to make it possible for them to be as cooperative with their physician as I guess I have been here!

Now, what did one have to watch for? This confrontation with death meant induced rage: Who has been the villain? "Was I the villain? I should not have taken my wife to that club. Somebody should have seen that there were proper protections against the fire"—and so on. First, accusations. Accusations, we learned later, often go against the surgeon who lost the patient or against the funeral director. So, increased hostility. Second, waves of sorrow and preoccupation with the image of the deceased. This image was often very disturbing—for instance, being in the fire. A variety of images in one's mind—and really, one of the worst pains there is, is sorrow. Having to suffer this, one gradually masters this pain, and gradually gets away from the inclination one has not to think about it, to be busy with getting the deceased out of one's mind—forgetting it—putting things away which belonged to him; moving into another place so that one will not be reminded of him. Or, one is busy with this aggression against people, looking for the villain but avoiding thinking of the patient. On the other hand, one may suffer through his mourning, and while one does that, do the essentials of grief work, which now becomes important for all people who are faced with a loss, including *losing themselves.*

This grief work has to do with the effort of reliving and working through in small quantities events which involved the now-deceased person and the survivor: the things one did together, the roles one had vis-à-vis each other, which were complementary to each other and which one would pass through day by day in the day's routine. Each item of this shared role has to be thought through, *pained* through, if you want, and gradually the question is raised, How can I do that with somebody else? And gradually the collection of activities which were put together in this unit with the person who has died can be torn asunder and be put onto other people. So it can be divided among other future role partners, who then become loved a little—not much, perhaps, at first—but become tolerable, with whom one can do things and have companionship.

This process is something which can be learned. Thus one can see some people do well, while others never learn it. If they don't learn it they often remain stuck in this early period of grieving, in the first phase of the grief process, in which one has a global relationship to the person lost—perhaps in heaven, perhaps in a picture on the wall. One speaks or prays to that image, sets a place for the person as an imaginary companion at the breakfast table, speaks to the children as if the person were still there, and cannot abandon the total image in favor of partial relationships to parts of that person.

Now I began with parts, when I spoke of losing one's uterus, rather than losing one's whole person. And I think it is important to keep in mind that this problem of relationship to a total entity of a person as compared to partial aspects of one's doing, or to parts of his or her own body, is one of the major themes which occurs in people who are confronted with impending death and who have in their body a dangerous tumor—or, for that matter, have had a heart attack or an amputation of the leg, lose their eyes, etc. In each of these situations, the "job," what we call *grief work*, arises: to think out the aspects of the new role which one has to play in life. With our uterus-deprived women, the question of a new sexual role arises: will I be a cold partner to my husband, or will he think I am, even if I'm not? And so the sexual role relationship threatens to be altered, has to be worked through, and often is neglected to be worked through. The person who loses a leg and has to be rehabilitated has to learn the role of a legless person, who will be received by other people in new role constellations—which must be acceptable to him and to the other persons because one of the ingredients of comfortable living is to have a reference group that accepts one's identity and accepts that network of roles in which one relates to them.

And so in a variety of medical events, which are witnessed by various departments, this process of grieving and of learning new roles takes place, and has to be achieved if one wants to be a mentally healthy griever. Out of this study of grief arose what is now called *community mental health*, where, instead of waiting for illnesses, one tries to find people who are in grief states in response to losses of various kinds, including medical losses, and helps them with these processes. This work is a form of preventive psychiatry or preventive medicine. If they get stuck in this process without knowing it, people then find themselves in a condition of being neurotics, or often psychotics, or angry, ugly persons whom nobody likes. They then become the patients from whom one turns away in the ward, to whom one doesn't talk, and who are so unpleasant and hostile that the social network which is necessary, on the ward perhaps more than in a good many other places, cannot be reestablished with them.

The patient who is caught in the confrontation with a severe impending loss, in this case of his own self, and who has to do *anticipatory grieving*, as we call it now, is facing a psychological job, which can be facilitated by those who look after him or be impeded inadvertently because one doesn't know what is going on; and so one comes out with some of the casualties of maladaptive grief processes. They then have to be handled one way or the other, and usually one is very unhappy with these people.

Now let us turn away from partial losses and think about losing of oneself in threatening death. Some time left, a little time left, a long time left?—how much, one doesn't know. How many impeding aspects are there in the situation? And one of the big things is uncertainty, as it was with our burn patients—the uncertainty about the timing of one's own loss. The problem then is the reaching out and clamoring for information from the physician that he often cannot give. One of the tensions between the patient and yourselves is that you cannot give the information which he wants and which in some way you really ought to be able to give him; but you have a lot of misgivings about giving him that. I went through this in a very big way indeed with my illness and the threat in my system. And so it is a matter of knowledge: information seeking is an essential part of the mentally healthy effort of adapting to a crisis situation.

Around this matter of information getting so many issues have arisen that a whole book has been written about it by Anselm Strauss, a sociologist, and a nurse friend of his. They write in great detail, having studied various hospitals, about the habitual "culture pattern" of communication of the doctors, nurses, and social workers vis-à-vis one another, the patient, and the family. The problem is what information to give to whom, to avoid contradictory information to different participants in a social orbit. Problems arise such as who ought to be the bearer of good or bad news. The relevant participants in this social orbit are likely to receive opposing messages, and the patient is confronted with contradictory information. Then his task is not to adapt to information, period!—but to figure out what is right and what is wrong. And so information getting and transmission is one of the important things.

The second thing is, what does one do with sorrow, the bad feelings? Patients who are confronted with impending loss are busy with weeping, with painful experiences; and there is an inclination in many medical cultures to consider the good patient as a brave patient, who doesn't show any misery and who—you might almost say—is nice to the doctor by not showing how upset he is because he doesn't want to make his friend the doctor upset. This is a very common reaction among patients. And so the problem is, how does one deal with the masses of emotion? Well, the important thing is that emotions can be displayed and emotions can be shared. Often the nurses are the ones who are the most skillful in this, in sharing the emotions, and who, however, then need a little backing from *their* friends in their social orbit when they go through too much of that. The nurses in the intensive care unit are especially endangered in that way, with such an immediate threat of death. And all these things happen very rapidly, over and over again, and they need help. For instance, in some of the intensive care units we now have nurses' groups, in which they tell each other about feelings such as "I killed that patient—I didn't watch out at the right moment," and that sort of thing, this sense of guilt about not having been properly available or not having used the right judgment. And so the problem of emotions arising and being displayed has to do not only with the patient but also with the caretaking staff: doctor, nurse, social worker, etc. —with their responses and with their sharing, with the patient and with their colleagues, and with themselves. And this emotional impact is a job to be done which takes time . . . And if you have to come to terms with your own demise, it also takes time.

A number of studies have now been done under the heading of terminal care, trying to figure out carefully what is the mode by which this job is done by patients under various circumstances. How is it different in the case of mentally healthy versus neurotic patients, and what devices does one learn from one patient that one can give to another patient. This matter of learning from sufferers and communicating with new sufferers about it has now become a part of psychiatry called *research on coping*. How do people cope with stress situations, such as impending death? And how can one tell other people confronted with such stress how it has been done by successful persons? And how can the means be taught most effectively?

Now, what sort of things have I, for instance, learned, and which did I use in my own coping? One thing which impressed me very much was a book by Hans Zinsser, who was a faculty member at Stanford some years ago—a man who died of leukemia at a relatively young age, when he thought he had only done about a third of what he was going to do. He had to grieve about himself. Since grieving means to review shared experiences, he reviewed those experiences which he had had with Hans Zinsser! He looked him up very carefully, and reconstructed his life, and out of this came one of the most fascinating books, called *As I Remember Him.* In it he describes this partly idealized, partly odd sort of person who was that wonderful guy Hans! Putting him there and loving him—and perhaps sometimes while he was writing, sorrowing a lot—he came to terms with the fact that this *was* once, and lives in memory, but in the future will not be there as an identity. It can only be represented by symbols, such as a book, or—there is a building named for me in Boston, the Lindemann Mental Health Center, which means an awful lot. So you have something which continues your identity's existence by a global attribute, a book or a building which then allows the survivors to remember those things which are pertinent to *you*, the particular person, just as at various stages of your anticipatory grieving you think about various aspects of that life which you are now reconstructing.

Now the reading of this book was a revelation to me and led me to wonder, in looking at grief patients, if they have similar tasks? They don't write books, but with members of their families, or the nurse, they have confidential exchanges about the sort of things they did with other people. They like to be visited by a lot of friends, as long as they don't feel too embarrassed about their emotions, and would like to pick up items in their lives which they shared with the future survivors. And they will rub in these experiences with the family and friends, so that they will be sure to remember when they are gone. So this constructing a collective surviving image of oneself which still will be there when one happens not to be there any more in the flesh is the core of grieving, which, if it is done well, is apt to become an admirable process—a fascinating process if one is lucky enough to witness it.

And every once in awhile one hears about some person who is confronted with a severe illness and is not going to live, who is an inspiration to somebody else. And from our observations, it is these people who do such a good job of recalling their own lives and their own shared experiences, constructing an image which is a tenable image of a human being.

Now if that is so, one can understand why in books dealing with terminal care, the authors are concerned that there is not enough contact between the patient and his family. The family gets into a conflict over whether to stay or not, how much to share in the patient's illness; whether these sometimes trite things which the patient brings up are worth the time of the patient and everybody else. And for the family, a very important problem may come up, which may have been mentioned here by David Kaplan and Dr. Fishman in connection with the mothers of leukemic children—namely, that one does one's grieving so well that one emancipates oneself from the person who is going to die and then has no relationship any more. The parents don't know whether to visit or whether to stay away; if they try to pull themselves out of the bondage they will feel they are disloyal. This problem of a relationship which may be severed too successfully becomes a difficult one for the anticipatory griever. Sometimes patients who have a terminal illness come to terms with this illness, are all settled; and then when people still come, they don't want to see them any more. One wonders what is the matter with them unless one is aware of the fact that a process has been going on, and one has to tap at what phase this process now is.

The next point is the problem of the model for this new kind of endeavor, coming to terms with one's own death. How have other people done it? Does one know somebody who was a good terminal patient? Therefore, the need to know other patients, knowing other people in a similar predicament, becomes so important. That's why some departments have developed groups of patients who meet each other, and why I found the experience in your waiting room helpful, where we got together in our funny little gowns and where you can see the typical evolution of a group process. People when they first come there are very stiff, they don't talk, "they really aren't sick but have just come in order to be irradiated"; finally someone dares to speak about leukemia; what a remarkable place this department is compared to other clinics where they may have been treated; *they* don't know yet what's wrong, but *they* are surely going to find out. So they are proud of the place, and having something to be proud of, they gradually begin to be proud of themselves, telling each other what good patients they are. And a little later, the problem is, can they tell each other what good grievers they are, and how they can come to terms with their death. That comes only after quite a while; it is likely to come first in a dyadic relationship; with a nurse or with a doctor whom one trusts. On the other hand, the learning from a model, perhaps doing it better than a model who doesn't do so well—that's the kind of thing one can have only in a group. And that is where the information we have assembled in psychiatry about group process is very important here, in this particular section of general medicine.

Having a model, then, for the grief process is the third item one hopes will be successfully managed in the person exposed to this need in his life. If it is done successfully, we rejoice with the patient; if he fails to do it, we hope there will be somebody who knows this sort of thing. And we have made great efforts to have not only psychiatrists but also our medical colleagues and our clergymen, who are often the persons chosen as communicators by physicians, know some of these aspects. I think . . . the thing that hits you is that . . . it is not just a naughty patient, or one who doesn't know what it is all about, but a patient who is caught up in not knowing how to do a certain psychological task.

Now I'm sure you don't often have a patient who is also a physician and a psychiatrist and who went through this, and so I shall say a little about some of these items of the work which indeed I have done somewhere, otherwise I couldn't talk with ease about it. They happened to align themselves in confrontation with a chordoma, one of the worst forms of tumor, which was discovered during an exploratory operation three years too late, having been misdiagnosed for three years as a virus or a disc. The surgeon, when he came to send me to radiation, saying he couldn't remove it, was so unhappy that *I* had to comfort *him*, that he had missed the boat. And he said, well, you have three or four years now, can you do with three or four years? Then it really hits you, and the thing that hits you is that you are not immortal. Because there is a curious conviction in some way in everybody that one is immortal. We can't really imagine ourselves dead. When you dream about death, you dream you are a perceiving dead person, and not a person who is nonexistent. And so you search for an image of what that is. There is a story about three clergymen who decided to check with each other, being sure that they would come back after three days; and one of them, being resurrected somehow, is supposed to tell his friends how it was, but all he can report is "totaliter aliter"—absolutely different!

And so one has to recoil from the nonexistence—and then say, what existence? Then the Zinsser model comes to one's mind—namely, the existence is the memory of the person who one was. One thinks back about the past, like mad! All the childhood experiences, boyhood experiences. I began to recall German poems I had memorized, and in terms of this poetry, relive past experiences. And as an older person looks back to an earlier period, just as Goethe in *Faust* looks back to the Ur-Faust, when he was a young man, he sees that that self which was there was interacting with other people as I do now, and I really am a chain of selves; one of them I am now, and in the future there will probably be just an agglomeration of these selves in the memory of other people.

And the next thing I did, which was so important for me as an anticipatory griever, was to actually look at the places of former experiences. I went to Germany and visited the places where I had grown up, the house of my birth; tried to find some people whom I had known then; went back to Heidelberg where I started my career; and did something which I should have done if I had stayed in Heidelberg instead of coming to the United States—that is, I gave a lecture to the medical students. It seemed important to make up for this opportunity which had been missed and which might not occur again. This making up for missed opportunities is a very important element, which anticipatory grievers can't do if they don't know they are going to die. As one knows from grief studies, unrelieved hostile relationships and quarrels which have not been redeemed are just as difficult an aspect of grieving as loving relationships which have led to a great attachment and a great loss of instinctual fulfillment. And therefore, getting quarrels straightened out with the people who are concerned is good not only for oneself who goes, but also for the people who stay afterwards. And to allow some people to have a fight with some of their relatives, maybe on the ward or in an appropriate room when they are in this particular period of life, rather than think "I must stop this right away and intervene" is a good thing to know.

And so, after dealing with the past and the present, the next thing is to get somehow a structure of the remaining future. Now that is where doctor, nurse, and the patient have to be so much together. So often you don't know exactly what to say. The problem is, how can you formulate the future in such a way that it is emotionally tolerable, that it is possible still to do certain things, and that there is an acceptable image of what happens after I am gone—that the people who are left here will have a tolerable life without me. What happens to the other people's grieving after I am gone, and what happens to the empty spot in the social system. Parents who leave children want to know how their children will grieve about them; what happens with the particular job and the particular income—that's where the social worker comes in—and with the particular place which one happens to have had as a buffer person between other people in a complicated social system. For example, one may have felt quite sure "that as long as I am there nothing can go wrong with the others." So one has to straighten that out. In other words, there has to be an opportunity to think about, recollect, and then enact those scenes which are unfinished business.

I really became hypomanic, in the sense that I raced around and wanted to do all the things that would be wonderful to do once more. In other words, see that people who are confronting death are not in an environment which is restrictive of *doing* possibilities; that they are still as mobile as is compatible with their ailments, and still as rich in possible experiences for a little while. I guess it isn't silly to make up for the things you won't have any more of later, and token fulfillment along that line can make an enormous difference.

These are the things to be worked at; and one can be a knowledgeable accomplice in this, as doctor, nurse and social worker, or one can stand there and be baffled: Why is the patient so ununderstandable? If the patient feels that you don't understand him, of course he often won't do certain aspects of his share of the treatment. Now one serious difficulty is that in an institution you don't have any time—I was amazed at how much time you people were able to take with me—and don't have the emotional resources to think of the patient as a suffering person who is going to die and lose himself, rather than as a specimen of a biological species with certain impairments which I luckily am able to fix up to a certain extent. "Maybe he, in my statistics, isn't one of the lucky ones, but I have a lot more who gradually can make up for him." Only "biological statistics" doesn't work for the patient; that is one of the things which requires an awful lot of altruism on the part of the patient who is just now very busy with narcissistic endeavors. But I think that once one understands this process, one can be surprised at how little actual time expenditure is needed to say the right word at the right time, and not too much; the right kind of affirmation that one accepts the patient with his particular style of coping; and in doing so forms what we call a therapeutic alliance with the patient—a companionship with the patient in the effort which he is making, rather than having him as the target of our ministrations.

24 · St. Christopher's Hospice

Cicely Saunders

*Dame Cicely Saunders, Medical Director of St. Christopher's
Hospice near London, has waged a lifelong war against the
needless pain and indignity which so often surround death. This
selection, which is excerpted from her annual report of St.
Christopher's, reviews some of the ways in which a contemporary
institution is developing programs for helping terminally ill
patients achieve a decent and "appropriate" death.*

*From St. Christopher's Hospice Annual Report 1971–72. Reprinted
by permission.*

WHAT IS A HOSPICE?

In one sense, St. Christopher's was founded when a
patient left us the first gift of all, back in 1948, but in a deeper one, it belongs to
a tradition stretching back to the hospices of the Middle Ages which welcomed the pilgrims who arrived hungry, tired, and sore as they crossed
Europe on the way to the various sites of pilgrimage. The word continued to
be used in France and was extended to hospices for the elderly, the incurable
and for foundlings (enfants trouvés). Mother Mary Aidenhead then took up
the title when she founded the Irish Sisters of Charity in the middle of the last
century, although the hospice at Harold's Cross, Dublin, was only dedicated
especially to the care of dying patients sixty-seven years ago. Her foundation
has long extended to several hospices, mainly concerned with the care of the
dying and the long-term sick. St. Joseph's Hospice, Hackney, was founded in
1905, but before it opened its doors the sisters were visiting the sick in their
homes, thus foreshadowing the domiciliary work we have now started at St.
Christopher's over the past three years.

The other tradition from which St. Christopher's springs is that of the
medieval hospital. Apart from the hospices which followed the pilgrim routes
and which were primarily for hospitality, there came to be others, located in
towns, "for the sick and poor" who were literally dying in the streets through
cold and malnutrition, and who were picked up from the gutters and brought
in for care and treatment. It was when these began to be staffed by professional physicians and surgeons that they took the name "hospital." The rich
were nursed and died at home, although at times they made arrangements to
spend their old age in a hospital, praying and preparing their souls for death;
a hospital would often have a special wing for such patients with private
rooms and many amenities. Poor patients, on the other hand, arrived *in
extremis* because they had nowhere else to go. Medical treatment was still
limited, and the chief comfort they could be offered was a religious consolation; they could contemplate the crucifix—"He suffered as I suffer now."

So the word originates back in time with the stopping places for pilgrims and extends through the French hospices and above all through the work of the Irish Sisters of Charity, to the present day. All the groups we have mentioned are gathered within our walls: the elderly residents in the Drapers' Wing; the Playgroup members—not foundlings but the children of staff—who come and cheer us all by their noisy play; those who need longer-term nursing than can be carried out in an ordinary hospital, and who make their home with us and give us all so much in friendship and life; and the very ill to whom we can give a great deal of treatment, often unexpected remission or even cure, but always, we hope, something of real comfort. The staff is, no doubt, more numerous than the monks of the hospice in the St. Bernard Pass, but I think that the way they involve themselves so deeply in the lives and problems of the patients and their families, the way they stay with us and bring their own families and friends to see us, and the way in which students come and come again combine to give us something of the busy, many-sided life of the medieval pilgrimage and its resting places.

The life of St. Christopher's is illustrated by the variety of announcements on the notice board. There is a diagram of the way the hospice finances have gone during these five years, with the mounting expenses (mainly consisting of the payments for salaries and wages of staff) met partly by monies from the regional board and the teaching hospitals and fully supplemented by the many good gifts we receive. There are frequent announcements of the birth of a baby to an ex-staff member, often set alongside the list of the anniversaries of patients who died during the same week a year ago. There is the chapel diary and notices of social and more serious meetings, and sometimes extras such as one never-to-be-forgotten notice, "As you know, the goldfish pond needs restocking . . ." Small things are very important. . . .

THE WORKING OF ST. CHRISTOPHER'S

People often ask us about the waiting list and are concerned at the number of applications they feel we must have to refuse. The situation has changed surprisingly little over the five years since we opened, and numbers have remained fairly constant. We have about 1,500 enquiries a year. Some 500 of these are about patients for whom St. Christopher's care has not been designed. We are often able to make suggestions about other organizations who may be able to help them. Sometimes we have heard that the chance to talk on the telephone has been all that was needed to help people to sort out their problems.

We help approximately two-thirds of the roughly 1,000 patient enquirers which remain. Most of those at home are visited before admission, and it is rare that we fail to admit a patient who is in distress which cannot be helped at home. Some of those who are never admitted include people who, having been given assurance that St. Christopher's will help if the time comes, remain well cared for in their own homes. One of the local family doctors has repeatedly said that he puts his patients on our list as a sort of insurance because he has found that the fact that the family are aware that St. Christopher's is in the background often means that admission will not be necessary.

The number of people we have been able to help has been increasing. During the first full year (1968) we admitted 380 patients, and during 1971 we admitted 489; during 1972, 519; and during 1973, 579.

The first voice on the telephone answering an enquiry from a member of family or the first person seen at the hospice is of great importance. The stewards and everyone at reception are the first people who are met as the hosts at St. Christopher's. The many jobs that they and the maintenance staff do around the hospice in keeping everything as a good gift should be kept is important, but their availability to meet any members of families, visitors, or any other enquirer who comes in is rightly put first by them. We have always tried to make it possible for each patient to see a doctor every day. . . .

All analgesics for patients with malignant pain should be given regularly, usually four hourly. The aim is to titrate the level of analgesia against the patient's pain, gradually increasing the dose until the patient is pain-free. At this stage the dose of analgesic will be given before the effect of the previous one has worn off and therefore before the patient may think it necessary. It is thus possible to erase the memory and fear of pain.

Since the opening of St. Christopher's Hospice considerable interest has been stimulated among nursing staff about the care of the dying and those with chronic pain, and we find that trained staff want to come and work with us to further their experience in this type of nursing. Obviously these trained nurses are not going to stay indefinitely, and therefore it means that we always have a need for this type of staff. One interesting fact has emerged and that is that there is an obvious place here for the young, who show a great interest and an amazing capacity for understanding the needs of our patients. Again, they do not stay longer than about a year as they either marry or move on.

The fact that we have a playroom for the children of the staff has played an enormous part in maintaining a continuity of staffing. This enables a married person, trained or untrained, who has a desire to come back to nursing or care for people, to return to a field of nursing where she has a tremendous amount to give and also finds satisfaction.

There have been times when in order to keep the wards running as they should we have been extended as far as we are able, but help has always come just when we were getting desperate. We have not employed agency nurses—the gaps that occur at holiday periods have been filled by volunteers or by the students and others who do much of their learning by working. . . .

People often say, "How can you work at St. Christopher's Hospice? It must be so depressing." This is just not true. It is a very happy place, but, of course, it has its moments of tension, its moments of distress; but amongst all this there is also joy and fulfillment. The work is hard and heavy, both physically and emotionally, but also very satisfying. Over the past five years the demands on the nursing staff have increased. When we started we based our ratio of staff on a 1–1 basis over twenty-four hours, but that has now been increased to 1.25–1 over twenty-four hours on a year-round basis. I think the fact that fourteen nurses have been with us for over five years and another twelve nurses for over four years emphasizes that there are people who really do want to nurse and that this type of nursing is rewarding. . . .

Referrals come to the staff medical social worker from the doctors, ward and clinic sisters, other staff, from patients themselves and their families, or from the social worker who arranges the admission. Numbers remain steady, at around ninety a year, with proportionately more men than women. Many contacts are necessarily short, and help when needed must be given immediately. Needs vary and are often practical—fares for visiting relatives can be heavy—advice over sorting personal and legal affairs is often needed, and a few patients and residents have been helped to have a holiday. But help is not only of a material kind. As with all the staff, the social worker's job is to listen, support, and counsel.

The social worker also organizes the Family Service Project, a study of the effects of bereavement, which is directed by Dr. Murray Parkes, and was started in May 1970. The purpose is to identify and offer help to any recently bereaved families or friends who may prove unlikely to be able to cope unaided with their grief and the stresses of life caused by their loss. Staff and volunteers visit to assess the need and to offer support, and if more specialized help is indicated, this can be arranged.

The work involved in keeping the records and arranging visits is cumulative. Out of approximately 750 records reviewed since the project started, 118 people have been visited or offered help, and once contact has been established by a visitor, it may continue over several months or occasionally years. . . .

It is good to know that we still have twenty-six volunteers who came to us soon after the hospice opened, and although many volunteers have had to leave us during the past five years, we have been able to maintain a steady flow of new helpers, and our numbers stay at around 100 to 110.

We use voluntary help in every department of the hospice, and this has now been extended to making the curtains and assembling the library for the new teaching and residential block. A team of volunteers also help to get the news letters distributed three or four times a year. . . .

TEACHING

During the year, we have been watching with interest developments on the second site and the rapid rise of the teaching and residential unit down the road. Even more important, though less spectacular, has been the steady growth in the amount of teaching undertaken in the hospice itself. More time has been spent over in-service training for new members of the staff and voluntary workers. We have had in all 2,383 visitors either for a day or for an afternoon visit. This number includes doctors, nurses, social workers, priests, and students of all sorts. There have been over 100 residential visitors

—people who have lived and worked with us and who have been able to learn from the patients and their families the problems of long-term illness and ways of coping.

All the members of the Hospice staff are involved in one way or another with the teaching. As the program develops it will still be based on experience in the wards. Nothing else can take the place of such experience. . . .

CLINICAL STUDIES AND RESEARCH

Our Department of Clinical Studies is gradually extending its work. The evaluation of analgesic (pain relieving) drugs continues, and one of the ward staff nurses has now joined the team as nurse observer. This is enabling us to look at well-established drugs and their use while patients are fully relieved and comfortable and to plan the treatment that suits them best. At the same time a number of other symptoms and their treatment are being considered. This is a long-term project which will eventually be fully reported in the medical press.

A marathon task is undertaken by the recorder (one of the doctors on our council) in making precis of the notes of all the patients who have been in the hospice. This enables us to keep records on a punch card system and to review the many facets of our work year by year. It gives valuable information on the demands for our care as well as our success in giving it, and the statistics compiled from these records have been used by the groups who are planning to enter this field.

Some people with cancer spend most of their illness in hospital, some are cared for at home, and others spend part of their time at home and part in hospital. Each pattern of care has advantages and disadvantages for the patient and for the family. We have been trying to assess these by visiting the surviving spouses of people who have died of cancer in two London boroughs and asking them for their opinion about each phase of the illness. Our analysis to date indicates that although patients are often sent into hospital because of painful symptoms, those who die at home will have more pain than those who die in hospital. From the relative's point of view nursing someone at home is often a time of severe stress, but there is reason to believe that, in the long term, people who have been able to care for someone in this way may find themselves coping with life rather better after bereavement than those who have never had the opportunity to do so.

This study is also enabling us to discover the comments, criticisms, and general attitudes of family members toward various aspects of the care provided by St. Christopher's Hospice. These comments are of particular value in helping us to improve our standards of care. . . .

TWO STORIES

Mr. P. was fifty-two and a proofreader for a national newspaper. He came to us from a teaching hospital with an unsolved problem of pain, unhappy and breathless.

He quickly settled to our regime of drugs, and pain was never a problem again. Mr. P. used the ten weeks he was with us to sort out his thoughts on life and faith, and he found his own way into peace. He was quiet and self-contained, but he enjoyed meeting students and visitors and he made good friends in the ward.

After Christmas I took him some copies of a photograph I had taken of him at one of our parties. I wanted to give it to him, he wanted to pay for it. We ended by each accepting something from the other. As we were discussing this I held my hand out. At this he held both his, palms upwards, next to mine and said, "That's what life is about, four hands held out together." After that we could discuss anything. Once I asked him what he thought about heaven. "If you believe in Him there's just no question," he said promptly. Pressed to go further he added, "It's not as if I could think of Him—like a breathing person—it's the same when you are going on a holiday—you don't know what it will be like when you get there, you just hope it will be nice."

Mr. P. became weary before he died, and though he was somewhat confused for a day or two, this quickly disappeared, and he was very peaceful till he died in his sleep one morning without a sign of distress, not even a sigh. I will never forget the picture of the hands he gave us. I cannot think of a better symbol for our aims for St. Christopher's.

Mr. A., a bricklayer of sixty-one came to the ward after Mr. P. left us. He had been visited at home for fifteen weeks before his admission. He was not very keen to let anyone into his flat, where he lived alone, protecting his independence even from his daughter. Throughout the weeks of his stay in St. Christopher's we had to help him maintain his fight for independence. Short of breath as he was, he would stamp up and down the stairs to the garden or the Pilgrim Room, pausing to look very critically at the progress of the Play Group Wing building on the way. He made many friends and established himself as escort and guide to a blind patient in his bay. His relationships with the other patients were often colourful but always kind. Bed was definitely not on his schedule, and he sat out beside it till his last day surrounded by the *Daily Mirror*, well spread out, ashtrays with endless cigarette ends and ash everywhere.

On his last day he was still in charge, dictating what he would let us give him and very much himself. In the evening he checked that Sister had his sons' phone number correctly. When the night nurses came on he said, "I may give you trouble tonight." He died quietly in his sleep early next morning.

25 ·

Some Aspects of Psychotherapy with Dying Persons

Edwin S. Shneidman

In this selection Dr. Shneidman outlines the ways in which working with a dying person (called clinical thanatology) is different from ordinary psychotherapy.

From Psychosocial Aspects of Terminal Patient Care, *edited by Charles A. Garfield. Copyright © 1978 by McGraw-Hill Book Company. Reprinted by permission of McGraw-Hill Book Company.*

From the psychosocial point of view, the primary task of helping the dying person is to focus on the *person*—not the biochemistry or pathology of the diseased organs, but a human being who is a living beehive of emotions, including (and especially) anxiety, the fight for control, and terror. And, with a dying person, there is another grim omnipresent fact in the picture: time is finite. The situation is dramatic, unlike that of psychotherapy with an essentially physically healthy person, where time seems "endless" and there is no push by the pages of the calendar. One of the main points of this chapter is that just as psychotherapy is, in some fundamental ways, clearly different from "ordinary talk," so working psychotherapeutically with a dying person involves some important differences from the usual modes of psychotherapy.

I

At the outset it is only reasonable that I indicate some issues that are fundamental to understanding any list of therapeutic suggestions. The "rules" for psychotherapy are rather easy to comprehend but their more meaningful application within the context of a stressful dying scenario has to take into account certain subtleties that lie behind the obvious and visible drama. We must look behind the apparent dying scenario if we wish to encompass the powerful and poignant psychological richness inherent in the dying drama. To be specific, I shall suggest that there are three aspects of the dying process that need to be kept in mind.

A. PHILOSOPHIC (MORAL-ETHICAL-EPISTEMOLOGICAL) ASPECTS OF THE DYING PROCESS

One can begin with the assertion that, typically, a death is a dyadic event, involving the chief protagonist (the dying person) and the survivors—basically an I-thou relationship. Toynbee (1969) has stated it succinctly:

The two-sidedness of death is a fundamental feature of death . . .
There are always two parties to a death; the person who dies and the

survivors who are bereaved . . . the sting of death is less sharp for the person who dies than it is for the bereaved survivor. This is, as I see it, the capital fact about the relation between living and dying. There are two parties to the suffering that death inflicts; and in the apportionment of this suffering, the survivor takes the brunt.

Often the situation is even more complicated, involving several persons as in the two vignettes below.

1. A physician asks me to see one of his patients. He tells me, beforehand that her numerous physical pains and complaints have absolutely no organic basis. I see her and talk with her. As much as I try to eschew simplistic diagnostic labels for a complicated human being, the tag of "agitated depression" seems to describe her rather accurately. She is complaining, pain filled; she wrings her hands; her brow is furrowed; she is restless; fidgety, tearful, woebegone. She looks older than her forty years.

   The story is this: Her wealthy husband has a terminal disease. He may very well be dead in a few years or even much sooner. He has told her that she makes him nervous and that he cannot stand her. He has placed her in a private nursing home. She hates that nursing home and wants to return to her own home. Coincidentally, he has employed a practical nurse to massage his muscular pains and also to act as chauffeur and "keeper" for his wife.

   At the end of my session with the wife, the nurse comes into the office to take her back to the nursing home. She is rather heavily made up, and has a striking figure. The picture is suddenly clear to me. The practical nurse is the husband's mistress. The wife has been evicted from her own home. "But, after all," says the doctor, "the poor man is dying."

2. A seventy-year-old man has cancer of the esophagus. He received a course of chemotherapy, which made him excruciatingly uncomfortable—nausea, vertigo, vomiting. Several weeks after the treatment he began to show memory loss, some confusion, and uncharacteristic irritability. A thorough neurological examination disclosed a malignant brain tumor. Another course of treatment was suggested. His son—a physician (neurologist) in another city (who was in daily telephone communication with his parents)—asked his father's doctor to forgo the treatments. To me, on the telephone, the son said: "What is the point of an unknown amount of possible good compared to an onerous treatment of absolutely uncertain benefit imbedded in a procedure which will give him a substantial amount of certain torture?" The local treating physician was incensed. The wife was in a quandary. The treating physician demanded that the patient be told "all the facts" and be permitted to make up his own mind. The physician-son retorted that his father, not being medically trained, was in no position to evaluate "all the facts," and more than that, his mind —specifically his brain—was no longer able to make the ordinary judgments of which he had been previously capable. As the mother's

psychotherapist, I marveled at the sad game of what I called "Who owns the body?"

Toynbee raises the question of who, in the total suffering a death inflicts, is hurt the most? The two criteria are comfort and dignity—their opposites are pain and humiliation (degradation).

Imagine for each of the two vignettes cited above, a chart in the shape of a circle. In each there seem to be four characters: in the first, the husband, the wife, the mistress, and the doctor; in the second, the father, the mother, the son, and the doctor. The second case is compounded by the fact that we do not know, from day to day, what the father can think or experience. How should the calculations of the percentages of dignity, self-esteem, well-being, comfort, sense of accomplishment, freedom from pain, and so on be made? Who should be given the largest percentage; who the least? Should, in the first case, the wife be scapegoated—given electric shocks for her "depression?" In the second case, should the treating physician's wishes—who may have the patient on some research protocol as part of a grant—supersede, in the name of science and possible help for future patients (not to mention the physician's narcissistic and professional investment in his research), the physician-son's emotional feelings about his father's dignity and comfort?

Far from being esoteric abstractions, these philosophic points touch on the deepest questions relating to death: Who have become the priests of death? What are the citizen's rights to "death with dignity"? When can a spouse or grown child say for a loved one, "Enough"?

B. SOCIOLOGICAL (SITUATIONAL) ASPECTS OF THE DYING PROCESS

Inasmuch as nowadays, the majority of terminally ill persons die in institutions—hospitals or nursing homes—it is appropriate to ask: What are the constraints of the social environment? The recent observations and reports of field sociologists such as David Sudnow, author of *Passing On* (1967) (an intriguing description of "what actually happens" in hospitals, especially in emergency rooms and the various uses to which fresh corpses are put), and Barney Glaser and Anselm Strauss, authors of *Awareness of Dying* (1965) and *Time for Dying* (1968) (with their enlightening concepts of "mutual pretense" and "dying trajectory"), teach us that a great deal "goes on" in the institutional interplay that is neither in the organizational chart nor in the brochure given to visitors.

Whether or not a person is resuscitated; how many minutes doctors and nurses spend in a dying person's room; whether a person will be "pronounced dead" on this hospital shift or that; whether or not interns will practice surgery on the dead body—all these occurrences, and others, are what realistic sociologists tell us about—and it behooves us to listen. In an understanding of the dying person, we need to include a keen situational view of the events.

Glaser and Strauss's concept of "the dying trajectory" deserves our close attention. In *Time for Dying* they say:

> When the dying patient's hospital career begins—when he is admitted to the hospital and a specific service—the staff in solo and in concert make initial definitions of the patient's trajectory. They expect him to linger, to die quickly, or to approach death at some pace between these extremes. . . . Since the definition of trajectory influences behavior, these differing definitions may create inconsistencies in the staff's care of and interaction with the patient, with consequent problems for the staff itself, family and patient.

When ordinary, well-functioning individuals are asked about what they consider to be most important to them if they were dying, they usually list "control"—having some measure of "say" over their own treatment and management—as the most important item (followed by relief from pain, which can, in the last analysis, also be subsumed under control). But we see that there are often conflicting agendas between the dying person and his or her fight for dignity (self-control, autonomy) and the hospital staff and their interest in assigning that person (called "patient") to certain roles, including even the pace or rate at which those roles are to be played.

In order to be a "good patient," one has to die on schedule, in accordance with the dying trajectory mapped by the staff. To die too early, unexpectedly, is an embarrassment to hospital staff; but what is more surprising (and of psycho-social interest), is that to linger too long, beyond the projected trajectory, can be an even greater embarrassment to hospital staff—and a great strain on the next of kin who may have premourned and set their mind's clock for a specific death date, which, if not met, becomes painfully overdue.

C. PSYCHOLOGICAL (CHARACTEROLOGICAL) ASPECTS OF THE DYING PROCESS

For the terminally ill person, the time of dying is a multiscened drama, with elements of Shakespearean tragedy and historical (introspective) pageant. It is probably true that each person dies idiosyncratically alone, "in a notably personal way," but nonetheless there are generalizations that can be made about the dying process. From a psychological point of view, the most interesting question is what are the psychological characteristics of the dying process.

In the current thanatological scene there are those who write about fewer than a half-dozen stages lived through in a specific order—not to mention the even more obfuscating writing of a life after death. My own experiences have led me to rather different conclusions. In working with dying persons I see a wide range of human emotions—few in some people, dozens in others—experienced in a variety of orderings, reorderings, and arrangements. The one psychological mechanism that seems ubiquitous is denial, which can appear or reappear at any time. (See Avery Weisman's *On Dying and Denying* (1972).) Nor is there any natural law that an individual has to achieve closure before death sets its seal. In fact, most people die too soon or too late, with loose threads and fragments of agenda uncompleted.

My own notion is more general in scope; more specific in content. It borrows from Adolph Meyer and Henry A. Murray in its spirit. My general hypothesis is that a *dying person's flow of behaviors will reflect or parallel that person's previous segments of behaviors, specifically those behaviors relating to threat, stress, or failure.* There are certain deep *consistencies* in human beings. Individuals die more-or-less characteristically as they have lived, relative to those aspects of personality which relate to their conceptualization of their dying. To put it oversimply: The psychological course of the cancer mirrors certain deep troughs in the course of the life—*oncology recapitulates ontogeny.*

What is especially pertinent is how individuals have behaved at some of the most stressful, least successful times in their lives—whether those incidents relate to stress in school, job, marriage, separations, loss, or whatever. The hypothesis further holds that people's previous macrotemporal patterns and coping mechanisms will give clues about their patterns of behavior when dying—fighting illness or surrendering to it, despairing, denying, and their combinations, as they become increasingly aware of the life-threatening situation.

II

I believe that working intensively with a dying person is different from any other human encounter. The main point is that when a clinical thanatologist (physician, psychologist, nurse, social worker, or any trained person) is working with a dying person, he or she is not just "talking." (There is, of course, an enormously important place for mere *presence*—which, after all, may be the most important ingredient in care—or for sitting in communicative silence, or for seemingly just talking about what may appear to be trivial or banal topics.)

Working with the dying person is a special task. A person who systematically attempts to help a dying individual achieve a more psychologically comfortable death or a more "appropriate death"—given the dire, unnegotiable circumstances of the terminal disease—is either a psychotherapist or is acting in the role of a psychotherapist. That role cannot be escaped. (This is not to say that many others—relatives, church members, neighbors—cannot also play extremely important roles). But the distinction between a *conversation* and a *professional exchange* is crucial; more than that, I now believe that working with dying persons is different from working with any other kind of individual and demands a different kind of involvement; and I am willing to propose that there may be as important a conceptual difference between ordinary psychotherapy with individuals where the life span is not an issue) and psychotherapy with dying persons as there is between ordinary psychotherapy and ordinary talk. The following paragraphs outline what I feel are some of the important nuances of these differences.

1. Ordinary talk or conversation

   In this kind of exchange which makes up most of human discourse, the focus is on the surface content (concrete events, specific details, abstract issues, questions and answers of content). The individuals are talking about what is actually being said: the obvious, stated meanings, and the ordinary interesting (or uninteresting) details of life. Further, the social role between the two participants is one of essential equality, sometimes tempered somewhat by considerations of age, status or prestige. But each of the two parties has the social right to ask the other the same kind of questions which he or she has been asked. Some examples of ordinary talk might be two friends conversing with one another about the events of the day, or two lovers whispering intimate thoughts to one another, or two businessmen closing a deal, or two neighbors simply chatting.

2. A hierarchical exchange

   In this kind of exchange the entire focus (like in a conversation) is on the manifest content—on what is being said—but the situation is marked by an explicit or tacit acknowledgment by the two parties that there is a significant difference of status between them; one of them is "superior" to the other. Questions asked or suggestions made or information transmitted or orders given by one would seem inappropriate if attempted by the other party. Examples would be the verbal exchange between a supervisor and subordinate, between an army officer and enlisted man, or between an oncologist and a patient in the doctor's office. The officer can order the enlisted man, but not vice versa; the doctor can examine the patient, but not vice versa. The doctor-patient relationship is an hierarchical one in that a doctor and a patient do not exchange roles.

3. A professional (e.g., psychotherapy) exchange

   Here the focus is on feelings, emotional content and unconscious meanings, rather than primarily on what is apparently being said. The emphasis is on the latent (between-the-lines) significance more than on the manifest and obvious content; on unconscious meanings, including double entendre, puns and slips of the tongue; on themes that run as common threads through the content rather than on the concrete details for their own sake. Perhaps the most distinguishing aspect of the professional exchange (as opposed to ordinary talk) is the occurrence of "transference"—wherein the patient projects onto the therapist certain deep expectations and feelings. These transference reactions often stem from the patient's childhood and reflect earlier patterns of reaction (of love, hate, dependency, suspicion, etc.) to whatever the therapist may or may not be doing. The therapist (like the doctor) is often invested by the patient with almost magical healing powers, which, in fact, can serve as a self-fulfilling prophecy and thus help the interaction become therapeutic for the patient. The roles of the two participants, unlike those in a conversation, are not coequal. The situation is hierarchical but the focus is not on the manifest content.

4. A thanatological exchange

A person who systematically attempts to help a dying individual achieve a psychologically comfortable death (or a more "appropriate" death or an "ego-syntonic" death)—given the dire, unnegotiable circumstances of the situation—is acting in a special role. (This is not to say that many others—doctors, nurses, relatives, dear friends, specially trained volunteers—cannot also play extremely important roles.) If the distinction between a conversation and a professional exchange is crucial, certainly the distinction between working with dying persons as opposed to working with any other kind of individual is a vital one. Working with a dying person demands a different kind of involvement. My position is that there may be as important a conceptual difference between ordinary psychotherapy and working with dying persons as there is between ordinary psychotherapy and ordinary talk. Below, I have attempted to limn out some of the important nuances of these differences.

III

I believe that every physician should be a clinical thanatologist, at least once (preferably early) in his or her career, dealing intensively (five or six days, for an *hour* each day) with the personal-human-psychological aspects of a dying person. This means sitting unhurriedly by the bedside and coming to know the dying person as a person—over and above the biochemistry, cytology, medicine, and oncology of the "case." This also means not avoiding the dying and death aspects of the situation, but learning about them, sharing them, being burdened by them, (and their enormous implications)—in a word, to share the intensity of the thanatalogical experience. It also means (1) working with the survivor-victims to help them survive better; (2) interacting with ward staff personnel (doctors and nurses) to help them cope better; and (3) being mindful of one's own countertransference so the thanatologist can survive better.

The reward of this onerous event—treating one person intensively as a paradigm of how one might optimally (if there were unlimited time and one had infinite psychic reserves) treat every dying person—is an enrichment experience that will illuminate all the rest of one's practice and will enable admittedly busy physicians to be enormously more effective in the necessarily briefer encounters with all their patients, terminal or otherwise. The proper role of the physician in the twentieth century is not only to alleviate pain and cure the sick but, when the situation requires it, to help people die better. And how can the physician really know "on the pulses" unless he or she carves out the time to gain the *intimate* experience of the psychological details of at least one or two intensive dying experiences?

Let me now list some of the specific characteristics of working with dying persons—as opposed to those who are "only" critically ill, sick, diseased, injured, or disturbed. What these add up to is the prefiguring of a new specialty—of import to all care givers and not limited to physicians—called thanatology.

What is special about thanatological work?

1. *The goals are different.* Because the time is limited, the goals are more finite. The omnipresent goal is the psychological *comfort* of the person, with, as a general rule, as much alleviation of physical pain as possible. With a terminal person, addiction is not the issue—yet many physicians are niggardly or inappropriately moral about the use of pain-relieving substances. We have much to learn from Dame Cicely Saunders, founder of St. Christopher's Hospice (near London), about the humane uses of morphine, alcohol, and other analgesics. Nor is psychological insight the goal. There is no rule that states that an individual must die with any certain amount of self-knowledge. In this sense, every life is incomplete. The goal—fighting the calendar of the lethal illness—is to "will the obligatory"; to make a chilling and ugly scene go as well as possible; to give psychological succor; to permit the tying off of loose ends; to lend as much stability to the person as it is possible to give.

2. *The rules are different.* Because there is a foreseeable (although tentative) death date in the finite future—a matter of months or weeks—the usual rules for psychotherapy can realistically be modified. The celerity with which the relationship between therapist and patient is made and the *depth* of that relationship can be of a nature that would be totally appropriate for a dying person, but, with an ordinary (non-dying) patient might appear unseemly or even unprofessional. But the "love" that flows between patient and therapist (and in the opposite direction also) when the patient is a dying person can be sustaining, even ennobling. One might ask what would happen if the patient were to have a remission, even recover. That is an embarrassment devoutly to be wished; in that rare case, the therapist would simply have to "renegotiate" the "contract" or understanding between the two of them. But intensive work with a dying person generally permits a depth of transference and countertransference that should not be done nor countenanced in perhaps any other professional relationship.

3. *It may not be psychotherapy.* Obviously, working with a dying person should, for that person, be psychotherapeutic. (Anything that might be iatrogenic should be avoided). But the process itself may be sufficiently

different from ordinary psychotherapy that it might very well merit a label of its own. What is important is that the process be flexible —which is somewhat different from eclectic—and be able to move with the dying person's shifts of needs and mood, efforts toward control, detours into denial, and so on. Working with a dying person contains elements of rather traditional psychotherapy, but it also is characterized by other kinds of human interaction, including rapport building, interview, conversation, history taking, just plain talk, and communicative silences.

4. *The focus is on benign intervention.* In thanatological work, the therapist need not be a *tabula rasa;* nor need the therapist be inactive. There can be active intervention, as long as it is in the patient's interests. These interventions can take the form of interpretations, suggestions, advice (when asked for), interacting with doctors and nurses on the hospital ward, interacting with members of the family, arranging for social work services, liaison with clergy, and so on. The notion that any intervention is an incursion into the patient's rights and liberties is rejected as a blunt idea that does not make the distinction between benign and malign activities. The clinical thanatologist can act as the patient's ombudsman in many ways—on the ward, in the hospital, and within the community.

5. *No one has to die in a state of psychoanalytic grace.* Putting aside the Jehovah or "savior complex" that is understandably present in many psychotherapists, there is underlying concern with "success" in the motivational system of any effective therapist. With a dying patient, therapists must realign their notions of what they can realistically do for that person. It is a process that no matter how auspiciously begun or effectively conducted always ends in death. We hear phrases like "death work," but we need to appreciate that very few individuals die right on psychological target with all their complexes and neuroses beautifully worked through. The therapist needs to be able to tolerate incompleteness and lack of closure. Patients never untangle all the varied skeins of their intrapsychic and interpersonal life; to the last second there are psychical creations and recreations that require new resolutions. Total insight is an abstraction; there is no golden mental homeostasis.

6. *"Working through" is a luxury for those who have time to live.* It follows from the above that people die either too soon or too late with incompleted fragments in their life's agenda. The goal of resolving life's problems may be an unattainable one; the goal of an "appropriate death"—Avery Weisman's felicitous concept—of helping the dying person to "be relatively pain free, suffering reduced, emotional and social impoverishments kept at a minimum . . . resolving residual conflicts, and satisfying whatever remaining wishes are consistent with his present plight and with his ego ideal." The best death is one that an individual would choose for himself or herself if the choice

were possible (even though the disease remained unnegotiable). Dying people can be helped to put their affairs in order—although everyone dies more-or-less intestate, psychologically speaking.

7. *The dying person sets the pace.* Because there are no specific substantive psychological goals (of having this insight or coming to that understanding), the emphasis is on process and on the thanatologist's continued presence. Nothing *has* to be accomplished. The patient sets the pace. This even includes whether the topic of death is ever mentioned—although, if permitted, it almost always will be. The therapist will note the usefulness of "the method of successive approximations," in which a dying person may say, over the course of many days, "I have a problem, an illness, a tumor, a malignancy, a cancer, a terminal metastasis." This is not a litany that needs to be recited. Different individuals get in touch with their illness at various points of candor. Any one of these points is equally good, as long as it is comfortable for that person.

8. *Denial will be present.* We have already characterized the notion of a half-dozen stages of dying as being oversimplistic and not true to life. In the most popular explication of this approach, denial is listed as the first stage ("No, it can't be me!"). But our disavowal of the idea of a half-dozen fixed stages of dying should not lead us into the error of neglecting the importance of the psychological mechanism of denial itself. Denial is not a stage of dying; it is rather a ubiquitous aspect of the dying process, surfacing now and again (at no predetermined regular intervals) all through the dying process. It is only human for even the most extraordinary human beings occasionally to blot out or take a vacation from their knowledge of their imminent end. It is probably psychologically necessary for dying people intermittently to rest their own deathful train of thoughts on a siding, off the main track that leads only to blackness or mystery. This means that the clinical thanatologist must be prepared for the dying person to manifest a rather radical change of pace. If the therapist will only ride with this transient denial, the dying person will—as surprisingly as he or she began it—abandon it and come back to some of the realities of the present moment.

9. *The goal is increased psychological comfort.* The main point of working with the dying person—in the visit, the give-and-take of talk, the advice, the interpretations, the listening—is to increase that individual's psychological *comfort.* The criterion of "effectiveness" lies in this single measure. One cannot realistically be Pollyannish or even optimistic; the therapist begins in a grim situation that is going to become even grimmer. The best that the therapist can hope to accomplish is to have helped the ill person in whatever ways it takes to achieve some increased psychological comfort. However, hope should never be totally abandoned.

10. *The importance of relating to nurses and doctors on the ward.* If the

dying work is done in a hospital—or wherever it is done—it cannot be conducted as a solo operation. It is of key importance that relatives and personnel on the ward be kept informed of the dying person's condition and needs, and more, that they be kept informed as to the guiding concepts that underlie this special therapeutic exchange. Like clinical research on a ward, thanatological work often goes best with the full cooperation of the chief nurse. It is understood that no one approaches a patient as a "patient care specialist"—the euphemism for clinical thanatologist—unless he or she has been asked to do so by the physician in charge of the case. Then such a person—who has been introduced to the patient by the regular doctor—acts as any consultant would act, the difference being in the frequency and duration of the visits.

11. *The survivor is the victim—and eventually the patient: the concept of postvention.* Arnold Toynbee wrote eloquently about his view that death was essentially a two-person event and that, in the summation of anguish, the survivor bore the brunt of the hurt. All that has been said above should now be understood in the context of advocating that almost from the beginning of working with the dying person, the clinical thanatologist ought to become acquainted with the main survivor-to-be, to gain rapport with that person, and to have an explicit understanding that the survivor will be seen in the premourning stages and then for a while, at decreasing intervals, for perhaps a year or so after the death. *Postvention*—working with survivor-victims — ought to be part of any total health-care system. It is not only humane; it is also good medical practice, for we know—especially from the work of Colin Murray Parkes (1972)—that a population of survivors (of any adult age) is a population at risk, having elevated rates of morbidity (including surgeries and other hospitalizations) and mortality (from a variety of causes of death) for at least a year or so after the death of a mourned person. Postventive care relates not only to "losses" in the survivor's life but also to other aspects of stress from which that mourner may be suffering.

12. *Just as the role of transference is paramount, the place of countertransference bears careful watching, and a good support system is a necessity.* A terminal person's dying days can be made better by virtue of "the joys of transference" that are projected on the thanatological therapist. The therapist, if able, should work for an intense transference relationship. But there is a well-known caveat: where there is transference, there is also countertransference—the flow of feeling from the therapist to the patient. The therapist is invested in the patient's welfare and is thereby made vulnerable. When the patient dies, the therapist is bereaved. And during the dying process, the therapist is anguished by the prospect of loss and a sense of impotence. Dealing with a dying person is abrasive work. The therapist is

well advised to have good support systems in his or her own life: loved ones, dear friends, congenial work, and peer consultants.

The other side of these injunctions is that a physician needs to take vacations from death. A gynecological oncologist, for example, might intersperse his or her practice with obstetrical cases, delivering babies as a balance for those patients who are dying of cancer of the uterus. Moreover, a physician in oncological practice should not fail to seek out psychological or psychiatric consultation for patients if they are significantly depressed or otherwise disturbed about dying and for *himself* (or herself) if there is any sense that one's own equanimity has been touched. This type of psychotherapeutic help might well be made a routine part of a physician's dealing with dying person's, lest the physician fall prey to the predictable consequences of the unusual psychological stresses that come from working constantly around and against death. (Shneidman, 1974, 1980)

References

Glaser, Barney G., and Strauss, Anselm. *Awareness of Dying.* Chicago: Aldine Publishing Company, 1965.

Glaser, Barney G., and Strauss, Anselm. *Time for Dying.* Chicago: Aldine Publishing Company, 1968.

Hinton, John. *Dying.* Baltimore: Penguin Books, 1967.

Parkes, Colin Murray. *Bereavement: Studies of Grief in Adult Life.* New York: International Universities Press, 1972.

Shneidman, Edwin S. *Deaths of Man.* Baltimore: Penguin Books, 1974. (First published by Quadrangle Books, 1973.)

Shneidman, Edwin S. Aspects of the Dying Process. *Psychiatric Annals* 7, no. 3 (March 1977).

Shneidman, Edwin S. *Voices of Death.* New York: Harper & Row, 1980.

Sudnow, David. *Passing On.* Englewood Cliffs, N.J.: Prentice-Hall, 1967.

Toynbee, Arnold, *et al. Man's Concern with Death.* New York: McGraw-Hill Book Company, 1969.

Weisman, Avery D. *On Dying and Denying.* New York: Behaviorial Publications, 1972.

PART VI
SELF-IMPOSED DEATH: SUICIDE

Contents

Ordinarily, we tend to think of death as a biological or adventitious event. Suicide falls outside that pattern and for that reason is generally the most enigmatic of all modes of death. In the last twenty-five years, there has been a great expansion of interest and effort in suicide prevention; the number of books and articles written about suicide has increased enormously and a whole new field of specialization—suicidology—has arisen. Numerous suicide prevention centers have been established. But suicide is a ubiquitous and intransigent issue and suicidal deaths remain the most cryptic of all deaths.

Compared to the other three modes of death (natural, accident, and homicide) suicide is the least frequent. Perhaps, then, some justification for an advertent focus on suicide in this volume ought to be made. That justification lies in the fact that suicide is, from the survivor's view, the most stigmatizing mode of death and, at the same time, it is clearly the most preventable.

In this part, the six chapters are authored by an unusual array of contemporary suicidologists including two philosophers, a sociologist, a psychiatrist, a psychologist, and a poet-critic.

26 · Feelings

A. Alvarez

A. Alvarez is not a professional suicidologist. He is a poet and drama critic. He has edited and written several books, of which the most interesting and important for this anthology is his book about suicide—The Savage God—in which, as perhaps only a literary man can, he discusses suicide in a broadly humanistic and deeply personal way.

The psychoanalytic theories of suicide prove, perhaps, only what was already obvious: that the processes which lead a man to take his own life are at least as complex and difficult as those by which he continues to live. The theories help untangle the intricacy of motive and define the deep ambiguity of the wish to die but they say little about what it means to be suicidal, and how it feels.

First and most important, suicide is a closed world with its own irresistible logic. This is not to say that people commit suicide, as the Stoics did, coolly, deliberately, as a rational choice between rational alternatives. The Romans may have disciplined themselves into accepting this frigid logic, but those who have done so in modern history are, in the last analysis, monsters. And like all monsters, they are hard to find. In 1735 John Robeck, a Swedish philosopher living in Germany, completed a long Stoic defense of suicide as a just, right and desirable act; he then carefully put his principles into practice by giving away his property and drowning himself in the Weser. His death was the sensation of the day. It provoked Voltaire to comment, through one of the characters in *Candide:* ". . . I have seen a prodigious number of people who hold their existence in execration; but I have only seen a dozen who voluntarily put an end to their misery: three Negroes, four Englishmen, four Genevois, and a German professor called Robeck." Even for Voltaire, the supreme rationalist, a purely rational suicide was something prodigious and slightly grotesque, like a comet or a two-headed sheep.

The logic of suicide is, then, not rational in the old Stoic sense. It scarcely could be, since there is almost no one now, even among the philosophers, who believes that reason is clean and straightforward, or that motives can ever be less than equivocal. "The desires of the heart," said Auden, "are as crooked as corkscrews." To the extent that suicide *is* logical, it is also unreal: too simple, too convincing, too total, like one of those paranoid systems such as Ezra Pound's Social Credit, by which madmen explain the whole universe. The logic of suicide is different. It is like the unanswerable logic of a nightmare, or like the science-fiction fantasy of being projected suddenly into another dimension: everything makes sense and follows its own strict rules;

yet, at the same time, everything is also different, perverted, upside down. Once one decides to take his own life he enters a shut-off, impregnable but wholly convincing world where every detail fits and each incident reinforces his decision. An argument with a stranger in a bar, an expected letter which doesn't arrive, the wrong voice on the telephone, the wrong knock at the door, even a change in the weather—all seem charged with special meaning; they all contribute. The world of the suicide is superstitious, full of omens. Freud saw suicide as a great passion, like being in love: "In the two opposed situations of being most intensely in love and of suicide, the ego is overwhelmed by the object, though in totally different ways." As in love, things which seem trivial to the outsider, tiresome or amusing, assume enormous importance to those in the grip of the monster, while the sanest arguments against it seem to them simply absurd.

This imperviousness to everything outside the closed world of self-destruction can produce an obsession so weird and total, so psychotic, that death itself becomes a side issue. In nineteenth-century Vienna a man of seventy drove seven three-inch nails into the top of his head with a heavy blacksmith's hammer. For some reason he did not die immediately, so he changed his mind and walked to the hospital, streaming blood.[1] In March 1971 a Belfast businessman killed himself by boring nine holes in his head with a power drill. There is also the case of a Polish girl, unhappily in love, who in five months swallowed four spoons, three knives, nineteen coins, twenty nails, seven window bolts, a brass cross, one hundred and one pins, a stone, three pieces of glass and two beads from her rosary.[2] In each instance the suicidal gesture seems to have mattered more than its outcome. People try to die in such operatic ways only when they are obsessed more by the means than by the end, just as a sexual fetishist gets more satisfaction from his rituals than from the orgasm to which they lead. The old man driving nails into his skull, the company director with his power drill and the lovelorn girl swallowing all that hardware seem to have acted wildly out of despair. Yet in order to behave in precisely that way they must have brooded endlessly over the details, selecting, modifying, perfecting them like artists, until they produced that single, unrepeatable happening which expressed their madness in all its uniqueness. In the circumstances, death may come but it is superfluous.[3]

Without this wild drama of psychosis, there is a form of suicide, more commonplace but also more deadly, which is simply an extreme form of self-injury. The psychoanalysts have suggested that a man may destroy himself not because he wants to die, but because there is a single aspect of himself which he cannot tolerate. A suicide of this order is a perfectionist. The flaws in his nature exacerbate him like some secret itch he cannot get at. So he acts suddenly, rashly, out of exasperation. Thus Kirillov, in Dostoevsky's *The Possessed*, kills himself, he says, to show that he is God. But secretly he kills himself because he knows he is not God. Had his ambitions been less, perhaps he would have only attempted the deed or mutilated himself. He conceived of his mortality as a kind of lapse, an error which offended him beyond bearing. So in the end he pulled the trigger in order to shed this mortality like a tatty suit of clothes, but without taking into account that the clothes were, in fact, his own warm body.

Compared with the other revolutionaries in the novel, Kirillov seems sane, tender-hearted and upright. Yet maybe his concern with godhead and metaphysical liberty consigned him, too, to the suburbs of psychosis. And this sets him apart from the majority of the inhabitants of the closed world of suicide. For them, the act is neither rash nor operatic nor, in any obvious way, unbalanced. Instead it is, insidiously, a vocation. Once inside the closed world, there seems never to have been a time when one was not suicidal. Just as a writer feels himself never to have been anything except a writer, even if he can remember with embarrassment his first doggerel, even if he has spent years, like Conrad, disguised as a sea dog, so the suicide feels he has always been preparing in secret for this last act. There is no end to his sense of *déjà vu* or to his justifications. His memory is stored with long, black afternoons of childhood, with the taste of pleasures that gave no pleasure, with sour losses and failures, all repeated endlessly like a scratched phonograph record.

An English novelist who had made two serious suicide attempts said this to me:

I don't know how much potential suicides *think* about it. I must say, I've never really thought about it much. Yet it's always there. For me, suicide's a constant temptation. It never slackens. Things are all right at the moment. But I feel like a cured alcoholic: I daren't take a drink because I know that if I do I'll go on it again. Because whatever it is that's there doesn't alter. It's a pattern of my entire life. I would like to think that it was only brought on by certain stresses and strains. But in fact, if I'm honest and look back, I realize it's been a pattern ever since I can remember.

My parents were very fond of death. It was their favorite thing. As a child, it seemed to me that my father was constantly rushing off to do himself in. Everything he said, all his analogies, were to do with death. I remember him once telling me that marriage was the last nail in the coffin of life. I was about eight at the time. Both my parents, for different reasons, regarded death as a perfect release from their troubles. They were very unhappy together, and I think this sunk in very much. Like my father, I have always demanded too much of life and people and relationships—far more than exists, really. And when I find that it doesn't exist, it seems like a rejection. It probably isn't a rejection at all; it simply isn't there. I mean, the empty air doesn't reject you; it just says, "I'm empty." Yet rejection and disappointment are two things I've always found impossible to take.

In the afternoons my mother and father both retired to sleep. That is, they retired to death. They really died for the afternoons. My father was a parson. He had nothing to do, he had no work. I begin now to understand how it was for him. When I'm not working, I'm capable of sleeping through most of the morning. Then I start taking sleeping pills during the day to keep myself in a state of dopiness, so that I can sleep at any time. To take sleeping pills during the day to sleep isn't so far from taking sleeping pills in order to die. It's just a bit more practical and a bit more craven. You only take two instead of two hundred. But during those afternoons I used to be alive and lively. It was a great big house but I never dared make a sound. I didn't dare pull a plug in case I woke one of them up. I felt terribly rejected. Their door was shut, they were absolutely unapproachable. Whatever terrible crisis had happened to me, I felt I couldn't go and say, "Hey, wake up, listen to me." And those afternoons went on a long time. Because of the war I went back to live with them, and it was still exactly the same. If I ever bumped myself off, it would be in the afternoon. Indeed, the first time I tried was in the afternoon. The second time was after an awful afternoon. Moreover, it was after an afternoon in the country, which I hate for the same reasons as I hate afternoons. The reason is simple: when I'm alone, I stop believing I exist.

Although the speaker is well into a successful middle age, the injured and rejected child she had once been still lives powerfully on. Perhaps it is this element which makes the closed world of suicide so inescapable: the wounds of the past, like those of the Fisher King in the legend of the Holy Grail, will not heal over—the ego, the analysts would say, is too fragile—instead, they continually push themselves to the surface to obliterate the modified pleasures and acceptances of the present. The life of the suicide is, to an extraordinary degree, unforgiving. Nothing he achieves by his own efforts, or luck bestows, reconciles him to his injurious past.

Thus, on August 16, 1950, ten days before he finally took sleeping pills, Pavese wrote in his notebook: "Today I see clearly that from 1928 until now I have always lived under this shadow." But in 1928 Pavese was already twenty. From what we know of his desolate childhood—his father dead when he was six, his mother of spun steel, harsh and austere —the shadow was probably on him much earlier; at twenty he simply recognized it for what it was. At thirty he had written flatly and without self-pity, as though it were some practical detail he had just noticed: "Every luxury must be paid for, and everything is a luxury, starting with being in the world."

A suicide of this kind is born, not made. As I said earlier, he receives his reasons—from whatever nexus of guilt, loss and despair—when he is too young to cope with them or understand. All he can do is accept them innocently and try to defend himself as best he can. By the time he recognizes them more objectively, they have become part of his sensibility, his way of seeing and his way of life. Unlike the psychotic self-injurer, whose suicide is a sudden fatal twist in the road, his whole life is a gradual downward curve, steepening at the end, on which he moves knowingly, unable and unwilling to stop himself. No amount of success will change him. Before his death Pavese was writing better than ever before —more richly, more powerfully, more easily. In the year before he died he turned out two of his best novels, each in less than two months of writing. One month before the end he received the Strega Prize, the supreme accolade for an Italian writer. "I have never been so much alive as now," he wrote, "never so young." A few days later he was dead. Perhaps the sweetness itself of his creative powers made his innate depression all the harder to bear. It is as though those strengths and rewards belonged to some inner part of him from which he felt himself irredeemably alienated.

It is also characteristic of this type of suicide that his beliefs do not help him. Although Pavese called himself a Communist, his politics permeate neither his imaginative work nor his private notebooks. I suspect they were merely a gesture of solidarity with the people he liked, against those he disliked. He was a Communist not because of any particular conviction, but because he hated the Fascists who had imprisoned him. In practice, he was like nearly everybody else in this present time: skeptical, pragmatic, adrift, sustained neither by the religion of the Church nor by that of the Party. In these circumstances, "this business of living"—the title of his notebooks—becomes peculiarly chancy. What Durkheim called "anomie" may lead to a social conception of man infinitely more impoverished than any religious formulation of his role as a servant of God. Yet since the decline of religious authority,[4] the only alternative to the ersatz and unsatisfactory religions of science and politics has been an uneasy, perilous freedom. This is summed up in an eerie note found in an empty house in Hampstead: "Why suicide? Why not?"

Why not? The pleasures of living—the hedonistic pleasures of the five senses, the more complex and demanding pleasures of concentration and doing, even the unanswerable commitments of love—seem often no greater and mostly less frequent than the frustrations—the continual sense of unfinished and unfinishable business, jangled, anxious, ragged, overborne. If secularized man were kept going only by the pleasure principle, the human race would already be extinct. Yet maybe his secular quality is his strength. He chooses life because he has no alternative, because he knows that after death there is nothing at all. When Camus wrote *The Myth of Sisyphus*—in 1940, after the fall of France, a serious personal illness and depressive crisis—he began with suicide and ended with an affirmation of individual life, in itself and for itself, desirable because it is "absurd," without final meaning or metaphysical justification. "Life is a gift that nobody should renounce," the great Russian poet Osip Mandelstam said to his wife when, in exile after his imprisonment, she proposed that they commit suicide together if Stalin's secret police took them again.[5] Hamlet said that the only obstacle to self-slaughter was fear of the afterlife, which was an unconvinced but Christian answer to all those noble suicides which the heroes of Shakespeare's Roman plays performed so unhesitatingly. Without the buttress of Christianity, without the cold dignity of a Stoicism that had evolved in response to a world in which human life was a trivial commodity, cheap enough to be expended at every circus to amuse the crowd, the rational obstacles begin to seem strangely flimsy. When neither high purpose nor the categorical imperatives of religion will do, the only argument against suicide is life itself. You pause and attend: the heart beats in your chest; outside, the trees are thick with new leaves, a swallow dips over them, the light moves, people are going about their business. Perhaps this is what Freud meant by "the narcissistic satisfactions [which the ego] derives from being alive." Most of the time, they seem enough. They are, anyway, all we ever have or can ever expect.

Yet such "satisfactions" can also be very fragile. A shift of focus in one's life, a sudden loss or separation, a single irreversible act can suffice to make the whole process intolerable. Perhaps this is what is implied by the phrase "suicide when the balance of mind was disturbed." It is, of course, a legal formula evolved to protect the dead man from the law and to spare the feelings and insurance benefits of his family. But it also has a certain existential truth: without the checks of belief, the balance between life and death can be perilously delicate.

Consider a climber poised on minute holds on a steep cliff. The smallness of the holds, the steepness of the angle, all add to his pleasure, provided he is in complete control. He is a man playing chess with his body; he can read the sequence of moves far enough in advance so that his physical economy—the ratio between the effort he uses and his reserves of strength—is never totally disrupted. The more improbable the situation and the greater the demands made on him, the more sweetly the blood flows later in release from all that tension. The possibility of danger serves merely to sharpen his awareness and control. And perhaps this is the rationale of all risky sports: you deliberately raise the ante of effort and concentration in order, as it were, to clear your mind of trivialities. It is a small-scale model for living, but with a difference: unlike your routine life, where mistakes can usually be recouped and some kind of compromise patched up, your actions, for however brief a period, are deadly serious.

I think there may be some people who kill themselves like this: in order to achieve a calm and control they never find in life. Antonin Artaud, who spent most of his life in lunatic asylums, once wrote:

> If I commit suicide, it will not be to destroy myself but to put myself back together again. Suicide will be for me only one means of violently reconquering myself, of brutally invading my being, of anticipating the unpredictable approaches of God. By suicide, I reintroduce my design in nature, I shall for the first time give things the shape of my will. I

free myself from the conditioned reflexes of my organs, which are so badly adjusted to my inner self, and life is for me no longer an absurd accident whereby I think what I am told to think. But now I choose my thought and the direction of my faculties, my tendencies, my reality. I place myself between the beautiful and the hideous. The good and evil. I put myself in suspension, without innate propensities, neutral, in the state of equilibrium between good and evil solicitations.[6]

There is, I believe, a whole class of suicides, though infinitely less gifted than Artaud and less extreme in their perceptions, who take their own lives not in order to die but to escape confusion, to clear their heads. They deliberately use suicide to create an unencumbered reality for themselves or to break through the patterns of obsession and necessity which they have unwittingly imposed on their lives.[7] There are also others, similar but less despairing, for whom the mere idea of suicide is enough; they can continue to function efficiently, and even happily, provided they know they have their own, specially chosen means of escape always ready: a hidden cache of sleeping pills, a gun at the back of a drawer, like the wife in Lowell's poem who sleeps every night with her car key and ten dollars strapped to her thigh.

But there is also another, perhaps more numerous class of suicide to whom the *idea* of taking their own lives is utterly repugnant. These are the people who will do everything to destroy themselves except admit that that is what they are after; they will, that is, do everything except take the final responsibility for their actions. Hence all those cases of what Karl Menninger calls "chronic suicide"—the alcoholics and drug addicts who kill themselves slowly and piecemeal, all the while protesting that they are merely taking the necessary steps to make an intolerable life tolerable. Hence, too, those thousands of inexplicable fatal accidents—the good drivers who die in car crashes, the careful pedestrians who get themselves run over—which never make the suicide statistics. The image recurs of the same climber in the same unforgiving situation. In the grip of some depression he may not even recognize, he could die almost without knowing it. Impatiently, he fails to take the necessary safety measures; he climbs a little too fast and without working out his moves far enough in advance. And suddenly, the risks have become disproportionate. For a fatal accident, there is no longer need of any conscious thought or impulse of despair, still less a deliberate action. He has only to surrender for a moment to the darkness beneath the threshold. The smallest mistake—an impetuous move not quite in balance, an error of judgment which leaves him extended beyond his strength, with no way back and no prospect of relief—and the man will be dead without realizing that he wanted to die. "The victim lets himself act," said Valéry, "and his death escapes from him like a rash remark . . . He kills himself because it is too easy to kill himself."[8] Whence, I suppose, all those so-called "impetuous suicides" who, if they survive, claim never to have considered the act until moments before their attempt. Once recovered, they seem above all embarrassed, ashamed of what they have done, and un-willing to admit that they were ever genuinely suicidal. They can return to life, that is, only by denying the strength of their despair, transforming their unconscious but deliberate choice into an impulsive, meaningless mistake. They wanted to die without accepting the responsibility for their decision.

Every so often the opposite of all this occurs: there is a cult of suicide which has very little to do with real death. Thus early-nineteenth-century romanticism—as a pop phenomenon rather than as a serious creative movement—was dominated by the twin stars of Thomas Chatterton and Goethe's Young Werther. The ideal was "to cease upon the midnight with no pain" while still young and beautiful and full of promise. Suicide added a dimension of drama and doom, a fine black orchid to the already tropical jungle of the period's emotional life. One hundred years later a similar cult grew up around the *Inconnue de la Seine*. During the 1920s and early 1930s, all over the Continent, nearly every student of sensibility had a plaster cast of her death mask: a young, full, sweetly smiling face which seems less dead than peacefully sleeping.

The girl was in fact genuinely *inconnue*. All that is known of her is that she was fished out of the Seine and exposed on a block of ice in the Paris morgue, along with a couple of hundred other corpses awaiting identification. (On the evidence of her hair style, Sacheverell Sitwell believes this happened not later than the early 1880s.) She was never claimed, but someone was sufficiently impressed by her peaceful smile to take a death mask.

It is also possible that it never happened at all. In another version of the story a researcher, unable to obtain information at the Paris Morgue, followed her trail to the German source of the plaster casts. At the factory he met the *Inconnue* herself, alive and well and living in Hamburg, the daughter of the now-prosperous manufacturer of her image.

There is, however, no doubt at all about the cult around her. I am told that a whole generation of German girls modeled their looks on her.[9] She appears in appropriately aroused stories by Richard Le Gallienne, Jules Supervielle and Claire Goll, and oddly enough, since the author is a Communist, was the moving spirit behind the heroine of *Aurélian*, a long novel which Louis Aragon considers his masterpiece. But her fame was spread most effectively by a sickly though much-translated best seller, *One Unknown*, by Reinhold Conrad Muschler. He makes her an innocent young country girl who comes to Paris, falls in love with a handsome British diplomat—titled, of course—has a brief but idyllic romance and then, when milord regretfully leaves to marry his suitably aristocratic English fiancée, drowns herself in the Seine. As Muschler's sales show, this was the style of explanation the public wanted for that enigmatic, dead face.

The cult of the *Inconnue* seemed to attract young people between the two world wars in much the same way as drugs call them now: to opt out before they start, to give up a struggle that frightens them in a world they find distasteful, and to slide away into a deep inner dream. Death by drowning and blowing your mind with drugs amount, in fantasy, to the same thing: the sweetness, shadow and easy release of a successful regression. So the cult flourished in the absence of all facts, perhaps it even flourished because there were no facts. Like a Rorschach blot, the dead face was the receptacle for any feelings the onlooker wished to project into it. And like the Sphinx and the Mona Lisa, the power of the *Inconnue* was in her smile—subtle, oblivious, promising peace. Not only was she out of it all, beyond troubles, beyond responsibilities, she had also remained beautiful; she had retained the quality the young most fear to lose—their youth. Although Sitwell credits to her influence an epidemic of suicide among the young people of Evreux, I suspect she may have saved more lives than she destroyed. To know that it can be done, that the option really exists and is even becoming, is usually enough to relieve a mildly suicidal anxiety. In the end, the function of the romantic suicide cult is to be a focus for wandering melancholy; almost nobody actually dies.

The expression on the face of the *Inconnue* implies that her death was both easy and painless. These, I think, are the dual qualities, almost ideals, which distinguish modern suicide from that of the past. Robert Lowell once remarked that if there were some little switch in the arm which one could press in order to die immediately and without pain, then everyone would sooner or later commit suicide. It seems that we are rapidly moving toward that questionable ideal. The reason is not hard to find. Statistics, for what they are worth, show that in Great Britain, France, Germany and Japan there has been an enormous increase in death by drugs. In a brilliant essay entitled "Self-Poisoning," Dr. Neil Kessel has written:

> In every century before our own, poisons and drugs were dissimilar. Poisons were substances which should not be taken at all, the province not of physicians but of wizards. Their properties verged upon the magical. They were, indeed, "unctions bought of mountebanks." By the second half of the nineteenth century, science had displaced sorcery and poisons were purchased from the chemist, not the alchemist. But they still differed from drugs. Drugs, with few exceptions, though recognized to produce undesirable actions if taken in excess, were not considered lethal agents and were not used to kill. The growth of self-poisoning has come about in the train of a rapid rise in the number of highly dangerous preparations employed therapeutically, together with a great contemporaneous increase in prescribing.
>
> The effect of this medical resolution has been to make poisons both readily available and relatively safe. The way has thus been opened for self-poisoning to flourish . . . Facilities for self-poisoning have been placed within the reach of everyone.[10]

Along with the increase in suicide by drugs has gone a proportionate decrease in the older, more violent methods: hanging, drowning, shooting, cutting, jumping. What is involved, I think, is a massive and, in effect, a qualitative change in suicide. Ever since hemlock, for whatever obscure reason, went out of general use, the act has always entailed great physical violence. The Romans fell on their swords or, at best, cut their wrists in hot baths; even the fastidious Cleopatra allowed herself to be bitten by a snake. In the eighteenth century the kind of violence you used depended on the class you belonged to: gentlemen usually took their lives with pistols, the lower classes hanged themselves. Later it became fashionable to drown yourself, or endure the convulsions and agonies of cheap poisons like arsenic and strychnine. Perhaps the ancient, superstitious horror of suicide persisted so long because the violence made it impossible to disguise the nature of the act. Peace and oblivion were not in question; suicide was as unequivocally a violation of life as murder.

Modern drugs and domestic gas have changed all that. Not only have they made suicide more or less painless, they have also made it seem magical. A man who takes a knife and slices deliberately across his throat is murdering himself. But when someone lies down in front of an unlit gas oven or swallows sleeping pills, he seems not so much to be dying as merely seeking oblivion for a while. Dostoevsky's Kirillov said that there are only two reasons why we do not all kill ourselves: pain and the fear of the next world. We seem, more or less, to have got rid of both. In suicide, as in most other areas of activity, there has been a technological breakthrough which has made a cheap and relatively painless death democratically available to everyone. Perhaps this is why the subject now seems so central and so demanding, why even governments spend a little money on finding its causes and possible means of prevention. We already have a suicidology; all we mercifully lack, for the moment, is a thorough-going philosophical rationale of the act itself. No doubt it will come. But perhaps that is only as it should be in a period in which global suicide by nuclear warfare is a permanent possibility.

Notes

1 See S. A. K. Strahan, *Suicide and Insanity* (London, 1893), p. 108.

2 See G. R. Fedden, *Suicide: A Social and Historical Study* (London: Peter Davies, 1938), p. 305.

3 A perfect example of a suicide which summed up a man's whole life and yearnings occurred in March 1970. A body was found jammed in a crevice one hundred feet down the sheer cliffs near Land's End. It was dressed in full "City gentleman's" uniform: pinstriped trousers, black jacket, polished shoes and bowler hat. Over the dead arm was a neatly rolled umbrella. The man, who carried no identification, was looking westward, out to sea. He had died from an overdose of sleeping pills. The police eventually discovered that he was a much Anglicized and Anglophile American who had lived and worked in London for a long time. His marriage had gone on the rocks and he had finally left his wife. He had chosen Land's End to die because that was the point nearest America. By jamming himself in the rock, he was able to gaze west toward the States until he lost consciousness.

Another, though less odd, example is that of a young American climber, very gifted and graceful, who was badly depressed at breaking up with his girl. One Saturday morning he called on friends who lived near the Shawangunks, a popular outcrop north of New York City. He seemed quite relaxed and played in the garden with the friends' small children, of whom he had always been fond. Then he drove over to the cliffs, which are vertical and between two and three hundred feet high, and jumped off. Physical perfectionist to the last, he performed as he fell an immaculate swan dive.

4 "What undermined the Christian faith was not the atheism of the eighteenth century or the materialism of the nineteenth—their arguments are frequently vulgar and, for the most part, easily refutable by traditional theology—but rather the doubting concern with salvation of genuinely religious men [like Pascal and Kierkegaard], in whose eyes the traditional Christian content and promise had become 'absurd.' " (Hannah Arendt, *The Human Condition* [Chicago, 1958, and London, 1958–1959, p. 319.)

5 Mandelstam was, in fact, rearrested and died in a forced-labor camp somewhere in Siberia. Yet right up to the end he refused his wife's alternative: "Whenever I talked of suicide, M. used to say: 'Why hurry? The end is the same everywhere, and here they even hasten it for you.' Death was so much more real, and so much simpler than life, that we all involuntarily tried to prolong our earthly existence, even if only for a brief moment—just in case the next day brought some relief! In war, in the camps and during periods of terror, people think much less about death (let alone about suicide) than when they are living normal lives. Whenever at some point on earth mortal terror and the pressure of utterly insoluable problems are present in a particularly intense form, general questions about the nature of being recede into the background. How could we stand in awe before the forces of nature and the eternal laws of existence if terror of a mundane kind was felt so tangibly in everyday life? In a strange way, despite the horror of it, this also gave a certain richness to our lives. Who knows what happiness is? Perhaps it is better to talk in more concrete terms of the fullness or intensity of existence, and in this sense there may have been something more deeply satisfying in our desperate clinging to life than in what people generally strive for." (Nadezhda Mandelstam, *Hope Against Hope* [New York, 1970], p. 261.)

6 *Artaud Anthology*, ed. by Jack Hirschman (San Franciso, 1965, and Great Horwood, 1967), p. 56.

7 Perhaps the most famous example is that of the distinguished scholar who had worked for years on the definitive edition of one of the gloomier American novelists. Maybe the long, deadening grind and obsessional detail got to him in the end. Add to that the even deeper gloom of McCarthyism and vague hints of a private scandal. It doesn't matter. One afternoon he finally put all his papers in order, paid every bill to the last cent, wrote farewell letters to all his friends saying he was sorry, put out food and milk for his cat, packed an overnight case and carefully locked his apartment. Down in the street he mailed the letters—they would arrive too late—and then took a taxi downtown. He checked into a scruffy hotel and took a room on an upper floor. Every last meticulous detail had been attended to; he had added the final footnote to his own life. Then his whole obsessionally controlled, minutely organized universe exploded like a grenade. He hurled himself across the room and crashed through the window he hadn't even bothered to open. He burst, lacerated, into free space and smashed onto the sidewalk.

8 Paul Valéry, *Oeuvres* (Paris, 1962), Vol. II, pp. 610–11.

9 I owe this information to Hans Hesse of the University of Sussex. He suggests that the *Inconnue* became the erotic ideal of the period, as Bardot was for the 1950s. He thinks that German actresses like Elisabeth Bergner modeled themselves on her. She was finally displaced as a paradigm by Greta Garbo.

10 Neil Kessel, "Self-Poisoning," in E. Shneidman, (Ed.), *Suicidology: Contemporary Developments* (New York: Grune & Stratton, 1976), p. 346.

Margaret Pabst Battin

*Margaret Pabst Battin is associate professor of philosophy at the
University of Utah. She is the author of several articles touching
on the philosophical, ethical, and legal aspects of death and dying,
including suicide. In the piece below, Professor Battin gives us a
learned exposition of the concept of a rational suicide. It is an idea
that is central to any comprehensive discussion of human
self-destruction.*

From Ethical Issues in Suicide *by Margaret Pabst Battin.
Copyright © 1982 by Prentice-Hall, Inc. Reprinted by permission of
Prentice-Hall, Inc., Englewood Cliffs, New Jersey.*

Although traditional moral arguments still inform
many of the pre-critical assumptions we make about suicide, they have fallen
into disuse. We now tend to treat suicide as the product of mental illness, or
as a desperate dangerous "cry for help" used by someone who does not really
want to die. Both of these views suggest that the traditional moral arguments
no longer have relevance either for persons contemplating suicide or for
bystanders who would intervene. But these views sidestep a crucial issue:
can suicide ever be a *rational* act? If so, we may need to reconsider our moral
assessment of suicide. That an act is rational does not mean, of course, that it
is also morally good, but to find potentially rational an act we had thought
could only be crazy may invite reinspection of our views. This means both
that we may wish to reassess the the traditional arguments concerning
suicide, and that we may want to approach the moral issues from a contemporary viewpoint.

THE CHARACTERIZATION OF "RATIONAL SUICIDE"

To determine whether suicide can ever be rational, we must first define a
rational act; then we must decide whether suicide could ever fit such a
definition. Perhaps none of our acts are ever *wholly* rational, in that they are
never wholly free from emotion, training, circumstantial coercion, or other
arational components. Yet we readily distinguish between things which we
choose rationally to do, or which it is rational for us to do, and alternative acts
which could be done in the same circumstance but are not rational acts. The
question, then, is this: can suicide be as rational as our other "rational" acts?

"Rational suicide" may seem easy to characterize in negative terms. Presumably, it is suicide in which the individual is not insane, in which the
decision is reached in unimpaired, undeceived fashion, and in which the
choice made is not a bad thing for that individual to do. Alternatively, one
might attempt to characterize "rational suicide" in positive terms. Choron,
for instance, asserts:

"Rational" here implies not only that there is no psychiatric disorder but also that the reasoning of the suicidal person is in no way impaired and that his motives would seem justifiable, or at least "understandable," by the majority of his contemporaries in the same culture or social group.[1]

Choron's claim that the rational suicide's motives must seem "justifiable" or "understandable" to "the majority of his contemporaries in the same culture or social group," however, overlooks the fact that in contemporary culture, suicide has been a phenomenon very heavily enveloped in taboo; the majority of almost any individual's contemporaries within this culture will find suicide unjustified, whatever the circumstances, except perhaps in terminal illness. Consequently, we can hardly appeal to the criterion Choron suggests; it will only reflect the existing taboo. As an alternative, we shall attempt to construct a set of criteria for rationality which will be independent as possible of the prevailing suicide taboo.

These criteria fall into two broad groups. The first three, ability to reason, realistic world view, and adequacy of information, are what might be called the "nonimpairment" criteria. The final two, avoidance of harm and accordance with fundamental interests, are what might be called the "satisfaction of interests" criteria in that they assure us that a rational decision is one which serves the agent's own interests, both in avoiding harm and achieving his goals. We typically speak of a decision as "rational" or "rationally made" if it is made in an unimpaired way; we also speak of a decision as "rational" or as "the rational thing for someone to do" if it satisfies his interests in avoiding harm and achieving his goals. The question of rational suicide, then, may be restated as a compound issue: can suicide be chosen in a rational way, and can it be the rational thing for a particular person to do?

The five criteria we will use to assess the rationality of suicide are the same criteria we would use to assess any other act of choice. Of course, such a list of criteria will itself invite philosophic dispute. There is little consensus among philosophers on the precise characterization of rationality in general, and so no agreement on what might count as standards for a rational suicide or for a rational choice of any sort. Nor is there agreement on which of these conditions, if any, are necessary for rationality, and whether any combination of them is jointly sufficient. Rather than divert ourselves with these preliminary difficulties, however, we shall simply posit the five rationality criteria to be discussed, and suggest that a suicide which is rational will meet all or most of them. Rational suicide may be quite rare in contemporary culture; the pressing question is whether there can be, by even an approximate set of criteria, any such thing as rational suicide at all.

CRITERIA FOR RATIONAL SUICIDE

Ability to reason

Traditionally, a rational person has been defined as one who has the use of reason, or the ability to reason; a rational decision is one in the reaching of which reason is employed. But to say that a person is able to reason implies at least two distinct things: 1) that in moving from the premises from which he begins to the conclusion he reaches he maintains good logical form—that is, he doesn't make mistakes in logic—and 2) that he can see the consequences of the positions he adopts or of the actions he plans to take.

Suicidologists Shneidman and Farberow have examined a large number of suicide notes collected from the Los Angeles County Coroner's Office, and on this basis attempt to recreate what they call "suicidal thinking."[2] Suicidal thinking, they claim, involves both syntactic and semantic fallacies, the most characteristic of which is a confusion between "oneself as experienced by oneself," and "oneself as experienced by others." For instance, in the quite typical bit of reasoning, "People who kill themselves get attention; I will kill myself; therefore I will get attention," the prospective suicide uses the pronoun 'I' to refer to himself *as experienced by himself* in the second premise, but in the conclusion he uses it to refer to himself *as he will be experienced by others* after he is dead. What this equivocation disguises is the fact that 'I' who is now doing the experiencing and is now eager for attention is not the same 'I' as the one who will get attention: after death, the 'I' who now craves attention will not be present to experience it.

This error in reasoning is very closely related to the second condition for 'being able to reason': a person who has the use of reason is one who can see, at least to some degree, not only the logical but also the causal consequences of his beliefs, statements, and actions. The "rational suicide" is one who is able to foresee the probable consequences of this act of suicide, both for others and for himself. It may, of course, be very difficult to foresee with full accuracy the impact of one's suicide on others, but there is one consequence of suicide which can be foreseen with certainty: the individual who commits suicide will be dead.

But this is precisely what a great many suicides do not accurately foresee; they tend to assume that even after death, they will continue to have experiences, to interact with other persons, and to play some continuing causal role in the world. This is characteristic of psychotic suicides. Some researchers also suggest that almost all child suicides are "irrational" in this way; influenced perhaps by television and cartoon figures who die but revive unharmed, children are not able to think of themselves as dead, but instead think of the death that follows suicide as a kind of sleep from which they will reawaken.

Many adults, too, do not accurately foresee the consequences of suicide, namely, that they will be dead. Freud claims that this is true of all people, insofar as the human unconscious "believes itself immortal."[3] Others point to the fact that when we imagine ourselves dead, we characteristically imagine an external view. This view typically shows our own dead body surrounded by grieving relatives or located in a grave, but this view itself presupposes a subject of experiences, and so shows that we do not accurately imagine death.[4]

Joyce Carol Oates points out another kind of error in reasoning committed by those who are unduly influenced by romantic literary accounts of death:

they conceive of death in what she calls "metaphorical" terms: as alluring, inviting, liberating, and deep. A metaphor like Jung's "the profound peace of all-knowing non-existence," Oates thinks, breeds tragic error:

> To so desperately confuse the terms of our finite contract as to invent a liberating Death when it is really brute, inarticulate Deadness that awaits—the "artist" of suicide is a groping, blundering, failed artist, and his art-work a mockery of genuine achievement.[5]

Most common among the errors in reasoning committed by those who kill themselves or attempt to do so, however, may be the kind of assumption underlying much of so-called "dyadic" suicide.[6] In these suicides, the intention of the individual is to injure, manipulate, insult, or impress the important other person in his life. "I'll get even with you," is an expression typical of the dyadic suicide; so is "I'll make you love me after all," or "I'll make you finally see how much you really need me." But, some suicidologists claim, this kind of assumption is fundamentally irrational in suicide contexts, since if the gesture is effective there will be no "I" to appreciate that fact.

Most suicide attempts, and some completed suicides, are of this dyadic form,[7] and thus subject to the kind of fallacy in reasoning which such motivation invites. But this does not establish that all such suicide is irrational. A person may in fact succeed in "getting even" with another even though he is no longer available to appreciate that fact: for instance, an intolerant parent may "get even" with a wayward child by striking him from his will, even though the will does not go into effect until after the parent has died. Similarly, we can imagine cases in which a person intends to "get even" with someone else by suicide, even though he knows that he will be unable to savor his success and that his own sacrifice will be great; although such cases may be infrequent, they can in principle occur.

There are, in addition, two important classes of suicides which are not necessarily irrational. First, for those individuals whose religious or metaphysical beliefs include the possibility of a sentient afterlife, it is not irrational to assume that one will have continuing experiences or relationships after suicide. And, second, some individuals place little or no value on themselves as subjects of experiences or participants in relationships, but place great importance on the ways in which they are viewed by others. Typically, reputation and honor are paramount to these individuals; continuing experience is not. These individuals too rarely confuse the notion that they will be viewed in a certain way after death with the erroneous notion that they will be able to observe or experience this view; such suicides are not irrational in this respect. The religious suicides . . . might be taken as examples of this first class of exceptions; Lurcretia or the Japanese suicides of honor as examples of the second.

To establish in a positive way, however, that some suicides meet the criterion of "ability to reason" may prove more difficult, for a detractor can always claim such individuals must have made some other fundamental error in reasoning. But this, I think, is often a symptom of the *post hoc* argumentation so common in discussions about suicide. It might be equally difficult to prove that we reason in nondefective ways in making other important life-choices: do we avoid all equivocation? Do we have adequate conceptions of the future? It is very easy to grant that some, perhaps even most, suicides do reason in fallacious ways—the juvenile and psychotic suicides who do not understand that they will be dead, the romantic adults who glamorize death, the get-even revenge-seekers who assume that they themselves will continue to exert influence on their survivors. But although we may readily grant this point, this is not to establish that all suicides commit these errors. In the absence of any compelling evidence to the contrary, we must simply leave open the possibility that some persons do choose suicide in preference to continuing life on the basis of reasoning which is by all usual standards adequate.

Realistic world view

We may assume that a rational decision is one based upon a realistic view of the world; this criterion is closely related to that of ability to reason. Many types of suicide are clearly highly irrational in this respect. For instance, suicides among schizophrenics are quite often based on bizarre beliefs about the nature of the world, and the methods employed in such cases can be equally bizarre. A schizophrenic may throw himself from a window believing that he will be transformed into a bird; this sort of suicide is irrational because it results from a world view which is very clearly false.

In less severe sorts of disorders, an individual may have a relatively realistic picture of the world as a whole but fail to have a realistic conception of his own life situation, including his identity, his position in the world, and his particular talents and disabilities. Some milder afflictions are quite common: extremely low self-esteem and the overly inflated ego. As these conditions become increasingly pronounced we are increasingly likely to say decisions made on such bases are irrational.

For Jerome Motto, whether an individual has a realistic assessment of his life situation is crucial in determining the psychiatrist's approach towards the prospective suicide. Acknowledging that the psychiatrist, like anyone else, can offer only his own perception of reality, he nevertheless claims that

> Some persons have a view of reality so different from mine that I do not hesitate to interfere with their right to suicide. Others' perceptions are so like mine that I cannot intercede. The big problem is that large group in between.[8]

The notion that rational suicide requires a realistic world view, however, raises difficulties concerning suicides based on strong religious convictions. In Chapter One we discussed metaphysical and religious doctrines which assert the existence of an afterlife, often including continuing sensation, intellection, and heightened spiritual experience. Yet we are reluctant to call holders of these religious beliefs "irrational," even though no evidence supports their beliefs. Consequently, we find it difficult to term irrational a suicide performed in order to enter into this state. Similarly, it is difficult to label irrational a great variety of institutional suicides, even though the world view involved is different from our own. For instance, among certain African groups, it was common for kings to kill themselves or have themselves killed, either after a fixed term or at the first signs of debility, in order to promote their transformations into the next stages of divinity. The Scandinavian peoples practiced suicide in the belief that those who died by violence, rather than allowing themselves to succumb to sickness, age, or captivity, were assured of a place in Valhalla. Many primitive religions have held that an individual reaches the afterlife in the same condition in which he or she leaves this one; suicide is frequently practiced in these societies to avoid degenerative disease, senility, and so forth. Some religiously motivated suicides are irrational in the extreme, but, as H. J. Rose puts it,

> ... religious suicides are not always maniacs ... Nor can one justly class as maniacs those persons who hold that by killing themselves they can attain future happiness ... or will return to life in this world stronger or wiser than before.[9]

While suicide in these cases is similar to that of the psychotic, in that both are based on apparently unrealistic world views, it is clear that the rationality or irrationality of an individual's views of the world is relative to the environment in which he lives. We term the schizophrenic who thinks he can fly "irrational" because he has come to have this belief in a culture which offers no evidence for it; in the context of religious cultures, however, we do not usually label "irrational" those who adopt the views of the group, even if we believe them wrong. No doubt we take odd metaphysical beliefs as evidence of irrationality not because they are any more false than usual metaphysical beliefs, but because we suspect that the person who has odd beliefs, unlike his peers, has them because of some mental disability: he has reacted in an "abnormal" way to the cultural dogmas of his society. This issue may, of course, raise larger questions of rationality and irrationality within cultural and religious systems,[10] but it is important for our present examination because so much suicide is associated with it. In order that a suicide count as rational, it is only necessary that it be based on a world view which is consonant with the surrounding culture; we do not consider whether the world view of the culture as a whole is realistic or not. There may of course be considerable variation in world views within a culture; contemporary western culture, for instance, includes both those whose view of the universe is materialistic and those whose view includes spiritual entities; individuals of neither sort would be counted *irrational* in a suicide predicated upon such beliefs, though adherents of the opposite view would surely regard them as foolish.

Adequacy of information

A rational action is one performed not only in accordance with acceptable logical principles and based on a realistic world view, but one also based on adequate information. This third criterion is the basis of many claims that suicide can never be rational.

One quite poignant type of inadequately informed suicide is the person who reasons that if he has a painful terminal illness he will be better off to put an end to his life, and on the basis of a puzzled glance by his physician, or imagined but undiagnosed pains wrongly assumes he is dying. One of the Los Angeles suicide notes collected by Shneidman and Farberow reflects this sort of irrationality:

> Dearest Mary. This is to say goodbye. I have not told you because I did not want you to worry, but I have been feeling bad for 2 years, with my heart. I knew that if I went to a doctor I would lose my job. I think this is best for all concerned. I am in the car in the garage. Call the police but please don't come out there. I love you very much darling. Goodbye. Bill[11]

A large number of similar cases, frequently involving fear of cancer, occur each year; in comparatively few of them is there any evidence of malignancy. An analogous type of case, also quite frequent, involves fear of pregnancy.

The suicide who mistakenly fears a terminal disease or unwanted pregnancy is a special case of a more general type: the suicide whose act, though not necessarily the project of illogical thinking or a distorted world view, is based on inadequate or faulty information. This may be information about present circumstances: the author of the suicide note just cited, for instance, displays inadequate information about his own present physical condition, in that he has not had his alleged heart trouble diagnosed by a doctor. But he also displays inadequate information about the future: he believes that he will be fired if he consults a doctor, and he no doubt also believes, though he does not say so explicitly in his note, that his heart condition will involve progressive deterioration, dependency, and pain.

Inadequate information about present circumstances may involve simple ignorance of some important fact—that help is on the way, that a reprieve has been granted, or that a drug to reverse one's condition has just been synthesized—or it may involve distortion of all information about one's circumstances and environment, ranging from the slightly unrealistic to the gross dislocations of the schizophrenic.[12] Of course, we do not consider choices irrational if they are made in the absence of important relevant information which one has no way of knowing or cannot be expected to have: a suicide committed to avoid torture is not therefore irrational if help turns out to have been on the way but the victim had no way of knowing that this was the case. We tend to judge a choice inadequately informed only if it has been made without a substantial attempt to obtain information from reliable sources, or if it involves distortion of whatever information is actually available; the same criterion applies in suicide.

Some choices are irrational because the agent does not have access to adequate information from outside sources; but in another very large group of cases, the inadequacy of information is due to factors within the agent himself. This is particularly conspicuous in depression. In his widely re-printed paper "The Morality and Rationality of Suicide," Richard Brandt describes the way in which depression can constrict normal information-gathering processes when one approaches a decision, and result in reasoning which is impaired.

In the first place, depression, like any severe emotional experience, tends to primitivize one's intellectual processes. It restricts the range of one's survey of the possibilities. One thing that a rational person will do is compare the [future] world-course containing his suicide with his best alternative. But his best alternative is precisely a possibility he may overlook if, in a depressed mood, he thinks only of how badly off he is and does not contemplate plans of action which he has not at all considered.[13]

Thus, a depressed person's view of the range of possibilities for alternative actions may be severely restricted. His judgment about probabilities may be seriously affected: he may pessimistically select data upon which he forms a gloomy self-image, subconsciously suppressing data which lead to a more optimistic prediction. Good things in the future tend to seem less significant than bad things occurring now; this is the familiar goal-gradient phenomenon, under which we agree to read a paper or visit an unpleasant relative a year in advance, though we would not dream of committing ourselves to do so in just a month. Finally, depression tends to warp our recollections about our preferences for and enjoyment of certain types of things: when depressed we may be quite unmoved by things or prospects which would normally excite us, and the focal object of the depression, say a jilting lover, failing health, or a dwindling fortune, tends to assume all-consuming importance. In short, depression, because of its characteristic effects on the way in which it affects our preferences, can seriously interfere with the "rationality" of a decision. This observation is often used to promote a general argument against suicide: as we have seen, many researchers claim that depression is present in the majority of suicide cases. Thus, it is inferred, most if not all suicide is irrational.

However, although a great many suicides in depression involve inadequate information, not all depressive suicides are irrational in this way. Not all predictions of the future are inadequately informed, even when associated with depression. There are some situations in which the narrow view produced by depression cannot be greatly broadened. For instance, depression is a frequent concomitant of Parkinson's Disease, and the Parkinson's victim is likely to see his future as extremely bleak. But the future may in fact be quite bleak. Severe parkinsonism may mean decreasing mobility, conspicuous tremors, fixation of the eyes, unintelligible speech, and ultimately nearly total incapacitation. On the other hand, much parkinsonism responds dramatically to levadopa therapy. There may even be compensation: L-dopa often acts as an aphrodisiac in male patients, and many Parkinson's victims have extraordinarily satisfying sex lives. But for the patient for whom levadopa therapy is medically ineffective, for whom other side effects are too great or for whom increased sexuality is a burden, the future is dismal, and although he may be distorting information, he may nevertheless have an adequate view of what the future is likely to bring.

Inadequacy of information about the future may also affect suicide decisions even where depression is not involved. Much suicide is undertaken to avoid future evils: physical or mental suffering, torture, falls from honor, the discovery of misdeeds, bankruptcy, old age, or even boredom. But in the real world it is difficult to be certain exactly what will occur, and one can never be entirely sure that a particular event will happen.[14] Effective suicide means certain death, whereas torture, bankruptcy, or boredom are, at worst, only likely.

This component of our rationality criteria is often used as an explicit argument against suicide. Josephus, under pressure from the remnants of the Jewish forces at Jotapata to initiate a mass suicide in which he would be obliged to participate, attempts (unsuccessfully) to convince them to surrender to the Romans rather than kill themselves:

> What is it we fear that prevents us from surrendering to the Romans? Is it not death? And shall we then inflict upon ourselves certain death, to avoid an uncertain death, which we fear, at the hands of our foes? ... in my opinion there could be no more arrant coward than the pilot who, for fear of tempest, deliberately sinks his ship before the storm.[15]

Josephus' underlying argument, that the future is never fully certain, is fed not merely by exorbitant hope, but by many actual occurrences: history is full of tales of narrowly missed cataclysms, impossible rescues, stays of execution, and miraculous cures of hopeless disease. Dostoevsky was spared from a firing squad after the rifles were already loaded, cocked, and aimed. Indeed, there is great epistemological sense in which no future event is entirely certain. We do, of course, know that certain sequences of events have always occurred in the past and that fundamental physical laws predict that they will do so in the future, but we can never be certain that our formulations of these laws are fully accurate, or that our descriptions of events are entirely complete.

This argument is most pressing in medicine. Few physicians would agree that any particular case is *absolutely* certainly hopeless: though physicians are well acquainted with fatal diseases, they are also familiar with cases in which patients unpredictably and quite inexplicably recover. This is true of advanced malignancies, organ failures, and near-flat EEG's, as well as other sorts of illnesses; spontaneous recoveries can and do occur. If it is possible that the feared event—whether slaughter by the Romans, execution by a firing squad, or death by cancer—may not after all occur, then, according to this argument, suicide is irrational: it brings about certain death in a case where it is not entirely certain.

But this does not succeed as an argument against the rationality of suicide in general. Although there may be some chance of a striking change in the future—the rescue, the reprieve, the cure—it is not therefore rational to act in accordance with these hopes, or irrational to choose to avoid what the future is highly likely to bring. It is rational to bank on a likely event, not a highly unlikely one. The terminal patient may survive an extended period of severe pain and recover entirely, but it is irrational for him or others to behave as though this were going to occur; the very strong chance is that it will not.

It is important to see clearly the consequences of the anti-suicide argument here. When the claim that future circumstances are never fully certain is used as an argument against suicide, it condemns the potential suicide to almost certain suffering by encouraging an irrational hope.[16] In terminal-illness situations, this is almost always the case. To insist that the victims of extremely serious burns or irreversible cancers ought to stay alive because there is a slight chance that they will survive may mean that a few persons who would otherwise have ended their lives do survive; but it will also mean that many, many others will die in greater suffering than they might otherwise have chosen to undergo. Users of the "there's always hope" argument against suicide, although beginning from a premise which is technically true, must accept responsibility for the suffering they cause in offering unrealistic hopes as well as for the pleasure of those whose remote hopes come true.

One might object that although it is not rational to *believe* that the unlikely event will actually occur, it can nevertheless be rational to act in accord with that belief: one can rationally bet a penny to win a million dollars, even though the likelihood of winning is extremely small. In betting pennies for millions, this is certainly true. And it is true that the rationality of a wager depends on the attractiveness of the stakes; indeed, if a million dollars is an attractive win, surviving with one's life is even more so. But the rationality of a wager is also a function of the magnitude of the likely loss, and this is where the cases diverge. If you bet a penny to win a million, what you almost certainly will lose is the single penny. But when someone is encourged to forgo suicide on the outside chance that he may survive an ordinarily painful and fatal condition, the likely loss is considerably more than a penny: it is an end of one's life in perhaps excruciating physical and emotional pain.

Thus, the "there's always hope" argument against suicide is a particularly dangerous one in practice, especially when it is used to override someone's choice of an earlier, less painful death. For every individual who, foregoing suicide when his situation seemed hopeless, survives to a complete and full life, countless more die in misery. Suicide to avoid likely future evils, then, is not irrational as a calculation of future interest; where the likely loss is great enough, to bet against such evils would be folly, to act to avoid them wise.

This, of course, applies only to future evils whose likelihood we can predict with a strong degree of assurance. Many of the future evils for which suicide may be contemplated cannot be predicted with any real degree of confidence, and many fears are based on only the flimsiest evidence. Firm diagnoses are sometimes wrong, and many seemingly secure predictions of future catastrophes are false. Of course, it would be irrational to end one's life to avoid a future evil foreseen on only scanty evidence, or where there is some substantial chance the future evil will not occur. However, there may be exceptions, such as when the future evil predicted is so calamitous that no chance of other experience outweighs the risk of suffering it. For instance, if we were to assume that the paranoia associated with certain illnesses would preclude suicide after the onset of symptoms adequate to diagnose the disease, one might suggest—if the end stages of the disease often involves severe dementia as well as physical deterioration—that suicide on the basis of even slight, insidious early symptoms, in the presence of genetic or other risk, might be a rational choice. Virginia Woolf's suicide appeared to be of this form.

A separate but very closely related issue regards the difficulty for the prospective rational suicide of accurately predicting how he will *react* to predictable future events.[17] A financial magnate may be able to accurately predict forthcoming ruin and poverty, but may be quite unable to tell whether he will resent or—released from his responsibilities and a heavily material life—perhaps enjoy it. A person severely injured in an accident may accurately forsee a life involving severe physical limitations, but not realize that they will constitute little hindrance to his real cerebral interests. Reactions to past though perhaps dissimilar evils may provide some basis for predicting one's own reactions to future evils, but one's prediction may be warped by depression and other strong emotional states; some future evils turn out to be "not so bad" after all. But this fact does not make avoidance of future evils theoretically mistaken. The problem of predicting one's reactions to future events is a general problem not confined to suicide; it is equally a problem in setting positive goals. Yet we do not consider it irrational to set positive goals, even if we cannot be sure how we will respond to attainment of them. What the prospective rational suicide must calculate is just how damaging it will be to him if things turn out as he fears, and whether this risk is offset by the possibility of other, better outcomes.

Finally, there is a general sense in which, as we have seen earlier, no suicide decision can be adequately informed—since, as Philip Devine has pointed out, we can never have knowledge of what death actually is: suicide is a leap into the wholly unknown.[18] Strictly speaking, this argument is correct. But each individual will have his firm convictions of what is to come after death; just as we do not consider beliefs irrational which are consonant with the beliefs of the individual's cultural group, so we do not count as irrational a choice made with respect to alternatives about which the individual, in concert with his religious group, believes himself fully informed. The traditional Christian believer cannot be said to lack adequate information in his choice of suicide over life: he knows perfectly well he will burn in the fires of hell (though we might count him irrational for making such a choice). The general sense in which we are inadequately informed about the nature of death is part of the sense in which we are inadequately informed about the metaphysical character of the universe and about which religious claims, if any, are true. This does not show the suicide's act any more inadequately informed, or less rational, than any of our other important moral choices.

Avoidance of harm

We also widely assume that an action, to be rational, must accord with the agent's own interests in the protection of his person and body from harm. For instance, self-mutilators strike us as irrational, since they cause themselves harm; suicides may strike us in the same way, since we assume that it is in one's own prudential interests to remain alive.

It may be argued, however, that death is not a harm to the individual who is dead. The process of painfully dying or knowing one is going to die, of course, can constitute an extraordinary harm, but once dead, the individual no longer exists, and therefore is no longer harmed. For this reason, the suicide, provided he selects a reasonably painless and expeditious method of carrying out his plan, cannot be said to act contrary to his own prudential interests, since he does himself no harm. In fact, R.M. Martin argues that even the suicide which is hastily planned, irrationally chosen, or undertaken for wholly inadequate reasons is not a harm to that individual, since that individual is dead.

> The man who believes that death will bring him to paradise will not be disappointed; not because he will go to paradise, but because there won't be any *him* left after his death to be disappointed. Neither will the man who kills himself because he falsely believes he has a terminal disease regret his decision. The man who didn't know about therapy won't be worse off than he could have been had we intervened, after his suicide, since he won't exist at all. And the man who had the fleeting desire to kill himself and did won't suffer as a result of his desire's being only a fleeting one, as the man who went to live in the woods would.[19]

We might object as we suggested in discussing the value of life, that if a view like this were correct, it would be no harm to someone else to kill him either, at least if we can do it quickly, painlessly, and without warning. But we do think that to kill someone, even quickly, painlessly, and without warning, is to harm *him;* death is a harm, and a harm to the person whose death it is. Are we correct in thinking so? One way in which we might make sense of his assumption is to understand "harm" not simply in terms of bodily injury or discomfort, but also in terms of deprivation of pleasures, satisfactions, and other goods,[20] or what we called the *praemium vitae.* It is wrong to kill someone—even though swiftly, painlessly, and without his knowing it— because he is thereby deprived of these goods. Indeed, since killing him deprives him of *all* such goods, killing him is the greatest harm. Similarly, it can also be argued, since suicide too will deprive one of pleasures, satisfactions, and the other goods of life, it must also be a harm. Thus, since it is irrational to do an act which constitutes a harm to oneself (unless of course some greater good is thereby to be obtained), it is irrational to commit suicide.

Thus suicide, viewed this way, is always irrational, even if logically chosen on the basis of adequate and correct beliefs, because it brings about the greatest possible harm. But this view, although widespread, may not be correct. Note that we have defined "harm" in terms of the deprivation of *goods:* pleasures, satisfactions, and whatever else life may make possible. We do not ordinarily think it a harm to be deprived of evils: pain, suffering, terror, or want; and we do not count it irrational when one acts to avoid harm. If so, then surcease suicides, undertaken to avoid either physical or emotional harm, are not irrational after all: they serve to avoid harms, not to deprive one of goods.

It is certainly clear that we count most harm-avoiding activities as rational.
But this does not tell us whether harm-avoiding *suicides*, as distinguished
from other harm-avoiding activities, can be considered rational. The answer

depends in part on whether we consider death or suffering to be the greater
evil. If death is the greater evil it is irrational to seek it, even if suffering can
thereby be avoided; if, on the other hand, suffering is viewed as the worst
thing that can befall a human being, then death undertaken to avoid it is not
irrational.

We might try to resolve this issue by counting life in itself as a good,
regardless of the kinds of experiences or suffering it involves; this is a version
of the view that life has intrinsic value. Thus, we consider it a benefit to save
someone's life, even though his life may involve pain. But we do not always
consider preserving life a good, as Philippa Foot's examples may show:

> Suppose, for instance, that a man were being tortured to death and
> was given a drug that lengthened his sufferings; this would not be a
> benefit but the reverse. Or suppose that in a ghetto in Nazi Germany a
> doctor saved the life of someone threatened by disease, but that the
> man once cured was transported to an extermination camp; the
> doctor might wish for the sake of the patient that he had died of the
> disease.[21]

Life, she grants, is *normally* a benefit to the person whose life it is, but this
is not always so; there may be cases in which it is better for a person to die
earlier than later. Presumably, then, life is a harm if it consists wholly of
harmful or painful experiences; if it is rational to avoid harm, then it is
sometimes rational to avoid life.

Of course, it is not rational to avoid harm when there is some purpose to be
served by undergoing it: we rationally submit to dental pain in order to
prevent decay. This is precisely the view many Catholic writers take in
arguing against the rationality (and moral permissibility) of surcease
suicides. . . . The contemporary Catholic doctrine, first explicated with reference to suicide by Mme. de Staël and later by Paul-Louis Landsberg, teaches
that enduring even severe pain and suffering is of important spiritual value.
The Christian should regard suicide as depriving himself of a possible
good—suffering—and thus causing himself harm. Thus, the Christian may
rationally choose to endure the pain, while his non-Christian counterpart
may rationally choose to evade it.

This distinction rests, of course, on the thesis that pain and suffering may
serve some further purpose. As we've noted earlier, even within the Christian
religious tradition some thinkers distinguished between "constructive" and
"destructive" pain, or pain which serves some further purpose and permits
some further spiritual growth, as against pain which does not. A similar
secular distinction between productive and destructive pain can also be
drawn on the basis of other purposes which may be served. It may be easy to
distinguish pain which serves some further purpose from pain which does
not in cases like childbirth, dentistry, or first-aid treatment for accident
victims. It might be harder to make this distinction in cases of severe burn
treatments or repeated amputation, and perhaps impossible in terminal

cancer or in burn cases where survival is unprecedented. No doubt one would be tempted to formulate a kind of rule-of-thumb approximation: the longer-term and less transitory the pain threatens to be, and the dimmer the outlook for pain-free recovery, the more rational an attempt to avoid the pain by suicide.

Fortunately, enormous progress has been made in the medical control of pain; new drugs and methods of anesthesia and analgesia are under continuous development. Perhaps most promising in this respect is the Hospice movement's technique of pain prevention in terminal illness, which is based on administration of pain-relief mixtures on a scheduled basis prior to need, designed to anticipate and prevent pain rather than subdue already occurring pain.[22] Presumably, it would not be rational to choose suicide in order to avoid pain when in fact there will be little or none; we are already beginning to see the day when terminal cancer will be, as are kidney stones and gout, another outmoded example of irremediable pain.

Presumably, it would also be irrational to choose suicide to avoid pain when, although the pain itself serves no further purpose, another positive experience may occur which it is rational to seek. Lael Wertenbacker describes the cancer death of her husband as involving episodes of extreme pain, but describes the pain-free periods between those episodes as times of remarkable intimacy and preciousness.[23] Hospice workers often report that the most valued human relationships arise in the period between diagnosis and death. Literature, too, offers many accounts of experience of great spiritual depth and importance even in the immediate accompaniment of severe pain: for instance, the experience of (religious) enlightenment which occurs two hours before the death by cancer of the title figure in Tolstoi's *The Death of Ivan Ilych*.[24] Nevertheless, some kinds of pain are simply resistant to treatment, or occur in locations (for example, battlefields or remote territories) where treatment is unavailable, or in establishments (some hospitals, nursing homes, and unhappy families) where treatment is only erratically or ineptly offered, and preclude experience of any other sort. In some of these situations suicide may be the rational choice.

Furthermore, not all suffering is a matter of pain. The Hospice program is extremely effective in controlling physical pain, but reports much less success with other problems like difficulty in swallowing. Then, too, much physical pain is accompanied by severe emotional pain, and it is not always easy to differentiate the two. But it is important to discriminate between them because our responses to suicide based on avoidance of physical and of emotional pain are often quite different. We regard both as in principle transitory. Yet we recognize, and are beginning to acknowledge as grounds for suicide, a category of terminal physical pain which we do not recognize in cases of emotional suffering. However, many psychotics live in considerable mental agony, and can expect no cure; though contemporary society is beginning to acknowledge suicide as a remedy in cases of irremediable, terminal physical pain, it does not respect a suicide decision reached by a person suffering permanent and irreversible psychosis.

Of course most emotional pain, like most physical pain, *is* transitory, and will recede to permit other intrinsically valuable experience in the future.

Mme. de Staël remarks:

> Observe, after a period of ten years, a person who has sustained some
> great privation, of whatever nature it may be, and you will find that
> he suffers and enjoys from other causes than those from which ten
> years ago his misery was derived.[25]

The transitoriness of most depression can hardly be emphasized strongly
enough, since depression is so widely associated with suicide. Yet one can
also imagine cases of permanent emotional pain, either circumstantially
caused, as in lasting public disgrace or social ostracism, or produced by an
individual's own psychological constitution, as in untreatable depression or
psychosis. Robert Burton, in 1621, says of "melancholics" or the mentally ill
that:

> In the day time they are affrighted still by some terrible object, and
> torn in pieces with suspicion, fear, sorrow, discontents, cares, shame,
> anguish, &c. as so many wild horses, that they cannot be quiet an
> hour, a minute of time, but even against their wills they are intent, and
> still thinking of it, they cannot forget it, it grinds their souls day and
> night, they are perpetually tormented, a burden to themselves, as Job
> was, they can neither eat, drink, nor sleep.[26]

Modern psychotherapeutic drugs have done a good deal to change this, but
they have by no means eradicated the sufferings of mental despair and illness
from the face of the earth. In many cases of mental suffering, suicide may be
an irrational choice, since most such suffering is transitory and treatable, and
suicide precludes the real possibility of having other, subsequent experience
which it is rational to seek. Nevertheless, where the possibility of such other
experience is small, suicide—in mental illness as well as physical illness—
appears to be the prudent, rational choice.

This indicates a remaining problem: if we do acknowledge the rationality
of surcease suicide in cases where pain and suffering, either mental or
physical, serve no further purpose, it is still not clear what degree the pain
and suffering must reach before it becomes rational to avoid them by death.
Contemporary western culture appears to assume that only intense, unrelenting, and terminal physical pain makes death a rational choice, if ever. The
Stoics, on the other hand, admitted both physical and emotional suffering as
legitimizing reasons for suicide, and held that any modest preponderance of
pain of either sort was sufficient to make death the rational choice. They did,
of course, school themselves to resist pain, but did not hold that only severe
or terminal pain could provide a reason for suicide. Seneca remarks:

> And there are many occasions on which a man should leave life not
> only bravely but for reasons which are not as pressing as they might
> be—the reasons which restrain us being not so pressing either.[27]

Need pain be terminal, or need it reach excruciating levels before it is rational to avoid it by suicide? Again, one might attempt to formulate a rule-of-thumb answer; it would depend on the amount of *other* experience permitted by the pain, and whether this other experience is of intrinsic value. A person seized by periodic episodes of intense physical pain may neverthe- less have important experience during the pain-free intervals (the Werten- backer case); so may a person seized by intense psychological distress (Virginia Woolf). On the other hand, a person subjected to low-grade but unremitting physical or emotional pain (say, chronic headache or perma- nent endogenous depression) may have no experience not infected by the pain. Hume remarks on the man who is

> cursed with such an incurable depravity or gloominess of temper as must poison all enjoyment and render him equally miserable as if he had been loaded with the most grievous misfortunes.[28]

Suicide, he says, cannot be held against such a man.

Accordance with fundamental interests

In general, we regard an act as rational only if it is in accord with what we might call one's "ground-projects" or basic interests, which themselves arise from one's most abiding, fundamental values.[29] Sometimes these "ground- projects" or fundamental interests are self-centered ones, in the sense that they are concerned with the acquisition or arrangement of things for the benefit of ourselves; sometimes, however, they are altruistic, and concerned with the benefit of someone or something else. Thus, an individual's ground- projects may involve acquiring a bigger house, getting a better job, or learning various skills (though for some people such projects may be superficial ones only); they may also involve working for a cause, initiating reforms, or other projects of social improvement. They may even be malevolent: what is at immediate issue here is the rationality of an act, not its moral character.

An act which conflicts with the satisfaction of one's ground-projects or fundamental goals is usually held to be irrational; an act intended to satisfy them is not. To put this another way, an act can be said to be rational in the sense that it is an effective means to a given end; the moral character of the end is not at issue.[30] For instance, if a person has been working for years, say, for a liberal political cause, has attended party meetings and organized campaigns, but votes for the conservative candidate when there is no politi- cally expedient reason to do so, we say that that person has acted "irration- ally"; we would also say that he acts irrationally if he does not vote at all. In fact, he acts rationally only if he votes for the liberal candidate, since it is the success of the candidate which is his goal. If a person has multiple but conflicting ground-projects, we will say that it is rational to act to satisfy the most basic of these. Suicide, since it puts an end to life, appears to thwart the satisfaction of all one's basic projects or ground interests, and so appears to be irrational in every case.

It is true that one cannot satisfy certain kinds of interests if one is dead, and the satisfaction of many ground-projects requires the continuing exist- ence of the agent. One cannot satisfy one's project to live in a bigger house if one does not live, nor can one perfect one's skills when dead. But not all ground-projects require the continued existence of the agent: one's most important project may be essentially altruistic or centered on others, and can perhaps be satisfied even if one is dead. So, for instance, parents whose fundamental goals include putting their children through college can have this ground-project satisfied, even if they are no longer alive. One's ground-projects can sometimes even be satisfied if one kills oneself for them, as for instance in the parent who kills himself in order to donate an organ and thus ensure the survival of his child. We have already mentioned a number of cases of self-sacrificial and martyrdom suicide, including Cato and Captain Oates, in which an individual relinquishes his life in order that his fundamental goals with respect to someone else or some cause be satisfied.

Suicides which might appear to satisfy an individual's basic goals, however, are often said to be irrational on psychological grounds. For instance, as Margolis points out, although General Custer clearly entertained a fundamental interest in the success of his forces at Little Bighorn, his bravery is sometimes viewed as the symptom of a pronounced death wish, and therefore irrational.[31] Norman Morrison, the Quaker who burned himself to death to protest the Vietnam War, was said by some of the press to be insane.[32] Criticism of religious martyrs is often conducted in this way: self-sacrificial acts are frequently said to be impelled by hidden death wishes, neurotic desires to manipulate others, delusions of grandeur, or by outright psychosis. In many cases, no doubt, these claims are right. But this does not mean, of course, that it is always irrational to die for a cause. Even in the presence of obvious psychopathology, one might not want to call an act irrational when it serves its agent's fundamental ends.

One might object that to be dead precludes appreciation of the satisfaction of one's ground-projects or interests, and that therefore suicide can never be rational. An argument of this sort is hinted at by Choron in reporting the death of Paul Lafargue, son-in-law of Karl Marx, a physician who had become increasingly active in support of the socialist revolution in Russia. Lafargue had long planned to kill himself when he reached the age of seventy; he did so in 1911. Choron writes:

> There is considerable irony in Lafargue's suicide, for had he waited another six years (and there is no indication that he could not have lived that long), he would have seen the triumph of his cause in Russia in November 1917.[33]

But it is obvious that although his suicide precludes Lafargue's knowing or appreciating the fact that his guiding interest in the success of social revolution was satisfied, that interest was nevertheless in fact satisfied, whether Lafargue was alive or not. And since Lafargue's interest was in the triumph of the revolution, not in his appreciation of it, there appears to be no reason to think that Lafargue's suicide ran counter to his own most basic interests. According to this criterion, it cannot be said to have been an irrational act.

Furthermore, there may be cases in which not the life but the death of the agent is required to promote the ground-projects which he has himself adopted. One thinks for instance of Socrates, facing the hemlock. Given his fundamental commitment to preserving the laws of Athens, to escape execution would be to thwart satisfaction of those interests. Hence, he allows himself to be killed. Similarly, only by suicide could Saul satisfy his fundamental interests in protecting him from humiliation and torture by the Philistines, and thus preserving the dignity and honor of the Jews. Likewise, only by suicide could Cato promote his interests in the freedom of his people. The figures and their cases are familiar; now we also see the sense in which their suicides are the *rational* consequences of their commitment to certain abiding purposes. Suicide is, in these cases, the only effective means of achieving their paramount ends. Bernard Williams writes:

> It is worth noting here that there is no contradiction in the idea of a man's dying for a ground-project: quite the reverse, since if death really is necessary for the project, then to live would be to live with it unsatisfied, something which, if it really is his ground-project, he has no reason to do.[34]

Suicide may also be rational if it is the only effective means by which one can avoid change in the ends one has—even if those ends would be changed by oneself. For instance, imagine a person whose fundamental ground-project is to live his life in a way that is kind, generous, and humane: it is central to him to be morally good. But now suppose, as Dan Wikler suggests,[35] that such a person is captured by the Nazis, and is commanded to do a certain morally repugnant task. He is convinced by their psychologist that if he goes ahead and does it, the psychologist will turn him into the kind of person who enjoys doing morally repugnant things—just the kind of person he earlier least wanted to be.

Would suicide to avoid forcible alterations of his fundamental ground-projects be rational? This is a very difficult question to answer; we must remember that it is closely connected with the issue of predicting one's reactions to future events. We have not held that it is irrational to act on the basis of preferences one does not now have but predictably will have in the future. The business executive who falls from favor may not now, as we suggested in earlier analogous cases, find satisfaction in the notion of selling shoes for a living; but he may (predictably, if he knows himself well enough) find satisfactions in life as a shoe salesman in the future. There, we said that it would be irrational to discount future preferences and commit suicide now; here we seem to be saying that future preferences may (and should) be rationally discounted, and that suicide to avoid Nazi reprogramming can indeed be the rational choice.

Is there a conflict here? Only an apparent one, I think; the difficulty lies in the fact that in the one case, it is a genuinely *fundamental* ground-project—living a life which is morally good—which is at risk. In the other, the character of one's occupation may not be a matter of fundamental ground-project, though obtaining satisfaction from one's employment may be. If the erstwhile business executive were a person to whom executive status is genuinely central, we might grant that the choice of suicide when executive status is irrevocably closed to him might be the rational choice; but such cases are rare. The person for whom living a morally good life is central, on the other hand, cannot lightly discard this commitment as just another evanescent goal.

This notion permits us to see that suicide may be rational, insofar as it permits satisfaction of one's goals or fundamental interests, even for individuals who do not have commitments to other persons or groups, or to institutions, principles, or causes. Some individuals' primary goals or interests are connected with other persons and things; for some individuals, however, the most fundamental interest involves self-understanding, self-revelation, and perhaps self-perfection. This is not to be confused with naive interests in self-protection or the usual prudential interests in avoiding harm; rather, these interests arise when the individual finds himself and his own character the focus of his major concerns. It is a trait we admire in novelists, poets, and religious visionaries; it is a trait that is shared, perhaps, by many lesser folk. But there is a familiar problem: if one's basic goals are self-centered, can suicide ever be rational, when that self will no longer exist?

In one type of case this seems immediately obvious: the case in which the individual's basic goal or concern is in some way connected with the act of dying, so that suicide will bring about this experience. This focus is common among the Romantics, especially Novalis and Rilke, and it is inherited to some degree by the Existentialist movement; death in these traditions is sometimes described as a central, culminating event, a kind of final "peak experience." James Hillman, a contemporary psychoanalyst who shares the view that death is the most important and culminating event in life, but also holds that death is followed by a personal afterlife, writes:

> The impulse to death need not be conceived as an anti-life movement; it may be a demand for an encounter with absolute reality, a demand for a fuller life through the death experience.[36]

This need not involve the kind of misleading metaphor described by Joyce Carol Oates, though of course such misleading metaphors are prevalent; if one's metaphysical or religious conceptions lead one to believe that this culminating experience can be attained through suicide, and if, furthermore, attaining that experience is the central focus of one's life, then suicide in order to attain it would seem to count as a rational action. Whether life continues afterward or not is irrelevant once this utmost experience has been achieved.

However, religious and poetic lore aside, the real issue concerns whether suicide can be a rational choice for someone whose interests and fundamental goals are self-centered. One is included to think not. But there are cases when self-interests of this sort will be undermined or thwarted if death does not intervene, and in these cases suicide may be the rational choice. The Nazi-reprogramming case is one such circumstance. But there may be others on a much less conspicuous scale. Imagine, for instance, a pianist for whom perfection of keyboard technique has been his central, abiding interest since early youth. As this pianist ages and arthritis sets in, he finds it increasingly difficult to play well. If he kills himself, of course, his interests are not furthered, since he no longer exists as the referent of his piano-playing interests. But if he does not commit suicide and the arthritis becomes increasingly crippling, his long-term self-interest in perfection of his piano style will be increasingly undermined. No Nazi reprogramming is involved; the villain here is age.

Of course, he might simply stop playing the piano; this would be to live with an interest unsatisfied. Better still, he might succeed in releasing himself from piano playing as a central interest; still better, he might adopt another interest, say, composing, or writing music-theory books, and in his way avoid continued frustration of his original interests. Robert Schumann transferred his interests to composing after a finger sling he had devised jammed his right hand early in his performing career.

This, of course, is all well and proper for interests which are replaceable, or which can be relinquished. But we are talking about central interests and fundamental ground-projects, not peripheral ones; *fundamental* self-referential interests cannot be simply dropped, replaced, or forgotten whenever circumstances arise which make their satisfaction impossible. For instance, the maintenance of honor may be a central interest for some people, as it clearly was in classical Rome and in Japan. For some, it may be possible to discard one's interest in honor when one's honor is compromised, but if the interest is central, or if it is the product of long-term cultural influences, to discard it will not be easy. Or, imagine a person whose fundamental interests involve achieving a clear view of the world, or unimpaired rationality: when such a person feels insanity coming on, suicide may be the rational choice, as Plotinus recommended[37] and Virginia Woolf practiced.[38] If these cases are accepted, still others will occur. For instance, if it is correct to describe Ernest Hemingway's macho, tough-guy image as a central self-interest, then even the incursions of middle age might begin to thwart satisfaction of that interest. His suicide is generally viewed as pathological, in part a failure of the psychiatric sciences but in part also the product of his inflexibility in changing roles; under our criteria, however, it may count as rational.[39]

This is a general point about the rationality of altering one's life circumstances, activities, and goals in response to setbacks or hindrances, mishaps, unfortunate events, unfulfilled expectations, and so forth. It is almost universally assumed that to do so is rational; that is, the rational thing to do in the face of some unavoidable and irreversible setback is to alter one's life so as to accommodate oneself to the change. But the suggestion here is that if the concerns, interests, and fundamental ground-projects which one may be forced to relinquish are genuinely central, it may not be rational to let them go. These are the cases in which suicide may be a rational alternative.

This argument can be applied to distinct groups of people, particularly the aged. To those individuals for whom independence, status as contributing members of society, and/or the ability to experience intensely are central interests, old age will quite likely prove to be a condition which hinders satisfaction of their most basic interests. For some of these individuals, the original basic interests may prove not to be so basic after all, and may be fairly readily replaceable. Some older people find new satisfaction in being nurtured, in occupying a position as senior but not executive member of the family, or in active reminiscence of their earlier years. These are the individuals who "adjust well" to major life changes. But for some, abandonment of one's earlier concerns for autonomy, self-reliance, and activity may prove impossible, or categorically distasteful, and for these individuals the mental and physical limitations of old age may serve only to thwart their most basic interests. Of course, in many cases, it may be very hard to distinguish these situations from those in which individuals are fearful or defensive about altering relatively peripheral interests; this is the kind of distinction which continuing counseling might facilitate. But not all cases of refusal to "adjust" involve merely peripheral interests; in some cases it is much more the central interests which are at stake, and to thwart these is to thwart what it is that the individual essentially lives for. "The worst death for anyone is to lose the center of his being," Hemingway had said, "Retirement is the filthiest word in the English language."[40]

We are often tempted to claim that the preservation of one's one life is the most fundamental and basic of all ground projects; this is, no doubt, in part what is intended by the claim that self-preservation is man's most fundamental instinct and law. But it is quite obvious that some individuals place other projects and concerns above their interests in self-preservation. This becomes clear in forced-choice tests, as for instance the apostasy-or-torture choice offered many early Christians. Some chose one, some the other, but we may assume that when confronted with this choice, each individual revealed what at heart were his or her most basic goals: some wished to stay alive, some wished to see God. Similar forced-choice situations may reveal, in any case of apparent multiple ground interests, which one is really more fundamental. If one's basic ground-projects can be furthered only by one's own death, or if they will be thwarted by one's remaining alive, suicide in these cases appears to be the rational choice.

Of course, suicide to accomplish a ground-project is rational only if that ground-project can be fulfilled regardless of one's own existence. However, many ground-projects we think of as independent of our own existence may not really be so. For instance, I may have dedicated my life to writing an article which could, in fact, be completed equally well by someone else; if so, the article is a ground-project which is independent of my own existence. If, for whatever reasons, my own suicide would implement the completion of this article (by somebody else), while my staying alive would impede it, I would not be irrational, at least on these grounds, to kill myself. But, as John Perry (working on his own article) says, "I want not merely that this article be completed, but that it be completed by me."[41] Our involvement in even the most noble of projects often tends to be quite personal in this way, even though we are often unwilling or unable to admit it; but it is just this fact of personal involvement that precludes suicide as a rational choice in the accomplishment of that goal.

Finally, as David Wood points out,[42] suicide may also be rational even when it is not a means for accomplishment of some goal. He distinguishes between *instrumental suicide*, which is intended to bring about certain effects, and what he calls *expressive suicide*, in which the meaning of the act is its whole purpose. As an example, he suggests the suicide (by jumping) of an architect who pioneered highrise apartments, and realizes too late what he has done. The suicide will not accomplish the demolition of the highrises, nor prevent future entrepreneurs from building them. Nor will the suicide prevent future harms to this person (he will not be condemned, or rejected from the Architects' Society; and his remorse will diminish with time), or preclude forcible alterations in his fundamental ground-projects (his project remains, as it was, to contribute to the quality of human life). His suicide may not accomplish any good, or forestall any evil. Yet because of its capacity to express the central concern of this particular man, we may see it as a rational act. Not all expressive suicides are rational acts; they may suffer, as Wood suggests, from lack of genuine feeling, or from irrelevance of suicide as form of expression. But some acts of suicide may escape these difficulties, and even though not performed in order to produce some benefit or avoid some substantial harm, nevertheless count as rational acts.

One last issue presents itself in considering the concept of "rational suicide." In cases in which suicide, whether because it prevents harm, accomplishes goals, or expresses what is central to a human being, is a rational choice, is it always also rational to choose to remain alive? Is suicide, if it is rational in given circumstances, sometimes *the* rational choice, or is it always merely *a* rational choice among others? Clearly, when strategies other than suicide will equally well prevent harms, accomplish goals, or express a person's deepest convictions, staying alive and using these other strategies will be an at least equally rational choice. But where other strategies will not succeed, suicide may be the only rational thing to do. This issue will have crucial practical consequences for the theory of rational suicide.

Notes

1 Jacques Choron, *Suicide* (New York: Charles Scribner's Sons, 1972), pp. 96–97.

2 Edwin S. Shneidman and Norman L. Farberow, "The Logic of Suicide," in Shneidman and Farberow, eds., *Clues to Suicide* (New York: McGraw-Hill, 1957), pp. 31–40.

3 Sigmund Freud, *Thoughts for the Times on War and Death,* Chapter Two: "Our Attitude Towards Death," *The Standard Edition of the Complete Works of Sigmund Freud* (London: The Hogarth Press, 1915), 14, pp. 273–302, p. 289: "It is indeed impossible to imagine our own death; and whenever we attempt to do so we can perceive that we are in fact still present as spectators. Hence the psycho-analytic school could venture on the assertion that at bottom no one believes in his own death, or, to put the same thing in another way, that in the unconscious every one of us is convinced of his own immortality."

4 See, e.g., Shneidman and Farberow, "The Logic of Suicide" *(op. cit.),* p. 33, and, for the same notion in a philosophic context, Thomas Nagel, "Death," *Nous,* 4, no. 1 (1970), pp. 73–80. As a *Gedankenexperiment* to support this claim, one might also notice that it is typically much more difficult to imagine oneself dead and cremated than dead and buried.

5 Joyce Carol Oates, "The Art of Suicide," *The Re-evaluation of Existing Values and the Search for Absolute Values,* Proceedings of the Seventh International Conference on the Unity of the Sciences (Boston, 1978); also in M. Pabst Battin and David J. Mayo, eds., *Suicide: The Philosophical Issues* (New York: St. Martin's Press, 1980), pp. 161–168.

6 The term is Edwin Shneidman's; see his "Classifications of Suicidal Phenomena," *Bulletin of Suicidology* (July 1968), pp. i–9.

7 According to Ronald Maris, in *Pathways to Suicide* (Baltimore: Johns Hopkins University Press, 1981), p. 291, most completed suicides are escapist; the remainder, and almost all nonfatal attempts, are aggressive.

8 Jerome Motto, "The Right to Suicide: A Psychiatrist's View," *Life-Threatening Behavior*, Vol. 2, no. 3 (Fall 1972), reprinted in Battin and Mayo, eds., *Suicide: The Philosophical Issues (op. cit.),* pp. 212–19.

9 H. J. Rose, "Suicide (Introductory)," in *Encyclopaedia of Religion and Ethics* (New York: Charles Scribner's Sons, 1925), p. 22.

10 For instance, Dan Wikler, in a private communication, observes: "Suppose that someone grew up in a society believing some religion but was isolated within that society and was never transmitted the dominant religious belief. Suppose then that this person, quite on his own, began to believe these things. It would seem to me that we would have evidence that this person was irrational, even though his beliefs were precisely consonant with those of the dominant group, in this case. Similarly, someone who went on the warpath because of a belief in Valhalla would be suspect here even though his beliefs are quite consonant with the beliefs in another culture." Wikler's conclusions are consistent with the view presented here.

11 Shneidman and Farberow, *Clues to Suicide (op. cit.),* Note 3A, p. 200. The names of the authors of these genuine suicide notes have been changed by Shneidman and Farberow for publication.

12 See Jerome A. Motto, "The Right to Suicide: A Psychiatrist's View," *Life-Threatening Behavior,* 2, No. 3 (Fall, 1972), pp. 183–88. Motto discusses, among other things, the psychiatrist's conception of "realistic life-assessment" and its use in suicide situations.

13 Richard B. Brandt, "The Morality and Rationality of Suicide," in Seymour Perlin, ed., *A Handbook for the Study of Suicide* (Oxford: Oxford University Press, 1975), p. 380; a portion of this essay is reprinted as "The Rationality of Suicide" in Battin and Mayo, eds., *Suicide: The Philosophical Issues (op. cit.),* pp. 117–32.

14 See Antony Flew, "The Principle of Euthanasia," in A. B. Downing, ed., *Euthanasia and the Right to Death* (London: Peter Owen, 1969), p. 37.

15 Flavius Josephus, *The Jewish War* III 367–368 (New York: G. P. Putnam's Sons, 1927). Josephus, seeing that he was unable to persuade his companions to abandon their suicide plan and surrender, proposed that they all draw lots and kill one another in turn, so that "we shall be spared from taking our lives with our own hands" (III 389). Josephus drew the next-to-last lot; when each of those preceding had been killed in turn, Josephus persuaded the man behind him that they should both remain alive. This episode is often taken to cast doubt on the sincerity of Josephus' views concerning suicide.

16 See Flew's discussion of the fallibility of medicine and the consequences of this circumstance, "The Principle of Euthanasia" *(op. cit.),* pp. 37–40.

17 See Brandt's discussion in "The Morality and Rationality of Suicide" *(op. cit.),* especially in the section titled "Whether and When Suicide is Best or Rational for the Agent."

18 Philip Devine, *The Ethics of Homicide* (New York: Cornell University Press, 1979), pp. 24–28.

19 *Robert M. Martin, "Suicide and False Desires," in Battin and Mayo, eds., Suicide: The Philosophical Issues (op. cit.),* pp. 144–50, quotation from earlier version.

20 This is the strategy Nagel uses in his paper "Death" *(op. cit.).*

21 Philippa Foot, "Euthanasia," *Philosophy and Public Affairs,* 6 (Winter 1977), p. 88.

22 Hospice, founded and directed by Cicely Saunders, is a movement devoted to the development of institutions for providing palliative but medically nonaggressive care for terminal-illness patients. In addition to its extraordinary contribution in developing methods of prophylactic pain control, according to which analgesics are administered on a scheduled basis in advance of experienced pain, Hospice has also emphasized attention to the emotional needs of the patient's family. An account of the theory and methodology of Hospice can be found in a number of the publications of Cicely Saunders, including "The Treatment of Intractable Pain in Terminal Cancer," *Proceedings of the Royal Society of Medicine* 56 (1963),

p. 195, and "Terminal Care in Medical Oncology," in K. D. Bagshawe, ed., *Medical Oncology* (Oxford: Blackwell, 1975), pp. 563–76. A careful assessment of potentials for abuse of the Hospice system may be found in John F. Potter, M.D., "A Challenge for the Hospice Movement," *The New England Journal of Medicine* 302, no. 1 (Jan. 3, 1980), 53–55.

23 Lael Tucker Wertenbacker, *Death of a Man* (Boston: Beacon Press, 1974); see also two other intimate accounts of deaths by cancer, Jessamyn West's *The Woman Said Yes* (New York: Harcourt Brace Jovanovich, 1976), and Derek Humphrey with Ann Wickett, *Jean's Way* (London, Melbourne, New York: Quartet Books, 1978).

24 Leo Tolstoi, "The Death of Ivan Ilych," in *The Death of Ivan Ilych and Other Stories* (New York: New American Library, 1960).

25 Mme. de Staël-Holstein [Anne Louise Germaine (Necker), the baroness Staël-Holstein], "Reflections on Suicide," in George Combe, *The Constitution of Man, considered in relation to external objects*, "Alexandrian Edition" (Columbus: J. and H. Miller, 18–?), p. 102.

26 Robert Burton, *The Anatomy of Melancholy* (1621), (New York: Farrar and Rinehart, 1927), p. 368.

27 Seneca, *Letters from a Stoic (Epistulae Morales)*, tr. Robin Campbell (Baltimore: Penguin Books, 1969), Letter 77, p. 125.

28 David Hume, "Essay on Suicide" (1776) in *The Philosophic Works of David Hume* (Edinburgh: Printed for Adam Black and William Tait, and Charles Tait, 1826), p. 567.

29 The notion of *ground project* is developed by Bernard Williams in "Persons, Character and Morality," in *The Identities of Persons*, Amelie Oksenberg Rorty, ed. (Berkeley and Los Angeles: University of California Press, 1976), pp. 197–216.

30 This is the Rawlsian value-free notion of rationality, originally a purely economic notion; rationality is "taking the most effective means to given ends." John Rawls, *A Theory of Justice* (Cambridge, Mass.: Belknap/Harvard, 1971), p. 14.

31 Joseph Margolis, *Negativities* (Columbus, Ohio: Charles E. Merrill, 1973), p. 24.

32 Pretzel, describing the death of Norman Morrison (see Chapter II, footnote 78), concludes that we do not have adequate data to determine whether this self-immolation should count as a rational suicide.

33 Choron, *Suicide (op. cit.)*, p. 101. Lafargue's suicide was a joint one with his wife, Karl Marx's daughter.

34 Williams, "Persons, Character and Morality" *(op. cit.)*, p. 209.

35 Private communication.

36 James Hillman, *Suicide and the Soul* (New York: Harper & Row, 1964), p. 63; emphasis his.

37 Plotinus, *Enneads* I.4 and I.9, tr. A. H. Armstrong (Cambridge, Mass.: Harvard University Press, 1966), see esp. note 1, pp. 324–35.

38 Quentin Bell's *Virginia Woolf: A Biography* (New York: Harcourt Brace Jovanovich, 1972), provides the text of the note Virginia Woolf left for her husband Leonard on the morning she drowned herself: "I feel certain I am going mad again. I feel we can't go through another of those terrible times. And I shan't recover this time. I begin to hear voices, and I can't concentrate. So I am doing what seems the best thing to do . . ." (p. 226).

39 Thomas Szasz, in his "The Ethics of Suicide," *The Antioch Review*, 31 (Spring 1971), pp. 7–17, says that Hemingway was "demeaned" by the "psychiatric indignities inflicted on him" (p. 13). Also see Paul Pretzel, "Philosophical and Ethical Considerations of Suicide Prevention," *Bulletin of Suicidology*, 2 (July 1968), pp. 31–32, and Maris, *Pathways to Suicide (op. cit.)*.

40 A. E. Hotchner, *Papa Hemingway* (New York: Random House, 1966), p. 228.

41 John Perry, "The Importance of Being Identical," in Rorty, ed., *The Identities of Persons (op. cit.)*, pp. 67–90; see p. 79.

42 David Wood, "Suicide as Instrument and Expression," in Battin and Mayo, eds., *Suicide: The Philosophical Issues (op. cit.)*, pp. 151–60.

Edwin S. Shneidman

In this selection from the journal Life-Threatening Behavior, *Shneidman reports on a study in which a "blind analysis" was conducted of thirty cases—five suicides, ten natural deaths, and fifteen living persons. The analysis was conducted in terms of perturbation and lethality. The results indicated that suicide is a discernible part of a life-style, and the suicide of a fifty-five-year-old could be predicted by the time that individual was thirty. Various psychodynamic hypotheses are offered to account for these findings.*

From Life-Threatening Behavior, *Vol. 1, No. 1, Spring 1971. Reprinted by permission.*

INTRODUCTION AND BACKGROUND

The two principal assertions in this paper are (a) that discernible early prodromal clues to adult suicide may be found in longitudinal case history data and (b) that it is useful to conceptualize these premonitory clues in terms of *perturbation* and *lethality.*

The data from which evidence for these assertions was obtained are those of the longitudinal study of 1,528 gifted people initiated by Lewis M. Terman in 1921.[1] Terman and his coworkers searched the public schools of the cities of California for exceptionally bright youngsters. His purposes were "to discover what gifted children are like as children, what sort of adult they become, and what some of the factors are that influence their development" (Oden, 1968). That study, begun over a half-century ago, continues to this day.

Of the original 1,528 subjects, 857 were males and 671 were females. The sample was composed of children (mean age 9.7 years) with Stanford-Binet IQs of 140 or higher—the mean IQ was over 150—and an older group of high school students (mean age 15.2 years) who scored within the top 1 percent on the Terman Group Test of Mental Ability. The present analysis will be limited to male subjects, of whom approximately 80 percent were born between 1905 and 1914.

An enormous amount of data has been collected. At the time of the original investigation in 1921–22, the information included a developmental record, health history, medical examination, home and family background, school history, character trait ratings and personality evaluations by parents and teachers, interest tests, school achievement tests, and the like. Subsequently, there has been a long series of systematic follow-ups by personal field visits: in 1924, 1925, 1936, 1940, 1945, 1950, 1955, and 1960. Another follow-up study is planned for the near future. In the field studies (1921, 1927, 1940, and 1950), subjects and their families were interviewed, and data from intelligence tests, personality tests, and questionnaires were obtained.

The Terman studies have catalyzed two generations of thought, research, attitudinal changes, and educational developments. Detailed descriptions of the subjects at various ages, as well as summaries of the important findings, are available in a series of publications authored by Professor Terman and his chief coworker, Melita Oden (Oden, 1968; Terman, 1925, 1940; Terman & Oden, 1947, 1959). Among longitudinal studies (Stone & Onque, 1959) the Terman Study is unique in many ways, including the extent to which its staff has continued to maintain contact with the subjects for over half a century. As of 1960, only 1.7 percent of the 1,528 subjects had been lost entirely.

Almost everyone in the psychological and pedagogical worlds now knows the basic findings of the Terman Study: that intellectually gifted children —far from being, as was once thought, spindly, weak, and maladjusted or one-sided—are, on the whole, more physically and mentally healthy and successful than their less-than gifted counterparts. An unusual mind, a vigorous body, and a well-adjusted personality are not incompatible.[2]

A mortality summary for the Terman gifted group is as follows: In 1960 —when the median age was 49.6—there had been 130 known deaths, 83 male and 47 female. The mortality rate was 9.8 percent for males and 7.2 percent for females—8.6 percent for the total group. According to Dublin's life tables (Dublin, Lotka, & Spiegelman, 1949), 13.9 percent of white males, 10.1 percent of white females, and 12 percent of a total cohort who survive to age eleven will have died before age fifty. In 1960, the figures indicated a favorable mortality rate in the Terman group lower than the general white population of the same age.

By 1960, 110 of the 130 Terman group deaths—61 percent—had been due to natural causes. (Cardiovascular diseases ranked first with males, and cancer was first among females.) Accidents accounted for nineteen male deaths, while only five females died in accidents. Five men had lost their lives in World War II. There were no homicide victims. One death was equivocal as to mode and could not be classified. As of 1960, suicide was responsible for fourteen male and eight female deaths; by 1970 there were twenty-eight known deaths by suicide—twenty men and eight women.

An inspection of the listing of suicidal deaths (table 1) suggested that there were several subgroups: student suicides, thirty- and forty-year suicides, and middle-age suicides. Among the twenty-eight suicides—of both sexes, ranging in age from eighteen to sixty-three (a forty-five-year span), year of death from 1928 to 1968 (forty years), using a variety of lethal methods (pills, poison, drowning, guns)—there was a subgroup of five persons—numbers 14 to 18—all of whom were male, Caucasian, with IQ's over 140, born about the same time (between 1907 and 1916), four of whom committed suicide within a year of each other (1965 or 1966), were in the "middle period" of their lives (ages at death forty-three, fifty, fifty-one, fifty-three, and fifty-eight), and used the same method (all gunshot). This special subgroup seemed to offer a unique opportunity for an especially intensive investigation.[3]

A listing of all those subjects who had died indicated that there were ten other males, born about the same time (1910 to 1914) as the five suicides, who had died of natural causes (either cancer or heart disease) during the same years that four of the five suicides had killed themselves (1965–66). The opportunity for a natural experiment, using blind analyses, was evident.

TABLE 1

THE TWENTY-EIGHT SUICIDES AS OF 1970

	Age at suicide	Year of birth	Year of suicide	Marital status	Education	Occupational level	Method of suicide
Men							
1.	18	1910	1928	S	High school	Student	Poison
2.	19	1916	1935	S	2 years college	V	Gunshot
3.	24	1908	1932	S	AB +	Graduate student	Drowning
4.	28	1910	1938	S	MA	II	Poison
5.	33	1913	1946	M^2, D	High school	III	Barbiturate
6.	34	1913	1947	S^*	2 years college	III	Carbon monoxide
7.	35	1904	1939	S	Ph.D.	I	Gunshot
8.	37	1909	1946	M	1½ years college	II	Poison
9.	42	1905	1947	M^2, D^2	2 years college	II	Not known
10.	42	1916	1958	M^2, D^2	AB + 3 years	I	Barbiturate
11.	45	1911	1956	M	3 years college	II	Barbiturate
12.	45	1911	1956	M	AB, MA, LLB	IV	Carbon monoxide
13.	45	1913	1958	M	MD +	I	Poison
14.	43	1910	1953	M^4, D^4	2 years college	II	Gunshot
15.	50	1916	1965	M, D	BS	—	Gunshot
16.	51	1915	1966	M^2, D^2	High school	III	Gunshot
17.	53	1913	1966	M	LLB	I	Gunshot
18.	58	1907	1966	M^3, D^2	2 years college	I	Gunshot
19.	61	1905	1966	S	MA	I (retired)	Barbiturate
20.	63	1905	1968	M^2, D^1	Ph.D.	I	Barbiturate
Women							
1.	22	1914	1936	S	2 years college	Student	Gunshot
2.	30	1905	1935	S	AB	Librarian	Carbon monoxide
3.	30	1913	1943	M	2 years college	Housewife	Gunshot
4.	32	1917	1949	W	3 years college	Physical therapist	Barbiturate
5.	37	1916	1953	M^5, D^4	2 years college	Writer	Barbiturate
6.	40	1915	1955	M, D	3 years college	Housewife	Barbiturate
7.	44	1910	1954	M	MA	Housewife	Barbiturate
8.	44	1910	1954	M, D	BS	Social Worker	Barbiturate

I. Professional; II. Official, managerial, and semiprofessional; III. Retail business, clerical, sales, skilled trades, and kindred; IV. Agricultural and related; V. Minor business, minor clerical, and semiskilled occupations.

Thirty cases were selected to include the five suicides, the ten natural deaths, and fifteen individuals who were still alive. The latter two subgroups were matched with the five suicides in terms of age, occupational level, and father's occupational level. That these three subgroups are fairly well matched is indicated by the information in table 2. (The reader should keep in mind that all thirty subjects were male, Caucasian, Californian middle- and upper-middle-class, had IQ's over 140, and were members of the Terman Gifted Study.) Each folder was edited by Mrs. Oden so that I could not tell whether the individual was dead or still alive. (Death certificates, newspaper clippings, and other "death clues" were removed.) The cases came to me, one at a time, in a random order. Although I was "blind" as to the suicide-natural death-living identity of each case, I did know the total numbers of cases in each subgroup.

TABLE 2

OCCUPATIONS AND AGES FOR THE SUICIDE,
NATURAL DEATH, AND LIVING SUBJECTS

	Suicide (N=5)	Natural (N=10)	Living (N=15)
Occupational level			
I — Professional	2	5	7
II — Official, managerial, semiprofessional	2	4	6
III — Retail business, clerical and sales, skilled trades	1	1	2
Fathers' occupational level			
I — Professional	–	2	5
II — Official, managerial, semiprofessional	4	6	6
III — Retail business, clerical and sales, skilled trades	–	1	4
IV — Agricultural and related occupations	–	–	–
V — Minor business or clerical and semiskilled	1	1	–
Year of birth			
1907	1	–	–
1908	–	–	–
1909	–	–	–
1910	1	1	3
1911	–	3	3
1912	1	1	4
1913	–	2	1
1914	–	3	3
1915	1	–	1
1916	1	–	–

RATING OF PERTURBATION (THE LIFE CHART)

The cases were analyzed in terms of two basic continua (by which every life can be rated): perturbation and lethality. Perturbation refers to how upset (disturbed, agitated, sane-insane, discomposed) the individual is—rated, let's say, on a 1 to 9 scale[4]—and the latter to how likely it is that he will take his own life. (Lethality is discussed in the next section below.) For each of the thirty cases a rough chart of the individual's perturbation in early childhood, adolescence, high school, college, early marriage, and middle life was made. Clues were sought relating to tranquility-disturbance especially evidences of any *changes* and variations in the levels of perturbation. An attempt was made to classify the materials under such headings as "Early prodromata," "Failures," and "Signatures"—each explained below.

A "life chart" was constructed for each case, roughly following the procedures developed by Adolf Meyer (1951, 1952). In each case the folders were examined more or less chronologically in an attempt to order the materials in a temporal sequence while keeping in mind a number of related skeins.

One example of perturbation (from an individual who turned out to be among the five homogeneous suicides): A high school counselor wrote about one young man that he was "emotionally unstable, a physical roamer and morally erratic, excellent to teachers who treat him as an adult but very disagreeable to others." At the same time, the home visitor wrote: "I like him tremendously; he is better company than many teachers." Ten years later the subject himself wrote: "My gifts, if there were any, seem to have been a flash in the pan."

Early prodromata

Under this category were included early important interpersonal relationships, especially with the subject's father and mother. The folder materials contained ratings by the subject of his attitudes and interactions with each of his parents. Some information relating to relationships with parents may be of special interest. In the 1940 questionnaire materials—when the modal age of the male subjects was 29.8 years—there was a series of questions concerning earlier conflict and attachment to mother and father. The responses of the five individuals who, as it turned out, made up the homogeneous suicide group seemed to have three interesting features: (a) in answer to the question "Everything considered, which was your favorite parent—father, mother, had no favorite?" only one of the five answered "father"; (b) in answer to the question about the amount of conflict between the individual and his father and the individual and his mother, two of the five indicated moderate to severe conflict with the mother; (c) the one suicide who was most obviously rejected by his father (and who indicated that he had had conflict with him) was the only one (of the five) to indicate that "there has been a person . . . who had had a profound influence on his life." He wrote: "My father, I think, has been responsible for a code of ethics stressing honesty and fair dealing in all relations." It was this man's father who insisted that he come into the family business and then called him stupid when he, for reasons of his own temperament, did not show the same amount of aptitude for business that his (less bright) older brother demonstrated.

In general, for the five suicidal subjects, for reasons that are not completely clear, it seemed that the relationships with the father were more critical than the relationships with the mother. It may be that any exceptionally bright, handsome young child tends to be mother's darling and, for those same reasons, tends to be father's rival—hence the built-in psychological tendency for there to be more friction between father and son than between mother and son. (It all sounds vaguely familiar: I believe that there is a Greek play about this theme.)

In the perusal of the records, evidence of trauma or stress in early life was sought: the death of a parent, divorce of the parents, stress (either overt or subtle) between the parents, or rejection of the subject by either parent. In retrospect, I had in mind a continuum ranging from tranquil and benign at one end to stressful and traumatic at the other.

The folder materials indicated that at the time the study began practically all of the subjects were described in essentially positive terms. For example, among the five subjects who, as it turned out, were the five homogeneous suicides, the following early descriptions by the home visitor appeared: "Attractive boy, well built, attractive features, charming." "Round chubby boy; very sweet face." "Winning little fellow, very fine all-around intelligence. The mother has excellent common sense and much is due to her." "Friendly, cheerful, freckled boy." "Tall for his age."

At the beginning, the psychological picture for most Terman youngsters was benign. However, in two of five homogeneous suicide cases there were, at an early age, already subtle prodromal clues of things to come: "He is the constant companion of his father but he is not his father's favorite." (A few years later, at age fourteen, a teacher wrote about this child: "This boy's parents are of two minds; his mother is for college, his father thinks that college is of no value to a person who expects to take up the business. The boy does not show very much hardmindedness. His type is more the theoretical, he prefers ideas to matter.") During the same year, his mother wrote that the child's worst faults were "his lack of application and irresponsibility"— perhaps not too unusual at age fourteen.

Another example: A child is ranked by his mother as "average" in the following traits: prudence, self-confidence, optimism, permanence of mood, egotism, and truthfulness. We do not know, of course, how much of this is accurate perception or how much is self-fulfilling prophecy.

Still another example: At age fourteen there is a series of letters from the head of his boarding school. (The parents were away on an extended trip.) The headmaster wrote letters having to do with the boy's veracity, perhaps revealing his own special emphases: "We have every hope of making him a straightforward young man. We are people he cannot bluff, and with consistent vigilance the boy will be able to overcome his difficulties." A few years later his mother wrote: "His success will depend a good deal on his associates."

Least successful

In Melita Oden's (1968) monograph she presented a number of measures and comparisons between the 100 Terman subjects ranked as most successful and an equal number adjudged to be least successful. For each of the thirty

cases that I have analyzed, I tried to make some judgment along a success-failure continuum. In the end, eight cases were labeled as conspicuous successes and five cases as failures. As it turned out, none of those cases rated by me as "most successful" subsequently committed suicide, whereas three of the cases rated as "least successful" killed themselves.[5]

An example: a very bright young boy (IQ 180) who did very well in high school, both academically and in extracurricular activities. When he was fifteen years old Professor Terman wrote of him: "I think there is no doubt that he would make a desirable student at Stanford." Within a year, at age sixteen, he had entered Stanford and flunked out. Eventually, after working as a clerk, he returned to college after one year and graduated. He earned a law degree going to an evening law school. He then became an attorney in a large law firm. He was described as unsocial and shy. In his forties he says he was inclined to drink rather heavily, but not sufficiently to interfere with his work. His wife is described as vivacious and he as withdrawn. After a heart attack, his income suddenly became half of what he had been earning. He described himself as much less interested than his peers in vocational advancement or financial gain.

Signatures

In each case I looked for some special (albeit negative) indicators that might in themselves, or in combination, be prodromatic to suicide. For example, alcoholism, homosexuality, suicide threats, conspicuous achievement instability, depression, neurasthenia, and dyspnea could be listed. All five of the homogeneous suicides had one or more of these signature items. An additional eight (of the thirty cases) also had signature items. These items in themselves did not necessarily point to suicide, but when taken in combination with other features in the case they constituted an important aspect of the total prodromal picture.

Another example, this one emphasizing the lifelong instability of the individual: At age seven his mother wrote that "he is inclined to take the line of least resistance." At the same time, the teacher rated him high in desire to excel, general intelligence, and originality; average in prudence, generosity, and desire to know; and low in willpower, optimism, and truthfulness. She indicated that, though he came from a good home, he was inclined to be moody and sulky. At age eight his mother said he was strong-willed and liked to have his own way, that school was easy, and that he was making excellent grades. At age ten his parents divorced. At age twelve the teacher reported that he was not a very good student and was only doing fair work, that he had rather lazy mental habits. At age sixteen he graduated from high school with a C average. He did not attend college. In his twenties he became an artist. He was married. During World War II he was in the army. After the service he was unemployed and was described by his wife as "immature, unstable, irresponsible and extravagant." Because of his many affairs his wife, although stating she was fond of him, left him. She called him impulsive, romantic, and unstable. In his thirties he worked for a while as a commercial artist. He wrote to Professor Terman: "I am a lemon in your group." He indicated, as a joke, that his "hobby" was observing women from a bar stool. He remarried. He wrote to Professor Terman in relation to his art work that he "received much acclaim from those in the immediate audience," but that his works had not yet been displayed in any shows. His life was a series of ups and downs, some impulsive behaviors, and lifelong instability, although his status improved markedly in the late 1950s.

Apropos "up and downs" in general, any sudden *changes* in life status or life-style can be looked upon as suspicious (i.e., prodromal to suicide), especially a change which marks a decline of status, position, or income. Generally, in suicide prevention work, one views any recent changes in life-style as possible serious indicators of suicidal potential.

RATING OF LETHALITY (THE PSYCHOLOGICAL AUTOPSY)

In addition to the life chart, the second procedure employed was one that I had some years before labeled "the psychological autopsy." This procedure is a retrospective reconstruction of an individual's life that focuses on lethality, that is, those features of his life that illuminate his intentions in relation to his own death, clues as to the type of death it was, the degree (if any) of his participation in his own death, and why the death occurred at that time. In general, the main function of the psychological autopsy is to help clarify deaths that are equivocal as to the *mode* of death—usually to help coroners and medical examiners decide if the death (which may be clear enough as to cause of death, e.g., asphyxiation due to drowning or barbiturate overdose) was of an accidental or suicidal mode. Clearly, the *psychological* autopsy focuses on the role of the decedent in his own demise.

In the last few years, a number of individuals have written on this topic: Litman and his colleagues (Litman, Curphey, Shneidman, Farberow, & Tabachnick, 1963) have presented a general overview of its clinical use; Curphey (1961) has written of the use of this procedure from the medicolegal viewpoint of a forensic pathologist; and Weisman and Kastenbaum (1968) have applied this procedure to study the terminal phase of life. Elsewhere (Shneidman, 1969b), I have indicated that three separate types (and uses) of the psychological autopsy can be discerned. Each is tied to answering a different primary question as follows: (a) why did the individual commit suicide? (b) why did the individual die at this time? and (c) what is the most accurate mode of death in this case? Given a death which is clear as to *cause* of death but which is equivocal as to *mode* of death, the purpose of this type of psychological autopsy is to clarify the situation so as to arrive at the most accurate or appropriate mode of death—what it "truly" was. This original use of the psychological autopsy grew out of the joint efforts of the Los Angeles County chief medical examiner-coroner (then Dr. Theodore J. Curphey) and the staff of the Los Angeles Suicide Prevention Center as an attempt to bring the skills of the behavioral sciences to bear relevantly on the problems of

equivocal deaths. In those 10 percent of coroner's cases where the **329**
mode of death is questionable or equivocal, this equivocation usually
lies between the modes of accident and suicide. Here are three simplified
examples:

1. *Cause of death:* asphyxiation due to drowning. Woman found in her
   swimming pool. Question: did she "drown" (accident), or was it intentional (suicide)?
2. *Cause of death:* multiple crushing injuries. Man found at the foot of a tall
   building. Question: did he fall (accident), or did he jump (suicide)? Or,
   even, was he pushed or thrown (homicide)?
3. *Cause of death:* barbiturate intoxication due to overdose. Woman found
   in her bed. Question: would she be surprised to know that she was dead
   (accident), or is this what she had planned (suicide)?

An outline for a psychological autopsy is presented in table 3.

TABLE 3
OUTLINE FOR PSYCHOLOGICAL AUTOPSY

1. Identifying information for victim (name, age, address, marital status, religious practices, occupation, and other details)
2. Details of the death (including the cause or method and other pertinent details)
3. Brief outline of victim's history (siblings, marriage, medical illnesses, medical treatment, psychotherapy, previous suicide attempts)
4. "Death history" of victim's family (suicides, cancer, other fatal illnesses, ages at death, and other details)
5. Description of the personality and life-style of the victim
6. Victim's typical patterns of reaction to stress, emotional upsets, and periods of disequilibrium
7. Any recent—from last few days to last twelve months—upsets, pressures, tensions, or anticipations of trouble
8. Role of alcohol and drugs in (a) overall life style of victim and (b) in his death
9. Nature of victim's interpersonal relationships (including physicians)
10. Fantasies, dreams, thoughts, premonitions, or fears of victim relating to death, accident, or suicide
11. Changes in the victim before death (of habits, hobbies, eating, sexual patterns, and other life routines)
12. Information relating to the "life side" of victim (upswings, successes, plans)
13. Assessment of intention, i.e., role of the victim in his own demise
14. Rating of lethality
15. Reactions of informants to victim's death
16. Comments, special features, etc.

In the usual application of the psychological autopsy, the procedure is to
interview close survivors (relatives and friends) of the decedent in order to
reconstruct his role in his own death. In the present study, I was, of course,
limited to an examination of folder materials.

All the criteria that have been discussed above—perturbation, including early prodromata, failure, and signatures—were combined into one judgment of that individual's lethality, that is, the probability of his committing suicide in the present or the immediate future. In this process of judgment I was guided by two additional governing concepts: (a) the key role of the significant other and (b) the concept of a partial death (or chronic suicide or "burned out" life).

The crucial role of the significant other

In an adult who is suicide prone, the behavior of the significant other, specifically the wife, seems either lifesaving or suicidogenic. My reading of the cases led me to feel that the wife could be the difference between life and death. In general, a wife who was hostile, independent, competitive, or nonsupporting of her husband who had some of the suicidal prodromata seemed to doom him to a suicidal outcome, whereas a wife who was helpful, emotionally supportive, and actively ancillary seemed to save a man who, in my clinical judgment at least, might otherwise have killed himself.

To the extent that these global clinical impressions of the important role of the spouse, in some cases, are correct, then, in those cases, there is an equal implication for suicide prevention, specifically that one must deal actively with the significant other. A regimen of therapy or a program of education must not fail to include the spouse; indeed it might be focused primarily on the spouse and only secondarily on the potential suicide victim. Of course, the conscious and unconscious attitudes of the wife toward her husband must be carefully assessed. In a situation where the wife is deeply competitive (and might unconsciously wish him dead), using her as an auxiliary therapist would at best be an uphill climb. It is possible that in some cases a separation might be a lifesaving suggestion. All the above is not to impugn the wife; rather it is to involve her appropriately. It could very well be that, had the study focused on female suicides, the above prescription would be in relation to the complementary role of the husband.

The concept of a partial death

This concept is well known in suicidology. In the technical literature it was given its most well known presentation by Karl Menninger (1938) in *Man against Himself.* On valid psychological grounds it denies the dichotomous nature of psychological death and asserts that there are some lives that are moieties and only partial existences. Henry Murray (1967) expands this theme in his paper "Dead to the World":

> When I chose the phrase "dead to the world," I was thinking of a variety of somewhat similar psychic states characterized by a marked diminution or near-cessation of affect involving both hemispheres of concern, the inner and the outer world. Here it is as if the person's primal springs of vitality had dried up, as if he were empty or hollow at the very core of his being. There is a striking absence of anything but the most perfunctory and superficial social interactions; output as well as intake is at a minimum . . .

I have been talking about a diminution or cessation of feeling, one component of consciousness, on the assumption that this condition is somewhat analogous to a cessation of the whole of consciousness. If the cessation of feeling is temporary it resembles sleep; if it is permanent (a virtual atrophy of emotional life) it resembles death, the condition of the brain and body after the home fires of metabolism in the cortex have gone out. In a feelingless state the home fires are still burning but without glow or warmth.

That last statement about the home fires burning led me to think of a "burned out" person—a person whose whole life was a kind of chronic suicide, a living death, a life without ambition and seemingly without purpose.

In the lethality ratings of the thirty cases, those that gave me the greatest difficulty were the chronic, nonachieving, "partial death" lives. I decided that I would rate this type of person among the first twelve in lethality, but not among the first five. I did this with the conviction that this very style of living was in itself a kind of substitute for overt suicide; that in these cases, the *raison d'être* for committing overt suicide was absent, in that the truncated life itself was the significant inimical act (Shneidman, 1963).

RESULTS OF BLIND CLINICAL ANALYSES

On the day that I completed the blind analysis of the thirtieth case I wrote a memorandum to Professor Sears that included the following:

> My analysis of the data and possibly the data themselves do not permit me to state with anything like full confidence which five cases were suicidal. The best that I can do—from my subjective ratings of each individual's perturbation and lethality—is to rank order eleven of the cases as the most likely candidates for suicidal status. I should be somewhat surprised if any of the other nineteen individuals committed suicide. The rank order for suicide potential is as follows . . .

Then we—Mrs. Oden, Mrs. Buckholtz, and I—met to "break the key."

The facts revealed that the individual whom I had ranked as number 1 had, in fact, committed suicide, my number 2 had committed suicide, number 3 was living, number 4 had committed suicide, number 5 had committed suicide, and number 6 had committed suicide. Numbers 7 and 9 were living; numbers 8, 10, and 11 had died natural deaths. For the statistical record, the probability of choosing four or five of the five suicide cases correctly by chance alone is 1 out of 1,131—significant at the .000884 level. Obviously, the null hypothesis that there are no discernible prodromal clues to suicide can be discarded with a fair degree of confidence.

Table 4 presents a summary of the blind analysis data in terms of a brief vignette, signature items, success-failure ratings, perturbation ratings, lethality ratings, and suicide probability ranking for all thirty subjects. (The "Post-

TABLE 4

BLIND RATINGS AND OUTCOMES FOR THIRTY MATCHED MALE SUBJECTS

No.	Notable characteristics	Signatures	Life success	Pertur-bation	Lethal-ity	Suicide rank	Postscript
1	NP hospitalization; divorced; great perturbation: talks of suicide at 15 and 20	Suicide threats	C-	7-8	High	1	Committed suicide
2	Deaf; professional; low drive for worldly success	Nonachiever	C	3-4	Low	12+	Living
3	Flunked out of college; obtained LLB; shy; ups and downs; drop in income; alcohol	Alcohol; ups and downs	C	6-7	High	2	Committed suicide
4	Insurance man in heart attack rut	–	B	3-4	Low	12+	Died—heart
5	Ambitious bank officer	–	B	3-4	Low	12+	Died—cancer
6	Brilliant professor of medicine; textbook author; good life	–	A	1-2	Low	12+	Died—cancer
7	Set back at adolescence by home stresses; obese; no college aspirations; withdrawn; low-level job; underachiever; stabilized	Underachiever; stabilized	C-	6-7	?	11	Died—heart
8	Physician; too high standards for people; tones down	–	B+	5-6	Low	12+	Died—heart
9	Hard-driving rancher; dominated by mother	–	B	5-6	Low	12+	Died—cancer
10	Stable geologist; steady life	–	A	1-2	Low	12+	Living
11	Lithographer; brilliant; no family back-up; underachiever	Underachiever	C	5-6	Low	12+	Living
12	Multimarried, emphysemic; inventor; ups and downs	Dyspnea; failure	C	6-7	High	4	Committed suicide
13	Scion of business fortune; straight success line; father helpful and supportive	–	A	4-5	Low	12+	Living
14	Quietly successful in own small business; tranquil life	–	B	3-4	Low	12+	Living
15	Had all advantages; did rather well but not superlatively	–	B	3-4	Low	12+	Living
16	Neurasthenic; esoteric mother; underachiever; chronic suicide	Depression; neurasthenia	C-	6-7	?	7	Living

No.	Description						Outcome
17	Artist; unstable; flighty; impetuous; willful	Instability	B-	7-8	?	5	Committed suicide
18	Insurance man; stable life; interesting siblings	—	B	3-4	Low	12+	Living
19	Brilliant child and siblings; needed a father; stabilized by second wife	—	B	4-5	Low	12+	Living
20	Pleasant man; pleasant life; pleasant family; likes work	—	B	2-3	Low	12+	Living
21	Early genius; hiatus; never fully recovers; wife commits suicide	—	B	5-6	Mdn	12+	Died—heart
22	Shy, depressed artist; multiple illnesses; making it	Depression; ill	B	6-7	?	9	Living
23	Unhappy; forced into father's business; rejected by father; always second to sibling 4 divorces; unstable; downhill; alone	Depression; instability	B+	7-8	?	6	Committed suicide
24	Average school administrator; ordinary stresses	—; —	B	4-5	Low	12+	Living
25	Well-adjusted, stable attorney; great relationship with father; good life success	—	A	2-3	Low	12+	Living
26	Depressed engineer; hypomanic wife; his job holds him	Depression	B	6-7	Mdn+	8	Died—cancer
27	Scientist; brilliant beginning; wife drains him; good but not great	—	B+	3-4	Low	12+	Living
28	Engineer; overcame adolescent crisis and parents' divorce; good marriage; has grown steadily	—	B	4-5	Low	12+	Died—heart
29	Author; asthmatic; depressed; strong support from wife	Dyspnea; depression	A-	5-6	?	10	Died—cancer
30	Professional; stormy life; alcoholic; competing wife	Alcohol; instability	B-	6-7	?	3	Living

script" information was not available to me when I made these ratings and was added to the chart after all the other ratings and rankings had been made.)

Much of my analysis of these thirty cases was inferential, sometimes even intuitive—which is to say that not every clue or cognitive maneuver can be recovered, much less communicated. But for what it is worth, I deeply believe that a number of experienced professional persons could have done as well. Indeed, I feel that the volumes of information generated in the past twenty years by suicidologists furnish the working concepts and the background facts for making precisely this kind of (potentially lifesaving) judgment every day of the year in the practical clinical situation. Knowledge of this sort is now an established part of the new discipline of suicidology.

One striking result was that among those who committed suicide in their fifties, the pattern of life consistent with this outcome seemed clearly discernible *by the time they were in their late twenties.* The data subsequent to age thirty served, in most cases, primarily to strengthen the impression of suicidal outcome that I had formulated at that point. Those relatively few cases in which this earlier impression was reversed in the thirties and forties had one or two specific noteworthy elements within them: (a) a psychologically supporting spouse or (b) a "burning out" of the individual's drive and affect. In the latter cases, this condition of psychological aridity and successlessness seemed to be the price for continued life.

What were some of the main clinical impressions relating to adult suicide in this gifted male group? In the briefest possible vignette, my main overall clinical impression might be formulated in this way: the *father,* even in his absence, *starts* the life course to suicide; *school and work* (and the feelings of inferiority and chronic low-grade hopelessness) *exacerbate* it; and the *wife* can, in some cases, effect the *rescue* from it (or otherwise play a sustaining or even a precipitating role in it).

Among the five homogeneous suicides, three types of suicidal prodromata—relating to instability, trauma, and control—could be differentiated.

Instability

In general, suicide is more likely to occur in a life where there has been instability (rather than stability). As used here, instability is practically synonymous with perturbation.

Chronic instability Evidences of chronic, long-term instability would include neuropsychiatric hospitalization, talk or threat of suicide, alcoholism, multiple divorces, and any unusually stressful psychodynamic background—even though these bits of evidence occurred in as few as one of the five cases. Examples: Mr. A: NP hospitalization, divorce, talk of suicide at 15 and at 20; Mr. B: unstable personality, divorced, flighty behavior, few stabilizing forces; Mr. C: unhappy man, rejected by father, always second-best, four marriages, highly perturbed.

Recent downhill course   A recent downhill change that occurs in a career
marked by ups and downs, that is, a generally unstable life course, was
characteristic of suicidal persons. Specifically, these changes include a
marked sudden decrease in income, sudden acute alcoholism, a change in
work, and divorce or separation, especially where the wife leaves the husband for another man. In general, a sudden, inexplicable change for the
worse is a bad augury. This means that in an individual with an up-and-down
history, the most recent bit of information can be singularly irrelevant, if not
outright misleading. Examples: Mr. D: highly recommended for university,
flunked out of college, went back to school, earned an LL.B. degree, shy,
alcoholic, sudden drop in income, up and down course, does not "burn out";
Mr. E: inventor, multiple marriages, up and down course, severe emphysema.
(N.B., dyspnea can be an especially incapacitating symptom and has been
related to suicide in special ways [Farberow, McKelligott, Cohen, & Darbonne, 1966].)

Trauma

Early childhood or adolescent trauma   Examples would include acute rejection by one or both parents, lack of family psychological support, and
separation or divorce of the parents. A crisis in adolescence can turn a life
toward lower achievement.

Adult trauma   This includes poor health, such as asthma, emphysema,
severe neurosis, obesity, and multiple illnesses. Another major type of adult
trauma relates to the spouse, either rejection by the wife for another man or
being married to a hyperactive (and competing) wife, who has changed from
the woman he married. Examples: Mr. F, a depressed engineer whose
top security job in aerospace holds him together; and Mr. G, who has a
complicated, hypomanic, and successful wife toward whom he is deeply
ambivalent.

Controls

Outer controls   These are the compensations or stabilizing influences in
individuals who, without these assets from other than within themselves,
would be more perturbed than they are and might commit suicide. Examples: the stabilizing work of Mr. F, mentioned above; the stabilizing wife of
asthmatic Mr. H, a woman who nurses him and keeps the world from
inappropriately intruding upon him or exhausting him. She husbands his
limited energies.

Inner controls   These inner controls are not the usual strengths or positive
features or assets of personality or character. They are the negative inner
controls of default. One such is what occurs in some individuals who are
perturbed early in their lives, who, if they survive, stabilize or simmer down or
"burn out" in their fifties or sixties.

Examples: Mr. J: He was psychologically traumatized during adolescence by home stresses. He has no hobbies, no college aspirations, is withdrawn, and works as a mechanic and caretaker. Mr. K: Extremely high IQ. He is neurasthenic, has a mother with esoteric tastes, experiences back and shoulder pains just like his father, and is unable to hold a job as a professional. He calls himself "an unsuccessful animal." He ends up working as a clerk in a large company. His stance is that—to use an example from Melville—of a contemporary Bartleby ("I prefer not to"), what Menninger (1938) has called a "chronic suicide," where the truncated life itself can be conceptualized as a partial death.

DISCUSSION

Whereas the clinical challenge is to be intuitive, to display diagnostic acumen, and to manifest therapeutic skill, the scientific challenge is to state theory and to explicate facts in a replicable way. I feel obligated to address myself to the theoretical side of this issue.

I shall begin with low-level theory, that is, an explication of the specific items that guided my thinking in choosing the individuals whom I believed had committed suicide. Some ten items were in my mind: (1) early (grammar school, adolescence, or college age) evidences of instability, including dishonesty; (2) rejection by the father; (3) multiple marriages; (4) alcoholism; (5) an unstable occupational history; (6) ups and downs in income; (7) a crippling physical disability, especially one involving dyspnea; (8) disappointment in the use of one's potential, that is, a disparity between aspiration and accomplishment; (9) any talk or hint of self-destruction; and (10) a competitive or self-absorbed spouse. In summary, this low-level theoretical explication states that a bright male Caucasian who committed suicide in his fifties was apt to be: rejected by his father, adolescently disturbed, multimarried, alcoholic, occasionally unsettled or unsuccessful, disappointed in himself and disappointing to others, unstable, lonely, and perturbed with a penchant for precipitous action.

At a somewhat deeper level, and thus more theoretical, are the elements of rejection, disparity between aspiration and accomplishment, instability, and perturbation. At a still deeper level (and even more theoretical) is the notion that the suicidal person is one who believes that he has not had his father's love and seeks it symbolically without success throughout his life, eventually hoping, magically, to gain it by a singular act of sacrifice or expiation. The most theoretical formulation might be stated as follows: those gifted men who committed suicide in their fifties did not have that internalized viable approving parental homunculus that—like a strong heart—seems necessary for a long life.

It is interesting to reflect that the five gifted suicidal persons of this study constituted an essentially nonpsychotic group. This assertion is not to gainsay that each of them was severely perturbed at the time of the suicide, but they were not "crazy"; that is, they did not manifest the classical hallmarks of psychosis such as hallucinations, delusions, dereistic thinking, and the like.

Their perturbation took the form—prior to the overt suicidal act—of alcoholism, other than one marriage (single, divorced, or multiple marriages), and chronic loneliness, occupational ups and downs, impetuosity and impulsivity, and inner (as well as overt) agitation. Although, as it is in most suicidal persons, one can suppose that their thought processes were circumscribed ("tunnel vision") and tended to be dichotomous ("either a happy life or death"), there was no direct evidence to indicate that they were psychotically bizarre or paleological (Shneidman, 1969a).

As has been noted by Oden (1968), the "magic combination" for life success among the gifted is not a simple one. For suicide also the equation is a combination of obvious and subtle elements. Many factors, none of which alone seems to be sufficient, appear to coexist in a suicidal case. And, as in any equation, there are factors on both the positive (life-loving, biophilic, suicide-inhibiting) and the negative (death-loving, necrophilic, suicide-promoting) sides.

In the algebra of life and death, the wife may play an absolutely vital role, holding her spouse to life or, at the worst, stimulating or even provoking him to suicide. Every suicidologist knows that suicide is most often a two-person event, a dyadic occurrence, and for this reason, if no other, the management and prevention of suicide almost always has to involve the significant other. With high suicide risk gifted males, my impression is that the most important lifesaving task is not directly to the potentially suicidal person, but through the wife—especially in concert with the family physician.

Currently, there is a small number of retrospective studies seeking to establish some of the early precursors of suicide among special populations presumed to be intellectually superior, specifically physicians and university graduates. A few words about each.

Blachly and his colleagues (Blachly, Disher, & Roduner, 1968) have made an analysis of 249 suicides by physicians reported in the obituary columns of the *Journal of the American Medical Association* between May 1965 and November 1967. Deaths from suicide exceeded the combined deaths from automobile accidents, airplane crashes, drowning, and homicide. The mean age of the suicidal group was forty-nine. Blachly and his associates mailed questionnaires to the next of kin (usually the widow); about 30 percent of the inquiries were returned, many with extensive comments. The suicide rate varied greatly among the medical specialties, ranging from a low of 10 per 100,000 among pediatricians to a high of 61 per 100,000 among psychiatrists. A résumé of Blachly's main findings is presented in table 5.

Paffenbarger and his associates (Paffenbarger & Asnes, 1966; Paffenbarger, King, & Wing, 1969) have completed analyses of over 50,000 medical and social histories (including physical and psychological evaluations) of former male students at the University of Pennsylvania and at Harvard covering a thirty-four-year period from 1916 to 1950. Their original focus was on individuals who subsequently died of coronary heart disease. The data drew their attention to those who had committed suicide—whom they then compared with their nonsuicidal cohorts. The 4,000 known deaths included 225 suicide deaths. Their findings relative to suicide point to paternal depri-

TABLE 5

SUMMARY OF FINDINGS OF THREE STUDIES OF PRECURSORS OF SUICIDE

Present clinical impressions*	Blachly's tabular results	Paffenbarger's statistical findings
a. early (before 20) evidences of instability, including dishonesty	a. mentally depressed or disturbed	a. college education of father
b. actual or felt rejection by the father	b. prior suicidal attempt or statement of suicidal intent	b. college education of mother
c. multiple marriages	c. heavy drinker or alcoholic	c. father professional
d. alcoholism	d. drug addiction or heavy drug user	d. father died
e. an unstable occupational history	e. "inadequate" financial status	e. parents separated
f. ups and downs in income (not to mention ups and downs in mood)	f. death of close relative in decedent's childhood	f. cigarette smoker in college
g. a crippling physical disability, especially one involving dyspnea	g. suicide of relative	g. attended boarding school
h. disappointment in the use of potential, i.e., a disparity between aspiration and accomplishment	h. seriously impaired physical health	h. college dropout
i. any talk or hint of self-destruction		i. nonjoiner in college
j. a competitive or self-absorbed spouse		j. allergies
		k. underweight
		l. self-assessed ill health
		m. self-consciousness
		n. subject to worries
		o. feelings of being watched or talked about
		p. insomnia
		q. secretive-seclusiveness
		r. "anxiety-depression" index (including nervousness, moodiness, exhaustion, etc.)

*Of course, not all of these features occurred in any suicidal case; conversely, some of these features occurred in as few as one suicidal case. It was the "total impression" that counted most.

vation through early loss or death of the father, loneliness and underjoining in college, dropping out of college, and feelings of rejection, self-consciousness, and failure during the college years.

Dr. Caroline Thomas (1969)—like Paffenbarger, a cardiologist—studied the causes of death among 1,337 former medical students of the Johns Hopkins University School of Medicine from 1948 to 1964. Her project—as did Paffenbarger's—began as a study of the precursors of coronary heart disease but, in light of the data (fourteen suicides among the thirty-one premature deaths shifted to include precursors of suicide.

What may be of especial interest in table 5 are the common elements or threads in the findings of these three projects and the clinical findings of this present study. To what extent these findings relate only to the intellectually superior and to what extent they are ubiquitous is a matter for further study; nonetheless it is not premature to say that, on the basis of currently known data, it would appear that the common findings would seem to have general application.

Notes

1 This study was conducted while the author was a Fellow at the Center for Advanced Study in the Behavioral Sciences, 1969-70. Arrangements were made for confidential access to the research records by Professor Robert R. Sears who, with Professor Lee J. Cronbach, is one of the two scientific executors of the Terman Study. The data themselves are the property of Stanford University. The author is especially grateful to Mrs. Melita Oden and Mrs. Sheila Buckholtz, long-time staff members of the Gifted Study, for their extensive help in preparing relevant data for his use and for advice and guidance along the way.

2 As part of the Terman Study of the Gifted, Catharine M. Cox (1926) completed a comprehensive retrospective study of the childhood intelligence of 301 historically eminent men born after 1450. Of the individuals discussed in her study, 119 were thought to have I.Q.'s of 140 or higher. (As examples, here are some names—1 person in each of the five-step I.Q. intervals from 140 to 190: Carlyle, Jefferson, Descartes, Hume, Pope, J. Q. Adams, Voltaire, Schelling, Pascal, Leibnitz, and J. S. Mill.) As to suicide among this extraordinary group, so far as can be ascertained, only 1 of the 301 eminent men died by killing himself—Thomas Chatterton, at age 17.

3 In the technical literature on suicide, one does not find many anamnestic or case history reports for individuals who have *committed* suicide. (Materials for attempted suicides are another story; the data for them are far more plentiful.) Only four sources—spread over a half-century—come to mind: Ruth Cavan's (1928, pp.198–248) extensive diaries of two young adults, Binswanger's (1958) detailed report of 33-year-old Ellen West, Kobler and Stotland's (1964, pp. 98–251) extensive reports of four hospitalized patients—ages 23, 34, 37, and 56—in a "dying hospital," all of whom committed suicide within the same month, and Alvarez' (1961) annotated bibliography.

4 The following point must be strongly emphasized: a basic assumption in this entire scheme is that an individual's orientations toward his cessation are biphasic; that is, any adult, at any given moment, has (a) more or less long-range, relatively chronic, pervasive, habitual, characterological orientations toward cessation as an integral part of his total psychological makeup (affecting his philosophy of life, need systems, aspirations, identification, conscious beliefs, etc.); and (b) is also capable of having acute, relatively short-lived, exacerbated, clinically sudden shifts of cessation orientation. Indeed, this is what is usually meant when

one says that an individual has become "suicidal." It is therefore crucial in any complete assessment of an individual's orientation toward cessation to know both his habitual *and* his at-that-moment orientations toward cessation. (Failure to do this is one reason why previous efforts to relate "suicidal state" with psychological test results have been barren.)

5 Among the twenty men who committed suicide, at least three were considered outstandingly successful by gifted group standards: two in the 1960 study and one who died in 1938 who had a brilliant record until his death at the age of twenty-eight. Conversely, three were considered least successful: two in 1940 (they had died before 1960) and one in the 1960 evaluation (Oden, 1968).

References

Alvarez, W. C. *Minds That Came Back*. Philadelphia: Lippincott, 1961.

Binswanger, L. The Case of Ellen West. In R. May, E. Angel, & H. F. Ellenberger (Eds.), *Existence*. New York: Basic Books, 1958. Pp.237–364.

Blachly, P. H., Disher, W., & Roduner, G. Suicide by Physicians. *Bulletin of Suicidology*. December 1968, 1–18.

Cavan, R. S. *Suicide*. Chicago: University of Chicago Press, 1928.

Cox, C. M. The Early Mental Traits of Three Hundred Geniuses. *Genetic Studies of Genius*. Vol. 2. Stanford: Stanford University Press, 1926.

Curphey, T. J. The Role of the Social Scientist in the Medicolegal Certification of Death from Suicide. In N. L. Farberow & E. S. Shneidman (Eds.), *The Cry for Help*. New York: McGraw-Hill, 1961.

Dublin, L. I., Lotka, A. J., & Spiegelman, M. *Length of Life*. New York: Ronald Press, 1949.

Farberow, N. L., McKelligott, W., Cohen, S., & Darbonne, A. Suicide among Patients with Cardiorespiratory Illnesses. *Journal of the American Medical Association*, 1966, 195, 422–28.

Kobler, A., & Stotland, E. *The End of Hope*. New York: Free Press of Glencoe, 1964.

Litman, R. E., Curphey, T. J., Shneidman, E. S., Farberow, N. L., & Tabachnick, N. D. Investigations of Equivocal Suicides. *Journal of the American Medical Association*, 1963, 184, 924–29.

Menninger, K. A. *Man against Himself*. New York: Harcourt, Brace, 1938.

Meyer, A. The Life Chart and the Obligation of Specifying Positive Data in Psychopathological Diagnosis. Reprinted in E. E. Winters (Ed.), *The Collected Works of Adolf Meyer*. Vol. 3. Baltimore: Johns Hopkins Press, 1951. Pp. 52–56.

Meyer, A. Mental and Moral Health in a Constructive School Program. Reprinted in E. E. Winters (Ed.), *The Collected Works of Adolf Meyer*. Vol. 4. Baltimore: Johns Hopkins Press, 1952. Pp. 350–70.

Murray, H. A. Dead to the World: The Passions of Herman Melville. In E. S. Shneidman (Ed.), *Essays in Self-Destruction*. New York: Science House, 1967.

Oden, M. H. The Fulfillment of Promise: 40-year Follow-Up of the Terman Gifted Group. *Genetic Psychology Monographs*, 1968, 77, 3–93.

Paffenbarger, R. S., Jr., & Asnes, D. P. Chronic Disease in Former College Students. III. Precursors of Suicide in Early and Middle Life. *American Journal of Public Health*, 1966, 56, 1026–36.

Paffenbarger, R. S., Jr., King, S. H., & Wing, A. L. Chronic Disease in Former College Students. IX. Characteristics in Youth that Predispose to Suicide and Accidental Death in Later Life. *American Journal of Public Health*, 1969, 59, 900–908.

Shneidman, E. S. Orientations toward Death: A Vital Aspect of the Study of Lives. In R. W. White (Ed.), *The Study of Lives*. New York: Atherton Press, 1963. Reprinted, with discussion, in *International Journal of Psychiatry*, 1966, 2, 167–200; and in Shneidman, E. S., Farberow, N. L., & Litman, R. E., *The Psychology of Suicide*. New York: Science House, 1970.

Shneidman, E. S. Logical Content Analysis: An Explication of Styles of "Concludifying." In G. Gerbner et al. (Eds.), *The Analysis of Communication Content*. New York: John Wiley & Sons, 1969(a).

Shneidman, E. S. Suicide, Lethality and the Psychological Autopsy. In E. S. Shneidman & M. J. Ortega (Eds.), *Aspects of Depression*. Boston: Little, Brown & Co., 1969(b).

Stone, A. A., & Onque, G. C. *Longitudinal Studies of Child Personality*. Cambridge: Harvard University Press, 1959.

Terman, L. M. *Genetic Studies of Genius: I. Mental and Physical Traits of a Thousand Gifted Children*. Stanford: Stanford University Press, 1925.

Terman, L. M. Psychological Approaches to the Biography of Genius. *Science*, October 4, 1940, 92, 293–301.

Terman, L. M., & Oden, M. H. *Genetic Studies of Genius: IV. The Gifted Child Grows Up*. Stanford: Stanford University Press, 1947.

Terman, L. M., & Oden, M. H. *Genetic Studies of Genius: V. The Gifted Child at Mid-Life*. Stanford: Stanford University Press, 1959.

Thomas, C. B. Suicide among Us: Can We Learn to Prevent It? *Johns Hopkins Medical Journal*, 1969, 125, 276–85.

Weisman, A. D., & Kastenbaum, R. The Psychological Autopsy: A Study of the Terminal Phase of Life. *Community Mental Health Journal Monograph*, 1968, 4, 1–59.

29 · Philosophers on Suicide

Jacques Choron

The late Jacques Choron was a distinguished philosopher and a long-time student of self-destructive phenomena. Most recently he had been a Fellow at the Suicide Prevention Center in Los Angeles and a Fellow at the Center for Studies of Suicide Prevention at the National Institute of Mental Health in Rockville, Maryland. He is the author of Death and Western Thought *and* Modern Man and Mortality, *among other books. In the following selection from* Suicide, *Choron provides an encyclopedic survey of major Western philosophers' attitudes and reflections on the topic of suicide.*

Philosophers have at different times rejected, condoned, or advocated suicide, and done so on grounds that were not necessarily philosophical but rather psychological although their attitudes toward suicide necessarily reflected their views on life and death. But no generalization of any kind is possible in this connection, since even a negative view of life did not always serve as an argument in favor of suicide. Moreover, the belief in immortality does not make death necessarily attractive, and the conviction that death is total annihilation does not always make it an object of terror. Thus we often find that immortalists condemn suicide, and those who think death to be final condone or even recommend it. On the whole, however, philosophers seem to have been instrumental in bringing about the permissive and tolerant view of suicide that generally prevails today. Thanks to them, no one seriously challenges the individual's right to dispose of his life as he sees fit, society does not enforce the penalties which may still be on the books, and even religious sanctions are often waived under some pretext or other. As an indirect result of this humane and enlightened attitude toward suicide, it has become possible to initiate efforts to help the suicidal individual instead of punishing him.

PYTHAGORAS

The attitude toward suicide of the earliest Greek philosophers, those usually termed "Pre-Socratics," is not known, since none of their works survived independently and the quotations from them found in later philosophers make no reference to suicide. The only exception is Pythagoras (born probably in 570 B.C.). According to Plato, he was opposed to suicide, even though he taught that man is a stranger in this world and his soul is in the body as in a tomb.[1] The cause of his prohibition of suicide lies in his doctrine of transmigration of the soul (reincarnation), borrowed from Orphic cults. Being immortal but "fallen," the soul is imprisoned in the body where it undergoes a process of atonement and purification, and on the success of this process depends whether the soul at death will return to its divine origin or transmigrate into another body, to resume or continue its penitential path toward liberation. To interfere with this process by voluntary—that is, premature—death is to revolt against the divine law. One must wait until God releases the soul from its bonds. Thus, even though life is a probation and, as such, clearly acknowledged as an ordeal, suicide is inadmissible.

PLATO

Plato (427–347 B.C.) took over from Pythagoras the notion of the immortal and imprisoned soul, as well as the condemnation of suicide. The latter is expressed in the *Phaedo*, when Socrates, who has been condemned to die by drinking hemlock, remarks to his friends, "No man has the right to take his own life, but he must wait until God sends some necessity upon him, as he has now sent upon me."[2]

Plato does not accept the Pythagorean view that life is a penal servitude for sins committed in previous existences and that men have no right to avoid doing penance, but he too considers that man is a "chattel" of God, the way a slave is a "chattel" of his owner, and therefore may not dispose of his own life. This view is binding on the true philosopher, even though he has "the desire for death all his life long."[3] This much misunderstood phrase refers to the Platonic notion that true knowledge is possible only when the soul is free from the body, whose senses are obstacles in the way of discovering "the real." Thus, a person who pursues true knowledge "rehearses" death in the

sense that he endeavors to approach in life the ideal state of knowing which
can be achieved only after death. He does this by concentrating on his soul
and turning away his attention from the body. But this does not imply that
the philosopher ought to expedite his death. He, too, must patiently wait
until it pleases God to bring about, or decree, the release of the soul.

The reason why one ought not to put an end to one's life ahead of its
divinely ordained expiration is that by committing suicide man contradicts
God's will, and in doing so forfeits his chance for a pleasant afterlife. Socrates,
who firmly beleives in the immortality of his "true self," his "soul," expresses
the hope that he will find himself after death in the company of the most
worthy men of the past.[4] He does so because, among other reasons, he sees
his manner of dying not as a suicide but as self-execution, which is only
another form of capital punishment, to which he has been condemned, no
matter how unjustly, by his judges.

Thus, although for Plato immortality is not a gift of God, but the natural
endowment of each and every soul, not all the souls will enjoy the same fate
in their future existence because each retains its intrinsic tendencies for
good and evil; Plato even mythologizes about the different lot of the virtuous
and the wicked souls.

In any case, Plato thought that suicide ought to be punished by the state,
even though he allows some exceptions. In *The Laws* he writes:

> But what of him ... whose violence frustrates the decree of Destiny by
> self-slaughter though no sentence of the state required this of him, no
> stress of cruel and inevitable calamity has driven him to the act, and
> he has been involved in no desperate and intolerable disgrace, the
> man who thus gives unrighteous sentence against himself from mere
> poltroonery and unmanly cowardice? Well, in such a case, what
> further rites must be observed, in the way of purification and
> ceremonies of burial, it is for Heaven to say; the next of kin should
> consult the official canonists as well as the laws on the subject, and
> act according to their direction. But the graves of such as perish thus
> must, in the first place, be solitary ... further they must be buried
> ignominiously in waste and nameless spots ... and the tomb shall be
> marked by neither headstone nor name."[5]

ARISTOTLE

Plato's most outstanding pupil, Aristotle (384–322 B.C.), the only philosopher
whose fame and influence at certain periods of history overshadowed Plato's,
employed in his quest for knowledge an entirely different principle, that of
empirical science, and eventually rejected nearly all of Plato's metaphysics,
including especially his theory of eternal "Ideas" and his doctrine of the
immortality of the soul. But on suicide he took a position as negative as
Plato's. Indeed he was even more uncompromising than his teacher in that
he seems to have rejected any exceptions or mitigating circumstances.
However, Aristotle in his numerous works devotes to suicide only two brief

passages in the fifth book of his treatise on Ethics. The first reference is in connection with the discussion of virtues and vices. He speaks of courage in terms of concern with death, "which is the most terrible of all things; for it is the end, and nothing is thought to be any longer either good or bad for the dead," and defines a brave man as one "who is fearless in face of a noble death" [that is, death in battle] and in "all emergencies that involve death" because of a sense of honor. Then he concludes:

> But to die to escape from poverty or love or anything painful is not the mark of a brave man, but rather a coward; for it is softness to fly from what is troublesome, and such a man endures death not because it is noble but to fly from evil.[6]

The other reference to suicide is in connection with the question "whether a man can treat himself unjustly." Aristotle writes:

> . . . one class of just acts are those acts in accordance with any virtue which are prescribed by the law; e.g. the law does not expressly permit suicide, and what it does not expressly permit, it forbids. Again, when a man in violation of the law harms another (otherwise than in retaliation) voluntarily, he acts unjustly, and a voluntary agent is one who knows both the person he is affecting by his action and the instrument he is using; and he who through anger voluntarily stabs himself does this contrary to the right rule of life, and this the law does not allow; therefore he is acting unjustly. But towards whom? Surely toward the state, not towards himself. For he suffers voluntarily, but no one is voluntarily treated unjustly. This is also the reason why the state punishes; a certain loss of civil rights attaches to the man who destroys himself, on the ground that he is treating the state unjustly.[7]

The intent of these passages is clear enough. Suicide is a cowardly act. Since it deprives the state of a citizen, it is a crime similar to a soldier's desertion of his post. It is also an amoral act (contrary to the "right rule of life"), and on both accounts should be punished. However, the punishment is not too severe—merely "a certain loss of civil rights." Perhaps Aristotle would not have justified any punishment at all had he taken the more enlightened view that the law does not necessarily forbid what it does not expressly permit.

Curiously enough, when, after the death of his former pupil, Alexander the Great, Aristotle had to flee Athens and soon thereafter suddenly died in exile at the age of sixty-two, there were persistent rumors that he had committed suicide. Their truth, like that of most such stories involving philosophers, is suspect.

EPICURUS

The political unrest and spiritual crisis in Athens toward the end of the fourth century B.C. appears to have favored a change in the philosophical outlook on life. In addition to the Platonists, the "'Peripatetics" (as the followers of Aristotle were called), and some less important groups like the Cynics and the Cyrenaics, two important new philosophical schools were founded. In 307 B.C. Epicurus (341–270 B.C.), born on the island of Samos of Athenian parents, established his "garden," and in 300 B.C. Zeno of Citium (336–265 B.C.), a Phoenician, began to teach on the "Painted Porch" *(stoa poikile)* and became the founder of Stoicism.

It would be difficult to find two personalities more different than the gentle and gregarious Epicurus and the austere, even ascetic Zeno. No wonder they produced two very different philosophies. But their aim was on the whole the same—to enable man to cope with life's vicissitudes and to come to terms with death.

Epicurus's view of the task of philosophy is expressed in his statement that "vain is the word of that philosopher which does not heal any suffering of man."[8] He taught that the two great afflictions of man are the fear of the gods and the fear of death. The former is unfounded, because, although gods exist, they do not interfere in human affairs. As for the fear of death, this "most terrifying of all ills is nothing to us, since as long as we exist, death is not with us, but when death comes, then we do not exist."[9] Once this is understood, nothing stands in the way of man's happiness, which consists in peace of mind and the health of the body. As long as the latter is unimpaired, life is enjoyable, since bodily pleasure is the highest good, and mental pleasure is derived from and related to it. Epicurus was opposed to suicide, even in misfortune, which "we must heal by the grateful recollection of what has been and by the recognition that it is impossible to make undone what has been done."[10]

While "the many at one moment shun death as the greatest of evils, at another yearn for it as a respite from the evils of life . . . the wise man neither seeks to escape life nor fears the cessation of life, for neither does life offend him nor does the absence of life seem to be an evil."[11] Epicurus's negative attitude toward suicide is perhaps best expressed in his sarcastic comments about the statement by the poet Theognis that it is best not to be born but "once born make haste to pass the gates of Death." For, if he really means it, why does he not pass away out of life? For nothing stops him if he really made up his mind to do so. "But if he speaks in jest, his words are idle."[12]

Epicurus's most ardent admirer, the Roman poet Titus Lucretius Carus (99–53 B.C.), the author of the didactic poem *De Rerum Natura* (On the Nature of Things), which is the most comprehensive exposition of materialism in antiquity, and of Epicurean teachings, was less negative toward suicide. But he condemned it if it was committed for the wrong reasons. Denouncing his contemporaries' greed and lust for power, which he attributed to their fear of death, Lucretius is particularly scornful of those who "sacrifice life itself for the sake of statues and titles" and points out that "often from fear of death mortals are gripped by such a hate of living . . . that with anguished hearts they do themselves to death. They forget that this very fear is the fountain-head of their troubles."[13] However, those who find no flavor in life should not hesitate to take leave of it. Taking up Epicurus's argument against those who are complaining about the inevitability of death, he asks:

Why do you weep and wail over death? If the life you have lived till now has been a pleasant thing ... why then, you silly creature, do you not retire as a guest who has had his fill of life and take your carefree rest with a quiet mind? Or, if all your gains have been poured profitless away and life has grown distasteful, why do you seek to swell the total? ... Why not rather make an end of life and labor?[14]

Lucretius himself is supposed to have committed suicide, but although this version of his death is widely accepted, its only source is St. Jerome (born c. A.D. 340). Jerome's source, in turn, was the *Chronicles* of Eusebius of Caesarea (died c. A.D. 325) who, in his report for the year A.D. 95, mentions that "the poet T. Lucretius is born, who later went insane after drinking a love philter, in his lucid moments wrote some books which were amended by Cicero, and who committed suicide at age forty-four."

THE GREEK STOICS

The decisive change toward approval of suicide was made by Epicurus's great rival, Zeno. While Epicurus accepted the atomism of Democritus but taught that the world is ruled by chance, the Stoic school retained Democritus's doctrine of natural necessity, that the future is inevitably fixed in advance, and that the universe is ruled by divine *logos* (reason), of which man's rational part is a reflection. Thus, to live "according to Nature" is to live according to reason which is a reliable guide to correct action. And while for Epicurus the highest good was pleasure, Zeno proclaimed it to be virtue. The question of suicide, however, is, for the Stoics' "wise man," not one of moral right or wrong, but of a rational decision as to what is preferable in a given situation, life or death.

Legend has it that Zeno himself committed suicide in his old age. According to one version, when walking along the road he tripped and broke his toe. Interpreting this accident as God's sign that he had lived long enough, he went home and killed himself. Another version has it that he lay on the road holding his breath until he died. His successor, Cleanthes, is also said to have been a suicide. When he developed a boil on his gum he was advised by his physician to refrain from eating for two days. But although his condition improved rapidly and he was told to resume taking normal nourishment, "having gone so far in the path of death, he persisted to the end."[15]

Actually, the stoic position with regard to suicide was in some repects an enlargement of that of Plato. As has been mentioned, Plato allowed exceptions from the general rule in a number of circumstances which were "objectively" intolerable and irremediable. The philosophers of the so-called middle stoa, in particular Panaetius (185–110 B.C.) and Posidonius (135–51 B.C.) replaced objective by subjective criteria, substituting for external compulsion an overwhelming inner conviction. The Stoic who finds it no longer possible to live "according to reason" interprets this as an intimation from God (or "Nature") that it is time to depart from life. This does not mean, however, that suicide should be a rash act resulting from a momentary impulse or a temporary confusion of values; it should be carried out or rejected only after due deliberation. But, as was already indicated, for the Stoic suicide completely lost its moral reprehensiveness; it ceased to be a crime or a sin, and in time the only problem, particularly in imperial Rome, was how to commit it most gracefully and casually, parading one's courage and fortitude.

THE ROMAN STOICS

The most forceful statements of the Stoic position on suicide are those of the Roman Stoics, the wealthy and politically influential Seneca (4 B.C.–A.D. 65) and the former slave, Epictetus (A.D. 50–132). Some typical pronouncements by Seneca, made in one of his famous "Letters to Lucilius," are: "Living is not the good, but living well. The wise man, therefore, lives as long as he should, not as long as he can ... he will always think of life in terms of quality not quantity." More specifically referring to suicide, he says: "Dying early or late is of no relevance, dying well or ill is ... Even if it is true that 'while there is life, there is hope' life is not to be bought at any cost." But Seneca does not believe that one should try to escape the executioner's sword by committing suicide, and he echoes Lucretius's statement that it is folly to die for fear of dying. Yet if one death involves torture and the other is easy and simple, there is no reason why one should not choose the latter. He takes issue with "even professed philosophers who assert that a man may not do violence to his own life, and pronounce it sinful for a man to be his own executioner. We must wait, they say, for the end Nature has decreed. The man who says this does not see that he has blocked his way to freedom. Eternal law has never been more generous than in affording us so many exits to one entry. . . . The situation of humanity is good in that no one is wretched except by his own fault. If you like, live; if you don't like, you can go back where you came from." And he concludes: "To live by violence is unfair, to die by violence is the fairest of all."[16]

Seneca committed suicide by opening his veins; this, as has been mentioned, was on orders of his former pupil, the emperor Nero, who suspected Seneca of being implicated in a plot to assassinate him. Seneca's wife insisted on dying with her husband but was saved at the last moment at Nero's order.

Epictetus's position was much less radical than that of Seneca. Not only the times had changed. Stoicism having become the dominant philosophy, suicide had become extremely prevalent among the higher ranks of Roman society. A restraining voice was obviously needed, and Epictetus provided it. He was well suited to do so, not being a "radical" like Zeno, or a proud "aristocrat" like Seneca. Aware of the broad interpretation of the justifications for suicide, he warns that suicide for trifling reasons is inadmissible. He presents the problem in an imaginary dialogue with his disciples: "You come saying: 'Epictetus, we can bear no longer to be bound with the fetters of this wretched body, giving it meat and drink and rest and purgation. . . . Suffer us to depart to the place whence we came, suffer us to be released from these bonds.' . . . Hereupon, I answer: 'Men as you are, wait upon God. When he gives the signal and releases you from your service, then you shall depart to Him.'" And he cites the example of Socrates as showing the only proper attitude.[17]

As has been noted, "departure" for the Stoics must be "reasonable." To make his point, Epictetus compares one's life situation to being in a smoke-filled room. "If only moderately, I will stay; if there is too much smoke, I will go. . . ." However, while emphasizing that one should not be hasty in committing suicide, he also reminds his followers of the consolation which the possibility of suicide offers to suffering humanity.

> To sum up: remember the door is open. Be not a greater coward than the children, but do as they do. When things do not please them, they say, "I will not play anymore." So when things seem to you to reach that point, just say "I will not play anymore" and so depart, instead of staying to make moan.[18]

MONTAIGNE

The permissiveness of ancient philosophers toward suicide was completely obliterated by the uncompromising attitude of the Christian Church, which has already been discussed in some detail. Only after the philosophical thought had regained a modicum of independence from theology with the rediscovery of classical literature which served as a prelude to the Renaissance could a dialogue over suicide be resumed.

The great French essayist Michel de Montaigne (1533–1592) contributed the first significant discussion of suicide to conclude with a decisive departure from the Church's blanket prohibition. He devotes a whole chapter of his *Essays*, "Custom of the Isle of Cea [Kea]" to the topic of suicide. The title refers to the alleged custom, already mentioned, of making poison available free to all persons who desired to kill themselves and were able to give valid reasons to the court for doing so. Montaigne also mentions, without giving any source, the existence of the same custom in ancient Marseilles.

Montaigne begins by presenting the position of those who hold that there are many situations which are worse than death. He quotes Seneca, one of his favorite philosophers, and describes the Stoic view on suicide and death:

> Death is a very sure haven, which should never be feared, and often sought . . . the more voluntary a death is the most beautiful it is. . . .
> Life depends on the will of others—death on our own will.

As to the religious prohibition of suicide, he argues that "God gives us sufficient dispensation when he puts us in a situation where life becomes worse than death." Referring to the extension of the commandment "Thou shalt not kill" to suicide, he adds, "I don't break the law made for crooks, when I take away my own property—thus I am not obliged to conform to the law made for murderers when I deprive myself of my own life."

Montaigne objected to the idea that one had to ask permission to commit suicide. He considered the act to be foolish, not immoral, but he is very careful to present this view in such a way as not to offend the Church. He therefore proceeds to present the opposite view: We ought not to quit "the worldly garrison" without the express permission of the One who has put us there. When we do so we are deserters who are punished for it in the hereafter. He points out the great doubt which undermines the first position: "Which occasions are sufficient to justify a man in killing himself?" There are many delusions which mislead not only individuals but entire populations into doing away with themselves, whereas one should never give up as long as there is a glimmer of hope. He admits that perhaps there are no inconveniences great enough that one should die in order to escape them. Moreover, no one is capable of determining precisely at what point we ought to give up hope, and he mentions that Pliny considered only a stone in the bladder, and Seneca only "the prolonged disturbance of the soul," as valid reasons to kill oneself. Montaigne also discusses the much-debated question of whether a woman should commit suicide to protect her chastity. On the face of it, he seems to agree with the view that she ought to go to this extreme and cites the canonization of Pelagia and Sophronia. But, typically for him, he cannot refrain from presenting the possible soundness of the opposite view by telling a supposedly true story of a woman who, after having been raped by several soldiers, exclaimed, "Thanks be to God that at least once in my life I was completely sated without having sinned."

Becoming serious again, Montaigne considers instances when one desires death not in order to escape miseries and affliction on this earth but in the hope of a greater bliss in the hereafter. He quotes St. Paul's wish to die in order to be with Christ, pointing out that this shows how erroneous it is to ascribe all suicides to despair.

Only at the very end of the chapter does Montaigne discuss "the custom of Cea." He appears to be in sympathy with it. He concludes his discussion of suicide by saying: *"La douleur insupportable et une pire mort me semblent les plus excusables incitations"* [unbearable pain and a worse death seem to be the most excusable incentives].[19]

DESCARTES

The negative views of suicide of the French mathematician and philosopher René Descartes (1596–1650) are found in his letters to Princess Elizabeth, the unhappy and neurasthenic daughter of the deposed Elector of the Palatinate.[20] In the letter of October 6, 1645, he touches on the subject of the influence which the knowledge of the immortality of the soul and the happiness which awaits her in the beyond have on those who are bored with earthly existence. He is referring here to those who are not "true" Christians, since he holds that true believers cannot be bored in this life and are certain of immortality. But to seek an escape in suicide is to succumb to the false notion that in this life evil prevails, whereas even in the greatest calamity and most intense discomfort one can always be content if one uses one's reason properly. A more forceful statement against suicide, and the reason for its rejection, are found in the letter of November 3, 1645. Here Descartes modestly disclaims precise knowledge of the state of the soul after it leaves the body at death. He suggests that if we put aside for the moment what religion tells us and rely solely on natural reason, the most rosy expectations will always be mere conjectures, not certainties. However, reason tells us not only that there are more good things in this life than evil ones but also that we should not give up something uncertain. "Thus reason seems to me to teach us that we should not really fear death, but also that we should never seek it."[21]

Descartes evidently realized that his assertion that the good in life out-weighs the bad needed some justification. In the letter of January 1646[22] he explained that what he means is that we should attribute little importance to things which do not depend on our own free choice, and that those things which do so depend we can always render good if only we know how to use them properly. Moreover, with the help of reason all the evil that comes our way from the outside can be prevented from causing more sadness than is evoked by watching similar disasters on the stage. Descartes admits, howev-er, that in order to be able to react in this way one has to be a true philo-sopher. Nevertheless, he holds that even those who let themselves be over-whelmed by their passions still believe in the depths of their souls that there is more good than evil in the world. Even though they may call for death to deliver them when they suffer great pain, they do not really want to die. Those who seriously want to die and kill themselves do so because of an error in judgment, not at all because of considered reasoning. In any case, Nature does not impose negative feelings about life on people, whereas it is natural to prefer the good of this life to its evils.

SPINOZA

There is no condemnation of suicide in Spinoza, nor is there advocacy of it. As a matter of fact, he devotes so little space to the subject that one may wonder how a thinker for whom the goal of philosophy was "the attainment of continuous supreme and unleading happiness" could have neglected what in many instances appears as the dreadful consequence of unhappiness.

However, what Spinoza does say about self-destruction in general ex-plains his brevity. His position is extremely interesting, particularly when compared with the current views on self-destructive propensities.

> ... No one, I say, from the necessity of his own nature, or otherwise than under compulsion from external causes, shrinks from food or kills himself ... That a man, from the necessity of his own nature, should endeavor to become non-existent is as impossible as that something should be made out of nothing.[23]

This amounts to no more and no less than a categorical denial of a natural impulse for self-destruction.

This is the direct consequence of the famous principle stated in Proposi-tion VI of the third book of the *Ethics:* "Everything, in so far as it is in itself, endeavours to persist in its own being."[24] As is made clear in Proposition VII, this endeavour *(conatus)* for self-preservation is determined from the necessity of the divine nature by which all things exist. This principle, as far as Spinoza is concerned, covers both inanimate objects and animate beings, including man. It is important to realize that the *Conatus in suo esse perseverendi* (the drive to self-preservation) is not an act of free will; Spinoza describes it as the innate love of each person for himself.

The denial of a natural impulse of self-destruction deserves some scrutiny, particularly in view of the present-day tendency to assert the existence of such an impulse as a basic trait of the human psyche; Freud, in his theory of the death "instinct" in all living things, went so far as to endow it with "ontological" status as a cosmic force, "Thanatos," locked in eternal struggle with "Eros."

The principle of self-preservation as a basic law of nature has a long and venerable history. It goes back to the Peripatetic school as well as to the Stoics who held that the animal's first impulse (appetite) is for self-preservation. St. Augustine, St. Thomas Aquinas, and the Scottish theologian Duns Scotus (1265?–1308) reiterated the assertion that every natural thing (everything that exists), desires its own existence, and many Renaissance philosophers variously restated this, so that the principle of self-preservation had become practically a philosophical axiom by the time Spinoza expounded it. His term *"conatus"* had already been used by Cicero as an equivalent of "appetite," both of these being translations of the Greek term ορμή, and Spinoza equates this term with "force" *(vis)*. Recently the similarity with Freud's "libido," of which *conatus* is asserted to be an ancestor, has been pointed out. There are other similarities between Spinoza's and Freud's psychological views, and as late as 1910 (at the meeting on student suicide held in Vienna) Freud wondered "how it becomes possible for the extraordinarily powerful life instinct to be overcome." His subsequent attempt of explanation by stipulating the existence of an equally powerful death instinct is no less "metaphysical" than Spinoza's assertion of the impossibility of a self-destructive "conatus." What makes suicide possible for Spinoza is physical or psychological compulsion, which may be overt or latent but is always "external."

FRENCH EIGHTEENTH-CENTURY PHILOSOPHERS

The eighteenth-century French *philosophes* take, on the whole, a distinctly permissive view of suicide, which ranges, depending on their philosophical position, from unconditional approval to certain reservations based on sociological considerations.

Thus the materialist and atheist Baron Paul Henri Dietrich d'Holbach (1723–1789) unconditionally approves suicide, a view which follows naturally from his idea that death is the supreme remedy for all human ills. Not only is suicide not against nature, it actually carries out nature's verdict. Nature, far from rejecting the suicidal individual, has labored thousands of years to create the very iron which will cut short his years. Nor is suicide a crime against society, since the contract between it and the individual is made for mutual benefit, and therefore if society cannot make life tolerable to the individual, the latter is no longer bound by the contract. Moreover, an unhappy man is a burden to his fellow men, and his voluntary departure a good solution all around.[25]

The deist Voltaire (1694–1778) insists that individual circumstances, not dogma or preconceived ideas and superstition, must decide whether the suicide acted properly or wrongly, praiseworthily or damnably. Typically, he infuses common sense as well as wit and irony into his generally tolerant view of suicide by ridiculing "romantic" suicides and by explaining that his own suicide is very improbable since he is drawing liberal life pensions from two monarchs and would hate to have them benefit from his premature death.

What is new in Voltaire is that he used empirical material—reports of historical suicides as well as contemporary newspaper accounts—in order to draw conclusions about suicide in general. Thus he found that suicide is more frequent in cities than in rural areas. He attributed this to the greater leisure of city dwellers, who have more time to think and therefore are more prone to melancholia. He also thought that suicidal tendencies, like other moral characteristics, are inherited, and that some suicides are due to a desire for revenge.[26] These conclusions were widely accepted by subsequent students of suicide, and although the first three have been discarded in recent times, the motive of revenge has been recognized and even stressed.

Somewhat earlier, Montesquieu (1689–1755) in his *Lettres Persanes* (1721), castigated the barbaric laws against suicide. Usbek, the Oriental voyager who is his imaginary spokesman, ridicules the moral, religious, and legal sanctions imposed on people who kill themselves. He argues that life is a gift, and that once it ceases to give us pleasure we can return it. Suicide does not hurt society, nor does it disturb the beauty and order of the world, since the body is destined to perish in any event, and the soul remains unimpaired.[27]

Surprisingly, Denis Diderot (1713–1784) in his article on "suicide" in the *Encyclopédie* (1765), takes an antisuicide position. He says that it is unnatural, since it goes against the instinct of self-preservation, transgresses the divine law as embodied in the teachings of the Church, and is antisocial. Some have surmised that this reflected, not Diderot's actual opinion, but his desire to avoid trouble with the authorities. However, Diderot also presents the arguments for the opposing position; probably he simply wanted to present a balanced account in keeping with the scientific spirit of the *Encyclopédie*. He insists that suicide cannot be called a crime if it is committed, as it often is, in the state of insanity or deep depression—*"melancolie noire."*[28] In this assertion he anticipates the position of the French alienists of the nineteenth century. His friend and collaborator, the great mathematician Jean d'Alembert (1717?–1783), was even further ahead of his time in emphasizing particularly the harm suicide did to the survivors.

The Encyclopedists and their circle can be credited with having contributed to the subsequent morally neutral attitude toward suicide and to its recognition as a danger to the mental health of the community, thus preparing the way for present-day efforts toward its prevention.

The most influential statement of a pro-suicide position was made by

Rousseau in the twenty-first letter of his novel, *La Nouvelle Héloise* (1761). Its

hero, the young St. Preux, explains to his friend Lord Edouard his reasons for
justifying suicide. It is man's natural right to seek what is good for him and
flee what is bad, as long as it does no harm to others. But the brunt of the
argument is aimed at squaring the right to suicide with the belief in God.
Since God has endowed man with reason precisely for the purpose of
enabling him to choose what is best for him, man has to listen to it, and
reason tells us that an unhappy life must be remedied as much as a sick body:
"If it is permitted to seek a cure for gout, why not for life?" Suicide does not
alienate us from God and is not a sin, since in killing ourselves we merely
destroy our bodies and bring our immortal souls closer to God. If St. Preux
had believed differently he would not want to die. He recognizes one restriction only—that people who have duties to others should not commit suicide.
As to himself, he is neither a magistrate, nor has he a family to support, so that
nothing stands in his way.[29]

Rousseau, whose own life was extremely unhappy, was rumored to have
eventually committed suicide, but this seems doubtful. What seems certain,
however, is that Rousseau discussed suicide at length with David Hume
(1711–1776), the great English philosopher whose ungrateful guest he was in
1766/67.

HUME

Hume's essay "On Suicide" (published only in 1777, a year after his death, and
promptly suppressed) is the most forceful and best-reasoned statement in
English, and perhaps in any language, of the Enlightenment's position on the
subject. He concentrates on refuting the view that suicide is a crime. To be so
defined, it must be a transgression of our duty either to God, or our neighbor,
or to ourselves. As to the first, he argues that God has established general and
immutable laws by which all that makes up the universe is governed. Once
this had been done, however, there is no event, no matter how important in
the eyes of men, which is exempted from these laws or which He has
"particularly reserved for his own immediate action and operation." But as
the inanimate parts of creation carry on without regard to men, these in turn
are "intrusted with their own judgment and discretion . . . and may employ
every faculty with which they are endowed, in order to provide for their ease,
happiness, or preservation." If this is so, "what is the meaning of the principle
that a man, who, tired of life, and haunted by pain and misery, bravely
overcomes all the natural terrors of death, and makes his escape from this
cruel scene . . . [is] encroaching on the office of the divine providence, and
disturbing the order of the universe?" To assume this is plainly false, because
it presupposes that human life has a special value in the scheme of things.
But—and here Hume makes the famous assertion which put him into sharp
opposition to the traditional religious position—"the life of a man is of no
greater importance to the universe than that of an oyster."[30]

This statement is of particular importance for an inquiry into the possible
relationship between the denial of a "cosmic" or transcendent meaning of

human life and suicide. An argument often advanced is that if human life has no such meaning, it is not worth while, and since such a view may lead to despair and even to suicide, it must be wrong and life must have such an ultimate meaning.

One of the most frequent arguments against suicide compares it to the desertion of the post to which each individual has been assigned by Providence. Hume counters this by questioning the validity of the analogy. He argues that one's birth is due to a long chain of causes, many of which depend upon voluntary actions of men. "Since Providence guided all these causes, and nothing happens without its consent," the same applies to a man's death, even a voluntary one. Hume invokes in this connection the Stoic view that when pain and sorrow gain the upper hand over one's will to live, this may be a clear indication that Providence is recalling us from our post.

Turning to the second aspect, suicide as a crime against society ("one's neighbor"), Hume argues that by committing suicide one does not harm society but merely ceases to do good, which, if an injury at all, is "the lowest kind of injury." In any case, one is not obliged to do a small good to society if this causes great harm to oneself. Moreover, a man tired of life is often a burden to society since he hinders other useful members from being even more useful.

As to the third "criminal" aspect of suicide, transgression against oneself, no one can deny that suicide is often consistent with self-interest, particularly in cases where old age, sickness, and misfortune make life a burden.

Hume concludes by stating his belief that no one throws away his life as long as it is worth keeping and by declaring that "prudence and courage should engage us to rid ourselves at once of existence when it becomes a burden." By following this rule one actually renders a service to society by setting an example which, if followed by all, would preserve man's chance for happiness while making possible release from suffering and misery.

KANT

Immanuel Kant, who devoted most of his efforts to disproving Hume's skepticism, which for him meant the end of philosophy, disagreed also with his position on suicide. Kant's reasons for condemning suicide follow from his view of man as belonging not only to the realm of "phenomena" but also to that of "things in themselves" (noumena), and from the central place "duty" occupies in his ethics. Not surprisingly, it is his discussion of "the duties of man toward himself" that contains his discussion of suicide.[31]

As a natural being, as an "animal creature," man's first duty is self-preservation, and suicide therefore is a vice (which interestingly Kant puts into the same category as gluttony and the "unnatural" exercise of the sex drive, by which he probably meant sexual intercourse not solely devoted to procreation). But man is also a moral being, embodying the dignity of humanity in his person, and his being a person (Persoenlichkeit) lays upon him even more strictly the duty of preserving his life. This is the essence of Kant's criticism of the Stoic position on suicide. Since it seems nonsensical that a man can offend himself, the Stoics considered it as superiority in the true philosopher to be able to withdraw from life at his own discretion with a tranquil soul. But, argues Kant, precisely this courage, this inner strength not to fear death and to know something which man can value higher than his life, should serve as an even stronger reason for not destroying a being with powers capable of triumphing over the strongest emotions. In Kant's view, to annihilate the subject of morality in its own person is equivalent to destroying morality itself, to disposing of the moral person, which is an end in itself, as a means for attaining a purpose of one's own choosing. By doing so, man would be degrading the humanity inherent in his person *(homo noumenon)* in whose safekeeping man the phenomenon has been entrusted.

Although Kant's discussion of suicide occupies only a couple of pages, he closes it with some provocative questions: Is heroic suicide (to save one's country) or deliberate martyrdom by sacrificing one's life for the sake of mankind's salvation to be considered suicide? Is it permissible to escape a death sentence by killing oneself, even when a higher authority commands it as Nero did in the case of Seneca? How about a monarch who carries a poison so that in case of his capture he may spare his country the necessity of accepting disadvantageous conditions for his release? Or a person who, bitten by a rabid dog and knowing his condition to be incurable (this was written before Pasteur), kills himself to avoid endangering others? Or someone who accepts a smallpox vaccination and thus risks his life (in Kant's day vaccination was considered unsafe) for the sake of possibly saving it? However, in asking these questions Kant was obviously less concerned with a proper definition of suicide than with the challenge which such suicides, especially those committed for moral reasons, present to his main argument against suicide.

SCHOPENHAUER

The father of modern pessimism, Arthur Schopenhauer (1788–1860), who saw himself as the heir of Kant, occupies a very original position with regard to suicide. Readers of his magnum opus *The World as Will and Idea* (1818) are frequently surprised to find that he does not consider suicide as a logical conclusion to be drawn from his unrelenting and uncompromising indictment of human existence. "Whoever is oppressed with the burden of life, whoever desires life and affirms it, but abhors its torments, such a man has no deliverance to hope from death, and cannot right himself by suicide."[32]

The reason for this view is to be sought in Schopenhauer's metaphysics. Modifying Kant's position that the real reality, the "thing in itself," is unknowable, Schopenhauer asserts that it can be known, and that it discloses itself, through insight into our own real essence, as "Will," a blind, relentless, and universal striving which expresses itself in organic nature, and consequently also in man, as the "will to live." Since, according to Schopenhauer, this will to live is at bottom the source of all our suffering, misery, and pain, salvation can be achieved only by denying it. But this denial is not achieved through dying, since "our true nature, the Will, is indestructible." This is the reason that he says, in order to explain why suicide is not a genuine solution for the human predicament, that "suicide denies only the individual not the species" and "the willful destruction of the single phenomenal existence is a vain and foolish act; for the *thing in itself* remains unaffected by it, even as the rainbow endures, however fast the drops which support it for the moment may change."[33]

Far from being the result of a loss of the will to live, suicide is, on the contrary, "a phenomenon of strong assertion of will . . . the suicide wills life, and is only dissatisfied with the conditions under which it presents itself to him. He therefore by no means surrenders the will to live, but only life."[34]

Nevertheless, although he insists that suicide is a vain and foolish act, Schopenhauer vigorously defends the right of every individual to voluntary death. In his *Parerga und Paralipomena* [Odds and Ends] written in 1851, he states: "It is obvious that everyone has no more undeniable right than that to his own personality and life."[35] He suggests that the clergy should be challenged to show by what biblical authority and by what philosophical argument it arrogates to itself the right to brand as a crime an act committed by so many honored and loved people. Is Hamlet's soliloquy, he asks, the meditation of a criminal? And he was incensed by the suppression of the essay in which Hume effectively disposed of the arguments against suicide.

However, Schopenhauer declares that "the only really cogent moral reason against suicide" is that given in his own principle work. This has been outlined in preceding paragraphs, but Schopenhauer himself summed it up thirty years later: "It consists in that suicide is opposed to the achievement of the highest moral goal, in that it substitutes an imaginary deliverance from this vale of tears for the real one."

In general, Schopenhauer says, men put an end to their existence as soon as the terrors of life outweigh the terrors of death. These latter, however, are considerable and stand "like watchmen before the exit door." Perhaps there is no man living who would not have already done away with himself if the end were merely something purely negative, a sudden cessation of existence. Yet there is something "positive" to it, the destruction of the body. And the body shrinks before annihilation precisely because the body is the manifestation of the will to live.

Schopenhauer concludes his brief essay on suicide with the interesting thought that perhaps suicide can be interpreted also as an experiment, a question which man puts to Nature; namely, what change death brings about in man's existence and knowledge. But the suicide wants to obtain the answer by force, which is clumsy and self-defeating, since it eliminates the consciousness which has to receive the answer.

The Italian poet Giacomo Leopardi (1798–1837) was the other outstanding pessimist of the nineteenth century next to Schopenhauer (whose writings he probably did not know). But while Schopenhauer admitted and defended the right of every person to kill himself, Leopardi denies it. In an imaginary dialogue between the Neo-Platonist Plotinus and his disciple Porphyry, he presents the same argument as did Madame de Stael: man ought not to refuse to submit "to that portion of suffering of our race which destiny has appointed to us."[36]

It is interesting that there was actually a discussion of suicide between Plotinus and Porphyry, which the latter recorded and which was quite different from Leopardi's version.

> One day Plotinus noticed that I had the intention of departing this life. He came to me (I lived in his house) and he told me that my desire to commit suicide was not at all reasonable but stemmed from a morbid melancholia, and suggested that I undertake a voyage. I followed his advice and traveled to Sicily. ... In this manner I was delivered from my craving for death, but this prevented me from staying at Plotinus's side until his death.[37]

NIETZSCHE

Friedrich Wilhelm Nietzsche (1844–1900), the German philosopher who was influenced by Schopenhauer more than by any other thinker, nevertheless went his own way in many respects, and nowhere as radically as in his opposition to Schopenhauer's denigration of life. "Suffering is no argument against life," he writes to a friend, "and no pain has been able or shall be able to tempt me into giving a false testimony about life as I recognized it."[38]

At the same time Nietzsche was not opposed to suicide: "The thought of suicide is a strong consolation: it helps to get over many a bad night."[39] The meaning of this cannot be in doubt. For a man who suffered from terrible headaches and recurring blindness which forced him to give up at thirty-two a brilliant academic career, and who knew not only almost constant physical pain but mental torture and abysmal loneliness, the thought that if his condition became unbearable there was always suicide as a way out must be indeed a comforting one.

Other statements make his affirmative position with regard to suicide even more obvious. "Suicide is man's right and privilege," he writes in *The Dawn of Day (Morgenröte)*.[40] He is against interference with suicide. In *Human All-Too-Human* he writes: "Prevention of Suicide: There is a justice according to which we take a man's life, but there is none whatsoever when we deprive him of dying: this is only cruelty."[41] And in *Thus Spake Zarathustra:* "Many die too late, and some die too early. The maxim: die at the right time still sounds foreign to us."[42]

One may see a contradiction between Nietzsche's unconditional, even passionate affirmation of life and his defense of suicide. Psychologically this could be understood as resulting from his ambivalent attitude toward death, which appeared to him sometimes as an enemy and at other times as a friend. In any case, his *"amor fati"*—the acceptance of one's fate—is not compatible with the Dionysian attitude that when such a life becomes impossible one should put an end to it voluntarily, rather than to accept meekly a "living death." Moreover, Nietzsche's world of "Eternal Recurrence" where "all things return eternally, and we ourselves have already been numberless times," is "the world of eternal self-creation and eternal self-destruction."[43] Suicide as a manner of death would seem to conform better to

such a world than natural demise, particularly since *all* deaths are conquered by the "eternal return of the same."

HARTMANN

Another German, Eduard von Hartmann (1842–1906), author of the once
famous and influential *Philosophy of the Unconscious* (1869, English translation 1884), claimed that Schopenhauer's pessimism was not sufficiently well
founded. Hartmann did not consider Schopenhauer his teacher but assigned
this honor to Kant. Nevertheless there are important similarities between his
philosophy and that of Schopenhauer.

Surprisingly enough Hartmann agrees with Gottfried Wilhelm von Leibnitz (1646–1716) that this is the best of all possible worlds. According to
Hartmann, it is so because, if a better world were possible, the all-powerful
Unconscious would have brought it about. Hartmann sees intelligence and
purpose at work, not only in nature but also in history, which, far from being a
meaningless change, shows a definite, if not always unhampered, progress
toward a definite goal set by the "great Unconscious," which is similar to
Schopenhauer's "Will."

But, while this world can be said to be the best possible one, it is not
therefore necessarily good, and Hartmann proceeds to demonstrate that life
is essentially undesirable. He argues that happiness, toward which everything strives and which is the only discoverable purpose of life, forever eludes
man. Life is a continuous disappointment. However, Hartmann does not
advocate escape from life. On the contrary, he enjoins man to reconcile
himself to life as it is and to give up his illusions that happiness can be
attained, either in this world or in the hereafter, since he is not born to be
happy but to serve the ends of the Unconscious, which is "cosmic redemption." Although evolution occurs, it only brings with it a multiplication of
pains and a heightened sensitivity to them. Thus, as Hartmann sees it, the
redemption of a world doomed to ever-increasing suffering is no more and
no less than the extinction of that world.[44]

According to Hartmann, "the principle of absolute teleology" shows that
the final aim of all is "the deliverance of the absolute from transcendental
misery, and the return to its painless peace by means of the immanent
torment of the world evolution."[45] To help in this task is man's supreme duty,
since only man's consciousness can make salvation possible. The more
consciousness deepens and expands the clearer becomes the discovery that
life is essentially evil and futile. With the growth of intelligence and the
evolution of mankind, the conviction of this fact is bound to spread and
eventually to take possession of all men. Then, by a common act of will,
humanity (or a race of supermen that will succeed it on this planet) will
decree its own extinction and along with it the disappearance of the world of
which man is the consummation. Existence will be "hurled back" into the
Unconscious again.

What all this boils down to as far as suicide is concerned is that, instead of
seeking escape through individual suicide, man must help in the "suicide" of

mankind. The difference between Hartmann and Schopenhauer is that the latter, while considering suicide a "vain and foolish" act, recognized everyone's right to commit it, whereas Hartmann denies this right as going against man's supreme obligation to help God (or "the great Unconscious") to achieve self-deliverance.

CAMUS

Although not strictly a philosopher in the sense of the other thinkers discussed in this chapter, the French novelist and essayist Albert Camus (1913–1960) deserves special consideration because of his concern with suicide. In the opening sentence of his brilliant essay *The Myth of Sisyphus* (1942), Camus declares that "there is but one truly serious philosophical problem, and that is suicide." What he actually means is that since human life appears to be devoid of meaning (and Camus is convinced that it is), it is not only legitimate but most relevant to ask whether it does not "logically" follow that life is not worth living and therefore suicide the only proper response to life's meaninglessness. His unequivocal answer to this question is that, although life has no meaning, suicide is not justifed.

A large part of *The Myth of Sisyphus* is devoted to a description of "the Absurd" and the sources of the feeling of meaninglessness or "absurdity" of life. Camus makes various and often contradictory statements about the Absurd, for which he does not offer a definition since he considers futile any attempt at doing so. But what emerges as the main root of the experience of the Absurd is the conflict between man's moral demands and the world's indifference to them which is what Pascal meant when he complained that it is the "silence" of the infinite expanse of the universe which frightened him. The "most obvious of all absurdities," however, is death, which for Camus is total annihilation. In the final accounting its "bloodstained mathematics" proves the ultimate vanity, the utter meaninglessness, of human existence.

How, then, does Camus justify his rejection of suicide? First he calls attention to the confusion between the statements that life is not worth living and that it is meaningless. It is a mistake to assume that "refusing to grant meaning to life necessarily leads to declaring that it is not worth living. In truth, there is no necessary common measure between these two judgments."[46] The absence of meaning not only does not compel one to commit suicide, but, as Camus asserts, "life will be lived all the better if it has no meaning." To live truly is to be constantly and keenly aware of the Absurd, a state which Camus likens to the state of revolt in which there is a constant confrontation between man and the world he challenges relentlessly. This is the "metaphysical revolt" which despite "the certainty of a crushing fate" avoids "the resignation that ought to accompany it."[47] It is this revolt that gives life its value and confers majesty on it; it is essential "to die unreconciled and not of one's free will" and to preserve to the bitter end one's integrity, and one's pride "the sight of which is unequaled."[48] This appeal to human pride is what, in the end, Camus opposes to the temptation of suicide. Here Camus clearly shows the influence of Nietzsche. Nihilism does not lead to despair but on the contrary is transformed into a proud stance of defiance and triumph over man's fate. In *Nuptials*, a collection of essays written a year before *The Myth of Sisyphus*, he celebrates the joys of life which made it worth living. As Philip Thody correctly points out, in his book on Camus, "it is because Camus, unlike Kafka, Kierkegaard and Sartre, feels instinctively that although the world may at times appear indifferent and strange, he is basically at home in it on the physical plane, that all his logic leads to a rejection of suicide."[49]

Obviously, the mere appeal of human pride and the reference to the joys of life might have little effect on one who finds life unbearable, feels defeated by it, in short is convinced that it is not worth the trouble. But Camus's question whether the awareness of the absurdity of life is "an invitation to death," to which he gives a negative answer, evokes the related question of whether the conviction that life has no meaning is a factor in suicide.

Notes

1 Plato, *Phaedo*, 62 b, translated by Benjamin Jowett (in Plato, *Republic and Other Works*, New York: Doubleday, Dolphin Books).

2 *Ibid.*, 64 c.

3 *Ibid.*, 64 a.

4 *Ibid.*, 63 c.

5 Plato, *The Laws*, 873, translated by A. E. Taylor (London: J. M. Dent & Sons, 1934).

6 Aristotle, *Nicomachean Ethics*, translated by W. D. Ross, 1115 a, 25, and 1116, 10.

7 *Ibid.*, 1138 a, 5.

8 H. Usener, ed., *Epicurea*, Fragment 221 (Leipzig, 1887); English translation in Whitney J. Oates, *The Stoic and the Epicurean Philosophers*, (New York: Random House, 1940), p. 31 (the Epicurus fragments are translated by C. Bailey).

9 Oates, *op. cit.*, Epicurus, Letter to Menoeceus, p. 31.

10 *Ibid.*, p. 43.

11 *Ibid.* p. 31.

12 *Ibid.*

13 Lucretius, *On the Nature of the Universe*, translation by Ronald Latham (Baltimore: Penguin Books, 1951), book III, 61.

14 *Ibid.*, book III, 916.

15 Cicero, *De Finibus Bonorum et Malorum* (45 B.C.), VII, 28, 176.

16 Seneca, Letter to Lucilius, no. 70, in *The Stoic Philosophy of Seneca*, translated by Moses Hadas, (Garden City, N.Y.: Doubleday Anchor Books), pp. 202 ff.

17 Oates, *op. cit.*, Epictetus, *Discourses*, translated by P. E. Matheson, book I, chapter IX.

18 *Ibid.*, book I, chapter XXIV, 9.

19 Michel de Montaigne, *Essais*, edited by Albert Thibaudet, Bibliothèque de la Pléiade (Paris: Nouvelle Revue Francaise, 1946), book II, chapter 3.

20 René Descartes, *Oeuvres et Lettres*, Bibliothèque de la Pléiade (Paris: Gallimard, 1963), p. 1219.

21 *Ibid.*, p. 1220.

22 *Ibid.*, p. 1225.

23 Benedict de Spinoza, *Ethics*, IV, note to Proposition XX, in *The Chief Works of Benedict de Spinoza*, translated by R. H. M. Elwes (New York: Dover Press, 1951), vol. II, p. 203.

24 *Ibid.*

25 Baron Paul Henri Dietrich d'Holbach, *Systeme de la nature, ou les lois du monde physique et du monde moral* (1770); English translation *The System of Nature; or The Laws of the Moral and Physical World* (London, 1795); first American edition (New York, 1835).

26 Voltaire, "Of Suicide," in *Works*, translated by T. Smollett, 4th ed. (Dublin, 1772), vol. XVII, pp. 165 ff.

27 Montesquieu, *Persian Letters*, nos. 76 and 77, in *Complete Works* (London, 1777), vol. III.

28 Denis Diderot *et al.*, *Encyclopédie* (Classiques Larousse series).

29 Jean-Jacques Rousseau, *La Nouvelle Héloise* (Larousse).

30 David Hume, "On Suicide," *Essays, Moral, Political and Literary*, new ed. (New York: Oxford University Press, 1963), p. 590.

31 Immanuel Kant, *Metaphysik der Sitten* (Metaphysics of Morals) (1797), Part II.

32 Arthur Schopenhauer, *The World as Will and Idea*, translated by T. B. Haldane and J. Kemp (London: Routledge & Kegan Paul, 1883), vol. I, p. 362.

33 *Ibid.*, vol. I, p. 515.

34 *Ibid.*

35 *Ibid.*, *Parerga und Paralipomena*, 2nd part, chapter XIII, in Collected Works, 5 vols. (Leipzig: Inselverlag), vol. V, p. 332 ff.

36 Giacomo Leopardi, *Essays, Dialogues and Thoughts*, translated by James Thomson (New York, 1905).

37 "The Life of Plotinus by Porphyry," in Plotinus, *The Enneads*, vol. I.

38 Friedrich Nietzsche, "Letter to Malwida Meysenburg," January 14, 1880, in *Gesammelte Briefe* [Collected Letters], Elizabeth Förster-Nietzsche, Peter Gast *et al.*, eds., 5 vols. (Leipzig, 1900–1909); the same thought is expressed in *Die Unschuld des Werdens—Aus dem Nachlass* [The Innocence of Becoming—Posthumous Writings] (Stuttgart: Kröner Verlag, 1956), vol. I, p. 254.

39 Nietzsche, *Beyond Good and Evil (Jenseits von Gut und Böse*, 1886; Stuttgart: Kröner Verlag, 1953), aphorism 157, p. 89.

40 Nietzsche, *The Dawn of Day (Morgenröte*, 1881; Stuttgart: Kröner Verlag, 1953), p. 210.

41 Nietzsche, *Human All-Too-Human (Menschliches Allzumenschliches*, 1877–78; Stuttgart: Kröner Verlag, 1954), aphorism 88.

42 Nietzsche, *Thus Spake Zarathustra (Also Sprach Zarathustra*, 1883; Stuttgart: Kröner Verlag, 1956), part I, p. 76.

43 Nietzsche, *The Will to Power (Der Wille zur Macht*, 1888; Stuttgart: Kröner Verlag, 1952), p. 697.

44 Eduard von Hartmann, *Zur Geschichte und Begründung des Pessimismus* [History and Justification of Pessimism] (Berlin: Carl Dunker, 1880).

45 Eduard von Hartmann, *Ethische Studien* [Ethical Studies] (Leipzig: Hermann Haacke, 1898), p. 189.

46 Albert Camus, *The Myth of Sisyphus*, translated by Justin O'Brien (New York: Alfred A. Knopf, Vintage Books, 1955), p. 7.

47 *Ibid.*, p. 40.

48 *Ibid.*, p. 43.

49 Philip Thody, *Albert Camus* (New York: Grove Press, 1957), p. 12.

30 · Definitions of Suicide

Jack D. Douglas

*Jack D. Douglas is professor of sociology at the University of
California at San Diego. Douglas's book* The Social Meanings of
Suicide *is a scholarly contemporary treatise on suicide from a
sociological point of view. It can be called neo-Durkheimian in that
Douglas begins with a discussion of Durkheim's theories of
suicide and then expands his own position to make it more
comprehensive and more contemporary. In the following appendix
from that book, Douglas writes from a psychological point of view,
expanding the various dimensions of such concepts as initiation,
motivation, intention, volition, will, and willing, and synthesizing
psychological and sociological theory.*

From The Social Meanings of Suicide *by Jack D. Douglas.
Copyright © 1967 by Princeton University Press. "Appendix II," pp.
350–383, reprinted by permission of Princeton University Press.*

THE FORMAL DEFINITIONS OF "SUICIDE"

Suicide is clearly a subject of considerable interest to
many of the disciplines concerned with human behavior. As long as this is
simply the immediate, practical interest of preventing individual deaths, the
problem of defining "suicide" and any related terms is either unrecognized
or, if it is recognized, can be handled relatively simply: the definition can be
given ostensibly (i.e., in terms of the real-world cases that concern the
definer). However, as soon as one becomes concerned with the more abstract
problem of *explaining* suicide, he immediately faces the problem of giving
some reasonably clear and distinct definition to the term.

Even the most cursory survey of the vast literature on suicide will quickly
lead one to conclude that the students of suicide have not very often been
able to agree on how to define the term. Probably the basic reason for this
continual disagreement over the definition is the complex family of meanings
given to the term in Western culture by everyday usage and, consequently, by
all the forms of literature. There are, in fact, certain arguments over the
meaning of suicide that have not changed much throughout the entire
history of Western culture.[1]

There are, presumably, many other reasons as well for the proliferation of
different definitions of suicide in the literature. But the important point is
that these many definitions exist and that significant progress in this field of
study will continue to be greatly hampered until the students of suicide
become clearly aware of the many different potential meanings of the term
"suicide" and of the empirical and theoretical justifications normally given
for each fundamental dimension's being included in the definitions. The
following is an attempt to present these fundamental dimensions of meaning
and to analyze the justifications given for using "suicide" in each sense.

FUNDAMENTAL DIMENSIONS OF MEANINGS IN THE DEFINITIONS OF SUICIDE

JACK D. DOUGLAS

When one considers the many different conceptual treatments of suicide it becomes reasonably clear that there are several fundamentally independent but related dimensions that are included in different combinations and to varying degrees in most, if not all, of the definitions:[2]

1. the *initiation* of an act that leads to the death of the initiator;

2. the willing of an *act* that leads to the death of the willer;

3. the willing of self-destruction;

4. the loss of will;

5. the *motivation to be dead (or to die)* which leads to the initiation of an act that leads to the death of the initiator;

6. the *knowledge* of an actor that actions he initiates tend to produce the objective state of death.

These dimensions are not entirely "pure": some of them do overlap. But, they also seem to cover most of the important dimensions of meanings found in formal definitions of suicide in the Western world. They do not, however, completely cover such definitions. It is possible to give at least three other dimensions that have been given in formal definitions: (1) The degree of central integration of the decisions of an actor who decides to initiate an action that leads to the death of the actor; (2) the degree of firmness or persistibility of the decision (or willing) to initiate an act that leads to the death of the initiator; and (3) the degree of effectiveness of the actions initiated by the actor in producing his own death. The first of these is, in fact, of considerable historical importance because it covers most of the argument over whether or not "insane" individuals can commit suicide.[3] I have, however, chosen to exclude it from consideration for three reasons: first, the subject is immense in itself; second, modern students of suicide have largely agreed that it is not a worthwhile argument; and, third, we have considered some parts of the argument in our considerations of whether an individual can ever be rightly said to kill his "self." The other two are not given separate consideration because they occur infrequently and because they have been largely dealt with under the major dimensions.

1. Suicide as the initiation of an act leading to one's own death

The act initiated need not be an act that leads directly to one's death. Indeed, the act may simply be an act that *objectively* places the actor's life in danger, whether he wills it or not, whether he knows it or not.[4] There are varying degrees of *objective indirection* or *uncertainty*[5] possible in the sequence of actions initiated by an actor that objectively places his life in jeopardy, whether the end result is death or not.

This dimension covers about the broadest range of referents of any of the dimensions used in the definition of suicide. In some ways it would certainly seem on *prima facie* grounds to cover too much to be of much value in a theory of suicide. The *initiation of the act* may well be a *necessary* dimension in the definition, but it does not distinguish between something called "suicide" and phenomena called "accidents" and "mistakes." Such a general definition would hardly seem useful for any theory other than one that is concerned with the cosmological forces leading to an individual's blind fulfillment of his fate.[6] But, on more careful consideration, it would seem that there are three excellent reasons for retaining this most general conceptual dimension for at least potential use in the theory of suicide.

First, there are many cases of *ego-initiated death* (or near death) in which it would be very difficult, if not impossible, to show that the individual had *intended* consciously to kill himself or had *decided to die* by his own actions; yet it can be shown that the individual has nearly killed himself many times by deadly acts; and, furthermore, that the individual has many motives toward death. Consider, for example, a case of attempted "suicide" (i.e., ego-initiated deadly acts) studied by Zeckel. This twenty-four-year-old girl almost succeeded in killing herself with gas, yet "when conscious she said she could not remember intending to commit suicide." She does remember, however, several previous experiences of fugues and amnesias. Her deadly act occurred after a (psychosomatic?) coughing spell which seems associated with her guilt feelings about an attack of asthma that sent her fiancé to the hospital. This guilt response is very similar to certain very strong guilt responses she learned as a child in her relation to her father.[7] Such guilt feelings might well have produced the fugue state in which she initiated the act that nearly killed her. Such a fugue state might, indeed, be a necessary factor in her initiation of a deadly act against herself; for, while conscious, her values and fears might have effectively blocked the act. A definition of suicide (and attempted suicide) as necessarily being the result of a *conscious* or *intentional* or *knowledgeable decision* would immediately exclude such extremely interesting phenomena as found in Zeckel's case. Such phenomena may, of course, be quite anomalous; but it is precisely these extreme and rare phenomena that frequently add most to our understanding.

The second justification concerns the age-old argument as to whether animals commit suicide or any form of "self destruction." Some students of suicide have maintained that only one man can commit suicide because, as Montaigne said, "Only man can hate himself." Most have maintained that animals cannot commit suicide because they cannot *know* of the relations between their acts and the consequences of their acts.[8] Such arguments may well hold in considerations of lemming marches to the sea or of mythical, incestuous horses; but there are some extremely well-documented (even experimental) cases of animal "self-destructive" behavior. Consider, for example, the case of the Macacus Rhesus Monkey named Cupid.[9] Cupid was conditioned to be dependent on Psyche (a Macacus Cynomologus monkey) and to have a monogamous sexual relationship with her. He was then conditioned, though with some and only partial success, to have a sexual relationship with Topsy (a Macacus Rhesus). Then Psyche was returned to Cupid, who resumed their sexual relation, but with a good bit of attention to almost immediately began biting his foot and lacerating his body. This "self-destructive" behavior seems very definitely related to a high degree of conflict, possibly even "guilt"; and there can be no doubt that he quickly learned the relation between biting and torn (painful) flesh. That this response is similar to many "appeal" attempted suicides[10] of human beings is seen in the fact that Cupid would only bite and lacerate himself when being *looked* at by Topsy or the experimenter. There is further evidence, of an even more carefully controlled experimental nature, that animals do, both partially and wholly, destroy themselves in situations very similar to those in which human beings destroy themselves. The Russian psycho-physiologists, for example, have found that as the degree of neurotic conflict (and consequent neurotic disorganization) increases in animals subjected to neurosis-inducing conditioning, the tendency to "self-referent" behavior, which is largely "self-destructive," increases.[11] Such behavior is remarkably similar to hypereridism[12] in human beings. Since such animal behavior is more subject to experimentation than similar human behavior, there is excellent reason for attempting to determine precisely the similarities rather than defining such data on animals out of consideration of the theory of suicide.

It should be noted, of course, that the *failure to initiate acts* that are objectively necessary to life is as important to this definitional dimension of suicide as the *positive* initiation of acts.[13] Simone Weyl's refusal to eat enough to keep herself alive during World War II was intended to heighten her identification with the suffering people of her homeland, France. But this negative act, this not eating, is certainly an initiation of acts that indirectly led to her death, especially since she initiated acts against the acts of attending doctors.[14]

2. Suicide as the willing of an act that leads to the death of the willer

The conceptual dimension of willing a deadly act, which is more or less equivalent to the *intention* to kill the self, is certainly one of the most frequently given as a necessary and (less frequently) sufficient definition of suicide. Halbwachs' definition, for example, includes the dimension *of intention* as necessary (though not sufficient).[15] The justification for this definition lies in the conception of the *self* or the individual's *being* as essentially *volitional*. The argument has generally been vague, but the fundamental line of reasoning seems simple enough:

1. suicide is synonymous with "the destruction of the self by the self";
2. the *self* is the *willing* or *volitional* factor of mind (-body);
3. therefore, suicide is synonymous with "the destruction of the will by the will" (or the intentional destruction of one's self).

Of course, since the will was generally considered to be distinct from the body, it would be necessary to add the factor of willed *acts* and to speak of suicide as the *willing of a state of the world* that acts back upon the will to destroy it:

No entity can lose a character by virtue of a reflexive act which presupposes the presence of that character. It is thus incorrect to speak of a man taking his own life; one should rather speak of his putting himself in a state so that his life can be taken from him. . . . By itself (a living being) forms a closed system. . . . It cannot by an act of its own produce the Relative Nothing which is its negation.[16]

In these conceptions of suicide as the willing of acts that lead to the willer's destruction, we are presented with the problem of *unity* of the self. Since the will was normally considered to be *unitary*, conceptions of suicide as *willing* the destruction of the *will* (i.e., *self*) run into the problem of explaining how a unity can be against itself. But these problems will be considered later, especially under the section concerned with the degree of central integration.

In considering the dimension of *intention* (or willing) in the initiation of acts that lead to one's death (or near death) it is most important to note that there are specific cases of self-initiated death in which the victim is, in a very real sense, the *victim of himself*. In these cases the individual *knows* that he is killing himself and *wills*, as far as can be determined, to stop himself from killing himself, but to no avail. Consider, for example, the case of a young English mother who continued to suffer intermittent attacks of depression even after a prefrontal leucotomy. She initiated deadly but unsuccessful acts against herself three times during depression. She realized (or *believed*, if one wishes to be sceptical) that she had strong impulses to kill herself and fought against them. She expressed confidence that she would be able to stop herself in any new attempts because she had in the first three attempts. But in a fourth initiation of a deadly act against herself (aspirin consumption) she died.[17] Such cases frequently involve *compulsion* and/or *hysteria*.[18] Compulsion especially seems to be a very important factor in producing the non-intentional, *partial and progressive* initiation of acts over a number of years that lead to one's death. Arthur Rimbaud is an example of a man who spent a lifetime doing a great number of things that progressively destroyed him; yet his sole (conscious) *intention* in all of these acts was to find security for himself. He seems to have realized after, and sometimes during, the acts that they were destroying him, yet he could not seem to stop himself from performing them.[19] At its greatest intensity a *compulsion* may turn reason to its support and certainly when a man is in the full possession of his compulsion he wills to live the compulsion even if it should result in his death. But it cannot be said that he has willed or intended the actions associated with the compulsion. He may fight these actions, may consider them utterly abhorrent and will to oppose them at all cost. Only when he has been swept up by the ecstasy of the doing does the will turn to the complete support of the compulsion:

Pure reason advised him to take this step. But pure reason has its sophistries; in this case it was in league with his lurking passion. The hope of winning a return to Russia at roulette may well have been the immediate pretext that brought him to the casino again; but what held him there afterward was the irresistible attraction of gambling itself. For once he had begun, it did not matter whether he won or lost; every incident, every circumstance at the gaming table served him equally as a fresh stimulus to go on gambling. If he won, his winning was a sign to go on; if he lost, he could not rest until he had won back his losses. "The principal thing is the game itself," he confessed.

To his three afflictions—exile, poverty, and illness—there was added a fourth: the obsessive passion for gambling that had its source in the depths of his own nature. It was this that completed the doom of his life in exile.

As in a Greek tragedy, from then on all evil hazards intertwined, all the conflicts mounted inexorably toward disaster. As though the hostile goddess of fate, Ate, were punishing him for the *Hybris* with which he attempted to bend fortune to his will, his pursuit of a coup at roulette carried him headlong to destruction. . . .

He had already passed through many an inferno; but this moral hell into which he was driven by his "cursed vice" and his "all to passionate nature" was worse than anything else. Tormented by shame and repentance, he resolved again and again to leave off gambling, that "diabolical possession, that self-poisoning" by his own imagination, and to live at Anya's side for his work alone. "I shall have only the one goal in view; to finish the novel swiftly and successfully. I will put my whole soul into the work. If it succeeds, we are saved."

But he could not escape.[20]

There are, then, cases of ego-initiated acts that kill ego (with varying degrees of *directness*) without ego's willing or intending to perform the acts, nevertheless willing to kill himself. These cases seem of potentially great value for a theory of suicide and self-destruction. It would seem, therefore, that the dimension of *willing* or *intending* an act that leads to the death of the willer should not be considered a *necessary* dimension of suicide; yet it would be unwise to overlook the significance of this dimension for the theory of suicide.

Some students of suicide have assumed that there exists some continuum relationship between the most fleeting thought or image of suicide and the act of committing suicide.[21] The continuum relationship is generally thought to be determined by lesser and greater degrees of *intent* to kill oneself. Other students have tried to show that attempted suicides are further or closer to the act of suicide in terms of the *degree of lethality of the attempt*, which is thought to be determined by the degree of *intent* to act in a manner that will lead to one's death.[22] Such a very close relation between intention and action has not actually been found in studies of ego-initiated deadly acts. In their study of English mental patients, for example, Stengel and Cook found that:

1. only among the (medically determined) "absolutely dangerous" attempts is the degree of intent maximal in a majority of cases;
2. in one-fifth of the "absolutely dangerous" attempts there is only medium intent;
3. serious intent is frequently associated with only a medium danger;
4. lowest danger is generally associated with medium to low intent;
5. degree of danger in attempt varies (partially independently of degree of intent) with respect to mental disorder syndrome.[23]

But, at the same time that intention and danger of attempt cannot be shown to vary with respect to each other in more than a roughly monotonic fashion, there is, nevertheless, ample evidence to suggest that intention, as determined by the previous *expression* and *demonstration* of intention, is generally present to some degree in those who initiate actions that kill themselves.

But, if there is no proof of a strictly monotonic relation between degree of *intent* and degree of danger of the act initiated by ego against himself, there is, nevertheless, some evidence that those who die by their own acts have most frequently given previous *expressions* of *intention* to kill themselves:

1. in a retrospective study of suicide in a VA hospital from 1949–1959, Pokorny found that only eleven of the forty-four had given no previous *expression of intention* to commit suicide; of the thirty-five, seven had attempted suicide before;[24] eight gave indirect "hints," and eight very direct expressions of intention to commit suicide;[25]
2. in a study of 152 New Hampshire mental patients who committed suicide in 1955–56, Vail found that fifty-three per cent had made either overt expressions of intention to commit suicide or had made previous "attempts."[26]

Of course, it is most important to note that the studies of Pokorny and Vail do not contain controls so that there may be an equally large (or even larger) population who *express an intention* to commit suicide, to initiate deadly acts against themselves, but do not actually do so. Indeed, in a study of "attempted suicides" and "suicide threats" in a VA Mental Hospital Farberow found both great personality differences between the two populations and great differences in their *actions*. Most of those who threaten to commit suicide do not actually do so. Some, however, very definitely do.[27]

We are, then, left uncertain as to the relations between expressions of intent, actual intent, and actions. In such matters it seems best to take the counsel of Schneider: "We see it as dangerous to try to establish at all cost any straight agreement between the act of suicide and the thoughts and motives of suicide."[28] Gaupp and others had previously established the necessity of distinguishing between "motives" ("the reasons which appear in the consciousness of the person in question") and "causes" ("the driving powers behind the act which very often do not become conscious").[29] We have seen here that we must distinguish not only between "subjective estimates" and "objective estimates" of the *causes* of suicide, but also between "subjective estimates" and *actions* and between actions and *consequences* (degree of danger, etc.). Some researchers have, indeed, considered intention to be most generally characteristic of suicide, but have implied that the term "suicide" is actually descriptive of actions rather than intention itself: "Some people undoubtedly commit suicide by 'accident,' i.e., as the result of a suicidal gesture that miscarried."[30] This conceptual approach is quite different from that of the researchers who consider *intention* a necessary dimension of suicide. These latter researchers would exclude any such phenomena as "accidental suicide," though they might consider them to be "pseudocides."[31]

To distinguish between intended suicide and accidental suicide that results from dangerous actions initiated by ego with the intention of eliciting a response (e.g., sympathy or control) not only involves the assumption that the *meaning core* of "suicide" is the intention to die by one's own (positive or negative) actions, but also the assumption that *intention* is not merely a *willing* but a *decision* involving more or less *effective expectations*, both social and non-social.[32]

The students of suicide and attempted suicide have come increasingly to realize that suicidal phenomena can not only be *meaningful* in the Durkheimian sense (see below), but also in the sense that *the individuals performing these acts expect that their acts will not only have consequences upon their bodies but upon their relations to significant others as well—individuals committing dangerous acts against themselves are not only concerned with the past, with the loss of social ties or of a hated love object,[33] but also with the future.*

In a study in St. Louis of individuals who had committed dangerous acts against themselves Schmidt found that approximately 35% of them had previously communicated their *intention* to commit suicide. But, whereas Vail and Pokorny stopped with determining the "expression of intention," Schmidt determined the social targets of these communications to be friends and relatives in the vast majority of cases.[34] In an even more specific set of studies Jensen and Petty have tried to show that those committing dangerous acts against themselves very frequently intend a specific significant alter to save them. For example, one man who did succeed in killing by carbon-monoxide asphyxiation had left many notes around the house indicating the need to check the insurance and had left a Chekhov book open at a case of suicide. Jensen and Petty hypothesize that this man's "plans for rescue" failed because his wife failed to respond to all of the obvious cues.[35] Such cases would seem to indicate that many individuals who die by the acts they intend to perform may intend something very different from dying.[36] They may have decided to run the *risk* of dying from their acts in order, by their destructive actions, to produce certain responses on significant alters.[37]

3. The willing of self-destruction
The intention to destroy oneself as opposed to the intention simply to initiate actions that lead to the (objective) death of the individual (body) involves far

more of the problem of the *unity of the self.* If the self is considered to be unitary,[38] then the objections of Hegel, Weiss, and others to the idea of a *self negating itself* becomes far more significant. Most men who have considered *ego-initiated* deadly acts have considered the "self" to be, in some way, unitary, and have almost always agreed in some way that "there can be no possible suicide of our being." There were a few who considered the possibility that a unitary self might have death as its unitary (and, thus, "natural") end. Spinoza was one of those few:

> If it agreed better with a man's nature that he should hang himself, could any reason be given for his not hanging himself? Can such a nature possibly exist? If so, I maintain (whether I do or do not grant free will), that such an one, if he sees that he can live more conveniently on the gallows than sitting at his own table, would act most foolishly, if he did not commit suicide.[39]

Yet even Spinoza came to the conclusion that the unitary "self" cannot actually destroy itself, cannot will its own end: "All persons who kill themselves are impotent in mind, and have been thoroughly overcome by external causes opposed to their nature." The assumptions and reasoning behind Spinoza's conclusion that "self-destruction" is against the nature of man are very similar to those of Hegel: "Spinoza would see a death instinct as inadequate: the very nature of man is appetite (unconscious) and desire (conscious) . . . a death urge, an urge to return to no desire, is self contradictory."[40] As previously intimated, then, the reason for considering "self-destruction" to be impossible was not simply that the "self" was considered to be unitary, but that the "self" was considered to be *essentially will* or *willing.* "Self-destruction" on the most fundamental level would mean, then, that the will had willed non-willing, that intention had produced non-intention. This clearly seemed logically absurd as long as the "self" was assumed to be unitary over time. Of course, the denial of the logical possibility of "self-destruction" did not necessarily lead to a denial of the logical possibility of "suicide." As long as "suicide" was defined as an act against the body that objectively produced (body) death, it was quite logically possible, perhaps even most logically correct, to maintain that "suicide," rather than being a "self-destruction," is actually an affirmation of the self: "Suicide is a strong affirmation of the will to live, not a denial of will" (Schopenhauer).[41]

"Self-destruction" could, however, be shown to be logically possible (1) by denying that the "self" is essentially the "will" or "willing," or (2) by denying that the "self" is *unitary over time,* or (3) by denying the "self" to be fundamentally unitary.

Western thinkers found it almost impossible to escape the assumption that a man will not "will" what he knows to be "bad" for himself, i.e., in terms of the balancing of his own pleasure and pain expectations. To the Greeks and Romans suicide was preeminently a "rational" action intended to either increase one's happiness[42] or decrease one's unhappiness. There was hardly any thought of self-destruction.[43] As the "will" assumed an increasingly central position in the conception of the "self," the concept of "self-destruction" became increasingly logically contradictory.

The development of psychology and sociology in the nineteenth and twentieth centuries contributed a great deal to the unseating of the "will" from the core of man. The extreme "willfulness" of Faust, the Romantics, and the early nihilists has largely given way to an *externalized conception of man*, of which the *oversocialized* conception of man is only one type.[44] Some of the early sociologists, especially Max Weber, saw man as a *chooser* (and, thus, a "willer") in a pluralistic social universe;[45] but this partially-internal-and-partially-external conception of man has given way before an increasingly externalized conception of man by sociologists. This externalized conception of man has quite naturally led to a conception of the "self" in terms of "complementary expectations" which are considered to be "constitutive rather than merely regulative of human nature."[46]

Once the "self" has been divested of "will" and made over in the image of a social structure it can quite *logically* be hypothesized that "self-destruction" not only exists but is *directly* related to "status integration" or to "status deprivation." But such an approach cannot leave conceptual room for the question as to whether "status disintegration" is the *cause* of "self"-destruction or itself merely one possible outcome of personality developments that also produce "suicide."

Many psychologists and psychiatrists, especially psychoanalysts, use the term "self" as a core term in their theories; but they have come to use "self" to mean very much the same thing the externalizing sociologists mean by it.[47] An alternative term used to mean much the same thing is "identity," which is what Erikson has called a "psychoanalytic sociological" term.[48] Used in this sense "self-destruction" (or "identity-destruction") becomes not only logically possible, but is frequently considered to be the primary factor in suicide:

> ... the "wish to die" is only in those rare cases a really suicidal wish, where "to be a suicide" becomes an inescapable identity choice in itself.[49]

These psychological theorists did not, however, discard "will." "Will" has been increasingly incorporated into the concept of "ego,"[50] which has been considered to be the fundamental "choosing" factor that produces the "self" or the "identity":

> In this paper, we are concerned with the *genetic continuity* of such a self-representation—a continuity which must lastly be described to the work of the ego. No other inner agency could accomplish the selective accentuation of significant identifications throughout childhood; and the gradual integration of self-images in anticipation of an identity.[51]

The psychoanalysts do not consider "ego-destruction" to be any more logically possible than the philosophers and psychologists who used "self" to mean approximately the same thing as "ego" considered "self-destruction" to be logically possible. Their fundamental (largely implicit) assumptions concerning the *adaptive* nature of human choice have prevented their considering "ego-cide" or "ego-destruction" to be possible.

One type of psychological theory that has a great deal in common with psychoanalysis but which has partially broken through this *conceptual barrier* is *existential analysis*. In existential analysis an individual's *existence* covers not only *will* (or the fundamental *choice* functions) but also "self" (or "identity"); yet ego-initiated death, is considered to be not only possible but quite frequently actual:

> Existential analysis cannot be content with the psychological judgment that the suicide of Ellen West is to be explained by the motive of her suffering of torture and the wish arising therefrom to end this torture; nor can we be satisfied with the judgment that her festive mood in the face of death is to be explained by the motive of her anticipating the certain end of this torture and the joy over this end. These judgments fall back on the motive as a final basis for explanation, whereas for existential analysis the motives too are still problems. For us it remains a problem how to understand that these motives become effective, in other words, how they could become motives at all.
>
> From the standpoint of existential analysis the suicide of Ellen West was an "arbitrary act" as well as a "necessary event." Both statements are based on the fact that the existence in the case of Ellen West had become ripe for its death, in other words, that the death, this death, was the necessary fulfillment of the life-meaning of this existence. This can be demonstrated by existential analysis, but conclusive evidence calls for insight into the kind of temporality which this existence engendered.[52]

There is no conceptual contradiction involved in "existence-destruction," in part because the existence included not only "will" or "choice" but also the ongoing situation as experienced by the willer. This brings in the possibility (and, in the case of Ellen West, the actuality) of changes in the "self" (or "identity") over time, which brings us to the consideration of the logical status of "self-destruction" when the self is not *unitary over time*.

Jung is one of the psychologists who conceives of the "self" as unitary by definition. The "self" is the directive *mechanism* of the personality that holds together the many different and even conflicting tendencies of the personality. This "self" may even be one or a few dominant motives.[53] But Jung maintains that this "self" *may not be unitary over time*, that this unitary mechanism may be destroyed or may simply change (especially "oscillate") over time; and that this dissolution or change of the "self" over time may lead to suicide.[54]

Jung maintains that this tendency to suicide results largely from an internal conflict within the "self" (especially a conflict involving a *slight* predominance of introversion over extroversion), a conflict which tends to produce a very great deal of tension which, in turn, produces an "equivalence of alternative paths" of which suicide is one. Jung considers suicide to be the result of following a *decision-path* made up of links connected by critical junctures (decisions) which are determined by "feeling-values" that approach each other as the tension (affect) level increases.[55]

But, though Jung's *dynamic* conception of the "self" makes it logically possible for ego-initiated deadly acts to be the result of a destruction of one "self-concept" by another "self-concept," it would not seem that Jung's conception of the "self" would give rise to the logical possibility of a *"self" that decides against itself, that decides in favor of a loss to itself.*[56]

Alfred Adler's theory of suicide offers little more hope in this direction. Adler considers the individual personality to be dynamic, " . . . a unified and unique whole, at all times directed by one over-all striving . . . a striving for a goal of success."[57] Adler does consider suicide to be "a striving on the useless side,"[58] but this is an objectively determined "uselessness," not a subjectively realized loss to the "unified and unique whole." Indeed, Adler maintains most explicitly that the individual commits suicide to increase his gains, to win over significant others, especially the most significant other.

Freud's theory of suicide is both *instinctual* and *psycho-social*. On the instinctual level he conceived of suicide as a result of the triumph of the "death urge" *(Thanatos)* over the "life urge" *(eros)*. On the most fundamental level the ego is involved in a conflict between these two opposite urges; should the "death urge" win out, the *id* becomes directed toward death and suicide is the end result.[59] On the most fundamental level this death-directedness was even conceived of as a natural process of organic running-down, a process truly beyond the pleasure (and displeasure) principle.[60] Yet this does not mean that Freud considered "self-destruction" (i.e., "ego-destruction") to be an actuality. The instinctual death-directedness is confirmed to the libidinal level, the level "below" the "self" (or "ego").

On the psycho-social level Freud considered suicide to be the result of an *introjected conflict* between the libidinal motivation to kill a loved-and-hated object and the superego-founded guilt resulting from this motivation to kill, a guilt which is made ineluctable by the death of the loved-and-hated object.[61] Suicide is simply a self-initiated death that is either unconsciously or consciously drive-determined. Suicide is not seen as a decision by the ego or self to act destructively toward the self or ego. Rather, suicide involves the ego or self only insofar as the ego or self fails to resolve the conflict between the id and the superego.

Otto Rank's treatment of suicide is both quite similar and quite dissimilar to Freud's. Rank maintained that self-initiated death is the result of a fundamental conflict within the self or ego, a conflict between the fear of living and the fear of dying that is inborn as fear but learned as fear of:

> It seems, therefore, as if fear were bound up somehow with the purely biological life process and receives a certain content only with the knowledge of death. . . . The individual comes to the world with fear, and this inner fear exists independently of outside threats, whether of a sexual or other nature. It is only that it attaches itself easily to outer

experiences of this kind; but the individual makes use of them therapeutically since they objectify and make partial the general inner fear. Man suffers from a fundamental dualism, however one may formulate it, and not from a conflict created by forces in the environment that might be avoided by a "correct bringing-up" or removed by later reeducation (psychoanalysis).[62]

Rank believed that this "ambivalent conflict of life fear and death fear" produced, in neurotic extremes, an *action strategy* based on the bargaining of life for *non-death:* the neurotic individual inhibits his life and, thereby, slowly kills himself *in order to avoid death.* The basic goal which is the primary determinant of the individual's willing (or deciding) to inhibit life is that of *non-death.* The decision to seek this goal by this means may *incidentally* produce the individual's death, but death is not his goal. Moreover, the decision is quite in agreement with the pleasure or, rather, with the displeasure, principle. It would, then, seem that Rank's theory does not even go *beyond* the pleasure principle, to the extent that Freud's theory does; and Freud's theory merely circumvents the pleasure principle by hypothesizing most instinctual *tendencies*—though not individual behavior—to be independent of the pleasure-displeasure principle.

Most depth-psychological theories, then, lead one necessarily, by definition, to conclude that the individual cannot will the destruction of the self (or ego). Freud's theory allows for the destruction of the self as a result of willing in favor of the instinctual tendencies other than *eros,* which is the tendency to pleasure and away from displeasure. But even Freud believed that man decided fundamentally in favor of *eros,* if only he can come to know what will gratify *eros* and what will not. In going "beyond" the pleasure principle, Freud did not go against it: he did not believe that man could will self-displeasure or fight against self-pleasure for its own sake. Masochism led Freud and others to believe that men can and frequently do will suffering for the self, but they have seen this willing of self-suffering as being the result of expectations of "secondary gain," either through "victory through defeat"[63] or "less defeat through preemptive punishment."[64]

The identification of the self (or ego) with willing and the basic assumption (or theoretical principle) that willing is in the direction of pleasure and away from displeasure (or pain) have been two fundamental factors in the development of the theories of suicide. The identification of self with willing has made many definitions of suicide illogical and has led, as well, to narrowly restrictive "willful" definitions of suicide. The opposite—to exclude will from the determining factors of human action—has led to externalized definitions of suicide or the failure to give any definition of suicide other than "that which officials are supposedly counting when they make estimates of suicide rates." The tendency to assume, either explicitly or implicitly, that suicide involves willing and willing is determined by pleasure and pain has produced a strong hedonic strain in most theories of suicide, a strain which seems to grossly underestimate the complexity of human action.

The evidence clearly shows both factors to be of significance in determining actions initiated by an individual that lead to his own death. But there

375

JACK D. DOUGLAS

seems little justification for *defining* suicide in terms of them.

4. The definition of suicide in terms of the loss of will

There have been many reported cases of death resulting from a simple "giving up the ghost" or losing of the will to live:

> Death and all that belongs to it is full of significance to these people. They are not afraid of it *per se*, they have no dread of its approach; in fact, given provocative reasons, they welcome death. I have seen several young men and women lie down and die as anyone lies down and sleeps. It was not suicide by poison and they committed no violent act nor did anyone else; they just died.[65]

Cannon even attempted to explain voodoo deaths in terms of a psychic giving-up that results in physiological giving-up (i.e., endocrinological stress-response breakdown).[66]

The important question here, however, is the degree to which suicide is defined in terms of a loss of will as opposed to the degree to which the loss of will is hypothesized to be a cause of suicide: in general, it seems that there has been little tendency for theorists to slip into *defining* suicide in terms of the loss of will, though, as usual, there certainly exists a tendency for some theorists to misuse their terms in such a manner that they at least seem to be using such a definitional identification.

Theorists such as Kennan have suggested that there are some individuals who are quitters and that these quitters account for many suicides.[67] Bergler has hypothesized that inner passivity, masochistically tinged, is the primary causal factor producing suicide.[68] But such approaches do not lead to any definition of suicide in terms of a loss of will.

Davidson goes a bit further toward the identification of suicide with the loss of will, but he is really stating a theoretical relation between the two.[69] He maintains that at the point of suicide the individual has reached the limits of his resources and has lost his goals. The immediate situation acts as a "dominant" that restricts the field of consciousness to such an extent that there is inattention to life itself. Organic depression sets in and prevents the higher nervous system centers from complying with and controlling the incoming impulses in order to choose an action. The individual ceases to will, giving way to imagination, with the result that normal, automatic rejection of what is unhealthy fails.

Durkheim very briefly considered such giving-up suicides in a footnote.[70] He considered them to be a special *type* of suicide and called them *fatalistic suicides*. He was not delineating *giving-up* or *loss of will* as a potential causal factor in suicide. He was *defining* a special type that involved a failing to will that was known by the individual to be fatal. Death from ego-initiated acts that are fatalistic in nature were subsumed under the term of suicide.

The work of Lewis is an example of those theories which come close to *identifying* all suicide with the *loss of will*.[71] This tendency, especially in the case of Lewis, is largely the result of a biological approach to suicide in terms of the failure of the will to self-preservation. Such approaches seem to suffer from a simple inability to clearly recognize (or state) the difference between a *statement of identification* and a *statement of cause.* When Achille-Delmas says that suicide *is* "the perversion of the instinct of self-preservation" we can be rather sure from the context that he does not mean that they are synonymous, one and the same thing.[72] But when Lewis makes a very similar statement it is not clear from the context that he does not mean that suicide and the loss (or failure) of the will to live are the same thing.

There has been no adequate justification given thus far by any theorist for a definition of suicide in terms of a loss of will (to live or to anything). Efforts to do so largely slip into a definitional solution to the problems involved in explaining deaths resulting from ego-initiated acts. It is, of course, possible that the loss of will is important in causing suicide, but there is at present no reason to make the two synonymous.

5. Suicide defined in terms of the motivation to be dead which leads to the initiation of acts that lead to the death of the initiator

Such a definition of suicide is very similar to the colloquial conception of suicide as death resulting from a wish or desire to be dead. This definition is obviously very similar to the treatment of suicide in terms of the intention to die and the resulting acts and their consequences. The main difference is that a definition of suicide which involves the factor of motivation involves a postulated *affective association* between the expected consequences and the acts, whereas a definition simply in terms of intention may involve only the postulation of the *cognitive relation* between expectations and actions. It is important to recognize the clear distinctions between intention and motivation.[73] The distinction is at least of analytic and probably of concrete significance. For example, O'Neal's findings of greater "intention" to die by one's own acts in the aged[74] may be quite compatible with the hypothesis that the young are more motivated to die in their deadly acts but, as Yap has suggested, fail more because of the behavioral disturbances produced by the high affect involved.[75]

In general, many of the same criticisms may be made of the definition in terms of intentions. It should be noted, of course, that both are multi-dimensional definitions: each involves an internal state, external action, and the externally perceived consequence of death. Consequently, they both suffer from the disadvantage of any multi-dimensional definition: it is almost impossible to use it in a fundamental theory since the dimensions may covary independently of each other with respect to other variables.

Both Deshaies and Schneider recognized the theoretical necessity of considering the factor of *motivation to die* in their definition of suicide. They decided to include the dimensions of *act, consequence,* and *consciousness* in their definition, but specifically excluded any dimension of *motivation to die* as necessary: "Suicide is the act of killing oneself in a continually conscious manner, taking death as a means or as an end."[76] Schneider definitely does believe that *motivations* are of great importance in leading to suicide. He does not, however, believe that any *motivation to die,* any desiring of death as a goal in itself,[77] is involved in producing or leading to suicide. To include the dimension of the *motivation to die* in the definition of suicide would actually eliminate Schneider's entire theory.[78] But there is a more basic reason for their rejection of the dimension of motivation from the definition of suicide. Suicide is the variable to be explained, the dependent variable. It must, therefore, be easily observable, easily measured by sense perceptions. To Schneider, as to almost all theorists, the *actions* are *givens* (or *easily gottens*) by sense perceptions; and one seeks to explain these givens by finding unseen variables, or *inferred variables*, that come before the givens, the *act-states*.[79] It can be objected, of course, that the inclusion of the factor of consciousness in the definition of suicide largely vitiates this purpose; and there seems to be a good bit of truth to this charge. Surely the specification of consciousness (or of knowledge) is already the first step in giving an explanation in the above sense. The justification, of course, lies in the greater definitional purity achieved by cutting away unconscious or accidental acts, presumably with the expectation that this greater definitional purity will lead to a more valid theory. The inclusion of the factor of consciousness has many of the same difficulties as the factor of intention—such as the exclusion of phenomena that very clearly involve the other two dimensions (of deadly act and deadly consequence) but only minimally or not at all the factor of consciousness. But it should further be noted here that the inclusion of any factor that links the individual's acts and their consequences to an internal state has already set the stage by definition for a theory in terms of motivation[80] and, of course, especially in terms of motivation to die or to be dead. Such definitional stage setting is, of course, an integral part of any highly developed theory applied to a highly worked-over field of phenomena; but it is most important that the highly differentiated and complexly integrated field of observations be the guides to the definitions and not the definitions the guides to observation and theory.

6. The knowledge of an actor that actions he initiates tend to produce the objective state of death

In the twentieth century most psychiatrists and psychologists who have studied suicide have tended to define the term in terms of intention, motivation, willing, or similar terms. Sociologists, on the other hand, have tended to assume, either implicitly or explicitly, that Durkheim's definition was the only correct one. Like the psychiatrists and psychologists, Durkheim assumed that suicide must be limited to deaths which are in some way meaningful to the social actors initiating the actions that result in their deaths. However, whereas the psychiatrists and psychologists have been primarily concerned with volitional or affective meanings, presumably because of their conviction that suicidal actions are the result of one's volitional or affective state, Durkheim and sociologists have generally tried to limit the meanings entirely to the cognitive meanings:

> Suicide, we say, exists indeed when the victim at the moment he commits the act destined to be fatal, knows the normal result of it

with certainty. This certainty, however, may be greater or less. Introduce a few doubts, and you have a new fact, not suicide but closely akin to it, since only a difference of degree exists between them. Doubtless, a man exposing himself knowingly for another's sake but without the certainty of a fatal result is not a suicide, even if he should died, any more than the daredevil who intentionally toys with death while seeking to avoid it, or the man of apathetic temperament who, having no vital interest in anything, takes no care of health and so imperils it by neglect. Yet these different ways of acting are not radically different from true suicide. They result from similar states of mind, since they also entail mortal risks not unknown to the agent, and the prospect of these is no deterrent; the sole difference is a lesser chance of death. Thus the scholar who dies from excessive devotion to study is currently and not wholly unreasonably said to have killed himself by his labor. All such facts form a sort of embryonic suicide, and though it is not methodologically sound to confuse them with complete and full suicide, their close relation to it must not be neglected.[81]

Durkheim had three major reasons for defining suicide in terms of knowledge and it seems worthwhile to give some brief consideration to each justification.

First, and probably most important for Durkheim, there was the methodological reason: Durkheim believed that intention (and, presumably, any factor of will or emotion) is much too subtle to infer on any large scale. This argument had some very serious consequences for Durkheim's whole work on suicide,[82] but he is clearly right in arguing that intention and willing are more difficult to infer than is knowledge of consequences. In fact, it seems clear that most definitions in terms of emotion or will or intention involve both the assumption that knowledge of consequences can be inferred and an additional assumption that willing or feeling about the consequences can be inferred. On the other hand, Durkheim seems to have been clearly wrong in thinking that the difficulty in inferring knowledge of consequences is of a different order from inferring the other kinds of information. It simply involves less information of the same type (information about what is "in the head" of the social actor), so that it has what Durkheim otherwise considered to be a grave disadvantage: it was highly inclusive. Durkheim's implicit assumption in his argument seems clearly to be that the act of suicide must be treated as something very rational, so that the student of suicide can simply reason about whether or not any man of average rationality would know that certain actions lead with a high degree of certainty to death. If one actually considered only cases of self-initiated death in which the individual was acting quite "rationally," there would be relatively few cases to consider, so that one would have *defined* the problems out of existence.

Second, Durkheim was very concerned with eliminating accidental deaths from consideration, while including all other self-initiated deaths. Durkheim believed that all knowledgeable "renunciations of life" constitute a class of phenomena for scientific investigation:

Whether death is accepted merely as an unfortunate consequence, but inevitable given the purpose, or is actually itself sought and desired, in either case the person renounces existence, and the various methods of doing so can be only varieties of a single class. They possess too many essential similarities not to be combined in one generic expression, subject to distinction as the species of the genus thus established. Of course, in common terms, suicide is pre-eminently the desperate act of one who does not care to live. But actually life is none the less abandoned because one desires it at the moment of renouncing it; and there are common traits clearly essential to all acts by which a living being thus renounces the possession presumably most precious of all. Rather, the diversity of motives capable of actuating these resolves can give rise only to secondary differences. Thus, when resolution entails certain sacrifice of life, scientifically this is suicide; of what sort shall be seen later.

The common quality of all these possible forms of supreme renunciation is that the determining act is performed advisedly; that at the moment of acting the victim knows the certain result of his conduct, no matter what reason may have led him to act thus. All mortal facts thus characterized are clearly distinct from all others in which the victim is either not the author of his own end or else only its unconscious author.[83]

Such a rationalistic argument as this tends to be confusing: on the surface it might well seem reasonable, yet it is not satisfying. The fundamental problem is simply that Durkheim did not give any justification for treating the "knowledgeable renunciation of life" as the only boundary determinants of a class of phenomena. Why not argue with Halbwachs that an action that takes death as a means is categorically different from one that takes death as an end in itself? Durkheim's method of determining what constitutes a class of phenomena seems to have been simply choosing whatever seemed to him reasonable, without specifying why it seemed reasonable. This is not a very valuable method of defining a theoretical variable.

Third, Durkheim seems to have believed that common usage of the term suicide was in agreement with his definition and that this constituted a reason for rejecting any definition in terms of intention:

Indeed, if the intention of self-destruction alone constituted suicide, the name suicide could not be given to facts which, despite apparent differences, are fundamentally identical with those always called suicide and which could not be otherwise described without discarding the term.[84]

This seems to be an assumption that the term has a *necessary meaning* that the scientist must get at, rather than a meaning which he gives it, and that Durkheim's definition is the only one that has gotten at the necessary meaning. As we have already noted, officials in the nineteenth and in the twentieth centuries have generally thought that intention or volition is a part of the everyday meaning of the term and they have used it in that way. Most people in everyday life probably use the term similarly. Consequently, it is hard to see what Durkheim could mean in arguing that those acts always called suicide have the properties he has attributed to the term suicide but not the property of intention. Presumably, he simply did not look carefully enough at the way in which the term is used.[85]

Thus, using "suicide" to mean self-initiated death with knowledge of consequences but without the constraint of establishing intention is not satisfactory. On the other hand, it should be clear that knowledge and intention (or will, etc.) can vary independently and must be treated independently. This brings us to the conclusion of our whole argument.

CONCLUSION

Most students of suicide who have taken the problem of defining suicide seriously have tried to specify some *fundamentum divisionis* of the phenomena *which they have already implicitly accepted as being the relevant phenomena on the basis of everyday usage of the term.* Their failure to recognize that their definitions are thus already partially determined by the everyday meanings has led to a great deal of confusion. Instead of recognizing that their realm of phenomena has been primarily determined by the everyday, *concrete* meanings of the term (especially as used by officials and doctors), with the consequence that their attempts to specify a *fundamentum divisionis* is partially predetermined by these everyday, concrete meanings, the students of suicide have tried to analyze these predetermined phenomena in terms of *ad hoc, abstract criteria (e.g., homogeneity) of what constitutes a* fundamentum divisionis *in any science.* The *ad hoc* nature of the selection of these criteria has been largely unrecognized by the students of suicide; each student has felt that there is something *inherently, necessarily* correct about his own criteria. The result has been endless, confusing, unresolvable arguments over defining suicide.

Moreover, the students of suicide have usually ignored the question of the *theoretical value* of their definitions (except insofar as the whole idea of a *fundamentum divisionis* is seen to constitute, or reveal the way to *the* most theoretically valuable definition of terms). They have not apparently considered the possibility that even if they were able to arrive at some systematic set of pure (or disjunct) definitions to cover the "relevant" phenomena, these definitions could still prove quite useless in building any worthwhile theories. It would seem instead that *the best strategy in such scientific work is to develop observations, descriptions, definitions, measurements, and theories simultaneously, each molding the other.*

Making use of our discussions of the many attempts to define "suicide," applying the strategy just proposed to the matter of defining "suicide," and accepting as we have argued in this work that the everyday meanings of "suicide" are not merely *implicit* determinants of our definitions of "suicide" (as in earlier works) but are themselves information of the first importance, we can arrive at some conclusions about the definitions of "suicide" that should prove useful in studying "suicide."

First, a student of suicide should not expect to *begin* with a clear and distinct definition of what he is studying: he must begin with open-ended, largely unexpressed definitions (or meanings) of suicide. He must begin with his own (and other's) common-sense or everyday understanding of the term.

Second, he must attempt at once to determine just what these everyday meanings are; but he must try to determine these *concretely*, that is, the way the term(s) is used in the treatment of actual cases.

Third, his increasingly formal definition(s) of suicide (i.e., his attempts to close this open-ended approach to defining the term) must be made within the context of attempts to explain the suicidal phenomena: explanation and definition must modify each other.

Notes

1 For example, the arguments of Augustine and his opponents concerning whether "martyrs" were "suicides" involved almost the same disagreements found in the arguments between Durkheim, Halbwachs, and others over whether "self-sacrifices" are to be considered "suicides." (On Augustine see W. E. H. Lecky, *History of European Morals from Augustus to Charlemagne*, New York: Braziller, 1955. For a résumé of the twentieth-century dispute see G. Deshaies, *Psychologie du Suicide*, Paris: Presses Universitaires de France, 1947, pp. 4–5.)

2 Karl Menninger (*Man Against Himself*, New York: Harcourt, Brace, and Company, 1938) has tried to show that *every* suicide has (to different degrees) a desire (a) to die, (b) to kill, and (c) to be killed. Such attempts to deal with the most *fundamental* necessary and sufficient dimensions of all suicides are rare in the literature on suicide. Frequently the most fundamental dimensions of *description* and *decision making* are thrown into a pastiche of factors that includes supposed causes such as "loss of a family member at an early age" or "unresolvable conflict." (See, for example, Ruth S. Cavan, *Suicide*, Chicago: University of Chicago Press, 1928).

3 This was the major concern with the definition of suicide in the nineteenth century.

4 The popular use of "suicide" is frequently of this sort. See, for example, H. W. Rose, *Brittany Patrol: The Story of the Suicide Fleet*, New York: Norton, 1937; and W. Westover, *Suicide Battalions*, New York: Putnam's, 1929.

5 This *objective* uncertainty must be distinguished very clearly from the *subjective* (decisional) uncertainty of number (6), the sort of decisional uncertainty that Durkheim recognized in his considerations of the definition of suicide (see below).

6 Some students of suicide have, to be sure, been largely concerned with just such a factor as "fate," though generally it is a natural-selection mediated "fate." See, for example, N. D. C. Lewis, "Studies on Suicide," *Psychoanalytic Review*, xx (July, 1933) 241–273; and *Psychoanalytic Review*, xxi (April, 1934) 146–153.

7 A. Zeckel, "Hypnotherapy in a Case of Amnesia with Suicide Attempt," *Psychiatric Quarterly*, 25 (1951), pp. 484–499. It is an unanswered question as to whether this girl was conscious when turning on the gas and has since repressed the memory or was unconscious at the time of the act. I have inferred, contrary to Zeckel's unsupported assumption, that this was a fugue state, not merely amnesia.

8 See, for example, Durkheim's argument against the "suicide" of Aristotle's incestuous horse (Emile Durkheim, *Suicide: A Study in Sociology* [1897], tr. by J. A. Spaulding and G. Simpson, New York: The Free Press, 1951, p. 45).

   In a similar vein, Hegel has said, "I possess my life and my body only in so far as my will is in them; *an animal cannot maim or destroy itself, but a man can.*" (T. M. Knox, *Hegel's Philosophy of Right*, Oxford, 1942, p. 43).

9 This case is reported in O. L. Tinklepaugh, "The Self-Mutilation of a Male Macacus Rhesus Monkey," *Journal of Mammology*, 9 (1928).

10 See E. Stengel and N. G. Cook, *Attempted Suicide*, London: Oxford University Press, 1958; and N. L. Farberow and E. S. Shneidman, *The Cry for Help*, New York: McGraw-Hill, 1961.

11 L. N. Norkina, "The Production of Experimental Neurotic States in the Lower Apes," in Reprinted, Translated from Russian: *The Central Nervous System and Human Behavior*, U.S. Department of Health, Education, and Welfare, 1960, pp. 718–727.

12 See P. M. Yap, "Hypereridism and Attempted Suicide in Chinese," *Journal of Nervous and Mental Disease*, 127 (July, 1958), pp. 34–41.

13 See Durkheim's discussion of *positive* and *negative* acts in *Suicide*, p. 42.

14 Some students of suicide have called this negative initiation of acts "physiological suicide." See G. N. Raines and S. V. Thompson, *Suicide: Some Basic Considerations*, U.S. Naval Hospital, Bethesda, Md., 1950.

15 M. Halbwachs, *Les Causes du Suicide*, Paris: Felix Alcan, 1930, pp. 451–480.

16 P. Weiss, *Reality*, Princeton, New Jersey: Princeton University Press, 1938, p. 167.

17 See Case 20 in E. Stengel and N. G. Cook, *Attempted Suicide*, pp. 73–74.

18 See G. Zilboorg's discussion of compulsion and hysteria in cases of "suicide" in "Differential Diagnostic Types of Suicide," *Archives of Neurology and Psychiatry*, 35 (January, 1936) pp. 270–291.

19 See Henry Miller, *The Time of the Assassins*, London: Spearman, 1956. This work is a brilliant critical biography of Rimbaud and his work. Miller specifically maintains that Rimbaud spent his adult life destroying himself.

20 René Fueloep-Miller, *Fyodor Dostoevsky*, New York: Scribner's, 1950, pp. 25, 28, 29.

21 For a discussion of such factors see P. B. Schneider, *La Tentative de Suicide*, Paris: Delachaux, 1954, pp. 9–43.

22 See, for example, C. Catalano-Nobili and G. Cerquetelli, "Il Suicido: Studio Statistico e Psicopatologico," *Rassegna di Neuro-Psichiatr.*, 4 (1950) pp. 22–87.

23 E. Stengel and N. G. Cook, *Attempted Suicide*. It might be noted that from a study of six hundred "attempted suicides" at Bellevue H. Hendin estimated that one-third of the men and one-half of the women had a minimum *actual intent* to kill themselves. ("Attempted Suicide: A Psychiatric and Statistical Study," *Psychiatric Quarterly*, 24 [1950], pp. 39–46.) But the basis for Hendin's estimates is unclear.

24 From the above discussion, of course, it is obvious that an attempt to "commit suicide" cannot be used directly to infer any intent—unless one is being merely tautologous.

25 A. D. Pokorny, "Characteristics of Forty-Four Patients Who Subsequently Committed Suicide," *Archives of General Psychiatry*, 2 (March, 1960) pp. 314–323.

26 D. J. Vail, "Suicide and Medical Responsibility," *American Journal of Psychiatry*, May (1959) pp. 1006–1010.

27 N. L. Farberow, "Personality Patterns of Suicidal Mental Hospital Patients," *Genetic Psychology Monographs*, XLII (1950) 3–79.

28 P. B. Schneider, *op. cit.*

29 See K. G. Dahlgren, *On Suicide and Attempted Suicide*, Lund, 1945. pp. 19–20. It is very interesting to note what Lichtenberg said concerning these matters as early as 1799:

> If suicides gave their reasons for the act in set terms, not much light would be thrown on the matter. But this is precisely what everyone who hears of a suicide tries to do. All he really accomplishes is to reduce the case to his own language, thus making it something different from the reality. (G. C. Lichtenberg, "Reflections.")

30 P. G. Daston and G. A. Sakheim, "Prediction of Successful Suicide from the Rorschach Test, Using a Sign Approach," *Journal of Projective Techniques*, 24 (December, 1960) pp. 355–362.

31 F. Lendrum ("A Thousand Consecutive Cases of Suicide," *American Journal of Psychiatry*, 13 [1933], pp. 479–500), for example, excluded seven "pseudocides" from his study of Detroit "attempted suicides."

32 It is of interest to note here that Kant maintained that the mind is reducible to three fundamental faculties: (1) the faculty of *knowledge*, (2) the faculty of *feeling* pleasure and pain, and (3) the faculty of *desire*. (See *Critique of Judgment*, Oxford: Oxford University Press, 1952, pp. 4 and 15.) Most of the fundamental definitions of "suicide" consider the operation of one of the faculties to be critical: (1) Durkheim favored "knowledge," (2) Lendrum *et al.*, "desire," (3) Schilder *et al.* ("Death and Dying," *Psychoanalytic Review*, 70 [1933], pp. 135–185), pleasure and displeasure. It is only with the introduction of *decision* or choice that "monistic-faculty" theories are transcended.

33 Almost all psychoanalytic theories are as deficient in this respect as Durkheim's theory, but Sandor Rado is a great exception: see his discussion of the "appeal" nature of "melancholia" and "suicide" in *Psychoanalysis of Behavior*, New York: Grune and Stratton, 1956, pp. 40–46.

34 E. H. Schmidt, *et al.*, "Evaluation of Suicide Attempts as a Guide to Therapy," *Journal of the American Medical Association*, 155 (June 5, 1954), pp. 549–557.

35 V. W. Jensen and T. A. Petty, "The Fantasy of Being Rescued in Suicide," *Psychoanalytic Quarterly*, XXVII (1958) 327–39. Jensen and Petty have even given a detailed description of a chronic paranoid schizophrenic who "committed suicide" only after having made three unsuccessful "attempts to be rescued."

36 Actually, of course, this has long been recognized by many observers. Consider, for example, the statement by Ximenes Doudon, a French Romantic: "I do not say that it is cowardly to kill oneself, because that moral antithesis has always made me laugh, but I do say that there is a desire to create an impressing, personally experienced justification." Quoted in O. Brachfeld, *Inferiority Feelings*, New York: Grune and Stratton, 1951, p. 130.

37 See J. M. A. Weiss, "The Gamble with Death in Attempted Suicide," *Psychiatry*, 20 (1957), pp. 17–25.

38 Quite obviously, few men who have considered the "self" (or the "soul" as many earlier students called it) to be unitary have considered the "self" to be *monolithic*. They have considered the "self" to be made up of many parts, but of parts which in some way make up a whole, a unity.

39 Spinoza, *Correspondence with Blyenbergh*, XXXVI.

40 L. S. Feuer, *Spinoza and the Rise of Liberalism*, Boston: Beacon Press, 1958, p. 213. That Spinoza's view is still held by some can be easily seen from a few statements by O. Lodge in a recent *Fortnightly Review:* "Surely no one wishes to injure his essential self. . . . Self injury is unnatural though in certain moods it is possible."

41 Quoted in J. Sully, *Pessimism*, London: Henry and King, 1877.

42 Cleombrotus is probably the best example of a Greek's killing himself to increase his happiness: "And he who, to enjoy Plato's Elysium, leaped into the sea, Cleombrotus." (Milton, *Paradise Lost*, Bk. III)

"Suicide is *unlawful* when committed for the sake of the body, but rational when committed for the sake of the soul, since this is sometimes advantageous to it." (Plotinus, *First Ennead*, Bk. 9.)

43 It is of interest to note that even the Apostle said that "No one ever hated his own flesh." (Discussed by A. Girard *et al.*, in "Justice" in *The Virtues and States of Life*, ed. A. M. Henry, Chicago: Fides, 1957, pp. 360–361). That many Christian thinkers continued to see "suicide" as essentially a "rational" act and, if intended to help others, as morally right, is demonstrated by the fact that St. Jerome and the Venerable Bede even included Christ among the Suicides. (See H. R. Fedden, *Suicide: A Social and Historical Study*, London: Davis, 1938, p. 10.) For a full treatment of the tremendous conflict that raged among Christian thinkers concerning the

descriptive and moral nature of "suicide" see W. E. H. Lecky, *History of European Morals from Augustus to Charlemagne*, New York: Appleton, 1869.

44 See Dennis H. Wrong, "The Oversocialized Conception of Man," *American Sociological Review*, 26 (April, 1961), pp. 183–193.

45 "Weber saw social life as a polytheism of values in combat with one another, and choices were possible among these values." (Talcott Parsons, "Introduction" to *From Max Weber: Essays in Sociology*, New York: Oxford, 1946, p. 70.)

46 D. Wrong, *op. cit.* This conception of the "self" is not only central to the Durkheim-Parsons line of sociological theory, it is also central to the line of theory and research that has developed from the theories of "self" (and "self concept") of Cooley and Mead: see, for example, the recent work of W. R. Rosengren, "The Self in the Emotionally Disturbed," *The American Journal of Sociology*, LXVI (March, 1961), pp. 454–463.

47 See, especially, H. S. Sullivan's theory of the "self-system" (*The Interpersonal Theory of Psychiatry*, New York: W. W. Norton, 1953) and P. Schilder's theory of "fluctuating self-experiences" (*The Image and Appearance of the Human Body*, New York: International Universities Press, 1951).

48 "It has not escaped the reader that the term identity covers much of what has been called the self by a variety of workers. . . ." (Erik H. Erikson, "The Problem of Ego Identity," in *Identity and Anxiety*, M. R. Stein *et al.* [(Eds.], Glencoe: The Free Press, 1960, pp. 37–88.)

49 *Ibid.* Erikson gives an example of a young woman whose mother had conditioned her to feel both that death is better than prostitution and that she herself had strong tendencies in that direction. When (falsely) arrested for prostitution she hanged herself, closing her suicide note with the words: "Why I achieve honor only to discard it. . . ."

50 It is best to consider this incorporation as still an on-going process. In the beginning Freud conceived of the ego as entirely cognitive. Only later did he consider the ego to have "drive energy" of its own, which was necessary for ego to take over entirely the functions of "will."

51 E. Erikson, *op. cit.*

52 Ludwig Binswanger, "The Case of Ellen West," in Rollo May *et al.* (Eds.), *Existence*, New York: Basic Books, 1958, pp. 294–295. Binswanger's analysis of Ellen West is both one of the best documented and most brilliant analyses of an individual's suicide. Though Binswanger's analysis of Ellen West's "suicide" is very creative in that it goes so far beyond most of what has been done in this direction before, it should, nevertheless, be noted that his analysis has a great deal in common with the German view of "oceanic suicide": ". . . the desire to escape from one's individuality, whether through love, through death, or through music—a tendency which has led to tragic consequences in the German history of the nineteenth and twentieth centuries—is an essentially formless and nihilistic desire to succumb to the chaos of the universe." (Leo Spitzer, "Three Poems on Ecstasy," in *A Method of Interpreting Literature*, Northampton, Mass.: Smith College Press, 1949, p. 56.) "Aus dem Leben, wie aus seinem Keime, Wächst der ewige Würzer nur." (Schiller, "Melancholie an Laura," quoted in J. R. Frey, "Schiller's Concept and Poetic Treatment of Death," *Journal of English and German Philology*, LVIII [October, 1959], pp. 557–588.)

53 See C. G. Jung, *Psychological Types*, New York: Pantheon Books.

54 The anguished feeling of lacking unity that results from radical, rapid changes (or oscillations) in one's "self" has been excellently expressed by Virginia Woolf in *The Waves:* "I have no face . . . other people have faces. . . . Their world is the real world. The things they lift are heavy. They say Yes, they say No; whereas I shift and change. . . ." Virginia Woolf seems to have suffered precisely such shifts in "self" and she committed suicide in a manner that might reasonably lead one to believe that she was seeking an "oceanic unity" of self:

> She walked out into the sea until she became a part of the river and sea. She was tired of the land. And being tired of the time, too, she turned her back on it and walked into a timeless beyond named eternity.

(Carl Sandburg, "Virginia Woolf's Personal Decision," in *Home Front Memo.)*

55 C. G. Jung, *Psychiatric Studies*, New York: Pantheon, 1957, pp. 120–124.

56 Jung was probably partly prevented from conceiving of suicide in such terms because of the close relation between his conception of "self" and the earlier (see above) conception of the "will." He even quotes the following excerpt from Schopenhauer in his discussion of "suicide": "Man ever does what he wills, and does so by necessity; that is because he *is* what he wills; for from what he is there follows by necessity everything he will ever do." *(Ibid.)* Such an approach is not only partially tautologous; it is also completely opposed to the decisional approach that synthesizes across the *personality-situation nexus* (see below).

57 Alfred Adler, "Suicide," *Journal of Individual Psychology*, 14 (May, 1958) pp. 57–62.

58 H. L. Ansbacher, "Suicide: The Adlerian Point of View," in Farberow and Shneidman, pp. 204–220.

59 See S. Freud, *Beyond the Pleasure Principle.*

60 See J. C. Flügel, "Death Instinct, Homeostasis and Applied Concepts," *International Journal of Psychoanalysis* (Supplement), 34, pp. 43–74; and L. Saul, "Freud's Death Instinct and the Second Law of Thermodynamics," *International Journal of Psychoanalysis*, XXXIX (1958) 323–325.

61 See S. Freud, "Mourning and Melancholia."

62 Otto Rank, *The Myth of the Birth of the Hero*, New York: Vintage Books, 1959.

63 Theodore Reik, *Masochism and Modern Man.*

64 Sandor Rado, *Psychoanalysis of Behavior*, New York: Grune and Stratton, 1956.

65 Reported by J. H. Holmes and quoted in G. Zilboorg, "Suicide," *American Journal of Psychiatry*, 92 (May, 1936) pp. 1347–1368.

66 W. B. Cannon, "Voodoo Death," *The American Anthropologist*, 44, no. 2 (1942) pp. 169–182.

67 George Kennan, "The Problem of Suicide," *McClure's Magazine*, 31 (1908) pp. 218–229.

68 Bergler, *Inferiority Feelings.*

69 G. M. Davidson, "The Mental State at the Time of Suicide," *Psychiatric Quarterly, Supplement*, 15 (1941) pp. 41–50.

70 *Suicide*, p. 276, fn. 25.

71 N. D. C. Lewis, "Studies on Suicide," Parts I and II, *Psycho-Analytic Review*, XX (July, 1933) 241–273 and XXIL (April, 1934) 146–153.

72 F. Achille-Delmas, *Psychologie Pathologique du Suicide.*

73 In general the distinction is not even recognized. Prisco, for example, seems to include both under the term "voluntary": "Suicide is the voluntary action by which one takes away his own life." (Quoted in "Suicidio," *Encyclopedia Universal Ilustrada*, LVIII, pp. 559–574.) The failure to make any such distinction can clearly be seen in the following quotation from Dublin and Bunzel: "An immense resistance, both objective as well as subjective, must, however, first be overcome. Yet in spite of all the safeguards provided by instinct and social sanctions, the death motive does often gain the ascendancy. There are many people who voluntarily seek death, sometimes on apparently slight provocation, even though they would seem to have every incentive to live." Louis Dublin and Bessie Bunzel, *To Be or Not to Be*, New York: Harrison Smith and Robert Haas, 1933, p. 5.

74 P. O'Neal *et al.*, "A Psychiatric Study of Attempted Suicide in Persons over Sixty Years of Age," *Archives of Neurology and Psychiatry*, 75:3 (March, 1956) pp. 275–284.

75 P. M. Yap, "Suicide in Hong Kong," *Journal of Mental Science*, 104 (April, 1958) pp. 266–301; and "Hyperiridism and Attempted Suicide in Chinese," *Journal of Nervous and Mental Diseases*, pp. 34–41.

76 G. Deshaies, *Psychologie du Suicide.*

77 In discussions of this sort one runs into the problem of the distinction between what one *chooses* or *wants* (given reality) and what one *prefers* or *would like to have* (if only reality were amenable). For a recent theoretical treatment of the definitional problems involved here see

Francis W. Irwin, "On Desire, Aversion, and the Affective Zero," *Psychological Review,* 68 (September, 1961) pp. 293–301.

78 Such a definition would also exclude from suicide all cases of "appeal suicide" and "escape suicide."

79 The belief that science should start from the most easily observable and/or measurable variables and proceed to explain these variables in terms of less easily (or less immediately perceived and/or measured) variables is related to, and is probably largely derived from, the widely-held belief that "... Science begins with what is most obvious..." (Bernard Bosanquet, *A History of Aesthetic,* New York: Meridian Books, 1957, p. 5.) It is important to remember that this approach in scientific theory is a *strategy* for doing research and theory, not a criterion of validity. The difficulty is that the immediacy of perceptibility is to some degree at least a first-stage criteria of reliability in scientific theory and, thereby, tends to come to seem a full-fledged criterion of validity.

80 The precise definition of motivation is, of course, problematic; but the best definition for our general purposes seems to be that of McClelland: "... a strong affective association, characterized by an anticipatory goal reaction and based on past association of certain cues with pleasure or pain." (Quoted from David C. McClelland, *Studies in Motivation,* New York: Appleton-Century-Crofts, Inc., 1955, p. 226.)

81 *Suicide,* 45–46.

82 For example, he made it impossible for himself to reasonably make use of official statistics to test his theory of suicide as defined by himself, simply because officials who collected the statistics generally define suicide in terms of intention or volition.

83 *Suicide,* pp. 43–44.

84 *Ibid.*

85 Halbwachs used precisely the same sort of "verbal realism" argument to arrive at a conclusion in opposition to Durkheim's conclusion: "If we do not allow one thus to separate the collection of suicides into two types so different from each other that one does not see how and why one would reunite them into one type, it is, first of all, because we do not believe that, if they were naturally and essentially different, one would give them the same name and that society would react in the same way in the presence of them." (Halbwachs, *op. cit.,* pp. 406–407).

Erwin Stengel

*The late Erwin Stengel was professor of psychiatry at the
University of Manchester in England. Before he fled from Nazi
Germany he had a career as a psychiatrist in that country. The
following selection is now considered to be a standard definition of
the suicide attempt. Stengel distinguishes the various degrees of
seriousness possible in a suicide attempt, identifying danger to life
as the criterion for evaluating apparently suicidal acts.*

The conventional notion of a genuine suicidal act is
something like this: "A person, having decided to end his life, or acting on a
sudden impulse to do so, kills himself, having chosen the most effective
method available and having made sure that nobody interferes. When he is
dead he is said to have succeeded and the act is often called a successful
suicidal attempt. If he survives he is said to have failed and the act is called an
unsuccessful suicidal attempt. Death is the only purpose of this act and
therefore the only criterion of success. Failure may be due to any of the
following causes: the sense of purpose may not have been strong enough; or
the act may have been undertaken half-heartedly because it was not quite
genuine; the subject was ignorant of the limitations of the method; or he was
lacking in judgment and determination through mental illness." Judging by
those standards only a minority of fatal and very few non-fatal suicidal acts
would pass muster, as both serious and genuine. The rest have to be dismissed as poor efforts, some of which succeeded by chance rather than
design. Obviously, this approach cannot do justice to a very common and
varied behavior pattern.

If a visiting scholar from one of the inhabited planets came to earth to
study the human species, he would sooner or later notice that some humans
sometimes commit acts of self-injury. He would observe that occasionally
this self-damaging behavior causes the person's death, but it would hardly
occur to him that this relatively rare outcome is the main purpose of that
behavior. Having been taught that careful observation of as many subjects as
possible is essential before one draws conclusions about the purpose of a
certain type of behavior, and having also learned that the subjects' explanations can be highly misleading, he would watch as many such acts as
possible, together with their antecedents and consequences, without preconceived ideas, over a fairly long period. His report on his observations
would read like this: "There are some humans who damage themselves more
or less badly and in about one in eight cases the damage is so severe that they
die. Whatever the outcome, most of them give a hint or a clear warning to one
or several of their fellow humans well before the act telling them that they are

thinking of killing themselves. Those fellow humans may or may not take notice of this warning. But once a person is found to have committed an act of self-damage there is invariably a great commotion among the other humans. They clearly show that they wish the act had never been committed. They do everything to keep him alive and to undo the damage that he did to himself. They go even further than this. While they usually do not show much concern about and sympathy with the suffering of fellow humans, an act of self-injury by one of themselves seems to make them take a profound and most active interest in him, at least for a time. They behave as if they had to help him and put him on his feet. As a result, his situation is transiently or permanently transformed for the better. These helpful reactions are particularly marked in the members of his family group but the larger community to which the human belongs also takes part.

"If one looked at the acts of self-damage alone one would be led to believe that self-destruction is their only purpose. But if one considers certain antecedents and the consequences of these acts, this simple explanation cannot be sustained. Why should these humans so often warn others of their intention to damage themselves, especially as they must know that this kind of behavior is dreaded in their family group and the community? They must also know that, once they have injured themselves, everybody will be upset and will want to help them, and if they should die, many other humans will feel they ought to have helped them. It looks as if their peculiar behavior cannot be derived from one single tendency but is probably due to a combination of at least two tendencies, one of which might be the urge to self-damage and possibly self-destruction, the other the urge to make other humans show concern and love and act accordingly. There are other peculiar features in the self-damaging behavior of humans, but these seem the most important."

The purpose of this fictitious report from unprejudiced space is to bring home the need for a new and very careful look at suicidal behavior. The most striking difference between the conventional view of suicidal acts and that of the unprejudiced observer lies in his emphasis on the reactions of the environment. The possibility of such reactions and their occasional exploitation has long been known, but this is believed to occur only in suicidal attempts regarded as non-genuine. All genuine suicidal acts are understood to aim at death alone. It is this notion which the uncommitted observer refuses to accept. On what facts does he base his challenge?

DEFINING THE SUICIDAL ATTEMPT

The death of a person by suicide gives rise to a great number of questions all of which are concerned with facts and events preceding the act. This is why all suicide research has been retrospective, like any other post-mortem investigation. As such, it has considerable limitations because the chief source of information is no longer available. Only in a minority of cases can records such as hospital case notes be obtained which are of help in the reconstruction of the antecedents. Usually one has to rely on whatever information the victim left behind and on hearsay. Attempted suicides have often been used for research into the causes and motives of suicide, the

assumption being that they are minor suicides. Therefore, investigations of suicidal attempts were purely retrospective and concerned with the same problems as those of suicide. This line of inquiry is perfectly legitimate and necessary, but until recently research workers ignored the obvious difference between suicides and attempted suicides, i.e. that the former are all dead while the latter are alive. At least, they have survived the suicidal act.

Studies into the fate of people who attempt suicide have been carried out only during the last two decades. They are the follow-up investigations undertaken by Dahlgren at Malmö, by Pierre B. Schneider at Lausanne and by Stengel and his associates at London. These studies have thrown light on how many members of large groups of people who had attempted suicide finally killed themselves.

The London team also investigated the social significance and effects of suicidal attempts. They started from the hypothesis that those who attempted and those who committed suicide constituted two different groups or "populations." They set themselves the task of investigating the following questions: What is the relationship between the two populations: those who commit suicide and those who attempt suicide? How many kill themselves later, and what makes them liable to do so? How does the suicidal attempt affect the patient's mental state? If suicide was motivated by a crisis in human relations, were those modified by the suicidal attempt, and if so, how? What is the effect of the suicidal attempt on the patient's group and what are their reactions to it? Sociologists have stated that suicide is due to social disintegration and isolation. Do these factors hold good for the suicidal attempt, and, if so, are they influenced by it? Some of these questions are of immediate practical interest for the clinician. The study of others might help us to understand the function of the suicidal attempt in our society.

Research carried out since these questions were first posed in 1952 makes it possible to answer some of them tentatively today.

The *definition* of what constitutes a suicidal attempt is far from simple. If a person is taken to hospital in a drowsy or comatose state, having left a suicide note behind, and if he admits that he wanted to take his life, there is no problem about the nature of his action. However, if another person, having been admitted in a similar condition denies suicidal intentions and contends that he took an overdose by mistake, or because he wanted to have a good sleep, is he to be regarded as a suicidal attempt? Or if a teenager, after a row with her boy-friend, swallows a boxful of her mother's sleeping pills in his presence, with the obvious intention of impressing him, is she to be classed as a suicidal attempt? Or was this only a demonstrative suicidal gesture or threat? In practice the layman's answer to this question will depend on the effect of the pills and on the reactions of the environment. If the girl falls into a coma, has to be rushed into hospital and survives, the incident will be called a suicidal attempt. If she dies it will be a case of suicide. But if the boy-friend has the presence of mind to make her drink a tumbler of concentrated salt water immediately after she has swallowed the tablets and thus to make her vomit them before absorbed, the whole episode may be over in a few minutes and be dismissed as just another lovers' tiff. However, it will be remembered if she should repeat the act at some later date, perhaps with a less harmless outcome. This example illustrates that the degree of damage and even the outcome of a suicidal act may depend on outside intervention, irrespective of the seriousness of the suicidal intent.

Many people deny suicidal intention after an act of self-damage, because they feel ashamed and guilty. They may not want to tell the truth, or their intention may have been confused at the time. It is generally believed that most if not all people who commit suicidal acts are clearly determined to die. The study of attempted suicides does not bear this out. Many suicidal attempts and quite a few suicides are carried out in the mood "I don't care whether I live or die," rather than with a clear and unambiguous determination to end life. A person who denies, after what seems an obvious suicidal attempt, that he *really* wanted to kill himself, may be telling the truth. Most people, in committing a suicidal act, are just as muddled as they are whenever they do anything of importance under emotional stress. Carefully planned suicidal acts are as rare as carefully planned acts of homicide. Many are carried out on sudden impulse, although suicidal thoughts were usually present before. At any rate, the person concerned cannot be the sole guide to the interpretation of his conduct. Doctors and others who have to make up their minds about acts of self-damage have to adopt a definition like this: "A suicidal attempt is any act of self-damage inflicted with self-destructive intention, however vague and ambiguous. Sometimes this intention has to be inferred from the patient's behavior." For the clinician it is safer still to regard all cases of potentially dangerous self-poisoning or self-inflicted injury as suicidal attempts whatever the victim's explanation, unless there is clear evidence to the contrary. "Potentially dangerous" means in this context: believed by the "attempter" possibly to endanger life. For instance, if a person who is ignorant of the effects of drugs takes double or three times the prescribed dose, this might have to be regarded as a suicidal attempt because in taking that overdose the person took a risk which may have proved fatal. However, if a doctor or a nurse took the same dose, the act may not be regarded as a suicidal attempt but only as a gesture. The same applies to injuries with cutting instruments, and to other means of self-damage. To draw an example from literature, the blind Gloucester's jump in *King Lear* from what he thought to be the cliffs of Dover was subjectively a serious suicidal attempt, but in reality quite harmless.

Was it a serious suicidal attempt? This is a question immediately asked in every case by everybody who gets to know about the attempt. The question may have various meanings. It may refer to the chances of survival while the outcome is still in the balance. As the term suicidal attempt is . . . used only for non-fatal suicidal acts, this version of the question need not be discussed here.

There is a good deal of confusion about the criteria of the seriousness of a suicidal attempt, even among experts. Should the degree of self-inflicted damage, i.e. the depth of the coma, the amount of blood lost, in short, the degree of the danger to life, be the sole yardstick? If so, a carefully planned act of self-destruction which was prevented from taking effect by timely intervention may have to be classed as harmless.

Some writers call an attempt serious if it caused severe physical dysfunction or if the suicidal intention was serious. But, there is another aspect which has to be taken into account, i.e. the possibility of intervention from the environment. A lethal dose of a narcotic taken with genuine intent in a situation in which immediate counter-measures can be instituted may not seriously endanger life. On the other hand, a relatively small overdose taken half-heartedly by a person in poor health in a situation where help is not available may be fatal. If danger to life is to be the criterion of the seriousness of a suicidal attempt three aspects have to be taken into account: (1) the potential threat to vital bodily functions; (2) the degree of the suicidal intent; and (3) the social constellation at the time of the attempt, i.e. the chances of intervention from the environment. The majority of the fatal or almost fatal suicidal acts have a high rating in at least two of those three criteria. To give an example: a suicidal attempt by a person who takes a heavy overdose of sleeping tablets with strong suicidal intention in his home and is found unconscious by a member of his family will not rank as highly on the seriousness scale as a similar attempt undertaken in a hotel room or on a lonely moor. From this point of view, only a minority of suicidal acts, fatal and non-fatal, qualify for top scores. Ettlinger and Flordh, two Swedish investigators, found that of 500 attempted suicides only four per cent could be regarded as well planned, but only seven percent were more or less harmless.

PART VII
THE SURVIVORS
OF DEATH:
GRIEVING AND
MOURNING

Contents

To be a survivor, to have suffered a grievous loss of someone close, is a terrible plight. If grief is not an illness, often its effects are so severe that it might as well be one. Grief and mourning are powerful and stressful emotional states that can touch off unconscious psychological reactions that actually jeopardize the individual's life. A recent study shows that loss of a loved one is absolutely at the top of the list of stressful, abrasive, and disruptive events that can happen to someone. For a while—at least a year or so—the grieving person is an individual "at risk," more apt not to take adequate care of him or herself, more apt to be sick and hospitalized, and even more apt to die or be killed.

One of the most interesting psychological-philosophical issues related to mourning is Toynbee's question of whether or not one should wish to survive a person that one truly loves in order to take the burden of bereavement upon oneself. That question is one of those bittersweet unanswerable issues which, in all but a few instances, is resolved by external forces.

Currently there is much-needed and overdue concern with widows and widowers, bereaved parents, orphaned children, who have, by and large, been rather neglected. This section concerns itself with the psychological needs of the mourners and grievers who are left behind.

This part consists of four chapters that include philosophic reflections, clinical essays, and a personal account. The writers are an author-essayist, a philosopher-mathematician, a psychologist, and a psychiatric social worker.

32 ·

A Grief Observed

C. S. Lewis

C. S. Lewis was known to students at Cambridge University as a brilliant scholar and tutor, and to the world as an observer, author, and essayist of unusual distinction. His works include The Screwtape Letters, The Allegory of Love, Mere Christianity, The Chronicles of Narnia *(an acknowledged classic of fantasy), and his famous science fiction trilogy* (Out of the Silent Planet, Perelandra, *and* That Hideous Strength). *Born in Northern Ireland in 1898, he died at Oxford in November 1963. C. S. Lewis had the rare gift of translating the concepts of Christianity into the language and context of the everyday world.*

Reproduced below is the first chapter of a poignant essay, written under the following circumstances: In April 1956, Lewis, a confirmed bachelor, married Joy Davidman, an American poet with two small children. After four brief, intensely happy years, Lewis found himself alone again and inconsolable. To defend himself against the loss of belief in God, Lewis began a journal that became an eloquent statement of rediscovered faith. He freely confesses his doubts, his rage, and his awareness of human frailty, and finally is able to find the way back to life.

No one ever told me that grief felt so like fear. I am not afraid, but the sensation is like being afraid. The same fluttering in the stomach, the same restlessness, the yawning. I keep on swallowing.

At other times it feels like being mildly drunk, or concussed. There is a sort of invisible blanket between the world and me. I find it hard to take in what anyone says. Or perhaps, hard to want to take it in. It is so uninteresting. Yet I want the others to be about me. I dread the moments when the house is empty. If only they would talk to one another and not to me.

There are moments, most unexpectedly, when something inside me tries to assure me that I don't really mind so much, not so very much, after all. Love is not the whole of man's life. I was happy before I ever met H. I've plenty of what are called "resources." People get over these things. Come, I shan't do so badly. One is ashamed to listen to this voice but it seems for a little to be making out a good case. Then comes a sudden jab of red-hot memory and all this "common-sense" vanishes like an ant in the mouth of a furnace.

On the rebound one passes into tears and pathos. Maudlin tears. I almost prefer the moments of agony. These are at least clean and honest. But the bath of self-pity, the wallow, the loathsome sticky-sweet pleasure of indulging it—that disgusts me. And even while I'm doing it I know it leads me to misrepresent H. herself. Give that mood its head and in a few minutes I shall have substituted for the real woman a mere doll to be blubbered over. Thank

God the memory of her is still too strong (will it always be too strong?) to let me get away with it.

For H. wasn't like that at all. Her mind was lithe and quick and muscular as a leopard. Passion, tenderness and pain were all equally unable to disarm it. It scented the first whiff of cant or slush; then sprang, and knocked you over before you knew what was happening. How many bubbles of mine she pricked! I soon learned not to talk rot to her unless I did it for the sheer pleasure—and there's another red-hot jab—of being exposed and laughed at. I was never less silly than as H.'s lover.

And no one ever told me about the laziness of grief. Except at my job—where the machine seems to run on much as usual—I loathe the slightest effort. Not only writing but even reading a letter is too much. Even shaving. What does it matter now whether my cheek is rough or smooth? They say an unhappy man wants distractions—some thing to take him out of himself. Only as a dog-tired man wants an extra blanket on a cold night; he'd rather lie there shivering than get up and find one. It's easy to see why the lonely become untidy; finally, dirty and disgusting.

Meanwhile, where is God? This is one of the most disquieting symptoms. When you are happy, so happy that you have no sense of needing Him, so happy that you are tempted to feel His claims upon you as an interruption, if you remember yourself and turn to Him with gratitude and praise, you will be—or so it feels—welcomed with open arms. But go to Him when your need is desperate, when all other help is vain, and what do you find? A door slammed in your face, and a sound of bolting and double bolting on the inside. After that silence. You may as well turn away. The longer you wait, the more emphatic the silence will become. There are no lights in the windows. It might be an empty house. Was it ever inhabited? It seemed so once. And that seeming was as strong as this. What can this mean? Why is He so present a commander in our time of prosperity and so very absent a help in time of trouble?

I tried to put some of these thoughts to C. this afternoon. He reminded me that the same thing seems to have happened to Christ: "Why hast thou forsaken me?" I know. Does that make it easier to understand?

Not that I am (I think) in much danger of ceasing to believe in God. The real danger is of coming to believe such dreadful things about Him. The conclusion I dread is not, "So there's no God after all," but, "So this is what God's really like. Deceive yourself no longer."

Our elders submitted and said, "Thy will be done." How often had bitter resentment been stifled through sheer terror and an act of love—yes, in every sense, an act—put on to hide the operation?

Of course it's easy enough to say that God seems absent at our greatest need because He *is* absent—non-existent. But then why does He seem so present when, to put it quite frankly, we don't ask for Him?

One thing, however, marriage has done for me. I can never again believe that religion is manufactured out of our unconscious, starved desires and is a substitute for sex. For those few years H. and I feasted on love; every mode of it—solemn and merry, romantic and realistic, sometimes as dramatic as a thunderstorm, sometimes as comfortable and unemphatic as putting on your soft slippers. No cranny of heart or body remained unsatisfied. If God were a substitute for love we ought to have lost all interest in Him. Who'd bother about substitutes when he has the thing itself? But that isn't what happens. We both knew we wanted something besides one another—quite a different kind of something, a quite different kind of want. You might as well say that when lovers have one another they will never want to read, or eat—or breathe.

After the death of a friend, years ago, I had for some time a most vivid feeling of certainty about his continued life; even his enhanced life. I have begged to be given even one hundredth part of the same assurance about H. There is no answer. Only the locked door, the iron curtain, the vacuum, absolute zero. "Them as asks don't get." I was a fool to ask. For now, even if that assurance came I should distrust it. I should think it a self-hypnosis induced by my own prayers.

At any rate I must keep clear of the spiritualists. I promised H. I would. She knew something of those circles.

Keeping promises to the dead, or to anyone else, is very well. But I begin to see that "respect for the wishes of the dead" is a trap. Yesterday I stopped myself only in time from saying about some trifle, "H. wouldn't have liked that." This is unfair to the others. I should soon be using "what H. would have liked" as an instrument of domestic tyranny; with her supposed likings becoming a thinner and thinner disguise for my own.

I cannot talk to the children about her. The moment I try, there appears on their faces neither grief, nor love, nor fear, nor pity, but the most fatal of all non-conductors, embarrassment. They look as if I were committing an indecency. They are longing for me to stop. I felt just the same after my own mother's death when my father mentioned her. I can't blame them. It's the way boys are.

I sometimes think that shame, mere awkward, senseless shame, does as much towards preventing good acts and straightforward happiness as any of our vices can do. And not only in boyhood.

Or are the boys right? What would H. herself think of this terrible little notebook to which I come back and back? Are these jottings morbid? I once read the sentence "I lay awake all night with toothache, thinking about toothache and about lying awake." That's true to life. Part of every misery is, so to speak, the misery's shadow or reflection: the fact that you don't merely suffer but have have to keep on thinking about the fact that you suffer. I not only live each endless day in grief, but live each day thinking about living each day in grief. Do these notes merely aggravate that side of it? Merely confirm the monotonous, tread-mill march of the mind round one subject? But what am I to do? I must have some drug, and reading isn't a strong enough drug now. By writing it all down (all?—no: one thought in a hundred) I believe I get a little outside it. That's how I'd defend it to H. But ten to one she'd see a hole in the defense.

It isn't only the boys either. An odd by-product of my loss is that I'm aware of being an embarrassment to everyone I meet. At work, at the club, in the street, I see people, as they approach me, trying to make up their minds whether they'll "say something about it" or not. I hate it if they do, and if they don't. Some funk it altogether. R. has been avoiding me for a week. I like best the well-brought-up young men, almost boys, who walk up to me as if I were a dentist, turn very red, get it over, and then edge away to the bar as quickly as they decently can. Perhaps the bereaved ought to be isolated in special settlements like lepers.

To some I'm worse than an embarrassment. I am a death's head. Whenever I meet a happily married pair I can feel them both thinking, "One or other of us must some day be as he is now."

At first I was very afraid of going to places where H. and I had been happy—our favorite pub, our favorite wood. But I decided to do it at once—like sending a pilot up again as soon as possible after he's had a crash. Unexpectedly, it makes no difference. Her absence is no more emphatic in those places than anywhere else. It's not local at all. I suppose that if one were forbidden all salt one wouldn't notice it much more in any one food than in another. Eating in general would be different, every day, at every meal. It is like that. The act of living is different all through. Her absence is like the sky, spread over everything.

But no, that is not quite accurate. There is one place where her absence comes locally home to me, and it is a place I can't avoid. I mean my own body. It had such a different importance while it was the body of H.'s lover. Now it's like an empty house. But don't let me deceive myself. This body would become important to me again, and pretty quickly, if I thought there was anything wrong with it.

Cancer, and cancer, and cancer. My mother, my father, my wife. I wonder who is next in the queue.

Yet H. herself, dying of it, and well knowing the fact, said that she had lost a great deal of her old horror at it. When the reality came, the name and the idea were in some degree disarmed. And up to a point I very nearly understood. This is important. One never meets just Cancer, or War, or Unhappiness (or Happiness). One only meets each hour or moment that comes. All manner of ups and downs. Many bad spots in our best times, many good ones in our worst. One never gets the total impact of what we call "the thing itself." But we call it wrongly. The thing itself is simply all these ups and downs: the rest is a name or an idea.

It is incredible how much happiness, even how much gaiety, we sometimes had together after all hope was gone. How long, how tranquilly, how nourishingly, we talked together that last night!

And yet, not quite together. There's a limit to the "one flesh." You can't really share someone else's weakness, or fear or pain. What you feel may be bad. It might conceivably be as bad as what the other felt, though I should distrust anyone who claimed that it was. But it would still be quite different. When I speak of fear, I mean the merely animal fear, the recoil of the organism from its destruction; the smothery feeling; the sense of being a rat in a trap. It can't be transferred. The mind can sympathize; the body, less. In one way the bodies of lovers can do it least. All their love passages have trained them to have, not identical, but complementary, correlative, even opposite, feelings about one another.

We both knew this. I had my miseries, not hers; she had hers, not mine. The end of hers would be the coming-of-age of mine. We were setting out on different roads. This cold truth, this terrible traffic-regulation ("You, Madam, to the right—you, Sir, to the left") is just the beginning of the separation which is death itself.

And this separation, I suppose, waits for all. I have been thinking of H. and myself as peculiarly unfortunate in being torn apart. But presumably all lovers are. She once said to me, "Even if we both died at exactly the same moment, as we lie here side by side, it would be just as much a separation as the one you're so afraid of." Of course she didn't *know*, any more than I do. But she was near death; near enough to make a good shot. She used to quote, "Alone into the Alone." She said it felt like that. And how immensely improbable that it should be otherwise! Time and space and body were the very things that brought us together; the telephone wires by which we communicated. Cut one off, or cut both off simultaneously. Either way, mustn't the conversation stop?

Unless you assume that some other means of communication—utterly different, yet doing the same work, would be immediately substituted. But then, what conceivable point could there be in servering the old ones? Is God a clown who whips away your bowl of soup one moment in order, next moment, to replace it with another bowl of the same soup? Even nature isn't such a clown as that. She never plays exactly the same tune twice.

It is hard to have patience with people who say, "There is no death," or, "Death doesn't matter." There is death. And whatever is matters. And whatever happens has consequences, and it and they are irrevocable and irreversible. You might as well say that birth doesn't matter. I look up at the night sky. Is anything more certain than that in all those vast times and spaces, if I were allowed to search them, I should nowhere find her face, her voice, her touch? She died. She is dead. Is the word so difficult to learn?

I have no photograph of her that's any good. I cannot even see her face distinctly in my imagination. Yet the odd face of some stranger seen in a crowd this morning may come before me in vivid perfection the moment I close my eyes tonight. No doubt, the explanation is simple enough. We have seen the faces of those we know best so variously, from so many angles, in so many lights, with so many expressions—walking, sleeping, laughing, crying, eating, talking, thinking—that all the impressions crowd into our memory together and cancel out into a mere blur. But her voice is still vivid. The remembered voice—that can turn me at any moment to a whimpering child.

Bertrand Russell

*Bertrand Russell, British philosopher, mathematician, and essayist,
was one of the most intellectually gifted individuals of our century.
His many works, characterized by wit, clarity, and vivid metaphor,
are known throughout the world. In this selection, taken from his
book* Why I Am Not a Christian, *Russell, in his typical
no-nonsense, pungent prose, attacks the notion of survival after
death.*

Before we can profitably discuss whether we shall con-
tinue to exist after death, it is well to be clear as to the sense in which a man is
the same person as he was yesterday. Philosophers used to think that there
were definite substances, the soul and the body, that each lasted on from day
to day, that a soul, once created, continued to exist throughout all future
time, whereas a body ceased temporarily from death till the resurrection of
the body.

The part of this doctrine which concerns the present life is pretty certainly
false. The matter of the body is continually changing by processes of nutri-
ment and wastage. Even if it were not, atoms in physics are no longer
supposed to have continuous existence; there is no sense in saying: this is the
same atom as the one that existed a few minutes ago. The continuity of a
human body is a matter of appearance and behavior, not of substance.

The same thing applies to the mind. We think and feel and act, but there is
not, in addition to thoughts and feelings and actions, a bare entity, the mind
or the soul, which does or suffers these occurrences. The mental continuity
of a person is a continuity of habit and memory: there was yesterday one
person whose feelings I can remember, and that person I regard as myself of
yesterday; but, in fact, myself of yesterday was only certain mental occurrences which are now remembered and are regarded as part of the person
who now recollects them. All that constitutes a person is a series of experiences connected by memory and by certain similarities of the sort we call
habit.

If, therefore, we are to believe that a person survives death, we must believe
that the memories and habits which constitute the person will continue to be
exhibited in a new set of occurrences.

No one can prove that this will not happen. But it is easy to see that it is
very unlikely. Our memories and habits are bound up with the structure of
the brain, in much the same way a river is connected with the riverbed. The
water in the river is always changing, but it keeps to the same course because
previous rains have worn a channel. In like manner, previous events have

worn a channel in the brain, and our thoughts flow along this channel. This is the cause of memory and mental habits. But the brain, as a structure, is dissolved at death, and memory therefore may be expected to be also dissolved. There is no more reason to think otherwise than to expect a river to persist in its old course after an earthquake has raised a mountain where a valley used to be.

All memory, and therefore (one may say) all minds, depend upon a property which is very noticeable in certain kinds of material structures but exists little if at all in other kinds. This is the property of forming habits as a result of frequent similar occurrences. For example: a bright light makes the pupils of the eyes contract; and if you repeatedly flash a light in a man's eyes and beat a gong at the same time, the gong alone will, in the end, cause his pupils to contract. This is a fact about the brain and nervous system—that is to say, about a certain material structure. It will be found that exactly similar facts explain our response to language and our use of it, our memories and the emotions they arouse, our moral or immoral habits of behavior, and indeed everything that constitutes our mental personality, except the part determined by heredity. The part determined by heredity is handed on to our posterity but cannot, in the individual, survive the disintegration of the body. Thus both the hereditary and the acquired parts of a personality are, so far as our experience goes, bound up with the characteristics of certain bodily structures. We all know that memory may be obliterated by an injury to the brain, that a virtuous person may be rendered vicious by encephalitis lethargica, and that a clever child can be turned into an idiot by lack of iodine. In view of such familiar facts, it seems scarcely probable that the mind survives the total destruction of brain structure which occurs at death.

It is not rational arguments but emotions that cause belief in a future life.

The most important of these emotions is fear of death, which is instinctive and biologically useful. If we genuinely and wholeheartedly believed in the future life, we should cease completely to fear death. The effects would be curious, and probably such as most of us would deplore. But our human and subhuman ancestors have fought and exterminated their enemies throughout many geological ages and have profited by courage; it is therefore an advantage to the victors in the struggle for life to be able, on occasion, to overcome the natural fear of death. Among animals and savages, instinctive pugnacity suffices for this purpose; but at a certain stage of development, as the Mohammedans first proved, belief in Paradise has considerable military value as reinforcing natural pugnacity. We should therefore admit that militarists are wise in encouraging the belief in immortality, always supposing that this belief does not become so profound as to produce indifference to the affairs of the world.

Another emotion which encourages the belief in survival is admiration of the excellence of man. As the Bishop of Birmingham says, "His mind is a far finer instrument than anything that had appeared earlier—he knows right and wrong. He can build Westminster Abbey. He can make an airplane. He can calculate the distance of the sun . . . Shall, then, man at death perish utterly? Does that incomparable instrument, his mind, vanish when life ceases?"

The bishop proceeds to argue that "the universe has been shaped and is governed by an intelligent purpose," and that it would have been unintelligent, having made man, to let him perish.

To this argument there are many answers. In the first place, it has been found, in the scientific investigation of nature, that the intrusion of moral or aesthetic values has always been an obstacle to discovery. It used to be thought that the heavenly bodies must move in circles because the circle is the most perfect curve, that species must be immutable because God would only create what was perfect and what therefore stood in no need of improvement, that it was useless to combat epidemics except by repentance because they were sent as a punishment for sin, and so on. It has been found, however, that, so far as we can discover, nature is indifferent to our values and can only be understood by ignoring our notions of good and bad. The universe may have a purpose, but nothing that we know suggests that, if so, this purpose has any similarity to ours.

Nor is there in this anything surprising. Dr. Barnes tells us that man "knows right and wrong." But, in fact, as anthropology shows, men's views of right and wrong have varied to such an extent that no single item has been permanent. We cannot say, therefore, that man knows right and wrong, but only that some men do. Which men? Nietzsche argued in favor of an ethic profoundly different from Christ's, and some powerful governments have accepted his teaching. If knowledge of right and wrong is to be an argument for immortality, we must first settle whether to believe Christ or Nietzsche, and then argue that Christians are immortal, but Hitler and Mussolini are not, or vice versa. The decision will obviously be made on the battlefield, not in the study. Those who have the best poison gas will have the ethic of the future and will therefore be the immortal ones.

Our feelings and beliefs on the subject of good and evil are, like everything else about us, natural facts, developed in the struggle for existence and not having any divine or supernatural origin. In one of Aesop's fables, a lion is shown pictures of huntsmen catching lions and remarks that, if he had painted them, they would have shown lions catching huntsmen. Man, says Dr. Barnes, is a fine fellow because he can make airplanes. A little while ago there was a popular song about the cleverness of flies in walking upside down on the ceiling, with the chorus: "Could Lloyd George do it? Could Mr. Baldwin do it? Could Ramsay Mac do it? Why, NO." On this basis a very telling argument could be constructed by a theologically minded fly, which no doubt the other flies would find most convincing.

Moreover, it is only when we think abstractly that we have such a high opinion of man. Of men in the concrete, most of us think the vast majority very bad. Civilized states spend more than half their revenue on killing each other's citizens. Consider the long history of the activities inspired by moral fervor: human sacrifices, persecutions of heretics, witch-hunts, pogroms leading up to wholesale extermination by poison gases, which one at least of

Dr. Barnes's episcopal colleagues must be supposed to favor, since he holds pacifism to be un-Christian. Are these abominations, and the ethical doctrines by which they are prompted, really evidence of an intelligent creator? And can we really wish that the men who practiced them should live forever? The world in which we live can be understood as a result of muddle and accident; but if it is the outcome of deliberate purpose, the purpose must have been that of a fiend. For my part, I find accident a less painful and more plausible hypothesis.

34 · The Process of Mourning and Grief

Lily Pincus

The late Lily Pincus was a social worker who lived and practiced in England. She was a founder of the Institute for Marital Studies at the Tavistock Institute for Human Rights in London. Among the books she has co-authored are Marriage: Studies in Emotional Conflict and Growth, Social Casework in Marital Problems, *and* Shared Phantasy in Marital Problems. *The following chapter from* Death and Family *contains Mrs. Pincus's reflections on grief and separation anxiety, and she relates her experiences to the theoretical formulations about loss by the English psychoanalyst Melanie Klein.*

An increasing number of psychological studies in recent years reflect a growing interest in grief and bereavement. This trend appears to be due partly to an attempt to break down social taboos about death and mourning. Recent uncertainties about boundaries between mental health and mental illness also may have made it more urgent to conceptualize distinctions between normal and pathological mourning, and between grief and illness. However, since the nature of mourning is so manifold, and the reactions of individual personalities vary so widely, a comprehensive definition is difficult to find. To cope with this problem, attempts have been made to break down the process of mourning into observable phases, and although the number of phases and the emphases on them varies in different studies, a picture is now emerging which is helpful for understanding and assessment.

All studies agree that *shock* is the first response to the death of an important person, and that shock will be particularly pronounced at sudden unexpected death. It may find expression in physical collapse . . . , in violent outbursts . . . , or in dazed withdrawal, denial, and inability to take in the reality of death. . . .

Mourners often complain that they were not prepared for what it would be like: "Why did nobody warn me that I would feel so sick . . . or tired . . . or exhausted?"; "Nobody ever told me that grief felt so like fear"; "I wish I had known about the turmoil of emotions." But can anybody tell or warn, can books really help? Or is grief one of those emotional learning situations in which theory makes sense only after the experience?

Yet here I am, writing a book about grief and mourning, hoping that even if it does not help the problems of immediate bereavement, it may help toward creating a climate in which these are not increased by the bewildered and uncomprehending responses of others. And that once the state of shock and confusion is over, the mourner's shame and anxiety about his irrational behavior may be lessened by the knowledge that this is the universal and natural response to grief and loss, and that he is not only entitled to have and express these feelings, but that it would be wrong and perhaps harmful not to do so.

The attempts of the bereaved to cope with this first phase of shock and confusion will vary with his temperament and situation. He may be completely numbed and apathetic or he may be overactive. For physical shock, rest and warmth are the recognized methods of treatment, yet the most frequent advice given for the emotional shock of grief is to "keep going," "get busy." This "remedy" may not only set the scene for a denial of loss and pain and subsequent pathological development, but it is likely to lead to all sorts of disasters. I know from my own experience and that of others the frightening and exhausting results of the innumerable blunders of those first busy days—the things mislaid, lost, wrongly addressed, and so on, and the agonizing attempts to retrieve them. For example, having collected my husband's most important papers from his lawyer, I managed to throw them into a strange letter box. Why, then, this advice to "get busy"? Does it express the adviser's fear of getting involved in the mourner's pain? Geoffrey Gorer says, "Giving way to grief is stigmatized as morbid, unhealthy, demoralizing. The proper action of a friend and well-wisher is felt to be distraction of a mourner from his/her grief."[1]

There may also be in this desire to distract a recognition that the newly bereaved who finds it difficult to rest and sleep even at night is unlikely to be able to relax, and therefore it is better to "keep going." The mourner's restlessness may be his anxiety about having to acknowledge that he is alone, abandoned. What he may need most is the physical comfort of another person's presence, and in our modern condition of isolation such comfort often is not available.

The most common "solution" for widows and widowers is to fill the empty space in the double bed with a child. As the need for warmth and comfort will last beyond the usually short phase of shock, this "replacement," which may well meet the child's conscious or unconscious wishes to take the place of the dead parent in relation to the living one, may induce a situation which later could become difficult to resolve, and could lead to neurotic problems and dependence. Often a pet is used to mitigate the misery of lonely nights. A more satisfactory solution was found by one widow, who after an initial period of sleeplessness could happily go to sleep cuddling a bolster, just like a baby who needs a teddy bear to go to sleep without his mother. Why not acknowledge and satisfy without shame the baby needs stirred up by bereavement?

Usually the phase of acute shock lasts only a few days and is followed by what one might call a *controlled phase*, in which arrangements have to be made and the funeral faced and endured, and during which the mourner is surrounded and supported by relatives and friends. This period of support and the form it takes vary not only according to tradition, culture, and social and religious group, but also in the interpretation of the supportive function. This may support the mourner's super-ego with expressed or implicit demands for mature behavior or it may support the mourner's regressive needs with the expectation that he give vent to grief. In either case the presence and sympathy of others, the "special" position in which he finds himself, will give the mourner a sense of safety. He may literally feel that the others will see to it that things do not get out of control, that life goes on.

The real pain and misery makes itself felt when this controlled phase, and the privileges that went with it, is over, and the task of testing reality, coming to terms with the new situation, and the painful withdrawal of libido from the lost person begin. It is then that the mourner feels lost and abandoned and attempts to develop defenses against the agonies of pain. *Searching* for the lost person, an almost automatic universal defense against accepting the reality of the loss, may go on for a long time. C. M. Parkes quotes from a catalogue to an exhibition of the works of Kaethe Kollwitz:

> Over a number of years, K. Kollwitz worked on a monument for her young son who was killed in October 1914. His death became for her a sort of personal obligation. Two years later she noted in her diary: "There is a drawing made, a mother letting her dead son slide into her arms. I could do a hundred similar drawings, but still can't seem to come any closer to him. I'm still searching for him as if it were in the very work itself that I had to find him."[2]

Searching is the principal behavior pattern evoked by loss. Children and animals search for the absent object. The bereaved adult, even if he is aware of the irrational component in his behavior, keeps on searching for his dead, during unguarded moments, in hallucinations, and especially in his dreams. My neighbor Andrew . . . is a vivid example. Again and again in his dreams he tried, with great urgency, to get to a place where he might find his lost wife. His dreams were a wish for a miracle.

Most people are not aware of their need to search but express it in restless behavior tension, and loss of interest in all that does not concern the deceased. These symptoms lessen as bit by bit the reality of the loss can be accepted and the bereaved slowly, slowly rebuilds his inner world. Yet I wonder whether the impulse to search for the lost person ever completely disappears. Even for those bereaved who have successfully built a new life, search for the lost love object persists at moments of great strain, weakness, or illness, just as the dying person often recalls memories of his childhood and appears to be searching for his first love objects, his parents.

As the bereaved becomes more relaxed, and tension, frustration, and pain decrease, *searching* may lead to *finding* a sense of the lost person's presence. C. S. Lewis says in *A Grief Observed:*

> . . . as I have discovered, passionate grief does not link us with the dead but cuts us off from them. This becomes clearer and clearer. It is just at those moments when I feel least sorrow—getting into my morning bath is one of them—that H [his wife] rushes upon my mind in her full reality, her otherness. Not, as in my worst moments, all foreshortened and patheticized and solemnized by miseries, but as she is in her own right. This is good and tonic.[3]

For me it took years before I could experience this "tonic" of Fritz's presence, and it is a wonderful surprise that this is increasing as time goes on. It happens most often on waking (when he used to come in with my breakfast tray, and now does so in my vision) or at night, when I go to sleep. It has nothing of the supernatural about it, and is a reassuring, gratifying experience which feels absolutely realistic. Other widows have told me of the same experience and of it becoming more frequent as they relax in their new life and the "pining" stops or at least decreases. For whatever the mitigating experiences, depression and despair will come and go, reappearing—if all goes well—at longer intervals, staying for shorter spells. If mourners can accept and understand this, they will feel less pain and anxiety about "relapses."

There are no timetables for what have been called phases of mourning, nor are there distinct lines of demarcation for the various symptoms of grief which find expression during these phases. For the bereaved, the most alarming and bewildering aspects of grief are those in which he can no longer recognize himself, for example, the often irrational anger and hostility, which may be quite alien to the mourner's usual behavior and may make him feel that he is going insane. I still remember with shame my own completely mad anger when an otherwise loved relative carried an umbrella for an occasion on which I found it inappropriate. Anger and hostility may take quite irrational forms and be directed not only against the medical people who looked after the deceased, but against the nearest and dearest, including the dead person himself. They express the ambivalence of the mourner toward all these people but most especially, and most painfully, toward the lost person who is causing him so much distress by his abandonment. One of the aspects of this distress is that neither the love for the lost person nor the person himself was perfect. "A stable adjustment to another's death involves assimilating both the loved and the hated elements of his personality. As a consequence the bereaved must experience some self-hate, some self-accusation, some guilt."[4]

Here we can perhaps see most clearly the repetition of childhood responses toward the loved parent who, when he leaves the child, is hated and becomes the object of murderous fantasies. Ambivalence toward the absent mother or the dead person is more than just mixed feelings about them. Mixed feelings may be based on a conscious, realistic assessment of the imperfect nature of these people; ambivalence only becomes a conscious process with difficulty, by overcoming resistances. Its pain is caused by contradictory and interdependent feelings of love and hate for the same person. The infant has to cope with the terror that his hate will kill his mother, and that he will then lose her forever. The adult mourner who has lost his loved object forever relives the infantile terror that his hate and lack of love have brought about the loss.

Ambivalence is inseparable from guilt, and there is always guilt at the death of an important person—guilt about what has been said or not said, done or not done, justified guilt and guilt which has no rational justification. Perhaps the most painful and confusing guilt is about the moments—however fleeting—of triumph that the other one is dead, and I am alive! Yet just as with mixed feelings, guilt can also be based on realistic regrets about insufficient care and concern for the dead. Often it is a mixture of justified and unjustified feelings, and it is this mixture which makes it so difficult to live with guilt.

We all know situations in which a mourner who has behaved very badly toward the person who died can find relief for his guilt only by devoting his life to paying restitution. Uncle Jack, the uncle of a friend of mine, was such a person. While his wife, Molly, was alive, he had given her a miserable time. Until she married her grumpy, bad-tempered husband, Molly was a lively and charming woman. The couple had two sons and lived in Yorkshire where Uncle Jack bought farms and converted them into small holdings. Before or during the conversion periods, he lived with his family in makeshift arrangements. Their home was sometimes in the manor house, empty, barely furnished, with splendid marble fireplaces but no money to provide heat in the winter; sometimes they had to make do in shacks on the building site. In either case, they were always on the move, never settled, never had a comfortable home. The frequent moves also involved frequent changes of schools for the boys and, as a result, poor educational records, which contributed to their insecurity and aggressiveness.

In addition, there was never any money, not so much because Uncle Jack did not have any as that he needed what he had for new conversions and persuaded his wife that he could not spare anything for the household. It was she who had to earn what the family needed, and as a trained school-teacher, she managed to do this. But the frequent moves naturally also affected her jobs, and made her life unbearably hard, especially since her husband never acknowledged the difficulties he made for her. Whenever she had a problem finding a new job or had to accept an inferior, badly paid one, he blamed her incompetence.

There was no sign of love or mutual concern between the parents. The only affection in the household was between mother and sons. The boys were sorry for their mother and hated their mean, bad-tempered father.

The gay, beautiful Molly, turned into a sad, prematurely aged wife, and at the age of fifty suddenly, without fuss, she died of a stroke in her classroom.

From the moment of his wife's death, Uncle Jack was desolate. He immediately stopped all work, lost all interest in his farms, and bought a house next to the churchyard where Molly was buried. In one of the ground floor rooms he had a special window made so that he could look out on Molly's grave. He had the most expensive, most impressive memorial built for his wife, whom throughout their married life he had neglected and humiliated. Now he liked to think and talk of her, as of a cherished, very special, very important person. For the rest of his life, six full years, he sat by the window staring at her grave.

When Uncle Jack died, not yet sixty, he had not really been ill but simply gave up his futile life. His one wish was to be buried next to his wife, and to share with her the V.I.P. memorial which he had built in idealization of her and which was to reflect some glory on himself. Such idealization of the deceased may express an attempt at restitution and a defense against the pain of guilt.

Often idealization is closely linked to identification with the lost person. Identification appears to be a feature in all cases of bereavement, varying only in degree, and can be seen as one aspect of the necessary task of internalizing the lost person. It gives comfort to the mourner, makes him feel close to the deceased, and thus mitigates somewhat the pain of loss. . . .

It is well known that mourners often get the illness which led to the death of a close person. Habits and interests of the deceased may be taken over indiscriminately. A woman in her forties was never interested in gardening before losing a brother who had been a passionate gardener. After his death she compulsively got up every day at sunrise to tend the garden, since she felt this was what her brother wanted her to do.

A hitherto rather dull wife whose witty husband had died surprised herself and all around her by her newly acquired gift of repartee. She tried to explain this by saying alternately, "I have to do it for him now" or, "It isn't really me, he speaks out of me" (like a ventriloquist). This same woman, partner in a very good, loving marriage, told me that she had always been amused by her husband's patient peeling of the top of his boiled egg, while she used to cut it off. "Now," she said, "I just cannot bring myself to cut the top off, I have to peel it off patiently."

Another woman, who had always been upset (and often nagging) about her husband's bad table manners, developed these same manners after his death. Freud says: "If one has lost an object or has to give it up, one often compensates oneself by identifying oneself with it."[5] Identification with those aspects of the bereaved's personality which have been previously rejected (such as the bad table manners) may be an attempt at restitution, at repairing the rejection. Identification and restitution, anger, hostility, and guilt may all be interwoven during the mourning process. There are no distinct boundaries or timetables. Identification with the lost object, in Freud's sense, is a filling up, a replenishment of the self, in order to become a stronger, better integrated, more separate person. It is quite distinct from the identification with a marriage partner that . . . implies a weakening, a giving-up of the self.

Perhaps the most important and critical, and also the most painful and bewildering, phase of grief is *regression*. . . . People who believe strongly in self-discipline and control may be puzzled by regressive behavior in themselves and others. The bereaved may feel frightened and ashamed of the childish and irrational actions which neither he nor the people around him seem able to understand. What he needs most are sympathy and loving acceptance, which will make him feel secure. If these are lacking, the mourner is in great danger of getting struck in the regression which may then lead to illness. The fear that the regression will last forever probably causes anxiety to all bereaved people. In my case material as well as in encounters I have not reported, people have said, "I felt like I was going insane"; "I was terrified that things were beyond my control." The terror of these people is not just because they behaved in a childish way, but because of the compulsion to do it.

We have seen earlier how in grief the mourner falls back on methods which in childhood helped to control and master pain. Regressive behavior is one of these. The three-year-old who starts wetting and soiling again after the birth of a rival sibling is asking for extra care and attention. Both the small child who wants to be a baby again and the adult in pain learn to use regression in their new situation to gain comfort and love. If the desired response is forthcoming, the toddler can move on and make a step toward growth, become the "big" brother or sister. The regression of the adult mourner can alternate with expressions of exceptional maturity and self-discipline (as in the case of the woman who gave in to her most infantile needs when she wrapped herself in a soaking hot bathtowel, but showed outstanding strength and control by reading one of the lessons at her husband's memorial service). Regression in grief must be seen and supported as a means toward adaptation and health.

THE PHASE OF ADAPTATION

There are two points on which all studies of grief and mourning agree. I have already mentioned the first, that shock is the initial response to bereavement. The second is much more difficult to define. It is the fundamental importance of being able to mourn and to "complete the mourning process." What exactly does this mean?

We have seen that the course of mourning cannot be predicted because it depends on many factors, such as the relationship between the lost person and the survivor, the circumstances of the death, the external situation, and the inner resources of the bereaved. Therefore, however much we learn about patterns of mourning, they will take different forms with each individual. The precondition for a person to "complete" his mourning process must be that he is allowed to mourn in his own way and time.

There is no norm for mourning and no norm for adaptation; nor can there be any definite time limit for either. The time mentioned in studies for the various phases and for the total process of mourning is too short to fit the needs of many mourners. One year, comprehending the full circle of the seasons with their birth and death symbols, may be the most meaningful "objective" period of time for the completion of the mourning process, although I have known mourners who after the loss of their partners suffered from episodes of depression, despair, and regressive setbacks for well over two years and later made exceptionally good adaptations to a new life. Even then, periods of despair and grief as well as searching may recur in special external or internal situations, such as an anniversary or illness. These recurrences should not be regarded as pathological. The only valid criteria for pathological grief is that the mourner is unable to cope with his life. In any case, there is never just a continuous progress with a definite date for adaptation, and periods of apparently good recovery may well be followed by periods of pathology.

Physicians are familiar with means for alleviating pain and supporting the natural healing powers of physical wounds. But for the wound caused by the loss of a loved person there has been great uncertainty in our time and culture as to how far and in what way help can be given. Medical or psychotherapeutic help will be required only in exceptional cases, but in the loneliness and isolation of modern society every mourner needs special sympathy and support from the people around him.

The mourning process, like the process of physical healing, involves the healing of a wound, a new formation of healthy tissue. In mourning, however, the cause of the injury, the loss of an important person, must not be forgotten. Only when the lost person has been internalized and becomes part of the bereaved, a part which can be integrated with his own personality and enriches it, is the mourning process complete. With this enriched personality the adjustment to a new life has to be made.

It is often the bereaved who has never been able to face his own death who cannot successfully survive bereavement. As Boswell wrote in his *Life of Samuel Johnson:* "Our fear of death is so great, that the whole of life is but keeping away the thoughts of it." In 1755, after his wife's death, he wrote: "I have ever since seemed to myself broken off from mankind; a kind of solitary wanderer in the wild of life, without any direction, or fixed point of view; a gloomy gazer on the world to which I have little relation."[6] Repressed or delayed mourning may contribute to such a condition, and may lead to an impoverished life.

In his major contribution to the theme of grief in "Mourning and Melancholia," Freud makes clear that

> although grief involves grave departures from the normal attitude to life, it never occurs to us to regard it as a morbid condition and hand the mourner over to medical treatment. We rest assured that after a lapse of time it will be overcome, and we look upon any interference with it as inadvisable or even harmful.

"What is the task which the work of mourning performs?" Freud asks — and answers, "The testing of reality, having shown that the loved person no longer exists, requires forthwith that all the libido shall be withdrawn from its attachments to this object." In other words, faced with the fact of death, the bereaved has to withdraw his emotional attachment from the deceased.

Freud then speaks of the struggle which arises from this demand, a struggle which can be so intense "that a turning away from reality ensues, the object being clung to through the medium of hallucinatory wish-psychosis."

The difficulty of facing another's death is sometimes so strong as to make the acceptance of reality impossible. An example of hallucinatory wish-psychosis would be Mrs. Green's vision of her husband flying in through the hospital window to visit her. But as Freud says, "The normal outcome is that deference for reality gains the day ... Why this process of carrying out the behest of reality bit by bit, which is in the nature of compromise, should be so extraordinarily painful is not at all easy to explain in terms of mental economics. It is worth noting that this pain seems natural to us."[7]

Melanie Klein, whose contribution to the subject is pre-eminent, goes some way toward answering Freud's question about mental economics:

> The pain experienced in the slow process of testing reality in the work
> of mourning seems to be partly due to the necessity, not only to
> renew the links to the external world and thus continuously
> re-experience the loss, but at the same time, and by means of this, to
> rebuild with anguish the inner world which is felt to be in danger of
> deteriorating and collapsing.[8]

In "Mourning and Melancholia" Freud stresses as the paramount task in mourning the withdrawal of libido from the dead person, and lays no emphasis on the other, perhaps even more important part of the task, that of internalizing the lost love object. This is probably because his concern in this work is to contrast the relative normality of the process of mourning with the relatively pathological state of melancholia. At that time, Freud was not primarily interested in mourning as such. Later on, in "Mourning and Melancholia," and still more clearly in *The Ego and the Id* (1923), he put forward the notion that the withdrawal of the libido that attaches one person to another can only take place when the lost person is reinstated with the Ego.

Abraham, in his *Short Study of the Development of the Libido*, says, "The loved object is not gone, for now I carry it within myself and can never lose it."[9] This process of internalizing the dead, taking the deceased into oneself and containing him so that he becomes part of one's inner self, is the most important task in mourning. It does not happen immediately; for a varying span of time the bereaved is still in touch with the external presence of the lost person. Once the task of internalizing has been achieved, the dependence on the external presence diminishes and the bereaved becomes able to draw on memories, happy or unhappy, and to share these with others, making it possible to talk, think, or feel about the dead person.

From the moment life begins through all the phases of child development, human growth depends on accepting and mastering loss—loss of the safety in the womb, loss of the breast, loss, real, fantasied or threatened. Melanie Klein (in her paper "Mourning and Its Relationship to Manic-depressive States") sees the "infantile depressive position" (the sadness which we can sometimes see in the expression of a preverbal baby who seems to tell us that he is frightened and feels lost because the "good" mother has deserted him and has become "bad") as the first response to the threat of loss, a threat which rouses feelings of hate toward the loved mother, whose loss is feared. The contradicting feelings for the same person, which are struggling inside the baby, are his first frightening experience of ambivalence. They set the scene for all the future struggles in this major human predicament, to come to terms with ambivalence, and the contradicting forces which make up the inner and outer worlds.

To cope with loss, the child has to take into itself the object whose absence frightens him—in other words, in order not to get too bewildered by the mother's comings and goings, the infant has to set up a permanent mother inside himself. If the real mother is felt to be more threatening than reassuring, or if the child feels her absence more than her presence, the internalized mother will be a "bad" instead of a "good" object. Melanie Klein sees success at establishing an internal "good" object in early childhood as a precondition for the ability to tolerate later anxiety about loss and separation. In adult mourning the fears of losing the internalized "good" parent are revived through the death of a loved person. This is what the mourner means when he says, "I have not only lost my husband (wife), I have lost everything good; I have lost myself." In the process of mourning, the bereaved will repeat the same defenses used in the infantile depressive position to master "bad" objects and the feelings they arouse, and to restore the "good" ones, in order to be able to cope with the ambivalence about the dead person who has deserted him. Just as the frightened child has to set up a permanent mother inside himself, the adult mourner has to internalize, take into himself, his loved object so that he will never lose it.

Klein's point that the child's internal "good" object is a precondition for the ability to tolerate loss and separation is taken further by John Bowlby's studies on separation.[10] Bowlby stresses the concepts of attachment and loss, and sees separation anxiety in early childhood as the main key to understanding the mourning process. Separation anxiety expresses dread of some unspecified danger, either from the outside or from mounting internal tension, and dread of losing the object believed capable of protecting or relieving one. The baby's first response to this threat is protest and screaming: followed, if the threat is not removed, by withdrawal, apathy, and despair.

Separation anxiety will be reactivated in all subsequent fears of losing a person to whom a deep attachment exists. It is a natural process and the basis for mourning. If a child has not experienced separation anxiety, this indicates that he has not been able to develop a true attachment, and his ability to cope with loss through mourning will be crippled. So will be his chances to internalize the lost person as part of the mourning process, and to strengthen his own identity with the support of the internalized object. In short, to tolerate separation anxiety and to mourn are signs of the healthy personality who is capable of deep attachment. Without real attachments, secure autonomy cannot be achieved.[11]*

---

*I would like here to express my indebtedness to Colin Murray Parkes and to Yorick Spiegel, who through their untiring and sustained research have made major contributions to our knowledge in this field, and whose findings I have widely used. Yorick Spiegel, *Der Prozess des Trauerns* (Munich: Kaiser Verlag, 1973).

I also want to mention those autobiographical publications which focus on the loss of a marriage partner and which have helped me to link the increased knowledge of processes of mourning with the individual mourner and his unique experience: C. S. Lewis, *A Grief Observed* (New York: Seabury Press, 1963); Mary Stott, *Forgetting's No Excuse* (London: Faber and Faber, 1973); Sarah Morris, *Grief and How to Live With It* (New York: Grosset & Dunlop, 1972).

Notes

1 *Death, Grief and Mourning in Contemporary Britain* (London: Cresset Press, 1965), p. 130.

2 Colin Murray Parkes, *Bereavement: Studies of Grief in Adult Life* (New York: International Universities Press, 1973), p. 39.

3 London: Faber and Faber, 1961, pp. 44–45.

4 John Hinton, *Dying* (Baltimore: Penguin Books, 1967), p. 181.

5 Sigmund Freud, *New Introductory Lectures* in *Complete Psychological Works of Sigmund Freud (Standard Edition)*, trans. and ed. James Strachey (London: Hogarth Press, 1953–66), distributed in the United States by the Macmillan Co., vol. 22, p. 86.

6 James Boswell, *Life of Johnson*, R. W. Chapman and C. B. Tinker, eds. (New York: Oxford University Press, 1953), pp. 416, 196.

7 Sigmund Freud, *Standard Edition*, vol. 14, p. 244.

8 "Mourning and Its Relationship to Manic-depressive States," *International Journal of Psycho-Analysis* 21 (1940): 125.

9 Karl Abraham, "A Short Study of the Development of the Libido," in *Selected Papers* (London: Hogarth Press, 1924), p. 437.

10 *Attachment and Loss*, vol. I, *Attachment* (New York: Basic Books, 1969).

11 John Bowlby, "Pathological Mourning and Childhood Mourning," *Journal of the American Psycho-Analytic Association:* II (1963): 500.

35 · Postvention and the Survivor-Victim

Edwin S. Shneidman

The following selection is taken from Deaths of Man. *Here Shneidman introduces the view of the survivor as a victim and discusses working with survivors for several months after the death of a loved one—a type of therapy he calls "postvention."*

A person's death is not only an ending: it is also a beginning—for the survivors. Indeed, in the case of suicide the largest public health problem is neither the prevention of suicide (about 25,000 suicides are reported each year in the United States but the actual number is much higher, probably twice the reported rate) nor the management of suicide attempts (about eight times the number of reported committed suicides), but the alleviation of the effects of stress in the survivor-victims of suicidal deaths,

whose lives are forever changed and who, over a period of years, number in the millions.

This is the process I have called "postvention": those appropriate and helpful acts that come *after* the dire event itself (1971, 1974, 1975). The reader will recognize prevention, intervention, and postvention as roughly synonymous with the traditional health concepts of primary, secondary, and tertiary prevention, or with concepts like immunization, treatment, and rehabilitation. Lindemann (1944) has referred to "preventive intervention in a four-year-old child whose father committed suicide"; it would be simpler to speak of postvention.

Postvention, then, consists of activities that reduce the aftereffects of a traumatic event in the lives of the survivors. Its purpose is to help survivors live longer, more productively, and less stressfully than they are likely to do otherwise.

It is obvious that some deaths are more stigmatizing or traumatic than others: death by murder, by the negligence of oneself or some other person, or by suicide. Survivor-victims of such deaths are invaded by an unhealthy complex of disturbing emotions: shame, guilt, hatred, perplexity. They are obsessed with thoughts about the death, seeking reasons, casting blame, and often punishing themselves.

The recent investigations of widows by Dr. C. M. Parkes (1970) are most illuminating. The principal finding of his studies is that independent of her age, a woman who has lost a husband recently is more likely to die (from alcoholism, malnutrition, or a variety of disorders related to neglect of self, disregard of a prescribed medical regimen or commonsense precautions, or even a seemingly unconscious boredom with life) or to be physically ill or emotionally disturbed than a nonwidowed person. The findings seem to imply that grief is itself a dire process, almost akin to a disease, and that there are subtle factors at work that can take a heavy toll unless they are treated and controlled.

The striking results have been intuitively known long before they were empirically demonstrated. The efforts of Erich Lindemann (1944), Gerald Caplan (1964), and Phyllis R. Silverman (1969) to aid survivors of "heavy deaths" were postventions based on the premise of heightened risk in bereaved persons. Lindemann's work (which led to his formulations of acute grief and crisis intervention) began with his treatment of the survivors of the tragic Coconut Grove nightclub fire in Boston in 1942, in which 499 persons died. Phyllis Silverman's projects, under the direction of Gerald Caplan, have centered around a widow-to-widow program. These efforts bear obvious similarities with the programs of "befriending" practiced by the Samaritans, an organization founded by the Reverend Chad Varah (1966; 1973) and most active in Great Britain.

On the basis of work with parents of adolescent (fifteen- to nineteen-year-old) suicides in Philadelphia, Herzog (1968) has enumerated three psychological stages of postventive care: (1) resuscitation: working with the initial shock of grief in the first twenty-four hours; (2) rehabilitation: consultations with family members from the first month to about the sixth month; and (3) renewal: the healthy tapering off of the mourning process, from six months on.

A case can be made for viewing the sudden death of a loved one as a disaster and, using the verbal bridge provided by that concept, learning from the professional literature on conventionally recognized disasters—sudden, unexpected events, such as earthquakes and large-scale explosions, that cause a large number of deaths and have widespread effects. Martha Wolfenstein (1957) has described a "disaster syndrome": a "combination of emotional dullness, unresponsiveness to outer stimulation and inhibition of activity. The individual who has just undergone disaster is apt to suffer from at least a transitory sense of worthlessness; his usual capacity for self-love becomes impaired."

A similar psychological contraction is seen in the initial shock reaction to catastrophic news—death, failure, disclosure, disgrace, the keenest personal loss. Studies of disastrous ship sinking by P. Friedman and L. Lum (1957) and of the effects of a tornado by A. F. Wallace (1956) both describe an initial psychic shock followed by motor retardation, flattening of affect, somnolence, amnesia, and suggestibility. There is marked increase in dependency needs with regressive behavior and traumatic loss of feelings of identity, and, overall, a kind of "affective anesthesia." There is an unhealthy docility, a cowed and subdued reaction. One is reminded of Lifton's (1967) description of "psychic closing off" and "psychic numbing" among the *Hibakusha*, the survivors of the atomic bomb dropped on Hiroshima:

> Very quickly — sometimes within minutes or even seconds — *Hibakusha* began to undergo a process of "psychic closing off"; that is, they simply ceased to feel. They had a clear sense of what was happening around them, but their emotional reactions were unconsciously turned off. Others' immersion in larger responsibilities was accompanied by a greater form of closing off which might be termed "psychic numbing." Psychic closing off could be transient or it could extend itself, over days and even months, into more lasting psychic numbing. In the latter cases it merged with feelings of depression and despair. . . . In response to this general pattern of disintegration, *Hibakusha* did not seem to develop clearcut psychiatric syndromes. To describe the emotional state that did develop they frequently used a term which means a state of despondency, abstraction or emptiness, and may be translated as "state of collapse" or "vacuum state." Also relevant is a related state . . . a listlessness, withdrawn countenance, "expression of wanting nothing more," or what has been called in other contexts "the thousand-mile stare." Conditions like the "vacuum state" or "thousand-mile-stare" may be thought of as apathy but are also profound expressions of despair: a form of severe and prolonged psychic numbing in which the survivor's responses to his environment are reduced to a minimum—often to those necessary to keep him alive—and

in which he feels divested of the capacity either to wish or will . . . related forms of psychic numbing occur in people undergoing acute grief reactions as survivors of the deaths of family members—here vividly conveyed in a psychiatric commentary by Erich Lindemann (1944):

"A typical report is this, 'I go through all the motions of living. I look after my children. I do my errands. I go to social functions, but it is like being in a play; it doesn't really concern me. I can't have any warm feelings. If I would have any feelings at all I would be angry with everybody' . . . The absence of emotional display in this patient's face and actions was quite striking. Her face had a masklike appearance, her movements were formal, stilted, robotlike, without the fine play of emotional expression."

All this sounds remarkably like Henry Murray's (1967) description of partial death, those "psychic states characterized by a marked diminution or near-cessation of affect involving both hemispheres of concern, the inner and the outer world."

Postventive efforts are not limited to this initial stage of shock, but are more often directed to the longer haul, the day-to-day living with grief over a year or more following the first shock of loss. Postvention is in the honored tradition of holding a wake or sitting *shiva*; but it means more. Typically it extends over months during that critical first year, and it shares many of the characteristics of psychotherapy: talk, abreaction, interpretation, reassurance, direction, and even gentle confrontation. It provides an arena for the expression of guarded emotions, especially such negative affective states as anger, shame, and guilt. It puts a measure of stability into the grieving person's life and provides an interpersonal relationship with the therapist which can be genuine, in that honest feelings need not be suppressed or dissembled.

An example may be useful: Late one afternoon a beautiful nineteen-year-old girl was stabbed to death by an apparent would-be rapist in a government building. Within an hour her parents were hit between the eyes with the news (and this is the way these matters are usually handled) by two rather young, well-meaning, but inexperienced policemen. The victim was the couple's only child. Their immediate reactions were shock, disbelief, over-whelming grief, and mounting rage, most of it directed at the agency where the murder had occurred.

A few days later, right after the funeral, they were in the office of a high official who was attempting to tender his condolences when the mother said in an anguished tone: "There is nothing you can do!" To which, with good presence of mind, he answered that while it was true the girl could not be brought back to life, there was something that could be done. Whether he knew the term or not, it was postvention that he had in mind.

I began seeing the parents, usually together, sometimes separately. The principal psychological feature was the mother's anger. I permitted her to voice her grief and to vent her rage (sometimes even at me), while I retained the role of the voice of reason: empathizing with their state, recognizing the legitimacy of their feelings when I could, but not agreeing when in good conscience I could not agree. I felt that I was truly their friend, and I believed they felt so too.

A few months after the brutal murder, the mother developed serious symptoms that required major surgery, from which she made a good recovery. I had insisted that each of them see a physician for a physical examination. Although the mother had had similar difficulty some years before, the situation raises the intriguing (and unanswerable) question in my mind whether or not that organic flurry would have occurred in her body if she had not suffered the shock of her daughter's death. Whatever the answer to that may be, I doubt very much that she would have recovered so well and so rapidly if she had received no postventive therapy.

The parents had an extraordinarily good marriage. Many relatives gave them emotional support. The husband, more laconic and more stoic, was my principal cotherapist—although I did not forget his needs and saw him alone occasionally, when for example, his wife was in the hospital.

Several months after the tragedy the parents seemed to be in rather good shape, physically and emotionally, everything considered. They still had low-level grief, and no doubt always will. But what is most important for this discussion is that each of them has stated that the process of working through their grief was made easier for them and that the outcome was better and more quickly achieved (though not with undue haste) as a result of our postventive sessions, that something of positive value had been done for them, and that they felt that something of this nature ought to be done for more people who found themselves in similar situations.

Quite a few months have passed since the homicide, and the murderer has still not been apprehended. If an arrest is ever made, it will inevitably present renewed conflicts for the girl's parents, and a new question will be raised: Should someone also be concerned with the welfare of the parents of the accused after his arrest?

Most deaths occur in the hospitals, and the dying patient is often isolated and his awareness clouded by drugs. (We nowadays rarely see our loved ones die "naturally" at home—a common event a few generations ago.) The topic of death is an especially unpleasant one for medical personnel. Death is the enemy; death represents failure. It has been noted that physicians constitute one of the few groups (along with policemen and combat soldiers) licensed to take lives in our society; at the same time, however, relatively few physicians deal with dying patients (consider the vast numbers of orthopedists, dermatologists, obstetricians, pediatricians, psychiatrists, and other specialists who deal with conditions that only rarely result in death) and are therefore ill equipped to teach others about death comfortably and meaningfully.

From the point of view of the staff-patient relationship vis-á-vis death, there are essentially three kinds of hospital wards or services. They can be labeled benign, emergent, and dire. A benign ward is one on which deaths are not generally expected and the relationship between staff and patient may be of short or long duration: obstetrical services, orthopedic wards, psychiatric wards. A death on such a service is a sharp tragedy and cause for special self-examination. The reaction is both to loss of a person and to loss of control. The staff, typically, is not so much in mourning as in a state of shock at administrative and professional failure.

Emergency services are quite different. These are the hospital emergency room and the intensive care unit. Here death is not an uncommon experience but the relationship between staff and patient is short lived; the patient is hardly known as a person, and there is typically no time for meaningful interpersonal relationships to develop: the focus is on physiological functioning. Patients are often unconscious and almost always acutely ill. Death on such a service is not mourned as deep personal loss. It is a "happening," distressing but seldom totally unexpected. The staff—often self-selected—must be inured to the constant psychological toll of working in such a setting. The dangers are callousness, depression, and even acting out, especially in the forms of alcoholism, drug abuse, and heightened sexual activity.

It is the dire service that poses the most stressful problems for physicians and nurses. On such a ward the patients have grim prognoses (and are often doomed when they come to the ward, their illnesses diagnosed as cancer, leukemia, scleroderma, or whatever), and they remain there for an extended period of time, long enough for personal relations to be formed and for them to be known, loved, and then mourned as "real" human beings. Physicians practicing specialties dealing with fatal conditions—certain hematologists, oncologists, radiologists, and so on—know death all too intimately. Often there is not a week that is free of a death. The psychological stresses on such a service may be even greater for nurses, for they face the problem of giving intimate care, risking personal investment, and then dealing with loss.

Consider the following case: A thirty-year-old man was admitted to a hospital ward diagnosed as having leukemia in the terminal stage. He had an unusual combination of physical and personality characteristics that made him an especially "difficult" patient—not difficult in behavior, but difficult to see grow more ill and die: he was handsome, good-natured, alert; he had a keen sense of humor and was flirtatious with nurses, and through intermittent spells of depression and concern with dying he was remarkably brave, reassuring doctors and nurses and telling them not to worry about him or take it so hard. (It would have been much easier for them if he had been difficult in the usual sense—querulous, demanding, complaining; then they might have accommodated more easily to his death.)

As a consultant on the ward, I visited him each day, having been asked to see him because of his depression. He talked openly about the topic of death and his fears of pain, aloneness, and loss, and specifically about his own death and its meaning for his wife and children. These sessions were, by his own account, very meaningful to him. It was the kind of death work that is not unusual in this kind of circumstance. But what was of special professional interest was the behavior, both before and after his death, of a nurse and of his physician.

The nurse, an exceptionally attractive young woman, grew to like the patient very much, with feelings that seemed to strike deeper than routine professional countertransference. I once witnessed a fascinating scene in which the nurse was massaging the patient's back while his wife stood stiffly off to one side; it was an interesting question as to who, at that moment, "owned" the dying patient. (But this nurse was extraordinarily good with the wife, taking her out to dinner, helping her with her young children, making, in a friendly and noncompetitive way, a number of practical arrangements for her.) After the young man's death there were several mourners for whom postvention was necessary, and the nurse was one of them. She grieved for one she had loved and lost, and her grief was sharpened and complicated by its somewhat secret and taboo nature.

The reaction of the physician in the case, a hematologist in this forties, was rather different but no less intense. We had planned to get together after the patient's death to discuss, I thought, interesting features of the case and possible plans for future collaborative efforts. Instead, he came into my office and announced that the young man's death had been the last straw. He was sick and tired of having all the doctors in the country dump their dying patients on him. He wondered how I could bear to see the young man every day while he was dying, and I countered candidly that I had wondered the same thing about him. Mainly he wanted a safe arena in which to vent his feelings about having had enough of death and dying for a while. Within a few weeks he followed his announced intention of making a major change in his professional life: he accepted a faculty position in a medical school in another state and in a specialty other than hematology.

In my own postventive work I have come to at least a few tentative conclusions:

1. Total care of a dying person needs to include contact and rapport with the survivors-to-be.

2. In working with survivor-victims of dire deaths, it is best to begin as soon as possible after the tragedy; within the first seventy-two hours if possible.

3. Remarkably little resistance is met from survivor-victims; most are willing to talk to a professional person, especially one who has no ax to grind and no pitch to make.

4. The role of negative emotions toward the deceased—irritation, anger, envy, guilt—needs to be explored, but not at the very beginning.

5. The professional plays the important role of reality tester. He or she is not so much the echo of conscience as the quiet voice of reason.

6. Medical evaluation of the survivors is crucial. One should be alert for possible decline in physical health and in overall mental well-being.

Three brief final points: Postvention can be viewed as prevention for the next decade or for the next generation; postvention can be practiced by nurses, lawyers, social workers, physicians, psychologists, and good neighbors and friends—thanatologists all; and a comprehensive total health program in any enlightened community will include all three elements of care: prevention, intervention and postvention.

References

Caplan, Gerald. *Principles of Preventive Psychiatry*. New York: Basic Books, 1964.

Friedman, Paul, and Lum, L. Some Psychiatric Notes on the *Andrea Doria* Disaster. *American Journal of Psychiatry* 114 (1957):426–32.

Herzog, Alfred A. Clinical Study of Parental Response to Adolescent Death by Suicide with Recommendations for Approaching the Survivors. In Norman L. Faberow (Ed.), *Proceedings of the Fourth International Conference for Suicide Prevention*. Los Angeles: Delmar Publishing Co., 1968.

Lifton, Robert Jay. *Death in Life: Survivors of Hiroshima*. New York: Random House, 1967.

Lindemann, Erich. Symptomatology and Management of Acute Grief. *American Journal of Psychiatry* (1944): 141–48.

Murray, Henry A. Dead to the World: The Passions of Herman Melville. In Edwin S. Shneidman (Ed.), *Essays in Self-Destruction*. New York: Science House, 1967.

Parkes, Colin Murray. The First Year of Bereavement: A Longitudinal Study of the Reaction of London Widows to the Death of Their Husbands. *Psychiatry* 33 (1970):444–67.

Shneidman, Edwin S. Prevention, Intervention and Postvention of Suicide. *Annals of Internal Medicine* 75 (1971):453–58.

Shneidman, Edwin S. *Deaths of Man*. New York: Penguin Books, 1974.

Shneidman, Edwin S. Postvention: The Care of the Bereaved. In Robert O. Pasnau (Ed.), *Consultation-Liaison Psychiatry*. New York: Grune and Stratton, 1975.

Silverman, Phyllis R. The Widow-to-Widow Program: An Experiment in Preventive Intervention. *Mental Hygiene*. 53 (1969):333–37.

Varah, Chad. *The Samaritans*. New York: Macmillan, 1966.

Varah, Chad. *The Samaritans in the 70's*. London: Constable, 1973.

Wallace, A. F. *Tornado in Worcester: An Exploratory Study of Individual and Community Behavior in an Extreme Situation*. Washington, D.C.: National Research Council, 1956.

Wolfenstein, Martha. *Disaster: A Psychological Essay*. New York: Macmillan, 1957.

PART VIII
TWENTIETH-CENTURY MEGADEATH

Contents

Anyone who knows anything knows that we live in an era more perilous than any previous time. Suddenly, in the 1940s we developed a "gadget," a procedure, whereby we could destroy the present, expunge the future, and erase the past. Politicians speak of megadeath and overkill as though they were discussing menus. The blind lead the bewildered and those top leaders with access to specially built government bombshelters speak with the most passionate intensity. If we don't solve this issue—or, more directly stated, if we muff it—nothing else may much matter.

This part also contains reminders of megadeaths in the twentieth century short of global nuclear destruction: genocide, the Holocaust, the 110 million murders committed so far in this century by organized governments. The past is almost unspeakable; there may be no future to speak of and no voices to speak of it.

The four chapters in this part are by an author-essayist, an anguished survivor, a social psychiatrist, a psychologist, and an important government official.

420

36 · Agents of Death

Gil Elliot

Gil Elliot was born in Scotland in 1931 and studied at Glasgow and Sussex universities. In his remarkable work The Twentieth Century Book of the Dead, *from which this selection is taken, Elliot details the 110 million murders committed by governments in this century.*

From The Twentieth Century Book of the Dead, *by Gil Elliot. Copyright © 1972 by Gil Elliot. Reprinted by permission of Ballantine Books, a Division of Random House, Inc., and Penguin Books, Ltd.*

DEATH MACHINES

In considering violent or untimely death, it is the manner and means of death—not the general phenomenon of death itself—that are of primary philosophical interest.

Can the manner and means of violent death be reduced to a knowable mechanism—a "death machine"?

Of the ways in which we can think of knowing or understanding such a death machine, one is to "know all the facts," another is to ask the question, "how does it relate to me?"

To know the facts is desirable. To know *all* the facts about such a phenomenon as the death machine would clearly be an absurd pretension. Yet, "waiting for science to establish all the facts" is the everyday limbo of the game of factual knowledge. Whilst playing this waiting game we are supposed to suspend the judgment of values, and even to neglect that most sensitive tool of inquiry, sharpened by experience, alert to survive, vivid in its brief life: intuition. Intuition, or the practice of relating oneself to the object in the immediacy of experience, is, like life itself, "unreliable." It seems that the certainties of science are worth waiting for. But when these so-called certainties appear they are pluralistic, as conflicting, as subject to opinion as anything else. In short, the procedures of "objective" inquiry are just as much modified by self and by fantasy as those of subjective inquiry. The difference is that in the first case the part played by the self is concealed from the observer, and often from the would-be scientist himself.

Shelley said that the poet is the "unacknowledged legislator" of the world. In our grim times the chief unacknowledged legislator has been the subjective fantasy of political leaders, academic theorists, social groups masquerading as "objective reality," "historical necessity," "political realism," "value-free judgment," "scientific objectivity," and so forth.

The death machine, then, is partly a factual object—an ever-incomplete accretion of facts; and partly a philosophical object—uncertain of definition yet conceived as a whole to which I relate myself, so intuitively that the "I" itself will become, if necessary, subject to analysis as part of the death machine!

We might manage a preliminary definition, or at least tease out some of the relevant parts, of the death machine if we look at those versions of it which [can be] loosely identified with different areas of macroviolence. The *war machine*, the *total-war machine*, and the *total-state machine* are pretty well factual objects, identifiable in terms of organization, weapons, production, deployment of plans and personnel.

I took the war machine of the First World War as the type of the twentieth-century war machine. What characterizes it most is a change in the nature of the *alienating process*. War was traditionally a conflict between two alienated sides, "enemies." During the First World War even the men in the trenches ceased to believe that the enemy was the men in the other trenches. The alienating process of the modern war machine divides men into two subjective environments: the physical environment of the victim (the death environment) and the technological environment of the systems and machines which produce death. Some have perceived this in terms of class alienation. According to this view, the killing systems and machines are within the conscious control of the leaders and generals, and it is their class alienation from the poor that prevents them from using restraint in the use of these systems against the chief victims, the ordinary soldiers who without their uniforms are, of course, the poor. I am sure that this process—which I shall call *natural alienation* when I discuss it below in the context of the nature machine—is relevant to a discussion of how the modern war machine came into being, or evolved. The other view is that the machines and systems inhabit a faceless environment of their own, and dominate their users. However it evolved in the first place, it is this, which we can fairly call *technological alienation*, that remains and persists as the most characteristic feature of the twentieth-century war machine.

It is also characteristic of the war machine that the same man, the soldier, operates the killing systems as well as being their victim. The *total-war* machine extends the alienation principle, for here death environments are also created for people who are not themselves involved in operating the killing systems, that is civilians shot, starved, or bombed, soldiers and civilians enclosed in camps. Here the alienation between the environment of the killing system—military or administrative—and the environment of the victim is total. The same is true of the total-state machine, with one additional refinement. The alienated identity of the victim is not merely created by the technological sweep of the machine, as it is in the total-war machine. In this case, before the victim is included in the killing technology (the labor camp, the mass execution, the deportation) a paranthropoid identity, such as class enemy or enemy of the people, is created for him out of the ideology of the total-state machine. That is to say, *ideological alienation* precedes the technological alienation.

The essential difference between the war machine and the total-war machine is one of *consciousness*. Traditionally war was a ritual in which certain qualities such as bravery, generalship, morale, cunning contributed to the symbolic outcome known as "victory." Where ritual and symbol broke down you had chaotic, meaningless conflicts such as the Thirty Years' War. The First World War was *not* this chaotic, meaningless thing, not merely the war of attrition and exhaustion. It was a case—*the* case—of ritual and symbol being outstripped and replaced by a new logic of war. But it was not yet a conscious logic. Total war as it developed thereafter was a *conscious* departure from the natural order provided by ritual and symbol. But how conscious? and how true has the logic of the new order been to the human consciousness?

As we know, the raw material of total war, and hence the chief premises of its logic are, one, vast numbers of people and, two, machines.

The vast numbers were first represented by the figure of the citizen-soldier, who reached his apotheosis in the First World War. By the Second World War he was already outstripped, in numbers participating, by the plain *citizen*. The next total war will involve very few soldiers as against citizens. Thus the logic of numbers reaches its conclusion, that total war is war between citizens not soldiers. But this logic cannot sustain a theory of war. "Soldiers" means a selective, limited number of people who can be used for purposive action. "Citizens" has no such finite, purposive meaning. It can only mean either "all citizens" or "citizens at random to an infinite number." It is an inchoate principle which cannot sustain a theory of conflict.

The responsibility for providing a rationale of total war thus devolves heavily upon the machines, and the logic of the machines is utterly fascinating. We should remember, first, that the machines of modern warfare are not merely horrid excrescences, nightmarish extrusions of the human mind. That is what they become in action, but purely as machines they are truly representative of us and the times we live in. The force of unprecedented numbers; impersonal answers to the demands of conflicting egos; the development of solutions under pressure; economical concentration of human ingenuity—all of these are represented and symbolized in our machines of warfare. They are our champions on the field of conflict.

It is part of the genius of living things that violence, when not directed to survival (food, protection), is economical in its effects. The biological response to conflict between equals is an instinctive ritual which (a) recognizes and respects the reality of the conflict or disagreement, and (b) reduces the struggle to symbolic dimensions. Animals fighting their own kind have a system of signals symbolizing defeat, victory, submission which allow the conflict to be resolved far short of irreparable physical harm. Human society is far too complex for such patterns to remain in a pure form, but they still survive at the roots of individual behavior. So far as group conflict is concerned, the most economical fighting ritual is that where two champions symbolize two numerous groups of people and fight on their behalf.

When it comes to the *machine as champion*, not only does the machine lack these reductive qualities: its response to the conflict situation is purely quantitative. Where there are two machines confronting one another, there will be soon four, and so on. The symbol or champion becomes greater in importance than what it represents. As the number and power of the machines increase, so does the number of people involved. But . . . the logic of numbers in the context of total war cannot sustain a rationale of conflict. Once again we reach a logical *impasse.* There is only one logical path left, and that is that the machines should fight one another *without the involvement of people.*

There are I think two possible reasons why we do not proceed with this logic and have a War of the Machines. One is the difficulty of arranging it; but I cannot believe this would be an insuperable obstacle. The other reason, and I believe the valid one, is that it would be absurd. For two opposing sides to contemplate arranging a War of the Machines would expose the absurdity of the logic of conflict by destructive machinery, and hence must lead to the dismantling of the machinery. But this is something that we could not bear to contemplate. So great is our spiritual and material investment in the machines, so much do they truly champion our values, so little do we have the wit or resourcefulness to devise other symbols to represent us in our conflicts, that we cannot face up to the logic of what we are doing. So the people and the machines continue to grow in numbers, the function of the people being to lend verisimilitude to the War of the Machines. Thus we achieve the poor man's version of sanity, which is the physical acceptance of whatever happens to exist, supported by whatever rationalization can be concocted at the moment.

. . . How true [has] the logic of total war been to the human consciousness? Well, it is a straightfoward denial of consciousness, of course. If the machines are looked upon as the objective results of thought, and in their development as the repositories of an objective logic, then the objective conclusion they display is, as demonstrated above, the need for their own destruction or dismantling. Consciousness demands that we draw this conclusion and act upon it. Indeed, if looked upon in this way the machines of war might provide the basis for a complete rationale of the place of conflict in human society, and of the destruction of human life in particular. In this case they would perform a useful rationalizing function, and would actually take human practice a progressive step beyond the simple logic of survival which governs the instinctive rituals of fighting. But, in the denial of this consciousness, we leave ourselves in that limbo known as the world of objective reality: a world of external objects in which the human being has no greater value than any other object displacing the same physical volume of space, a mental environment as hostile to the survival of life as a concentration camp.

What is the difference between the "nature machine" and these man-made death machines? Well, the *nature machine* is the mechanics of what used to be called, rather smugly, the balance of nature. It was a kind of long-term death machine for the poor in their environment, in the form of disease, epidemic, and shortage of food; tendencies that were exacerbated from time to time by natural disasters such as flood and crop failure, and by degenerate relationships between alienated classes. But the balance of nature was kept in the sense that life triumphed conspicuously over death.

On the basis of this definition we can draw some comparisons between death in the natural environment and in the man-made environment. By "natural environment" I mean the context of living when the world society as a whole was preindustrial. Many of the same conditions apply to present-day "underdeveloped" countries. But remember that however pre- or nonindustrial a society may be today, it almost certainly possesses two basic ingredients of the man-made environment: modern medicine, which may drastically reduce the deathrate and increase the population; and, at the least, rapid access to sophisticated military technology in the world community. The essential elements of the new man-made life and death.

If we think of untimely deaths in the natural environment as being the "violence of nature" then by far the greatest proportion came from *microviolence*, by which I mean the regular, widely distributed incidence of disease, infant mortality, malnutrition. Because of the gradual, pervasive nature of microviolence we tend to lack direct ways of apprehending its magnitude. For the same reason its impact is taken and absorbed by those directly affected by it: it does not *apparently* affect the structures of society as a whole. The macroviolence of nature—floods, famine, pestilence — had more apparent, dramatic impact, but in fact the quantitative effects were much smaller; and macroviolence was not institutionalized and given a continuous existence as it is in the man-made environment. The same was true of the macroviolent forms of fighting, which retained an inherent *reductive capacity;* whilst in the man-made environment, where the propensity to fight is invested in machines, the problem of reduction is divorced from instinct, ritual, and commonsense and is a problem of men and machines, and which control which.

The chief reason the effects of microviolence are unapparent is because it is an essential *part* of the social structure. The "balance of nature" depends upon it. So does the large-family structure and hence the specialized roles of men and women. Natural microviolence has a macroviolent impact only when the possibility of stopping it is perceived—then it promotes change or revolution; and when it *has* been stopped—then it promotes (in default of birth control) a population explosion with future implications of macroviolence.

The alienation process in the natural environment has the same roots as in the man-made environment, but develops in a radically different way. *Natural alienation* begins as a good and necessary separation of vigorous social elements from their bondage to the earth. As this separation flowers into the skills and arts of social management the classes formed from it, whether aristocratic or middle class, become physically alienated not only from the earthier aspects of themselves but from the people associated with the earth;

hence the despised class of *peasants*. In spite of this actual circumstance, of people living as it were in separate worlds, the Christian ethos claims to unite them. The people are spiritually united in God, and even physically united in a romanticized version of nature. When this unified consciousness is challenged or threatened we have *religious alienation*, the victims being in the post-Reformation period *minority Christian* denominations, in the turbulent and insecure seventeenth century *witches*, and persistently throughout the Christian centuries the *Jews*.

Physical and spiritual alienation is thus, in the natural environment, natural and religious, and in the man-made environment, technological and ideological. The victims are similar and the relevant psychological patterns seem to be very much the same. Peasants and Jews are major victims of both types of environment; they are the link as it were between the paranthropoid identities of one kind of society and the other. The great difference is in the kind of violence they bring about. The natural environment contained a continual microviolence which took a regular toll of human life and from time to time escalated sufficiently through plague, famine, and the chaos of war to give society a nasty jolt, but it preserved the balance of nature and never at any time threatened the existence of the human species. The man-made environment has brought microviolence impressively under control, but it threatens to disturb the balance of nature through industrial activity affecting the atmosphere, through the destruction of living species, and through uncontrolled increases in human population; it has brought macroviolence to a level which disastrously upsets the stability of societies, destroys morals, and threatens the continued existence of the human species.

Another link between the two environments is the *death-breeding machine* which at its most chaotic combines the violence of nature with that of technology. If technology is nature moulded by consciousness then we might expect this machine to contain a progression from a less-conscious to a more-conscious process. Certainly human consciousness is embedded in technology, yet apologists of modern war tend to present the technology as a massive simulation of nature about which little can be done; and it does seem more like a progression from blind nature to blind technology. If we extend the meaning of the *death-breeding process* to signify the active principle of all macroviolent systems, we shall see however that some are more conscious than others. Also we should remember that technology proceeds from a knowable first cause: man or, more specifically, scientific man. The death-breeding process leads to the final peak of the *total-death machine*, that which threatens the apocalyptic end and absolutely final appearance of . . . us.

What about . . . us? the celluloid lovers continually ask each other as we catch our breaths in the dark of the cinema, and that is also the question of the total-death machine. I suppose total death is some kind of absolute value and the philosophical core of the man-made death machine. Looking at the death machine as a philosophical entity, we might see the *nature machine* as the basic source of all; the *death-breeding process* as the active principle with its question about consciousness; and *total death* as the final question.

In the natural environment nature is supposed to unite society in happy worship of God. In the man-made environment technology is supposed to unite society in happy worship of Science. But if we look at the technologies of macroviolence we shall soon see that the reality is very different.

TECHNOLOGIES OF MACROVIOLENCE

Of the 110 million man-made deaths calculated in this century, sixty-two million died in conditions of *privation*, forty-six million from guns and bombs, or *hardware*, and two million from *chemicals*. In separating or *chemicals* as a category on its own I am thinking of the future as well as reflecting the century's progress from the heavy metal industries to the advances in the chemical industries which are such a significant part of our present-day scene. The familiar association of large-scale killing with factory production is not merely a colorful metaphor. Given the scale of modern killing technologies, their parallel development with that of industrial research and methods is inevitable. Hence the latest developments in killing methods are those associated with the fashionable science of the moment, biology.

Privation technologies

The basic kinds of privation technologies are I think best expressed as operating in *enclosed, semienclosed* and *diffuse* areas.

Enclosed privation areas

Camp privation is a highly conscious process, involving collection and movement of people, and selective identity of the victim. The systems of the killing technology are various: camp administration, collection or concentration system, and the wider governmental system directing all. Where the secret police system is a power in the land these functions are vertically integrated.

Deaths from privation technologies 62 million		
ENCLOSED	SEMIENCLOSED	DIFFUSE
Camp privation	City privation	Rural or mixed privation
20 million	16 million	26 million

But the people who perform the different functions, even if belonging to the same organization, differ from one another, partly in class and outlook, certainly in their spatial relationship with the victim. Where there is no curb on the power of the state (the first condition for camp privation), the state's victims are passed on *notionally* by those who make the rules, *administratively* by those who run the identification and collection system, and *physically* by the camp administration and guards. They are delivered from one set of people to the next. Arbitrary brutality occurs in those who are brutal by nature. But when the conditions notionally or administratively laid down are inhuman, and are supervised by the kind of people who survive by obeying orders, then the system is brutal and that is a more powerful force than arbitrary brutality. The most powerful force of all is physical neglect.

ENCLOSED PRIVATION AREAS

Camp privation

Enclosed ghetto, 1 m. deaths

Concentration camp, 2.5 m. deaths

Prisoners-of-war camp, 4.5 m. deaths

Labour camp, 12 m. deaths

The *enclosed ghettoes* of Poland—Warsaw, Lodz, Lublin—were used as camps. They were sealed off city areas in which people from outside were concentrated. They were virtually total-death environments. They are unique as enclosed privation areas in which the identity of the victim was not selective as to age and sex (although it is true that less severe privations have been suffered by entire families in transit camps for deported populations and in displaced person camps for refugees).

The German *prisoner-of-war camps* for Russians were the only enclosed privation areas with entirely male populations. Some of these camps were certainly places of total death. They are the most extreme example of sheer physical neglect, more powerful in its effects (cannibalism, for instance) than enforced human pressures.

Although the degeneration of conditions in the German *concentration camps* was possibly due to the secret police arm in particular, the German camps as a whole reflected the policy of the government over a period and hence to a very large extent the society as a whole. Racist attitudes were responsible for the ghettoes, and for the treatment of Slav prisoners of war in a way different from people of other races. The German camp system in its developed form was possible only as the result of military conquest, and with military cooperation. Nine-tenths of the victims were foreigners. Any individual actions leading to their presence in the camps were committed in response to military aggression. In the chain of people who pass on victims from one to the other, the military acted as delivery men to the secret police, not only in the case of some of the concentration camp victims, but also in the case of the Russian prisoners of war.

Whilst the German camp system lasted little more than the duration of the war, the Russian *labor camps* have the distinction of being a permanent assertion of a national system of injustice, traditional in its present form for over fifty years. This is the only camp system where privation has been imposed on people for more than about five years. Hence the environments created by the system—virtually a conscious re-creation of the microviolence of nature—are unique. Within the system, all on a large scale, are a survival environment, a random-death environment, and a total-death environment. There are certain special camps where people are deprived of liberty but otherwise not harassed. There are the camps of the survival environment, which Solzhenitsyn's novel describes as *The First Circle*. Beyond this there is the second circle, of the labor camp proper and the random-death environment. Beyond that there is the third circle, the camps of the far north and east and the total-death environment: Komi, Karaganda, Vorkuta.

Semienclosed privation areas   Privation technologies in semienclosed areas emphasize the vulnerability of cities. A city cannot adapt itself to military strategies. It cannot pretend it is not a city, disguise itself as a forest, grow its own food on the sly, and so on. Its citizens depend upon organizational structures and if these are interfered with so is the life of the citizen. Once disruption gets beyond a certain stage there is nothing much that can be done about it. Total war and total revolution bring the random-death environment to the city.

SEMIENCLOSED PRIVATION AREAS

City privation

Unenclosed ghetto, 1 m. deaths

Siege, 1 m. deaths

Occupation, 6 m. deaths

Civil dislocation, 8 m. deaths

The *unenclosed ghettoes of* eastern Poland and the Baltic States were subject to harassment and pressures from the occupying forces, for racialist reasons, which turned them into total-death environments. The purely military pressures of *siege* almost did the same for Leningrad. On a larger and somewhat more diffuse scale, the cities of Russia became areas of random death from privation during the *dislocation* of the civil war period and again under the pressures of military *occupation* during the Second World War.

The victims of city privation are of course families in their normal habitats; in time of war their identities are selective to the extent that the younger men are being killed elsewhere.

Diffuse privation areas   It's amazing in how many different ways the life can be squeezed out of people. It had never occurred to me that a sizable number of people might have died in *transit* — in the sheer bungling inefficiency of forced movement. Think of the way human beings have been driven and herded back and forth across Europe and Russia in our century. Deportation of peasants to Siberia. Trains to the labor camps. Deportation of Russian and Ukrainian slave laborers to Germany. Trains from every corner of Europe to the ghettos and death camps. Rail journeys and forced marches of prisoners of war.

DIFFUSE PRIVATION AREAS

Rural or mixed privation

Combat, 1 m. deaths

Transit, 1.5 m. deaths

Economic blockade, 2 m. deaths

Man-made famine, 5 m. deaths

Scorched earth, 5 m. deaths

War dislocation, 12 m. deaths

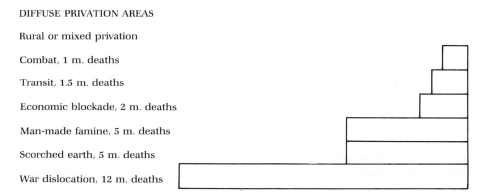

Privation deaths among soldiers in *combat* conditions include the typhus and wound infections of the First World War, the freezing hardship and disease of the Second World War in Russia, the starvation and typhus of the China War and amongst other ill-equipped armies throughout the century, the malarias and jaundices of Western soldiers in the East.

You would imagine that *diffuse* privation would have a larger element of the accidental about it, if only because of the sheer difficulty of getting at people in far-flung rural areas. But not so. *Economic blockade*, as practiced against the Germans in the First World War, against the Biafrans in the Nigerian Civil War; *man-made famine*, as engineered against the Russian peasants during the collectivization; *scorched earth* tactics, as used by the Germans in Russia and the Japanese in China. They are all highly conscious and deliberate methods of destroying people; killing technologies.

Most of these highly conscious technologies tend to produce an immediate random-death environment. In the case of the general *war dislocation* in China and other places where a slow privation was diffused over a vast population, you might say that the privation deaths were an intrusion into a survival environment, that is to say, a social climate in which death is not random but people still have some room to survive by their own efforts.

Listing these technologies, as objective parts of the death machine, is not difficult. But how can I, as an individual, relate myself to these? Perhaps we all tend to feel we ought to attempt to relive the sufferings of the dead. Apart from the self-delusion involved in such an attempt, it is difficult to see what object is served by it. It certainly doesn't bring back the dead or heal their agony or expiate the crimes of which they are the victims. In fact, if you read some of the basic factual accounts of the intensest death environments such as concentration or death camps—as you must do, if you hope to reach any understanding of the human story—you will probably have an *involuntary* "reliving" of suffering in any case. The experience of most people I have talked to on this subject agrees with my own—that the simple factual detail of such accounts is so horrifying that it is only bearable for a few pages at a time. Herein I think lies the salutary and sole purpose of "reliving" such sufferings: the perception of the unbearable. If it is bearable something phony is going on, either on the part of the writer or of the reader.

I cannot then truly relate myself to these technologies of macroviolence through the simulated emotions, feelings, and sufferings of the flesh known as "reliving." But I *can* suffer these structures of reality—these terms descriptive of real event—to enter the mind undistorted by specific color, myth, or image.

Indeed it would be difficult enough to describe the *ghetto*, the *blockade*, the *scorched earth*, the *famine*, in terms of image or metaphor—for these are the basic realities which provide image and metaphor for the rest of ordinary existence. They are the bare bones of reality. Nor is there much need, in order to convey their reality, to explain in great detail how the *siege* or *occupation* comes into being and works its effects, for the bones of death are easily enough achieved. There is nothing extraordinary about any of these—they could be organized by a wise child if there were a wise child willing to organize millions of deaths. If we were describing some complex social fabric where a million conflicting interests were maintained in a living pattern then there would be some call for depth of study . . . but when it comes to the *prison camp*, the *concentration camp*, the *labor camp*, all of these share that cretinous unity of human purpose whereby success and failure achieve the same end of destruction and death. These are the bones, these technologies of the past and those death systems latent in our present, that form the skeleton structure of the death machine.

If it is true that in the twentieth century man has finally come face to face with his own skeleton, it is a structure such as this that he is looking at. I would have the *intellect*, not simulated feelings but the perceiving *mind*, to suffer that skeleton.

Hardware technologies

Military experts tend to assert that in twentieth-century conflicts many more deaths have been caused by the big guns than by small arms. In this generalization there is an important truth and an important untruth. Quantitatively, the statement is not true. According to my calculations deaths from hardware technologies divide roughly as follows:

Deaths from hardware technologies 46 million			
BIG GUNS	AERIAL BOMBS	SMALL ARMS	DEMOGRAPHIC (mixed)
18 million	1 million	24 million	3 million

But the *significant* untruth lies in the implication that as deaths from the big guns increase, deaths from small arms might, or do, or by some logic should, decline in numbers. Not only is this a demonstrably false proposition, but it is the very opposite that is true. As deaths from big guns increase, they also help to bring about an *increase* in deaths from small arms. This is the important truth about the death potential of the big guns. It is not a question of a particular type of weapon being chosen for military reasons, or of one type making another type obsolete. It is a question of big guns *creating an environment* of death on the scale of macroviolence. In this environment small arms and other death technologies not only flourish but also tend to increase to the same scale of macroviolence.

Big guns   Basing itself on the general nature of the First World War and on some evidence suggesting the preponderance of wounds to be from the effects of exploding shells, expert opinion concludes that "90 percent" or "three-quarters" of the deaths came from the big guns. We may modify that proportion if we assume that experts tend to think exclusively in terms of combat deaths, chiefly in terms of the major theaters of war and mainly of the most characteristic set-piece battles. On the basis of a ten million total, at least two million deaths (from the economic blockade and from soldier disease) were outside of combat. If we think of the early part of the war when the machine gun was used intensively, of the massed cavalry charges of the Russian front and the heavy losses on the Italo-Austrian front, as well as continuous small engagements and sniping throughout the war, it becomes at least possible that as many as three million may have died from small arms fire.

Even if the proportion of deaths from the big guns was as low as five million out of ten, the experts are certainly correct in emphasizing the overwhelming significance of these weapons. The big guns created a physical and mental environment, a list of whose effects on the human race would break the spirit of any computer. The mechanical scale of the big guns determined strategy and the general context in which twentieth-century conflict would take place. The big guns decided that the characteristic form of killing in the twentieth century would be repetitive massacre, with a minimum of felt conflict. Thus the nature of the *small arms* killings in the First World War was predetermined by the big guns. In the first place, whether they amounted to one or three million, the number was greater than the number killed by small

BIG GUNS

China, 1 m. deaths

Other conflicts, 2 m. deaths

Rest of the Second World War, 5 m. deaths

Second World War, Russians, 5 m. deaths

First World War, 5 m. deaths

arms in any previous war. Secondly, probably the majority took the form of repetitive massacre in situations created by the logic of the big guns.

In the First World War the big guns were heavier and the distinction between them and small arms was cruder than in the Second World War. Rifles and machine guns—dominated, like the minds of generals, by the big guns—did the work of big guns. That is to say, they were frequently used for massacre in situations where big guns might as well have been used. In the Second World War big guns were generally lighter and the range of weapons wider. Some were even portable. Weapons had been rationalized to meet the techniques of massacre.

The big guns and, later, the mechanized battlefield created a technological environment which men accepted as a simulation of nature, a force which could not ultimately be controlled by men but only guided in certain directions. We can see this development also in the smaller conflicts of the century. The forces which govern the incidence of conflict and the scale of death are still localized, traditional ones: genuine if senseless conflicts, death occurring on a scale with at least some reference to the objects of struggle. But in the post-Second World War period, as the world situation casts its shadow more and more on local conflicts, so the great technological environment of large-scale death is imported into them and the localized effects diminish in importance.

In China, the physical environment created by the big guns has not existed to a very large extent at all. In China, of course, the natural environment was sufficiently deteriorated not to require the massive technological creation of a death environment.

Small arms   The use of small arms is much wider than the limits of formal wars or conflicts. Big guns are used within the context of a formal war, and indeed often dominate the context and create their own environment. This is probably not true of small arms. There is always, I believe, a controlling system or factor stronger than the weapons themselves. This is clearly evident in the case of *formal executions*, where the legal or pseudolegal process decides death for every individual; death is certified in advance. Execution can be by a number of means—strangling, guillotine, hanging—as well as by shooting. But it seems unlikely that the executions of this century would have reached such numbers without the rifle and pistol. Pulling a

SMALL ARMS

Formal execution, 4 m. deaths

Massacre, 6 m. deaths

Combat, 14 m. deaths

trigger is so easy. The uniquely twentieth-century characteristic of these killings is the scale on which they have occurred. The sinister auspices of state interrogations, trials, summary executions are not new, they are as old as human records. The scale is quite new, and it is of course the scale of military operations and massacre.

If the massacre by big gun and the massacre by formal execution are rationalized by their apparent connections with traditional human activities —"fighting" and "war," "punishment" and the "legal process"—at least in the massacre by massacre there are no such hypocrisies to obscure the simple truth. Administrative or military orders, men with guns, selected victims, killing: that's the simple recipe. In listing five major areas of massacre with small arms, I shall indicate associated areas where massacres on a smaller scale have occurred, and the approximate figures relate to all the areas mentioned.

The last and largest category of small arms deaths is those that occurred in military *combat*. My impression is that, on the basis of about fourteen million deaths, half of these would be in the two world wars, and the other half in other wars including those of China. Of the small arms deaths in the First World War it is likely the preponderance were in situations where the massed firepower of small arms were used as a means of massacre auxiliary to that of the big guns. This would also be true of Russian combat deaths in the Second World War, and somewhat less true of deaths on other fronts. In the spectrum of smaller wars over the century the pattern would be more erratic. It is probably safe to say that at least half of all the deaths from small arms in the

RECIPE FOR MASSACRE

Administrative or military orders	Men with guns	Selected victims	Number killed
Suppression of minority and other *ad hoc* orders	Turkish Army and others in "small" wars	Armenians and others	1m.
Enforced collectivization and other administrative tasks	Russian Secret Police	Peasants, camp prisoners, etc.	1m.
Reprisal orders and other law-and-order measures	German Army	People, random selected	2m.
Orders to suppress and destroy Jewry and other groups	German Secret Police	Jews, Gypsies, old and sick people	1m.
Other *ad hoc* orders	Japanese army and other armies in the Second World War	Peasants and others	1m.
		Approximate total	6m

major and minor wars had the characteristics of massacre in environments dominated by big guns.

It becomes necessary to make a distinction between formal combat and what we understand by conflict. Presumably, in conflict in the individual sense, there is some kind of equation such as equal opportunity for both parties or at least a feeling of such, or that the outcome should be dependent on some kind of skill. Conflict in this sense does not exist where people die from privation, or from the big guns, or from the various massacres of small arms. Only in about half the deaths from small arms in combat situations is there the remotest possibility of a conflict situation having existed. If we add to this the category of demographic violence where there is clearly a large element of conflict, we have a figure of about ten million deaths where a situation of conflict *might* have existed; that is to say, in less than 10 percent of all the man-made deaths of the century.

Demographic violence   Each of the three cases I have noted, the Russian Bread War, the Chinese antibourgeois campaigns, and the Indian Partition riots—accumulating to a minimum of three million deaths—might be looked upon as escalated forms of microviolence. That is to say, to some extent they have the character of ordinary civil violence. Yet in each case there is a macroelement in the organizational structure of the event as well as in its incidence, in the form of instruction or recommendation from the center. In each case an official pronouncement, coming at a time of transition between two systems of government, leads to a violence which reflects the clash between the two forms of government. This reminds us that even in an age of macroviolence the violence of "the people" remains microviolent, that is taking the form of frequent individual and occasional mob violence which *never* approaches the dimensions of macroviolence *except when organized by the state*. Feelings of violence in the people are only united into a mass in the fantasy of scholar and politician. Thus we have the grotesque paradox that many respectable statesmen, in their fear of "the people" or "the masses" or "disorder," recommend that the best way to keep them off the streets is to put them in uniform—the very action that unites vast numbers of people in the potential of macroviolence!

The very exceptional nature of demographic violence in the spectrum of macroviolence—the fact that it involves hand-to-hand fighting reflecting direct conflict, aggression, fear, and struggle in the individual—leads to a necessary question. Do the technologies of macroviolence, with a few exceptions, lead to situations, and ultimately to a general situation, in which violence may explode or proliferate without reference to conflict, aggression, fear, or struggle? Can macroviolence become completely divorced from human psychology and motivation? If it can, then it calls for a completely new dimension of inquiry, for most studies of violence assume a link with aggression, conflict, frustration, boredom, and other human conditions.

Aerial bombing   The number of deaths [from aerial bombing] may be a good deal in excess of the one million I have calculated, but it is most unlikely to be more than two million. The peak level of deaths for an individual city is

about 200,000 and the main victims were Dresden, Hiroshima, and Nagasaki, chief targets of Allied terror bombing in the Second World War. The deliberate bombing of civilians was the chief source of deaths in volume, and other cities attacked in this way during the Second World War (including the Sino-Japanese war) were: Coventry and other English cities; Rotterdam and other Dutch cities; Warsaw and other Polish cities; Stalingrad and other Russian cities; Shanghai and other Chinese cities; Frankfurt and other German cities; Tokyo and other Japanese cities.

In the bombing of cities the technologies of violence are destroying the technologies of peace. In the early days, bombing was similar to the shelling of a city, that is the city happened to crop up in the strategic plans. By the time we reach the atom bomb, Hiroshima and Nagasaki, the ease of access to target and the instant nature of macroimpact mean that both the choice of city and the identity of the victim have become completely randomized, and human technology has reached a final platform of self-destructiveness. The great cities of the dead, in numbers, remain Verdun, Leningrad, and Auschwitz. But at Hiroshima and Nagasaki the "city of the dead" is finally transformed from a metaphor into a literal reality. The city of the dead of the future is our city and the victims are—not French and German soldiers, nor Russian citizens, nor Jews—but all of us without reference to specific identity.

Chemicals and other advanced technologies

About the asphyxiation of between one and two million people by poisonous fumes in specifically prepared chambers and vans, there is little to be said that has not already been said. It should be studied in direct physical detail as recorded in several books and the reader will then find if he has not already done so that there is no need to compare it with anything else in order to get it "into perspective." Since then science and technology have proliferated the technologies of macroviolence to the extent that every new technological development has a death application as well as a life use. If you explore the ocean bed and contemplate its human uses you also devise a means of devastating the ocean bed. If you discover how to isolate germs and viruses for protective purposes you also proceed to concentrate them into a technology for killing a million people. If you can deaden the nerves to lessen surgical pain you can also paralyze the nerves for hostile purposes, and modify your technology to produce various degrees of agony and types of death. Whilst scientific discoveries and technologies often remain hypothetical and open ended for a considerable time while their life uses are being explored, the death application has the advantage of unquestionable effectiveness. The technology can thus instantly become a closed system and acquire that aura of magic and power which has been sought through the ages of villains, charlatans, psychopaths, and fools. Thus, for instance, the attempt to connect the subtle detail and variety of human behavior with physiological processes is delicate—difficult—hypothetical—frustrating— open ended. But if you approach it from the angle of the *death application*, you can most certainly by drugs and surgery ensure the deadening of great areas of human behavior, and thus become a magician freed from irritating difficulties.

Such is the romanticization of technology, like the old romanticizing of nature, that the technologies of macroviolence are actually glamorized in modern fiction, with the glossy inanity with which overfed, stupid aristocrats used to dress up as swains and shepherdesses. These corruptions are beginning to eat back at technology so that, in addition to the city of the dead as a future arena of self-destructiveness, we have the possibility of human technology destroying itself at the source . . .

VALUES: NEGATIVE AND POSITIVE

Seeking an *answer to death* is perhaps the greatest wild-goose chase of human existence. Yet from time to time a new attitude if not solution arises out of our experience. Such an attitude is latent in the connection between *violence* and *death* which, although apparently an obvious one, has not yet been fully expressed in terms of recent experience. Violence in the twentieth century has produced the new phenomenon of *total death*. As an *idea*, total death has existed—in mental pictures of *the day of judgment, doomsday, the end of the world*—at least since the formulation of the great religions. As a *reality* attainable by human means, the science of which is a permanent unalterable part of knowledge, it originates in the notorious half century from which we are just emerging. *Can* we emerge from the nightmare of reality and vision created in that period? We cannot create a retrospective order for the chaos of the actual events. Can we escape from the chaos of the idea that is left to us? *Total death* could mean the obliteration of particular cities, or countries, or regions; it could mean the collapse of world civilization or the death of the species; or it could mean the total death of the mind within a variety of physical parameters. *Total death* might be brought about by a wide range of means; by the carefully considered destruction of selected millions; by the direct and secondary effects of pollution or overcrowding; by a death-breeding mixture of every kind of human motivation acting on machineries and systems which are beyond the control of living creatures. *Total death* has a time span overwhelming the convenient human notion of time. It can "happen" in an instant, in a few days; it can have the monthly, yearly rhythms of traditional warfare or it could create a chronic long-term disruption of seasons of nature and the years of human life. Its possibility is tomorrow, or in the next two hundred years, or at any "time" in the future. *Total death* is a hard, scientific, and immediate reality at the same time as being a speculative idea in search of a philosophy. No existing mental structures, of science, philosophy, or religion, are adequate to contain it.

Death after all is a powerful reality. It is one of two or three fundamental ideas that condition the human attitude to existence. I think we should find, if we examined them in the cool comparative way that is now becoming possible, that some of the great religions have gravely distorted truth in order to accommodate the idea of death—to explain it away, to dodge its straight-

forward implications. A common result is the identification of *death* with *evil*,
or with an unknowable darkness or *chaos*. Hence the rejection in the mind of
death as a reality. Hence the reluctance of those who write with such vigor
the history of the machines and systems of violence to mention the facts of
death and to include these in their historical interpretations. Hence *our* need
to *reject the assumption that reality is chaos*, to insist on *the possibility of
knowing the truth about the deaths that result from our behavior*, to *structure
our knowledge of death and deaths and total death* and bring the facts into the
light of day. *Bringing into light of day* is what happens to the soul after death,
according to the *Egyptian Book of the Dead*. I made a distinction, between
ancient books of the dead and the present one, of *necromancy* and *necrology*,
as an indication of the different structures of knowledge of different ages. As a
deeper level of truth the distinction is, I admit, a mere quibble. *Our* bringing
into the light of day is different in structure but reaches the same end.

Our structure of knowledge is founded in fact. Yet the exposition of total
death in terms of fact explodes the ethos of factual knowledge that is so
characteristic of our age!

Total death explodes the simple *myths* of belligerent nationalism. It reduces the death formulas of *religion* to absurdity. As an idea, it cannot be
relegated to those rarefied spheres of *philosophy* where all ideas are made
silly and ineffectual by the cleverness of philosophers. There is too much
grim reality in it for that. As a practical reality, aspects of total death can be
governed on a factual basis by a discipline such as *ecology*. But the full reality
cannot, for it is too much beyond the predictable, its time span is too
unwieldy, to be contained within the factual parameters of a scientific discipline.

It is not surprising that the idea of total death should crash through
established structures of thought. It is the intellectual legacy of a violence
that crashed through the physical structures of human societies for half a
century. Those who used to live by the *Tibetan Book of the Dead* would not be
surprised: yet some of our most "modern," "scientific," "brilliant" minds
seem to imagine that we can go on living just as before, with the degradation
and nothingness of the public experience expressed in terms of the historical
myths and clichés that preceded it! But total death is not simply a myth-
destroying reality. It disrupts more than those *intellectual* forms of mediation
between man and his surroundings—religion, philosophy, scientific disciplines—already mentioned. It tears apart in the mind some of the forms of
physical mediation that are most dearly cherished by the advanced societies.
Principal among these is the arms pile.

The notion that national "defense" rests in the accumulation of suicidal
weaponry is the final surrealism of the factual ethos, for total death is itself
the mocking product of this delusion.

And this great scientific proof—that there is no ultimate physical "protection" against one's surroundings—calls in question the whole area of "factual" mediation between man and his surroundings as expressed in technology.

Fact is not superior to myth. Technology is not more efficient than religion.

However much factual and technical knowledge we acquire, we shall always have to live with the unpredictable. These are the immediate implications of total death. That is why, although this exploratory study is grounded in fact and systems, the intellectual tools I am most familiar with as a child of my age, it also indicates the possibility of *knowing* this area of reality through myth and through speculative philosophy, and future students may develop the subject in these directions, taking the factual grounding for granted.

It is easy to italicize a few phrases, more difficult to predict how they are to be absorbed into the fabric of existence. The student of total death will not expect immediate technical spin-off from his researches, for he knows the time span of total death is not that of a generation nor of a lifetime, but of a civilization. A great deal of fuss is made about the pace at which "modern ideas" succeed one another. But these are ideas used as technology, as closed systems of thought. The open-ended idea takes longer to absorb, it continues to breed and stimulate further thought. It was in the nineteenth century that the idea of men as gods came to us, and we still do not know what it means. The turbulence of our own century has produced advances in the idea of consciousness which we have hardly begun to absorb. And in the aftermath of that turbulence we have perforce to change our idea of death.

The discoveries of science and the rapid production of ideas-as-technology are very important and powerful and capable of bringing about the most significant historical events, such as the end of the world and endless other adjustments to life. No one can deny the impressiveness of that claim.

But with the above three ideas alone—god, consciousness, death—and the new interpretations of them afforded by recent experience, it would be possible to build a high civilization, and that is something different.

In our own period we are in the midst of a movement to recover inner values. Among these the values of death must be recycled into our vision of totality so that we may live truly in the world of life and death.

Elie Wiesel

Elie Wiesel was a child when he was thrown into the nightmare world of the Nazi concentration camps. The story of this experience is told in his searing book Night. *The final three sections of that book are reproduced below. The tenderness between the boy and his father is the human (and angelic) counterpoint to the inhuman (and devilish) environment in which they tried to survive.*

7

Pressed up against the others in an effort to keep out the cold, head empty and heavy at the same time, brain a whirlpool of decaying memories. Indifference deadened the spirit. Here or elsewhere—what difference did it make? To die today or tomorrow, or later? The night was long and never ending.

When at last a gray glimmer of light appeared on the horizon, it revealed a tangle of human shapes, heads sunk upon shoulders, crouched, piled one on top of the other, like a field of dust-covered tombstones in the first light of the dawn. I tried to distinguish those who were still alive from those who had gone. But there was no difference. My gaze was held for a long time by one who lay with his eyes open, staring into the void. His livid face was covered with a layer of frost and snow.

My father was huddled near me, wrapped in his blanket, his shoulders covered with snow. And was he dead, too? I called him. No answer. I would have cried out if I could have done so. He did not move.

My mind was invaded suddenly by this realization—there was no more reason to live, no more reason to struggle.

The train stopped in the middle of a deserted field. The suddenness of the halt woke some of those who were asleep. They straightened themselves up, throwing startled looks around them.

Outside, the SS went by, shouting:

"Throw out all the dead! All corpses outside!"

The living rejoiced. There would be more room. Volunteers set to work. They felt those who were still crouching.

"Here's one! Take him!"

They undressed him, the survivors avidly sharing out his clothes, then two "gravediggers" took him one by the head and one by the feet, and threw him out of the wagon like a sack of flour.

From all directions came cries:

"Come on! Here's one! This man next to me. He doesn't move."

I woke from my apathy just at the moment when two men came up to my father. I threw myself on top of his body. He was cold. I slapped him. I rubbed his hands, crying:

"Father! Father! Wake up. They're trying to throw you out of the carriage. . . ."

His body remained inert.

The two gravediggers seized me by the collar.

"Leave him. You can see perfectly well that he's dead."

"No!" I cried. "He isn't dead! Not yet!"

I set to work to slap him as hard as I could. After a moment my father's eyelids moved slightly over his glazed eyes. He was breathing weakly.

"You see," I cried.

The two men moved away.

Twenty bodies were thrown out of our wagon. Then the train resumed its journey, leaving behind it a few hundred naked dead, deprived of burial, in the deep snow of a field in Poland.

We were given no food. We lived on snow; it took the place of bread. The days were like nights, and the nights left the dregs of their darkness in our souls. The train was traveling slowly, often stopping for several hours and then setting off again. It never ceased snowing. All through these days and nights we stayed crouching, one on top of the other, never speaking a word. We were no more than frozen bodies. Our eyes closed, we waited merely for the next stop, so that we could unload our dead.

Ten days, ten nights of traveling. Sometimes we would pass through German townships. Very early in the morning usually. The workmen were going to work. They stopped and stared after us, but otherwise showed no surprise.

One day when we had stopped, a workman took a piece of bread out of his bag and threw it into a wagon. There was a stampede. Dozens of starving men fought each other to the death for a few crumbs. The German workmen took a lively interest in this spectacle.

Some years later, I watched the same kind of scene at Aden. The passengers on our boat were amusing themselves by throwing coins to the "natives," who were diving in to get them. An attractive, aristocratic Parisienne was deriving special pleasure from the game. I suddenly noticed that two children were engaged in a death struggle, trying to strangle each other. I turned to the lady.

"Please," I begged, "don't throw any more money in!"

"Why not?" she said. "I like to give charity. . . ."

In the wagon where the bread had fallen, a real battle had broken out. Men threw themselves on top of each other, stamping on each other, tearing at each other, biting each other. Wild beasts of prey, with animal hatred in their eyes; an extraordinary vitality had seized them, sharpening their teeth and nails.

A crowd of workmen and curious spectators had collected along the train. They had probably never seen a train with such a cargo. Soon, nearly everywhere, pieces of bread were being dropped into the wagons. The audience stared at these skeletons of men, fighting one another to the death for a mouthful.

A piece fell into our wagon. I decided that I would not move. Anyway, I knew that I would never have the strength to fight with a dozen savage men! Not far away I noticed an old man dragging himself along on all fours. He was trying to disengage himself from the struggle. He held one hand to his heart. I thought at first he had received a blow in the chest. Then I understood; he had a bit of bread under his shirt. With remarkable speed he drew it out and put it to his mouth. His eyes gleamed; a smile, like a grimace, lit up his dead face. And was immediately extinguished. A shadow had just loomed up near him. The shadow threw itself upon him. Felled to the ground, stunned with blows, the old man cried:

"Meir. Meir, my boy! Don't you recognize me? I'm your father . . . you're hurting me . . . you're killing your father! I've got some bread . . . for you too . . . for you too. . . ."

He collapsed. His fist was still clenched around a small piece. He tried to carry it to his mouth. But the other one threw himself upon him and snatched it. The old man again whispered something, let out a rattle, and died amid the general indifference. His son searched him, took the bread, and began to devour it. He was not able to get very far. Two men had seen and hurled themselves upon him. Others joined in. When they withdrew, next to me were two corpses, side by side, the father and the son.

I was fifteen years old.

In our wagon, there was a friend of my father's called Meir Katz. He had worked as a gardener at Buna and used to bring us a few green vegetables occasionally. Being less undernourished than the rest of us, he had stood up to imprisonment better. Because he was relatively more vigorous, he had been put in charge of the wagon.

On the third night of our journey I woke up suddenly and felt two hands on my throat, trying to strangle me. I just had the time to shout, "Father!"

Nothing but this word. I felt myself suffocating. But my father had woken up and seized my attacker. Too weak to overcome him, he had the idea of calling Meir Katz.

"Come here! Come quickly! There's someone strangling my son."

A few moments later I was free. I still do not know why the man wanted to strangle me.

After a few days, Meir Katz spoke to my father:

"Chlomo, I'm getting weak. I'm losing my strength. I can't hold on. . . ."

"Don't let yourself go under," my father said, trying to encourage him. "You must resist. Don't lose faith in yourself."

But Meir Katz groaned heavily in reply.

"I can't go on any longer, Chlomo! What can I do? I can't carry on. . . ."

My father took his arm. And Meir Katz, the strong man, the most robust of us all, wept. His son had been taken from him at the time of the first selection, but it was now that he wept. It was now that he cracked up. He was finished, at the end of his tether.

On the last day of our journey a terrible wind arose; it snowed without ceasing. We felt that the end was near—the real end. We could never hold out in this icy wind, in these gusts.

Someone got up and shouted:

"We mustn't stay sitting down at a time like this. We shall freeze to death! Let's all get up and move a bit. . . ."

We all got up. We held our damp blankets more tightly around us. And we forced ourselves to move a few steps, to turn around where we were.

Suddenly a cry rose up from the wagon, the cry of a wounded animal. Someone had just died.

Others, feeling that they too were about to die, imitated his cry. And their cries seemed to come from beyond the grave. Soon everyone was crying out. Wailing, groaning, cries of distress hurled into the wind and the snow.

The contagion spread to the other carriages. Hundreds of cries rose up simultaneously. Not knowing against whom we cried. Not knowing why. The death rattle of a whole convoy who felt the end upon them. We were all going to die here. All limits had been passed. No one had any strength left. And again the night would be long.

Meir Katz groaned:

"Why don't they shoot us all right away?"

That same evening, we reached our destination.

It was late at night. The guards came to unload us. The dead were abandoned in the train. Only those who could still stand were able to get out.

Meir Katz stayed in the train. The last day had been the most murderous. A hundred of us had got into the wagon. A dozen of us got out—among them, my father and I.

We had arrived at Buchenwald.

8

At the gate of the camp, SS officers were waiting for us. They counted us. Then we were directed to the assembly place. Orders were given us through loudspeakers:

"Form fives!" "Form groups of a hundred!" "Five paces forward!"

I held onto my father's hand—the old, familiar fear: not to lose him.

Right next to us the high chimney of the crematory oven rose up. It no longer made any impression on us. It scarcely attracted our attention.

An established inmate of Buchenwald told us that we should have a shower and then we could go into the blocks. The idea of having a hot bath fascinated me. My father was silent. He was breathing heavily beside me.

"Father," I said. "Only another moment more. Soon we can lie down—in a bed. You can rest. . . ."

He did not answer. I was so exhausted myself that his silence left me indifferent. My only wish was to take a bath as quickly as possible and lie down in a bed.

But it was not easy to reach the showers. Hundreds of prisoners were crowding there. The guards were unable to keep any order. They struck out right and left with no apparent result. Others, without the strength to push or even to stand up, had sat down in the snow. My father wanted to do the same. He groaned.

"I can't go on. . . . This is the end. . . . I'm going to die here. . . ."

He dragged me toward a hillock of snow from which emerged human shapes and ragged pieces of blanket.

"Leave me," he said to me. "I can't go on. . . . Have mercy on me. . . . I'll wait here until we can get into the baths. . . . You can come and find me."

I could have wept with rage. Having lived through so much, suffered so much, could I leave my father to die now? Now, when we could have a good hot bath and lie down?

"Father!" I screamed. "Father! Get up from here! Immediately! You're killing yourself. . . ."

I seized him by the arm. He continued to groan.

"Don't shout, son. . . . Take pity on your old father. . . . Leave me to rest here. . . . Just for a bit, I'm so tired . . . at the end of my strength. . . ."

He had become like a child, weak, timid, vulnerable.

"Father," I said. "You can't stay here."

I showed him the corpses all around him; they too had wanted to rest here.

"I can see them, son. I can see them all right. Let them sleep. It's so long since they closed their eyes. . . . They are exhausted . . . exhausted. . . ."

His voice was tender.

I yelled against the wind:

"They'll never wake again! Never! Don't you understand?"

For a long time this argument went on. I felt that I was not arguing with him, but with death itself, with the death that he had already chosen.

The sirens began to wail. An alert. The lights went out throughout the camp. The guards drove us toward the blocks. In a flash, there was no one left on the assembly place. We were only too glad not to have had to stay outside longer in the icy wind. We let ourselves sink down onto the planks. The beds were in several tiers. The cauldrons of soup at the entrance attracted no one. To sleep, that was all that mattered.

It was daytime when I awoke. And then I remembered that I had a father. Since the alert, I had followed the crowd without troubling about him. I had known that he was at the end, on the brink of death, and yet I had abandoned him.

I went to look for him.

But at the same moment this thought came into my mind: "Don't let me find him! If only I could get rid of this dead weight, so that I could use all my strength to struggle for my own survival, and only worry about myself." Immediately I felt ashamed of myself, ashamed forever.

I walked for hours without finding him. Then I came to the block where they were giving out black "coffee." The men were lining up and fighting.

A plaintive, beseeching voice caught me in the spine:

"Eliezer ... my son ... bring me ... a drop of coffee...."

I ran to him.

"Father! I've been looking for you for so long. ... Where were you? Did you sleep? ... How do you feel?"

He was burning with fever. Like a wild beast, I cleared a way for myself to the coffee cauldron. And I managed to carry back a cupful. I had a sip. The rest was for him. I can't forget the light of thankfulness in his eyes while he gulped it down—an animal gratitude. With those few gulps of hot water, I probably brought him more satisfaction than I had done during my whole childhood.

He was lying on a plank, livid, his lips pale and dried up, shaken by tremors. I could not stay by him for long. Orders had been given to clear the place for cleaning. Only the sick could stay.

We stayed outside for five hours. Soup was given out. As soon as we were allowed to go back to the blocks, I ran to my father.

"Have you had anything to eat?"

"No."

"Why not?"

"They didn't give us anything ... they said that if we were ill we should die soon anyway and it would be a pity to waste the food. I can't go on any more...."

I gave him what was left of my soup. But it was with a heavy heart. I felt that I was giving it up to him against my will. No better than Rabbi Eliahou's son had I withstood the test.

He grew weaker day by day, his gaze veiled, his face the color of dead leaves. On the third day after our arrival at Buchenwald, everyone had to go to the showers. Even the sick, who had to go through last.

On the way back from the baths, we had to wait outside for a long time. They had not yet finished cleaning the blocks.

Seeing my father in the distance, I ran to meet him. He went by me like a ghost, passed me without stopping, without looking at me. I called to him. He did not come back. I ran after him:

"Father, where are you running to?"

He looked at me for a moment, and his gaze was distant, visionary; it was the face of someone else. A moment only and on he ran again.

Struck down with dysentery, my father lay in his bunk, five other invalids with him. I sat by his side, watching him, not daring to believe that he could escape death again. Nevertheless, I did all I could to give him hope.

Suddenly, he raised himself on his bunk and put his feverish lips to my ear:

"Eliezer ... I must tell you where to find the gold and the money I buried ... in the cellar. ... You know...."

He began to talk faster and faster, as though he were afraid he would not have time to tell me. I tried to explain to him that this was not the end, that we would go back to the house together, but he would not listen to me. He could no longer listen to me. He was exhausted. A trickle of saliva, mingled with blood, was running from between his lips. He had closed his eyes. His breath was coming in gasps.

For a ration of bread, I managed to change beds with a prisoner in my father's bunk. In the afternoon the doctor came. I went and told him that my father was very ill.

"Bring him here!"

I explained that he could not stand up. But the doctor refused to listen to anything. Somehow, I brought my father to him. He stared at him, then questioned him in a clipped voice:

"What do you want?"

"My father's ill," I answered for him. "Dysentery . . ."

"Dysentery? That's not my business. I'm a surgeon. Go on! Make room for the others."

Protests did no good.

"I can't go on, son. . . . Take me back to my bunk. . . ."

I took him back and helped him to lie down. He was shivering.

"Try and sleep a bit, father. Try to go to sleep. . . ."

His breathing was labored, thick. He kept his eyes shut. Yet I was convinced that he could see everything, that now he could see the truth in all things.

Another doctor came to the block. But my father would not get up. He knew that it was useless.

Besides, this doctor had only come to finish off the sick. I could hear him shouting at them that they were lazy and just wanted to stay in bed. I felt like leaping at his throat, strangling him. But I no longer had the courage or the strength. I was riveted to my father's deathbed. My hands hurt, I was clenching them so hard. Oh, to strangle the doctor and the others! To burn the whole world! My father's murderers! But the cry stayed in my throat.

When I came back from the bread distribution, I found my father weeping like a child:

"Son, they keep hitting me!"

"Who?"

I thought he was delirious.

"Him, the Frenchman . . . and the Pole . . . they were hitting me."

Another wound to the heart, another hate, another reason for living lost.

"Eliezer . . . Eliezer . . . tell them not to hit me. . . . I haven't done anything . . . Why do they keep hitting me?"

I began to abuse his neighbors. They laughed at me. I promised them bread, soup. They laughed. Then they got angry; they could not stand my father any longer, they said, because he was now unable to drag himself outside to relieve himself.

The following day he complained that they had taken his ration of bread.

"While you were asleep?"

"No. I wasn't asleep. They jumped on top of me. They snatched my bread

... and they hit me ... again. ... I can't stand any more, son ... a drop of water...."

I knew that he must not drink. But he pleaded with me for so long that I gave in. Water was the worst poison he could have, but what else could I do for him? With water, without water, it would all be over soon anyway....

"You, at least, have some mercy on me...."

Have mercy on him! I, his only son!

A week went by like this.

"This is your father, isn't it?" asked the head of the block.

"Yes."

"He's very ill."

"The doctor won't do anything for him."

"The doctor *can't* do anything for him, now. And neither can you."

He put his great hairy hand on my shoulder and added:

"Listen to me, boy. Don't forget that you're in a concentration camp. Here, every man has to fight for himself and not think of anyone else. Even of his father. Here, there are no fathers, no brothers, no friends. Everyone lives and dies for himself alone. I'll give you a sound piece of advice—don't give your ration of bread and soup to your old father. There's nothing you can do for him. And you're killing yourself. Instead, you ought to be having his ration."

I listened to him without interrupting. He was right, I thought in the most secret region of my heart, but I dared not admit it. It's too late to save your old father, I said to myself. You ought to be having two rations of bread, two rations of soup....

Only a fraction of a second, but I felt guilty. I ran to find a little soup to give my father. But he did not want it. All he wanted was water.

"Don't drink water ... have some soup...."

"I'm burning ... why are you being so unkind to me, my son? Some water..."

I brought him some water. Then I left the block for roll call. But I turned around and came back again. I lay down on the top bunk. Invalids were allowed to stay in the block. So I would be an invalid myself. I would not leave my father.

There was silence all around now, broken only by groans. In front of the block, the SS were giving orders. An officer passed by the beds. My father begged me:

"My son, some water. ... I'm burning. ... My stomach...."

"Quiet, over there!" yelled the officer.

"Eliezer," went on my father, "some water...."

The officer came up to him and shouted at him to be quiet. But my father did not hear him. He went on calling me. The officer dealt him a violent blow on the head with his truncheon.

I did not move. I was afraid. My body was afraid of also receiving a blow.

Then my father made a rattling noise and it was my name: "Eliezer."

I could see that he was still breathing—spasmodically.

I did not move.

When I got down after roll call, I could see his lips trembling as he

murmured something. Bending over him, I stayed gazing at him for over an
hour, engraving into myself the picture of his blood-stained face, his shattered skull.

Then I had to go to bed. I climbed into my bunk, above my father, who was
still alive. It was January 28, 1945.

I awoke on January 29 at dawn. In my father's place lay another invalid. They
must have taken him away before dawn and carried him to the crematory. He
may still have been breathing.

There were no prayers at his grave. No candles were lit to his memory. His
last word was my name. A summons, to which I did not respond.

I did not weep, and it pained me that I could not weep. But I had no more
tears. And, in the depths of my being, in the recesses of my weakened
conscience, could I have searched it, I might perhaps have found something
like—free at last!

9

I had to stay at Buchenwald until April eleventh. I have nothing to say of my
life during this period. It no longer mattered. After my father's death, nothing
could touch me any more.

I was transferred to the children's block, where there were six hundred of
us.

The front was drawing nearer.

I spent my days in a state of total idleness. And I had but one desire—to
eat. I no longer thought of my father or of my mother.

From time to time I would dream of a drop of soup, of an extra ration of
soup. . . .

On April fifth, the wheel of history turned.

It was late in the afternoon. We were standing in the block, waiting for an
SS man to come and count us. He was late in coming. Such a delay was
unknown till then in the history of Buchenwald. Something must have
happened.

Two hours later the loudspeakers sent out an order from the head of the
camp: all the Jews must come to the assembly place.

This was the end! Hitler was going to keep his promise.

The children in our block went toward the place. There was nothing else
we could do. Gustav, the head of the block, made this clear to us with his
truncheon. But on the way we met some prisoners who whispered to us:

"Go back to your block. The Germans are going to shoot you. Go back to
your block, and don't move."

We went back to our block. We learned on the way that the camp resistance organization had decided not to abandon the Jews and was going to
prevent their being liquidated.

As it was late and there was great upheaval—innumerable Jews had passed themselves off as non-Jews—the head of the camp decided that a general roll call would take place the following day. Everybody would have to be present.

The roll call took place. The head of the camp announced that Buchenwald was to be liquidated. Ten blocks of deportees would be evacuated each day. From this moment, there would be no further distribution of bread and soup. And the evacuation began. Every day, several thousand prisoners went through the camp gate and never came back.

On April tenth, there were still about twenty thousand of us in the camp, including several hundred children. They decided to evacuate us all at once, right on until the evening. Afterward, they were going to blow up the camp.

So we were massed in the huge assembly square, in rows of five, waiting to see the gate open. Suddenly, the sirens began to wail. An alert! We went back to the blocks. It was too late to evacuate us that evening. The evacuation was postponed again to the following day.

We were tormented with hunger. We had eaten nothing for six days, except a bit of grass or some potato peelings found near the kitchens.

At ten o'clock in the morning the SS scattered through the camp, moving the last victims toward the assembly place.

Then the resistance movement decided to act. Armed men suddenly rose up everywhere. Bursts of firing. Grenades exploding. We children stayed flat on the ground in the block.

The battle did not last long. Toward noon everything was quiet again. The SS had fled and the resistance had taken charge of the running of the camp.

At about six o'clock in the evening, the first American tank stood at the gates of Buchenwald.

Our first act as free men was to throw ourselves onto the provisions. We thought only of that. Not of revenge, not of our families. Nothing but bread.

And even when we were no longer hungry, there was still no one who thought of revenge. On the following day, some of the young men went to Weimar to get some potatoes and clothes—and to sleep with girls. But of revenge, not a sign.

Three days after the liberation of Buchenwald I became very ill with food poisoning. I was transferred to the hospital and spent two weeks between life and death.

One day I was able to get up, after gathering all my strength. I wanted to see myself in the mirror hanging on the opposite wall. I had not seen myself since the ghetto.

From the depths of the mirror, a corpse gazed back at me.

The look in his eyes, as they stared into mine, has never left me.

Robert Jay Lifton and Eric Olson

Robert Jay Lifton is professor of psychiatry at Yale University. This selection, taken from Living and Dying *(written with Eric Olson), discusses the effects of the Hiroshima explosion not only on those who survived that blast and experienced what the authors call "psychic numbing," but on the rest of humanity as well.*
Eric Olson, who was a graduate student at Harvard when he wrote this selection with Dr. Lifton, has earned his Ph.D. degree and is a psychology instructor in the department of psychiatry at Harvard Medical School. He is also affiliated with the Cambridge Hospital.

The 17th century was the century of mathematics, the 18th that of the physical sciences, and the 19th that of biology. Our 20th century is the century of fear.

> — Albert Camus, from
> *Neither Victims Nor Executioners*

The sun can't hold a candle to it.

Now we're all sons of bitches.

> —Two reactions of nuclear
> scientists to the first atomic bomb test

Early in the morning of August 6, 1945, the United States dropped on the Japanese city of Hiroshima the first atomic bomb ever used on a human population. The destruction and chaos wrought by that bomb were so immense that it has never been possible to make a precise count of the number of people killed. Most estimates are in the range of 100,000 to 200,000 people. Even for the hundreds of thousands who experienced the bombing but remained alive, the vision and taint of nuclear holocaust left lifelong scars.

The bomb was unexpected; it came as people went about their morning chores of making and eating breakfast and preparing to go to work. Suddenly a blinding flash cut across the sky. There were a few seconds of dead silence and then a huge explosion. Enormous clouds formed and then rose upward in a gigantic dark column. The clouds leveled off and the whole formation resembled an enormous black mushroom.

Those who have seen atomic explosions speak of their awesome and frightening beauty. On that Japanese summer morning, the beauty was immediately eclipsed by the experience of an overwhelming encounter with death. Normal existence had suddenly been massively invaded by an eerie and unknown force. An area of total destruction was created extending for two miles in all directions, and 60,000 buildings within the city limits were demolished.

The reaction of the survivors was at first a sense of being totally immersed by death. Houses and buildings leveled, the sight of dead bodies, the cries and moans of the severely injured, and the smell of burning flesh all combined to leave a permanent death imprint of staggering power.

Among the survivors there quickly developed a profound kind of guilt. This guilt was related both to having remained alive while others (including loved ones and neighbors) died, and to the inability to offer help to those who needed it. All of this became focused in a question that remained at the center of a lifelong struggle for the survivors: "Why did I remain alive when he, she, they died?" And this question itself sometimes became transformed into the haunting suspicion that one's own life had been purchased at the cost of the others who died: "Some had to die; because they died I could live." This suspicion led to a feeling among survivors that they did not deserve to be alive and that one could justly remain alive only by coming in some way to resemble the dead.

The Japanese survivors became psychologically numb, their sensitivities blunted by guilt and by an inability to resume meaningful activity amid the chaos. The boundary separating life from death no longer seemed distinct. By becoming numb, the survivors blocked their awareness of the pain and suffering and effected a kind of compromise between life and death.

The survivors' lives were made even more difficult by a susceptibility to various forms of disease and weakness to which their exposure to atomic radiation made them vulnerable. Many of those exposed have had to struggle to live with maimed bodies; all have had to live with the incredible end-of-the-world image of nuclear holocaust.

For us, now, the image of Hiroshima symbolizes the possibility that what has happened once can happen again. By today's standards, that first atomic bomb was a very small one. The difficulty of imagining the human suffering that followed in the wake of its use is multiplied many times over in trying to contemplate what a world war with atomic weapons would be like now.

The atomic bomb was the product of an extraordinary research program carried out during World War II. In the beginning there had been little confidence that an atomic bomb could actually be made. But the suspicion that German scientists were attempting to put such a weapon into the hands of Hitler led the United States to undertake an all-out effort.

In 1939, a letter to President Roosevelt was drafted by Albert Einstein encouraging full support for a scientific program that would lead to the development of the atomic bomb. Research installations were established at a number of places throughout the country, and work went ahead with unprecedented commitment. By July 1945, the first atomic bomb was ready for testing in the New Mexico desert. So intense was the effort to create the

few physicists at Los Alamos were inclined to raise moral questions about the

weapon they made.

The bomb worked. Suddenly, it became possible for one plane to deliver a single bomb, the explosive power of which previously would have required two thousand bombs. All who watched were awestruck by what they saw; the experience had a religious quality. Men had released through the bomb a source of power literally beyond imagining. It seemed that the use of this powerful device could bring the war to a rapid conclusion and could in peacetime yield untold energy, and would thus transform the nature of both war and peace.

All these things were possible. But what was immediate and overwhelming was the sheer majesty and power of the bomb itself. Robert Oppenheimer, director of the research project that produced the bomb, later remembered his thoughts at the time of the explosion:

> At that moment . . . there flashed into my mind a passage from the Bhagavad-Gita, the sacred book of the Hindus: "I am become Death, the Shatterer of Worlds!"

Another observer at the time used such phrases as "mighty thunder" and "great silence" to describe his response, and went on to speak in clearly religious language:

> On that moment hung eternity. Time stood still. Space contracted to a pinpoint. It was as though the earth had opened and the skies had split. One felt as though he had been privileged to witness the Birth of the World.

Others had more cynical responses: "Now we're all sons of bitches," and, more simply, "What a thing we've made." Still others spoke of "the dreadful," "the terrible," "the dire," and "the awful."

"This is the greatest thing in history!" was President Truman's response upon hearing of the bomb's successful use in Hiroshima, which seemed to portend a rapid end to the war. And a newspaper report at the time described the force as "weird, incredible, and somehow disturbing."

If we understand the experience of religious conversion as involving a changed image of the cosmos and man's place within it, then certainly the responses of those early witnesses to atomic power would qualify as religious. There was a sense of a "new beginning," of making contact with the infinite and the feeling that life would never be the same again. The bomb took on qualities of a deity, a god whose strange and superhuman power would change the course of human history.

After it became clear that this atomic god was real, the scientists who had unleashed it began to diverge in their responses to the new power. As in any situation, most went on with their professional "business as usual." Some assumed a sense of mission in committing themselves to controlling the use of this threatening force. Others identified themselves with the force, became converts to the religion of nuclearism, and dedicated themselves to propagating the new faith.

Nuclearism is a peculiar, twentieth-century disease of power. We would do well to specify it, trace its roots, and see its connection with other forms of religious and immortalizing expression. Nuclearism is a form of totalism. It yields a grandiose vision of man's power at a historical time when man's precarious sense of his own immortality makes him particularly vulnerable to such aberrations.

Man has always attached deep emotion to his tools. As extensions of his own body and capacities, they have provided him with an image of himself. The centrality of technology to twentieth-century culture has increased this tendency to define life in terms of the tools and techniques that have so deeply transformed the world. In this sense, nuclearism is a manifestation of two underlying contemporary inclinations: to deify tools, and to seize whatever symbols are available in the desperate search for a sense of significance.

The career and personal struggles of Robert Oppenheimer reveal the tensions that have existed in relation to nuclear weapons. Oppenheimer directed the vast and complex research effort at Los Alamos. He and those with whom he worked were convinced that if the bomb could be developed quickly, its availability would hasten the end of the war and could even rid the world of war permanently. Certain nuclear scientists in Chicago who had completed their contribution to the bomb research project tried to raise moral questions about the bomb's use. Oppenheimer, however, remained committed and resisted such reflection. He did not agree that the bomb should merely be "demonstrated" to frighten the enemy into submission rather than be actually used on a human population.

It was not until 1949, when the vastly more powerful hydrogen bomb was nearly completed, that Oppenheimer began to reexamine his convictions. He continued to work on weapons research, and even came to favor the development of small "tactical" hydrogen bombs. But he became concerned that the idea of a "super" H-bomb seemed "to have caught the imagination, both of the congressional and military people, as the answer to the problem posed by the Russians' advance." With his characteristic brilliance, Oppenheimer then began to expose the dangers involved in letting the bomb dominate all thinking on international relations.

Oppenheimer had been a national hero during and just after the war, when he was widely credited with the success of the atomic bomb research project. But when he began to raise questions about nuclearism and underwent what we might call "nuclear backsliding," he was forced to submit to extreme public humiliation in the form of a long government investigation of his "Americanism" and was eventually denied a security clearance. His earlier strong advocacy of the bomb and his national standing made his subsequent doubts all the more dangerous to those who remained proponents of nuclearism.

Edward Teller, another physicist important in early bomb research who later became known as "the father of the hydrogen bomb," is representative of the opposite sequence. In 1945, Teller opposed the use of the atomic bomb without warning. After the war, he vehemently objected to the moral reservations expressed by other scientists toward the idea of making nuclear weapons. Teller advocated maintaining an "adventurous spirit" in fully exploring the possibilities of atomic weapons—which now meant "his" H-bomb—and he believed that "we would be unfaithful to the tradition of Western civilization if we shied away from exploring what man can accomplish." This combination of ethical blindness and extreme technicism, not just in Teller but in many others as well, inspired the subtitle of the film *Dr. Strangelove, or How I Stopped Worrying and Learned to Love the Bomb.*

No one could argue that the power of the atomic bomb is not impressive, or that it does not readily engender a sense of awe both for nature's power and man's capacity for technological mastery. But the danger of the nuclearist position is that the bomb's power and its limitations are never clearly examined. The terms that were used by the scientists in referring to the bomb—terms such as "the gadget," "the thing," "the device," or simply "It"—served to blunt a continuing awareness of the bomb's deadly purpose. The bomb became enmeshed in utopian hopes for total salvation that seemed otherwise unattainable. Man's own place in the scheme of things was devalued and made subordinate to the demands of the weapon.

The early discussion of bomb shelters and diplomacy in the postwar period are examples of the perversions of logic to which the bomb led. It became clear that the United States could not fully defend itself from nuclear attack in case of another major war. An anxious debate ensued in which the chief issue was whether there would be any survivors of a major nuclear conflagration—shelters or no shelters. Also involved was the question of whether, considering the world into which they would emerge, the survivors would envy the dead. Teller argued that there *would* be survivors and that democratic ideals would survive with them. He insisted that "realistic thinking" demanded facing up to the possible consequences of the use of atomic weapons.

Given the experience of those who actually did survive the atomic bomb in Hiroshima, the question about survivors in this debate was never properly posed. The important question is not "Would there be survivors?" or "Would the survivors envy the dead?" but rather "Would the survivors themselves feel *as if* dead?"

Nuclearist thinking pervaded the field of diplomacy. There was a feeling that "the big atomic stick" (as Edward Teller called it) could solve the political problems of the world. There is no doubt that the presence of nuclear weapons did exercise a deterrent effect in international relations immediately following World War II. But a weapon too awesome and frightening to be used could not be a permanently effective deterrent. Statesmen began to realize that an arsenal consisting only of nuclear weapons would make the punishment for international violations more destructive than the crime. As one writer put it, a policeman armed only with an atomic bomb could not even prevent a housebreaking unless he were willing to sacrifice the entire city in doing so. It is even possible that the restraint on all-out war created by nuclear weapons made smaller, more prolonged conflicts like Vietnam more likely.

Nuclearism involves a failure of the imagination—a failure to conceive in human terms the meaning of the weapons—and the embrace as a means of man's salvation of that which most threatens it. Nuclearism provides an apocalyptic alternative to the already impaired modes of symbolic immortality while itself further undermining the viability of these modes. Nuclearism propels us toward use of the weapons and, equally dangerous, undermines man's capacity to confront the problems they raise.

Each of the modes of symbolic immortality has been affected by the dislocations of the nuclear era. Even without the actual deployment of these weapons, their very existence poses a profound threat to our perceptions of living and dying. The possibility that the human species can annihilate itself with its own tools fundamentally alters the relationship of human imagination to each mode of symbolic continuity.

The biological (and biosocial) mode is perhaps most obviously affected. The assumption of "living on" in one's descendants is made precarious. The aspiration of living on in one's nation is also undermined, for no longer do national boundaries offer the protection and security they once did. National security becomes identical with international security, which is dependent upon the partial relinquishment by each nation of its own exclusive claim on the allegiance of its citizens.

Because ultimate issues of life and death have become more urgent and more problematic, the theological mode has also become problematic. A rational-scientific age had already made commitments of religious faith and the meaning of God difficult issues for many people. Theological imagery of transcending death becomes a dubious promise if the assurance of some form of earthly survival is not also given. If there are none (or few) left among the biologically living, then the image of spiritual survival loses much of its symbolic and comforting power. It is precisely these threats to the belief in salvation that may account for the burgeoning of fundamentalist groups and the insistence of these groups upon the most narrow and literal—one might say desperate—forms of biblical faith.

In Japan after the explosion of the atomic bomb, neither Eastern nor Western religious imagery seemed capable of providing an acceptable explanation or formulation of the meaning of the disaster. The bomb experience seems to have wounded that deep layer of human confidence and trust to which religious symbolism appeals. No conventional religious expression was adequate to reestablish a sense of trust and continuity.

Partly as a response to this impasse, religious language has come to emphasize the sacred quality of man's earthly commitments and the religious importance of responsible political action. At the same time, there has been a revival of fundamentalist and occult religion—a manifestation of the increased plausibility of apocalyptic visions. Who can now say that an image of the end of the world is merely a religious pipe dream meant to frighten people into submission?

Theological imagery has developed in two contrasting directions. There

has been a movement toward naturalism, in which religious imagery is more
humanistic and closer to observable process. But there has also been a rise of visionary and doom-prophesying religious forms, in which salvation is made conditional upon total repentance. In either case, man's new demonic technological capacity (if not demonic human psychological potential) always threatens to overwhelm and render futile the attempt to immortalize man's spiritual attainments.

Immortality through the creative mode depends upon the conviction that one's works will endure. But what lasts anymore? The existence of nuclear weapons, together with the breakdown of the many forms of collective symbolization and ritual we have discussed, raise doubts about the permanence of any contributions to human culture. The fear is that nothing will last and that, therefore, nothing matters.

This concern about the viability of particular social forms and even about historical continuity itself creates an undercurrent of anxiety and mistrust that is generally not directly felt. But this concern is expressed in the increased need of young people to have a sense of the immediate human impact of their work and has resulted in heightened interest in careers involving teaching, legal practice, social work, and medicine. With regard to scientific work, as more questions are raised about the ethics of various scientific projects, the individual scientist is less able to undertake research without consideration of the lethal or life-enhancing potentials of the new knowledge he may unearth.

These questions and threats lead to a greater reliance upon the fourth mode—that of nature—for an image of permanence. But we now know that nature is all too susceptible to both our weapons and our pollution. Joan Baez's mournful tones in the song "What Have They Done to the Rain?" and Bob Dylan's desperate anger in "A Hard Rain's A-gonna Fall" both suggest a vision, shared by all of us in some degree, of ultimate nuclear violation of our planet.

In the face of this vision, explorations of outer space take on a special symbolic urgency. In these explorations we seek to extend our natural environment almost to infinity. But it would be the most wishful kind of illusion to see in these explorations, or in speculation about life on other planets, a solution to the problems of human continuity on our own endangered planet.

The impairment of these four modes of symbolic immortality has led to a greater reliance on the mode of experiential transcendence. This mode is closely related to immediate sensation. It is therefore less vulnerable to being impoverished by misgivings about historical durability, on which the other modes are more dependent. The resort to pleasure seeking or mystical experience is common in historically dislocated times. In our own time, we have witnessed great preoccupation with intensified forms of experience through drugs, sex, music, meditation, dance, nature, and even politics.

Beyond enabling one to live more fully in the present, the experiential mode lends itself to something more—to engaging death anxiety directly by experimenting with risk. Almost as artists become a community's conscience by exploring the extremities of the community's unfaced danger, the active pursuit of experiential transcendence plays with fears of death by inviting them, even encouraging them.

In this respect, there may be a strange parallel between nuclearism and the intense forms of experience that many people are now seeking. The most perverse response to the existence of a doomsday machine would be to love the bomb itself joyously: the nightmare of oblivion experienced as ecstasy. This is the malignant phenomenon that the film *Dr. Strangelove* carries even further and portrays in a powerfully bizarre image: a cowboy euphorically riding an atomic bomb as it soars from the plane toward glorious explosion.

Fanciful as this image appears, it has an eerie psychological plausibility. Expressed boldly, there may be a need to destroy one's world for purposes of imagined rebirth, a need which lends itself either to suicidal obliteration or to transformation and regeneration. This need takes advantage not only of every variety of individual and social aggression, but fits as well with the psychological principle of touching death, either imaginatively or literally, as a precondition of new life. Thus, nuclear weapons can achieve vivid symbolic representation in our minds precisely because of their promise of devastation.

The ultimate threat posed by nuclear weapons is not only death but meaninglessness: an unknown death by an unimaginable weapon. War with such weapons is no longer heroic; death from such weapons is without valor. Meaninglessness has become almost a stereotyped characterization of twentieth-century life, a central theme in modern art, theater, and politics. The roots of this meaninglessness are many. But crucial, we believe, is the anxiety deriving from the sense that all forms of human associations are perhaps pointless because subject to sudden irrational ends. Cultural life thus becomes still more formless. No one form, no single meaning or style appears to have any ultimate claim. The psychological implications of this formlessness are not fully clear; while there seem to be more life choices available, fewer are inwardly compelling.

Such broad historical themes as these can influence even the most fundamental of human relationships—the nurturing bond between mother and child. No mother can fully escape the general threat to the continuity and significance of life, nor the resulting death anxiety. Nor can she avoid transmitting these doubts to her offspring. Erik Erikson has emphasized the importance for the child of gaining a sense of "basic trust" early in life. Lack of such a firm sense of basic trust can undermine one's self-confidence for life and can prevent an individual from fulfilling his creative potential. Such childhood deficiencies may result from a lack of parental trust, from misgivings in the parents about the meaning and significance of their own lives.

Fundamental attitudes like these are communicated to children in subtle ways from their earliest days on. The importance of symbolic impairments in parents, such as a lost sense of immortality, in producing individual-psychological difficulties in children has not been much examined. But it is in such ways as this that the psychohistorical themes that characterize an era—like unfaced death anxiety in our time—become enmeshed in the psychological lives of individuals from one generation to another.

We began this discussion by describing some of the psychological struggles of those who survived the atomic bomb in Hiroshima. Those struggles involved guilt, numbing, and a continuing effort to give form and meaning to radically disrupted lives. Perhaps we can achieve little more than a glimmer of the excruciating tensions such extraordinarily painful lives have involved. But in another sense we are all survivors of this century's holocausts.

In cultivating and making clear to ourselves our own status as survivors, we become more fully part of the century in which we live. In doing so we open ourselves to the experience of pain and to the imagery and anxiety of death. We glimpse at such moments the necessity for personal and social transformation in the interest of continued survival and new meaning. The urgency of the tasks of reconstruction are then pressed upon us—though the forms our efforts must take are never fully clear.

39 · A Proposal for International Disarmament

George F. Kennan

George F. Kennan, formerly United States ambassador to Russia and Yugoslavia, is professor emeritus at the Institute for Advanced Study at Princeton and the author of many books, including Russia Leaves the War *and* Memoirs, 1925–1950 *(both of which were awarded the Pulitzer Prize and the National Book Award). He has received a number of honors, including the Albert Einstein Peace Prize (1981) and, most recently, the peace prize awarded by the German book trade in Frankfurt (October 1982). For many years, Professor Kennan has been a member of the American Academy of Arts and Letters, serving as president of that academy from 1968 to 1972, and he is currently co-chairman of the American Committee on East-West Accord. "A Proposal for International Disarmament" is the speech that Professor Kennan delivered on receipt of the Albert Einstein Peace Prize, outlining a realistic plan which might, if adopted, literally save the world. Its importance can hardly be overestimated.*

From The Nuclear Decision: Soviet-American Relations in the Atomic Age *by George F. Kennan. Copyright © 1976, 1980, 1981, 1982 by George F. Kennan. Reprinted with permission of Pantheon Books.*

Adequate words are lacking to express the full seriousness of our present situation. It is not just that we are for the moment on a collision course politically with the Soviet Union, and that the process of rational communication between the two governments seems to have broken down completely; it is also—and even more importantly—the fact that the ultimate sanction behind the conflicting policies of these two governments is a type and volume of weaponry which could not possibly be used without utter disaster for us all.

For over thirty years, wise and far-seeing people have been warning us about the futility of any war fought with nuclear weapons and about the dangers involved in their cultivation. Some of the first of these voices to be raised were those of great scientists, including outstandingly that of Albert Einstein himself. But there has been no lack of others. Every president of this country, from Dwight Eisenhower to Jimmy Carter, has tried to remind us that there could be no such thing as victory in a war fought with such weapons. So have a great many other eminent persons.

When one looks back today over the history of these warnings, one has the impression that something has now been lost of the sense of urgency, the hopes, and the excitement that initially inspired them, so many years ago. One senses, even on the part of those who today most acutely perceive the problem and are inwardly most exercised about it, a certain discouragement, resignation, perhaps even despair, when it comes to the question of raising the subject again. The danger is so obvious. So much has already been said. What is to be gained by reiteration? What good would it now do?

Look at the record. Over all these years the competition in the development of nuclear weaponry has proceeded steadily, relentlessly, without the faintest regard for all these warning voices. We have gone on piling weapon upon weapon, missile upon missile, new levels of destructiveness upon old ones. We have done this helplessly, almost involuntarily: like the victims of some sort of hypnotism, like men in a dream, like lemmings heading for the sea, like the children of Hamlin marching blindly along behind their Pied Piper. And the result is that today we have achieved, we and the Russians together, in the creation of these devices and their means of delivery, levels of redundancy of such grotesque dimensions as to defy rational understanding.

I say redundancy. I know of no better way to describe it. But actually, the word it too mild. It implies that there could be levels of these weapons that would not be redundant. Personally, I doubt that there could. I question whether these devices are really weapons at all. A true weapon is at best something with which you endeavor to affect the behavior of another society by influencing the minds, the calculations, the intentions, of the men that control it; it is not something with which you destroy indiscriminately the lives, the substance, the hopes, the culture, the civilization, of another people.

What a confession of intellectual poverty it would be—what a bankruptcy of intelligent statesmanship—if we had to admit that such blind, senseless acts of destruction were the best use we could make of what we have come to view as the leading elements of our military strength!

To my mind, the nuclear bomb is the most useless weapon ever invented. It can be employed to no rational purpose. It is not even an effective defense against itself. It is only something with which, in a moment of petulance or panic, you commit such fearful acts of destruction as no sane person would ever wish to have upon his conscience.

There are those who will agree, with a sigh, to much of what I have just said, but will point to the need for something called deterrence. This is, of course, a concept which attributes to others—to others who, like ourselves, were born of women, walk on two legs, and love their children, to human beings, in short—the most fiendish and inhuman of tendencies.

But all right: accepting for the sake of argument the profound iniquity of these adversaries, no one could deny, I think, that the present Soviet and American arsenals, presenting over a million times the destructive power of the Hiroshima bomb, are simply fantastically redundant to the purpose in question. If the same relative proportions were to be preserved, something well less than 20 percent of those stocks would surely suffice for the most sanguine concepts of deterrence, whether as between the two nuclear super-powers or with relation to any of those other governments that have been so ill-advised as to enter upon the nuclear path. Whatever their suspicions of each other, there can be no excuse on the part of these two governments for holding, poised against each other and poised in a sense against the whole Northern Hemisphere, quantities of these weapons so vastly in excess of any rational and demonstrable requirements.

How have we got ourselves into this dangerous mess?

Let us not confuse the question by blaming it all on our Soviet adversaries. They have, of course, their share of the blame, and not least in their cavalier dismissal of the Baruch Plan so many years ago. They too have made their mistakes; and I should be the last to deny it.

But we must remember that it has been we Americans who, at almost every step of the road, have taken the lead in the development of this sort of weaponry. It was we who first produced and tested such a device; we who were the first to raise its destructiveness to a new level with the hydrogen bomb; we who introduced the multiple warhead; we who have declined every proposal for the renunciation of the principle of "first use"; and we alone, so help us God, who have used the weapon in anger against others, and against tens of thousands of helpless noncombatants at that.

I know that reasons were offered for some of these things. I know that others might have taken this sort of a lead, had we not done so. But let us not, in the face of this record, so lose ourselves in self-righteousness and hypoc-risy as to forget our own measure of complicity in creating the situation we face today.

What is it then, if not our own will, and if not the supposed wickedness of our opponents, that has brought us to this pass?

The answer, I think, is clear. It is primarily the inner momentum, the independent momentum, of the weapons race itself—the compulsions that arise and take charge of great powers when they enter upon a competition with each other in the building up of major armaments of any sort.

This is nothing new. I am a diplomatic historian. I see this same phe-nomenon playing its fateful part in the relations among the great European powers as much as a century ago. I see this competitive buildup of arma-ments conceived initially as a means to an end but soon becoming the end itself. I see it taking possession of men's imagination and behavior, becoming a force in its own right, detaching itself from the political differences that initially inspired it, and then leading both parties, invariably and inexorably, to the war they no longer know how to avoid.

This is a species of fixation, brewed out of many components. There are fears, resentments, national pride, personal pride. There are misreadings of the adversary's intentions—sometimes even the refusal to consider them at all. There is the tendency of national communities to idealize themselves and to dehumanize the opponent. There is the blinkered, narrow vision of the professional military planner, and his tendency to make war inevitable by assuming its inevitability.

Tossed together, these components form a powerful brew. They guide the fears and the ambitions of men. They seize the policies of governments and whip them around like trees before the tempest.

Is it possible to break out of this charmed and vicious circle? It is sobering to recognize that no one, at least to my knowledge, has yet done so. But no one, for that matter, has ever been faced with such great catastrophe, such inalterable catastrophe, at the end of the line. Others, in earlier decades, could befuddle themselves with dreams of something called "victory." We, perhaps fortunately, are denied this seductive prospect. We have to break out of the circle. We have no other choice.

How are we to do it?

I must confess that I see no possibility of doing this by means of discussions along the lines of the negotiations that have been in progress, off and on, over this past decade, under the acronym of SALT. I regret, to be sure, that the most recent SALT agreement has not been ratified. I regret it, because if the benefits to be expected from that agreement were slight, its disadvantages were even slighter; and it had a symbolic value which should not have been so lightly sacrificed.

But I have, I repeat, no illusion that negotiations on the SALT pattern—negotiations, that is, in which each side is obsessed with the chimera of relative advantage and strives only to retain a maximum of the weaponry for itself while putting its opponent to the maximum disadvantage—I have no illusion that such negotiations could ever be adequate to get us out of this hole. They are not a way of escape from the weapons race; they are an integral part of it.

Whoever does not understand that when it comes to nuclear weapons the whole concept of relative advantage is illusory—whoever does not understand that when you are talking about absurd and preposterous quantities of overkill the relative sizes of arsenals have no serious meaning—whoever does not understand that the danger lies, not in the possibility that someone else might have more missiles and warheads than we do, but in the very existence of these unconscionable quantities of highly poisonous explosives, and their existence, above all, in hands as weak and shaky and undependable as those of ourselves or our adversaries or any other mere human beings: whoever does not understand these things is never going to guide us out of this increasingly dark and menacing forest of bewilderments into which we have all wandered.

I can see no way out of this dilemma other than by a bold and sweeping departure, a departure that would cut surgically through the exaggerated anxieties, the self-engendered nightmares, and the sophisticated mathematics of destruction in which we have all been entangled over those recent years, and would permit us to move, with courage and decision, to the heart of the problem.

President Reagan recently said, and I think very wisely, that he would "negotiate as long as necessary to reduce the numbers of nuclear weapons to a point where neither side threatens the survival of the other."

Now that is, of course, precisely the thought to which these present observations of mine are addressed. But I wonder whether the negotiations would really have to be at such great length. What I would like to see the president do, after due consultation with the Congress, would be to propose to the Soviet government an immediate across-the-boards reduction by 50 percent of the nuclear arsenals now being maintained by the two superpowers; a reduction affecting in equal measure all forms of the weapon, strategic, medium-range, and tactical, as well as all means of their delivery: all this to be implemented at once and without further wrangling among the experts, and to be subject to such national means of verification as now lie at the disposal of the two powers.

Whether the balance of reduction would be precisely even—whether it could be construed to favor statistically one side or the other—would not be the question. Once we start thinking that way, we would be back on the same old fateful track that has brought us where we are today. Whatever the precise results of such a reduction, there would still be plenty of overkill left—so much so that if this first operation were successful, I would then like to see a second one put in hand to rid us of at least two-thirds of what would be left.

Now I have, of course, no idea of the scientific aspects of such an operation; but I can imagine that serious problems might be presented by the task of removing, and disposing safely of, the radioactive contents of the many thousands of warheads that would have to be dismantled. Should this be the case, I would like to see the president couple his appeal for a 50 percent reduction with the proposal that there be established a joint Soviet-American scientific committee, under the chairmanship of a distinguished neutral figure, to study jointly and in all humility the problem not only of the safe disposal of these wastes but also of how they could be utilized in such a way as to make a positive contribution to human life, either in the two countries themselves or—perhaps preferably—elsewhere. In such a joint scientific venture we might both atone for some of our past follies and lay the foundation for a more constructive relationship.

It will be said this proposal, whatever its merits, deals with only a part of the problem. This is perfectly true. Behind it there would still lurk the serious political differences that now divide us from the Soviet government. Behind it would still lie the problems recently treated, and still to be treated, in the SALT forum. Behind it would still lie the great question of the acceptability of war itself, any war, even a conventional one, as a means of solving problems among great industrial powers in this age of high technology.

What has been suggested here would not prejudice the continued treatment of these questions just as they might be treated today, in whatever forums and under whatever safeguards the two powers find necessary. The conflicts and arguments over these questions could all still proceed to the heart's content of all those who view them with such passionate commitment. The stakes would simply be smaller; and that would be a great relief to all of us.

What I have suggested is, of course, only a beginning. But a beginning has to be made somewhere; and if it has to be made, is it not best that it should be made where the dangers are the greatest, and their necessity the least? If a step of this nature could be successfully taken, people might find the heart to tackle with greater confidence and determination the many problems that would still remain.

It will also be argued that there would be risks involved. Possibly so. I do not see them. I do not deny the possibility. But if there are, so what? Is it possible to conceive of any dangers greater than those that lie at the end of the collision course on which we are now embarked? And if not, why choose the greater—why choose, in fact, the greatest—of all risks, in the hopes of avoiding the lesser ones?

We are confronted here, my friends, with two courses. At the end of the one lies hope—faint hope, if you will, uncertain hope, hope surrounded with dangers, if you insist. At the end of the other lies, so far as I am able to see, no hope at all.

Can there be—in the light of our duty not just to ourselves (for we are all going to die sooner or later) but of our duty to our own kind, our duty to the continuity of the generations, our duty to the great experiment of civilized life on this rare and rich and marvelous planet—can there be, in the light of these claims on our loyalty, any question as to which course we should adopt?

In the final week of life, Albert Einstein signed the last of the collective appeals against the development of nuclear weapons that he was ever to sign. He was dead before it appeared. It was an appeal drafted, I gather, by Bertrand Russell. I had my differences with Russell at the time as I do now in retrospect; but I would like to quote one sentence from the final paragraph of that statement, not only because it was the last one Einstein ever signed, but because it sums up, I think, all that I have to say on the subject. It reads as follows:

We appeal, as human beings to human beings: Remember your humanity, and forget the rest.

A few years ago, the British–South African psychiatrist Michael A. Simpson published Dying, Death and Grief: A Critically Annotated Bibliography and Source Book of Thanatology and Terminal Care *(New York and London: Plenum Press, 1979). The main part of the book consists of several hundred annotated references on death and dying. Simpson has evaluated each of these by awarding them from one to five stars, where five stars means "highly recommended; buy and read." Below are reproduced 31 (of 708) books to which he has given his highest rating. The citations and comments are arranged alphabetically by author from Simpson's book, which itself deserves a five-star rating.*

A Death in the Family. James Agee. Bantam, New York. PB.

Pulitzer Prize–winning novel dealing with the effects of the sudden death of a young father on a close-knit family.

Kinflicks. Lisa Alther. Chatto & Windus, London, 1976. Penguin, 1977. PB. A. A. Knopf, New York (Random House Canada), 1975. Signet, New York, 1977. Also 'Haut-Kontakte' Ullstein Verlag, Berlin, 1977.

"My family has always been into death," it begins. At long last someone who had something new to say about death in America and a sparkling style to say it in. The story of Ginny Babcock is not merely brilliantly funny and poignant as a novel (It's a cliché for a reviewer to admit to laughing aloud, but the occurrence is still rare enough to be worth recording). It is also a fine account of varying responses to death; and of the dying, from idiopathic thrombocytopenic purpura, of Ginny's mother, for whom death was a demon lover for whose assignation one must be ready. "The trick was in being both willing to die and able to do so at the same time. Dying properly was like achieving simultaneous orgasm."

The Savage God. A. Alvarez. Weidenfeld & Nicolson, London, 1972. 250 pp. Bantam, New York. PB.

A study of attitudes toward suicide and death through history and literature, and the fascination this theme has had for writers at all times. Includes an account of his relations with Sylvia Plath, and her suicide and his own suicide attempt.

Ethical Decisions in Medicine. Howard Brodie. Little, Brown & Co., Boston, 1976. 340 pp.

Probably the best available book on medical ethics. Soundly organized with clearly stated objectives and self-evaluation components. Proposes a concise method for dealing with ethical problems and provides many lucid examples of its use. It examines key issues including informed consent, determination of the quality of life, ethical participation, allocation of scarce resources, euthanasia, and allowing to die. As some recent thanatology research has breached some of the principles of ethical research in human beings, everyone involved in this area could benefit from reading this book, which will also provide a valuable basis for teaching the subject.

The Sanctity of Social Life: Physicians' Treatment of Critically Ill Patients. Diana Crane. Russell Sage Foundation, New York, 1975. 286 pp.

A uniquely valuable study based on extensive interviews, observations, hospital record audit, and detailed questionnaires. Rather than pontificating on what ought to be done, Crane describes what doctors actually do for the critically ill. She shows that while withdrawal of treatment is widespread in some types of case, positive euthanasia is rare. Both adults and children seem to be regarded as "treatable" while they retain the potential for interacting in some meaningful way with others. A much-needed antidote to the usual speculative literature on this subject, with commendable detail and objectivity.

A Very Easy Death. Simone de Beauvoir. Penguin Books, Harmondsworth, 1969. 92 pp. Celo Press, Burnsville, N.C., 1965. 139 pp. Warner PB, New York, 1973.

Unreservedly recommended. A brilliant and unforgettable account of her mother's death in France, a death that was anything but easy. Deeply moving description of a proud woman's clinical humiliation and the conflicting love and hostility her daughter experienced in confronting the death.

New Meanings of Death. Ed. Herman Feifel. McGraw-Hill, New York, 1977.

A splendid volume—even more interesting and accessible than Feifel's 1959 classic. Includes Feifel on death in contemporary America; Kastenbaum on death and development through the life span; Bluebond-Langner on meanings of death to children; Shneidman on death and the college student; Weisman on the psychiatrist and the inexorable; Garfield on the personal impact of death on the clinician; Saunders on St. Christopher's Hospice; Kelly on Make Today Count; Kalish on death and the family; Leviton on death education; Lifton on immortality, Simpson on death and poetry; Gutman on death and power; Shaffer and Rodes on death and the law.

Death, Grief & Bereavement: A Bibliography 1845–1975. Compiled by Robert Fulton with others. Arno Press, New York, 1976. 253 pp.

The most comprehensive and reliable bibliography of the literature on death, grief and bereavement in print. Some 4,000 entries, mainly journal articles, indexed by subject, with nearly eighty classifications.

Talking About Death. E. A. Grollman. Beacon Press, Boston. 1970. 30 pp. PB.

Strongly recommended. A beautiful book, probably the best available for use in discussing death with children. Well-illustrated and constructed; simple, direct, honest.

Talking About Death: A Dialogue Between Parent & Child. Earl A. Grollman. Beacon Press, Boston. 1976. 98 pp.

Simply excellent. A new edition of the excellent earlier version with a greatly expanded guide to parents on how to use it and to discuss death with children. Lists some resources such as organizations, cassettes, films, books. Explicit and observant.

Dying. John Hinton. Pelican Books, Harmondsworth & Baltimore, 1967. 2nd edition, 1972. 220 pp.

Succinct and highly capable review of existing knowledge on attitudes to death, what dying is like, terminal care and mourning based on a thorough review of the literature up to the 1960s and the author's own experience. Compact.

Gramp. Mark and Dan Jury. Grossman Publishers (Viking Press), New York, 1976. 152 pp. Illustrated. PB.

Simply superb. A moving, honest and direct account of the dying of Frank Tugend, as recorded in photographs and words, by a family who made his death an act of love. Arteriosclerotic dementia led to a gruelling three-year deterioration. On February 11, 1974, aged eighty-one, he removed his false teeth and announced that he was no longer going to eat or drink. The family decided to respect his wishes and not hospitalize him. Three weeks later, he died at home. Death with dignity? Perhaps, though not how most people picture it. An invaluable, unromanticized corrective to the stickily sentimental nature of too much death literature.

The Psychology of Death. Robert Kastenbaum and Ruth Aisenberg. Springer Publishing Co. New York, 1972. 500 pp. Duckworth, London, 1974. Concise Edition, Springer, New York, 1976. 434 pp. PB.

Quite simply the very best book on the psychology of death, and one that is unlikely to be improved on for some time. Very well organized and highly useful to any professional or scholar involved in work related to death. A truly critical review; stimulating, eclectic and honest. Looks at concepts of and attitudes towards death, developmentally and clinically, and the relevant cultural milieu; also thanatomimesis, longevity, suicide, murder, accidents, and illness. Stylish, yet straightforward and not self-conscious. Strongly recommended.

Catastrophic Diseases: Who Decides What? A Psychosocial and Legal Analysis of the Problems Posed by Hemodialysis and Organ Transplantation. Jay Katz and Alexander Morgan Capron. Russell Sage Foundation, New York, 1975. 295 pp.

*A highly able explanation of important issues, extending and complementing both Katz's earlier work (*Experimentation with Human Beings, *1972) and Fox and Swazey's recent book (1974). The authors explore the nature and effects of catastrophic illness, and such goals and values as the preservation of life, reduction of suffering, personal integrity and dignity, pursuit of knowledge, economy and public interest. There's a cogent account of the development and present status of the technical procedures and a study of the characteristics, authority and capacity of the physician-investigators and patient-subjects, the functions of informed consent, and limitations of consent. The stages of decision making are reviewed, the activities of professional and public institutions involved; and proposals for the formulation of policy regarding the allocation of resources and selection of donors, the administration of such major medical interventions at local and national levels, with a review of decisions and consequences. Lucid, readable, fascinating and challenging.*

On Death and Dying. Elisabeth Kübler-Ross. Macmillan, New York, 1968. 250 pp. Tavistock, London, 1973, paperback edition.

Strongly recommended. A classic and highly influential work, in which Dr. Ross advanced her model of the "five stages" in the progress of the dying patient. Interesting and humane, with sound practical advice and transcripts of some interviews.

A Grief Observed. C. S. Lewis. Faber and Faber, London. 1961/1973. 60 pp. PB. Seabury Press, New York.

"No one ever told me that grief felt so much like fear" ... An outstandingly honest, naked observation of a widower's grief. Begun, without plans for publication, as a means of self-therapy, written informally in odd notebooks, during his first weeks alone. Unique, moving, memorable.

The American Way of Death. Jessica Mitford. 1963. 280 pp. Simon and Schuster, New York, 1963. Fawcett/Crest PB $1.95.

Justly famous, witty, well-documented and merciless exposure of the multi-million-dollar death industry and American funeral practices.

Death and the Family: The Importance of Mourning. Lily Pincus. Pantheon Books, New York, 1974. 278 pp. Vintage PB, 1976. Faber, London.

Written by a social worker with great experience in marital and family therapy; a brilliant book, sensitive and well written, always readable, wise and human. A genuine, fresh and substantial contribution to the understanding and therapy of bereavement and the dying family. Highly recommended.

The Bell Jar. Sylvia Plath. Bantam, New York, PB.

A brilliant novel, autobiographical in many respects, about a nineteen-year-old girl who attempts suicide, finding life difficult to bear. One of the best evocations of suicidal thinking in literature.

Jewish Reflections on Death. Jack Riemer. Schocken Books, New York, 1974. 184 pp.

An eloquent anthology of great interest and value to Jew and non-Jew alike. The laws of Judaism, especially with regard to bereavement, show great psychological and spiritual wisdom, giving a structure to grief that relates to death firmly and realistically as a normal part of life. These essays give a clear account of the beauty and insight of the traditional procedures for the business of mourning and also explore the modern problems relating to death, from the Jewish experience, of suffering and solace. An unusually interesting book. A short glossary of Hebrew terms used would aid the comprehension of non-Jewish readers.

Loss and Grief: Psychological Management in Medical Practice. Ed. B. Schoenberg, A. C. Carr, D. Peretz, and A. H. Kutscher. Columbia University Press, New York, 1970. PB 400 pp.

Strongly recommended. Deals with the broader issues of reactions to loss of different kinds, including loss of limb, organ, sensory loss or loss of sexual function; also with the reactions to death in the patient, family, and the health care team. A very high standard of contributions from a distinguished group of authors. A forty-five item annotated bibliography.

The Facts of Death. Michael A. Simpson. Spectrum/Prentice-Hall, 1979. 250 pp. approx.

An eloquent and warm practical book for families and helpers. Reviews succinctly what we know about the nature of death and dying, patient's rights, how to manage one's own death and to cope with the dying of another; death and children; suicide; how to cope with a suicidal person, and with one's own suicidal impulses; bereavement and grief; funerals, and how to plan one's estate and funeral, and how to avoid the Terminal R.I.P.-off. Maybe they told you the facts of life: this is what they left out.

Cancer Ward. A. Solzhenitsyn. Bantam, New York, 1969. 560 pp.

A great novel, about life in the cancer ward of a Russian hospital, that defies any brief review.

Death Inside Out. Ed. P. Steinfels and R. M. Veatch. Hastings Center Report. Harper Forum Books. Harper and Row, New York. Fitzhenry and Whiteside, Canada. 1975. 150 pp. PB.

One of the more refreshing books on death. Elegant, clear thinking, critical, thoughtful and stimulating. Principally concerned with philosophical, ethical and historical issues rather than practical and personal problems. One of the comparatively few books of genuine intellectual interest in the field. Includes Ariès's "Death Inside Out." again, and Ivan Illich on the political uses of natural death; Eric Cassell on dying in a technological society; William May on the metaphysical plight of the family (the great family secret: God is dead); Robert Morison on death: process or event? Paul Ramsey on the indignity of "death with dignity"; David Smith on letting some babies die; and other works by Leon Kass and Tristram Engelhardt.

Passing On: The Social Organization of Dying. David Sudnow. Prentice-Hall, Englewood Cliffs, N.J., 1967. 176 pp. PB.

Excellent sociological study of death in a county hospital and its management by the staff; including counting of deaths and their visibility, social death, preparing and moving bodies, how we announce death and bad news; uses of a corpse, etc. Fascinating reading, introducing a new way of looking at what we do. Strongly recommended.

The Death of Ivan Illych. Leo Tolstoy. New American Library, New York. PB. And other editions.

Strongly recommended. Brilliant account of the death of a bourgeois Russian judge, with probably more insight into the psychology of death than any other major author.

Man's Concern with Death. Arnold Toynbee et al. Hodder and Stoughton, London, 1968. 280 pp.

One of the early and persisting classics of the death literature. Among its competent chapters are several by Ninian Smart on philosophical and religious concepts, Keith Mant on the medical definition of death, Simon Yudkin on death and the young, and Eric Rhode on death in twentieth century fiction. But best of all are the splendid chapters by Arnold Toynbee, erudite and elegant and superbly literate. The epilogue, a moving account of Toynbee's personal experience and his feelings about the imminent prospect of death, is especially poignant reading.

Johnny Got His Gun. Dalton Trumbo. Bantam, New York. PB.

A powerful antiwar novel; a nineteen-year-old World War I veteran has been left, after multiple injuries, blind, speechless, and limbless. He beats out messages on his pillow with his head, begging to be taken out of his hospital room, to show the world a survivor of Every War.

The Book (On the Taboo Against Knowing Who You Are). Alan Watts. Vintage Books, New York, 1972. 146 pp. PB.

A classic, elegantly, lucidly and wittily written book. Dealing with the delusion of the lonely separate ego alienated from the universe, with his usual skillful understanding of Eastern and Western religions and philosophies. Offers a *coherent philosophical style which genuinely deals with fear of death and a manner of coming to terms with life. Highly recommended.*

On Dying and Denying. Avery Weisman. Behavioral Publ., New York, 1972.

A very significant study of "terminality," concentrating on the central role of denial. Very competent and illustrated with many clinical examples. Of the highest quality both intellectually and practically.

Helping Your Children to Understand Death. Anna M. Wolf. Revised edition, 1973. Child Study Press, New York, 64 pp. PB.

Possibly the best book available to help parents and children talk about death. Simple but not simplistic, wise but not know-all, and soundly practical. Well grounded in child development and family dynamics, it deals sensibly with the common questions of children and parents. Issues of faith, inescapable in this area, are considered from the viewpoint of the major faiths; other matters covered include suicide, assassination and war, and hypocrisy. Very highly recommended to all who deal with children, have children, or have been children.

EXTENSIVE
BIBLIOGRAPHIES

There are many bibliographies relating to death and suicide. Here is a listing of several of the more extensive contemporary lists.

Corr, Charles A. "Books for Adults: An Annotated Bibliography." In *Helping Children Cope with Death: Guidelines and Resources*, edited by H. Wass and C. A. Corr, pp. 77–93. Washington, D.C.: Hemisphere, 1982. 44 references.

Des Pres, Terrence. "Bibliography: Original Testimony." In *The Survivor: An Anatomy of Life in the Death Camps*, pp. 249–254. New York: Pocket Books, 1977. 79 references.

Farberow, Norman. *Bibliography on Suicide and Suicide Prevention: 1897–1957; 1958–1967*. Rockville, Md.: National Institute of Mental Health, 1969. 203 pp. 2202 references.

Fulton, Robert. *Death, Grief and Bereavement: A Bibliography, 1845–1975*. New York: Arno Press, 1976. 253 pp. 4,000 + references.

Kutscher, Austin H. *A Bibliography of Books on Death, Loss and Grief: 1935–1968*. New York: Health Science Publishing Corp. 1969. 84 pp. Approx. 1,200 references.

Simpson, Michael A. *Dying, Death and Grief: A Critically Annotated Bibliography and Source Book of Thanatology and Terminal Care*. New York: Plenum, 1979. 288 pp. 708 references.

Wass, H., Corr, C. A., Pacholski, R. A., and Sanders, C. M. *Death Education: An Annotated Resource Guide*. Washington, D.C.: Hemisphere, 1980. 303 pp. 500 + references.

NAME INDEX

Page numbers in italic indicate a selection by this author.

SUBJECT INDEX